# FROMMER'S

## COMPREHENSIVE TRAVEL GUIDE

# COLORADO 1ST EDITION

by John Gottberg

**PRENTICE HALL TRAVEL**

NEW YORK • LONDON • TORONTO • SYDNEY • TOKYO • SINGAPORE

**FROMMER BOOKS**

Published by Prentice Hall General Reference
A division of Simon & Schuster Inc.
15 Columbus Circle
New York, NY 10023

ISBN 0-13-334574-2
ISSN 1053-2463

Design by Robert Bull Design
Maps by Geographix Inc.

**FROMMER'S COLORADO, 1ST EDITION**

Editor-in-Chief: Marilyn Wood
Senior Editors: Alice Fellows, Judith de Rubini
Editors: Sara Hinsey, Paige Hughes, Lisa Renaud, Theodore Stavrou
Assistant Editor: Peter Katucki
Managing Editor: Leanne Coupe

# CONTENTS

# LIST OF MAPS

## INVITATION TO THE READERS

In researching this book, I have come across many wonderful establishments, the best of which I have included here. I am sure that many of you will also come across appealing hotels, inns, restaurants, guesthouses, shops, and attractions. Please don't keep them to yourself. Share your experiences, especially if you want to comment on places that have been included in this edition that have changed for the worse. You can address your letters to:

John Gottberg
*Frommer's Colorado*
c/o Prentice Hall Travel
15 Columbus Circle
New York, NY 10023

## A DISCLAIMER

Readers are advised that prices fluctuate in the course of time, and travel information changes under the impact of the varied and volatile factors that affect the travel industry. Neither the author nor the publisher can be held responsible for the experiences of readers while traveling. Readers are invited to write to the publisher with ideas, comments, and suggestions for future editions.

## SAFETY ADVISORY

Whenever you're traveling in an unfamiliar city or country, stay alert. Be aware of your immediate surroundings. Wear a moneybelt and keep a close eye on your possessions. Be particularly careful with cameras, purses, and wallets, all favorite targets of thieves and pickpockets.

# CHAPTER 1

# GETTING TO KNOW COLORADO

Colorado is the heartland of the Rocky Mountains, the backbone of North America. With more than 50 peaks that soar above 14,000 feet, it is the most highly elevated state in the United States, and perhaps the most spectacular. The Rockies— with their evergreen and aspen forests, their racing streams and rivers, their wealth of wildlife—lend themselves to recreation throughout the year, from summer hiking and rafting to winter skiing.

But Colorado is not *only* the mountains. It is also the wheat and corn fields of the vast eastern prairies, the high plateau country of the west, and the modern, sophisticated cities of the Front Range.

Take the time to see the sights of cosmopolitan Denver, the "Mile High City"; Colorado Springs, home of the U.S. Air Force Academy and U.S. Olympic Training Center; and the university towns of Boulder and Fort Collins. Indulge in luxury hotels, gourmet cuisine, and year-round recreation at thriving resort communities such as Aspen, Vail, and Steamboat Springs. Ride the narrow-gauge steam trains and relive the mining-boom days in rejuvenated towns such as Durango, Georgetown, and Cripple Creek, straight out of the Old West but alive with 20th-century verve. Immerse yourself in the natural and human-made wonders of national parks and monuments such as Mesa Verde, Rocky Mountain, Great Sand Dunes, Dinosaur, Black Canyon of the Gunnison, and Bent's Old Fort, each with its own unique fascination.

Get to know Colorado's people. Meet the hotelier in Denver and the cowboy in Craig, the ski instructor in Crested Butte and the Hispanic farmer in San Luis.

Come to Colorado for the seasons. Whatever you do, don't stay indoors. Enos Mills, an early 20th-century environmentalist who was the driving force behind the creation of Rocky Mountain National Park, said that a knowledge of nature is the basis of wisdom. In other words, get out and get smart. That's the essence of Colorado.

## 1. GEOGRAPHY & PEOPLE

First-time visitors traveling to Colorado may be awed by the looming wall of the Rocky Mountains. They come into sight a good 100 miles away, soon after drivers cross the state boundary with Kansas. East of the Rockies, a 5,000-foot peak is considered high; yet Colorado alone has 1,143 mountains above 10,000 feet,

**❓ DID YOU KNOW . . . ?**

- Colorado contains 75% of all land in the continental U.S. above 10,000 feet in elevation.
- The world's largest natural mineral hot-spring swimming pool is at Glenwood Springs.
- The world's highest automobile tunnel, the Eisenhower Tunnel, crosses the Continental Divide at 11,000 feet.
- The world's two largest known dinosaur skeletons were uncovered south of Grand Junction in the 1970s.
- Grand Mesa, east of Grand Junction, is the world's largest flat-top mountain and has more than 300 lakes on its plateau.
- The Granby Theatre at Grand Lake is the oldest summer resort theater in the United States.
- Four Corners Monument near Towaoc is the only place in America where visitors can stand in four states—Colorado, New Mexico, Arizona, and Utah—at once.
- Butch Cassidy robbed his first bank, in Telluride, in 1880.
- The key collection at the Baldpate Inn near Estes Park could unlock Hitler's desk, Mozart's wine cellar, Fort Knox, and Westminster Abbey.
- Great Sand Dunes National Monument contains the highest inland dunes in the U.S., rising to 700 feet.
- The highest suspension bridge in North America spans the Royal Gorge: 1,055 feet above the Arkansas River.
- The Pikes Peak Cog Railway, which climbs to 14,110 feet, is the world's highest cog road and the highest railroad in the U.S.
- Leadville, at 10,152 feet, is the highest city in North America.
- Pictographs found near Springfield, in the southeast, date from the A.D. 5th century and may be Celtic in origin.
- The mountainous area of Colorado is six times that of Switzerland.
- Denver gets more days of sunshine a year than San Diego or Miami.

including 53 over 14,000! Highest of all is Mount Elbert at 14,433 feet. The ridge of the Continental Divide zigzags more or less through the center of the 104,000-square-mile state.

Thanks to territorial legislators of the last century, Colorado is an almost-perfect rectangle, measuring some 385 miles east to west and 275 miles north to south. Its basic topography can be visualized by dividing the state into vertical thirds: The eastern third is plains, the midsection is high mountains, and the western third is mesa land.

That's a broad simplification, of course. The central Rockies, though they cover six times the mountain area of Switzerland, are not a single vast highland but are composed of a series of high ranges running in roughly north-south directions. The spectacular San Juans separate the southwestern corner from the rest of Colorado, with the result that it is culturally more akin to the Southwest than to the Rocky Mountains.

The westward-flowing Colorado River system dominates the western part of the state, with tributary networks including the Gunnison, Dolores, and Yampa-Green rivers. East of the Divide, the primary river systems are the South Platte, the Arkansas, and the Rio Grande, all flowing toward the Gulf of Mexico. Particularly in eastern Colorado, but also in the west, the rivers are not broad bodies of water like the Ohio or Columbia, or even like the Allegheny or Willamette. They are streams heavy with spring and summer snowmelt, and during much of the year, they are reduced on the dry prairies to mere trickles by the heavy demands of farm and ranch irrigation. Besides agricultural use, they are a prime wildlife habitat and a tremendous outdoor recreational resource.

The forested mountains are essential to retaining the precious water for the lowlands. Eleven national forests comprise 15 million acres of land, and there are 8 million acres controlled by the Bureau of Land Management also open for public recreational use. Another half million acres are within national parks, monuments, and recreation areas under the administration of the National Park Service. Besides all this, the state operates 30 state parks and recreation areas.

Colorado's name, Spanish for "red," comes from its red soil and rocks. Some of the sandstone agglomerates have become attractions in their own rights, such as the Red Rocks Amphitheatre west of Denver and the startling Garden of the Gods State Park in Colorado Springs.

Of Colorado's 3.3 million people, some 80% live along the "Front Range," the I-25 corridor, where the plains meet the mountains. Denver, the state capital, has a population of about 500,000, with nearly another million in the metropolitan area. Colorado Springs has the second largest population with about 290,000 residents, followed by Pueblo (100,000), Boulder (84,000), Fort Collins (88,000), and Greeley (53,000).

It's important for all Colorado visitors to be aware of the state's high elevation at all times—for two reasons. The first is clothing: Don't come at any time of year, even in the middle of summer, without at least a warm sweater. The second is health: Don't push yourself too hard during your first few days. The air is thinner, the sun more direct. You should expect to sunburn more easily and stop to catch your breath more frequently.

# 2. HISTORY

The history of Colorado is a testimony to the human ability to adapt to and flourish in a difficult environment. This land of high mountains and limited water continues to challenge its inhabitants even today.

Archeologists say the earliest inhabitants of Colorado migrated from the Bering Land Bridge about 12,000 B.C. Weapon points discovered in Folsom, New Mexico, just southeast of modern Trinidad, Colorado, established for the first time that prehistoric peoples hunted now-extinct mammals such as woolly mammoths. Stable farming settlements, evidenced by the remains of domestically grown maize, date from about 3,000 B.C.

Around the beginning of the Christian era, the early Anasazi people lived in shallow rock shelters, or pit houses, in the region of modern Durango. One of America's best-known pre-Columbian civilizations, they left behind distinctive basketwork. By about A.D. 700, Anasazi culture had expanded into elaborate cliff villages throughout what is now known as the Four Corners Region (where Colorado, New Mexico, Arizona, and Utah come together). Remnants of the cliff dwellers' culture, which was at its peak around A.D. 1000, are best observed at Mesa Verde National Park in southwestern Colorado.

By the time Spanish conquistadors, the first European visitors, arrived in the mid-16th century, the Anasazi had long since departed. Their cliff dwellings were abandoned around the 13th century for unknown reasons. In the Anasazis' place were two major nomadic Native American cultures: the mountain dwellers of the west, primarily Utes, and the plains tribes of the east, principally Arapahoe, Cheyenne, and Comanche.

# EXPLORATION & SETTLEMENT

Spanish colonists, having established settlements at Santa Fe, Taos, and other upper Rio Grande locations in the 16th and 17th centuries, didn't find Colorado's San Luis Valley as attractive for colonization. Not only was there a lack of financial and military support from the Spanish crown, but

## DATELINE

- **12,000 B.C.** First inhabitants include Folsom Man.
- **3,000 B.C.** Prehistoric farming communities.
- **A.D. 1,000** Anasazi cliff-dweller culture peaks in Four Corners Region.
- **Late 1500s** Spanish explore upper Rio Grande valley, colonize Santa Fe and Taos.
- **1776** The U.S. achieves independence.
- **1803** The Louisiana Purchase includes most of modern Colorado.
- **1806–07** Capt. Zebulon Pike leads first U.S. expedition into Colorado Rockies.
- **1822** William Becknell establishes Santa Fe Trail.
- **1828–32** Bent's Fort built on Arkansas River.
- **1842–44** Lt. John C. Frémont and Kit Carson explore Colorado and American West.
- **1848** Treaty of Guadalupe Hidalgo ends Mexican War, adds American

*(continues)*

## DATELINE

Southwest (including much of Colorado) to U.S.

- **1858** Gold discovered in modern Denver.
- **1859** Gen. William Larimer founds Denver; major gold strikes in nearby Rockies.
- **1861** Colorado Territory proclaimed.
- **1862** Colorado cavalry wins major Civil War battle at Glorieta Pass, N.M.
- **1862** Homestead Act.
- **1863–68** Utes obtain treaties guaranteeing 16 million acres of western Colorado land.
- **1864** Hundreds of innocent Cheyennes killed in Sand Creek Massacre; University of Denver becomes Colorado's first institution of higher education.
- **1866** Territorial legislature passes doctrine of prior appropriation for water rights.
- **1867–74** Longhorn cattle ranching dominates eastern plains.
- **1869–72** John Wesley Powell leads expeditions down the Green and Colorado rivers.
- **1870** Kansas City–Denver rail line completed; agricultural commune of Greeley estab-

*(continues)*

the fierce, freedom-loving Comanches and Utes wouldn't be roped into servile hacienda life.

Nevertheless, the Spanish still held title to southern and western Colorado in 1803, when U.S. President Thomas Jefferson paid $15 million to buy the vast Louisiana Territory from Napoleon. The tract included the lion's share of modern Colorado, to the sources of the Arkansas and Platte rivers near the Continental Divide.

To explore the hinterlands, Jefferson commissioned a company of 16 soldiers, led by Capt. Zebulon Pike. Pike and his party left St. Louis in June 1806. By the end of November, they were camped at the foot of the landmark mountain that today bears the captain's name: Pikes Peak. They continued west until they were arrested by Spanish soldiers for trespassing on the Rio Grande. In July 1807, after being taken to Santa Fe for questioning and to Chihuahua, Mexico, for jailing, Pike and his men were released to American authorities.

Pike's eyewitness account of previously inaccessible Santa Fe was of major interest to Americans. When Mexico won its independence from Spain in 1821 and dropped the ban against trade with other countries, William Becknell led a pack train from St. Louis to Santa Fe and sold his wares for seven times their original cost. Becknell returned the following year, establishing the Santa Fe Trail.

To mesh the growing Santa Fe trade with eastern demands for Rocky Mountain furs, Bent's Fort was built on the Arkansas River (near modern La Junta) between 1828 and 1832 by brothers William and Charles Bent and their partner, Ceran St. Vrain. In 1838 a second outpost, Fort St. Vrain, was built on the South Platte River east of modern Denver. A road linked the two with Fort Laramie on the North Platte.

Many of the furs were provided by "mountain men," self-reliant adventurers including Kit Carson, Jim Bridger, Lucien Maxwell, and Tom Fitzpatrick. Making their livings mainly as trappers and guides, these men forged a mutual understanding with the Native American tribes and became legends in their own times.

The fur boom collapsed around 1840. By that time, Missouri Sen. Thomas Hart Benton was pushing his doctrine of "Manifest Destiny." Benton believed that control of the West Coast would wrest the fabled trade with Asia from the British and other European powers.

Americans had been generally apathetic to western expansion ever since an 1820 expedition led by Maj. Stephen Long had labeled the high plains of eastern Colorado as "the great American desert." In 1842, in hopes of reversing public opinion, Benton sent his son-in-law, Lt. John Charles Frémont, to map the Oregon Trail from the Missouri River up the North Platte to the Continental Divide. Frémont was so taken by the country that he returned in 1843 to plot a new route. Employing Carson and other mountain men as his guides and hunters, he took his party across the Continental Divide to Oregon, south through the Sierra Nevada to the Mojave Desert, and back across Utah and Colorado to Bent's Fort. In the fall of 1844, after 18 months and 5,000 miles of traveling, they returned to St. Louis. Jessie Benton Frémont wrote and published the expedition's story based on her husband's letters and journals, and it caused great excitement among the American public. The Mormon migration to Utah and the rush of easterners to the Columbia River country were almost direct consequences of John Frémont's expedition and Jessie Frémont's hyperbole. (It enhanced John's fame, as well: 12 years later, in 1856, he narrowly lost the U.S. presidential election to Democrat James Buchanan.)

Meanwhile, Texas had declared its independence from Mexico in 1844. Within 3 years President James Polk had found an excuse to invade Mexican territory. In the summer of 1847, Gen. Stephen Kearny and an army of 1,700 men paused at Bent's Fort en route to Santa Fe, which they conquered in August without a shot being fired. From there, Kearny marched west to California, which he took in December. The treaty of Guadalupe Hidalgo on February 2, 1848, set the U.S.–Mexico frontier close to its present boundary. (A small piece of Arizona and New Mexico was added in 1853.)

Modern Colorado was split between the territories of Utah (in 1850), which extended from the California border to the Continental Divide; New Mexico (in 1850), including Bent's Fort and the southeast; Kansas (in 1854), from the Divide east to Missouri; and Nebraska (in 1854), including the South Platte valley of the northeast.

Arapahoe County was among those created within the Kansas Territory, extending over 150 miles east from the Continental Divide to the 103rd meridian. It was populated almost exclusively by plains tribes until 1858, when gold seekers discovered flakes of the precious metal in sands near the junction of Cherry Creek and the South Platte. General William Larimer established Denver adjacent to the site, naming it after Kansas Gov. James Denver.

The Cherry Creek strike was literally a flash in the gold-seeker's pan, but strikes in the nearby mountains in early 1859 were much more significant: at Clear Creek, near what would become Idaho Springs; and in a quartz vein at Gregory Gulch, which led to the founding of Central City. When word got back East that summer, 50,000 pioneers hurried to "Pikes Peak or Bust."

## THE TERRITORY

Abraham Lincoln was elected president in November 1860. Congress, then dominated by Republicans eager to please the wealthy gold-mine owners, created the Colorado Territory on February 28, 1861. The new territory absorbed neighboring sections of Utah, Nebraska, and New Mexico to fill out the boundaries that the state still has today.

Lincoln's Homestead Act of 1862 brought much of the public domain into private ownership, and led to the platting of Front Range townships, starting with Denver in 1861.

Controlling the Native American peoples was a priority of the territorial government. A treaty negotiated by Tom Fitzpatrick at Fort Laramie in 1851 had guaranteed the

## DATELINE

lished by Nathan Meeker; Colorado State University opens.
- **1871** Gen. William Palmer founds Colorado Springs.
- **1876** Colorado becomes 38th state.
- **1877** University of Colorado opens in Boulder.
- **1878** Little Pittsburg silver strike launches Leadville mining boom, Colorado's greatest.
- **1879** Milk Creek Massacre by Ute warriors leads to tribe's removal to reservations.
- **1882** Overnight millionaire Horace Tabor becomes Colorado lieutenant-governor.
- **1890** Sherman Silver Purchase Act; gold discovered at Cripple Creek, leading to state's biggest gold rush.
- **1891** America's first forest reserves established.
- **1892** Colorado Fuel and Iron Company founded in Pueblo, and becomes major national steel producer.
- **1893** Women win right to vote; silver industry collapses following repeal of Sherman Silver Purchase Act.
- **1896** Bimetallist Sen. Henry Teller *(continues)*

## 6 • GETTING TO KNOW COLORADO

entire Pikes Peak region to the nomadic plains tribes, but that had been made moot by the rush of settlers in the late 1850s. The Fort Wise Treaty of 1861 exchanged the Pikes Peak territory for 5 million fertile acres of Arkansas Valley land, north of modern La Junta. But when the Arapahoes and Cheyennes continued to roam their old hunting grounds, conflict was inevitable. Frequent rumors and rare instances of hostility against settlers gave the Colorado cavalry sufficient reason to attack a peaceful settlement of Cheyennes—flying Old Glory and a white flag—in November 1864. About 200 Cheyennes, two-thirds of them women and children, were killed in what has become known as the Sand Creek Massacre.

The Cheyennes and Arapahoes vowed revenge, and launched a campaign to drive whites from their ancient hunting grounds. Their biggest triumph was the destruction of the town of Julesburg in 1865. But the cavalry, bolstered by returning Civil War veterans, forced the two tribes into reservations in Indian Territory (now Oklahoma) by the Medicine Lodge Creek Treaty of October 1867. The cavalry nailed the coffin on the few remaining renegades with victories over the Cheyennes near Wray (1868) and Sterling (1869).

Mining was at a standstill in 1864 when William Gilpin, who had served as the first territorial governor from 1861 to 1862, bought the million-acre Sangre de Cristo grant embracing the San Luis Valley. Intending to sell parcels to European investors on speculation, he hired Brown University chemistry professor Nathaniel Hill to evaluate its mineral wealth.

Hill saw greater potential for the Central City area—if he could develop a smelting process to reduce its gold, silver, and copper ores to concentrates. After a transatlantic research trip to Wales and discussions with a Cornish metallurgist, he opened a smelter in Black Hawk in 1867. It was an immediate success. It not only attracted investment from the East but set the stage for the large-scale spread of mining throughout Colorado in years to come.

When the first transcontinental railroad was completed in 1866, the Union Pacific went through Cheyenne, 100 miles north of Denver. Such entrepreneurs as William Loveland, the founder of Golden—a town 14 miles west of Denver that shared the territorial capital until 1867—promoted a rail link with Cheyenne. Finally, former Gov. John Evans (1862–65) and banker Jerome Chaffee hired Gen. William J. Palmer, director of the Kansas Pacific Railroad, to build a Kansas City–Denver railroad. It was completed in 1870.

Water and land issues also were an important focus. The territorial and federal legislatures in 1866 passed what was called the Colorado Doctrine of prior appropriation, later adopted throughout the Rockies. It held that during times of near-drought, when a stream's low flow didn't provide sufficient water for every farm along its route, priority for beneficial use was given on a seniority basis to the first persons to file a claim to a farm along that stream.

One of the most important developments in Colorado

agriculture was conceived not in Denver, but in New York. *New York Tribune* editor Horace Greeley sent his farm columnist, Utopian idealist Nathan Meeker, to establish an agrarian prairie commune to be known as Union Colony in 1870. Meeker recruited more than 200 pioneers from all walks of life, purchased a tract on the Cache la Poudre River from Evans's and Chaffee's Denver Pacific Railroad, and called his community Greeley in honor of his patron.

The potentially fertile soil needed irrigation to be productive. Colonist E. S. Nettleton devised a canal system that revolutionized high-altitude agriculture. A series of long ditches ran parallel to the Cache la Poudre but fell at a more gradual rate than the river, irrigating many thousands of acres of barren land.

Farther east, the prairie grasses provided fine grazing for herds of longhorn cattle. The largest livestock empire was that of John Wesley Iliff, who bought 2,000 longhorns at $10 a head in 1867, sold them for $35 a head, and soon became a millionaire with 650,000 acres of land in northern Colorado. He brought the public domain into private ownership by reversing the intent of the Homestead Act, as his employees signed their land over to him in a sort of neofeudal autocracy. To assure his empire's security, he stationed armed foremen at all nine of his ranches.

Other stockmen imitated Iliff's success. But numerous factors led to the cattle industry's rapid demise. As more and more longhorns populated the plains, competing with sheep for the prairie grasses, their price rose dramatically. Barbed wire, invented in 1874, soon surrounded farms and railroad tracks, further diminishing the animals' range. Soon they were branded as disease carriers and banished from Colorado entirely.

## DATELINE

- **1958** U.S. Air Force Academy opens at Colorado Springs.
- **1964** National Wilderness Preservation Bill enacted.
- **1988** Sen. Gary Hart, a frontrunner for Democratic presidential nomination, withdraws from race after a scandal.
- **1991** Denver awarded major-league baseball franchise for 1993, making it the 15th U.S. city with three major professional sports.

## STATEHOOD

Colorado had already begun moving in the direction of statehood during the Civil War years but it wasn't until August 1, 1876, that Colorado became the 38th state. Coming less than a month after the United States' 100th birthday, it was natural that Colorado should become known as "the Centennial State." John Routt was elected the first governor.

The state's new constitution gave the vote to African Americans, but not to women, despite the strong efforts of the Colorado Women's Suffrage Association. This was mildly surprising: The feminist movement was particularly strong in the state. Since Julia Holmes had donned "bloomers" to climb Pikes Peak in 1858, women had played an active if behind-the-scenes role in Colorado's growth. The suffragettes finally succeeded in winning the vote in 1893, 3 years after Wyoming became the first state to offer universal suffrage.

At the time of statehood, most of Colorado's vast western region was still occupied by some 3,500 mountain and plateau dwellers of a half-dozen Ute tribes. Unlike the plains tribes, their early relations with white explorers and settlers had been peaceful and unpressured. Their great Chief Ouray, leader of the Uncompahgre Ute tribe of the Southwest, had negotiated treaties in 1863 and 1868 that guaranteed them 16 million acres, or most of western Colorado. In 1873, Ouray agreed to sell the United States one-fourth of that acreage in the mineral-rich San Juan Mountains in exchange for hunting rights and $25,000 in annual annuities.

But a mining boom that began in 1878 led to a flurry of intrusions into Ute territory and stirred up a "Utes Must Go!" sentiment fueled by editorials in the *Denver Tribune*. Tension grew until, in September 1879, Greeley founder Nathan Meeker (then a Native American agent), cavalry Maj. Thomas Thornburgh, and 20 other men were killed in the Milk Creek Massacre near the modern-day town **of**

Meeker. The incident convinced the U.S. Senate that the safety of Americans was more important than appeasing the tribes. The Utes were moved in 1880 to small reserves in southwestern Colorado and Utah. Their vacated lands were opened to settlement in 1882.

The Milk Creek Massacre is remembered for the rescue of Thornburgh's surviving but besieged troops by the African American Company D of the Ninth Cavalry. Their action was considered a turning point toward better white-black relations during an especially difficult period.

# THE MINING BOOM

On April 28, 1878, when August Rische and George Hook hit a vein of silver carbonate 27 feet deep on Fryer Hill in Leadville the real mining boom began. They called their strike the Little Pittsburg.

Perhaps the stir over the strike wouldn't have been so great had not Rische and Hook 8 days earlier traded one-third interest in whatever they found for a basket of groceries from storekeeper Horace Tabor, the mayor of Leadville and a shrewd entrepreneur. Tabor was well acquainted with the Colorado "law of apex," which said that if a ore-bearing vein surfaced on a man's claim, he could follow it wherever it led, even out of his claim and through the claims of others. Within a few months, Hook and Rische sold out; Senator Chaffee and financier David Moffat bought in; and the Little Pittsburg Consolidated Mining Company was earning $8,000 a day.

Tabor, a legend in Colorado, typifies the "rags-to-riches" success story of a common working-class man. A native Vermonter, he had mortgaged his Kansas homestead in 1859 and moved west to the mountains, where he had been a postmaster and storekeeper in several hamlets before Leadville. He was 46 when the Little Pittsburg strike was made. By 50, he was the state's richest man and its Republican lieutenant-governor. His love affair and marriage to Elizabeth "Baby Doe" McCourt, a young divorcee for whom he left his assiduous wife, Augusta, became both a national scandal and the subject of numerous books, even an opera.

The Leadville strike was the greatest of many claims that led to the peopling of the Colorado Rockies. The construction of towns and transportation of mineral wealth was made easier by the narrow-gauge Denver & Rio Grande Railroad. This network was the brainchild of Gen. William Palmer, who had founded the resort of Colorado Springs in 1871 after leaving the Kansas Pacific Railroad directorship. Pueblo, Alamosa, Leadville, Durango, Silverton, Grand Junction, and other communities were linked to Denver by various D&RG spur routes by 1882.

But trouble loomed. Silver was being produced faster than the market could absorb it, causing an unstable partnership in the silver-and-gold exchange upon which the U.S. monetary system was based. The limited commitment of the Sherman Silver Purchase Act of 1890 forced the Treasury Department to pay more for silver than it was worth on world markets. When the act was repealed in 1893, the Colorado silver industry collapsed. Every silver mine and smelter in the state closed down. Thousands lost their jobs, and many resorted to crime and violence to get food for their families. Even Horace Tabor found himself penniless.

But while silver's value was on the wane, gold's was rising. In the fall of 1890, a cowboy named Bob Womack found gold in Cripple Creek as it flowed through a cow pasture on the southwestern slope of Pikes Peak. He sold his so-called El Paso Lode to Winfield Scott Stratton, a carpenter and amateur geologist. Stratton's mine earned him a tidy profit of $6 million by 1899, when he sold it to an English company for another $11 million. Cripple Creek turned out to be the richest gold field ever discovered, ultimately producing $500 million in gold.

Unlike the flamboyant Tabor, Stratton was an introvert and a neurotic. His fortune was twice the size of Tabor's, and it grew daily as the deflation of silver's value boosted that of gold. But he invested most of it back in Cripple Creek, searching for a fabulous mother lode that he never found. Ultimately, by the early 1900s, overproduction of gold began to drive the price of the metal back down, just as had happened to silver.

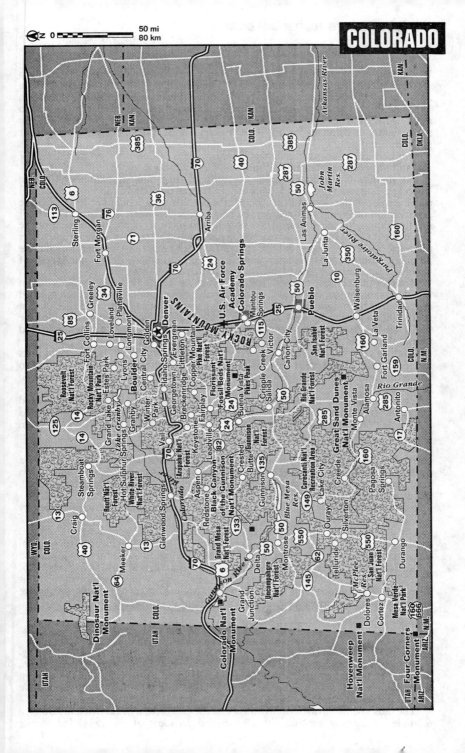

## ENVIRONMENTALISM & TOURISM

Exploration of Colorado had not ceased with Frémont's epic journey of 1843–44. In 1867 and 1868, natural scientist John Wesley Powell, a Civil War veteran with an amputated arm, scaled several of Colorado's 14,000-foot peaks. In 1869 and again in 1871–72, he led descents of the Green and Colorado rivers, becoming the first to travel through Arizona's Grand Canyon. His writings both as an explorer, and subsequently as director of the U.S. Geological Survey, influenced many later environmentalists.

Similarly influential was Ferdinand Hayden's *Atlas of Colorado,* produced in 1877 and still regarded as a leading authority on Colorado topography.

But modern Colorado environmentalism really began in September 1900, when Theodore Roosevelt made his first visit to the state as the Republican vice-presidential nominee. Soon after Roosevelt acceded to the presidency in September 1901, after the assassination of President McKinley, he began to declare more and larger chunks of the Rockies as forest reserves. Then he removed them from the jurisdiction of the Department of the Interior and placed them in the Department of Agriculture, under the aegis of the U.S. Forest Service. By 1907, when an act of Congress forbade the president from creating any new reserves by proclamation, nearly one-fourth of Colorado was national forest land—16 million acres in 18 forests.

Another project that reached fruition during the Teddy Roosevelt administration was the establishment of Mesa Verde National Park in 1906. The cliff dwellings and artifacts had been discovered by surveyors for mapmaker Hayden in the 1870s, but vandals and souvenir hunters were soon helping themselves. A feminist group, the Cliff Dwellers Association, arranged to lease the lands from the Ute tribes, who held title to them, and successfully lobbied for the park's creation.

Tourism grew hand-in-hand with the setting aside of public lands. Eastern tourists had been visiting Colorado since the 1870s, when Palmer founded his Colorado Springs resort and made the mountains accessible via his Denver and Rio Grande Railroad.

Estes Park was among the first resort towns to emerge in the 20th century, spurred by the visit in 1903 by Freelan Stanley. With his brother Francis, Freelan had invented the Stanley Steamer, a kerosene-powered automobile, in Boston in 1899. Freelan Stanley freighted one of his vehicles to Denver and drove the 40 miles via Longmont to Estes Park in less than 2 hours, a remarkable speed at the time. Finding the climate conducive to his recovery from tuberculosis, he returned in 1907 with a fleet of a dozen Stanley Steamers and set up a shuttle service to Estes Park from Denver. Two years later, having made extensive real-estate purchases, he built the Stanley Hotel, still a hilltop landmark today.

Stanley developed a friendship with Enos Mills, a young innkeeper whose property was more a workshop for students of wildlife than a business. A devotee of conservationist John Muir, Mills believed tourists should spend their Colorado vacations in the natural environment, camping and hiking. As Mills gained national stature as a nature writer and lecturer, he urged that the national forest land around Longs Peak, outside of Estes Park, be redesignated as a national park. In January 1915, the 400-square-mile Rocky Mountain National Park was created by President Woodrow Wilson; today it is one of America's leading tourist attractions, with more than two million visitors each year.

## THE MODERN ERA

World War I affected Colorado in much the same way it did the rest of the country. Some 43,000 Coloradans served in the armed forces, 1,000 of them dying. Back home, dry-land wheat farmers and sugar-beet producers made large profits. On the western slope, there was a small boom in the rare metal vanadium, a uranium ore derivative used in hardening steel.

The '20s saw the growth of highways and the completion of the Moffat Tunnel, a 6.2-mile passageway beneath the Continental Divide that (in 1934) led to the long-sought direct Denver–San Francisco rail connection. Of more tragic note was the worst flood in Colorado history. Pueblo was devastated when the Arkansas River overflowed its banks on June 1, 1921: 100 people were killed, and damage exceeded $16 million. The disaster led to the passage by the state legislature of a bill for flood control.

The Great Depression of the 1930s was a difficult time for many Coloradans, but it had positive consequences. The federal government raised the price of gold from $20 to $35 an ounce, reviving Cripple Creek and other stagnant mining towns. The Civilian Conservation Corps built roads and trails in the mountains. The Works Progress Administration employed tens of thousands in positions from construction to the arts. The Agricultural Adjustment Administration supported the farming communities. And the state's first Department of Public Welfare was created.

In 1934 the Taylor Grazing Act ended homesteading and initiated a schedule of fees for use of unoccupied public lands by ranchers, miners, and others. The federal act, which applied throughout the American West, provided the basis for the Bureau of Land Management, established in 1946.

World War II attracted many of the defense installations that are now an integral part of the Colorado economy. Camp Carson was built in 1942 (it was renamed Fort Carson in 1954) to house 37,000 soldiers on 60,000 acres south of Colorado Springs. Its subsidiary, Camp Hale, just north of Leadville, trained the 10th Mountain Infantry Division in cold-weather survival and military skiing. Ent Air Force Base, established in the Springs in 1942, evolved after the war into the Continental Air Defense Command (CONAD) and in 1957 to the North American Air Defense Command (NORAD). A military nerve center for the entire northern hemisphere, NORAD was moved in 1966 to *inside* Cheyenne Mountain, where several thousand communications specialists now work around the clock.

Colorado Springs is also the site of the $200-million U.S. Air Force Academy, authorized by Congress in 1954 and opened to cadets in 1958.

The war was also indirectly responsible for the other single greatest boon to Colorado's late 20th-century economy—the ski industry. Soldiers in the 10th Mountain Division, on leave from Camp Hale before heading off to fight in the Italian Alps, often crossed Independence Pass to relax in the lower altitude and milder climate of the 19th-century silver-mining village of Aspen. They tested their skiing skills against the slopes of Ajax Mountain, using a frightening boat-on-a-rope conveyance to climb the hill.

In 1945, Walter and Elizabeth Paepcke—he the founder of the Container Corporation of America, she a devoted conservationist—moved to Aspen and established the Aspen Company as a property investment firm. Skiing was already popular in New England and the Midwest, but had few devotees in the Rockies. (There was a famous ski jump at Steamboat Springs and smaller hills around Denver, Colorado Springs, and Leadville.) Paepcke bought a 3-mile chair lift, the longest and fastest in the world at the time, and had it ready for operation by January 1947. Soon, easterners were flocking to Aspen—and the rest is ski history. Paepcke soon established a summer music festival, the Aspen Institute for Humanistic Studies, and the Aspen Health Center to round out the town as a year-round resort.

During the postwar era, two of the environmentalists' greatest triumphs were the defeat in 1955 of the Echo Park Dam project and the rejection of the 1980 Winter Olympic Games, awarded Denver in 1974 by the International Olympic Committee.

The Echo Park Dam would have flooded the Yampa River's fossil-rich Lodore Canyon in the heart of Dinosaur National Monument. The dam was proposed by the states of Colorado, Wyoming, Utah, and New Mexico to help them make full use of their half of the river's flow, as guaranteed by the Colorado River Compact of 1922. (The other half of the flow was assigned to Colorado, Nevada, and Arizona.) Echo Park failed, but numerous other dams have been built, including Blue Mesa and Morrow Point dams on the Gunnison River and Dolores Dam on the Dolores River. More are on the way.

Environmentalists still hope to drive a final stake into the proposed Narrows Dam on the South Platte River near Fort Morgan.

# 3. FAMOUS COLORADANS

**Katherine Lee Bates** (1859–1929) College English teacher who wrote "America the Beautiful," one of the nation's best-loved patriotic hymns, in 1895. It was published in 1911.

**Molly Brown** (1868–1932) Oafish wife of Denver financier J. J. Brown whose heroism during the sinking of the *Titanic* in 1912 earned her international fame.

**M. Scott Carpenter** (1925– ) Boulder native and navy lieutenant who became the second U.S. astronaut to make an orbital space flight, in 1962, and who led Sealab teams in underwater living experiments in 1965 and 1967.

**John Chivington** (1821–94) Methodist minister and major in Colorado cavalry. He was a hero when he led "Gilpin's Lambs" to a key 1862 Civil War victory at Glorieta Pass, N.M.; an antihero in leading the cavalry in the 1864 Sand Creek Massacre.

**William "Buffalo Bill" Cody** (1846–1917) Buffalo hunter, U.S. Army scout, Indian fighter, and later an entertainer whose life came to symbolize the Old West. A memorial on Lookout Mountain, west of Denver, marks his grave.

**Jack Dempsey** (1895–1983) World heavyweight boxing champion, 1919–26; the "Manassa Mauler" grew up near Alamosa in the San Luis Valley.

**John Denver** (1943– ) Popular singer ("Rocky Mountain High"), a resident of Aspen.

**Frank Edbrooke** (1854?–1930?) Colorado's most noted architect, designer of many late 19th-century buildings.

**John Evans** (1814–97) Obstetrician, medical technologist, railroad builder; founder of Evanston, Ill., Northwestern University, and the University of Denver, who served as governor of Colorado Territory 1862–65.

**Douglas Fairbanks** (1883–1939) Swashbuckling Denver-born actor who was the "King of Hollywood" during the 1920s. He was a co-founder of United Artists Corporation.

**Gerald Ford** (1913– ) 38th U.S. President 1974–77, a part-time resident of Vail since 1970.

**William Gilpin** (1815–81) Colorado's first territorial governor, 1861–62; a Utopian visionary who also rode with John C. Frémont in 1843–44 and fought in the Mexican War.

**Scott Hamilton** (1959– ) World figure-skating champion 1981–84, and gold medalist in men's figure skating in the 1984 Winter Olympic Games at Sarajevo, Yugoslavia.

**Gary Hart** (1936– ) Democratic senator in 1980s, unsuccessful presidential candidate in 1984 and 1988.

**Helen Hunt Jackson** (1830–85) Author of *Ramona* and other noted novels, resident of Colorado Springs from 1875.

**Nathan Cook Meeker** (1817–79) *New York Tribune* farm columnist and Utopian transcendentalist. With the backing of Horace Greeley, he established the Union Colony of Greeley, which he headed, 1870–77. He died as a Ute agent in the Milk River Massacre of 1879.

**Enos Mills** (1870–1922) Early 20th-century environmentalist who was almost single-handedly responsible for the creation of Rocky Mountain National Park in 1915.

**Chief Ouray** (1833–80) Ute tribe leader who negotiated many wise treaties in the 1860s and 1870s, but lived to see his tribe restricted to reservations.

**Walter Paepcke** (1896–1960) Founder of the American Container Corporation who, with his wife, Elizabeth, established the Aspen Company in 1945 and created Aspen as a major winter-summer resort town.

**William J. Palmer** (1836–1909) Civil War general and railroad executive who built the Kansas City–Denver line in 1870; founded Colorado Springs as a resort in 1871; and built the narrow-gauge Denver & Rio Grande Railroad in the 1870s, leading to the growth of many mountain towns.

**Patricia Schroeder**   (1940–  ) First Colorado woman elected to Congress, Democratic member of the U.S. House of Representatives.

**Freelan Stanley**   (1849–1940) Inventor (with twin brother Francis) of the Stanley Steamer car; resident, hotelier, and promoter of Estes Park tourism in early 20th century.

**Henry M. Teller**   (1830–1900) Central City lawyer elected to the U.S. Senate in 1876. He split with the Republicans over bimetallism in 1893 and led a famous 23-delegate walkout from the party's national convention in 1896.

**Wallace "Buddy" Werner**   (1936–64) Steamboat Springs skier, national skiing champion and three-time U.S. Olympian who died in an avalanche in the Swiss Alps.

**Byron R. White**   (1917–  ) U.S. Supreme Court justice since 1962, born in Fort Collins. In the late 1930s he was an All-American football player at the University of Colorado.

**Paul Whiteman**   (1890–1967) Popular jazz musician of the 1920s and 1930s, known for a style of "symphonic jazz" best exemplified by George Gershwin's *Rhapsody in Blue.*

# 4. SPORTS & RECREATION

**SPECTATOR SPORTS**   Denver is a mecca for professional sports, with major-league football (the Broncos), basketball (the Nuggets), soccer (the Foxes), and in 1993, baseball (the Rockies of the National League). Area football fans also thrive on college sports; in fact, Colorado's three largest universities—Colorado (Boulder), Colorado State (Fort Collins), and Air Force Academy (Colorado Springs)—all won bowl titles in early 1991. In addition, the largest indoor rodeo in the U.S. is held as part of the National Western Stock Show in Denver in January.

**OUTDOOR SPORTS**   While 50,000 people might attend a football game on a given Saturday, hundreds of thousands others enjoy the state's outdoor wonderland.

Two-thirds of the Colorado Rockies are preserved within national forests, making them ideal for backpacking, camping, and other pursuits. More than 400 public campgrounds are maintained in the forests. Rocky Mountain National Park and an ample handful of designated wilderness areas—around Pikes Peak, Mount Evans, the San Juan Mountains, and near Steamboat Springs, Glenwood Springs, and Vail—offer true backcountry experiences.

**Fishing**   For anglers, many cold-water species live in the mountains, including seven kinds of trout (native cutthroat, rainbow, brown, brook, lake, kokanee, and whitefish), walleye, yellow perch, northern pike, tiger muskie, and bluegill. Warm-water sport fish (especially in eastern Colorado and in large rivers) include catfish, crappie, and bass—largemouth, smallmouth, white, and wiper.

The season is year round, except in certain specified waters. A 1-year license costs $20 for an adult nonresident (15 and over), $20 for a resident; 5-day licenses are $18 and 1-day licenses $5 for nonresidents and residents alike. Children under 15 are restricted to half the daily bag limit without a license. For **general information on fishing,** call 303/291-7533, or for up-to-date fishing reports, call 303/291-7534.

**Hunting**   Hunting license fees depend upon the animal being sought. An annual small-game license is $40 for nonresidents, $15 for residents. Big-game licenses vary in cost from $150 for nonresidents, $20 for residents, for deer or antelope, to $1,000 for nonresidents, $200 for residents, for moose or desert sheep. Elk, mountain lion, bear, mountain goat, and bighorn sheep are also game of renown. Anyone born in 1949 or later must display a hunter-education course card or certificate before they will be issued a license.

The main rifle-hunting season begins in late September and continues until mid-December each year. Dates vary by region and species. This season is preceded by a 6-week archery-hunting season (mid-August to late September) and a 10-day muzzle-loading-rifle season.

For **information** on large game, call 303/291-7529; small game, 303/291-7546; upland game birds, 303/291-7547; and waterfowl, 303-291-7548.

**Boating**    White-water rafting has become one of Colorado's most popular sports. The towns of Salida and Buena Vista, both located on the upper Arkansas River, have become known as rafting capitals.

Less excitable boating enthusiasts find lakes and rivers all over the state, from the world's highest anchorage at Grand Lake to waterskiing on various reservoirs on the eastern plains. Large craft take to Shadow Mountain, Granby, Dillon, Blue Mesa, and other reservoirs. Navajo State Recreation Area in the southwest gives access to a 35-mile-long reservoir straddling the New Mexico border.

**Bicycling**    Bicycling is popular everywhere, especially around Denver and Boulder. Maps and information on bike routes are available from the **Colorado Department of Highways,** 4201 East Arkansas Avenue, Room 235, Denver, CO 80222 (tel. 303/757-9313).

**Rockhounding**    Rockhounding is carried on in various areas for recovery of semiprecious gemstones and petrified woods that take a high polish. Chalcedony varieties of quartz are widespread throughout the state. Agatized fossil bones that can be cut and polished are also found. Gemstones include beryl, topaz, phenacite, and aquamarine. Gold is found in every major mining area, and there is also silver, lead, copper, zinc, molybdenum, and uranium. Gold panning is a popular pastime. Information is available from the Geology Museum at the **Colorado School of Mines,** 1500 Illinois Street, Golden, CO 80401 (tel. 303/273-3823).

**Skiing**    The most popular winter sport, of course, is skiing, dealt with extensively in subsequent chapters on individual resorts. You can telephone for **ski conditions** throughout Colorado by calling 831-7669.

**SOURCES OF RECREATIONAL INFORMATION**    Recreational information sources in Colorado include:

**Colorado Campgrounds Association** (private campgrounds), 5101 Pennsylvania Avenue, Boulder, CO 80303 (tel. 303/499-9343). A directory is available by mail.

**Colorado Division of Parks and Outdoor Recreation** (state parks, boating, RV, and snowmobile regulations), 618 State Centennial Building, 1313 Sherman Street, Denver, CO 80203 (tel. 303/866-3437).

**Colorado Division of Wildlife** (hunting and fishing regulations), 6060 Broadway, Denver, CO 80216 (tel. 303/297-1192 or 291-7529 for a recording that gives seasons and regulations). There are regional offices at 317 West Prospect Avenue, Fort Collins, CO 80526 (tel. 303/484-2836); 2126 North Weber Street, Colorado Springs, CO 80907 (tel. 719/473-2945); 711 Independent Avenue, Grand Junction, CO 81505 (tel. 303/248-7175); and 2300 South Townsend Avenue, Montrose, CO 81401 (tel. 303/249-3431).

**Colorado Geological Survey,** 1313 Sherman Street, Suite 715, Denver, CO 80203 (tel. 303/866-2611).

**Colorado Guides and Outfitters Association,** P.O. Box 31438, Aurora, CO 80041 (tel. 303/751-9274).

**Colorado Llama Outfitters and Guides Association,** 30361 Rainbow Hills Road, Golden, CO 80401 (tel. 303/526-0092, or 800/462-8234).

**U.S. Bureau of Land Management,** 2850 Youngfield Street, Lakewood, CO 80215 (tel. 303/236-2100).

**U.S. Fish and Wildlife Service,** P.O. Box 25486, Federal Center, Denver, CO 80225 (tel. 303/236-7904).

**U.S. Forest Service,** Rocky Mountain Region, 11177 West Eighth Avenue, Lakewood, CO 80225 (tel. 303/236-9431).

**U.S. Geological Survey** (topographical maps), P.O. Box 25286, Denver, CO 80225 (tel. 303/236-7477).

**U.S. National Park Service,** P.O. Box 25287, Denver, CO 80225 (tel. 303/969-2000).

# 5. RECOMMENDED BOOKS

Perhaps the single best book for Colorado visitors to read before their arrival is James Michener's *Centennial* (New York: Random House, 1974). Not only does this historical novel tell the state's story in Michener's inimitable fashion, it creates an understanding of the struggles that have carried Colorado into the modern era.

For a comprehensive history, consult *A Colorado History* (Boulder: Pruett, 1988) by Carl Ubbelohde and others; a shorter read is *Colorado: A History* (New York: W. W. Norton, 1984) by Marshall Sprague. Robert G. Athearn's *The Coloradans* (Albuquerque, N.M.: University of New Mexico, 1982) describes the personalities and people who have shaped the state. If you're driving, two breezy reads are James McTighe's *Roadside History of Colorado* (Boulder: Johnson Books, 1989) and Halka Chronic's *Roadside Geology of Colorado* (Denver: Mountain Press, 1980).

Other notable books on the state are *Colorado* (New York: Bantam, 1981), by Dana F. Ross, part of the "Wagons West" series of frontier West novels; *Stampede to Timberline* (Boulder: Swallow, 1974), Muriel Sibell Wolle's 1949 classic account of Colorado ghost towns; and if you can find a reprint somewhere, *A Lady's Life in the Rocky Mountains,* Englishwoman Isabella Lucy Bird's scandalous 1879 account of her explorations.

When in Denver, anyone with an interest in books should visit the **Tattered Cover** bookstore, opposite the Cherry Creek Shopping Center at 2955 East First Avenue (tel. 303/322-7727). With more than 200,000 volumes on three floors, the store is so large, it provides maps to help you find your way through its collection.

# CHAPTER 2

# PLANNING A TRIP TO COLORADO

t's important to spend some time preparing for any journey, including a trip to Colorado. This chapter offers a variety of planning tools, including information on when to go, how to get there, how to get around once you're there, and some suggested itineraries.

## 1. INFORMATION

Start at the **Colorado Tourism Board,** 1625 Broadway, Suite 1700, Denver, CO 80202 (tel. 303/592-5410, or 800/433-2656). Request a "Vacation Kit" containing the official state vacation guide, map, events guide, and related information.

Other good advance information sources are the **Colorado Hotel and Motel Association,** 999 18th Street, Suite 1240, Denver, CO 80202 (tel. 303/297-8335); **Colorado Restaurant Association,** 899 Logan Street, Suite 300, Denver, CO 80203 (tel. 303/830-2972); **Colorado Dude & Guest Ranch Association,** P.O. Box 300, Tabernash, CO 80478 (tel. 303/887-3128); **Colorado Council on the Arts & Humanities,** 750 Pennsylvania Street, Denver, CO 80203 (tel. 303/894-2617); **Colorado Historical Society,** 1300 Broadway, Denver, CO 80203 (tel. 303/866-3682); **U.S. Forest Service Regional Headquarters,** P.O. Box 25127, Lakewood, CO 80025 (tel. 303/236-9431); and the **National Park Service Regional Headquarters,** P.O. Box 25287, Denver, CO 80225 (tel. 303/969-2000).

The tourist councils of the various cities and regions are listed in the appropriate chapters in this book.

## 2. WHEN TO GO

To hear a Coloradan tell it, the state has three seasons: winter, summer, and fall. Spring comes and goes so quickly: one day, usually in April, the sun has broken through and the snow is melting fast.

Along the Front Range, including Denver and Colorado Springs, summers are hot and dry, evenings pleasantly mild. Relative humidity is very low, and temperatures seldom rise above the 90s. Evenings start to get cooler by mid-September, but even as late as November days can as easily be warm as they can crisp. Winters are, surprisingly, warmer and less snowy than those of the Great Lakes or New England; golf courses, in fact, remain open year round! Denver boasts more than 300 sunny days a year, with more annual hours of sun than San Diego or Miami Beach.

Most of the state is considered semi-arid. The prairies average about 16 inches of precipitation annually; the Front Range, 14 inches; the western slope, only about 8 inches. The rain, when it falls, is commonly a short deluge: a summer afternoon thunderstorm.

# COLORADO CALENDAR OF EVENTS

## JANUARY

✪ ***Aspen/Snowmass Winterskol*** *This 5-day event includes a parade, fireworks, torchlight ski descent, freestyle skiing and ice-skating competition, skydiving, and more.* ***Where:*** *Aspen.* ***When:*** *3rd week.*

☐ **Ullrfest,** Breckenridge. A week-long festival in honor of Ullr, Norse god of snow. Parade, fireworks, torchlight display, ski competitions. 3rd week.

✪ ***Cowboy Downhill*** *Professional rodeo cowboys tame a slalom course, lasso a resort employee, and saddle a horse before crossing the finish line.* ***Where:*** *Steamboat Springs.* ***When:*** *2nd weekend.*

## FEBRUARY

☐ **Steamboat Springs Winter Carnival,** Steamboat Springs. The longest continuously observed winter carnival west of the Mississippi River includes a week of downhill and cross-country ski races, jumping, broomball, and "ski joring" street events. 1st full week.
☐ **Cajun Ski Week,** Winter Park. Mardi Gras gets a boost with more than 300 visiting Louisiana ski enthusiasts. There are races, parties, and, of course, a parade.
☐ **Loveland Valentine Remailing Program,** Loveland. More than 250,000 valentines are remailed from Loveland. Feb. 14.
☐ **Estes Park Cup,** Estes Park. Annual dog weight-pull competition.

## MARCH

☐ **San Juan Quadrathlon,** Telluride. Billed as the "ultimate physical challenge," this event combines competition in running, mountain biking, and skiing.
☐ **Crane Festival,** Monte Vista. Whooping and sandhill cranes returning to the San Luis Valley for the spring are welcomed by bus tours, wildlife art exhibits, and evening lectures by naturalists. Mid-March.
☐ **Easter Sunrise Service, Garden of the Gods,** Colorado Springs. Easter Sunday.
☐ **Winter Quarters,** La Junta. Life during the mid-19th-century fur-trading era at Bent's Old Fort is reenacted for 4 days and 3 nights.

## APRIL

☐ **Flauschink,** Crested Butte. Winter is "flushed" out and spring/summer greeted with a parade of polka music and a coronation ball. 1st or 2nd weekend.

## MAY

☐ **Southern Ute Tribal Bear Dance,** Southern Ute Indian Reservation, Ignacio. This traditional spiritual and social dance celebrates the coming of spring. Memorial Day weekend.
☐ **Territory Days,** Colorado Springs. The Old Colorado City historic district hosts a carnival, games, contests, and a prestatehood gunfight.

□ **Iron Horse Bicycle Classic,** Durango. Mountain bikers race the Durango & Silverton Railroad from Durango to Silverton. Memorial Day weekend.

## JUNE

✪ *Fibark Festival  North America's longest and oldest downriver kayak race is the focus of a 4-day festival. It includes live entertainment, foot and boat races, a parade, carnival rides, arts and crafts. **Where:** Salida. **When:** Mid-June.*

□ **Telluride Bluegrass Festival,** Telluride. Country and acoustic music are also performed at this 4-day festival, founded in 1974. 3rd full weekend of June.
□ **Springspree,** Colorado Springs. Downtown merchants and restaurateurs close their doors and move outdoors for 2 days. Late June.

## JULY

□ **Independence Day.** Parades, barbecues, fireworks, and other celebrations throughout the state. July 4.

✪ *Colorado State Mining Championship  Entrants from six states compete in old-style hand steeling, hand mucking, and spike driving, and newer methods of machine drilling and machine mucking. **Where:** Creede. **When:** July 4 weekend.*

✪ *High Country Folk Life Festival  American heritage celebration. Dulcimer and fiddle-playing contests, story tellers, folk art, crafts demonstrations. **Where:** Buena Vista. **When:** Mid-July.*

□ **Ducky Derby,** Montrose. Flotilla of yellow rubber ducks races down the Uncompahgre River. 1st Saturday.
□ **Last Trial of Alferd Packer,** Lake City. Western State College students reenact the trial of Packer, Colorado's most nefarious cannibal, in the courtroom where his trial took place. July 8.
□ **Skookum Day,** Fort Collins. Blacksmiths, craftspeople, and others demonstrate traditional crafts and trades in a day of historical re-creations.

## AUGUST

□ **Boom Days,** Leadville. Parade, carnival, street fair, live entertainment, food booths, mine-drilling competition. The highlight is a 22-mile pack-burro race. 1st weekend.
□ **Little Britches Rodeo,** Delta. National competition of all youth rodeo events. 2nd full week.
□ **Rocky Mountain Wine and Food Festival,** Winter Park. Colorado's finest chefs and many of America's best-known vintners offer their creations to benefit the National Sports Center for the Disabled. 3rd weekend.

✪ *Colorado State Fair  National professional rodeo, carnival rides, food booths, industrial displays, horse shows, animal exhibits, and entertainment by top-name performers. **Where:** Pueblo. **When:** Mid-August through Labor Day.*

□ **Pikes Peak Marathon,** Manitou Springs. Runners race up and down 14,110-foot Pikes Peak via the Barr Trail. 4th weekend.
□ **Telluride Jazz Festival,** Telluride. 1st full weekend.

## SEPTEMBER

□ **West Fest,** Copper Mountain. Music, art, and culture of the traditional American West are featured. Country-and-western performer Michael Murphey

("Wildfire") is the annual headliner, supported by cowboy poets, a mountain man rendezvous, artists, and craftspeople, as well as Native American weavers and dancers. Labor Day weekend.

☐ **Steamboat Vintage Auto Race & Concours d'Elégance,** Steamboat Springs. More than 200 classic cars in a mountain course; vintage aircraft fly-in; rodeo series finals. Labor Day weekend.

☐ **Meeker Classic Championship Sheepdog Trial,** Meeker. Sheepdogs corral flocks of sheep in timed competition. Dogs from across the nation compete. Weekend after Labor Day.

☐ **Vail Fest,** Vail. An Oktoberfest-style weekend with street entertainment, yodeling contest, 5km and 10km runs, dancing, games, and sing-alongs. 2nd weekend.

☐ **Chile Cookoff and Wild West Off Roaders Rodeo & Trail Drive,** Rifle. As four-wheel-drive teams tackle the backcountry, chile chefs match recipes in town.

☐ **Colorfest,** Durango and vicinity. Dozens of events focusing on fall colors. September and October.

☐ **Southern Ute Tribal Fair & Powwow,** Ignacio. Games, exhibits, horse show, parade, dancing. 2nd full weekend.

☐ **Autumn Equinox Festival,** Springfield. During the autumnal equinox, Crack Cave, a short distance from town, takes on Stonehenge-like qualities. On this date and on the spring equinox, the sun shines directly into the cave, highlighting ancient writings. Sept. 22.

## OCTOBER

☐ **Idaho Springs Festival of the Arts,** Idaho Springs. 1st full week.

## NOVEMBER

☐ **Christmas Card Lane,** Buena Vista. Giant Christmas cards from local merchants line Highway 24 at both ends of town. Thanksgiving through New Year's Day.

## DECEMBER

☐ **Celebration of Lights,** Vail. Month-long festival of music and holiday celebrations. Former President and Mrs. Gerald Ford, Vail residents, light the town Christmas Tree. Fireworks erupt at midnight on New Year's Eve.

☐ **Royal Gorge Bridge Christmas Celebration,** Cañon City. There are hay rides across the bridge, caroling performances, free cider, thousands of lights, and free evening admission. All month.

☐ **Christmas Tree Mountain Lighting,** Salida.

☐ **Carousel and Old Town Christmas,** Burlington. All month.

☐ **Posata,** Pueblo. A processional with a living nativity.

# DENVER CALENDAR OF EVENTS

## JANUARY

✪ *National Western Stock Show and Rodeo.* *The world's largest livestock show and indoor rodeo, beginning with a parade through downtown Denver. There are 23 rodeo performances, a trade exposition, western food and crafts booths, livestock auctions, and many country-and-western entertainers.* *Where:* *Denver Coliseum/ National Western Complex.* *When:* *2nd and 3rd weeks of January.* *How:* *Tickets $6–$12; write 4701 Marion St., Denver, CO 80216 (tel. 303/297-1166).*

## MARCH

- □ **Saint Patrick's Day.** The second largest Irish holiday parade in the United States features floats, marching bands, and more than 5,000 horses. Mar. 17.
- □ **Pow Wow.** More than 700 Native American dancers and musicians, representing some 70 tribes from 22 states, gather for this annual event. Arts and crafts are sold.

### APRIL

- □ **Arbor Day Celebration and Run,** Littleton.

### MAY

- □ **Cinco de Mayo Celebration,** Santa Fe Drive. May 5.
- □ **Riverfront Festival,** Littleton. 3rd full weekend.

### JUNE

- □ **Cherry Blossom Festival,** Sakura Square. Japanese food bazaar at Buddhist Temple, performances, demonstrations, arts and crafts. 2nd weekend.

✪ *Colorado Renaissance Festival*  Sixteenth-century England outdoor fair. **Where:** Larkspur. **When:** June and July weekends and holidays.

- □ **Juneteenth.** Five Points neighborhood celebration recalls the end of slavery in Texas. Parade, gospel singing, food, and entertainment. Mid-June.

### JULY

- □ **Independence Day.** Parades, fireworks, concerts. July 4.
- □ **Colorado Indian Market.** Jewelers, painters, potters, weavers, sculptors, dancers, musicians, and others from more than 90 Native American tribes hold their market at Currigan Exhibition Hall. 2nd weekend.

### SEPTEMBER

- □ **A Taste of Colorado.** Billed as "a festival of mountain and plain," this is Denver's largest celebration, with an annual attendance of about 400,000. Local restaurants serve house specialties; there are also crafts exhibits and free concerts from top-name acts. Labor Day weekend.
- □ **Larimer Square Oktoberfest.** Three-week festival re-creates Munich's famous beerfest. Three weekends in late September and early October.

### OCTOBER

- □ **Denver International Film Festival.** 2nd through 3rd Thursday.

### DECEMBER

- □ **World's Largest Christmas Lighting Display.** The Denver City and County Building is illuminated by 20,000 red, green, blue, and yellow floodlights.

# 3. HEALTH & INSURANCE

## HEALTH

Colorado's elevation—about two-thirds of the state is more than a mile above sea level—translates to less oxygen and lower humidity. This creates a unique set of problems for short-term visitors.

Get plenty of rest, avoid large meals, and drink plenty of nonalcoholic fluids, especially water. As you climb into the mountains, be wary of acute mountain sickness, which is characterized in its early stages by headaches, shortness of breath, appetite loss and/or nausea, tingling in the fingers or toes, and lethargy and insomnia. Ordinarily, it can be treated with aspirin and a slower pace. If it persists or worsens, descend to a lower altitude.

Because the sun's rays are more direct in the thinner atmosphere, they cause sunburn more quickly. Their potential for skin damage increases when they reflect off snow. Use a good sunblock.

Any time of year, keep yourself warm and your clothing dry. Hypothermia is most threatening in winter, but is not unheard of in the middle of a cold summer night.

## INSURANCE

Before starting your trip to Colorado, peruse your medical insurance policy to be certain you're covered when away from home. If you are not, buy a traveler's policy, available at banks, travel agencies, and automobile clubs. Coverage offered by many companies is relatively inexpensive. Besides medical assistance, including hospitalization and surgery, it should include the cost of an accident or death, loss or theft of baggage, costs of trip cancellation, and guaranteed bail in the event of a lawsuit or other legal difficulties.

# 4. WHAT TO PACK

It's impossible to offer this advice too often: *Travel as light as possible.*

Except perhaps for underwear and socks, carry no more than three changes of clothing. Ideally, you shouldn't have more than one suitcase and a small bag of essentials that fits neatly under an airplane seat or in the upper rack of a train or bus.

Be sure to pack a sweater and/or a rainproof jacket. Even in summer, it can get cold at night. You'll want shorts and a swimsuit (for hotel pools or mountain lakes) in the summer, and several layers of warm clothing, including gloves and wool hat, in winter. You won't need a coat and tie or an evening dress unless you're in the state on business or plan dinner at one of the handful of very elegant restaurants in Colorado. Certainly, formal wear is rarely seen in resort communities. No matter what your plans, a good pair of walking shoes is essential.

A few other easily forgotten items that could prove priceless during your stay: (1) a travel alarm clock, so as not to be at the mercy of your hotel for wakeup calls; (2) a Swiss army knife, which has a multitude of uses, from bottle opener to screwdriver for ski bindings; (3) a magnifying glass to read the small print on maps; and (4) a small first-aid kit (containing an antibiotic ointment, bandages, aspirin, soap, a thermometer, motion-sickness pills, and required medications).

# 5. TIPS FOR THE DISABLED, SENIORS & STUDENTS

## FOR THE DISABLED

The **Information Center for Individuals with Disabilities,** Fort Point Place,

27-43 Wormwood St., Boston, MA 02210 (tel. 617/727-5540), provides travel assistance and can also recommend tour operators; and **Mobility International USA,** Box 3551, Eugene, OR 97403 (tel. 503/343-1284), charges a small annual fee and provides travel information for those with disabilities. A useful book for handicapped travelers is *Access to the World, a Travel Guide for the Handicapped,* by Louise Weiss, which can be ordered from Henry Holt & Co. (tel. toll free 800/247-3912).

**Amtrak** will, with 24 hours' notice, provide porter service, special seating, and a substantial discount (tel. toll free 800/USA-RAIL). If you're traveling with a companion, **Greyhound/Trailways** will carry you both for a single fare (tel. toll free 800/531-5332).

An organized tour package can make life on the road much easier, and two well-established firms that specialize in travel for the disabled are: **Whole Person Tours,** P.O. Box 1084, Bayonne, NJ 07002 (tel. 201/858-3400); and **Evergreen Travel Service/Wings on Wheels Tours,** 4114 198th Street, Suite 13, Lynnwood, WA 98036 (tel. 206/776-1184).

# FOR SENIORS

Nearly all major U.S. hotel and motel chains now offer a **senior citizen's discount,** and you should be sure to ask for the reduction *when you make the reservation*— there may be restrictions during peak days—then be sure to carry proof of your age (driver's license, passport, etc.) when you check in. Among those chains that offer the best discounts are **Marriott Hotels** (tel. toll free 800/228-9290) for those 62 and over and **La Quinta Inns** (tel. toll free 800/531-5900) for ages 52 and over. You can save sightseeing dollars if you are 62 or over by picking up a **Golden Age Passport** from any federally operated park, recreation area, or monument. **Elderhostel,** 80 Boylston St., Boston, MA 02116 (tel. 617/426-7788 or 617/426-8056) also provides stimulating vacations at moderate prices for those over 60, with a balanced mix of learning, field trips, and free time for sightseeing. If you fancy organized tours, **AARP Travel Service** (see below) puts together terrific packages at moderate rates, and **Saga International Holidays,** 120 Boylston St., Boston, MA 02116 (tel. toll free 800/343-0273), arranges tours for single travelers over 60.

Membership in the following senior organizations also offers a wide variety of travel benefits: The **American Association of Retired Persons (AARP),** 1909 K St. NW, Washington, DC 20049 (tel. 202/662-4850); and the **National Council of Senior Citizens,** 925 15th St. NW, Washington, DC 20005 (tel. 202/347-8800).

Major sightseeing attractions and entertainments also often offer senior discounts—*be sure to ask when you buy your ticket.*

# FOR STUDENTS

Before setting out, use your high school or college ID to obtain an International Student Identity Card from the **Council on International Educational Exchange (CIEE),** 205 E. 42nd St., New York, NY 10017 (tel. 212/661-1414) or 312 Sutter St., Rm. 407, San Francisco, CA 94108 (tel. 415/421-3473). It will entitle you to several student discounts, although not as many as in many foreign countries. For economical accommodations, as well as a great way to meet other traveling students, join **American Youth Hostels,** Box 37613, Washington, DC 20013-7613 (tel. 202/783-6161); for a small fee, they'll send a directory of all U.S. hostels. One of the leading student travel tour operators is **Contiki Holidays,** 1432 E. Katella Ave., Anaheim, CA 92805 (tel. 800/626-0611), for ages 18 through 35. **Arista Student Travel Association, Inc.,** 11 E. 44th St., New York, NY 10017 (tel. 212/687-5121 or toll free 800/356-8861), caters to ages 15 to 20. Remember, too, to *always* ask about **student discount tickets** to attractions.

# 6. GETTING THERE

## INDIVIDUAL TRAVEL

**BY PLANE**  Denver's **Stapleton International Airport**—the seventh busiest in the United States with approximately 1,200 flights each day—maintains a toll-free information line: 800/AIR-2-DEN. This line offers information on flight schedules and connections, parking, ground transportation, current weather conditions, even local accommodations.

Although Stapleton Airport has been completely closed due to bad weather only three times in 20 years, it is often subject to flight delays or cancellations. This is mainly because its runways are too close together for modern Federal Aviation Administration regulations—and it's the main reason the city of Denver is constructing a new airport.

When the $2-billion Denver International Airport opens in 1993, 18 miles east of downtown, it will be the largest airport in the world, covering 53 square miles. An underground rail system will shuttle passengers to and from 206 gates, serving 12 runways.

**Airlines**  The "official" carrier for Colorado, and the one with the greatest number of connections to and from the state, is **Continental** (tel. 800/525-0280). The airline offers more than 140 nonstops to Denver from cities across the United States. It also serves Colorado Springs and Grand Junction, and its feeder line, **Continental Express,** visits numerous other Colorado towns and resorts.

Stapleton is also served by **America West** (tel. 800/247-5692), **American** (tel. 800/433-7300), **Delta** (tel. 800/221-1212), **Trans World** (tel. 800/221-2000), **United** (tel. 800/241-6522), **USAir** (tel. 800/428-4322), and eight foreign carriers. There's nonstop service to 107 cities. Delta and TWA also fly into Colorado Springs, and TWA lands in Pueblo as well.

**Regular Fares**  The least-expensive domestic airfares to Denver are usually **Maxi-Savers,** which generally require a 14-day advance purchase and a Saturday-night stayover. Next are **Super-Savers,** calling for a 7-day advance purchase and Saturday-night stayover. **APEX** (advance purchase excursion), followed by standard **coach, business class,** and **first class,** are other categories of ticket.

A *word of warning:* It's virtually impossible to get a low-cost air ticket to Denver at certain times during the height of the winter season, when you're competing with skiers. Most often, these are flights arriving in Colorado on a Saturday and/or leaving on a Sunday. The Christmas holidays and President's Day weekend are particularly busy.

**BY TRAIN**  **Amtrak** has two routes through Colorado. The *Zephyr,* which links San Francisco and Chicago, travels each direction three times daily. It passes through Grand Junction, Glenwood Springs, Kremmling, Winter Park, Denver, Fort Morgan, Sterling, and Julesburg en route to Omaha, Neb. Inquire at Union Station, 707 17th Street, Denver, CO 80202 (tel. 303/534-2812, or 800/872-7245).

The *Southwest Chief,* which runs once daily in each direction between Los Angeles and Chicago, travels from Albuquerque, N.M., via Trinidad, La Junta, and Lamar before crossing the southeastern Colorado border into Kansas. Inquiries can be directed to Amtrak, First Street and Colorado Avenue, La Junta, CO 81050 (tel. 719/384-2275).

You can get a copy of Amtrak's National Timetable from any Amtrak station, from travel agents, or by contacting Amtrak, 400 North Capitol Street NW, Washington, DC 20001 (tel. 800/USA-RAIL).

**BY BUS**  **Greyhound/Trailways** (tel. 303/292-6111) has an extensive network that reaches nearly every corner of the state, with daily connections nearly everywhere. **TNM&O Coaches** (Texas, New Mexico & Oklahoma Coaches; tel. 806/763-5389) covers much of the southern part of the state, including some communities that Greyhound does not visit.

**BY CAR** Some 1,000 miles of Interstate highways form a star on the map of Colorado, with its centerpoint at Denver. **I-25** crosses the state from south to north, extending from New Mexico to Wyoming; over its 300 miles, it transits nearly every major city of the Front Range, including Pueblo, Colorado Springs, and Fort Collins. **I-70** crosses from west to east, extending from Utah to Kansas, a distance of about 450 miles; it enters Colorado near Grand Junction, passes through Glenwood Springs, Vail, and Denver, and exits just east of Burlington. **I-76** is an additional 190-mile spur that begins in Denver and extends northeast to Nebraska, joining **I-80** just beyond Julesburg.

Visitors entering Colorado from the southwest may take **U.S. 160** (from Flagstaff, Ariz.) or **U.S. 550** (from Farmington, N.M.). Both routes enter the state near Durango.

The approximate mileage to Denver from various cities around the United States and Canada are shown in the accompanying table.

## PACKAGE TOURS

Among the operators offering tours to and within Colorado are the following:

**Around & About Tours & Events,** 9678-B East Arapahoe Road, Suite 121, Englewood, CO 80112 (tel. 303/694-6133). This destination-management company offers guide and personalized tour services.

**Colorado Tours,** P.O. Box 38214, Denver, CO 80238 (tel. 303/377-2587), offers a variety of services from hunting and fishing expeditions to luxury limousine tours.

**Destination Colorado,** 4100 East Mississippi Avenue, Suite 200, Denver, CO 80222 (tel. 303/757-5459, or 800/726-2929). Customized tours.

**Discover Colorado Tours,** 2401 East Street, Suite 204, Golden, CO 80401 (tel. 303/277-0129). Personalized individual and group scenic tours.

**National Reservations Network,** 11072 North Colo. 9 (P.O. Box 3670), Breckenridge, CO 80424 (tel. 303/453-9237, or 800/525-8583). Specializes in summer and winter resort vacations.

**Organizers Etc.,** 7373 South Alton Way, Suite B-100, Englewood, CO 80112 (tel. 303/771-1178, or 800/283-2754). Sports and recreation packages for individuals and groups.

# 7. GETTING AROUND

**BY PLANE** The leading in-state commuter network is **Continental Express** (tel. 800/525-0280), which connects Denver with Aspen, Durango, Gunnison, Montrose, Steamboat Springs, and Telluride. **United Express** (tel. 800/241-6522) and **Mesa Airlines** (tel. 800/637-2247) also fly to numerous smaller towns around Colorado.

**BY TRAIN** Amtrak's *Zephyr* is a convenient way to cross the state. It runs east to west (Julesburg–Denver–Grand Junction) and west to east three times daily in each direction. This route avoids the I-90 corridor between Glenwood Springs and Denver, and thus fails to serve such resorts as Vail and Breckenridge. It does, however, make a stop in Winter Park, making that the only ski resort in Colorado with direct rail service. For information, check at Union Station, 707 17th Street, Denver, CO 80202 (tel. 303/534-2812, or 800/872-7245). On winter weekends, the *Rio Grande Ski Train* plies the same route from Denver. Inquire at 555 17th Street, Denver, CO 80202 (tel. 303/296-4754).

Numerous scenic railroads, including a handful of narrow-gauge operations, are found throughout the state. Information on all can be obtained from **Colorado Scenic Rails Association,** 17155 West 44th Avenue (P.O. Box 641), Golden, CO 80402 (tel. 800/866-3690). They include the Leadville Colorado and Southern Railroad, the Limon Twilight Limited, and the Wyoming and Colorado Scenic Railroad; five narrow-gauge railroads (the Black Hawk and Central City, the Cripple Creek/Victor, the Cumbres & Toltec, the Durango-Silverton, and the Georgetown

# COLORADO DRIVING TIMES & DISTANCES

N

North Platte

Ogallala — 53 / 1:00

Colby — 23 / :30 — Oakley

Oakley — 81 / 1:31 — Garden City

Garden City — 66 / 1:16 — Liberal

Liberal — 39 / :47 — Guymon

Guymon — 126 / 1:36 — Dalhart

Bridgeport — 90 / 1:38 — Ogallala

Bridgeport — 72 / 1:22

Sterling — 88 / 1:39

Bridgeport — 40 / 1:00 — Sidney

Sidney — 43 / 1:00

Sterling — 48 / :55 — Fort Morgan

NEB. / COLO.

Colby — 111 / 2:08 — Kit Carson

Kit Carson — 99 / 1:54 — Lamar

KAN. / COLO.

Colby — 144 / 2:37 — Limon

Kit Carson — 56 / 1:05 — Lamar

Kit Carson — 62 / 1:12 — Limon

Lamar — 55 / 1:05 — La Junta

Lamar — 128 / 2:37 — Raton

Sidney — 100 / 1:51 — Cheyenne

Fort Morgan — 52 / :59 — Greeley

Fort Morgan — 71 / 1:23 — Denver

Limon — 88 / 1:42 — Denver

Limon — 74 / 1:29 — Colorado Springs

La Junta — 64 / 1:16 — Pueblo

La Junta — 74 / 1:21 — Walsenburg

La Junta — 102 / 1:59 — Raton

Raton — 61 / 1:12

Raton — 86 / 2:00 — Taos

Cheyenne — 52 / 1:05 — Greeley

Greeley — 54 / 1:10 — Denver

Greeley — 52 / 1:01 — Loveland

Denver — 68 / 1:20 — Colorado Springs

Colorado Springs — 42 / :49 — Pueblo

Pueblo — 48 / :58 — Walsenburg

Walsenburg — 61

Raton — 134 / 2:43

Cheyenne — 49 / :55 — Laramie

Cheyenne — 58 — Loveland

Loveland — 52 — Denver

Denver — 94 / 1:50 — Granby

Denver — 105 / 2:05 — Poncha Springs

Denver — 100 / 2:07 — Poncha Springs

Denver — 136 / 3:00 — Poncha Springs

Pueblo — 100 / 2:07 — Poncha Springs

Walsenburg — 73 / 1:31 — Alamosa

Walsenburg — 126

Taos — 105 / 2:30 — Alamosa

Laramie — 80 / 1:45 — Cheyenne

Laramie — 98 / 1:49 — Rawlins

Granby — 110 / 2:07 — Dowd

Granby — 121 / 3:00 — Craig

Poncha Springs — 77 / 1:38 — Alamosa

Rawlins — 118 / 2:30 — Craig

Rawlins — 111 / 2:03 — Rock Springs

Craig — 118 / 3:10 — Glenwood Springs

Craig — 155 / 3:15 — Grand Junction

Craig — 56 / 1:05 — Dowd

Dowd — 129 / 3:45 — Glenwood Springs

Glenwood Springs — 92 / 2:00 — Grand Junction

Poncha Springs — 126 / 3:52 — Montrose

Poncha Springs — 186 — Grand Junction

Poncha Springs — 150 / 3:04 — Durango

Alamosa — 150 / 3:04 — Durango

Rock Springs — 37 / :44 — Little America

Little America — 140 / 3:05 — Vernal

Vernal — 121 / 2:35 — Craig

Grand Junction — 60 / 1:15 — Montrose

Montrose — 108 / 2:24 — Durango

Montrose — 214 / 5:10 — Cortez

Durango — 46 / :57 — Cortez

Durango — 78 / 2:00 — Shiprock

Cortez — 42 / :51 — Shiprock

Grand Junction — 85 / 1:42 — Crescent Jct.

Cortez — 59 / 1:09 — Monticello

UTAH / COLO.

Monticello — 85 / 1:40 — Crescent Jct.

Monticello — 119 / 2:20 — Kayenta

Cortez — 99 / 1:58 — Chinle

Chinle — 119 / 2:35 — Shiprock

ARIZ.

UTAH / ARIZ.

Kayenta

LEGEND:
Lightface numbers indicate driving times
Boldface numbers indicate distances in miles
In this schematic we assume 68 miles will take an
average of 1 hours 20 minutes (excluding stops) driving
time

Loop); and two more specifically serving tourists, the Manitou and Pikes Peak Cog Railway and the Royal Gorge Scenic Railway.

**BY BUS**   Every sizable town in the state is accessible by either **Greyhound/ Trailways** (tel. 303/292-6111) or **TNM&O Coaches** (Texas, New Mexico & Oklahoma Coaches; tel. 806/763-5389).

**BY CAR**   Visitors who plan to drive their own car to and around Colorado should give their vehicle a thorough **road check** before starting out. The high elevation and mutable weather conditions can create special problems for an engine, and it can be life-threatening to be stranded in the heat or cold with a vehicle that does not run. Check your lights, windshield wipers, horn, tires, battery, drive belts, fluid levels, alignment, and other possible trouble spots.

Make sure your driver's license, vehicle registration, safety-inspection sticker, and auto-club membership (if you have one) are valid. Check with your auto insurance agency to make sure you're covered when out of state, and/or when driving a rental car. *You must carry proof of insurance.*

Unless otherwise posted, the **speed limit** on open roads is 65 m.p.h. (105kmph). Minimum age for drivers is 16. Safety belts are required for drivers and all front-seat passengers age 4 and over; children under 4 must use approved child seats.

Colorado law allows drivers to make a right turn at a red signal, after coming to a complete stop, unless posted otherwise.

**Gas** is readily available at service stations throughout the state. All prices are subject to the same fluctuations as elsewhere in the United States. Anticipate higher prices in mountain resort communities.

An **official state highway map** is distributed by the Colorado Tourism Board. Otherwise, you can get one from almost any oil company or (if you're a member) from the American Automobile Association (AAA).

You can get **information on road conditions** from the Colorado State Patrol. For the Rockies and west slope, call 303/639-1111; for the I-25 corridor and eastern plains, call 303/639-1234.

**Winter Road Closings**   Two notable Colorado highways are closed in winter. U.S. 34, the Trail Ridge Road through Rocky Mountain National Park, is the highest continuous highway in the world, crossing the Continental Divide at 12,183 feet. Colorado 82, over Independence Pass (elevation 12,095 feet) east of Aspen, is the main route between Denver and Aspen in the summer months. In addition, the Mount Evans Road (Colo. 103 and Colo. 5) from Idaho Springs (35 miles west of Denver) to the 14,264-foot summit of Mount Evans is the highest paved road in North America; it's open June to September only. The world's highest tunnel at 11,000 feet, the Eisenhower Tunnel, carries I-70 beneath Loveland Pass year round.

Snow tires or chains are often required when roads are snow-covered or icy, or during winter storms. Motorists planning travel over unimproved high-elevation roads at any time of year should inquire locally about conditions before attempting them.

**Information**   For additional information on driving in Colorado, contact the **Colorado State Patrol,** 700 Kipling Street, Lakewood, CO 80215 (tel. 303/239-4500); or the **Colorado Department of Highways,** 4201 East Arkansas Avenue, Denver, CO 80222 (tel. 303/757-9011). If you're planning to use a four-wheel-drive or off-road vehicle, you can communicate with the **Colorado Association of Four-Wheel Drive Clubs,** P.O. Box 1413, Wheat Ridge, CO 80034 (tel. 303/321-1266).

**Road Emergencies**   In case of an accident or road emergency, contact the State Patrol. **American Automobile Association** members can get free emergency road service wherever they are, 24 hours, by calling AAA's emergency number (tel. 800/336-4357). In Colorado, AAA headquarters is at 4100 East Arkansas Avenue, Denver, CO 80222 (tel. 303/753-8800, or 800/283-5222).

**Rental Cars**   Car rentals are available in every sizable town and city in the state, always at the local airport, and usually also downtown. Widely represented agencies include **Alamo** (tel. 800/327-9633), **Avis** (tel. 800/331-1212), **Budget** (tel. 800/527-0700), **Dollar** (tel. 800/228-9987), **General** (tel. 800/327-7607), **Hertz**

(tel. 800/654-3131), **National** (tel. 800/227-7368), and **Thrifty** (tel. 800/FOR-CARS).

**Major East-West Highways** Besides **I-70** and **I-76**, major east-west highways are **Colo. 14**, linking Fort Collins with both Steamboat Springs and Sterling; **U.S. 40**, connecting Denver with Salt Lake City, Utah, via Steamboat Springs; **Colo. 82**, between Glenwood Springs, Aspen, and Independence Pass; **U.S. 24**, starting in the Vail Valley and proceeding through Leadville and Buena Vista to Colorado Springs and east; **U.S. 50**, which leads from Grand Junction via Montrose, Gunnison, Salida, Canon City, Pueblo, and La Junta toward Wichita, Kans.; and **U.S. 160**, extending from Arizona through Durango and Alamosa to Walsenburg.

**Major North-South Highways** In addition to **I-25**, principal north-south highways are **U.S. 550**, which branches off from U.S. 50 in Montrose and transits Durango en route to Farmington, N.M.; **U.S. 285**, connecting Denver with Santa Fe, N.M., via Buena Vista, Salida, and Alamosa; **Colo. 9**, a straight shot from Breckenridge and Summit County to Cañon City; **Colo. 71**, which spans the eastern plains from Scottsbluff, Neb., via Brush and Limon to Rocky Ford; and **U.S. 385**, which follows Colorado's eastern border from Julesburg through Burlington and Lamar all the way to Odessa, Texas.

**BY BICYCLE** Bicycling is popular everywhere. You'll see many long-distance travelers, both on touring and mountain bikes. Maps and information on bike routes are available from the Colorado Department of Highways.

## SUGGESTED ITINERARIES

### IF YOU HAVE 1 WEEK

**Day 1:** Arrive in Denver, preferably late morning or early afternoon. Browse Larimer Square and the 16th Street Mall.

**Day 2:** In the morning, visit the Denver Art Museum, the Colorado History Museum, the U.S. Mint, and/or the State Capitol. After lunch, take the short drive to the university town of Boulder.

**Day 3:** Follow U.S. 36 to Estes Park, eastern gateway to Rocky Mountain National Park. From there, the spectacular Trail Ridge Road slips over the Continental Divide to Grand Lake, where you can camp or sleep under a more solid roof.

**Day 4:** Take U.S. 40 through the Winter Park resort community and over Berthoud Pass to Georgetown, one of the best preserved of Victorian mining towns. I-70 goes through the Eisenhower Tunnel to Frisco, where you can turn on Colo. 9 to charming Breckenridge.

**Day 5:** Colorado 9 runs southeast 100 miles in a near-straight line to Cañon City; see the magnificent Royal Gorge and the re-created western film town of Buckskin Joe. Proceed northeast to Colorado Springs for the evening.

**Day 6:** Spend a full day in Colorado Springs. Choose between the Pikes Peak Cog Railway, the U.S. Olympic Training Center, the Garden of the Gods, and other sights.

**Day 7:** Stop and visit the U.S. Air Force Academy on your way back to Denver, where your flight home awaits.

### IF YOU HAVE 2 WEEKS

**Days 1 and 2:** Same as above.

**Day 3:** Take Canyon Boulevard (Colo. 119) west to Nederland, then follow the foothills north on Colo. 72 and Colo. 7 to Estes Park. Camp out or stay in cabins on the wilderness fringe.

**Day 4:** In the morning, enjoy spectacular Trail Ridge Road through Rocky Mountain National Park, across the Continental Divide to Grand Lake. After lunch, proceed south on U.S. 40 to Winter Park, Berthoud Pass, and Georgetown, one of the best-preserved Victorian mining towns.

**Day 5:** I-70 and Colo. 91 will take you uphill to Leadville, Colorado's 2-mile-high city. See the historic district and National Mining Hall of Fame, then continue across Independence Pass to the famed resort town of Aspen.

**Day 6:** Give yourself a day in Aspen, to shop, sightsee, hike, bike, or just enjoy the clean mountain air.

**Day 7:** Drive to Montrose. The route follows the Roaring Fork River west to Carbondale, turns south along Colo. 133 through the quaint historic village of Redstone, and transits Delta with its Fort Uncompahgre. Try to complete the 140-mile drive by midafternoon, leaving yourself a few hours to visit Black Canyon of the Gunnison National Monument.

**Day 8:** It's 98 miles via the "Million Dollar Highway," U.S. 550, to Durango. En route, between the memorable old mining towns of Ouray and Silverton, you'll cross Red Mountain Pass through the San Juan Mountains. Durango's historic district is one of Colorado's largest and best preserved.

**Day 9:** Visit the Anasazi cliff dwellings of Mesa Verde National Park, about 40 miles west of Durango.

**Day 10:** Get an early start for the 150-mile drive across Wolf Creek Pass on U.S. 160 to Alamosa. Spend part of the afternoon at eerie Great Sand Dunes National Monument, 30 miles northeast of Alamosa.

**Day 11:** Head north to the rafting capital of Salida, then east on U.S. 50 to Cañon City. See the Royal Gorge, the re-created Old West town of Buckskin Joe, and other sights.

**Days 12 and 13:** Two full days in Colorado Springs (see Day 6 in "If You Have 1 Week," above). A worthwhile side trip is to Cripple Creek, a wonderful 19th-century hillside mining town and venue of legalized gambling.

**Day 14:** See Day 7 in "If You Have 1 Week," above.

# IF YOU HAVE 3 WEEKS

**Day 1:** Arrive in Denver, preferably late morning or early afternoon. Browse Larimer Square and the 16th Street Mall.

**Day 2:** Explore the State Capitol, U.S. Mint, Denver Art Museum, and numerous other museums, and City Park.

**Day 3:** Enjoy a leisurely day in Boulder. Stroll the Pearl Street Mall and University of Colorado campus, or visit the Celestial Seasonings tea factory for a guided tour!

**Day 4:** Take Canyon Boulevard (Colo. 119) west to Nederland, then follow the foothills north on Colo. 72 and Colo. 7 to Estes Park. Camp out or stay in cabins on the wilderness fringe.

**Day 5:** Spend the day in Rocky Mountain National Park. Dawdle across the Continental Divide on the Trail Ridge Road, and enjoy the sunset on Grand Lake.

**Day 6:** Take U.S. 40 south through the Winter Park resort community, over Berthoud Pass, to Georgetown, one of Colorado's best-preserved Victorian mining towns.

**Day 7:** Follow I-70 to Frisco, seat of Summit County, and detour on a 10-mile spur to Breckenridge. After lunch, return to I-70 and proceed west to Vail, considered America's most popular ski resort (and a booming summer resort as well).

**Day 8:** Take U.S. 24 south to Leadville, the state's highest city at over 10,000 feet elevation. See the historic district and National Mining Hall of Fame, then continue across Independence Pass to Aspen.

**Day 9:** Shop, sightsee, hike, bike, or just enjoy Aspen's clean mountain air.

**Day 10:** Drive to Montrose via Carbondale, the historic village of Redstone, Paonia, and Delta. Leave a few afternoon hours to visit Black Canyon of the Gunnison National Monument.

**Day 11:** The "Million Dollar Highway," U.S. 550 to Durango, passes through the picturesque historic mining towns of Ouray and Silverton and across Red Mountain Pass, an alpine locale worthy of Switzerland. You'll be in Durango 3 nights.

**Day 12:** Durango's historic district is one of Colorado's largest and best preserved, and its Durango & Silverton Narrow Gauge Railroad plies a magnificent route.

**Day 13:** This is a day of archeological discovery. Spend most of it at Mesa Verde

National Park, some 40 miles west, or at Ute Mountain Park, south of Cortez. Hovenweep National Monument and other sites are in the Cortez area.

**Day 14:** It's 150 miles on U.S. 160 via Wolf Creek Pass to Alamosa. Spend the afternoon at seemingly misplaced Great Sand Dunes National Monument, 30 miles northeast of Alamosa.

**Day 15:** Continue east again on U.S. 160 to Walsenburg, then pick up Colo. 10 to La Junta. After lunch, visit Bent's Old Fort National Historic Site, the reconstructed hub of a trading empire in the 1830s and 1840s. Proceed to Pueblo for dinner.

**Day 16:** Browse Pueblo in the morning, including the Rosemount Victorian House Museum and the Greenway Raptor Center. Then take U.S. 50 west to Cañon City, the Royal Gorge, and the western theme village of Buckskin Joe.

**Day 17:** Weather and road conditions permitting, take the graded gravel Florence–Victor road north to Cripple Creek, a noted 19th-century hillside mining town and venue of legalized gambling. Then continue on Colo. 67 and U.S. 24 north and east to Colorado Springs for the next 3 nights.

**Days 18 and 19:** There's plenty to fill 2 days in Colorado Springs: the Manitou and Pikes Peak Cog Railway, U.S. Air Force Academy, U.S. Olympic Training Center, Garden of the Gods rock formations, Cave of the Winds, museums, historic sites, and much more.

**Day 20:** Return to Denver for 1 last day. Complete your souvenir hunting at the Cherry Creek Shopping Center, or get out of town to historic Central City, the Coors Brewery at Golden, or Red Rocks Amphitheatre at Evergreen.

**Day 21:** Have a great flight home!

 **COLORADO**

**American Express** American Express Travel Agency, 555 17th Street, Anaconda Tower, Denver (tel. 303/298-7100), offers full member services and currency exchange. Open Monday through Friday from 8:30am to 5pm. To report a lost card, call 800/528-4800. To report lost traveler's checks, call 800/221-7282.

**Banks** Banks are typically open Monday through Thursday from 10am to 3pm and on Friday from 10am to 6pm. Drive-up windows may be open later. Some may also be open on Saturday morning. Most branches have cash machines available 24 hours (call 800/THE-PLUS for the location nearest you). Colorado National Bank is the state's oldest, and has branches seemingly everywhere.

**Business Hours** In general, Monday through Friday from 9am to 5pm. Many stores are also open on Friday night and Saturday; those in major shopping malls have Sunday-afternoon hours as well.

**Camera/Film** Film of all kinds is widely available at camera stores throughout the state, and simple repairs can be handled in the major cities.

**Drugstores** You'll find 24-hour prescription services available at selected **Walgreens** Drug Stores around the state. Prices at **Thrifty** and **Wal-Mart** outlets might be somewhat less. If you're having trouble getting a prescription filled, call the nearest hospital pharmacy.

**Electricity** As throughout the U.S., 110–115 volts, 60 cycles. AC.

**Emergencies** Throughout Colorado, the number to dial for police, fire, or medical emergencies is **911** or **0** for an operator.

**Language** You may hear a smattering of Spanish in the southern part of the state, but English is by far the dominant language spoken.

**Liquor Laws** The legal drinking age is 21. Except for 3.2% beer, sold in supermarkets and convenience stores Monday through Saturday from 5am to midnight, alcoholic beverages must be purchased in liquor stores. These are open Monday through Saturday from 8am to midnight. Beverages may be served in licensed restaurants, lounges, and bars Monday through Saturday from 7am to 2am and on Sunday and Christmas Day from 8am to 8pm.

**Mail** It takes 2 to 3 days for mail from major Colorado cities to reach other major American cities. Figure an extra day or two to/from smaller communities.

Domestic postage for letters is 29¢ for the first ounce, 23¢ per additional ounce, and 19¢ for a postcard. Postage to most foreign countries is 50¢ per half ounce (it's 40¢ per ounce to Canada, 35¢ per ounce to Mexico). Buy stamps and send parcels from post offices in any city, town, or village. Major-city post offices are open Monday through Friday from 8am to 4pm and on Saturday from 9am to noon; smaller communities often have limited hours.

You can have mail sent to you in any city or town in Colorado. Have it addressed to you, c/o General Delivery, Main Post Office, Name of City and ZIP Code. The post office will hold it for 1 month. You must pick it up in person and show identification (a passport or valid picture driver's license will suffice).

**Maps**   The official state highway map is published by the state Department of Highways and distributed by the Colorado Tourism Board. Many local visitors bureaus and chambers of commerce publish maps of their cities or regions. The American Automobile Association (AAA) supplies detailed state and city maps free to members.

**Newspapers/Magazines**   The state's two largest daily newspapers, both published in Denver, are the morning *Denver Post* and the afternoon *Rocky Mountain News*. Other cities and large towns, especially regional hubs, have daily newspapers, and many smaller towns publish weeklies. National newspapers like *USA Today* and the *Wall Street Journal* can be purchased in cities and major hotels.

**Pets**   Dogs, cats, and other small pets are accepted at many motels around the state, though not as universally in the larger cities. Some properties require owners to pay a damage deposit in advance.

**Police**   In emergency, dial 911. Police departments also have nonemergency lines; in Denver, for instance, call 303/575-3127.

**Radio/TV**   There are well over 100 AM and FM radio stations in Colorado, so if you have a car radio or other receiver, you'll never be far from the rest of the world. Denver has 10 television stations, including ABC, CBS, NBC, and PBS affiliates; Colorado Springs has five more; and other cities have their own stations. Cable or satellite service is available at most hotels.

**Safety**   Whenever you're traveling in an unfamiliar city or region, stay alert. Be aware of your immediate surroundings, and keep a close eye on your possessions. Be especially careful with cameras, purses, and wallets, all favorite targets of thieves and pickpockets. Some travelers feel safest wearing a moneybelt.

**Taxes**   Colorado state **sales tax** is 3.7%. Each county tacks an additional local tax on top of that. In Denver's Arapahoe County, for instance, it's 3.5% (a total of 7.2%); in Colorado Springs, 2.8% (total 6.5%); in Boulder, 2.53% (total 6.23%). Each county also charges a local **hotel tax** to support the tourism infrastructure and other industries.

**Telephone/Fax**   Colorado uses two telephone area codes. In most of the state, including Denver, the area code is 303. But the south-central and southeastern parts of the state—south and east from Leadville, including Colorado Springs—use area code 719.

Local calls are normally 25¢. Facsimiles can be transmitted by most major hotels at a nominal cost to guests.

**Time**   Colorado is on mountain standard time (7 hours behind Greenwich mean time), 1 hour ahead of the West Coast and 2 hours behind the East Coast. Daylight saving time is in effect from April to October.

**Tipping**   A tip of 50¢ per bag is appropriate for hotel valets and airport porters. If you're staying longer than a night or two in a hotel or motel, tip about $1 per night for maid service. Restaurant servers should get 15% to 20% of your bill for service.

**Water**   You *can* drink the water everywhere, but be cautious about lakes and streams when you're enjoying the great outdoors. The diarrhea-causing *giardia* parasite, primarily spread by livestock, has invaded many previously pristine bodies of water.

# CHAPTER 3

# FOR FOREIGN VISITORS

1. **PREPARING FOR YOUR TRIP**
2. **GETTING TO & AROUND THE U.S.**
- **FAST FACTS: FOR THE FOREIGN TRAVELER**

**A**ll overseas visitors to the state of Colorado must first satisfy the entrance requirements for a visit to the United States. This chapter is designed to make your trip planning as uncomplicated as possible.

## 1. PREPARING FOR YOUR TRIP

### NECESSARY DOCUMENTS

Most foreigners entering the United States must carry two documents: (1) a valid **passport,** expiring not less than 6 months prior to the scheduled end of their visit to the U.S.; and (2) a **tourist visa,** which can be obtained without charge at any American consulate. Exceptions are Canadian nationals, who must merely carry proof of residence, and British and Japanese nationals, who require a passport but no visa.

To obtain a visa, complete the visa application and submit a passport photo. Visa application forms are available from U.S. embassies and consulates as well as from airline offices and leading travel agencies. At most consulates it's an overnight process, though it can take longer during the busy summer period of June, July, and August. Those who apply by mail should enclose a large, self-addressed, stamped envelope, and expect a response in about 2 weeks.

In theory, a tourist visa (Visa B) is valid for single or multiple entries for a period of 1 year. In practice, the consulate that issues the visa uses its own discretion in granting length of stay. Applicants in good standing, who can supply the address of a relative, friend, or business acquaintance in the United States, are most likely to be granted longer stays. (American resident contacts are also useful in passing through Customs quickly.)

### MEDICAL REQUIREMENTS

New arrivals in the United States do not need any inoculations unless they are coming from, or have stopped over in, an area known to be suffering from an epidemic, especially cholera or yellow fever.

Anyone applying for an immigrant's visa must undergo a screening test for the AIDS-associated HIV virus, under a law passed in 1987. This test does not apply to tourists.

Any visitor with a medical condition that requires treatment with narcotics or other drugs, or with paraphernalia such as syringes, must carry a valid, signed prescription from a physician. This allays suspicions of drug smuggling by Customs and other officials.

### TRAVEL INSURANCE

Insurance for tourists is optional in the United States. Medical care is very costly, however, and every traveler is strongly advised to secure full insurance coverage before starting a trip.

For a relatively low premium, numerous specialized insurance companies will cover (1) loss or theft of baggage, (2) costs of trip cancellation, (3) guaranteed bail in the event of a lawsuit or other legal difficulties, (4) the cost of medical assistance (including surgery and hospitalization) in the event of sickness or injury, and (5) the cost of an accident, death, or repatriation. Travel agencies, automobile clubs, and banks are among those selling travel insurance packages at attractive rates.

# 2. GETTING TO & AROUND THE U.S.

**By Plane**   Nearly all major airlines, including those of the United States, Europe, Asia, Australia, and New Zealand, offer **APEX** (advance purchase excursion) fares that significantly reduce the cost of transoceanic air travel. This enables travelers to pick their dates and ports, but requires that they prepurchase their ticket, and meet minimum- and maximum-stay requirements—often 15 to 90 days. Season of travel and individual airline discounts also affect fares, but this is the most widely acknowledged means of cheap, flexible travel.

Some large airlines, including Delta, Eastern, Northwest, TWA, and United, have in the past offered foreign travelers special add-on discount fares under the name **Visit USA.** Though not currently available, they may be repeated in the future, and are worth asking a travel agent about. These tickets (which could be purchased overseas only) allowed unlimited travel between U.S. destinations at minimum rates for specified time periods, such as 21, 30, or 60 days. Short of bus or train travel, which can be inconvenient and time-consuming, this was the best way of traveling around the country at low cost.

**By Train**   Amtrak, the American rail system, offers a **USA Railpass** to non–U.S. citizens. Available only overseas, it allows unlimited stopovers during a 45-day period of validity. Fares vary according to the size of the region being traveled.

**By Bus**   Foreign students can obtain the **International Ameripass** for unlimited bus travel on Greyhound/Trailways throughout the U.S. and Canada. Available for 7 to 30 days, it can be purchased with a student ID and a passport in New York, Orlando, Miami, San Francisco, and Los Angeles.

**By Car**   Foreign visitors who plan to rent a car can visit an American Automobile Association (AAA) office to obtain a "touring permit," which validates a foreign driver's licenses.

For detailed information on travel by car, train, and bus, see "Getting Around" in Chapter 2.

 **FOR THE FOREIGN TRAVELER**

**Currency & Exchange**   In the American monetary system, 100 cents (¢) equal 1 dollar ($1).

Foreign visitors accustomed to paper money of varied colors and sizes should look carefully at the U.S. "greenbacks"—all **bills** are green, and all are the same size regardless of value. Aside from the numbers, Americans often differentiate them by the portrait they bear: The $1 bill ("a buck") depicts George Washington; the seldom-seen $2, Thomas Jefferson; the $5, Abraham Lincoln; the $10, Alexander Hamilton; the $20, Andrew Jackson. Larger bills, including the $50 (Ulysses S. Grant) and the $100 (William McKinley), are not welcome in payment for small purchases.

There are six **coins,** four of them widely used: 1 cent ("penny," of brown copper), 5 cents ("nickel"), 10 cents ("dime"), and 25 cents ("quarter"). The 50-cent piece ("half dollar") is less widely circulated and $1 coins—including the older, large silver dollar and the newer, small Susan B. Anthony coin—are rare.

If they're *in U.S. dollars,* **traveler's checks** are easily cashed in payment for goods or services at most hotels, motels, restaurants, and large stores. If they're *in a foreign currency,* the best exchange rates are offered by major banks. However, the best course of action is not to bring any foreign currency; the foreign-exchange bureaus common in other countries are largely absent from U.S. cities.

The most widely used method of payment by travelers in the United States is **credit cards.** In Colorado, VISA (BarclayCard in Britain, Chargex in Canada) and MasterCard (EuroCard in Europe, Access in Britain, Diamond in Japan) are accepted almost everywhere. American Express is taken by most establishments; Diners Club and Carte Blanche, by a large number; Discover, by an increasing number. EnRoute and JCB, the Japanese Credit Bank card, are beginning to come into favor as well.

Use of this "plastic money" reduces the necessity to carry large sums of cash or traveler's checks. Credit cards are accepted almost everywhere, except in food stores. Credit cards can be used for a deposit on a car rental, as proof of identity (often preferred to a passport) when cashing a check, or as a "cash card" for withdrawing money from banks that accept them.

**Customs & Immigration**  U.S. Customs allows each adult visitor to import the following, duty free: (1) 1 liter of wine or hard liquor; (2) 1,000 cigarettes or 100 cigars (*not* from Cuba) or 3 pounds of smoking tobacco; and (3) $400 worth of gifts. The only restrictions are that the visitor must spend at least 72 hours in the U.S., and must not have claimed the exemption on imported goods within the preceding 6 months. Importing food and plants is forbidden.

Foreign visitors may import or export up to $5,000 in U.S. or foreign currency, with no formalities. Larger amounts of money must be declared to Customs.

Visitors arriving by air, no matter what the port of entry, are well advised to be exceedingly patient and to resign themselves to a wait in the Customs and Immigration line. At busy times, especially when several overseas flights arrive within a few minutes of each other, it can take 2 or 3 hours just to get a passport stamped for arrival. Allow *plenty* of time for connections between international and domestic flights!

Border formalities by road or rail from Canada are relatively quick and easy.

**Embassies & Consulates**  Embassies in the U.S. for English-speaking foreign visitors include the **Australian Embassy,** 1601 Massachusetts Avenue NW, Washington, DC 20036 (tel. 202/797-3000); **Canadian Embassy,** 1746 Massachusetts Avenue NW, Washington, DC 20036 (tel. 202/785-1400); **Irish Embassy,** 2234 Massachusetts Avenue NW, Washington, DC 20008 (tel. 202/462-3939); **New Zealand Embassy,** 37 Observatory Circle NW, Washington, DC 20008 (tel. 202/328-4800); **U.K. Embassy,** 3100 Massachusetts Avenue NW, Washington, DC 20008 (tel. 202/462-1340). None of these countries has a consulate in Denver.

**Emergencies**  A single emergency telephone number, **911,** will put you in touch with police, ambulance, or fire department throughout most of Colorado. You can also obtain emergency assistance by dialing 0 (zero) for an operator.

**Legal Aid**  Those accused of serious offenses are advised to say and do nothing before consulting an attorney. Under U.S. law, an arrested person is permitted one telephone call to a party of his or her choice: Call your embassy! If you are pulled up for a minor infraction, such as a traffic offense, never attempt to pay the fine directly to a police officer. You may wind up arrested on the much more serious charge of attempted bribery. Pay fines by mail, or directly into the hands of the clerk of a court.

**Newspapers & Magazines**  Foreign publications may be hard to find in Colorado, with the exception of a rare few newsstands in Denver and Boulder. Your best bet for staying abreast of foreign news is to pick up a copy of the *New York Times* or an American weekly newsmagazine.

**Radio & Television**  See "Fast Facts: Colorado" in Chapter 2. Audiovisual media, with three coast-to-coast networks—ABC, CBS, and NBC—joined in recent years by the Public Broadcasting System (PBS) and the Cable News Network (CNN), play a major part in American life. Most accommodations in Colorado include a TV.

**Safety**  See "Fast Facts: Colorado" in Chapter 2.

**Taxes**  In the U.S., there is no VAT (Value-Added Tax) or other indirect tax at a national level. Colorado levies a 3.7% state tax on gross receipts, including hotel checks and shop purchases. Food is exempt. In addition, each city or county levies an additional lodging tax, usually 3% to 4%, to support the local tax base.

**Telephone & Fax**   Public telephone booths are easily found in cities like Denver and Colorado Springs, but may be more difficult to find in smaller towns. Stores and gas stations are your best bets. Hotels often add a per-call surcharge of up to 75¢ to your room bill, even though the standard charge for local calls is but 25¢.

Colorado has two **area codes:** 303 for Denver and the northern and western parts of the state; 719 for Colorado Springs and the south-central and southeastern regions.

For direct **overseas calls,** dial 011, followed by the country code (Australia, 61; Ireland, 353; New Zealand, 64; United Kingdom, 44; etc.), then the city code and the number of the person you are calling. For Canada and **long-distance** calls within the U.S., dial 1 followed by the area code and the number you want. For reversed-charge or collect calls, and for person-to-person calls, dial 0 (zero) instead of 1, then follow the same procedure as above, and an operator will come on the line. For long-distance directory assistance, dial 1, the area code you need, then 555-1212.

**Fax** service (for instant facsimile transmission) can be provided by major hotels at a nominal charge, or by business service centers in most towns and cities.

**Time**   The U.S. is divided into six time zones. From east to west, they are: eastern standard time (EST, 5 hours behind Greenwich mean time), central standard time (CST), mountain standard time (MST), Pacific standard time (PST), Alaska standard time (AST), and Hawaii standard time (HST). Keep time zones in mind when traveling or telephoning long distances in the U.S. For example, noon in New York City (EST) is 11am in Chicago (CST), 10am in Denver (MST), 9am in Los Angeles (PST), 8am in Anchorage (AST), and 7am in Honolulu (HST). Daylight saving time is in effect from the last Sunday in April through the last Saturday in October; this alters the clock so that sunrise and sunset are an hour later.

**Toilets**   Some foreign visitors complain that public restrooms are hard to find in the States. There are none on the streets, but most hotels, restaurants, bars, department stores, gasoline stations, museums, and other tourist attractions have them available. In a restaurant or bar, it's usually appropriate to order a cup of coffee or soft drink to qualify you as a customer.

**Yellow Pages**   There are two kinds of telephone directories available. The general directory is called the "white pages," and includes individuals and businesses alphabetically by name. The second directory, called *Yellow Pages,* lists all local services, businesses, and industries alphabetically by category, with an index in the back. Listings include not only the obvious, such as automobile repairs and drugstores (pharmacies), but also restaurants by cuisine and location, places of worship by religious denomination, and other information that a tourist might not otherwise readily find. The *Yellow Pages* also include city plans or detailed area maps and often show postal ZIP Codes and public transportation routes.

# DENVER

It's no accident that Denver is called "the Mile High City." When you climb the State Capitol steps, you're precisely 5,280 feet above sea level.

It wasn't intended to be that way. In fact, it could not have been more purely coincidental.

Denver, you see, is a fluke of history, one of the few cities ever built by man that was not on an ocean, lake, or navigable river, or even on an existing road or railroad, at the time of its founding.

In the summer of 1858, a few flecks of gold were discovered by eager Georgia prospectors where Cherry Creek empties into the shallow South Platte River. A tent camp quickly sprang up on the site (the first permanent structure was a saloon). When militia Gen. William H. Larimer arrived in 1859, he claim-jumped the land on the east side of the Platte, laid out a city, and—hoping to gain political favors—named it after James Denver, governor of the Kansas Territory, of which this land was then a part. He didn't know that Denver had already resigned.

Larimer's wasn't the only settlement on the South Platte. Three others claimed equal predominance. But Larimer, a shrewd man, had a solution. For the price of a barrel of whiskey, he bought out the other founders, and the name Denver stuck.

Although the gold found in Denver was but a teaser for much larger strikes in the nearby mountains, the community grew as a shipping and trade center with a milder climate than the mining towns it served. A devastating fire in 1863, a deadly flash flood in 1864, and Native American tribal hostilities in the late 1860s created many hardships. But the establishment of rail links to the east and the influx of silver from the rich mines to the west kept Denver going. Leadville silver and Cripple Creek gold made it a showcase city in the late 19th and early 20th centuries. The U.S. Mint built here in 1906 established Denver as a banking and financial center.

In the years following World War II, Denver mushroomed to become the largest city between the Great Plains and the Pacific coast, with about 500,000 residents and over 1.8 million in the metropolitan area. Today, it's a sprawling city, extending from the Rocky Mountain foothills on the west, far into the plains on the south and east. Denver is noted for its dozens of tree-lined boulevards; its 200 city parks, comprising more than 20,000 acres; and its architecture, from Victorian to sleek contemporary.

A boom brought on by energy development in the early 1980s added 16 new skyscrapers downtown. Denver has also begun construction of a new international airport, which, when completed in 1993, will be the largest in the world.

# 1. ORIENTATION

## ARRIVING

**BY PLANE** **Stapleton International Airport** is rated the sixth busiest in the world, serving 34 million passengers a year—10 times the population of Colorado—with about 1,200 flights daily. Yet it is just 8 miles, or 15 minutes by car or bus, from downtown Denver.

# ✓ WHAT'S SPECIAL ABOUT DENVER

## Architectural Highlights

- ☐ The State Capitol (1890–1908), a replica of the U.S. Capitol with a gold-plated dome.
- ☐ Brown Palace Hotel (1892), Frank Edbrooke's remarkable, triangular masterpiece.
- ☐ Larimer Square, Denver's oldest retail district, restored to its 19th-century spirit.

## Museums

- ☐ Denver Art Museum, with the world's largest Native American art collection.
- ☐ Denver Museum of Natural History, exhibiting skeletons of dozens of prehistoric creatures found in Colorado.
- ☐ Museum of Western Art, showing paintings and sculptures by O'Keeffe, Remington, and Russell.
- ☐ Black America West Museum, which documents the lives of African-American cowboys and pioneers.

## Historical Sites

- ☐ Molly Brown House (1889), Victorian home of the "Unsinkable" heroine of the *Titanic* disaster.
- ☐ Buffalo Bill's Grave and Museum, honoring the famous frontier scout and Wild West showman.
- ☐ Pearce-McAllister Cottage (1899), with its upstairs doll and miniatures museum.

## Industrial Tours

- ☐ The U.S. Mint, where more than five *billion* coins are produced yearly.
- ☐ Coors Brewing Company, the largest single brewing facility in the world.

## Events/Festivals

- ☐ National Western Stock Show & Rodeo, the world's largest cattle show and indoor rodeo, each January.

- ☐ A Taste of Colorado, where mountain and plain join for food and fun, Labor Day weekend.

## For the Kids

- ☐ Elitch Gardens, the Rockies' largest amusement park.
- ☐ Children's Museum of Denver, a hands-on experience to delight children and adults.
- ☐ Tiny Town, the oldest kid-size village in the U.S.

## Shopping

- ☐ Cherry Creek Shopping Center, the state's newest, largest, most fashionable indoor mall.
- ☐ 16th Street Mall, a granite-paved pedestrian promenade that runs one mile through the heart of downtown.
- ☐ Tivoli Denver, a 19th-century brewery transformed into a dining/shopping center.

## Parks

- ☐ City Park, 314 city-center acres that include a zoo, natural history museum, lakes and gardens, and golf course.
- ☐ Denver Botanic Gardens, impressive indoor-outdoor home to thousands of exotic and native plants.
- ☐ Denver Mountain Parks, encompassing 20,000 acres in the adjacent Rockies.

## Natural Spectacles

- ☐ Red Rocks Amphitheatre, a 9,000-seat outdoor theater set between spectacular 400-foot red sandstone rocks.
- ☐ The silhouette of the Rocky Mountains seen from any city skyscraper at sunset.

---

**Major airlines** serving Denver include American (tel. 595-9304, or 800/433-7300), America West (tel. 517-0738, or 800/247-5692), Continental (tel. 784-4800, or 800/525-0280), Delta (tel. 696-1322, or 800/221-1212), Mexicana (tel. 832-5454, or 800/531-7921), Midway (tel. 800/621-5700), Trans World (tel. 629-7878, or 800/

221-2000), United (tel. 398-4141, or 800/241-6522), and USAir (tel. 850-5440, or 800/428-4322).

**Regional and commuter airlines** connect Denver with other points in the state; they include Continental Express (tel. 800/525-0280); Mesa Airlines (tel. 800/637-2247); and United Express (operated by Aspen Airways, tel. 398-2150, or 800/727-7077).

Stapleton maintains a toll-free **information line:** 800/AIR-2-DEN. This line offers information on flight schedules and connections, parking, ground transportation, current weather conditions, even local accommodations. An information office is located between C and D concourses.

The **Airporter** limo bus service (tel. 321-3222) to and from city hotels costs $6 one way inside Denver, more to Boulder. **City buses** from the airport to downtown cost 75¢. **Taxis** run about $10 to $12.

When the $2-billion **Denver International Airport** opens in 1993, 26 miles east of downtown, it will be the largest airport in the world—more than twice the size of Manhattan Island! Passenger use is expected to increase to 51 million annually. An underground rail system will shuttle passengers to and from 206 gates, serving 11 runways. When the new airport opens, Stapleton will be closed to all air traffic.

**BY TRAIN** **Amtrak,** 17th Street and Wynkoop Street (tel. 893-3911, or 800/USA-RAIL), connects Denver with San Francisco and serves western Colorado from Denver to such points as Winter Park, Granby, Glenwood Springs, and Grand Junction. There are six arrivals and departures daily.

**BY BUS** **Greyhound/Trailways,** 1055 19th Street (tel. 292-6111) is the major bus service in Colorado. There are more than 60 daily arrivals and departures to towns, cities, and resort communities throughout the state.

Some parts of Colorado are also served by **TNM&O** (Texas, New Mexico & Oklahoma; tel. 806/763-5389). It arrives at, and departs from, the Greyhound/Trailways Denver bus depot.

**BY CAR** The principal highway routes into Denver are I-25 from the north (Fort Collins, Cheyenne) or south (Colorado Springs, Albuquerque); I-70 from the east (Burlington, Kansas City) and west (Grand Junction); I-76 from the northeast (Sterling). If you're driving into Denver from Boulder, take U.S. 36; from Salida and southwest, U.S. 285.

# TOURIST INFORMATION

The downtown tourist information office is at the **Denver Metro Convention and Visitors Bureau,** 225 West Colfax Avenue, Denver, CO 80202 (tel. 303/892-1505), across from the U.S. Mint. Ask for the "Official Visitors Guide," a 96-page booklet with a comprehensive listing of accommodations, restaurants, and all other visitor services in Denver and surrounding areas. The information center is open in summer, Monday through Friday from 8am to 5pm, on Saturday from 9am to 4pm, and on Sunday from 9am to 1pm; in winter, Monday through Friday from 8am to 5pm and on Saturday from 9am to 1pm.

Another information office, at Stapleton International Airport, is located between C and D concourses. It's staffed daily from 8am to 5pm year round, and brochures are available 24 hours a day. Still another information booth is on the 16th Street Mall at Curtis Street.

For visitors who run into difficulties of one kind or another, **Travelers Aid** has an office at 1245 East Colfax Avenue (tel. 303/832-8194) and another at Stapleton Airport (tel. 398-3873).

# CITY LAYOUT

You can never truly get lost in Denver, as long as you remember that the mountains—almost always visible—are to the west. All the same, it can be perplexing to get around a city of half a million people. Denver has the added confusion of an older grid system, oriented northeast-southwest to parallel the South Platte River, surrounded by a newer north-south grid system.

## MAIN ARTERIES & STREETS

It's probably easiest to get your bearings from Civic Center Park. From here, **Colfax Avenue**—U.S. 40—extends east and west as far as the eye can see. Ditto **Broadway,** which reaches north and south.

**DOWNTOWN DENVER**  North of Colfax and west of Broadway is the center of downtown Denver, where the streets use the old grid pattern. **16th Street,** a mile-long pedestrian mall, cuts northwest off Broadway just above this intersection. (Numbered streets parallel 16th to the northeast, all the way to 44th; and to the southwest, as far as 5th.) It's 17 blocks down 16th Street to Union Station on **Wynkoop Street,** at the far (northwest) side of downtown. Intersecting the numbered streets at right angles are **Lawrence Street** (one way northeast) and **Larimer Street** (one way southwest), 12 and 13 blocks, respectively, from the Colfax-Broadway intersection.

**I-25** skirts downtown Denver to the west, with access from Colfax or from **Speer Boulevard,** which winds diagonally along Cherry Creek past Larimer Square.

**OUTSIDE DOWNTOWN**  Outside the downtown sector, the pattern is a little less confusing. But keep in mind that the numbered *avenues* that parallel Colfax to the north and south (Colfax is equivalent to 15th Avenue) have nothing in common with the numbered *streets* of the downtown grid. In fact, any byway labeled an "avenue" runs east-west, never north-south.

## FINDING AN ADDRESS

**NORTH-SOUTH ARTERIES**  The thoroughfare that divides avenues into "east" and "west" is **Broadway.** Each block east or west adds 100 to the avenue address; thus a restaurant at 2115 East 17th Avenue is a little over 21 blocks east of Broadway—just beyond Vine Street.

Main thoroughfares that parallel Broadway to the east include Logan Street (400 block), Downing Street (1200 block), York Street (2300 block; it becomes University Boulevard south of 6th), Colorado Boulevard (4000 block), Monaco Parkway (6500 block), and Quebec Street (7300 block). Colorado Boulevard (Colo. 2) is the most significant artery, intersecting I-25 on the south and I-70 on the north. North-south cross streets that parallel Broadway west of Broadway include Santa Fe Drive (U.S. 85; 1000 block); west of I-25 are Federal Boulevard (U.S. 287 North, site of the city's main sports arenas; 3000 block), and Sheridan Boulevard (Colo. 95; 5200 block), the boundary between Denver and Lakewood.

**EAST-WEST ARTERIES**  Denver streets are divided into "north" and "south" at **Ellsworth Avenue,** about 1½ miles south of Colfax. Ellsworth is a relatively minor street, but it's a convenient breaking point because it's just a block south of First Avenue. With addresses increasing by 100 per block, that puts an address like 1710 Downing Street at the corner of East 17th Avenue. First Avenue, Sixth Avenue, Colfax (1500 block), 26th Avenue, and Martin Luther King Way (3200 block, running directly to the Stapleton Airport entrance) are the principal east-west thoroughfares. There are no numbered avenues south of Ellsworth. Major east-west byways heading south are Alameda Avenue (Colo. 26; 300 block), Mississippi Avenue (1100 block), Florida Avenue (1500 block), Evans Avenue (2100 block), Yale Avenue (2700 block), and Hampden Avenue (U.S. 285; 3500 block).

There are excellent Denver maps on the reverse side of the Official State Highway Map, and in the removable centerfold of the Denver Visitors Guide. Both are available free of charge from the Convention and Visitors Bureau (see "Tourist Information," above).

## NEIGHBORHOODS IN BRIEF

**Lower Downtown**   Downtown Denver can be divided into three subdistricts. Lower Downtown ("LoDo") is the oldest part of the city. It extends northwesterly from Lawrence Street to Union Station and from the shops of Tivoli Denver northeast to 19th Street. No skyscrapers are permitted in this historic preservation district, most of which dates from the late 19th century. Larimer Square is the most notable redevelopment project, but plans have been drawn for many more.

**Central Business District**   This extends along 16th Street, 17th Street, and 18th Street between Lawrence Street and Broadway. Here, the ban on skyscrapers certainly does not apply!

**Civic Center Park**   This area is at the southeast end of 15th Street, where Broadway and Colfax Avenue meet. This two-square-block oasis of green is surrounded by state and metropolitan government buildings, the Denver Art Museum, the Colorado History Museum, the U.S. Mint, and the public library.

**Capitol Hill**   Located just southeast of downtown and extending roughly from the State Capitol (Colfax and Lincoln) past the Governor's Mansion to East Sixth Street Avenue, and from Broadway to Cheesman Park (on Franklin Street) is Capitol Hill. The area preserves a great many Victorian mansions from the mining-boom days of the late 19th and early 20th centuries, including the Molly Brown House and the Grant Humphreys Mansion. There are no old wooden buildings: After the disastrous fire of 1863, the government forbade the construction of wooden structures until after World War II.

**Cherry Creek**   Home of the new Cherry Creek Shopping Center and Denver Country Club, this area extends north from East First Avenue to East Eighth and east from Downing Street to Steele Street. You'll find huge, ostentatious stone mansions here, especially around Circle Drive (southwest of Sixth and University)—this is where most of Denver's wealthiest families have lived for generations.

**Historic Districts**   There are 17 recognized historic districts in Denver, including Capitol Hill, the Clements District (around 21st Street and Tremont Street, just east of downtown), and Ninth Street Park in Auraria (off Ninth Street and West Colfax Avenue). **Historic Denver**, 1330 17th Street (tel. 303/534-1858), offers walking-tour maps of several of these areas.

**Glendale**   Denver fully surrounds little Glendale, an incorporated city in its own right. The center of a lively entertainment district, Glendale straddles Cherry Creek on South Colorado Boulevard south of East Alameda Avenue.

**Tech Center**   At the southern end of the metropolitan area is Tech Center, along I-25 between Belleview Avenue and Arapahoe Road. In this district, about a 25-minute drive from downtown, there are eight technological centers, headquarters of several international and national companies, and a handful of upscale hotels heavily oriented to the business traveler.

# 2. GETTING AROUND

**BY BUS**   The **Regional Transportation District (RTD)** (tel. 299-6000 for route and schedule information, 299-6700 for other business), calls itself "The Ride." It provides good service within Denver and its suburbs and outlying communities, including Boulder, Longmont, and Evergreen.

Local fares are $1 during peak hours (Monday through Friday from 6 to 9am and 3 to 6pm), 50¢ during off-peak hours. Exact change is required. Express fares start at $1.05; regional fares vary ($2.50 Denver–Boulder). Senior citizens pay only 15¢ off-peak, and children 5 and younger travel free.

The various routes have different schedules of frequency including time of last bus, which varies from 9pm to 1am. Maps of all routes are available at the RTD office, 1600 Blake Street, Monday through Friday from 8:30am to 5:30pm.

**Free buses** run up and down the 16th Street Mall between the Civic Center and Market Street every 90 seconds. There's also **free trolley service** between Tabor Center, Larimer Square, and Tivoli Denver.

**BY TAXI**   The main services are **Yellow Cab** (tel. 777-7777), **Zone Cab** (tel. 861-2323), and **Metro Taxi** (tel. 333-3333). Taxis can be hailed on streets, though it's best to either call or wait at a taxi stand outside a major hotel.

**BY CAR**   Visitors unfamiliar with the Denver traffic pattern may prefer to wait until they're ready to leave the city before renting a car. Rush-hour traffic, especially on I-25, is no fun, and most downtown hotels charge a sizable sum for parking.

**Parking**   Downtown parking-lot rates vary from 75¢ per half hour to $10 for all day. Rates climb with proximity to the 16th Street Mall and the central business district. Keep a handful of quarters, dimes, and nickels if you hope to use on-street parking meters.

**Car Rentals**   Rental agencies in Denver—some of which have offices in or near downtown, as well as at Stapleton Airport—include **Airways,** 6800 Smith Road (tel. 320-1102, or 800/423-ACAR); **Alamo,** 7500 East 41st Avenue (tel. 321-1176, or 800/327-9633); **Avis** (tel. 839-1280, or 800/331-1212); **Budget,** 7400 East 32nd Avenue (tel. 341-2277, or 800/222-6772); **Dollar,** 7450 East 29th Avenue (tel. 398-2323, or 800/228-9987); **General,** 3898 Monaco Parkway (tel. 320-1244, or 800/327-7607); **Hertz,** 7600 Martin Luther King Boulevard (tel. 355-2244, or 800/327-7607); **Mountain Express,** 3333 Quebec Street (tel. 377-6962, or 800/525-2880); **National** (tel. 321-7990, or 800/227-7368); **Payless,** 6100 Smith Road (tel. 399-2608, or 800/231-5537); **Superior,** 4385 Grape Street (tel. 321-2321 or 237-8106); **Thrifty,** 4000 Quebec Street (tel. 388-4634, or 800/FOR-CARS); and **USA,** 7850 East 40th Avenue (tel. 355-1955, or 800/833-1436).

**Rental of Other Vehicles**   Campers, travel trailers, and motor homes may be rented from **Cruise America,** 8950 North Federal Boulevard (tel. 426-6699, or 800/327-7778), or **Go Vacations of America,** 275 West 43rd Avenue (tel. 480-0100).

For the traveler seeking true luxury, several limousine services operate from Denver. Among them are **Admiral Limousines,** 8055 East Tufts Avenue, Suite 1450 (tel. 741-6464, or 800/828-8680), and **Colorado Limousine Service,** 1304 Ogden Street (tel. 832-7155, or 800/628-6655). Want to travel from Stapleton Airport to Aspen by limo? No problem!

**Final Notes**   For regulations and advice on driving in Colorado, see Chapter 2. The **American Automobile Association (AAA)** maintains an office in Denver at 4100 East Arkansas Avenue (tel. 753-8800, or 800/283-5222).

**ON FOOT**   Downtown Denver is a pleasure to explore on foot. It's only a little over a mile from end to end, and the pedestrian mall on 16th Street makes the walk especially easy. Outside downtown, the metropolis stretches mile after mile in all directions. It's wise to take a bus or taxi.

 **DENVER**

**American Express**   The American Express Travel Agency is located in the Anaconda Tower at 555 17th Street (tel. 303/298-7100). Open Monday through Friday from 8:30am to 5pm. Full member services and currency exchange are offered. To report a lost card, call 800/528-4800; to report lost traveler's checks, call 800/221-7282.

**Area Code**   The telephone area code in the Denver metropolitan area is 303.

**Baby-sitters**   The **YWCA of Metropolitan Denver** has a year-round Child Care Information Network (tel. 825-7141) with free information on part-time and drop-in child-care services. In summer, the **Summer Fun Day Camp,** 7710 West 35th Avenue, Wheat Ridge (tel. 232-9191), is an excellent option. Concierges and front desks at leading hotels can also arrange child care.

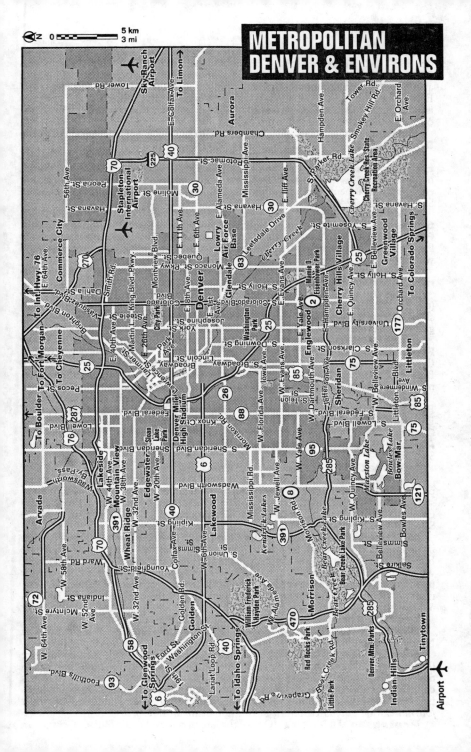

# METROPOLITAN DENVER & ENVIRONS

5 km
3 mi
0

**Banks**   Leading banks include **Colorado National Bank,** 918 17th Street (tel. 893-1862); **First Interstate Bank of Denver,** 633 17th Street, at California Street (tel. 293-2211); **United Bank of Denver,** 1700 Broadway (tel. 861-8811); and **The Women's Bank,** 821 17th Street (tel. 293-2265). **Money Express,** 907 East Colfax Avenue (tel. 830-CASH), offers 24-hour check cashing. Foreign currency is exchanged at **Deak International,** 1580 Court Place, downtown (tel. 571-0808), open Monday through Friday from 9am to 5pm.

**Dentist**   For referrals, call **Dial-4-Health** (tel. 443-2584), or visit the **Centre Dental Associates,** 1600 Stout Street, Suite 1370 (tel. 592-1133).

**Doctor**   For referrals, call **Dial-4-Health** (tel. 443-2584), or St. Joseph's Hospital's **Med Search** (tel. 866-8000). Minor illnesses and injuries are treated outpatient at **Downtown Health Care,** 1860 Larimer Street (tel. 296-2273). For emergency treatment, near downtown is **St. Joseph's Hospital,** 1835 Franklin Street (tel. 837-7240).

**Drugstores**   Reliable prescription services are available at **Walgreen's Drug Stores,** with an outlet on the 16th Street Mall at Stout Street (tel. 571-5316); or **Family Pharmacy,** 1724 South Chambers Road (tel. 695-1702), open daily from 9am to 10pm, with an emergency hotline open after hours. If it's 3 in the morning and you can't get your prescription, call a hospital.

**Emergencies**   For police, fire, or medical emergencies, call **911.** For **Colorado State Patrol** emergencies, call 303/239-4501.

**Eyeglasses**   At 999 18th Street, at Curtis Street, Suite 146, **The Visionary** (tel. 298-9398) can handle all routine and emergency optical and eye-care needs in short order. Outside downtown, you can get 1-hour replacement of lost or broken glasses at **Lenscrafter** stores in major shopping malls.

**Hairdressers/Barbers**   Downtown on the 16th Street Mall is **Shear Productions,** Republic Plaza, 303 16th Street (tel. 592-4247). Near the Cherry Creek Shopping Center is **Paul Garcia's,** 3000 East Third Avenue (tel. 333-5577). Both are full-service salons catering to men as well as women. **Fantastic Sams** has more than 20 salons in the Denver metropolitan area, offering haircuts for under $10.

**Hospitals**   Among Denver-area hospitals are **St. Joseph's Hospital,** 1835 Franklin Street (tel. 837-7240), just east of downtown; **Rose Medical Center,** 4567 East Ninth Street (tel. 320-2455), east of Colorado Boulevard; **Swedish Medical Center,** 501 East Hampden Avenue (tel. 788-6911), in Englewood; and **St. Anthony's Hospital,** 4231 West 16th Avenue (tel. 629-3721), west of Mile High Stadium.

**Information**   See "Orientation," above.

**Laundry/Dry Cleaning**   Nearly every major hotel offers valet drop-off and pickup service, but the charge can be steep. **Colorado Lace** is a reputable chain of self-service laundries with 20 locations in the Denver metropolitan area. One-day dry cleaning service is available at **La Petite Cleaners,** 2314 Sixth Avenue, at Josephine Street (tel. 377-7459), and many other locations.

**Libraries**   The **Denver Public Library,** 1357 Broadway (tel. 571-2000), has its main facility adjacent to Civic Center Park, abutting downtown. There are branches throughout the metropolitan area. The main library has a fine collection on western history and art, and has copy machines and computers available (for a fee) for public use. A local library card is required to check out material. Open Monday through Wednesday from 10am to 9pm, Thursday through Saturday from 10am to 5:30pm, and on Sunday from 1 to 5pm.

**Lost Property**   Consult the city police (tel. 575-3127).

**Maps**   Denver's largest map store is **Maps Unlimited,** 899 Broadway, at Ninth Street (tel. 623-4299).

**Newspapers/Magazines**   The state's two largest daily newspapers are the morning *Denver Post,* a broadsheet, and the afternoon *Rocky Mountain News,* a tabloid. There's also a widely read weekly, *Westword,* known as much for its controversial jibes at local politicians as for its entertainment listings. Best of all, it's free from newsstands. National newspapers such as *USA Today* and the *Wall Street Journal* can be purchased on the streets and at major hotels.

**Photographic Needs**   One of the largest photo shops is **Robert Waxman**

**Camera and Video,** with five locations including downtown at 913 15th Street (tel. 623-1155). Many professional photographers use **Pallas Photo Labs,** 700 Kalamath Street (tel. 893-0101), or **The Pro Lab,** 1200 West Mississippi Avenue (tel. 744-6126). Consult the experts at any of these shops for a full range of services, including repairs.

**Police** In emergency, dial **911.** For nonemergency needs, call 575-3127.

**Post Office** The **Main Post Office** is downtown at 1823 Stout Street, open Monday through Friday from 9am to 5pm. Denver offers full postal services 24 hours a day at two other locations: **Terminal Annex,** 1595 Wynkoop Street (tel. 297-6325), in LoDo, with 'round-the-clock window service including Express Mail dropoff; and the **Air Mail Facility: Stapleton Airport,** 3550 Roslyn Street (tel. 297-6745).

**Radio/TV** Two dozen AM and FM **radio stations** in the Denver area cater to all musical, news, sports, and entertainment tastes. Among them are KDEN (1340 AM) for all news, KMJI (100.3 FM) for light rock, KRFX (103.5 FM) for classic rock "oldies," KRXY (1600 AM and 107.5 FM) for contemporary rock, and KVOD (99.5 FM) for classical music. Denver has 10 **television stations;** they include KCNC (Channel 4), the NBC affiliate; KMGH (Channel 7), the CBS affiliate; and KUSA (Channel 9), the ABC affiliate. Other major stations are KWGN (Channel 2), an independent; and KRMA, Channel 6, the PBS affiliate. Cable or satellite service is available at most hotels.

**Safety** Denver is safe as large cities go, but use common sense when you visit. Stay alert. Be aware of your immediate surroundings, and keep a close eye on your possessions. Be especially careful with cameras, purses, and wallets, all favorite targets of thieves and pickpockets.

**Shoe Repairs** Right on the 16th Street Mall is **Shoe Biz,** in Republic Plaza at 303 16th Street (tel. 893-9686). Shoes and boots are quickly repaired, often while you wait.

**Taxes** Colorado state **sales tax** is 3.7%. Each county tacks on an additional local tax on top of that. In Denver, for instance, it's 3.5% (a total of 7.2%). The tax is lower in some neighboring counties, including suburbs. The **hotel tax** in Denver, added to room charges to support the tourism infrastructure and other industries, is 4.7%, bringing the total tax on rooms to 11.9%.

**Telephone/Fax** Local calls are normally 25¢. For directory assistance, dial 1-555-1212. Facsimiles can be transmitted by most major hotels at a nominal cost.

**Useful Telephone Numbers** **Poison control center** (tel. 629-1123), **rape assistance** (tel. 430-5656), **recorded road conditions** (tel. 639-1111 within a 2-hour drive of Denver, 639-1234 statewide), **recorded ski reports** (tel. 837-9907), **weather** (tel. 398-3964).

# 3. ACCOMMODATIONS

Even though Denver opened a spanking-new convention center in 1990, occupancy rates at city hotels remain low. That means visitors can frequently request, and obtain, a room rate lower than the one posted.

The rates listed here are the officially quoted off-the-street prices, or "rack rates," and don't take into account any individual or group discounts. Even in the upper price brackets, there are many ways to pay much less. Wise travelers seek reduced rates wherever they stay. Ask for corporate rates. If you don't work for a corporation, identify a big firm (a bank, for instance) and you'll save 20% to 35% off listed rack rates. Family emergencies warrant a medical rate. There are military rates and university rates. Travel-industry rates are 25% off in summer, half price in winter. Seniors almost always get at least 10% off. Weekend rates are often 50% lower than midweek business travelers' rates, especially in the low season. Speak up to save: If you don't ask, they won't ask you!

The chain hotels' national reservation services, usually reached through a toll-free telephone number, aren't authorized to offer special discounts, and will quote only standard rates. You're more likely to get a discounted rate if you call the hotel directly with your request. Any hotel manager will agree that it's better to sell a discounted room than not to sell it at all. In Denver, only during the National Western Stock Show the second and third weeks of January, and perhaps during occasional major conventions, are hotels likely to be close to full.

In these listings, the following categories define price ranges: very expensive, over $150 per night double; expensive, $110 to $150; moderate, $75 to $110; inexpensive, $40 to $75; budget, less than $40 per night double. An additional 11.9% tax is levied onto all bills, and is not included in the rates.

# DOWNTOWN

## VERY EXPENSIVE

**BROWN PALACE HOTEL, 321 17th St., Denver, CO 80202. Tel. 303/297-3111,** or 800/321-2599 in North America, 800/228-2917 in Colorado. Fax 303/293-9204. 205 rms, 25 suites. A/C TV TEL

**$ Rates:** $139–$199 single; $149–$214 double; $210–$825 suite. Weekend packages available. AE, CB, DC, DISC, JCB, MC, V. **Parking:** $10 per day.

The first open-atrium hotel in the U.S. opened in August 1892—and has never closed. This National Historic Landmark was the masterpiece of architect Frank Edbrooke, who designed it in Italian Renaissance style. Bounded by Broadway, 17th Street, and Tremont Place, the building is triangular in shape—though you'd never know it unless you looked down on it from a nearby office tower. A glass sunroof 10 stories above the Victorian lobby allows the rich wood paneling and Mexican onyx to glow. Original grillwork surrounds the mezzanine, and a huge American flag is suspended in the center of the atrium. Dwight Eisenhower kept the Western White House at the Brown Palace during his presidency, 1953 to 1961. His Eisenhower Suite has rich masculine decor, integrity, and even a dent in the fireplace trim said to have been made by an errant golf ball!

Standard rooms come in nine different Victorian decors, from peaches to carmines to deep greens. All have antique furnishings. Rooms have desks, remote-control TVs tucked away in armoires, and period prints on the walls. Local calls cost 50¢. (There's no access charge.) Oh, yes, the tap water's great: The Brown Palace has its own artesian wells!

**Dining/Entertainment:** Fine dining is in the Palace Arms (see "Dining," below). Ellyngton's serves breakfast ($4.75 to $10.25) and lunch (light grills and pastas, $6.50 to $15.75) daily from 7am to 2pm, and a Dom Perignon brunch on Sunday from 10:30am to 3:30pm. The Ship Tavern is open daily from 11am to 11pm for drinks and casual dining (steak and seafood, $7 to $16.50). Cocktails are served in the lobby and in Henry C's, a modern lounge adjoining Ellyngton's. The lobby also offers a Devonshire tea (with finger sandwiches, scones, and pastries) daily from 2 to 4:30pm for $8.50. Lunch is also served in the Brown Palace Club, for private members and hotel guests only.

**Services:** 24-hour room service, full concierge service, valet laundry, no-smoking rooms, turndown, robes, Crabtree and Evelyn amenities.

**Facilities:** United Airlines desk, jeweler, florist, barber, apparel shop, gift shop, newsstand; meeting facilities for 1,000.

**DENVER MARRIOTT—CITY CENTER, 1701 California St., Denver, CO 80202. Tel. 303/297-1300,** or 800/228-9290. Fax 303/298-7474. 571 rms, 41 suites. A/C TV TEL

**$ Rates:** $135–$145 single; $155–$165 double; $270–$475 suite. Weekend rates $89 single or double. AE, CB, DC, JCB, MC, V. **Parking:** $12 per day.

This tall black tower in the center of the financial district is oriented more to the business traveler than to the vacationer. Its lobby, simple and elegant with heavy use of marble and glass, is relatively small for a major hotel. An escalator leads down to the restaurant and lounge.

Rooms, appointed in shades of rust-red or lime-green, are not overly spacious. They have a king-size or two double beds, a table and chairs, a desk with a telephone (75¢ charge for local calls or long-distance access), a credenza with a color TV (and in-house movies), built-in radio, individual temperature control, and a full-mirror closet door.

**Dining/Entertainment:** Marjolaine's serves breakfast and lunch buffets, and an international menu selection for dinner ($9.95 to $16.95). Charms lounge also serves light lunch fare.

**Services:** Room service, valet laundry, safety-deposit boxes, baby-sitting, physician on call 24 hours, no-smoking floors, upgraded concierge level.

**Facilities:** Guest laundry, games room, gift shop/newsstand; fitness center with Universal and free weights, aerobics classes, pool, Jacuzzi, men's and women's saunas; meeting facilities for up to 2,300 people.

**HYATT REGENCY DENVER, 1750 Welton St., Denver, CO 80202. Tel. 303/295-1200,** or 800/233-1234. Fax 303/293-2565. 513 rms, 27 suites. A/C TV TEL
**$ Rates:** $140 single; $160 double; $310–$1,000 suite. Weekend rates $65 single or double. Children 18 and under stay free in parents' room. AE, CB, DC, DISC, JCB, MC, V. **Parking:** $10 per day.

The first thing visitors see when they enter the Hyatt is a pair of Belgian crystal chandeliers that seem to float on a mural of the sky painted on the lobby ceiling. It's a dramatic touch, but then, this is a dramatic property. The 26-story hotel is part of a four-building office-shopping-parking complex that also includes the 40-story Anaconda Tower. A glass-covered atrium links the quartet.

An art deco motif of light greens and mauves carries through the hotel to the guest rooms. There's a feeling of luxury here, with fabric wall coverings, long drapes, and marble-top oak dressers. Every room has soundproof windows that open, an individual thermostat, a well-lit desk, a color TV (in-room movies), direct-dial phones, an alarm clock, and an electric shoe polisher. Bathrooms are elaborate, with oversize bathtowels, a scale, radio extension speakers, even a telephone.

**Dining/Entertainment:** The Marquis restaurant has won *Travel/Holiday* magazine's fine dining award (see "Dining," below). McGuire's, for casual dining, is open Sunday through Thursday from 6am to midnight and on Friday and Saturday from 6am to 2am. Main dishes run $6.25 to $17.25, and there's a deli sandwich buffet Monday through Friday. The Lobby Lounge and Marquis Lounge both have nightly piano entertainment, the latter at a glass-top piano bar. Sky Court serves light meals and beverages daily from 11am to 4pm on the fourth-floor deck.

**Services:** Room service (during restaurant hours), valet laundry, half-hourly shuttle ($5 fee), no-smoking and concierge floors, Camp Hyatt program for children ($4 an hour).

**Facilities:** Athletic club; rooftop swimming pool (open summers), tennis courts, and jogging track; gift shop; meeting facilities for 1,500.

**WESTIN HOTEL AT TABOR CENTER, 1672 Lawrence St., Denver, CO 80202. Tel. 303/572-9100,** or 800/228-3000. Fax 303/572-7288. 407 rms, 13 suites. A/C MINIBAR TV TEL
**$ Rates:** $140–$170 single; $165–$195 double; $310–$1,050 suite. AE, CB, DC, DISC, MC, V. **Parking:** $10 per day self-park, $12 per day valet.

The focal point of the two-square-block Tabor Center shopping-and-office complex, the 19-story Westin bridges the historical gap between the central business district and lower downtown. Its contemporary design incorporates architectural elements of nearby Victorian-era structures. The third-floor lobby, reached by an elevator or a long escalator, features three-dimensional murals and modern fountains against a sand-tone background. Marble, brass, and bird's-eye maple wood add elegance.

The well-lit, spacious guest rooms, 75% of which have king-size beds, are appointed in muted shades of peach and gray, with 9-foot ceilings. Modern

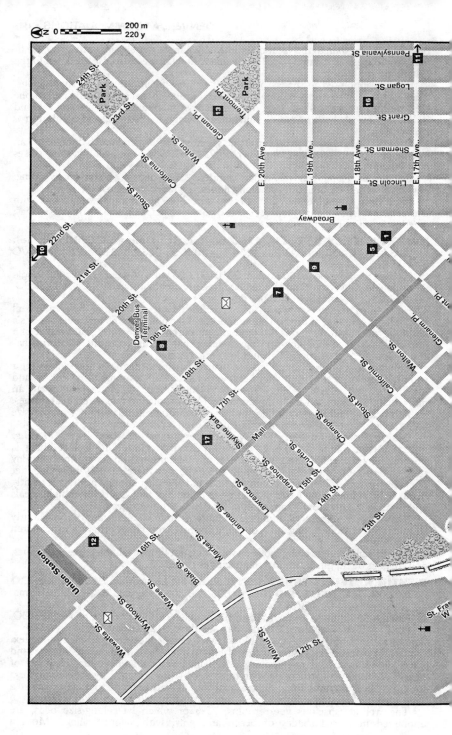

# DENVER ACCOMMODATIONS

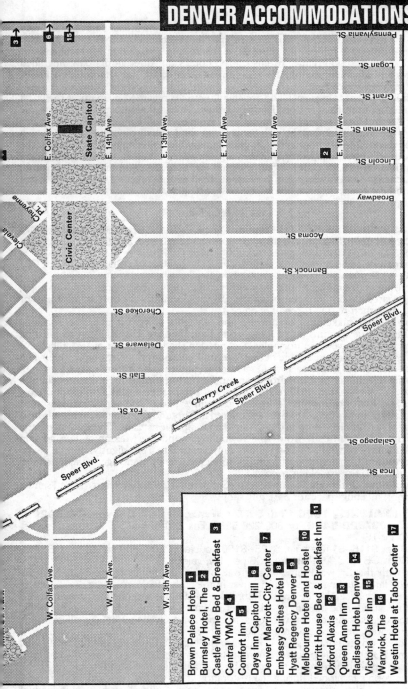

E. Colfax Ave.

State Capitol

E. 14th Ave.

E. 13th Ave.

E. 12th Ave.

E. 11th Ave.

E. 10th Ave.

Pennsylvania St.

Logan St.

Grant St.

Sherman St.

Lincoln St.

Broadway

Acoma St.

Bannock St.

Cherokee St.

Delaware St.

Elati St.

Fox St.

Galapago St.

Inca St.

Civic Center

Cheyenne Pl.

Cleve

Cherry Creek

Speer Blvd.

Speer Blvd.

Speer Blvd.

W. Colfax Ave.

W. 14th Ave.

W. 13th Ave.

Brown Palace Hotel **1**
Burnsley Hotel, The **2**
Castle Marne Bed & Breakfast **3**
Central YMCA **4**
Comfort Inn **5**
Days Inn Capitol Hill **6**
Denver Marriott-City Center **7**
Embassy Suites Hotel **8**
Hyatt Regency Denver **9**
Melbourne Hotel and Hostel **10**
Merritt House Bed & Breakfast Inn **11**
Oxford Alexis **12**
Queen Anne Inn **13**
Radisson Hotel Denver **14**
Victoria Oaks Inn **15**
Warwick, The **16**
Westin Hotel at Tabor Center **17**

Post Office ⊠   Church ✝

furnishings with English styling have black lacquer or tortoise-shell accents. Every room has a remote-control color TV (with pay movie channels), clock radio, and two phones—one on a full-size working desk. There's an 85¢ charge for local calls or long-distance access. Premier rooms on the hotel's top three floors have upgraded features and amenities, among them continental breakfast and afternoon cocktails, and a resident concierge.

**Dining/Entertainment:** The five-star Augusta is regarded by many as the finest hotel restaurant in Denver (see "Dining," below). A casual, contemporary bistro, the Tabor Bar and Grill, serves three meals daily from 6am to 11pm. There's a lively jazz piano bar nightly Monday through Saturday in the Lobby Lounge.

**Services:** 24-hour room service, valet laundry, no-smoking floors, rooms for the handicapped, turndown, complimentary shoeshine.

**Facilities:** Health club ($5 fee) with indoor/outdoor swimming pool, hot tub, sauna, exercise and weight room, and racquetball courts; meeting space for 800; gift shop; indoor connection to Tabor Center shopping arcade.

## EXPENSIVE

**EMBASSY SUITES HOTEL, Denver Place, 1881 Curtis St., Denver, CO 80202. Tel. 303/297-8888,** or 800/733-3366, 800/297-8888 in Colorado. Fax 303/298-1101. 337 suites. A/C MINIBAR TV TEL
**$ Rates** (including breakfast): $119 single; $129 double. AE, CB, DC, DISC, JCB, MC, V. **Parking:** $10 Mon–Fri, $7 Sat–Sun.

Every room in this modern building is either a one- or two-bedroom suite. The hotel, heavily geared toward long-term business travelers, occupies the bottom 19 stories of a 37-story structure (the top half is offices).

The interior makes use of mirrors and skylights to give it a bright, spacious appearance. Guest rooms also appear larger than they are, thanks again to mirrors. But the rooms are very comfortable: Decorated in shades of peach or teal, they have either a king-size or two double beds. (A second bedroom has just one double.) The remote-control TV is tucked away in an armoire, and each bedroom has a TV as well. There are telephones in the bedroom and in the parlor; local calls and access charges are 60¢. All rooms have small refrigerators, wet bars, coffeemakers, and clock radios.

**Dining/Entertainment:** The airy, gardenlike Plaza Café serves breakfast and lunch daily. Dinners ($9.50 to $15) are offered in Burgundy's, romantic with subdued lighting. The Club Deli is open daily from 8am to 8pm for snacks. There are two bars: the Piano Bar, open daily from 4pm to midnight, and the Mezzanine Bar, serving complimentary cocktails to hotel guests only, from 5 to 7pm nightly.

**Services:** Concierge, valet laundry, foreign-currency exchange, complimentary newspaper, 51% no-smoking rooms.

**Facilities:** Outdoor pool (open May–Sept), small 24-hour exercise room, sauna, whirlpool, meeting space for 350, gift shop.

**OXFORD ALEXIS, 1600 17th St. (at Wynkoop St.), Denver, CO 80202. Tel. 303/628-5400,** or 800/228-5838. Fax 303/628-5413. 74 rms, 7 suites. A/C TV TEL
**$ Rates:** $115–$140 single; $125–$150 double; $250–$400 suite. AE, CB, DC, DISC, JCB, MC, V. **Parking:** $9 per day, valet.

Along with the Brown Palace, this is one of the few hotels to have survived the sweeping land-clearing projects in Denver in the early 1980s. And like the Brown, it was designed by architect Frank Edbrooke a century ago. Behind a simple red sandstone facade, the interior of this lower downtown property boasts marble walls, carpeted floors, stained-glass windows, frescoes, and silver chandeliers, all of which were restored and exactly reproduced between 1979 and 1983, according to Edbrooke's original drawings. It is listed on the National Register of Historic Places.

Some 1,300 antique pieces were imported from England and France—armoires, Asian carpets, light fixtures, art deco chairs and tables, and bedsteads—to furnish the 81 large rooms fashioned during the restoration from the 200 original small rooms. No two are alike. Appointed in forest green or navy blue, they feature individual thermostats, hairdryers, dressing tables, large closets, and good amenities packages.

Some rooms have canopied beds and fireplaces; most have stocked minibars. There's bedside lighting, but electrical outlets are limited. Local phone calls are 75¢.

**Dining/Entertainment:** McCormick's Fish House (see "Dining," below) is open for three meals daily. The art deco Cruise Room Bar is open Monday through Saturday from 4:30 to 10pm. Its dinner menu is famous for Angus beef steaks. The Corner Bar, has enormous stained-glass panels on its back bar.

**Services:** 24-hour room service, valet laundry; downtown-area limousine service in 1937 Hudson; no-smoking and handicapped-accessible rooms; complimentary afternoon sherry at 4 in the lobby; complimentary morning paper and evening shoeshine; no-tipping policy except in restaurants.

**Facilities:** Health club and salon ($5 fee) with Universal and free weights, aerobics classes, steam room, Jacuzzi, and massage therapist; meeting space for 120; Sloans Gallery.

**RADISSON HOTEL DENVER, 1550 Court Place, Denver, CO 80202. Tel. 303/893-3333,** or 800/333-3333. Fax 303/623-0303. 674 rms, 66 suites. A/C TV TEL

**$ Rates:** $120–$140 single; $140–$160 double; $175–$250 suite. Weekend rates available. AE, CB, DC, DISC, JCB, MC, V. **Parking:** $10 per day, underground.

First constructed in 1960, the downtown Radisson underwent a $20-million renovation, reopening in 1990. Today it boasts more guest rooms than any other hotel in the seven-state Rocky Mountain region—and it's right beside the 16th Street Mall. Designed by renowned architect I. M. Pei, it has a unique exterior of glass and crushed rock that sparkles with flecks of gold whenever sunny. The lobby, one floor above street level, greets visitors with a strong use of marble and stainless steel in its decor.

Guest rooms are contemporary in appearance, though some have a strange configuration that renovators apparently were able to do nothing about. They're done in shades of rose or teal, with one king- or two queen-size beds, a table with wingback chairs, remote-control TVs, and telephones with voice messaging.

**Dining/Entertainment:** Finnegan's claims to be Denver's "only authentic" Irish dining and drinking establishment. Gaelic musicians perform nightly at 8pm. The international menu ($5.95 to $16.95) offers Irish specialties. It's open daily from 11am to 11pm, later for bar service. Windows serves a casual breakfast and lunch ($6.95 to $9.50) daily from 6:30am to 2pm. Katie's Ice Cream Parlour, located in an over-the-street bridge connecting the hotel to May's department store, is a delightful excuse to cater to a sweet tooth.

**Services:** Room service, valet laundry, no-smoking and concierge floors; business center with secretarial service.

**Facilities:** Health club with weight room, steam room, sauna, and heated outdoor swimming pool (open year round); meeting facilities for over 2,000.

**THE WARWICK, 1776 Grant St. (at E. 18th Ave.), Denver, CO 80203. Tel. 303/861-2000,** or 800/525-2888. Fax 303/832-0320. 145 rms, 49 suites. A/C TV TEL

**$ Rates** (including buffet breakfast): $94–$114 single; $104–$124 double; $124–$500 suite. Weekend rate $69 single or double. Children under 18 stay free in parents' room. AE, CB, DC, DISC, JCB, MC, V. **Parking:** $5 per day, underground.

One of three Warwicks in the U.S. (the others are in New York and Seattle), this elegant mid-size hotel is more characteristic of hostelries in Paris, where the corporate office is located. It's one of Denver's best bargains. The small but sophisticated lobby, in particular, has a European accent, with richly upholstered antique chairs and couches on marble floors.

Even standard rooms have a full private balcony, and all but a few have a refrigerator, wet bar, and dining table. Appointed in navy blue, forest green, or a muted rust tone, guest rooms have one king- or two queen-size beds, simple brass and mahogany furniture, antique hunting prints on the walls, cable TV in an armoire, clock radio, and telephone with two incoming lines—one for a modem connection. There's another phone in the bathroom. Local calls are 60¢.

**Dining/Entertainment:** The Liaison Restaurant and Lounge serves breakfast daily, lunch and dinner Monday through Friday. The fare is continental, though a Friday-night seafood buffet ($18.50) is a big draw. The lounge won a "Best of Denver" award for its hors d'oeuvres, served Monday through Friday from 4:30 to 7pm.

**Services:** 24-hour room service and concierge, valet laundry, courtesy limousine within a 5-mile radius, no-smoking rooms and rooms equipped for the handicapped, complimentary newspaper; baby-sitting and secretarial services (fee).

**Facilities:** Rooftop swimming pool (seasonal), gift shop, meeting space for 300, complimentary membership at adjacent athletic club.

## MODERATE

**THE BURNSLEY HOTEL, 1000 Grant St. (at E. 10th Ave.), Denver, CO 80203. Tel. 303/830-1000,** or 800/231-3915. 85 suites. A/C TV TEL
**$ Rates:** $95–$135 single or double; $225 penthouse suite. Weekend packages available. AE, CB, DC, MC, V. **Parking:** Free in hotel garage.
This member of the Small Luxury Hotels and Resorts group caters to visitors who seek a suite experience at a manageable price. Guest rooms feature fine furnishings and works of art, as well as monogrammed robes and imported toiletries. Most have living, dining, kitchen (with refrigerator), bedroom, and private patio areas. The hotel has a restaurant and jazz bar (called The Restaurant and The Bar), as well as a swimming pool, room service, and 24-hour concierge. Pets are permitted.

**CASTLE MARNE BED & BREAKFAST, 1572 Race St., Denver, CO 80206. Tel. 303/331-0621,** or 800/92-MARNE. 7 rms, 2 suites (all with bath).
**$ Rates** (including breakfast): $65–$100 single; $75–$110 double; $120–$145 suite. AE, CB, DC, MC, V. **Parking:** Ample street parking.
This impressive stone mansion, built in 1889, and a National Historic Landmark, has a gorgeous circular stained-glass peacock window and ornate fireplaces. It got its name from an owner whose son fought in the World War I Battle of the Marne. Denver's first indoor bathroom is still in operation in the Van Cise Room; the plumbing has been upgraded, but the clawfoot tub and marble vanity are the same. The John T. Mason Suite is named for a past owner, the curator of the Museum of Natural History; it displays part of his butterfly collection. The Presidential Suite has three rooms, each with a private fireplace, and a Jacuzzi solarium behind French doors. Guests enjoy a gourmet breakfast at one big table; there's afternoon tea as well. The inn also has a games room, library, gift shop, and a small office for business travelers' use. No smoking is permitted.

**MERRITT HOUSE BED & BREAKFAST INN, 941 E. 17th Ave., Denver, CO 80218. Tel. 303/861-5230.** 10 rms (all with bath). A/C TV TEL
**$ Rates** (including breakfast): $65–$85 single; $75–$95 double. AE, MC, V.
Located right in the middle of "Restaurant Row" on East 17th Avenue at Ogden Street, the Merritt House is another historic home. A handsome oak stairway leads from the parlor to guest rooms, each individually decorated with Victorian antiques or reproductions such as Alexander Graham Bell–style telephones, lamps that would make Thomas Edison proud, and cable TV—here known as "electric vision." All have private bath; the few with Jacuzzis are higher priced than those with simple showers. The house also boasts a glass-enclosed porch and a games room. A hearty breakfast is served in the morning, a glass of wine in the afternoon, and coffee throughout the day. Only children over 12 are accepted.

**QUEEN ANNE INN, 2147 Tremont Place, Denver, CO 80205. Tel. 303/296-6666.** 10 rms (all with bath). A/C TEL
**$ Rates** (including breakfast): $54–$99 single; $64–$109 double. AE, MC, V.
**Parking:** Private lot.
Attorney-history buff Charles Hillestad and his wife, Anne, bought this 1879 Victorian in the mid-1970s, and turned it into one of Denver's best-known bed and breakfasts. Located in the Clements Historic District, it was built by famed architect

Frank Edbrooke and stands opposite a small park only about five blocks from Edbrooke's Brown Palace Hotel. Fine art, antiques, and fresh flowers adorn the home. A dramatic oak stairway leads to two floors of distinctive rooms—including the Fountain Room, with its four-poster bed and luxurious sunken bathtub; the Aspen Room, occupying a rooftop turret and boasting walls painted in a continuous mural of autumn-colored aspens; and the Columbine Room, with a canopied bed and stained-glass windows overlooking the garden. Every room has a writing desk and a refrigerator. Free for guests are wine tastings, high teas, bowls of fresh fruit, and carafes of apéritif wines. Breakfast is an elaborate continental affair. Smoking is not permitted in the house

## INEXPENSIVE

**COMFORT INN, 401 17th St., Denver, CO 80202. Tel. 303/296-0400,** or 800/228-5150. 228 rms (all with bath). A/C TV TEL
**$ Rates** (including continental breakfast): $49–$65 single or double. AE, CB, DC, MC, V. **Parking:** $7 per day.
This may be Denver's best value in a modern, comfortable downtown accommodation. A private walkway over Tremont Place connects the Comfort Inn to the mezzanine of the Brown Palace Hotel—by which it was once owned as an annex. Rooms are adequate in size, and have all standard furnishings. The higher rooms in this 22-story hotel have great views, but they tend to overheat on hot summer days in spite of the air-conditioning system, so a lower-level room is preferable. Guests are treated to a free cocktail party with hot hors d'oeuvres at 5pm daily.

**DAYS INN CAPITOL HILL, 1150 E. Colfax Ave., Denver, CO 80218. Tel. 303/831-7700,** or 800/325-2525. 143 rms (all with bath). A/C TV TEL
**$ Rates** (including continental breakfast): $44–$54 single; $49–$60 double. Reduced weekend rates. AE, CB, DC, MC, V.
The brightly decorated rooms are reached from an interior corridor, and open onto a courtyard with a large swimming pool (open seasonally). There's also a casual restaurant and lounge here, and a complimentary shuttle to the airport and the State Capitol. Pets are welcome.

**VICTORIA OAKS INN, 1575 Race St., Denver, CO 80206. Tel. 303/355-1818.** 10 rms (1 with bath), 1 suite. A/C
**$ Rates** (including continental breakfast): $39–$69 single; $49–$79 double; $100 suite. AE, MC, V.
A European-style bed and breakfast across the street from the Castle Marne, this circa-1896 Victorian home has handsome oak floors accented by green carpeting. The nine upstairs rooms share baths; there's also a basement suite and a room with a private bath and fireplace on the main floor. Guests have kitchen and laundry privileges.

## BUDGET

**CENTRAL YMCA, 25 E. 16th Ave., Denver, CO 80202. Tel. 303/861-8300.** 189 rms (30 with bath). A/C TEL
**$ Rates:** $14–$24 single; $18–$30 double. MC, V.
Located just a block from the State Capitol, the Y offers clean, small, simple rooms—just big enough for a bed, a chair, and a dresser. Most share a bath down the hall; private baths are available. Overnight guests may use the Y's swimming pool, gymnasiums, sports courts, and workout rooms.

**MELBOURNE HOTEL AND HOSTEL, 607 22nd St., Denver, CO 80205. Tel. 303/292-6386.** 20 rms (all with bath); 38 beds (none with bath).
**$ Rates:** $8 bed; $15–$25 single; $22–$32 double. MC, V.
Backpackers enjoy this establishment, located six blocks from the bus station. There are dormitory rooms (with shared baths) and private rooms (with ceiling fans and their

own baths), all clean and secure. A common kitchen and laundry are open to all guests.

## OUTSIDE DOWNTOWN
### EXPENSIVE

**STOUFFER CONCOURSE HOTEL, 3801 Quebec St., Denver, CO 80207. Tel. 303/399-7500,** or 800/HOTELS-1. Fax 303/321-1966. 390 rms, 10 suites. A/C MINIBAR TV TEL
**$ Rates:** $125–$145 single; $135–$155 double; $185–$650 suite. AE, CB, DC, DISC, JCB, MC, V. **Parking:** Free.

Rated by Andrew Harper's *Hideaway Report* as the No. 1 airport hotel in the U.S., the Stouffer Concourse is a white double pyramid 12 stories high with a 10-story atrium. Tropical palms and fig trees rise beneath the central skylight, with vines draping from the balconies. A phone beside the reception desk underscores the hotel's commitment to service: It's a direct line to a red phone on the general manager's desk!

Each spacious room is appointed in peach and lime. It has two queen-size beds or one king-size, with an easy chair and ottoman, a desk with a telephone (75¢ for local calls), a large vanity, an armoire, and a private balcony. Coffee and a morning newspaper are delivered with the wakeup call. Three concierge floors have upgraded amenities, including a complimentary breakfast.

**Dining/Entertainment:** There's live light-jazz piano all day long at the Concorde Restaurant and Lounge, open daily from 6:30am to 11pm. Lunch entrees run $6.25 to $12.95; dinners—steaks and seafood in creative preparations—$12.25 to $19.50.

**Services:** 24-hour room service and concierge service, courtesy airport shuttle, no-smoking rooms and rooms equipped for the handicapped; incoming faxes are free, outgoing faxes have reduced rates, and there's no operator-assistance surcharge on phone bills.

**Facilities:** Indoor and outdoor swimming pools, whirlpool, steam room, full exercise room (Nautilus and free weights); meeting facilities for 1,300.

### MODERATE

**LOEWS GIORGIO HOTEL, 4150 E. Mississippi Ave., Denver, CO 80222. Tel. 303/782-9300,** or 800/345-9172. Fax 303/758-6542. 176 rms, 21 suites. A/C TV TEL
**$ Rates** (including continental breakfast): $99–$114 single; $109–$124 double; $160–$550 suite. Weekend rate $69 single or double. Children under 18 stay free in parents' room. AE, CB, DC, MC, V. **Parking:** Free.

Staying at Loews Giorgio is a little like taking a trip to Rome. Located just east of Colorado Boulevard and south of the community of Glendale, this is a black-steel and reflecting-glass tower on the outside—but inside, it's *bella Italia*. When it opened in 1987, the "ribbon" cut was a 20-foot strand of fettuccine. Columns are finished in faux marble and pillars are worked in faux wood grain. Renaissance-style murals and paintings look five centuries old. A library with a television, current newspapers and magazines, a carafe of complimentary Italian wine (5 to 10pm), and trays of Italian cookies is always open to guests.

Hotel owner Jack Naiman traveled to Italy to select antiques for the guest rooms. They include exquisite king-size and double beds with roll-top headboards. There's a wide use of colors (especially peaches and reds), floral patterns, Italian silk wall coverings, and marble-top furnishings. The desk offers a computer jack with its telephone (local calls are 50¢). All rooms have three phones and terry-cloth robes. The west-facing rooms have superb views of the Rocky Mountains.

The hotel offers a full range of services and dining and other facilities.

**SHERATON DENVER AIRPORT HOTEL, 3535 Quebec St., Denver, CO 80207. Tel. 303/333-7711,** or 800/325-3535. Fax 303/322-2262. 192 rms, 4 suites. A/C TV TEL
**$ Rates:** $90–$99 single; $90–$114 double; $150–$175 suite. Weekend rate $59

single or double. Children under 17 stay free in parents' room. AE, CB, DC, DISC, ER, JCB, MC, V. **Parking:** Free.

An 18,000-square-foot fenced backyard is an earmark of this eight-story hotel, across the street from Stapleton Airport. Guests use the grassy stretch for volleyball, barbecues, or just suntanning. Rooms are appointed in grays and greens, with light-wood furnishings and a king-size or two double beds. They have desks, direct-dial phones (local calls are 50¢), cable TVs, and clock radios. Suites have different themes: southwestern, Asian, executive, or traditional (with kitchen).

The hotel offers a full range of services and dining and other facilities.

## INEXPENSIVE

**ON GOLDEN POND BED & BREAKFAST, 7831 Eldridge St., Arvada, CO 80005. Tel. 303/424-2296.** 4 rms (all with bath). A/C

**$ Rates** (including breakfast): $40–$75 single or double. MC, V.

Ten acres of countryside surround this custom-built two-story brick home in the Rocky Mountain foothills 15 miles west of Denver. Verandas overlook a floating gazebo in a natural pond that attracts birds and other wildlife. Host Kathy Kula, a native of Germany, serves an extensive breakfast outdoors or indoors, and a *kaffeeklatsch* of coffee and pastries in the afternoon. Each guest room has a sliding glass door, which opens onto the veranda. Three of the rooms have private Jacuzzis; the Italianate Peacock Room has a king-size waterbed beneath a cathedral ceiling. All guests share a living room TV and fireplace, and a swimming pool and outdoor hot tub.

**THE HAMPTON INN, 3605 S. Wadsworth Blvd., Lakewood, CO 80235. Tel. 303/989-6900,** or 800/528-1234. 150 rms (all with bath). A/C TV TEL

**$ Rates** (including continental breakfast): $55–$63 single or double. Weekend rates $39 single or double. AE, CB, DC, MC, V.

Located on the southwestern edge of the metropolitan area, just south of U.S. 285 on Colo. 121, this pleasant motel offers rapid access to the foothills communities west of Denver. The rooms are well lit and brightly decorated, and feature king-size or double beds and plush lounge chairs.

## BUDGET

**MOTEL 6, 6 W. 83rd Pl., Thornton, CO 80221. Tel. 303/429-1550** or 505/891-6161 for central reservations. 121 rms (all with bath). A/C TV TEL

**$ Rates:** $26 single; $32 double. AE, DC, DISC, MC, V.

A no-frills accommodation, the Motel 6 has just enough amenities to make a night's stay comfortable. Rooms, though small, are clean; they have a phone and television; and there's even a swimming pool for summer afternoon dips. This Motel 6 is located off I-25 at Exit 219, north of Denver. There are others in the metropolitan area at 10300 South I-70 Frontage Road, Wheat Ridge, CO 80033 (tel. 303/467-3172); at 480 Wadsworth Boulevard, Denver, CO 80226 (tel. 303/232-4924); and near the airport at 12020 East 39th Avenue, Denver, CO 80239 (tel. 303/371-1980).

---

 ## FROMMER'S COOL FOR KIDS:

### HOTELS

**Hyatt Regency Denver** (see p. 45) The Camp Hyatt program introduces children to new friends and takes them on field trips while Mom and Dad shop or take in adult activities.

**Loews Giorgio Hotel** (see p. 52) Kids get a coloring book, crayons, and animal crackers when they arrive; there's also a special children's menu in the Tuscany Restaurant.

# 4. DINING

The categories below define a very expensive restaurant as one in which most dinner main courses are priced above $20; expensive, most dinner main courses $15 to $20; moderate, main courses $10 to $15; inexpensive, main courses $6 to $10; budget, main courses under $6.

## DOWNTOWN

### VERY EXPENSIVE

**AUGUSTA, in the Westin Hotel at Tabor Center, 1672 Lawrence St. Tel. 572-9100.**
   **Cuisine:** NEW AMERICAN. **Reservations:** Recommended.
**$ Prices:** Appetizers $4.75–$8; main courses $6.50–$12 at lunch, $13–$26 at dinner. AE, CB, DC, DISC, MC, V.
   **Open:** Lunch Tues–Fri 11:30am–2pm; dinner Tues–Fri 5:30–10pm, Sat 5:30–10:30pm.
Art deco decor and an open rotisserie spit draw immediate attention at this fine restaurant, selected as the best hotel restaurant in the city by *Denver Post* readers in 1990. Named for Horace Tabor's first wife, it has curving picture windows that overlook Skyline Park. Black-lacquered wood furnishings have melon-colored upholstery, accented by polished brass, etched-glass panels, potted palms, and fine china and crystal table settings.
   The menu emphasizes grilled and broiled dishes, in a gourmet new American style. Start with marinated silver salmon smoked over apple chips with caviar, or a cactus-cream seafood chowder. Main-course specialties include a rack of lamb in pecans and chestnuts, turkey breast poached in Gewurztraminer with a light curry-yogurt sauce, and a mixed grill of lobster, chicken, and beef tenderloin. The soufflé of the day is always popular.

**CLIFF YOUNG'S, 700 E. 17th Ave. Tel. 831-8900.**
   **Cuisine:** NEW AMERICAN. **Reservations:** Highly recommended.
**$ Prices:** Appetizers $8–$12; main courses $7.95–$14.95 at lunch, $17–$29 at dinner. AE, CB, DC, DISC, MC, V.
   **Open:** Lunch Mon–Fri 11am–2pm; dinner Sun–Thurs 6–10pm, Fri–Sat 6–11pm.
This is probably the one restaurant in the city that no one would argue if you labeled it "Denver's best." Spacious, elegant, dimly lit, it is sophisticated without being pretentious, like the ultimate upscale bistro. A classical pianist plays nightly, and is joined by a violinist Wednesday through Sunday. Young, who has a master's degree in philosophy and is a published poet, has developed a foundation of loyal local customers since he opened his restaurant in 1984. "It's my sensitivity for people," he says. That, the impeccable service, and the superb cuisine.
   Chef Dave Query's menu changes seasonally, while always focusing on Colorado products. Wild rice and duck cake with black-currant sauce is a heavenly appetizer; some swear by the rabbit terrine with pistachio nuts. Main dishes might include medallions of elk in a cherry-wine sauce, quail with a chestnut stuffing served with a dried-peach sauce, or pan-seared Atlantic salmon with macadamia and five-citrus butter.

**THE MARQUIS, in the Hyatt Regency Denver, 1750 Welton St. Tel. 295-5825.**
   **Cuisine:** CONTINENTAL. **Reservations:** Highly recommended.
**$ Prices:** Appetizers $6.75–$11.50; main courses $6.50–$13.50 at lunch, $17.50–$23.50 at dinner. AE, CB, DC, DISC, JCB, MC, V.
   **Open:** Lunch Mon–Fri 11:30am–2pm; dinner Mon–Sat 6–10pm.

A floor-to-ceiling brass wine rack greets diners at the restaurant entrance. Within, elegant suede wall coverings are adorned by gold-laminated sculptures. The ceiling is Belgian crystal set in brass. And everything else about the Marquis, a winner of *Travel/Holiday* magazine's fine dining award, underscores the luxurious atmosphere.

Start with shrimp amoureuses or a lobster bisque, continue with a Caesar salad prepared tableside, then sate your appetite with steak au poivre, spit-roasted duckling, or sole meunière. If you still crave a sweet, try the "floating islands"—poached meringue in vanilla sauce, topped with caramel and sliced almonds.

**PALACE ARMS, in the Brown Palace Hotel, 321 17th St. Tel. 297-3111.**
   **Cuisine:** INTERNATIONAL. **Reservations:** Highly recommended.
   **$ Prices:** Appetizers $6–$23.50; main courses $7.75–$17.50 at lunch, $18.50–$29 at dinner. AE, CB, DC, DISC, JCB, MC, V.
   **Open:** Lunch Mon–Fri 11:30am–2pm; dinner nightly 6–10pm.

The Palace Arms is a Napoleonic museum. Napoleon's own dueling pistols are mounted just inside the doorway, and a pair of papier-mâché golden eagles are parade decorations from the great Frenchman's march to Notre Dame to crown himself emperor. Behind glass are a full set of French military band figures, carved from wood by an imprisoned dollmaker. Replicas of battle flags, rich leather banquettes, 19th-century hunting prints, and ornate mirrors lend a strong European atmosphere.

The cuisine is an interesting combination of traditional American, new American, classical French, and southwestern influences. Start with a fresh lobster enchilada or pasta torta of chicken mousseline; follow with a wild-rice soup (with brandied almond cream). For the main course try sautéed breast of ringneck pheasant, roast loin of veal with sweetbreads and zucchini caponata, or canneloni of shrimp, lobster, scallops, and mussels. Flambés are a dessert specialty. The wine list is one of 42 around the world to receive *The Wine Spectator* magazine's award of excellence.

## EXPENSIVE

**THE BROKER RESTAURANT, 821 17th St., near Champa St. Tel. 292-5065.**
   **Cuisine:** STEAK/SEAFOOD. **Reservations:** Recommended.
   **$ Prices:** Lunch $7.95–$14.95; dinner $18.95–$29.95. AE, CB, DC, MC, V.
   **Open:** Lunch Mon–Fri 11am–2:30pm; dinner Sun–Thurs 5–10pm, Fri–Sat 5–10:30pm.

A huge vault in the basement of the old Denver National Bank building is the site of the Broker, fittingly located in the heart of the financial district. Diners enter through a circular 23-ton door and sit in cherry-wood booths once used by bank customers to inspect safety-deposit boxes. European antiques add to the Wall Street atmosphere.

Generous portions are an earmark of meals at the Broker. New York and Porterhouse steaks, tournedos Oscar and chicken Colorado, Alaskan king-crab legs and blackened catfish are just some of the house favorites. Nonmeat eaters are catered to with vegetarian Wellington. A 24-ounce bowl of steamed Gulf shrimp precedes all main dishes, and soup, green or spinach salad, baked bread, vegetables, and dessert are included with all meals. Tableside preparation of Caesar salad and cherries jubilee is also offered. The mammoth wine list (67 pages long) includes everything from regional maps to winery addresses, and is worth a visit in itself. Bottles run $14 to $2,000, the latter for a 1914 Château Lafite Rothschild.

**BUCKHORN EXCHANGE, 1000 Osage St., at W. 10th Ave. Tel. 534-9505.**
   **Cuisine:** ROCKY MOUNTAIN. **Reservations:** Recommended.
   **$ Prices:** Appetizers $4.25–$7.25; main courses $5.50–$12.50 at lunch, $14–$28 at dinner. AE, CB, DC, DISC, MC, V.
   **Open:** Lunch Mon–Fri 11am–3pm; dinner Sun–Thurs 5–10:30pm, Fri–Sat 5–11pm.

Denver's dining institution is located outside the downtown core, a few blocks south of the Ninth Street Historic District opposite the Rio Grande Railroad Yards.

0 200 m
220 y

24th St.
Park
23rd St.

Tremont Pl.
Park

Glenarm Pl.
Welton St.
California St.
Stout St.

22nd St.
21st St.
20th St.
Denver Bus Terminal
19th St.
18th St.
17th St.
Skyline Park
Mall

Pennsylvania St.
Logan St.
Grant St.
Sherman St.
Lincoln St.
E. 20th Ave.
E. 19th Ave.
E. 18th Ave.
E. 17th Ave.
Broadway

10

Welton St.
California St.
Stout St.
Champa St.
Curtis St.
Arapahoe St.
Lawrence St.
Larimer St.
Market St.
Blake St.
Wazee St.
Wynkoop St.
Wewatta St.

16th St.
15th St.
14th St.
13th St.
12th St.
Walnut St.

Union Station

St. Fran
W

17
22
6
8

4
20
7
1

18
9

2
3
13
19
12
14
23

# DENVER DINING

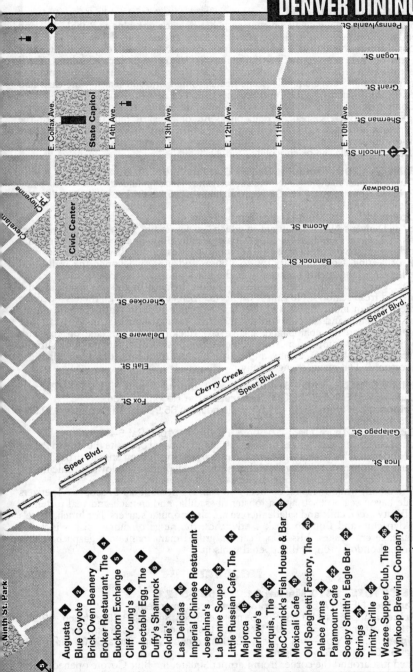

Augusta **1**
Blue Coyote **2**
Brick Oven Beanery **3**
Broker Restaurant, The **4**
Buckhorn Exchange **5**
Cliff Young's **6**
Delectable Egg, The **7**
Duffy's Shamrock **8**
Goldie's **9**
Las Delicias **10**
Imperial Chinese Restaurant **11**
Josephina's **12**
La Bonne Soupe **13**
Little Russian Cafe, The **14**
Majorca **15**
Marlowe's **16**
Marquis, The **17**
McCormick's Fish House & Bar **18**
Mexicali Cafe **19**
Old Spaghetti Factory, The **20**
Palace Arms **21**
Paramount Cafe **22**
Soapy Smith's Eagle Bar **23**
Strings **24**
Trinity Grille **25**
Wazee Supper Club, The **26**
Wynkoop Brewing Company **27**

Post Office  ✝■    ⊠ Church  ✝■

Founded in 1893 by Henry H. "Shorty Scout" Zietz—nicknamed by Sitting Bull and employed as a cowboy scout or hunting guide by such notables as Buffalo Bill and Theodore Roosevelt—it still occupies the same premises it did when Colorado Liquor License No. 1 was awarded. That certificate is still displayed over the 133-year-old hand-carved oak bar in the upstairs Victorian parlor and saloon. You'll have to search a bit to find it, though: Much more in evidence throughout the restaurant are 235 large animals (some heads, some full bodies) and more than 250 other taxidermy items, as well as a collection of 125 rare firearms.

Come to the Buckhorn to try Rocky Mountain oysters, smoked buffalo sausage, buffalo prime rib, elk steak, rabbit, pheasant, or alligator tail. If you're not the adventurous sort, you can also get steaks (a 24-oz. Porterhouse), chops, ribs, or a catch-of-the-day. Homemade bean soup comes with every meal, and dessert is old-fashioned apple pie or chocolate "moose."

**STRINGS, 1700 Humboldt St., at E. 17th Ave. Tel. 831-7310.**
   **Cuisine:** NEW AMERICAN. **Reservations:** Recommended.
   **$ Prices:** Appetizers $4.75–$8.25; main courses $6.25–$12 at lunch, $10.75–$20 at dinner. AE, CB, DC, MC, V.
   **Open:** Mon–Sat 11am–11pm, Sun 5–11pm.
Rated as Denver's No. 1 restaurant in which "to see and be seen," Strings welcomes guests in T-shirts as well as tuxedoes. It's especially popular among the before- and after-theater crowds. A casual establishment on Restaurant Row, Strings has two levels of seating. Contemporary music albums and posters decorate the walls, and large flower arrangements contrast with the black-and-white color scheme.

Chef Noel Cunningham, a native of Dublin, Ireland, orients his menu around pastas and fresh seafood. He calls it California Irish cuisine, though there's a definite northern Italian influence as well. Go for the penne bagutta (with chicken, mushrooms, broccoli, and a spicy tomato-and-basil rustica sauce), Strings pasta (with asparagus and cream, champagne, and caviar), duck breast rosé (char-broiled with wild rice, maple syrup, and a creamy date sauce), or swordfish tamara (with shrimp, bay scallops, mushrooms, capers, and beurre blanc). Unique meat and fish salads are also featured. The menu changes daily.

**TRINITY GRILLE, 1801 Broadway, at Tremont Place. Tel. 293-2288.**
   **Cuisine:** STEAK/SEAFOOD. **Reservations:** Recommended.
   **$ Prices:** Appetizers $4.50–$7.50; main courses $5.95–$9.95, at lunch, $10.95–$25.95 at dinner. AE, DC, MC, V.
   **Open:** Mon–Thurs 11am–10:30pm, Fri 11am–11pm, Sat 5–11pm.
Subdued elegance characterizes this fine restaurant, located opposite the Brown Palace Hotel and next door to the Museum of Western Art. In effect an upscale urban tavern, it boasts mahogany furnishings with brass trim, leaded-glass windows and tile floors, white linen tablecloths, and original artwork on the walls.

The menu, while focusing on beef and fish, is international in scope. Appetizers include bayou seafood sausage, a lobster quesadilla, and spinach-and-veal tortellini. The Trinity green chile and salade niçoise are also popular starters. For lunch, there's Brooklyn club and Boursin steak sandwiches; the range of dinner dishes includes Chesapeake crab cakes, Mississippi catfish, grilled mahi mahi with gazpacho salsa, schnitzel, London broil, and peppered venison.

## MODERATE

**BLUE COYOTE, 1410 Market St. Tel. 623-5171.**
   **Cuisine:** NEW WEST. **Reservations:** Recommended.
   **$ Prices:** Appetizers $3.95–$6.75; main courses $4.75–$8.75 at lunch, $9.95–$19.95 at dinner. AE, CB, DC, MC, V. 10% discount for cash payments.
   **Open:** Lunch Mon–Fri 11:30am–2:30pm; dinner Mon–Thurs 5:30–10pm, Fri–Sat 5:30–11pm, Sun 5–9pm.
Located just around the corner from Larimer Square, the Blue Coyote opened in late 1989 and quickly became a fixture in the city. A bighorn chandelier hangs over the bar, and a coyote-howling-at-the-moon motif recurs in etched-glass dividers. Spanish

classical guitar or contemporary jazz music plays continually. Each table is graced with a small potted evergreen.

Chef Jim Hay has made it his personal mission to define the term "New West cuisine." He focuses on creative preparations of Rocky Mountain fish and game with a bent toward southwestern ingredients: chile peppers, cilantro, piñon nuts, salsa, and tequila. The wild game medley, which varies nightly, might include elk, buffalo, rabbit, quail, and/or pheasant. Colorado striped bass, Blue Mesa turkey, and Phantom Canyon venison are favorites, and the Kiowa pie (Hay's answer to a shepherd's pie) is big with the lunch crowd.

**JOSEPHINA'S, 1433 Larimer St. Tel. 623-0166.**
   **Cuisine:** ITALIAN. **Reservations:** Recommended most nights; not accepted Fri–Sat.
$ **Prices:** Appetizers $3.50–$6.75; main courses $8.50–$15.95. AE, DISC, MC, V.
   **Open:** Sun–Thurs 11am–11pm, Fri–Sat 11am–midnight. **Closed:** Thanksgiving and Christmas.

A Larimer Square institution, Josephina's invokes nostalgia for decades past. Posters, neon lights, and early to mid-20th-century advertising signs decorate the walls of the bar. A wall-size mural of flappers from the Roaring '20s backs the bandstand (there's live rock or blues nightly). The adjacent dining room keeps the nostalgic feel, but it has carpets instead of a hardwood floor and white-linen service.

House specialties include fettuccine Josephina's (with chicken, tomatoes, and wine sauce), eggplant Parmigiana, and rack of veal chop, prepared a different way daily. There's a wide selection of seafood and pasta, including seafood Josephina's (scampi, bay shrimp, mussels, scallops, and clams on fettuccine) and pasta puttanesca (with sun-dried tomatoes, olives, red pepper, and garlic).

Josephina's has a secluded, romantic restaurant at 17th Avenue and Downing Street (tel. 860-8011) and a festive patio restaurant at 7777 East Hampden Avenue, Aurora (tel. 750-4422).

**LA BONNE SOUPE, 1512 Larimer St., Writer Sq. Tel. 595-9169.**
   **Cuisine:** FRENCH. **Reservations:** Recommended.
$ **Prices:** Appetizers $5.95–$7.95; main courses $5.25–$15.95 at lunch, $6.95–$17.95 at dinner. AE, CB, DC, MC, V.
   **Open:** Mon–Thurs 11am–10pm, Fri–Sat 11am–11pm, Sun noon–8pm.

A faithful replica of a French sidewalk bistro, this casual restaurant combines a patio café atmosphere with indoor seating that looks out onto Writer Square mall. Owner Shep Brown created it with the memory of his native Paris fresh in mind.

As the name suggests, soups are a meal in themselves. French onion, asparagus, and lamb, mushroom, and barley are always available, as is a soup du jour. Fondues (cheese, bourguigonne, and chocolate) are crowd pleasers. The plats du jour include poulet chasseur, crevettes provençales, and filet mignon au poivre.

**THE LITTLE RUSSIAN CAFE, 1424 Larimer St. Tel. 595-8600.**
   **Cuisine:** RUSSIAN. **Reservations:** Recommended.
$ **Prices:** Appetizers $3.50–$6.75; main courses at lunch $6–$9.50, dinner $8.50–$15.75. AE, CB, DC, DISC, JCB, MC, V.
   **Open:** Lunch Mon–Sat 11am–2:30pm; dinner Sun–Thurs 5:30–10pm, Fri–Sat 5:30–11pm.

A quiet, romantic restaurant set back in a Larimer Square arcade, Leningrad native Eugene Valershteyn's café is a touch of the old country . . . with a generous dose of the new, as well. Russian folk music shares air time with Dixieland jazz, and a uniformed mannequin plays the balalaika in a front window. Russian paintings and posters decorate the discreet, dimly lit dining room. There's also an outdoor patio.

Meals start with a shot of ice-cold vodka, followed by yazyk (spicy sliced beef tongue) or vareniki (potato-and-onion dumplings). They normally include a soup like shchi (cabbage, carrots, and celery in beef broth) or borscht (the famous beet-rich concoction). Among the main dishes are zharkoe (a beef-and-mushroom casserole), kurinyie kotlety (garlic-flavored chicken cutlets), nelma (a fish, carrot, and cheese casserole), and, of course, beef à la Stroganoff.

**MARLOWE'S, 16th St. at Glenarm St. Tel. 595-3700.**
   **Cuisine:** STEAK/SEAFOOD. **Reservations:** Recommended.
$ **Prices:** Appetizers $3.50–$13.50; main courses $5.95–$12.95 at lunch, $7.25–$18.95 at dinner. AE, CB, DC, MC, V.
   **Open:** Mon–Thurs 11am–11pm, Fri 11am–midnight, Sat 5pm–midnight.
Once called by *Cosmopolitan* magazine "one of the 10 hottest restaurant-bars in the country," Marlowe's has two levels of plant-surrounded seating beneath a vaulted ceiling and an outdoor patio on the 16th Street Mall, where seating seems always to be at a premium. Occupying a corner of the 1891 Kittredge Building, listed in the National Register of Historic Places, it features an antique cherry-wood bar, granite pillars, and plenty of open space for mixing.
   Many folks come here just for drinks and appetizers, like oysters Rockefeller, salmon brochette, and rumaki (baked chicken livers). There's an extensive choice of salads. Full meals, with salad, bread, and vegetables, include a Chicago-style veal rib chop, filet béarnaise, chicken marsala, poached Pacific salmon, and fish du jour.

**McCORMICK'S FISH HOUSE AND BAR, in the Oxford Alexis Hotel, 1659 Wazee St. Tel. 825-1107.**
   **Cuisine:** SEAFOOD. **Reservations:** Recommended.
$ **Prices:** Appetizers $2.95–$8.95; lunch and light dishes $4.95–$9.75; dinner $8.90–$21.95. AE, CB, DC, DISC, JCB, MC, V.
   **Open:** Breakfast Mon–Fri 6:30–10am; lunch Mon–Fri 11:30am–2:30pm; dinner Sun–Thurs 5–10pm, Fri–Sat 5–11pm; brunch Sat–Sun 7am–2pm.
Operating out of lower downtown's restored Oxford Alexis Hotel, an active part of city life since 1891, McCormick's is owned by the same seafood lovers who operate McCormick and Schmick's in Seattle and Jake's in Portland, Oregon. The restaurant maintains the turn-of-the-century theme with original stained-glass windows and skylights, oak booths, and a fine polished-wood bar.
   Seafood is flown in fresh daily, including Dungeness crab from Alaska, Goose Point oysters from Washington state, mussels from Maine, fresh yellowfin tuna from Hawaii, swordfish from California, rockfish from Oregon, and trout from Idaho.

## INEXPENSIVE

**IMPERIAL CHINESE RESTAURANT, 1 Broadway, at First Ave. Tel. 698-2800.**
   **Cuisine:** CHINESE. **Reservations:** Recommended.
$ **Prices:** Individual dishes $6–$13. AE, CB, DC, MC, V.
   **Open:** Mon–Thurs 11am–10pm, Fri 11am–10:30pm, Sat noon–10:30pm, Sun 4–10pm.
Spicy Szechuan and Hunan, hearty Mandarin, and delicate Cantonese items are offered at this restaurant, named by *Westword* readers as the best Chinese establishment in Denver 7 years running. A laughing Buddha and exquisite hand-carved wooden screens greet diners at the entrance, and inside, the mirrored ceiling and gold decor provide a regal atmosphere. You can't go wrong with anything here, but try the hot-and-sour soup, the sesame chicken, sweet-and-sour pork, or the Dungeness crab stir-fried with scallions and ginger. Seafood, in fact, is a specialty here, and the service is wonderfully attentive.

**MAJORCA, 777 E. 17th Ave. Tel. 830-1777.**
   **Cuisine:** MEDITERRANEAN. **Reservations:** Recommended.
$ **Prices:** Appetizers and tapas, $1.95–$7.95; dinner $7.25–$13.95. AE, CB, DC, MC, V.
   **Open:** Lunch Mon–Fri 11:30am–2:30pm; dinner Mon–Sat 5:30–10:30pm (bar service until midnight).
Tapas are light appetizers, no one plate of which is enough to make a meal, but which are very satisfying in variety and quantity. They are, in a word, "more-ish." So it's appropriate that this Mediterranean restaurant on Restaurant Row has architecture that's, well, Moorish. Tall arched windows, tile floors, decorative wrought iron, and

Mediterranean garden decor all fit the mood. The tapas range from applewood-smoked quail and lamb dolmas to mussels and clams Botticelli. The caponatta—roast eggplant with squash, peppers, and onions—is particularly good. Pastas, soups, salads, grilled sandwiches, and desserts round out the menu. Mediterranean-style dinners are served on the second floor, including steak cappricoso and cioppino.

## MEXICALI CAFE, 1453 Larimer St. Tel. 892-1444.

**Cuisine:** MEXICAN. **Reservations:** For parties of six or more; not accepted Wed–Fri at lunch or Fri–Sat at dinner.

**$ Prices:** Appetizers $2.75–$6.95; main courses $5.25–$11.95. AE, DISC, MC, V.

**Open:** Sun–Thurs 11am–10pm, Fri–Sat 11am–11pm.

The small burrito bar at the Larimer Square street entrance is misleading: The fiesta is at the bottom of the stairs. Mariachi music is piped through, and the bright orange-and-red decor may at first pop your eyes out. An orange 1947 Cadillac protrudes from one wall. The food is just as much fun: traditional foods like mesquite-roasted relleños, fajita burritos, and Santa Fe trail hash; rotisserie-turned meats like chile-rubbed chicken (with green-chile pesto) or Baja camarones (shrimp) in a spicy barbecue sauce.

## THE OLD SPAGHETTI FACTORY, 1215 18th St., at Lawrence St. Tel. 295-1864.

**Cuisine:** ITALIAN. **Reservations:** For large parties only.

**$ Prices:** Main courses $4.25–$9.50. AE, MC, V.

**Open:** Lunch Mon–Fri 11:30am–2pm; dinner Mon–Thurs 5–10pm, Fri–Sat 5–11pm, Sun 4–10pm.

Cable cars have long since ceased to be a part of the Denver scene, but they live on in the historic Tramway Cable building, with its 195-foot chimney. One of the trolley cars, in fact, is so much a part of this restaurant that there's seating inside it! The cheerful atmosphere of Victorian relics is a great place for a plate of spaghetti, served with a choice of five different sauces. Every meal includes salad, garlic butter, beverage, and spumoni ice cream.

## SOAPY SMITH'S EAGLE BAR, 1317 14th St. Tel. 534-1111.

**Cuisine:** AMERICAN. **Reservations:** For large parties only.

**$ Prices:** Lunch $3.95–$6.95; dinner $5.95–$18.95. AE, MC, V.

**Open:** Mon–Thurs 11am–10:30pm, Fri 11am–midnight, Sat noon–midnight (bar Mon–Sat until 1am).

Jefferson Randolph "Soapy" Smith was a con artist known throughout the American West, from Denver to Skagway, Alaska, in the late 19th century. This three-story western saloon wasn't in town when he was, but there are photos of him, as well as old Denver and nearby mining towns, set around the brick walls. Tourists, families, and businesspeople all enjoy this tavern, which gets increasingly rowdy as the night wears on. Burgers, chicken, steaks, and seafood, along with home-style items like pot roast, highlight the menu.

## WYNKOOP BREWING COMPANY, 1634 18th St., at Wynkoop St. Tel. 297-2700.

**Cuisine:** INTERNATIONAL. **Reservations:** For large parties.

**$ Prices:** Appetizers $1.25–$5.25; lunch $3.95–$7.25; dinner $4.50–$12.95. AE, DISC, MC, V.

**Open:** Lunch Mon–Sat 11am–3pm; dinner Sun–Thurs 5–10pm, Fri–Sat 5–11pm (brew pub Mon–Thurs 11am–1am, Fri–Sat 11am–2am, Sun 11am–midnight).

When the Wynkoop opened its doors in 1988 as Denver's first new brewery in more than 50 years, it started a mini-revolution. Nearly a dozen other small private breweries have since opened in Colorado, but the Wynkoop sets the standard. Located in a renovated LoDo warehouse across from Union Station, the brewery-restaurant was the brainchild of a pair of laid-off geologists who found the road to commercial success not too rocky. Free tours of the brewery, which turns out a variety of brews, are offered on Saturday between 1 and 5pm.

The food served here is surprisingly good—shepherd's pie filled with lamb and mashed potatoes, Spanish-style olla podrida stew, Uncompahgre black-bean cakes with rice, Greek salad, marinated shark steak, homemade apple-pecan sausage. There's a little of everything . . . and it all goes with beer.

## BUDGET

**BRICK OVEN BEANERY, 1007 E. Colfax Ave., at Ogden St. Tel. 860-0077.**
  **Cuisine:** AMERICAN.
  **$ Prices:** $2.95–$5.95. MC, V.
  **Open:** Mon–Sat 11am–8pm.
There's nothing fancy about this restaurant. Meals are dished up from a cafeteria line, which often extends all the way to the door. That in itself should tell you something. Meats are rotisserie-roasted, breads baked on the premises, salads and desserts homemade, malts and ice-cream sodas prepared 1950s style. And you can't argue with a leg of lamb dinner, a wild-rice meatloaf, or a half chicken with dressing and potatoes, salad and bread, for under $6.
  There are other branches at 10890 East Dartmouth Avenue and 8715 North Sheridan Street.

**THE DELECTABLE EGG, 1642 Market St. Tel. 572-8146.**
  **Cuisine:** AMERICAN.
  **$ Prices:** $2.95–$5.95. DC, MC, V.
  **Open:** Mon–Fri 6:30am–2pm, Sat–Sun 7am–2pm.
Every city should have a café like this one: eggs prepared 42 different ways, pancakes, waffles, and French toast . . . plus, for the after-11am lunch crowd, a variety of salads and sandwiches. You can get your eggs skillet fried, baked in a frittata, scrambled into pita pockets, smothered with chile or hollandaise, or any other way. About the only thing you can't get is a Denver omelet—here, it's called the "Mile High."
  The Delectable Egg has a second downtown location at 16th Street and Court Place (tel. 892-5720).

**DUFFY'S SHAMROCK, 1635 Court Place. Tel. 534-4935.**
  **Cuisine:** AMERICAN.
  **$ Prices:** Appetizers $2.25–$2.75; main courses $3.95–$9.25. AE, MC, V.
  **Open:** Daily 6:15am–1:15am.
In operation for more than three decades, this traditional Irish bar and restaurant with fast, cheerful service has been thriving at its present location since 1974. It specializes in Irish coffees and imported Irish beers. Daily specials may include prime rib, barbecued beef, fried prawns, or a stuffed bell pepper in Créole sauce. Sandwiches on every kind of bread are also offered: corned beef, Reuben, Braunschweiger, even a Dagwood. If you're still hungry after the sandwich, order the Duffy's special: hot raisin-and-custard pudding with blueberries, rice, and cream.

**GOLDIE'S, 511 16th St., at Glenarm Place. Tel. 623-6007.**
  **Cuisine:** DELI.
  **$ Prices:** $2.40–$4.95.
  **Open:** Mon–Fri 7am–5:30pm, Sat 10am–4pm.
A New York–style deli wedged between Marlowe's and the Paramount Café in the historic Kittredge Building, Goldie's features imported and kosher foods, with an emphasis on sandwiches . . . to eat there, or carry out on the 16th Street Mall. Consider the jive turkey, your swami's salami, Toulouse la Tuna, deliver de liver, or the Bronx blintz. Confused? Wait, there's more. Lox and lox of it.

**LAS DELICIAS, 439 E. 19th St., at Pennsylvania St. Tel. 839-5675.**
  **Cuisine:** MEXICAN.
  **$ Prices:** Main courses $5–$7. MC, V.
  **Open:** Mon–Sat 8am–9pm, Sun 9am–9pm.
Las Delicias occupies half a dozen interconnected rooms, all faced in plain red brick. The restaurant is a favorite among Hispanic families, who come back again and again. The food is always served with chips and spicy salsa. Tamales, burritos, tacos, and

other Mexican standbys are served, along with generous portions of carne asada and carne de puerco adovado. All dishes are served with plenty of fresh hot tortillas.

**PARAMOUNT CAFE, 511 16th St. Tel. 893-2000.**
   **Cuisine:** AMERICAN/MEXICAN.
   **$ Prices:** Lunch $2.50–$5.95; dinner $5.75–$6.95. AE, DC, MC, V.
   **Open:** Mon–Sat 11am–midnight.
The snack bar of Denver's historic Paramount Theatre, in the 1891 Kittredge Building, has been remodeled into one of the city's most popular restaurants. College-age servers in T-shirts (pink for women, yellow for men) move among an atmosphere of photos, posters, and other memorabilia of movies of the '40s, '50s, and '60s. The red vinyl soda fountain complete with an old jukebox has 44 bar stools, the most in the city. The menu features burgers and sandwiches, Tex-Mex burritos and nachos, and dinner favorites like country-fried chicken and a cheese-steak sandwich—as well, of course, as ice-cream sundaes and frozen margaritas.

**THE WAZEE SUPPER CLUB, 600 15th St., at Wazee St. Tel. 623-9518.**
   **Cuisine:** PIZZA/SANDWICHES.
   **$ Prices:** $2.95–$6.95, more for large pizzas. MC, V.
   **Open:** Mon–Sat 11am–1am.
A former plumbing-supply store in lower downtown, the Wazee is a Depression-era relic with a black-and-white tile floor and a bleached mahogany back bar. A hangout for jazz and pizza lovers (some say the pizza here is the best in the city),.it also serves an array of sandwiches from kielbasa to corned beef, buffalo to ham and cheese. There are 13 beers on draft. Don't miss the dumbwaiter used to shuttle food and drinks to the mezzanine floor: It's a converted 1937 garage door opener.

## OUTSIDE DOWNTOWN

### EXPENSIVE

**THE FORT, 19192 Colo. 8, off West Hampden Ave. (U.S. 285), Morrison. Tel. 697-4771.**
   **Cuisine:** ROCKY MOUNTAIN. **Reservations:** Recommended.
   **$ Prices:** Appetizers $3.95–$11.95; main courses $11.75–$28.95. AE, CB, DC, MC, V.
   **Open:** Dinner only, Mon–Fri 6–10pm, Sat 5–10pm, Sun 5–9pm. Special holiday hours.
There are many reasons to drive the 18 miles southwest from downtown Denver to visit The Fort. One is the atmosphere: The building is a full-scale reproduction of Bent's Fort, Colorado's first fur-trading post, hand-built adobe brick by adobe brick in 1962. The interior is equally authentic, and the staff are dressed as 19th-century Cheyenne-Native Americans. Another reason is owner Sam Arnold, a broadcast personality and master chef who opens champagne bottles with a tomahawk. He's had his menu translated into French, German, Spanish, Japanese, and Braille.

But the best reason is the food. The Fort built its reputation on high-quality, low-cholesterol buffalo, of which it serves the largest variety and greatest quantity of any restaurant in the world. There's buffalo steak, buffalo tongue, broiled buffalo marrow bones, and even "buffalo eggs"—hard-boiled quail eggs wrapped in buffalo sausage, which he served to Bryant Gumbel and Jane Pauley on *The Today Show*. Other house specialties are Taos trout, basted in a mint sauce and topped with bacon bits; "The Bowl of the Wife of Kit Carson," a spicy-hot chicken stew; broiled quail; and elk medallions with wild huckleberry sauce. Diehards can get beef steak.

**MATAAM FEZ, 4609 E. Colfax Ave. Tel. 399-9282.**
   **Cuisine:** MOROCCAN. **Reservations:** Recommended.
   **$ Prices:** Full dinners $21.75–$24. AE, CB, DC, MC, V.
   **Open:** Sun–Thurs 6–9:30pm, Fri–Sat 6–10:30pm.
A Moroccan restaurant out West is a rarity, and this one is in an authentic decor of low round tables, brass trays, and intricately designed wall tiles. Overhead is a bright-colored silk tent, and courses are served in running relays by waiters in caftans.

A traditional five-course dinner begins with lamb lentil soup and has three kinds of salad and b'stella, flaky egg-rich filo dough, and game hen smothered in a spicy 32-herb sauce and topped with crushed almonds, sugar, and cinnamon. Couscous is among other menu items. Lamb is prepared with honey, almond, eggplant, or onions; and there are various chicken specialties.

## MODERATE

**MOSTLY SEAFOOD, in King Soopers Shopping Center, 2223 S. Monaco Pkwy., at Evans Ave. Tel. 756-5541.**
  **Cuisine:** SEAFOOD. **Reservations:** Recommended.
$ **Prices:** Appetizers $4.95–$8.95; main courses $6.95–$11.95 at lunch, $9.95–$25.95 at dinner. MC, V.
  **Open:** Mon–Sat 11am–9pm, Sun 4–8pm.
They take their seafood seriously at this establishment. The atmosphere is bright and simple; the emphasis is on eating. Every catch is flown in fresh daily from the Pacific, Atlantic, or Gulf of Mexico. The menu offers a variety of steamed shellfish, spicy seafood stews, and fresh fish grilled, blackened, broiled, steamed, or fried. Specialties include a sautéed macadamia-nut ahi with taragon-mustard sauce, and a bouillabaisse of mussels, clams, crab, shrimp, and white fish. Daily specials always include a pasta and a stir-fry. Key lime pie is a recommended dessert.

There's another Mostly Seafood downtown in Republic Plaza on the 16th Street Mall at 303 16th Street (tel. 892-5999). Hours vary slightly.

**TRAIL DUST STEAK HOUSE, 7107 S. Clinton St., Tech Center. Tel. 790-2420.**
  **Cuisine:** STEAK. **Reservations:** For large groups only.
$ **Prices:** Appetizers $4–$7; main courses $8–$19. AE, DISC, MC, V.
  **Open:** Dinner only, Mon–Thurs 5–10pm, Fri–Sat 5pm–midnight, Sun noon–10pm.
Country music lovers flock to the Trail Dust, which serves up live dance music along with mesquite-broiled steaks and ribs nightly. Steaks come in sizes from 9 to 50 ounces, and are served with salad, beans, and ranch bread. Chicken and fish are also available. The unusual decor is comprised of necktie tips—if you let them clip yours off, you'll get a free drink.

To reach the Trail Dust, exit I-25 south at Arapahoe Road, drive one block east, and turn onto Clinton Street. There's a second Trail Dust at the north end of Denver: 9101 Benton Street, Westminster (tel. 427-1446), next to the Westminster Mall.

## INEXPENSIVE

**CASA BONITA, in the JCRS Shopping Center, 6715 W. Colfax Ave., Lakewood. Tel. 232-5115.**
  **Cuisine:** MEXICAN/AMERICAN. **Reservations:** For large parties only.
$ **Prices:** Lunch or dinner $6.95–$9.95. AE, CB, DC, DISC, MC, V.
  **Open:** Daily 11am–9:30pm.
A west Denver landmark, this is more a theme park than a restaurant! A peach-colored Spanish cathedral-type belltower greets visitors, who will find nonstop action inside: divers plummeting into a pool beside a 30-foot waterfall, puppet shows, a video arcade, Black Bart's Cave (a funhouse), and strolling mariachi bands. The food is served cafeteria style, which is truly an undertaking in a restaurant that seats 1,100! There's standard Mexican fare—enchiladas, tacos, tamales, and fajitas—along with country-fried steak, fried chicken, and fried fish. Hot sopaipillas, served at your table with honey, are delicious.

**PEARL STREET GRILL, 1477 S. Pearl St., at Florida Ave. Tel. 778-6475.**
  **Cuisine:** INTERNATIONAL. **Reservations:** For parties of six or more only.
$ **Prices:** Appetizers $3.25–$9.95; main courses $4.25–$7.95 at lunch, $5.95–$9.95 at dinner. AE, DC, MC, V.
  **Open:** Mon–Fri 11:30am–2am, Sat 11am–2am, Sun 11am–midnight; brunch Sat–Sun 11am–3pm.

This handsome bar and grill in the Washington Park neighborhood, just south of I-25 near the University of Denver, attracts a mixed bag of customers, from students to businesspeople to bikers. Inside, the atmosphere is modern, with a hardwood floor and oak furnishings. Outside is a big patio, adorned with flowers and packed throughout the summer. Soups, salads, and sandwiches are the lunchtime fare, including an outstanding Reuben and the "No Meat Treat." Dinner focuses on steak and seafood, such as the London broil and seafood fettuccine, as well as fajitas and a stir-fry "du jour." Brunch includes Cajun bubble-and-squeak, a New Orleans favorite. The bar offers 43 beers from 14 countries, including nine draft beers.

**T-WA INN, 555 S. Federal Blvd., near West Virginia Ave. Tel. 922-4584.**
   **Cuisine:** VIETNAMESE.
**$** **Prices:** Lunch $4.95–$11.95; dinner $6.95–$13.95. MC, V.
   **Open:** Sun–Thurs 11am–8:30pm, Fri–Sat 11am–10pm.
Denver's first Vietnamese restaurant is still its best. The decor is simple but pleasant, with Viet folk songs providing atmospheric background. Try the eggrolls, with shrimp and crab meat wrapped in rice paper; the hearty meat-and-noodle soups; the chicken salad; or the softshell crab. Vietnamese food, for the uninitiated, has similarities both to Thai and southern Chinese cooking.

## BUDGET

**BEACH GRILL RESTAURANT AND BAR, 5551 W. 88th Ave., Westminster. Tel. 428-7700.**
   **Cuisine:** AMERICAN.
**$** **Prices:** $2.95–$8.95. AE, MC, V.
   **Open:** May–Oct Tues–Sat 11:30am–2am.
Northwest Denver's favorite family fast-food establishment is this restaurant in the southeastern corner of Westminster Mall. On sunny days, as many as 500 people dine here at once, two-thirds of them on the all-season patio. Pizzas, burgers, and grilled sandwiches are the meals of choice. Try the Moon Doggie burger with sautéed mushrooms and onions.

**HEALTHY HABITS, 865 S. Colorado Blvd. Tel. 733-2105.**
   **Cuisine:** VEGETARIAN/DELI.
**$** **Prices:** $5.95–$8.95. AE, MC, V.
   **Open:** Daily 11am–9pm.
Greater Denver's finest salads are found inside this unpreposing cafeteria-style café just south of Exposition Street. The 60-item salad bar offers everything you'd expect, and more—like hearts of palm, artichoke hearts, avocadoes, herring, and chunks of tuna. Leave room for fresh fruit and a variety of pasta salads. The restaurant also has soup and pasta bars, and a fresh bakery section with wonderful cookies and muffins.

# SPECIALTY DINING

Establishments mentioned below without addresses and/or telephone numbers are discussed in detail above.
   **Local Favorites**   For local favorites, don't miss the **Buckhorn Exchange** or **The Fort,** both serving Rocky Mountain cuisine.
   **Hotel Dining**   The best is at the **Palace Arms** in the Brown Palace Hotel, **Augusta** in the Westin Tabor Center, and the **Marquis** in the Hyatt Regency.
   **Dining with a View**   If you like a view with your meal, consider **The Fort,** in the foothills 18 miles west of Denver: In the evening, it's fun to watch the city lights.
   **Dining Complexes**   There are two dining complexes in downtown Denver: the **Plaza Court Food Emporium,** in Republic Plaza at 370 17th Street, with fast-food outlets; and the **Tabor Center Food Court,** 1201 16th Street, between Larimer Street and Lawrence Street, with 18 booths serving everything from falafel to egg foo yung.

**After Theater**  The pre- and posttheater crowd appreciates the **theater café** in the Galleria of the Denver Performing Arts Complex, 14th Street at Curtis Street (tel. 623-7733). Make reservations for dinner, then return after the performance for dessert and coffee, and miss the traffic.

**Light Meals**  Light, casual, and fast food is readily found throughout the city. Personal favorites are **La Bonne Soup, Majorca, Soapy Smith's Eagle Bar, Duffy's Shamrock,** and **Healthy Habits.**

**For Breakfast**  Consider **The Delectable Egg, Duffy's Shamrock, McCormick's Fish House,** or **Las Delicias.** You can get a great **weekend brunch** at McCormick's or at Ellyngton's in the Brown Palace Hotel.

**Afternoon Tea**  Denver's best bet for an afternoon Devonshire tea is the lobby of the **Brown Palace Hotel.**

**Late-Night Dining**  Night owls have slim pickings in Denver after about 11pm. One of the best bets is **Bennigan's,** with seven locations around the metropolitan area—including one at 1699 South Colorado Boulevard, just off I-25 (tel. 753-0272). There are two in Lakewood, two in Aurora, and one each in Westminster and Tech Center. The international menu is served Monday through Saturday until 2am and on Sunday to midnight.

After the bars close, try **Jerusalem,** 1890 East Evans Avenue near the University of Denver (tel. 777-8828). An inexpensive Arabic café, it serves up huge portions of gyros and shish kebabs Monday through Friday until 4am and 24 hours on Saturday and Sunday.

**Picnic Fare**  My choice for picnic fare—especially if a picnic means people-watching on the 16th Street Mall—is **Goldie's.** Outside downtown, check out the **Bagel Deli,** with two locations, at 6217 East 14th Avenue, at Krameria Street (tel. 322-0350), and 6439 East Hampden Avenue, at Monaco Parkway (tel. 756-6667).

---

 **FROMMER'S COOL FOR KIDS:**
## RESTAURANTS

**Casa Bonita**  *(see p. 64)* If the kids' attention isn't on the tacos, they'll be enthralled by puppet shows, high divers, a funhouse, and a video arcade.

**The Old Spaghetti Factory**  *(see p. 61)* Dine inside an old trolley car, or take an adventure tour of the other fascinating turn-of-the-century antiques. And what child doesn't like spaghetti and spumoni?

**Buckhorn Exchange**  *(see p. 55)* Every species of large game animal you might imagine is mounted on the walls of this century-old restaurant once frequented by Buffalo Bill and Teddy Roosevelt.

**Brick Oven Beanery**  *(see p. 62)* Good, wholesome food and honest-to-gosh malted milks and ice-cream sodas appeal to the kid in all of us. They've even got peanut-butter-and-jelly sandwiches on the menu.

# CHAPTER 5

# WHAT TO SEE & DO IN DENVER

**D**enver's focal point, from a tourist's point of view, is Civic Center Park where Colfax Avenue meets Broadway. Here are the State Capitol, the U.S. Mint, the Denver Art Museum, the Colorado Historical Museum, and other important sites. What's more, the Civic Center is at the southeast corner of the square mile of downtown, in which lie the Colorado Convention Center and the Denver Center for the Performing Arts, Larimer Square, Union Station, most major hotels, and, of course, the principal shopping district.

Denver, therefore, is a great place for walkers. But don't restrict yourself to the downtown hub: Many more attractions are a 10 minutes' drive away, with others spread throughout the metropolitan area.

# 1. ATTRACTIONS

## SUGGESTED ITINERARIES

**IF YOU HAVE 1 DAY** Start at **Larimer Square,** Denver's birthplace. Have a casual breakfast in **The Market** and give yourself a self-guided walking tour of the historic sites. Then stroll the **16th Street pedestrian mall.** Your goal is the **State Capitol,** just across Broadway. En route, take a one-block detour to have an early lunch or a cup of tea at the **Brown Palace Hotel.** After seeing the Capitol, explore other Civic Center sites, including the Denver Art Museum.

**IF YOU HAVE 2 DAYS** Spend your first day as suggested above.

On day 2, take a drive west. Venture into the old mining towns in the Rocky Mountain foothills—atmospheric communities like **Central City, Idaho Springs,** and **Georgetown.** En route, visit the **Red Rocks Amphitheatre** near Morrison. On your return, tour the **Coors Brewery** in Golden.

**IF YOU HAVE 3 DAYS** Spend your first two days as suggested above.

On day 3, enjoy more of Denver. The city has numerous historic homes, beautiful parks, attractive new shopping centers, and several highly touted museums. I recommend the **Denver Museum of Natural History, the Museum of Western Art,** and the **Black American West Museum.**

**IF YOU HAVE 5 DAYS OR MORE** Spend days 1–3 as suggested above.

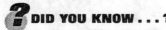

### DID YOU KNOW . . . ?

- Denver is exactly 1 mile high—the 15th step of the State Capitol Building is 5,280 feet above sea level.
- The first cheeseburger was grilled at Louis Ballast's Denver drive-in in 1944.
- Denver has the second-highest per capita number of college graduates of any major city in the U.S.
- Golda Meir, the former prime minister of Israel, attended North High School in Denver.
- The highest paved road in North America—to the top of 14,260-foot Mount Evans—is part of 20,000 acres of city parks.
- Douglas Fairbanks, the famous movie star of the '20s and '30s, was expelled from Denver's East High School.
- Denver receives more hours of sunshine per year than Miami Beach or San Diego.

On day 4, day-trip to nearby cities such as **Colorado Springs,** home of the Air Force Academy and the Pikes Peak Cog Railway, or **Boulder** and **Fort Collins,** both lively university towns.

For your fifth day, climb higher into the Rockies to resort communities like **Estes Park,** gateway to Rocky Mountain National Park, or **Breckenridge** and **Vail,** across the Continental Divide.

## THE TOP ATTRACTIONS

**DENVER ART MUSEUM, 100 W. 14th Pkwy. at Civic Center Park. Tel. 640-2793.**

This 10-story, 28-sided structure has a million shimmering glass tiles covering its exterior. Inside is the largest and oldest collection of Native American art of any art museum in the United States, as well as a large collection of western art, and 35,000 other art objects in seven curatorial departments.

The Native American collection consists of 20,000 pieces from 150 tribes of North America, covering a time span of some 2,000 years and valued at more than $25 million. Works are arranged geographically in 10 areas covering 22,000 square feet. The collection is growing not only through the acquisition of historic pieces, but by the commissioning of contemporary Native American artists.

Other exhibits include major collections of African, Oceanic, and early New World art, such as pre-Columbian artifacts, Spanish Colonial arts, some Spanish Peruvian works, and a group of southwestern *santos.* A solid representation of European artists includes works by van Dyck, Tintoretto, Rubens, Veronese, Monet, Renoir, Matisse, Modigliani, Degas, Chagall, and Toulouse-Lautrec. There are period rooms of art in French Gothic, English Tudor, and Spanish baroque styles, and Asian works from China, Japan, and India. At the top of the gallery floors is an exhibit of textiles and costumes from around the world.

Guided tours are available, and performing-arts events are frequently scheduled—including jazz most Wednesdays from 5 to 8pm, when the working day is over. A gift shop has unusual replicas of certain treasures displayed and many books on art and southwestern lore. A restaurant has an open patio for warm-weather lunches.

**Admission:** $3 adults, $1.50 students and seniors; free for everyone Sat.
**Open:** Tues–Sat 10am–5pm, Sun noon–5pm.

**DENVER MUSEUM OF NATURAL HISTORY, City Park, 2001 Colorado Blvd. Tel. 322-7009,** or 370-8257 for the hearing impaired.

This rambling three-story museum is the seventh-largest natural history museum in the United States. Exquisitely fashioned human and animal figures in more than 90 dioramas depict life on earth in various eras on four continents.

The first floor has articulated skeletons of mammals 50 million years old and displays on ancient Old World cultures and prehistoric American peoples. The second floor has a butterfly exhibit and sections devoted to Colorado wildlife, North American bears and sea life, and Australian ecology. This floor also has rooms showing artifacts of early Native American tribes from Alaska to Florida. The third-floor exhibits include displays of South American wildlife and the habitats of

Botswana, including a spectacular savannah diorama called "The Watering Hole."

The new Hall of Life offers hands-on studies of genetics, the wonder of birth, human anatomy, the five senses, fitness, and nutrition. The Coors Hall of Minerals displays semiprecious gemstones and minerals of the Southwest, including the largest gold nugget ever found in Colorado: the 8½-pound Tom's Baby.

The museum also houses the **IMAX Theater** (tel. 370-6300), which presents science- or technology-oriented films with sense-surround sound on a screen 4½ by 6½ *stories* in dimension; and the **Charles C. Gates Planetarium** (tel. 370-6351), which schedules frequent multimedia star programs and laser light shows.

**Admission:** Museum, $4 adults, $2 children under 13 and seniors; IMAX, $4.75 adults, $3.75 children and seniors; museum/IMAX combination, $7.50 adults, $5 children and seniors; planetarium, $3 adults, $2 children and seniors; museum/ planetarium combination, $6 adults, $3.50 children and seniors.

**Open:** Daily 9am–5pm. **Closed:** Christmas Day.

**UNITED STATES MINT, 320 W. Colfax Ave., at Cherokee St. Tel. 844-3582** or 844-3331.

The mint opened in 1863 and originally melted gold dust and nuggets into bars. In 1904 the office moved to the present site, and 2 years later began coinage operations in both gold and silver. Copper pennies began to be made a few years later. Silver dollars (containing 90% silver) were last manufactured in 1935; gold purchases were discontinued in 1968. In 1970 the coinage law changed and all silver was eliminated from dollars and half dollars: today they are made of a copper-nickel alloy.

Coins are made from prefabricated rolls of metal supplied by private dealers to the mint, which concentrates on the blanking function and on stamping the actual coins. The mint stamps more than 5 billion coins a year. A coin minted in Denver has a small *D* on it.

From the upstairs gallery, visitors watch coin metal stamped into coin blanks (both sides are stamped in a single stroke), then the coins are edge-rolled to make a raised rim. The next steps are inspection, weighing, counting, and bagging, before being stored in vaults to await shipment.

A visitor center has a machine that stamps blank coins, turning them into souvenir medals, and has various collectors' items in freshly minted coins on sale.

**Admission:** Free.

**Open:** 20-minute tours depart every half hour, Mon–Fri 8–11:30am and 12:30–3pm.

**COLORADO STATE CAPITOL, Broadway and E. Colfax Ave. Tel. 866- 2604.**

The building was built to survive 1,000 years. Constructed of granite from a Colorado quarry in 1886, the most salient feature is its gold dome, which rises 272 feet above the ground. The dome, first sheathed in copper, was replaced with 200 ounces of gold after a public outcry: Copper was not a Colorado product.

Murals depicting the history of the state, dating from 1940, adorn the walls of the first-floor rotunda. There is a fine view upward from here to the underside of the dome, a vertical distance of 180 feet. The rotunda, at the heart of the building, echoes the layout of the national Capitol in Washington, D.C. South of the rotunda is the governor's office, paneled in walnut and lighted by a massive chandelier.

Various levels of the interior of the Capitol may interest visitors. The basement has hearing rooms open to the public. On the first floor, the west lobby has a case showing moon rocks and another displaying dolls in miniature ball gowns as worn by various governors' wives. To the right of the main lobby, the governor's reception room is open to the public. The second floor has a hearing room, as well as main entrances to the public and visitor galleries to both the House and Senate. The **Colorado Hall of Fame** is located near the top of the dome, with stained-glass portraits of Colorado pioneers. Views from the dome on clear days are spectacular.

**Admission:** Free.
**Open:** 30-minute tours are offered year round (more frequently in summer), Mon–Fri 9am–4pm (last tour begins at 3:30pm).

## LARIMER SQUARE, 1400 block of Larimer St. Tel. 534-2367.

This was where Denver began. Larimer Street between 14th Street and 15th Street comprised the entire community of Denver City in 1858, with false-front stores, hotels, and saloons to serve gold seekers and other pioneers. In the mid-1870s it was the main street of the city, and the site of Denver's first post office, bank, theater, and street-car line. But by the 1930s the street had declined so badly that it was a "skid row" of pawn shops, gin mills, and flop houses. It had an impending appointment with the wrecking ball until 1965, when the entire block was purchased by a group of investors with a strong interest in historic preservation.

The Larimer Square project became Denver's first major historic-preservation effort. All 16 of the block's commercial buildings, constructed in the 1870s and 1880s, were renovated, providing space for streetside retail shops, restaurants, and nightclubs, and upper-story offices. A series of inner courtyards and open spaces were created. The project reached its climax in 1973 when Larimer Square was added to the National Register of Historic Places.

A self-guided walking tour pamphlet is available at the Larimer Square information booth, on the southeast side of Larimer Street near 15th Street.

# MORE ATTRACTIONS

## ARCHITECTURAL HIGHLIGHTS

### BROWN PALACE HOTEL, 321 17th St., at Tremont Place. Tel. 297-3111.

Designed in Italian Renaissance style by famed architect Frank Edbrooke, this was the first open-atrium hotel and the second fireproof building in the United States when it opened in August 1892. A National Historic Landmark, the building is triangular in shape, and is built of Colorado red granite and Arizona sandstone. Native Rocky Mountain animals are carved into the sandstone between the seventh-floor windows. Mexican onyx panels the lobby walls and white marble provides the flooring; elaborate cast-iron grillwork surrounds six tiers of balconies to the stained-glass ceiling high above the lobby. There's a remarkable Napoleonic collection in the Palace Arms restaurant; clipper-ship artifacts are exhibited in the Ship's Tavern.
**Admission:** Free.
**Open:** Daily 24 hours.

### D & F TOWER, 16th and Arapahoe Sts.

This 325-foot structure is a replica of the campanile of St. Mark's Basilica in Venice, Italy. When it was erected in 1910, it was the third-tallest building in the United States and the tallest west of the Mississippi River. The tower is especially beautiful when viewed from the fountains at either end of Skyline Park, which runs for three blocks along Arapahoe Street.

### TIVOLI DENVER, 901 Larimer St. Tel. 629-8712.

A landmark brewery for 105 years, from 1864 to 1969, this historic building was saved from demolition and developed into a shopping and entertainment complex in 1985. It is crowned by a seven-story tower patterned after a Bavarian castle, built in 1890 for storage of malt, barley, and hops. Two-story-high copper brewing kettles, a grain roll mill, and the power house are among remnants left behind by the old brewery. Historic photos and beer-label reproductions are further reminders.
**Admission:** Free.
**Open:** Mon–Sat 10am–9pm, Sun noon–5pm.

## HISTORIC BUILDINGS

**BYERS-EVANS HOUSE, 1310 Bannock St. Tel. 623-0709.**
    William N. Byers, who built this elaborate Victorian home in 1883, was the founder of the *Rocky Mountain News*. John Evans, who later owned it, was Colorado's second territorial governor. Restored to its present appearance during the era of World War I, the house contains original Evans family furnishings. Guided tours include a film about the Byers and Evans families and describe the architecture of the house. It's located just behind the Denver Art Museum.
    **Admission:** $2.50 adults, $1.25 seniors and children 6–16, free for children under 6.
    **Open:** Wed–Mon 11am–3pm.

**GRANT-HUMPHREYS MANSION, 770 Pennsylvania St. Tel. 894-2505.**
    Colorado Gov. James Grant built this 42-room mansion in 1902, and oil industrialist Albert Humphreys remodeled it in 1917. This is 15,000 square feet of Beaux Arts elegance, rich with period pieces. Groups often rent the building for private parties.
    **Admission:** $2 adults, $1 seniors and children 6–16, free for children under 6.
    **Open:** Tues–Fri 10am–2pm. **Closed:** Major hols.

**MOLLY BROWN HOUSE MUSEUM, 1340 Pennsylvania St. Tel. 832-4092.**
    The property of Historic Denver, Inc., the Molly Brown House Museum was designed by Denver architect William Lang and was built in 1889 of Colorado lava stone with sandstone trim. It was the residence from 1894 to 1932 of James and Margaret (Molly) Brown. The "unsinkable" Molly Brown became a national heroine in 1912 when the *Titanic* sank: She took charge of a group of immigrant women in a lifeboat and later raised money for their benefit. She was also the first preservationist of Denver, and in 1930 she bought the home of poet Eugene Field for the city.
    Restored to its 1910 appearance, the Molly Brown House has a large collection of turn-of-the-century furnishings and art objects, many the former possessions of the Brown family. A carriage house at the rear of the house is also open to visitors.
    **Admission:** $3 adults, $2 seniors over 65, $1 children 6–18, free for children under 6.
    **Open:** Apr–Sept, Tues–Sat 10am–4pm, Sun noon–4pm; Oct–Mar, Tues–Sat 10am–3pm, Sun noon–3pm. **Closed:** Major hols.

**PEARCE-McALLISTER COTTAGE, 1880 Gaylord St. Tel. 322-3704.**
    Whereas most of the historic homes in Denver are Victorian in architecture, this one is Dutch Colonial Revival. It was built in 1899 by Frederick J. Sterner for metallurgist Harold Pearce and his wife, Cara, who wanted an East Coast–style cottage. It was sold in 1907 to lawyer Henry McAllister, Jr., whose wife, Phebe, decorated the home in the popular Colonial Revival style of the 1920s. All the furnishings, down to books and tiny knickknacks, were bequeathed to the Colorado Historical Society, which used them to re-create the McAllisters' life-style. The house—located just west of City Park—also contains the **Denver Museum of Miniatures, Dolls, and Toys.**
    **Admission:** $2.50 adults, $2 seniors, $1.50 children 6–16, free for children under 6.
    **Open:** Wed–Sat 10am–4pm, Sun 1–4pm.

## MUSEUMS & GALLERIES
### Museums

**BLACK AMERICAN WEST MUSEUM AND HERITAGE CENTER, 3091 California St., at 31st St. Tel. 292-2566.**
    Nearly one-third of the cowboys in the Old West were black. Located in the heart of the Five Points neighborhood, this museum tells their story—along with the story

0 200 m
0 220 y

24th St.
Park
23rd St.
Glenarm Pl.
Welton St.
Park
Tremont Pl.
California St.
Stout St.

Pennsylvania St.
Logan St.
Grant St.
Sherman St.
Lincoln St.
E. 20th Ave.
E. 19th Ave.
E. 18th Ave.
E. 17th Ave.
Broadway

22nd St.
21st St.
20th St.
Denver Bus Terminal
19th St.
18th St.
17th St.
Skyline Park
Mall
Champa St.
Curtis St.
Arapahoe St.
15th St.
Lawrence St.
14th St.
Larimer St.
13th St.
Market St.
Blake St.
Wazee St.
Wynkoop St.
Union Station
16th St.
Wewatta St.
12th St.
Walnut St.
Welton St.
California St.
Stout St.
Glenarm Pl.
Tremont Pl.

St. Fran...
Wa...

# DENVER ATTRACTIONS

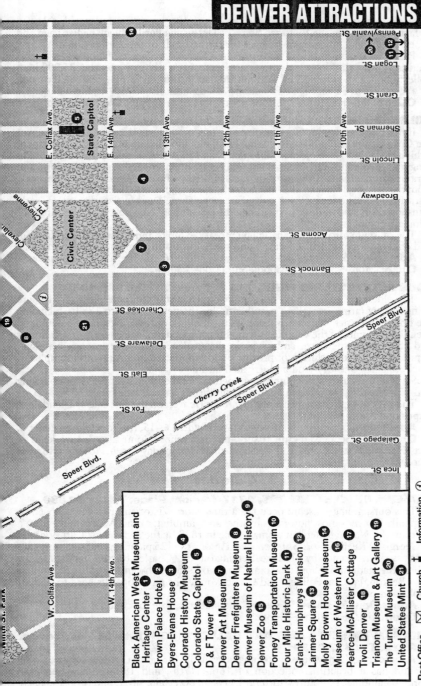

Black American West Museum and
Heritage Center ❶
Brown Palace Hotel ❷
Byers-Evans House ❸
Colorado History Museum ❹
Colorado State Capitol ❺
D & F Tower ❻
Denver Art Museum ❼
Denver Firefighters Museum ❽
Denver Museum of Natural History ❾
Denver Zoo ❶❺
Forney Transportation Museum ❶⓿
Four Mile Historic Park ❶❶
Grant-Humphreys Mansion ❶❷
Larimer Square ❶❸
Molly Brown House Museum ❶❹
Museum of Western Art ❶❻
Pearce-McAllister Cottage ❶❼
Tivoli Denver ❶❽
Trianon Museum & Art Gallery ❶❾
The Turner Museum ❷⓿
United States Mint ❷❶

Post Office ⊠   Church ✝◼   Information ⓘ

of black doctors, teachers, miners, farmers, newspaper reporters, and state legislators. In fact, it's lodged in the Victorian home of Dr. Justina Ford, a black pediatrician and gynecologist who practiced in Denver for the first half of the 20th century.

Paul Stewart, who still greets visitors in a Stetson, began collecting photographs, saddles, guns, clothing, and other artifacts as a hobby. Now the 35,000-item collection is acknowledged by the Smithsonian Institution for its great significance.

**Admission:** $2 adults, $1.50 seniors, 75¢ children 12–17, 50¢ children under 12. **Open:** Wed–Fri 10am–2pm, Sat noon–5pm, Sun 2–5pm. **Closed:** Major hols.

## COLORADO HISTORY MUSEUM, 1300 Broadway. Tel. 866-3682.

If this book's introductory section on history piqued your interest, this museum at the Civic Center is the place to come. The Colorado Historical Society's permanent exhibits include "The Colorado Chronicle," an 1800–1949 timeline that incorporates biographical plaques and a remarkable collection of photographs, news clippings, and various paraphernalia. Dozens of dioramas portray various episodes in state history, from the medieval Anasazi cliff-dweller culture through early settlement, including an intricate re-creation of 19th-century Denver. There's a life-size display of early transportation and industry, including heavy mining equipment and exhibits of mining techniques.

The museum also has fascinating temporary exhibits and an interesting gift shop, and offers series of in-house lectures and statewide historical and archeological tours.

**Admission:** $3 adults, $1.50 seniors and children 6–16, free for children under 6. **Open:** Mon–Sat 10am–4:30pm, Sun noon–4:30pm.

## FOUR MILE HISTORIC PARK, 715 S. Forest St. Tel. 399-1859.

The oldest log home (1859) still standing in Denver is the centerpiece of a 14-acre living-history farm. Everything is authentic for the period 1859 to 1883—including the house (a former stagecoach stop), its furnishings, outbuildings, farm equipment, even the costumes of the volunteers from Historic Denver, Inc. There are draft horses and chickens in the barn, and crops in the garden. A "phased interpretive plan" depicts the guided evolution of pristine prairie to cultivated farm, with examples of stock ranching and dry-land and irrigated farming.

Several times a season, volunteers in period dress engage in chores from plowing and blacksmithing to quilting and cooking (there's a small café here).

The park is 4 miles southeast of downtown Denver, on the east side of Glendale at Exposition Avenue.

**Admission:** $3 adults, $1.50 seniors and children 6–15, free for children under 6. **Open:** Apr–Sept, Wed–Sun 10am–4pm (last tour at 3pm); also 3rd weekend of Oct (Harvest Festival) and 2nd weekend of Dec (Holiday Open House). **Closed:** Oct–Mar.

## Galleries

## MUSEUM OF WESTERN ART, 1717 Tremont Place. Tel. 296-1880.

This outstanding museum occupies a three-story Victorian brick house that was originally Denver's most notorious brothel and gambling casino. Works range from a portrait of a Native American woman done in 1833 by the Swiss artist Carl Bodmer, to Georgia O'Keeffe's *Cow Skull on Red*. Among the 125 paintings and sculptures are classic western scenes by Frederic Remington and Charles Russell, landscapes by Albert Bierstadt and Thomas Moran, and works by 20th-century painters Thomas Hart Benton, Jackson Pollock, and Grant Wood. The gift shop sells hard-to-find art books and prints.

**Admission:** $4 adults, $2 seniors and students, free for children under 7. **Open:** Tues–Sat 10am–4:30pm.

## TRIANON MUSEUM AND ART GALLERY, 335 14th St., at Tremont Place. Tel. 623-0739.

A museum gallery where everything is available for sale to serious collectors, the Trianon has a beautiful collection of 16th-, 17th-, and 18th-century European works—paintings, sculptures, furniture, crystal, porcelain, silver, and bronzes. There are also some Asian treasures and a fine gun collection.

**Admission:** $1 adults and students, free for children under 12.
**Open:** Mon–Sat 10am–4pm.

## THE TURNER MUSEUM, 773 Downing St. Tel. 832-0924.

The Capitol Hill home of Douglas and Linda Graham houses one of the outstanding private art collections in the United States. Permanent exhibitions include watercolors and engravings of impressionist J. M. W. Turner and numerous land-scapes by Thomas Moran, whose work helped inspire the National Park Service. About 3,000 other works are shown on a revolving basis.

The best way to enjoy the collection is to dine within it. The Grahams serve three gourmet meals daily, by reservation: breakfast ($10), lunch ($12), and a candlelit dinner ($25). There's also a regular classical-music recital at 7:30pm the third Thursday of each month.

**Admission:** $5, including a 30-minute personalized tour.
**Open:** By appointment, daily 8am–9pm.

## MUSEUM OF OUTDOOR ARTS, 6312 S. Fiddler's Green Circle, Engle-wood. Tel. 741-3609.

Some 45 sculptures of various sizes and shapes are set about the Greenwood Plaza business park, adjacent to the Fiddler's Green Amphitheatre. In this museum without walls, rules, or hushed voices, they seem to blend into the environment. Located about 15 minutes' drive south of downtown Denver, it's a nice place to picnic. Call ahead for a guided tour or to obtain a self-guided tour map.

**Admission:** Free; guided tours, by appointment, $3 adults, $1 children 12 and under.
**Open:** Daily 8am–7pm.

# NEIGHBORHOODS

## FAR EAST CENTER, Federal Blvd., between W. Alameda and W. Missis-sippi Aves.

Denver's Asian community is focused along this strip, which burgeoned in the aftermath of the Vietnam War to accommodate throngs of Southeast Asian refugees, especially Thais and Vietnamese. Look for authentic restaurants, bakeries, groceries, gift shops, and clothing stores. The Far East Center building at Federal and Alameda is built in Japanese pagoda style.

## FIVE POINTS, 20th to 38th Sts. northeast of downtown.

The "five points" actually meet at 23rd Street and Broadway, but the cultural and commercial hub of Denver's African-American community covers a much larger area and incorporates four historic districts. Restaurants offer the likes of soul food, barbecued ribs, and Caribbean cuisine, while jazz and blues musicians and contempo-rary dance troupes perform in theaters and nightclubs. The Black American West Museum and Heritage Center is also in this neighborhood.

## LA ALMA/LINCOLN PARK, Santa Fe Dr., between W. Colfax and W. Sixth Aves.

Hispanic culture, art, food, and entertainment predominate along this strip, notable for its southwestern character and architecture. There are numerous restau-rants, art galleries, and crafts shops. Denver's annual Cinco de Mayo celebration takes place here each May.

## LOWER DOWNTOWN, Wynkoop St. to Market St. and 20th St. to Speer Blvd.

Twenty-two square blocks surrounding the Union Station contain numerous National Historic Landmarks and refurbished turn-of-the-century warehouses. Restaurants, galleries, antiques stores, and at least one outstanding hotel (the Oxford Alexis) operate in this district. See "Orientation" in Chapter 4, above.

## UPTOWN, Broadway to York St. (City Park) and E. Colfax Ave. to E. 23rd Ave.

Denver's oldest residential neighborhood is best known today for two things: It's bisected by 17th Avenue's "Restaurant Row" (see "Dining," in Chapter 4), and several of its classic Victorian and Queen Anne–style homes have been converted to bed-and-breakfasts (see "Accommodations," in Chapter 4).

## PARKS & GARDENS

**BARR LAKE STATE PARK, 13401 Picadilly Rd., Brighton. Tel. 659-6005** or 659-1160.

Some 18 miles northeast of Denver via I-76, this wildlife sanctuary of 2,500 acres comprises a prairie reservoir and surrounding wetlands. Motors are not allowed, but you can sail, paddle, or row, as well as fish. A 9-mile hiking and biking trail that circles the lake is popular in winter with snowshoers and cross-country skiers. A boardwalk from the nature center at the south parking lot leads to a good view of a heron rookery. Bird blinds along this trail offer wildlife observation and photography. Two picnic areas have tables and grills; there's a commercial campground opposite the park entrance.

**Admission:** $3 per vehicle.

**CASTLEWOOD CANYON STATE PARK, 13787 S. U.S. 85, Littleton. Tel. 688-5242.**

Steep canyons, a meandering stream, a waterfall, lush vegetation, and considerable wildlife bless this small park. The remains of Castlewood Canyon Dam can be seen; built for irrigation in 1890, it collapsed in 1933 and killed two people. The park, 30 miles south of Denver on Douglas County Road 51 east of Castle Rock, has picnic facilities and hiking trails.

**Admission:** $3 per vehicle.

**CHATFIELD STATE RECREATION AREA, 11500 N. Roxborough Park Rd., Littleton. Tel. 797-3986.**

Just 8 miles south of downtown Denver via U.S. 85, this park occupies 5,600 acres of prairie against a backdrop of the steeply rising Rocky Mountains. Chatfield Reservoir has a 26-mile shoreline that invites swimming, boating, fishing, and other water sports. The area also has 25 miles of paved bicycle trails, plus hiking and horseback-riding paths. In winter, there's ice fishing and cross-country skiing.

Rangers give guided interpretive walks in the park and host evening programs. An observation area on the south side of the park offers a view of a 27-acre nature-study grove, closed during nesting season because of its heron rookery. The park also has a model-airplane field, complete with paved runways.

There are 153 pull-through campsites with showers, laundry, and dump station. Various sites offer picnicking facilities.

**Admission:** $3 per vehicle; camping fee $7 daily.

**CHERRY CREEK STATE RECREATION AREA, 4201 S. Parker Rd., Aurora. Tel. 690-1166.**

Because Cherry Creek, the central attraction of the park, used to flood Denver, Cherry Creek Dam was built in 1953. The resulting 880-acre reservoir has become a mecca for 1.5 million visitors a year. Located at the southeast Denver city limits off I-225, the park has 3,900 acres of grounds.

Water sports include swimming, waterskiing, boating, and fishing. There's a fitness trail, dog-training area, rifle range, pistol range, and trap-shooting area. Six miles of paved bicycle paths and 10 miles of bridle trails circle the reservoir (horse rentals are offered). Rangers guide walks on a 1½-mile nature trail, and offer evening programs in an amphitheater. There's even a prairie dog colony with a special observation area. Winter-sports enthusiasts enjoy skating, ice fishing, and ice boating.

The park's 102 campsites include showers, laundry, and dump station, but no water or electrical hookups. Many lakeshore sites have picnic tables with grills.

**Admission:** $3 per vehicle; camping fee $7 daily.

**CITY PARK, E. 17th to E. 26th Ave., between York St. and Colorado Blvd.**

Denver's largest urban park covers 314 acres—96 square blocks—on the east side of Uptown. Established in 1881, and still containing Victorian touches, it includes two lakes (with boat rentals), athletic fields, playgrounds, tennis courts, picnic areas, even an 18-hole municipal golf course. In the summertime there are band concerts in the park. It's also the site of both the Denver Zoo and the Denver Museum of Natural History, with its planetarium and IMAX Theatre.

**Admission:** Free for park, although the zoo, museum, golf course, and other sites charge independently.

**Open:** Daily 24 hours.

## DENVER BOTANIC GARDENS, 1005 York St. Tel. 331-4000 or 331-4010 (24-hour recording).

These outstanding 20-acre outdoor and indoor gardens display plants native to the desert, plains, mountain foothills, and alpine zones; there's also a traditional Japanese garden, scripture garden (tying plants to biblical history), herb garden, home demonstration garden, water garden, and "wingsong" garden to attract songbirds.

Even in the cold of winter, the dome-shaped, concrete-and-Plexiglas Boettcher Memorial Conservatory houses 800 species of tropical and subtropical plants. Huge, colorful orchids and bromeliads share space with a collection of plants used for foods, fibers, dyes, building materials, and medicines. The Botanic Gardens also include a gift shop, library, and auditorium. Adjoining the gardens to the west is 20-square-block Cheesman Park.

**Admission:** May–Sept, $4 adults, $2 seniors and children 7–16; Oct–Apr, $3 adults, $1.50 seniors, $1 children; free for children under 7.

**Open:** Daily 9am–4:45pm. **Closed:** Christmas and New Year's days.

## DENVER MOUNTAIN PARKS, Department of Parks and Recreation, 1445 Cleveland Place. Tel. 575-2227.

Land in the mountains near Denver was acquired and set aside for recreational use by the city at the beginning of the 20th century. The 18 mountain parks are great places for hiking, picnicking, birdwatching, golfing, or lazing in the grass and sun.

The largest, **Genesee Park,** is 20 miles west of Denver off I-70; its 2,400 acres contain playgrounds, picnic areas with fireplaces, a softball field, a scenic overlook, and an elk and buffalo enclosure. Among the others are **Daniels Park,** 23 miles south of Denver via County Line Road and County Road 29, with similar facilities on 1,000 acres; and **Dedisse Park,** 2 miles west of Evergreen on Colo. 74, which has picnic facilities and a golf course. **Echo Lake Park** and **Red Rocks Park** are discussed later in this chapter (see "Easy Excursions from Denver"). The **Winter Park** ski resort, also a Denver park, has extensive coverage in Chapter 9 "The Northern Rockies."

## DENVER ZOO, City Park, 23rd Ave. and Steele St. Tel. 331-4110.

Four hundred species of animals, about 1,700 in all, live in this very spacious zoological park. The Bear Mountain exhibit, when it was built in 1918, was the first animal exhibit in the United States to be constructed of simulated concrete rockwork. At the other end of the timeline, Northern Shores (1991) allows underwater viewing of polar bears and sea lions; Tropical Discovery (1992) re-creates an entire tropical ecosystem under glass, complete with leopards and crocodiles, piranhas and king cobras. Exotic waterfowl inhabit several ponds, and 300 avian species live in Bird World, which includes a hummingbird forest and a tropical aviary.

A miniature train circles Children's Zoo near the zoo's west entrance. The rubber-tired Zooliner tours all zoo paths spring through fall. Rides are available as well on elephants and camels! Full meals are served at the Hungry Elephant, a zoo cafeteria with outdoor eating area. Many visitors bring picnic lunches and eat them on the expansive lawns.

**Admission:** $4 adults, $2 seniors and children 6–15 (accompanied by an adult), free for children 5 and under.

**Open:** Fall–spring, daily 10am–6pm; winter, daily 10am–5pm.

## ROCKY MOUNTAIN ARSENAL, Havana St. and E. 72nd Ave. Tel. 289-0132.

Once a place where the federal government manufactured chemical weapons such as mustard and chlorine gases, later the site of insecticide production, the Rocky Mountain Arsenal is now an environmental success story. Covering 27 square miles of open grasslands and wetlands north of Stapleton Airport, the RMA is home to deer, coyotes, various small mammals and reptiles, and thousands of birds—including (in winter) an estimated 100 bald eagles, making this one of the largest eagle nesting grounds in the lower 48 states.

There's a small information center and bald eagle viewing station on the site. Tours of wildlife resources and of waste-disposal cleanup operations are offered by the co-custodians, the U.S. Army and U.S. Fish and Wildlife Service.

**Admission:** Free.

**Open:** Daytime hours; tours by advance appointment.

**WASHINGTON PARK, S. Downing to S. Franklin Sts. and E. Virginia to E. Louisiana Aves.**

Named for its replica of George Washington's flower gardens at Mount Vernon, this 155-acre park also encompasses two lakes (Smith and Grasmere).

**Admission:** Free.

**Open:** Daily 24 hours.

# COOL FOR KIDS

Denver abounds with activities geared for children, and the listings below will appeal to young travelers of any age. In addition, some sights listed in the previous sections provide fun for the entire family. These include the Colorado History Museum, the Denver Art Museum, the Denver Museum of Natural History, the Denver Zoo, Four Mile Historic Park, and the U.S. Mint.

**BIG FUN, 920 S. Monaco Pkwy., near Leetsdale Dr. Tel. 369-4744.**

A high-tech indoor playground, Big Fun also offers two huge swimming pools and the Discovery Museum, with 35 hands-on science exhibits including the gyro, where kids and adults can experience the feeling of weightlessness. Kids must be 9 or older to be left alone; there's a special area for preschoolers.

**Admission:** $5.95 children 2–12, $2.95 adults.

**Open:** Mon–Sat 10am–9pm, Sun noon–6pm.

**CELEBRITY SPORTS CENTER, 888 S. Colorado Blvd. Tel. 757-3321.**

Older children are happy to spend the entire day at the 150,000-square-foot facility, built in 1960 by Walt Disney himself. Three five- and six-story water slides encircle part of the building. There's also an Olympic-size indoor swimming pool, 80 lanes of bowling, three arcade rooms with more than 300 video games and pinball machines, and numerous other activities. There are also two restaurants and a snack bar, as well as a bowling pro shop and a tavern for kids over 21. Younger children must be supervised, but child care is offered at no charge.

**Admission:** Free; attractions charge individually.

**Open:** Sun–Thurs 8:30am–midnight, Fri–Sat 8:30am–2am.

**CHILDREN'S MUSEUM, 2121 Crescent Dr. Tel. 433-7444.**

This is Denver's best hands-on experience. Children can assume the roles of shoppers and checkout clerks at a miniature Safeway supermarket, become news commentators at a mini TV studio, experience what it feels like to be physically disabled in various ways, or even explore bedtime fears. Then they can make a totem pole, get their faces painted, try a flight simulator, or check out the pinhole camera. The most popular exhibit is the ballroom, where a sea of 80,000 plastic balls await. The newest addition is a gigantic plastic mountain used for year-round ski lessons. Exhibits change frequently, and special events are scheduled throughout the year.

**Admission:** $2.50 Mon–Fri, $3 Sat–Sun, for children and adults; $1.50 seniors over 60; free for children under 2.

**Open:** Sept–May, Tues–Sun 10am–5pm; June–Aug, daily 10am–5pm (Tues 9–10am for preschoolers only). **Directions:** Take Exit 211 (23rd Avenue) east off I-25; turn right on Seventh Street, and again on Crescent Drive.

**ELITCH GARDENS, 4620 W. 38th Ave. at Tennyson St. Tel. 455-4771.**

Established in 1889, this traditional amusement park offers something for everyone. For the kids, there are two wooden roller coasters, including "The Twister," rated Number 3 in the world, and a steel-loop coaster. There's also a 1925 carousel, a log-flume ride, 16 other major rides, a miniature golf course, a 53-lane Skee Ball casino, and Miniature Madness, a child/adult participation area with kiddie rides, a maze, suspension bridges, and an outdoor children's theater. Adults enjoy the park's elaborate flower gardens, its regular outdoor concerts, and the oldest summer-stock theater in the United States. There are a dozen restaurants and snack bars in the park.

In 1994, Elitch Gardens will move from northwest Denver to a new 70-acre site on the banks of the South Platte River. It will add circus acts, musical revues, a dance pavilion, a brew pub, a rail heritage museum, and other attractions.

**Admission:** Gate admission with unlimited rides, $11 adults and children over 52 inches, $9 children under 52 inches, $6 children 3 and under; gate admission only, $5, free for children 3 and under (individual ride tickets can be purchased inside).

**Open:** Mid-Apr to May, Sat–Sun 10am–8pm; June–Labor Day, daily 10am–8pm.

### FUNPLEX, 9670 W. Coal Mine Ave., at Kipling St., Littleton. Tel. 972-4344.

A huge entertainment mall on the south end of Denver, Funplex offers two miniature golf courses, 40 bowling lanes, the Starport roller-dance rink, a large video arcade, billiards, Laserquest, an A&W Restaurant, and more.

**Admission:** Varies by activity, $2.50–$3.75 (discount packages available for more than one activity).

**Open:** Memorial Day–Labor Day, daily 11am–10pm; winter, daily 3:30–10pm. Skating Wed–Sun only; bowling closes at midnight.

### KIDSPORT, Stapleton International Airport, Main Terminal at Concourse C. Tel. 433-7444.

The Children's Museum operates KidsPort, a discovery center at the airport. It has hands-on educational and recreational exhibits on geography, world travel, and health; a horizontal rock-climbing wall; a "ballroom"; a play space for infants; and a gift shop.

**Admission:** $1.50 adults and children, free for kids under 2.

**Open:** Daily 9am–7pm.

### LAKESIDE AMUSEMENT PARK, I-70 and Sheridan Blvd. Tel. 477-1621.

Denver's newer amusement park (it dates from 1910) has 27 major rides, including three roller coasters: the Cyclone, Dragon, and Wild Chipmunk. There's also a 15-ride Kiddie Playland, Crystal Palace, and miniature golf course.

**Admission:** Gate admission, 75¢; unlimited rides, $6.95 Mon–Fri, $7.95 Sat–Sun and hols.

**Open:** May to early June, Sat–Sun and hols noon–11pm; mid-June to Labor Day, Mon–Fri 6–11pm, Sat–Sun and hols noon–11pm (Kiddie Playland, Mon–Fri 1–10pm, Sat–Sun and hols noon–10pm). **Closed:** Mon after Labor Day to Apr.

### TINY TOWN, 6249 S. Turkey Creek Rd. Tel. 790-9393.

The oldest kid-size village in America is just 30 minutes west of downtown Denver in the Rockies foothills. More than 80 buildings, all built at one-sixth scale, and a working railroad attract more than 60,000 visitors a year. The community was built in 1915 as a stagecoach stop, and has come back "from the dead" four times, after a fire and three floods. There's a snack bar and gift shop.

**Admission:** $2 adults, $1 seniors and children; train $1.

**Open:** Summer, daily 10am–7pm. **Closed:** Winter. **Directions:** Drive west on U.S. 285 (Hampden Avenue) and watch for the signs in Turkey Creek Canyon.

### WATER WORLD, 90th Ave. at Pecos St., Federal Heights. Tel. 427-SURF.

The largest publicly owned water park in the United States is this complex at the north end of the Denver metropolitan area. The park has pools with oceanlike waves, river rapids for inner-tubing, twisting water slides, a small children's play area, and other attractions—22 in all.

**Admission:** $11 adults, $10 children 4–12, free for seniors and children 3 and under.

**Open:** Memorial Day–Labor Day, Sat–Tues and Thurs 10am–6pm, Wed and Fri 10am–9pm. **Closed:** Winter. **Directions:** Take the Thornton exit (84th Avenue) off I-25 north.

## WALKING TOUR —— Downtown Denver

**Start:** Denver Information Center, Civic Center Park.
**Finish:** State Capitol, Civic Center Park.
**Time:** 2 to 8 hours, depending on how much time you spend shopping, eating, and sightseeing.
**Best Times:** Any Tuesday through Friday in late spring.

Start your tour of the downtown area at the Denver Information Center of the Denver Metro Convention & Visitors Bureau, opposite Civic Center Park on West Colfax Avenue at 14th Street. After collecting information about the city, cross to:
1. **Civic Center Park,** a two-square-block oasis featuring a Greek amphitheater, fountains, statues, flower gardens, and 30 different species of trees—two of which (it is said) were originally planted by Abraham Lincoln at his Illinois home.
   Overlooking the park on its east side is the State Capitol. On its south side, from east to west, are the:
2. **Colorado History Museum,** a staircaselike building with exhibits that make the state's colorful history come to life; the **Denver Public Library;** and the:
3. **Denver Art Museum.** Designed by Gio Pointi of Milan, Italy, the art museum is a 28-sided, 10-story structure that resembles a medieval fortress with a skin of over a million tiny glass tiles. Inside are 35,000 works of art, including the renowned Native American collection.
   On the west side of Civic Center Park is the:
4. **City and County Building,** decorated in spectacular fashion with a rainbow of colored lights during the Christmas season.
   A block farther west is the:
5. **U.S. Mint.** Modeled in the Italian Renaissance style, the building resembles the Palazzo Riccardi in Florence. Over 60,000 cubic feet of granite and 1,000 tons of steel went into its construction in 1904.
   Cross back over Colfax to the Information Center, then turn diagonally northwest up 14th Street. Four blocks ahead, on the left, is the:
6. **Colorado Convention Center,** with its impressive, five-story, steplike white facade. Opened in June 1990, the million-square-foot building contains a seven-acre exhibit room and the largest ballroom between Chicago and L.A.
   It's another two blocks up 14th to the:
7. **Denver Center for the Performing Arts,** covering four square blocks between 14th Street and Cherry Creek, Champa Street and Arapahoe Street. The complex is entered under a block-long, 80-foot-high glass archway. The center includes seven theaters, the nation's first symphony hall in the round, the world's only voice research laboratory, even a smoking solar fountain. Free tours are offered even when there's no performance scheduled.
   Two more blocks up 14th past the arts center is:
8. **Larimer Square,** Denver's oldest commercial district. The 18 restored turn-of-the-century Victorian buildings contain more than 30 shops and a dozen restaurants and clubs. Colorful awnings, hanging flower baskets, and quiet open courtyards accent the square, once home to such notables as Buffalo Bill Cody and Bat Masterson. Horse-drawn-carriage rides originate here for trips up the

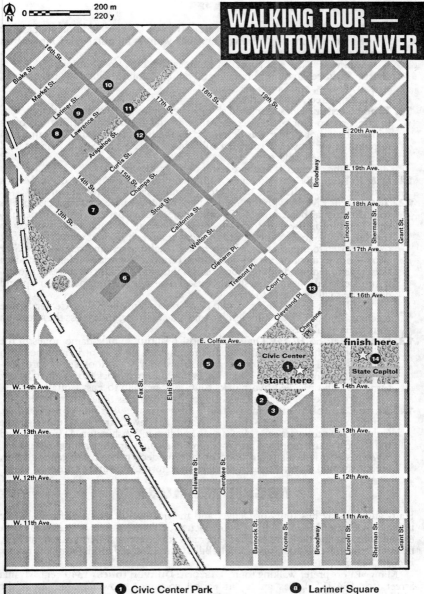

# WALKING TOUR — DOWNTOWN DENVER

0 — 200 m
0 — 220 y

N

16th St.
Blake St.
Market St.
Larimer St.
Lawrence St.
Arapahoe St.
Curtis St.
14th St.
15th St.
Champa St.
13th St.
Stout St.
California St.
Welton St.
Glenarm Pl.
Tremont Pl.
Court Pl.
Cleveland Pl.
Cheyenne Pl.
17th St.
18th St.
19th St.
E. 20th Ave.
E. 19th Ave.
E. 18th Ave.
E. 17th Ave.
E. 16th Ave.
Broadway
Lincoln St.
Sherman St.
Grant St.

E. Colfax Ave.

Civic Center
start here

finish here

State Capitol

W. 14th Ave.
E. 14th Ave.
Far St.
Elati St.

Cherry Creek

W. 13th Ave.
E. 13th Ave.

W. 12th Ave.
Delaware St.
Cherokee St.
E. 12th Ave.

W. 11th Ave.
Bannock St.
Acoma St.
Broadway
Lincoln St.
Sherman St.
Grant St.
E. 11th Ave.

Denver
COLORADO

1 Civic Center Park
2 Colorado History Museum
3 Denver Art Museum
4 City and County Building
5 U.S. Mint
6 Colorado Convention Center
7 Denver Center for the Performing Arts
8 Larimer Square
9 Writer Square
10 Tabor Center
11 D & F Tower
12 16th Street Mall
13 Brown Palace Hotel
14 State Capitol

16th Street Mall or through Lower Downtown. A new addition to Larimer Square is the Champion Brewing Company, with its unmistakable "Home Run Chewing Gum" wall mural.

A walkway at the east corner of Larimer and 15th leads through:

 **9. Writer Square,** another shopping-and-dining complex with quaint gas lamps, brick walkways, and outdoor cafés.

At 16th Street, cross to the:

**10. Tabor Center,** a glass-enclosed shopping complex of 70 shops on three levels. In effect a two-block-long greenhouse (with the Westin Hotel rising out of its midst), the Tabor Center was developed by the Rouse Company, the same firm responsible for Boston's Faneuil Hall, New York's South Street Seaport, and Baltimore's Harborplace.

The Tabor Center is anchored at its east end by the:

**11. D & F Tower,** a city landmark patterned after the campanile of St. Mark's Basilica in Venice, Italy, in 1910. Here, begin a leisurely stroll down the:

**12. 16th Street Mall,** with the State Capitol building in the southeast distance as your directional beacon. The $76-million pedestrian path is the finest people-watching spot in the city, from street entertainers to lunching office workers to travelers like yourself. Built of red and gray granite, it is lined with 200 red oak trees, a dozen fountains, festive banners, and a lighting system straight out of *Star Wars*—not to mention the outdoor cafés, restored Victorian buildings, modern skyscrapers, and hundreds of shops, restaurants, and department stores. Through it run sleek European-built shuttle buses, offering free transportation up and down the mall as often as every 90 seconds.

You'll walk seven blocks down 16th Street from the Tabor Center before reaching Tremont Place. Turn left, go one block farther, and across the street, on your right, you'll see the:

**13. Brown Palace Hotel.** One of the most beautiful grande-dame hotels in the United States, it was built in 1892 and features a nine-story atrium topped by a Tiffany stained-glass window. Step into the lobby for a look-see before continuing across Broadway on East 17th Avenue. Go two blocks to Sherman Street, turn right, and proceed two blocks south on Sherman to East Colfax Avenue.

You're back overlooking Civic Center Park, but this time, you're at the:

**14. State Capitol.** If you stand on the 13th step on the west side of the building, you're exactly 5,280 feet—1 mile—above sea level. Architects modeled the Colorado capitol after the U.S. Capitol building in Washington, D.C., and used the world's entire supply of rare rose onyx in its interior wainscoting. A winding, 93-step staircase leads to an open-air viewing deck beneath the capitol dome, with a sunny-day panorama from Pikes Peak to the Wyoming border.

# ORGANIZED TOURS

Half- and full-day bus tours of Denver and the nearby Rockies are offered by the ubiquitous **Gray Line,** P.O. Box 38667, Denver, CO 80238 (tel. 303/289-2841). A 6-hour tour, leaving the Denver Bus Center at 19th Street and Curtis Street, at 9am, takes in Denver, Red Rocks Park, Buffalo Bill's Grave, and old foothills mining towns. It costs $25 per person.

Many visitors prefer walking tours. **Historic Denver Tours,** 1340 Pennsylvania Street (tel. 534-1858), has guides in period costume, knowledgeable about the architecture and history of the time. They focus on historic districts like Lower Downtown and Capitol Hill, as well as historic homes. Reservations are required. Daily tours each summer morning cost $7 per person; a van tour combining tour highlights runs $12.

Back-road mountain tours departing from Denver to remote areas, reached on half- and full-day trips by four-wheel-drive vehicles, show visitors ghost towns, old mining camps, historic wagon trails, and other historic sites. Star treks on mountaintops at night can be arranged, as well as overnight camping and fishing trips. Among the firms offering these trips are **Best Mountain Tours by the Mountain Men,** 3003 South Macon Street, Aurora (tel. 750-5200), and **Scenic Mountain Tours,**

722 Julian Circle, Lafayette (tel. 665-7625). Destinations and daily availability vary. Typical rates are $35 per person for a 4½-hour tour, $60 for an all-day summer tour. Customized tour prices are considerably higher.

# 2. SPORTS & RECREATION

## SPECTATOR SPORTS

**AUTO RACING** The **Texaco/Havoline Grand Prix** brings top drivers to Denver annually, on the August weekend preceding Labor Day weekend. One of only five street races on the 17-race schedule of the CART/PPG Indy Car World Series, it features a 1.9-mile race course with 16 hairpin turns in front of top Denver attractions in the Civic Center area. The race is 152 miles, or 80 laps. For information, write 1100 Stout Street, Suite 300 (tel. 303/623-PRIX, or 800/477-PRIX).

Regular auto races are scheduled at **Lakeside Speedway,** Sheridan Boulevard at I-70 (tel. 477-1621). There are drag races April to September at the **Bandimere Speedway,** 3051 South Rooney Road, Morrison (tel. 697-6001, or 697-4870 for a 24-hour recording).

**BASEBALL** The **Colorado Rockies** will begin their initial season as a National League expansion franchise in 1993. The team will play its first 2 years at Mile High Stadium, home of the Denver Broncos football team, and in 1995 will move into new 43,000-seat Coors Field, under construction in Lower Downtown. The major-league baseball season runs from early April to the first week of October.

Meanwhile, the **Denver Zephyrs** of the minor-league American Association, a Milwaukee Brewers AAA farm team, will play their final season in 1992 at Mile High Stadium. Tickets are $3 to $7; call 433-8645 for information.

**BASKETBALL** The **Denver Nuggets** of the National Basketball Association play their home games at McNichols Sports Arena, 1635 Clay Street (tel. 893-DUNK). There are 41 home games a year between November and April, with playoffs continuing into June. Ticket prices range from $8 to $20.

The **University of Denver** plays a competitive college basketball schedule from late November to March.

**FOOTBALL** The **Denver Broncos** of the National Football League make their home at Mile High Stadium, 1900 Eliot Street (tel. 433-7466), part of a sports complex reached at Exit 210B of I-25. Single seats cost $19 to $30, but home games are sold out months in advance. Your best bet is to find someone hawking tickets outside the stadium entrance on game day.

You'll have better luck getting into a college game. The **University of Colorado** Buffaloes in Boulder play in the Big Eight Conference. For ticket information, call 492-5331. Other top college football teams in the area are at **Colorado State University** in Fort Collins and the **Air Force Academy** in Colorado Springs.

**GREYHOUND RACING** The **Mile High Kennel Club,** East 62nd Avenue and Colorado Boulevard, Commerce City (tel. 288-1591), has parimutuel dog races June to August, Monday through Saturday at 8:15pm and on Monday, Wednesday, and Saturday at 1:30pm. Admission is $1; reserved clubhouse seats are $3. When the local dog-racing season ends, off-track betting from other Colorado greyhound tracks continues.

**RODEO** The **National Western Stock Show and Rodeo,** with nearly $400,000 in prize money, is among the world's largest rodeos. It's held the second and third weeks of January at the Denver Coliseum, 4701 Marion Street (tel. 623-1166). (See Chapter 2, "Denver Calendar of Events," for details.) Rodeo sessions are generally Sunday through Friday at 2 and 7:30pm, and on Saturday at 11am, 3:30pm, and 8pm. Admission runs $6 to $12.

**SOCCER** The **Colorado Foxes** play in the American Professional Soccer League, which has an April-to-September season of 25 to 30 matches. Home matches are played at Jefferson County Stadium, Sixth Avenue and Kipling Street, Lakewood (tel. 840-1111). Ticket prices are $7 for adults, $4 for children 15 and under.

# RECREATION

Denver's proximity to the Rocky Mountains makes it possible to spend a day skiing, snowmobiling, horseback riding, hiking, river running, sailing, fishing, hunting, mountain climbing, or rockhounding—and be back in the city by nightfall. Within Denver itself, there are 85 miles of paved bicycle paths, 100 or more free tennis courts, and a score of golf courses. The city also boasts the world's largest sporting-goods store: **Gart Brothers Sports Castle,** on Broadway at 10th Avenue (tel. 861-1122). There are 30 other Gart Brothers outlets around the Denver area.

Campsites are easily reached from Denver, as are sites suitable for hang-gliding and hot-air ballooning. Campers enjoy many parts of the state, where half the land is in the public domain. Sailing is popular within the city at Sloans Lake and in Washington Park, and the Platte River is clear for many miles of river running in rafts, kayaks, and canoes.

The state and federal agencies, listed in Chapter 1, "Sports & Recreation," can help you with various aspects of outdoor recreation.

**BALLOONING** In the Denver area, try **Aero Cruise Balloon Adventures,** 2501 West 134th Circle, Broomfield (tel. 469-1243). A variety of options are available.

**BICYCLING** Denver is crisscrossed everywhere by paved bicycle paths, including a 10-mile stretch along the bank of the South Platte River and along Cherry Creek beside Speer Boulevard. All told, the city has 85 miles of off-road trails for bikers and runners. Bike paths link the city's 205 parks, and many city streets are marked with bike lanes. In all, the city has more than 130 miles of designated bike paths and lanes. Maps and information on bike routes in and beyond the Denver area are available from the **Colorado Department of Highways,** 4201 East Arkansas Avenue, Room 235, Denver (tel. 757-9313).

**Two Wheel Tours,** P.O. Box 2655, Littleton (tel. 303/798-4601, or 800/343-8940), offers half- and full-day bicycle tours of Denver, Vail, Mount Evans, and other Rocky Mountain destinations. Rates begin at $34.50 per person for a half-day Denver tour to $89.50 for a full-day descent of both sides of Vail Pass. Tours include breakfast, lunch, and hotel pickup and drop-off.

The **Clear Creek Bicycle Club,** 1431 Miner Street, Idaho Springs (tel. 303/567-9404), has a regular schedule of rides into the Rockies foothills from the old mining community.

**BOATING** Within the Denver city limits, both **Sloans Lake** (West 17th Avenue from Newton Street to Sheridan Boulevard) and **Smith Lake** in Washington Park (South Downing Street at East Center Avenue) are popular spots for punting. More serious boaters enjoy the powerboat marinas at **Cherry Creek State Recreation Area,** 4201 South Parker Road, Aurora (tel. 690-1166), 11 miles from downtown off I-225, and **Chatfield State Recreation Area,** 11500 North Roxborough Park Road, Littleton (tel. 303/794-8508), 16 miles south of downtown Denver off U.S. 85; and the facilities at **Barr Lake State Park,** 13401 Picadilly Road, Brighton (tel. 659-6005), 21 miles northeast of downtown via I-76. Motors aren't permitted on Barr Lake, so it's especially enjoyed by sailors and boardsailors.

For information on other boating opportunities, consult the Colorado Division of Parks and Outdoor Recreation, the National Park Service, or the U.S. Forest Service. (See Chapter 1, "Sports & Recreation," for addresses and telephone numbers.)

**BOWLING** Two of Denver's biggest bowling centers are the **Celebrity Sports Center,** 888 South Colorado Boulevard (tel. 757-3321), with 80 lanes, open daily from 8:30am to midnight; and the **Funplex,** 9670 West Coal Mine Avenue, Littleton (tel. 972-4344), with 40 lanes, open daily from 3:30pm to midnight (in summer, 11am to midnight).

**FISHING** A couple of good bets in the metropolitan area are **Chatfield Reservoir,** with trout, bass, and panfish, and **Cherry Creek Reservoir,** which boasts trout, walleye pike, bass, and crappie (see the addresses under "Boating," above). In all, there are more than 7,100 miles of streams and over 2,000 reservoirs and lakes in Colorado: for information, consult the Colorado Division of Parks and Outdoor Recreation; the Colorado Division of Wildlife; or the U.S. Fish and Wildlife Service. For information on licenses, see Chapter 1, "Sports & Recreation."

A couple of sporting goods stores that can provide more detailed information are **Uncle Milty's,** 4811 South Broadway, Englewood (tel. 789-3775), especially for local lakes and streams; and **Flyfisher Ltd.,** 252 Clayton Street (tel. 322-5014), particularly for higher mountain lakes and streams.

**GOLF** You'll often hear it said throughout the Front Range that you can play golf at least 320 days a year—that the sun always seems to be shining, and even when it snows, what little sticks melts quickly. With the resultant demand, the city of Denver operates seven municipal golf courses (for information on any of them, call the Denver Department of Parks and Recreation; tel. 575-2227): the **City Park Golf Course,** East 25th Avenue and York Street (tel. 295-4420); **Harvard Golf Course** (par 3), East Iliff Avenue and South Clarkson Street (tel. 744-9448); **Kennedy Golf Course,** 10500 East Hampden Avenue (tel. 751-0311); **Overland Golf Course,** South Santa Fe Drive and Jewell Avenue (tel. 777-7331); **Park Hill Golf Course,** 3500 Colorado Boulevard (tel. 333-5411); **Wellshire Golf Course,** 3333 South Colorado Boulevard (tel. 757-1352); and **Willis Case Golf Course,** West 50th Avenue and Vrain Street (tel. 575-2112). Greens fees for nonresidents at city courses are $12 for 18 holes, $8 for 9 holes, and $5.50 for the par-3 Harvard course. Call for hours, to reserve tee times, and to verify greens fees.

There are many more privately owned golf clubs and country clubs in the greater Denver area, many of which offer reciprocal memberships with clubs in other cities. Probably the best known is the exclusive **Castle Pines Country Club** at Castle Rock, midway between Denver and Colorado Springs off I-25; it's the site each August of a major PGA tournament.

For information on private clubs and other golf information, contact any of the following: **Colorado Golf Association,** 5655 South Yosemite Street, Suite 101, Englewood, CO 80111 (tel. 303/779-4563); **Colorado Golf Country USA,** 559 Second Avenue, Castle Rock, CO 80104 (tel. 303/688-8262); or **Colorado World of Golf,** 5500 East Yale Avenue, Denver, CO 80222 (tel. 303/758-0962).

**HIKING/BACKPACKING** The newly created **Colorado Trail** is a hiking and mountain-biking route winding 456 miles from Denver to Durango. Opened in 1988, it took 15 years to create with volunteer labor and funding from the Colorado Lottery. For information, write P.O. Box 260876, Lakewood, CO 80226 (tel. 303/526-0809).

For hikes specific to the Denver area, contact the city Department of Parks and Recreation (tel. 575-2227) for information on the 18 **Denver Mountain Parks.** Nearby state parks well known for their hiking trails are **Roxborough State Park,** 10 miles south of Littleton (tel. 973-3959), and **Golden Gate State Park,** 16 miles northwest of Golden (tel. 592-1502). Or contact any of the following state or federal agencies: Colorado Division of Parks and Outdoor Recreation, Colorado Division of Wildlife, National Park Service, U.S. Bureau of Land Management, and U.S. Forest Service. For topographic maps, consult either the Colorado Geological Survey or the U.S. Geological Survey. (See Chapter 1, "Sports & Recreation.")

**HORSEBACK RIDING** Horse enthusiasts can find a mount at **Stockton's Plum Creek Stables,** 7479 West Titan Road, Littleton (tel. 791-1966), near Chatfield Reservoir 15 miles south of downtown. Guided rides, by appointment only, are $10 per rider; children must be at least 7. Stockton's also offers hayrides and wintertime sleighrides.

Detailed information on longer trips can be obtained from the Colorado Guides and Outfitters Association, see Chapter 1, "Sports & Recreation."

**HUNTING** There's no hunting in the immediate Denver area, but opportunities abound in the foothills and plains. For information, consult the Colorado Division of

Wildlife, Colorado Guides and Outfitters Association, or U.S. Fish and Wildlife Service. (See Chapter 1, "Sports & Recreation.")

**OFF-ROAD VEHICLES** The best source of information is the **Colorado Association of Four-Wheel Drive Clubs** and **Colorado Off-Highway Vehicle Coalition,** P.O. Box 1413, Wheat Ridge, CO 80034 (tel. 303/321-1266 or 696-6835). The Colorado Division of Parks and Outdoor Recreation, U.S. Bureau of Land Management, and U.S. Forest Service can also offer suggestions. (See Chapter 1, "Sports & Recreation.")

**RECREATION CENTERS** The **Denver Department of Parks and Recreation** (tel. 331-4020) operates 37 rec centers around the city. Daily guest passes are available at many of them, at a price of $4 for adult nonresidents and $1 for anyone 17 or younger. Facilities may include basketball courts, indoor or outdoor swimming pools, weight rooms, and fitness classes. The following may be most convenient for out-of-town visitors: **Cook Park Recreation Center,** 7100 Cherry Creek Drive South (tel. 758-9887), with an outdoor pool; **Eisenhower Recreation Center,** 3300 East Dartmouth Avenue (tel. 758-9801), with an outdoor pool; **Martin Luther King, Jr., Recreation Center,** 3880 Newport Street (tel. 331-4034), with an indoor pool; **20th Street Recreation Center,** 1011 20th Street, between Arapahoe Street and Curtis Street (tel. 295-4430), with an indoor pool; and **Washington Park Recreation Center,** 701 South Franklin Street (tel. 777-9832), with an indoor pool.

Major private athletic clubs in downtown Denver include the **Athletic Club at Denver Place,** 1849 Curtis Street (tel. 294-9494), with an indoor pool, gymnasium, indoor track, racquetball courts, weight and exercise room, and aerobics classes; and the **International Athletic Center,** 1630 Welton Street (tel. 623-2100), with a major weight and cardiovascular training center, regular aerobics classes, and racquetball and squash courts.

**RIVER RAFTING** No one seriously rafts the South Platte through Denver (though there *is* a human-made kayak chute in downtown Denver). But the river is rafted nearer its source, along with many other rivers around the state during the mid-May to Labor Day season. Among rafting companies with headquarters in the Denver area are:

**Arkansas River Tours,** P.O. Box 20281, Denver, CO 80220 (tel. 303/333-7831, or 800/331-7238, 800/321-4352 in Colorado). Prices start at $29 for half-day trips on the Arkansas to $400 or more for trips of several days.

**Timber Rafting,** P.O. Box 905, Conifer, CO 80433 (tel. 303/670-0177, or 800/332-3381 in Colorado in summer only). One- and 2-day trips on the Colorado, Arkansas, or North Platte rivers run $49 to $179, or somewhat less midweek.

**Whitewater Encounters,** 1422 South Chambers Circle, Aurora, CO 80012 (tel. 303/751-0161). Rates are $29 to $129 for half-day or full-day trips on the Arkansas or Colorado.

**Whitewater Odyssey,** P.O. Box 2186, Evergreen, CO 80439 (tel. 303/674-3637). Two- and 3-day trips on the Colorado, North Platte, Rio Grande, and Rio Chama start at $139.

For more information on rafting, contact the **Colorado River Outfitters Association,** P.O. Box 1662, Buena Vista, CO 81211 (tel. 303/369-4632).

**SKIING** The nearest ski resorts to Denver are **Eldora Mountain Resort,** 45 miles west via Boulder (tel. 440-8700); **Loveland Basin and Valley,** 56 miles west via I-70 (tel. 571-5580); **Berthoud Pass,** 51 miles west via I-70 and U.S. 40 (tel. 670-1666); and **Winter Park,** 73 miles west via I-70 and U.S. 40 (tel. 892-0961 or 447-0588). Eldora and Winter Park boast nordic as well as alpine terrain. All areas are discussed in detail in subsequent chapters of this book.

Full information on skiing in the state can be obtained from **Colorado Ski Country USA,** 1560 Broadway, Suite 1440, Denver (tel. 837-0793), or the **Colorado Cross Country Ski Association,** P.O. Box 169, Winter Park, CO 80482 (tel. 303/887-2152).

Some useful Denver telephone numbers for skiers: **ski-area information** (tel.

831-7669), **mountain and snow conditions** (tel. 236-9435), **weather report** (tel. 398-3964), **road conditions** (tel. 639-1111).

**SNOWMOBILING** Get in touch with the **Mile Hi Snowmobile Club of Denver,** P.O. Box 26368, Denver, CO 80226.

**SWIMMING** If your hotel doesn't have a pool, visit a recreation center or athletic club (see above).

**TENNIS** The **Denver Department of Parks and Recreation** (tel. 575-2552) manages 120 tennis courts, 49 of them lit for night play. The most popular are in City Park, Washington Park, and Sloans Lake Park. For more information on tennis, contact the **Colorado Tennis Association,** 1201 South Parker Road, Suite 102, Denver (tel. 695-4116).

# 3. SAVVY SHOPPING

## THE SHOPPING SCENE

Most Denver visitors who are afoot concentrate their shopping along the 16th Street Mall and adjacent areas—including Larimer Square, the Shops at Tabor Center, Writer Square, and (just slightly farther away) Tivoli Denver.

For those with a vehicle, there are many more options, first and foremost of which is the huge new Cherry Creek Shopping Center south of downtown. There are many more suburban shopping malls, as well.

**Business hours** vary from store to store and from shopping center to shopping center. In general, it's safe to say that shops will be open Monday through Friday from 10am to 9pm, on Saturday from 10am to 6pm, and on Sunday from noon to 5pm.

## SHOPPING A TO Z

### ANTIQUES

**ANTIQUE GUILD, 1298 S. Broadway. Tel. 722-3359.** More than 200 dealers under one roof make this an antiques hunter's dream. You'll find fine European hardwood furniture, American primitive and pine furniture, china, glassware, stained glass, textiles, prints, objects in art deco and art nouveau styles, and much more. Open Monday through Saturday from 10am to 5:30pm and on Sunday from noon to 5pm.

### ARTS & CRAFTS

**COLORADO ARTIST-CRAFTSMEN CENTER, 1325 Curtis St. Tel. 893-8265.**

Located in the Denver Performing Arts Center Galleria, this gallery is an excellent place to get a feel for the work of contemporary regional artisans. Open Wednesday through Saturday from 11am to 7pm in summer, 11am to 8pm during theater season.

**CORE NEW ART SPACE, 1412 Wazee St. Tel. 571-4831.**

This Lower Downtown gallery features very contemporary, avant-garde, and "cutting-edge" art. Open Friday through Sunday from noon to 5pm.

**DENVER COOPERATIVE ARTS CENTER, 720 E. 18th Ave. Tel. 839-9439.**

Located Uptown near Restaurant Row, the co-op offers a representation of many area artists at highly reasonable prices.

**GALLERY ONE, 1512 Larimer St. Tel. 629-5005.**
Paintings, graphics, and sculptures by internationally recognized artists are offered at Writer Square. Open Monday through Saturday from 10am to 9pm and on Sunday from noon to 5pm. Also in Cherry Creek North Shopping Center.

**NATIVE AMERICAN TRADING COMPANY, 1301 Bannock St. Tel. 534-0771.**
This gallery offers weavings, ceramics, baskets, jewelry, and other Native American artifacts, as well as some contemporary paintings. Appropriately, it's across the street from the Denver Art Museum. Open Monday through Friday from 10am to 6pm and on Saturday from 11am to 4pm.

**PIRATE: A CONTEMPORARY ART OASIS, 3659 Navajo St. Tel. 458-6058.**
Across the South Platte in northwest Denver, Pirate treads the cutting edge in work of all types. Open on Friday from 7 to 10pm and on Saturday and Sunday from noon to 5pm.

**JOAN ROBEY GALLERY, 939 Broadway. Tel. 892-9600.**
Part of a four-gallery downtown complex known as Broadway Central Galleries, the Robey Gallery specializes in three-dimensional sculpture and wall art. Open Monday through Friday from 10am to 6pm and on Saturday from 10am to 4pm.

**CARL SIPLE GALLERY, 1401 17th St. Tel. 292-1401.**
Established national and emerging regional artists are represented at this beautiful gallery near Strings on Restaurant Row.

**THE SQUASH BLOSSOM, 1415 Larimer St. Tel. 572-7979.**
Southwestern-style paintings, Hispanic folk art and furniture, and jewelry, pottery, and weavings by Pueblo and Navajo peoples are presented at Larimer Square.

**TURNER GALLERY, 301 University Blvd. Tel. 355-1828.**
Colorado's oldest gallery specializes in traditional art forms, including oils and Colorado landscapes by contemporary and deceased American and European painters. Its collection also includes etchings, engravings, and antique botanicals. Open on Monday from 10am to 4pm and Tuesday through Saturday from 9am to 5:30pm.

## DEPARTMENT STORES

**JOSLIN'S, 16th Street Mall at Curtis St. Tel. 534-0441.**
Denver's oldest department store specializes in brand-name merchandise at value prices.

**MAY D & F, 16th Street Mall at Tremont Place. Tel. 620-7500.**
The Rocky Mountain region's largest retailer sells everything from clothing to kitchenware, sporting goods to children's toys. There are several stores in the Denver area, mainly in shopping malls.

## FASHIONS

**BANANA REPUBLIC, 535 16th Street Mall. Tel. 595-8877.**
This travel and safari merchandiser has developed a name for functional but attractive men's and women's wear.

**FASHION BAR, 16th Street Mall at Tremont Place. Tel. 620-9811.**
Women's clothing in a wide range of styles and prices are the specialty of Fashion Bars, found throughout Colorado.

**LAWRENCE COVELL, The Shops at Tabor Center. Tel. 595-8300.**
This upscale shop offers contemporary men's and women's fashions, including designer clothing by Giorgio Armani, Hugo Boss, Valentino, and Byblos.

**MILLER STOCKMAN, 1600 California St. at 16th Street Mall. Tel. 825-5339.**

In business since 1918, this purveyor of western wear stocks more than 400 pairs of cowboy boots.

**SHEPLERS, 8500 E. Orchard Rd., Tech Center. Tel. 773-3311.**

The world's largest western store and catalog merchant sells every piece of clothing you'll need. Also at 10300 Bannock Street, west off I-25, Northglenn (tel. 450-9999).

**UNITS, The Shops at Tabor Center. Tel. 892-9216.**

This specialty shop sells "one size fits all" mix-and-match fashions—shirts, skirts, pants, and so forth, that can be used to create a variety of outfits.

## FOOD

**ALFALFA'S, 201 University Blvd. Tel. 320-0700.**

Already an institution in the Denver area, this huge natural-foods store—50,000 square feet in area—helps perpetuate Coloradans' healthy life-styles. No food sold here contains any artificial flavoring or preservative, nor was any grown using pesticides, chemicals, or other additives. There's a juice and health-food bar as well. This Cherry Creek–area store opened in 1990; others are in Boulder and Littleton.

**STEPHANY'S CHOCOLATES, 4969 Colorado Blvd., north of I-70. Tel. 355-1522.**

Denver's largest manufacturer and wholesaler of gourmet confections is best known for the Denver Mint and Colorado Almond Toffee. In business for more than three decades, it offers tours by appointment. There are several retail outlets around the city.

## GIFTS & SOUVENIRS

**COLORADO PEDDLER, Writer Square, 15th and Lawrence Sts. Tel. 825-2932.**

Arts, crafts, and gift items made by more than 200 independent artisans, all of them Colorado residents, are retailed here. Jewelry, pottery, minerals, and gourmet foods are among them.

**LOKSTOK 'N BAREL, 1421 Larimer St. Tel. 825-3436.**

This Larimer Square outlet sells a variety of western and wildlife bronze sculptures, aspen vases, jewelry, antique toy reproductions, and more.

## JEWELRY

**JOHN ATENCIO, 280 Detroit St. Tel. 377-2007.**

A Cherry Creek–area dealer, Atencio carries one-of-a-kind, handcrafted gold jewelry. Many pieces are set with precious or semiprecious stones. Open Monday through Thursday from 10am to 5:30pm and on Friday and Saturday from 10am to 5pm.

**SHALAKO INDIAN ARTS, Tivoli Denver, 900 Auraria Pkwy. Tel. 592-1088.**

Native American jewelry is the specialty of this store, which also carries a variety of arts and crafts products. Open Monday through Saturday from 10am to 9pm and on Sunday from noon to 6pm.

## MALLS & SHOPPING CENTERS

**CHERRY CREEK SHOPPING CENTER, First Ave. between University Blvd. and Steele St. Tel. 388-2522.**

Saks Fifth Avenue, Neiman Marcus, and Lord & Taylor anchor this deluxe million-square-foot mall, which opened in August 1990 and drew more than 15 million shoppers in its first year. Across the street is Cherry Creek North, an upscale neighborhood retail area. Open Monday through Saturday from 10am to 9pm and on Sunday from noon to 6pm.

**LARIMER SQUARE, 1400 block of Larimer St. Tel. 534-2367.**

This restored quarter of old Denver (see "The Top Attractions" in "Attractions," above) includes numerous art galleries, boutiques, restaurants, and nightclubs. The Market is an excellent place to have breakfast or lunch, or sip on an espresso. Most shops are open Monday through Wednesday and on Friday and Saturday from 10am to 6pm, on Thursday from 10am to 9pm, and on Sunday from noon to 5pm.

**THE SHOPS AT TABOR CENTER, 16th Street Mall between Larimer and Arapahoe Sts. Tel. 534-2141.**

Some 70 specialty shops are in this two-block, glass-enclosed galleria. The Bridge Market offers a changing showcase of gifts and collectibles, while the PicNic Court has over a dozen dining opportunities. Open Monday through Saturday from 10am to 9pm and on Sunday from noon to 5pm.

**TIVOLI DENVER, 901 Larimer St. at Auraria Pkwy. Tel. 629-8712.**

Transformed from a 19th-century brewery (see "Architectural Highlights" in "Attractions," above), this exciting theme mall combines shops, restaurants, and nightclubs into one cohesive whole. Shops are open Monday through Saturday from 10am to 9pm and on Sunday from noon to 5pm. A free shuttle trolley runs throughout the day between Civic Center Park, Larimer Square, and Tivoli Denver.

## MARKETS

**DOG TRACK FLEA MARKET, 5150 E. 64th Ave., Commerce City. Tel. 289-7355.**

Located next door to the greyhound track, this market has more than 200 indoor selling booths and over 800 outdoor spaces selling old and new merchandise. Open year round, on Saturday and Sunday from 6am to 5pm; admission is 75¢, free for children under 12.

**MILE HIGH FLEA MARKET, 7007 E. 88th Ave., at I-76, Henderson. Tel. 289-4656.**

Though it's some 15 miles northeast of downtown Denver, this huge market attracts over a million shoppers a year to its 80 paved acres. Besides close-outs, garage sales, and seasonal merchandise, it has more than a dozen places to eat and snack. Open year round, on Wednesday, Saturday, and Sunday from 6am to 5pm. Admission is $1.50, free for children under 12.

# 4. EVENING ENTERTAINMENT

Denver's performing arts and nightlife scene, an important part of life in this sophisticated western city, is anchored by the four-square-block, $80-million Denver Performing Arts Complex, located downtown just a few blocks from major hotels. The complex contains nine theaters, a concert hall, and the nation's first symphony hall in-the-round; it is home to the Colorado Symphony, Colorado Ballet, Opera Colorado, and the Denver Center for the Performing Arts, the latter an umbrella organization for resident and touring theater companies.

In all, Denver has 30 theaters, more than 100 cinemas, and dozens of concert halls, nightclubs, discos, and bars. Numerous clubs offer country-and-western music; jazz, rock, and comedy acts are also popular.

Current **entertainment listings** can be found in special Friday-morning sections of the two daily newspapers, the *Denver Post* and the *Rocky Mountain News. Westword,* a weekly newspaper distributed free throughout the city every Wednesday, has perhaps the best listings of all; it focuses on arts, entertainment, and local politics.

Tickets for nearly all major entertainment and sporting events can be obtained from **TicketMaster** (tel. 290-TIXS for information). Credit-card orders can be placed on American Express, MasterCard, or VISA. There are cash-only TicketMaster outlets at selected Gart Brothers sporting-goods stores (including 10th

Street and Broadway), Dave Cook Sporting Goods, and Sound Warehouses. The agency adds a $3 charge to every ticket, in addition to the 10% city seat tax.

The **Ticket Bus,** an English double-decker on the 16th Street Mall at Curtis Street, sells tickets on a cash-only basis for many live theater performances as well as all events sold through TicketMaster. Half-price tickets may be available on the day of the performance. The Ticket Bus is open Monday through Friday from 10am to 6pm and on Saturday from 11am to 3pm.

Discount tickets are often available for midweek and matinee performances.

# THE PERFORMING ARTS
## MAJOR PERFORMING ARTS COMPANIES
### Classical Music & Opera

**COLORADO SYMPHONY ORCHESTRA, Denver Performing Arts Complex, 1031 13th St. Tel. 595-4388.**

Home for this international-caliber orchestra is Boettcher Concert Hall—the nation's first symphony hall in-the-round. Huge discs suspended from the ceiling help create perfect acoustics. The orchestra's classical concerts are interspersed with pops concerts, and occasionally there is a noted jazz soloist.

Concerts typically are scheduled on Thursday and Saturday at 8pm, on Friday at 6:30pm, and on Sunday at 2:30pm. During the summer season, the orchestra makes outdoor appearances at the Fiddler's Green Amphitheatre and other venues.

**DENVER CHAMBER ORCHESTRA, 1618 Glenarm Place, Suite 1360. Tel. 825-4911.**

Mozart and baroque festivals highlight the season for Denver's professional chamber orchestra, which offers most of its 20 annual performances either at the Trinity Church, 18th Avenue and Broadway, or at the Arvada Center for the Arts.

**OPERA COLORADO, 695 S. Colorado Blvd., Suite 20. Tel. 778-6464.**

Internationally renowed singers take the lead roles each spring during the opera's brief season. Both its operas (eight performances) are done in the round, with English surtitles, at the Boettcher Concert Hall in the Denver Performing Arts Complex. The schedule typically is 3 nights—a Tuesday, Friday, and Saturday—at 8pm, followed by a 2pm Sunday matinee.

**Prices:** Tickets, $15–$58.

### Theater Companies

**DENVER CENTER FOR THE PERFORMING ARTS, Denver Performing Arts Complex, 1245 Champa St. Tel. 893-4000,** or 893-DCPA for recorded information.

An umbrella organization for resident and touring theater, youth outreach, and conservatory training, the DCPA includes the following:

**Denver Center Theatre Company,** the largest professional resident theater company in the Rockies region. With 40 artists on its payroll, the troupe performs 8 to 12 plays in repertory from late fall to early spring in all four theaters of the Helen Bonfils Theatre Complex (tel. 893-4100). The company produces classical and contemporary dramas, innovative revivals of musicals, and premières of new plays.

Associated with the company is the **National Theatre Conservatory,** chartered by Congress in 1984, an institute of advanced theatrical education.

**Denver Center Productions** is comprised of Robert Garner/Center Attractions, which brings touring Best of Broadway shows like *Grand Hotel* and *Les Misérables,* and many Broadway-bound musicals, to the Auditorium Theatre; and Denver Center Media, an Emmy Award-winning film production arm.

The **Denver Center Recording and Research Center** does pioneering research on the voice, including environmental, physiological, and psychological effects.

**Prices:** Denver Center Theatre Company prices vary according to performance, $15–$25; Robert Garner/Center Attractions, $15–$50.

## Dance Companies

**COLORADO BALLET, 999 18th St., Suite 325. Tel. 298-0677.**

The city's sole professional resident company performs in the Auditorium Theatre at the Denver Performing Arts Complex. The classical program always includes *The Nutcracker* during the Christmas season, and another ballet in the spring.

**CLEO PARKER ROBINSON DANCE ENSEMBLE, 119 23rd St. Tel. 295-1759.**

A highly acclaimed multicultural ensemble, the Cleo Parker Robinson group performs in its own Shorter Church Building in the predominantly black Five Points neighborhood north of downtown. It offers 75 performances a year, many on tour.

## MAJOR CONCERT HALLS & ALL-PURPOSE AUDITORIUMS

**ARVADA CENTER FOR THE ARTS AND HUMANITIES, 6901 Wadsworth Blvd., Arvada. Tel. 431-3080.**

This multidisciplinary arts center is in use almost every day of the year for performances by its resident theater company; concert music and dance; historical museum and art-gallery exhibitions; and community education programs. The main auditorium seats 800.

The center is open Monday through Friday from 9am to 10pm, on Saturday from 9am to 5pm, and on Sunday from 1 to 5pm. Call for information on specific programs.

**DENVER PERFORMING ARTS COMPLEX, 14th and Curtis Sts. Tel. 893-4000.**

Covering four square blocks in downtown Denver from Cherry Creek to 14th Street and Champa Street to Arapahoe Street, the Performing Arts Complex is impressive even to those not attending a performance. Free guided tours of the complex are offered Monday through Friday at noon.

Components include the **Helen G. Bonfils Theatre Complex** (tel. 893-4000), with four theaters seating 157 to 547; the state-of-the-art **Arena Theatre** (tel. 575-2862), seating 2,800; the **Auditorium Theatre** (tel. 640-2862), seating 2,178; and the **StageWest** theater (tel. 623-6400), seating 240. It also contains the impressive **Boettcher Concert Hall** (tel. 640-2862), seating 2,629 for music-in-the-round performances of symphony and opera, as well as a restaurant and shopping promenade.

**FIDDLER'S GREEN AMPHITHEATRE, 6350 Greenwood Plaza Blvd., Englewood. Tel. 220-7000.**

Outdoor summer concerts at the Museum of Outdoor Arts feature national and international stars in rock, jazz, classical, and country milieus. (The 1991 Sunset Series featured Steve Winwood, Whitney Houston, Jimmy Buffett, Ray Charles, Styx, and Chicago.) There's also a pops subscription series presented by the Colorado Symphony Orchestra. The amphitheater has 7,500 reserved seats and room for another 10,500 on its spacious lawn. It's open May to September.

**MCNICHOLS ARENA, 1635 Clay St. Tel. 592-4700.**

Though this arena beside Mile High Stadium is home to the National Basketball Association's Denver Nuggets much of the year, it's also a perfect locale for concerts and other shows—many of which are moved here from outdoor amphitheaters when weather intervenes. There's seating for 18,500.

**PARAMOUNT THEATRE, 1621 Glenarm Place. Tel. 834-8336.**

A historic-preservation group bought this impressive early 20th-century downtown theater in 1978 and returned its gilded columns and emblazoned walls to their former glory. Now the 2,054-seat theater is a wonderful place to enjoy an eclectic series of jazz concerts, pop and folk performances, high-brow lectures, and films like the annual Warren Miller ski movies.

**RED ROCKS AMPHITHEATRE, Hogback Rd., Morrison. Tel. 572-4700.**

Denver's favorite venue for top-name outdoor summer concerts is set in the Rocky Mountain foothills, 12 miles from Denver via I-70 west. The amphitheater is flanked by 400-foot-high red sandstone rocks, and at night, with the lights of Denver spread across the horizon, the atmosphere is magical.

The Beatles performed here, as have top symphony orchestras from around the world. In 1991 the lineup featured Paul Simon, Sting, Bonnie Raitt, Andrew Dice Clay, a blues night headlined by B.B. King, and a country-and-western show with Clint Black and Merle Haggard.

The amphitheater seats 9,000; only 2,173 of which are reserved. There are an average of two shows a week from mid-May to mid-September; most begin at 7:30pm.

## THEATERS

**ARENA THEATRE, Denver Performing Arts Complex, 14th and Curtis Sts. Tel. 575-2862.**
The DPAC's new 2,800-seat theater opened in November 1991 with the touring production of Andrew Lloyd Webber's *Phantom of the Opera.* It will be the site for major stage productions.

**AVENUE THEATER, 2119 E. 17th Ave. Tel. 377-1720.**
Off-Broadway plays and musicals are presented in an intimate 100-seat theater. The company is best known locally for *Chicken Lips,* an improvisational comedy.

**EL CENTRO SU TEATRO, 4725 High St. Tel. 296-0219.**
A Hispanic theater and cultural center, El Centro presents Spanish-language productions on a regular basis.

**EULIPIONS CULTURAL CENTER, 2715 Welton St. Tel. 295-6814.**
This multicultural theater in the Five Points neighborhood specializes in works by African-American playwrights. It seats 300.

**GERMINAL STATE, 44th and Alcott Sts. Tel. 455-7108.**
In this 132-seat theater, plays by modern playwrights, such as Brecht, Albee, and Pinter, are presented.

**STAGE WEST, Denver Performing Arts Complex, 14th and Curtis Sts. Tel. 623-6400.**
Cabaret musical theater is offered on a regular basis.

## DINNER THEATERS

**ASCOT DINNER THEATRE, 9136 W. Bowles Ave., Littleton. Tel. 971-0100.**
This large (630-seat) dinner theater presents works from major Broadway musicals such as *Camelot, Evita, My Fair Lady,* and *The Sound of Music.* Open Wednesday through Sunday nights, it serves elegant, upscale dining with the performance.

**THE COUNTRY DINNER PLAYHOUSE, 6875 S. Clinton St., Englewood. Tel. 799-1410.**
A preshow buffet dinner is followed by live Broadway musicals and other productions, like *Steel Magnolias* and *It's a Wonderful Life.* The playhouse seats 481. Shows are Tuesday through Sunday nights, with matinees on Saturday and Sunday.

# THE CLUB & MUSIC SCENE

## NIGHTCLUBS & CABARETS

**BASIN'S UP, 1427 Larimer St. Tel. 623-7512.**
A well-established downtown rock emporium above Josephina's on Larimer

Square, Basin's Up features live rock bands playing Top-40 dance tunes Tuesday through Sunday nights from 9:30pm to 2am. A blues soloist performs Monday nights. The club, which attracts the 25-to-35 age group, features a sunken central seating area that looks up to the raised dance floor.
**Admission:** Free Sun–Wed, $5 Thurs–Sat.

**JAZZ WORKS, 1634 18th St. Tel. 297-0920.**
Lower Downtown's premier jazz venue is in the basement of the Wynkoop Brewing Company, with a side-alley entrance. The music starts Wednesday through Sunday at 8:30pm, and runs the gamut of jazz from mainstream to fusion to crossover, salsa to new age. Rhythm-and-blues artists sometimes perform as well.
**Admission:** $4–$6. Special events cost more.

## COMEDY CLUBS

**COMEDY WORKS, 1226 15th St. Tel. 595-3637.**
Tuesday is improvisation or new talent night at this Larimer Square club. But it's packed Wednesday through Sunday, when various touring big-name acts appear—many of whom may have appeared on HBO, Showtime, *Late Night with David Letterman,* or *Saturday Night Live.* Rosanne Barr performed here early in her career. There is also an adjoining café, Gibson's. Call for reservations.
**Admission:** $5–$10.

**GEORGE MCKELVEY'S COMEDY CLUB, 10015 E. Hampden Ave., at Havana St. Tel. 368-8900.**
This club is a little farther away—just within Denver's southeastern city limits—but it also draws top performers. Tuesday is new talent night; Wednesday is set aside for improv; headliners appear Thursday through Sunday.
**Admission:** $5–$8.

## COUNTRY MUSIC

**THE GRIZZLY ROSE, 5450 N. Valley Hwy. Tel. 295-1330.**
Consistently rated as the No. 1 country-and-western dance club in the Denver area, this huge establishment is just across the Adams County line off I-25, Exit 215. There's a 5,000-square-foot dance floor, largest in Colorado, beneath its one-acre roof, and it draws major national acts like Garth Brooks and Tanya Tucker for two-stepping. Bands perform every night of the week, with Sunday alone reserved for local entertainers. The café serves a full-service menu until last call at 1:30am.
**Admission:** $3–$15.

**PISTOL PETE'S SALOON, 2490 W. Hampden Ave., Sheridan. Tel. 761-6188.**
Pete serves up healthy portions of live country music for dancing on the south side Tuesday through Saturday nights.
**Admission:** Free Tues–Thurs, $1 Fri–Sat.

**URBAN COWGIRL SALOON, 9575 W. 57th Ave., Arvada. Tel. 420-4444.**
John Travolta has yet to make his entrance, but West Denverites come for music nightly, including top live acts Thursday through Saturday. The place opens daily at 9am and shuts down at 2am Thursday through Saturday.
**Admission:** Free Mon–Thurs, $2 Fri–Sat.

**CLUB ZANZA-BAR, 10601 E. Colfax Ave., Aurora. Tel. 344-2510.**
This eastside club presents country-and-western dance music by Straight Shot Wednesday through Sunday nights. Wednesday is ladies' night, highlighted by a dance contest. Hours are noon to 2am Monday through Saturday and 6pm to midnight on Sunday.
**Admission:** Free.

## ROCK MUSIC

**THE BROADWAY, 1082 Broadway. Tel. 860-7558.**

Malice in Wonderland, Pigmy Love Circus, and other "alternative rock" bands perform nightly.

**CRICKET ON THE HILL, 1209 E. 13th Ave., at Downing St. Tel. 830-9020.**

This Capitol Hill club, open daily at noon, offers live music every night. Tempos range from rock to blues to country-rock: Cricket characterizes itself as an "eclectic inner-city music emporium."

**Admission:** Free or $2–$5, depending on band.

**HERMAN'S HIDEAWAY, 1578 S. Broadway, near Mississippi Ave. Tel. 778-9916.**

Herman's is a local hideaway for the Washington Park–Denver University area crowd. There's live music Wednesday through Saturday nights, featuring contemporary rock groups such as The Subdudes and reggae from the likes of The Healers. Open daily.

**Admission:** $2–$15, depending on band.

**JIMMY'S GRILLE, 320 S. Birch St., at E. Alameda Ave. Tel. 322-5334.**

"Denver's reggae joint" is jumpin' when performers like Eek-a-Mouse, Burning Spear, or John Bayley are in town. More commonly, Mon, you'll hear bands like Monkey Siren. Tex-Mex cuisine is served Monday to Saturday at lunch and dinner. The club features a complimentary "Humpday" buffet on Wednesday from 5 to 8pm; ladies get free admission on Thursday, and pay only 50¢ for drinks after 7:30pm. Jimmy's opens at 11am Monday through Friday, and at noon on Saturday; it's open till 2am most nights. Closed Sunday.

**Admission:** Free or $3–$4, depending on night.

**XXIII PARISH, 2301 Blake St. Tel. 292-0816.**

Call it "23 Parish," so named for its cross street and its premises in a large former church. One of Denver's most popular nightclubs is actually two. The 30s and 40s crowd stays in the main sanctuary for classic rock on Tuesday, funk on Wednesday, R&B and reggae on Thursday, contemporary dance music on Friday and Saturday. Heavy-metal fanatics throng to the Garage, in an adjoining building, to hear visiting recording artists and top local bands. The action starts after 9pm.

**Admission:** $2–$13, depending on band.

## JAZZ, BLUES & FOLK MUSIC

**BURNSLEY HOTEL LOUNGE, 1000 Grant St. Tel. 830-1000.**

Here's soothing jazz that you can enjoy and still converse as it plays. A soloist appears on Wednesday and Thursday from 8:30 to 11:30pm, and joins a small combo on Friday and Saturday from 8:30pm to 12:30am. Open daily.

**Admission:** Free.

**EL CHAPULTEPEC, 1962 Market St. Tel. 295-9126.**

By 10pm on a weekend night, it's almost impossible to get through the door of this dive—there, I said it—on the edge of Lower Downtown. There's no room to dance, and you can hardly hear the music over the buzz of the crowd, but jazz at El Chapultepec has become a sort of late-night institution in Denver. Hispanic combos lean toward salsa rhythms.

**FALCONE'S, 1096 S. Gaylord St., at 11th Ave. Tel. 777-0707.**

This lively little club in the Washington Park neighborhood presents live jazz Wednesday through Sunday nights. Open daily from 5:30pm to 2am.

**Admission:** Two-drink minimum per person.

**THE MERCURY CAFE, 2199 California St., at 22nd St. Tel. 294-9281.**

It's hard to classify the Mercury in any one genre of music—or literature, for that matter. There's always live something Wednesday through Sunday, but the offerings range from avant-garde jazz to classical violin and harp, down-home blues to South American folk, progressive rock to, yes, poetry readings. Call ahead to find out who (or what) is playing at this downtown club.

**RALPH'S TOP SHOP, 2890 S. Zuni St., near W. Yale Ave. Tel. 762-1330.**

Bluegrass buffs meet here the first and third Thursdays of each month. Jam sessions start at 7:30pm; both pickers and listeners are welcome.

**Admission:** Free.

**YORK ST. CAFE AND BAR, 2239 E. Colfax Ave., at York St. Tel. 331-0533.**

Small progressive jazz combos play Wednesday through Saturday nights at this upbeat establishment near City Park. Open daily.

**Admission:** $3–$5 Fri–Sat.

## DANCE CLUBS & DISCOS

**ALFIE'S, 9700 E. Iliff Ave., near S. Parker Rd. Tel. 752-4990.**

Progressive rock plays nightly for dancing. A big draw here is the domestic bottled beer special: just $1, nightly from 8 to 11pm. Alfie's opens daily at 7pm.

**Admission:** $3 Fri–Sat.

**CLUB PEACHES & THE PIT, W. 38th Ave. and Wadsworth Blvd., Wheat Ridge. Tel. 420-8702.**

With two floors of dancing, partiers have a choice: live rock (Wednesday through Saturday) downstairs in The Pit, or hot dance tunes upstairs at Peaches. Popular with students, this dual club is open Monday through Saturday from 2pm to 2am and on Sunday from 4pm to midnight: 80 hours of dancing a week.

**Admission:** $1–$2.

**FISH DANCE, E. 17th Ave. at Clarkson St. Tel. 832-FISH.**

Stylized fish of various sizes, shapes, and forms are the motif of this "happening" club on Restaurant Row. Why fish? I don't know, but it's always busy—especially on Friday, when a huge free buffet of fresh food is set out from 4:30 to 8pm, with all drinks two-for-one. Ladies drink free on Tuesday from 9pm to 1am; well drinks, wine, and draft beer are free on Thursday from 11pm to midnight. Fish Dance is closed Sunday and Monday.

**Admission:** $1–$5, depending on night.

# THE BAR SCENE

The first permanent structure ever built on the site of modern Denver was a saloon, and the city hasn't lost a step in the century and a quarter since. Today there are sports bars, brew pubs, outdoor café bars, English pubs, Old West saloons, city-overlook bars, art deco bars, even bars that don't serve alcohol.

Glendale, an enclave completely surrounded by southeastern Denver where Colorado Boulevard crosses Cherry Creek, has long been recognized as headquarters for Denver's singles scene. An unusual zoning situation has resulted in over a dozen drinking establishments built into a small, concentrated area. Other "strips" can be found along East Hampden Boulevard, South Monaco Parkway, and along East and West Colfax Avenue.

Following are some popular bars and pubs:

**BULL & BUSH, 4700 S. Cherry Creek Dr., Glendale. Tel. 759-0092.**

This re-creation of a famous London pub offers good imported beer always, and Sunday Dixieland jazz by regional groups like the Boom Town Stompers.

**CRUISE ROOM BAR, in the Oxford Alexis Hotel, 1600 17th St., at Wynkoop St. Tel. 628-5400.**

Modeled after a bar aboard the *Queen Mary* in the 1930s, this charming hotel lounge has all the atmosphere of an ocean-going cruise ship.

**JACKSON'S HOLE SALOON, 990 S. Oneida St., at E. Leetsdale Dr. Tel. 388-2883.**

This huge sports bar boasts more than 100 television sets for every satellite game that any viewer could possibly want. "We cover the world in sports" is its motto. Couch potatoes also rave about its hamburgers. Other Jackson's Holes are on Kipling

Street at Sixth Avenue in Lakewood (tel. 238-3000), west of downtown, and in Thornton Town Center at 1001 Grant Street, Thornton (tel. 457-2100), north of Denver.

**MILE HIGH SALOON, 4451 E. Virginia Ave., Glendale. Tel. 399-5606.**

Sensitively termed "a gentlemen's cabaret," this is in fact Denver's most sophisticated strip bar. Besides the beautiful women who work there, it offers a full dinner menu and plenty of TVs for men who'd rather watch football.

**TUNETOWN, 3rd floor of Tivoli Denver, 900 Auraria Pkwy. Tel. 534-8441.**

Unlike most piano bars, which seem to play Duke Ellington, Barry Manilow, or "Alexander's Ragtime Band," this one focuses on goodtime sing-along rock 'n' roll. You can belt out "Johnny B Goode" or "Rock Around the Clock" Tuesday through Saturday nights.

**WYNKOOP BREWING CO., 1634 18th St., at Wynkoop St. Tel. 297-2700.**

The extremely popular microbrewery pub here is in a renovated 1899 mercantile building. You can even take a tour and see where those $2.40 pints of Sagebrush Stout and St. Charles VSB are being made.

# 5. EASY EXCURSIONS FROM DENVER

Golden, Georgetown, Idaho Springs, and Central City make up the fabled Gold Circle. The first big strikes came almost simultaneously near Central City and Idaho Springs in 1859. The Gold Circle towns boomed and died first with gold, again with silver . . . and now they're living a third boom cycle with tourism.

## GOLDEN

Golden, 12 miles west of downtown Denver via U.S. 6 or Colo. 58 off I-70, is better known for its Coors Brewery (founded in 1873) and the Colorado School of Mines (established in 1874) than for its years as territorial capital. About 15,000 people now live in the small city at the foot of the Rockies.

Major **annual events** are Buffalo Bill Days, the third weekend of July, and the Jefferson County Fair, in October. For tourist information, contact the **Greater Golden Area Chamber of Commerce,** 611 14th Street (P.O. Box 1035), Golden, CO 80402 (tel. 303/279-3113).

### WHAT TO SEE & DO

**HISTORIC GOLDEN**  Historic downtown Golden focuses around the **Territorial Capitol** in the Loveland Building at 12th Street and Washington Avenue. Built in 1861, it housed the first state legislature from 1863 to 1867, when the capital was moved to Denver. Today it contains the Mercantile Restaurant. The **Armory,** 13th Street and Arapahoe Street, is the largest cobblestone structure in the U.S.; 3,300 wagonloads of stone and quartz were used in its construction. The **Rock Flour Mill Warehouse,** 8th Street and Cheyenne Street, dates from 1863; it was built with red granite from nearby Golden Gate Canyon and has original cedar beams and wooden floors.

The **Golden DAR Pioneer Museum,** 911 10th Street in the Golden Municipal Building (tel. 279-3331), has an impressive collection of furniture, household articles, photographs, and other items, including a re-created 19th-century parlor and boudoir. It's open Memorial Day to Labor Day, Monday through Saturday from 11am to 4pm; the rest of the year, Monday through Saturday from noon to 4pm. Admission is free.

The **Astor House Hotel,** 822 12th Street (tel. 278-3557), charges $1 for hourly guided tours of the oldest stone hotel in Colorado, built in 1867. It's open in summer,

Monday through Saturday from 10am to 4pm; in winter, Monday through Saturday from 10am to 3pm. While there, obtain a walking-tour guide for the 12th Street Historic District.

The **Rocky Mountain Quilt Museum,** 1111 Washington Avenue (tel. 277-0377), has a changing collection of more than 100 antique and contemporary quilts, and teaches quilting classes. It's open Tuesday through Saturday from 10am to 4pm; admission is by donation.

### ADOLPH COORS BREWING COMPANY, 13th and Ford Sts. Tel. 277-BEER.

The world's single largest brewery (it employs nearly 10,000) conducts free 35-minute tours of its brewing facility, followed by free samples of its beer. The tour takes in Coors's own greenhouse, the barley-malting process, the gleaming copper brewing kettles, and much more. Children are welcome (though they aren't allowed to drink the beer, of course). Special tour arrangements can be made for disabled or foreign-speaking visitors. There's also a gift shop.

**Admission:** Free.

**Open:** June–Aug, Mon–Sat 10am–5pm; Sept–May, Mon–Sat 10am–4pm. **Closed:** Hols.

### BUFFALO BILL MEMORIAL MUSEUM, 987½ Lookout Mountain Rd. Tel. 526-0747.

William Frederick Cody, the most famous of all western scouts, is buried atop Lookout Mountain south of Golden. The adjacent museum has memorabilia from the life and legend of "Buffalo Bill," who rode for the Pony Express, organized buffalo hunts for foreign royalty, and toured the world with his Wild West Show. The museum, which is reached via Exit 256 from I-70, is in 66-acre Lookout Mountain Park, a Denver municipal park popular for picnicking.

**Admission:** $2 adults, $1.50 seniors, $1 children 6–15, free for children under 6.

**Open:** May–Oct, daily 9am–5pm; Nov–Apr, Tues–Sun 9am–4pm. **Closed:** Christmas.

### COLORADO RAILROAD MUSEUM, 17155 W. 44th Ave. Tel. 279-4591.

Occupying a replica of an 1880 railroad depot, this museum has an extensive collection of narrow- and standard-guage locomotives and cars. Inside are historical exhibits, including artifacts and photographs. It's located a mile east of Golden near Exit 265 of I-70.

**Admission:** $3.

**Open:** June–Aug, daily 9am–6pm; Sept–May, daily 9am–5pm. **Closed:** Thanksgiving and Christmas days.

### COLORADO SCHOOL OF MINES GEOLOGY MUSEUM, 16th and Maple Sts. Tel. 273-3815.

Exhibits of mining through history include a replica of a gold mine, gemstone and fluorescent metal displays, and a fascinating collection of mine lamps. Mineral specimens and books are sold in a small gift shop. The Colorado School of Mines, with an enrollment of about 2,500, is the nation's foremost college of mineral engineering, teaching mineral exploration, extraction, and refining.

**Admission:** Free.

**Open:** School year only, Mon–Sat 9am–4pm, Sun 1–4pm.

### FOOTHILLS ART CENTER, 809 15th St. Tel. 279-3922.

Housed in an 1872 Presbyterian church of Gothic architecture, this exhibition center for regional art developed out of the annual Golden Sidewalk Art Show. The center sponsors various other shows during the year, including the Rocky Mountain Watermedia Exhibition. The Roundel Gallery gift shop is stocked with articles from local artisans.

**Admission:** Free.

**Open:** Mon–Sat 9am–4pm, Sun 1–4pm.

### GOLDEN GATE CANYON STATE PARK, Golden Gate Canyon Rd., Colo. 46. Tel. 592-1502.

Hiking, fishing, and nature study are the main pursuits at this state park, about 15 miles northwest of Golden. The Panorama Point Overlook, reached by car, gives a view of 100 miles of the Continental Divide. The park visitor center, open year round, has an ecological and historical display, and schedules various summer nature programs. The 106-site Reverend's Ridge Campground has RV hookups; Aspen Meadow is reserved for tents only.

**Admission:** $3 per vehicle; campsites cost another $6 per vehicle per night.
**Open:** Daily year round.

### HERITAGE SQUARE, U.S. 40. Tel. 277-0040.

A shopping, dining, and entertainment village with a Wild West theme, Heritage Square features Victorian specialty shops that produce their goods and a music hall that stages daily melodramas. A 1½-mile train ride takes visitors aboard a miniature model of a period locomotive and passenger cars. Other rides include go-carts, bumper boats, a water slide, and in summer, a 2,350-foot alpine slide with bobsled-style carts. The Lazy H Chuckwagon serves dinner and presents a western-style show, and there's an ice-cream parlor and beer garden. It's located three-quarters of a mile south of the U.S. 6 and U.S. 40 interchange.

**Admission:** Free, but activities have their own charges.
**Open:** Memorial Day–Labor Day and Thanksgiving–Christmas, daily 10am–9pm; the rest of the year, daily 10am–6pm.

### JEFFERSON COUNTY CONFERENCE AND NATURE CENTER, 900 Colorow Rd., Lookout Mountain. Tel. 526-0855 or 526-0594.

A 110-acre estate with the English Tudor-style mansion of early 20th-century entrepreneur Charles Boettcher at its hub, the center is used for conferences and historical exhibitions. A 1¼-mile wheelchair-accessible nature trail winds through adjacent Ponderosa pine and mountain meadows.

**Admission:** Free.
**Open:** Conference center, Mon–Sat 8am–5pm or by appointment; nature center, Tues–Sun 10am–4pm; trails remain open until dark.

### MOTHER CABRINI SHRINE, I-70 Exit 259, Lookout Mountain. Tel. 526-0758.

A 22-foot statue of Christ stands at the top of a 373-step stairway, adorned by carvings representing the stations of the Cross and mysteries of the Rosary. Terra-cotta benches provide respites along the way. The shrine is dedicated to America's first citizen saint, St. Frances Xavier Cabrini, who founded the Order of the Missionary Sisters of the Sacred Heart. They have a convent here with a gift shop.

**Admission:** By donation.
**Open:** Summer, daily 7:30am–7:30pm; winter, daily 7:30am–5pm; gift shop, daily 9am–5pm.

### NATIONAL EARTHQUAKE INFORMATION CENTER, 1711 Illinois St. Tel. 236-1500.

The U.S. Geological Survey operates this facility to collect rapid earthquake information, transmit warnings via the Earthquake Early Alerting Service, and publish and disseminate earthquake data. Tours of 30 to 45 minutes can be scheduled.

**Admission:** Free.
**Open:** By appointment, Mon–Fri 9–11am and 1–3pm.

### RED ROCKS PARK AND AMPHITHEATRE, Hogback Rd., Morrison. Tel. 575-2638.

The road winds between spectacular 400-foot-high red sandstone spires and ledges at this area south of Golden. In their midst is the 9,000-seat Red Rocks Amphitheatre, famed for its wide-ranging summer concert series (see "Evening Entertainment," above). It is reached from the Morrison/Red Rocks exit off I-70.

**Admission:** Free except for scheduled concerts.
**Open:** Daily year round.

## WHERE TO STAY

**HOLIDAY INN—DENVER WEST, 14707 W. Colfax Ave., Golden, CO**

**80401. Tel. 303/279-7611,** or 800/HOLIDAY. 228 rms (all with bath). A/C TV TEL
$ **Rates:** $52–$63 single; $56–$66 double. Weekends $39. Ski packages available. AE, CB, DC, DISC, MC, V.

The highlight of this property is its Holidome Indoor Recreation Center—complete with indoor lap pool, miniature golf course, fitness center, whirlpool, saunas, sun beds, video arcade, and games room. The Dining Deck Restaurant serves three meals daily, and the Brass Rail Lounge offers live music Thursday through Saturday nights. There's also a coin-operated guest laundry. Guest rooms are extremely spacious, with all standard furnishings as well as a desk for business travelers. The hotel is just off I-70 at Exit 262.

**MOUNTAIN VIEW MOTEL, 14825 W. Colfax Ave., Golden, CO 80401.**
**Tel. 303/279-2526.** 34 rms, 2 suites (all with bath). A/C TV TEL
$ **Rates:** $26 single; $34–$36 double. AE, DC, DISC, MC, V.

A pleasant Budget Host hotel one block east of I-70 at Exit 262, the Mountain View offers tempting glimpses of the east slope of the Rockies. Rooms are simple but comfortable; there are eight kitchenette units (guests must provide their own utensils) and a pair of two-bedroom units. Facilities include a heated outdoor pool (seasonal) and a guest laundry. Pets are accepted with a $5 cleaning deposit.

### WHERE TO DINE

**BRIARWOOD INN, 1630 Eighth St., Golden. Tel. 279-3121.**
**Cuisine:** AMERICAN/CONTINENTAL. **Reservations:** Recommended.
$ **Prices:** Main courses $15–$25; lunch $9–$15. AE, CB, DC, MC, V.
**Open:** Lunch Mon–Fri 11am–2:30pm; dinner nightly 5:30–10pm; brunch Sun 10:30am–2:30pm.

One of the most celebrated restaurants in the greater Denver area, the Briarwood is noted for its gourmet food and attentive service. The decor is understated elegance— white linen and candlelight in an informal western atmosphere. Those who don't dine enjoy the cocktail lounge. The inn is at the junction of U.S. 6 and Colo. 58 west of downtown Golden.

# CENTRAL CITY/BLACK HAWK

The area once called "the richest square mile on earth" was hoping to approach that distinction again in late 1991 with the beginning of legalized casino gambling. Central City and its sister community of Black Hawk—along with Cripple Creek, west of Colorado Springs—have up to 2,000 slot machines, along with blackjack and poker, with a maximum bet of $5.

Located 35 miles west of Denver via I-70 or U.S. 6 and Colo. 119, **Central City** is at the head of Gregory Gulch, when John Gregory made Colorado's first major gold strike in 1859. By the 1870s the town had grown to become the most important trade and cultural center of the central Rockies. After a decline at the turn of the 20th century, an **Opera Festival,** started in the 1930s, revitalized the town.

Today Central City is a National Historic District with one of the finest collections of Victorian buildings in the West. Its main street has been used in many Western films, including the television mini-series *Centennial.*

The route to Central City from Denver goes through Clear Creek Canyon to **Black Hawk,** established in 1867 as the milling and smelting center for Central City ore. A mile farther, through Gregory Gulch, lies Central City. For information on attractions and travel services in either community, contact the **Central City Office of Public Relations,** City Hall (P.O. Box 249), Central City, CO 80427 (tel. 303/573-0247).

### WHAT TO SEE & DO

Begin a **walking tour** on lower Lawrence Street at the **Gilpin County Historical Museum** (tel. 582-5283). Formerly a high school, it now houses antiques and artifacts from the mining era. Admission is $3 for adults, $1 for children under 12. It's open June to August, daily from 9am to 5pm; September to November, Saturday and

Sunday from 9am to 5pm. The museum also operates the sporadically operational **Black Hawk & Central City Narrow Gauge Railroad.**

As you walk through town, you'll notice the solidity of the buildings. A great fire razed the town in 1874, after which stone and brick construction were exclusively used. An example of Cornish stone masonry is **St. Paul's Episcopal Church.** The granite **Raynold's Building** withstood the fire when the proprietor hung wet blankets over the windows and doors, thus preventing blasting powder kept in the cellar from blowing up the town. West on Eureka Street is the **Register-Call Building,** the oldest commercial building in the town still in use, housing the oldest newspaper in the state, a weekly. Interesting murals are on the walls of the **Masonic Temple** on the third floor of this building. Nearby, the oldest **city hall** in Colorado was originally built of logs in 1862 by the county sheriff, and over the years it has been used as a jail and courthouse. The second floor houses the **Gilpin County Art Gallery,** where an annual art exhibition is held. It's open in summer, daily from 11am to 5pm, with free admission. Farther west on Eureka Street is the **Gilpin County Courthouse.**

Beyond this are the **Thomas-Billings Home** and the **Lost Gold Mine,** both offering visitor tours. On the south side of Eureka Street are the famous **Opera House** and **Teller House** (see below for details on all four of these).

Main Street also has some old buildings worth the visitor's attention: the **Toll Gate Saloon** was originally a funeral parlor, and the **Old Gold Coin,** oldest bar in town, remains quite the way it looked a century ago. Jazz bands are frequent entertainers at the **Glory Hole Tavern,** location of the annual Central City Jazz Festival. On South Main Street is another old opera house—oldest in the state, in fact—now the **Belvidere Theater.**

**Walking tours** of Central City are led by the Gilpin Historical Society (tel. 582-5283) every day at noon, Memorial Day through Labor Day, and weekends September through November. Tours begin at the Teller House and cost $3 for adults, free for children under 12.

Visitors can tour the mines and museums of Central City year round.

In June, **Madame Lou Bunch Day** commemorates the sporting life of the last century with a bed race on Main Street and a Madam and Miners' Ball in the evening. After the July opera festival comes the August "trad jazz" festival. And at Christmas, there is the **March of the Singing Children,** led by Santa Claus on horseback, and a **Festival of Lights.**

Nearby **Black Hawk** is home to the best example of carpenter Gothic (or "gingerbread") architecture in the United States: the restored **Lace House,** 201 Gregory Street (tel. 582-5221). The house is open for tours in summer, daily from 9am to 4pm. Also in Black Hawk is the **Little Colonel Mine,** 301 Gregory Street (tel. 582-5559), which offers wheelchair-accessible tours daily from 10am to 5:30pm.

## LOST GOLD MINE, 231 Eureka St., Central City. Tel. 582-5913.

Visitors walk down the main shaft of an old mine, viewing actual veins of gold and seeing the original 19th-century tools used here. An airshaft lets light in from 125 feet above the mine. At the tour's conclusion, visitors can buy gold-nugget jewelry and other souvenirs from a gift shop.

**Admission:** $3.50 adults, $1.75 children 5–11, free for children under 4.

**Open:** Summer, daily 8am–8pm; winter, daily 10am–6pm.

## OPERA HOUSE, 120 Eureka St., Central City. Tel. 297-8306.

Built in 1878 by public subscription, the Opera House has walls of native granite 4 feet thick. Inside are three-dimensional murals lighted by a great crystal chandelier. Hickory chairs are inscribed with the names of historic Colorado characters and actors from all over the world who appeared on the Opera House stage. But the Opera House went into a gradual decline with the end of mining and was used for minstrel shows, wrestling matches, high-school graduations, and silent movies before being shuttered for a time.

Descendants of pioneer Coloradans reopened it for the first annual opera festival in 1932. The festival continues every year from early July through mid-August. In 1991 the operas presented were Puccini's *Tosca,* Strauss's *Die Fledermaus,* and

Gounod's *Romeo and Juliet*. Tickets run $19 to $41, depending on seating and performance dates. For tickets or information, call 292-6700.

**Admission:** $3 adults, $2.50 seniors and children; combined Opera House–Teller House tours, $4 adults, $3.50 seniors and children.

**Open:** Summer, daily 10am–2pm; the rest of the year, Thurs–Mon 10am–2pm.

**TELLER HOUSE, 110 Eureka St., Central City. Tel. 582-3200.**

Located next door to the Opera House, this was once the most elegant hotel between Chicago and San Francisco. It was built in 1872 by Henry Teller, one of Colorado's first senators. Visitors can see President Grant's room, Baby Doe Tabor's gold-plated suite, and rare antique furniture. The Teller House Bar is home of the *Face on the Barroom Floor*, recalling a poem about an artist's ill-fated love for a woman "with eyes that petrified me brain, and sunk into my heart." The truth of the drawing is less romantic; it was done as a joke by a Denver newspaper illustrator in 1936.

**Admission:** $3 adults, $2.50 seniors and children; combined Opera House–Teller House tours, $4 adults, $3.50 seniors and children.

**Open:** Summer, daily 10am–2pm; the rest of the year, Thurs–Mon 10am–2pm.

**THOMAS-BILLINGS HOME, 209 Eureka St., Central City. Tel. 582-5093** or 582-5011 evenings.

A handsome 1874 home in the American Renaissance style, this house was boarded up in 1917 with all the family furnishings inside, and was only reopened in 1986! Everything remains intact: quilts on the beds, clothes in the closets, family photos, 13 different styles of clocks, calendars dating from the 1870s. The architecture features Doric columns, pedimented windows, and a secluded patio terraced with a mortarless rock wall.

**Admission:** $2 adults, $1 seniors and children.

**Open:** June–Aug, daily 10am–5:30pm; Sept–Nov and Feb–May, Sat–Thurs 11am–4pm; Dec–Jan, Sat–Sun 11am–4pm.

## WHERE TO STAY

**GOLDEN ROSE INN, 102 Main St. (P.O. Box 157), Central City, CO 80427. Tel. 303/582-5060** or 825-1413. 22 rms, 4 suites (20 with bath).

**$ Rates:** June–Sept, $51–$85 single or double; $95–$120 suite. Oct–May, $40–$65 single or double; $74–$90 suite. AE, CB, DC, MC, V.

A gambling hall and saloon a century ago, this building is completely restored. The spacious lobby has a fireplace and elegant chandeliers. All rooms have antique furnishings and hand-printed wallpaper. Rooms are either European style (sharing a bath), American style (private bath), or Victorian parlor (oversize room with private bath and separate sitting area). TVs and phones are available on request. The hotel also has a hot tub and sauna, and a dining room serving continental cuisine.

## WHERE TO DINE

**TELLER HOUSE, 110 Eureka St., at Pine St., Central City. Tel. 582-3200** or 292-6500.

**Cuisine:** AMERICAN/CONTINENTAL. **Reservations:** Recommended.

**$ Prices:** Lunch $4–$10; dinner $7–$16. AE, CB, DC, MC, V.

**Open:** June–Sept, daily 11am–9pm; Oct–May, Fri–Sun 11am–9pm. **Closed:** Thanksgiving and Christmas days.

Ensconced in a historic 1872 hotel (see above), the Teller House serves an ample fare of sandwiches and pizza for lunch; steaks, seafood, and poultry for dinner. The five dining rooms are especially lively during summer opera season.

# IDAHO SPRINGS

The "Oh My God" dirt road winds dangerously from Central City through Virginia Canyon to Idaho Springs. Most visitors prefer to take I-70 directly to this community, 35 miles west of Denver. Site of a major gold strike in 1859, Idaho Springs today beckons visitors to try their luck at panning for any gold that may still remain. The **Argo Gold Mill and Museum,** 2350 Riverside Drive (tel. 567-2421), offers tours May through mid-October from 9am to sundown.

Lesser metals now provide miners their work in these hills: uranium, tungsten, zinc, molybdenum, and lead are worked, and there is a 5-mile-long tunnel linking some of these mines a third of a mile below ground.

The Colorado School of Mines in Golden uses the **Edgar Experimental Mine,** less than a mile north of Idaho Springs off Eighth Street (tel. 567-2911 or 273-3701), as a research area and facility for high-tech mining practices. Public tours of 45 to 60 minutes are offered throughout the year: mid-June through August, Wednesday through Saturday from 8am–4:30pm; other times by appointment.

Just outside of town at 302 Soda Creek Road is the **Indian Springs Resort** (tel. 567-2191), a great place for a soak in the hot springs after a long day of skiing or hiking. Lodging, meals, and weekend entertainment are also offered here.

Idaho Springs is the starting point for a 28-mile drive to the summit of 14,260-foot **Mount Evans.** Colorado 103 winds through Arapahoe National Forest, along Chicago Creek, to **Echo Lake Park,** another of the Denver mountain parks with fireplaces, hiking trails, fishing, and a shelter house. From here, Colo. 5—the highest paved auto road in North America—climbs to Mount Evans's summit. Only a pass between China and Pakistan is higher than this road. It is generally open from Memorial Day to Labor Day and is free.

# GEORGETOWN

A pretty village of Victorian-era houses and stores, Georgetown, 45 miles west of Denver on I-70 at an elevation of 8,500 feet, is named for an 1860 gold camp. But the town boomed more in the 1870s with silver. This is the best preserved of the foothills mining towns: It didn't suffer a major fire in its formative years. Perhaps to acknowledge their prayers, townspeople built eye-catching steeples on top of their firehouses, not their churches.

For information on attractions and travel services, contact the **Georgetown Chamber of Commerce,** P.O. Box 444, Georgetown, CO 80444 (tel. 303/567-4844), or the **Georgetown Society,** P.O. Box 667, Georgetown, CO 80444 (tel. 303/569-2840). A visitor information center, open in summer, is at Sixth Street across from the post office in Georgetown.

## WHAT TO SEE & DO

The **Georgetown–Silver Plume Mining Area,** including this community and the adjacent hamlet of Silver Plume, was declared a National Historic Landmark District in 1966. More than 200 of its buildings have been saved and restored through the efforts of the Georgetown Society, a nonprofit organization dedicated to preserving historic structures. The Hamill House and Hotel de Paris are open to public tours.

A convenient place to begin a **walking tour** of downtown Georgetown is the **Old County Courthouse** at Sixth Street and Argentine Street. Now the Community Center and tourist information office, it was built in 1867. Across Argentine Street is the **Old Stone Jail** (1868); three blocks south, at Third and Argentine, is the **Hamill House** (see below).

Sixth Street is Georgetown's main commercial strip. Walk east from the Old Courthouse to see, on your left, the **Masonic Hall** (1891), the **Fish Block** (1886), the **Monti and Guanella Building** (1868), and the **Cushman Block** (1874); and on your right, the **Hamill Block** (1881) and the **Kneisel & Anderson Building** (1893). The **Hotel de Paris** is at the corner of Sixth and Taos. Nearly opposite, at Sixth and Griffith, is the **Star Hook & Ladder Building** (1886), along with the town hall and marshall's office.

If you turn south on Taos Street, you'll find **Grace Episcopal Church** (1869) at Fifth Street, and the **Maxwell House** (1890) a couple of steps east on Fourth. Glance west on Fifth to see **Alpine Hose Company No. 2** (1874) and the **Courier Building** (1875). North on Taos Street from the Hotel de Paris are the **Old**

**Georgetown School** (1874), at Eighth Street; **First Presbyterian Church** (1874), at Ninth; **Our Lady of Lourdes Catholic Church** (1918), at Ninth; and the **Old Missouri Firehouse** (1870), at 10th and Taos.

If you turn west on Ninth at the Catholic church, you'll find two more historic structures: the **Bowman-White House** (1892), at Rose and Ninth, and the **Tucker-Rutherford House** (circa 1860), a miner's log cabin with four small rooms on Ninth Street at Clear Creek.

**Special events** during the year in Georgetown include a Fasching winter carnival in February; an antique fair and Swedish festival (Midsummer's Day) in June; an auction in Hamill House and house tours of private homes in August; an aspen festival in September; and a Christmas market with season foods, folk dancing, a Santa Lucia procession, and caroling in December.

**GEORGETOWN LOOP RAILROAD, Loop Dr. near Sixth St., Georgetown. Tel. 569-2403** or 279-6101 in Denver.

An 1884 railroad bridge serves this restored narrow-gauge line, which runs daily trips in summer between Georgetown and Silver Plume. The steel bridge is 300 feet long and 95 feet high, and was considered an engineering miracle a century ago. Though the direct distance between the terminals is 2.1 miles, the track covers 4.5 miles, climbing 638 feet in 14 sharp curves and switchbacks, and culminating with a 360° spiraling knot. Passengers may make round-trips from either end: The whole trip takes about 2½ hours, including a walking tour of the **Lebanon Mine and Mill,** which can be reached only by train.

**Admission:** $12.50 adults, $6.50 children 4–15, for train and mine tour; $9.50 adults, $5 children, for train ride only; no charge for children under 4 not occupying a seat.

**Open:** Memorial Day–Labor Day, daily; five weekends after Labor Day, Sat–Sun only. Departures from Georgetown at 11am and 12:20, 1:40, and 3pm; from Silver Plume at 10:20 and 11:40am, and 1, 2:20, and 3:40pm. There's no mine tour on the final run.

**HAMILL HOUSE, Third and Argentine Sts. Tel. 569-2840.**

Built in country Gothic Revival style, it dates to 1867, when it was owned by a silver speculator, William Hamill, and was the town's most ambitious residence. A carriage house and office occupy two stone structures behind the main house, and a delicately carved outhouse had two parts, one for the family and the other for servants. When acquired by the Georgetown Society in 1971, the house had the original woodwork, fireplaces, and wallpaper. An outstanding antique glass collection has been preserved. Restoration work on the upper stories is continuing.

**Admission:** $2.50 adults, $1.50 seniors and children.

**Open:** Memorial Day–Sept 30, daily 9am–5pm; Oct–May, Tues–Sun noon–4pm.

**HOTEL DE PARIS, Sixth and Taos Sts. Tel. 659-2311.**

The builder of the hotel, Louis Dupuy, once wrote an explanation of his desire to build a French inn so far away from his homeland: "I love these mountains and I love America, but you will pardon me if I bring into this community a remembrance of my youth and my country." The hotel opened in 1875 and soon became famous for its French provincial luxuriousness.

Today the hotel is a historic museum run by the National Society of Colonial Dames of America, whose members serve tea and coffee in the courtyard daily in warm weather. The hotel is embellished with many of its original furnishings: Haviland china, diamond-dust mirrors, a big pendulum clock, paintings and etchings of the past century, carved walnut furniture, lace curtains and draperies of tapestry, as well as Dupuy's considerable library. An antique stove and other cooking equipment occupy the kitchen; the wine cellar has some early wine barrels, with their labels still in place.

**Admission:** $2.50 adults, $1.50 seniors and children.

**Open:** Memorial Day–Sept 30, daily 9am–5pm; Oct–May, Tues–Sun noon–4pm.

## WHERE TO STAY

**BAEHLER RESORT SERVICES, 410 Third St. (P.O. Box 247), George-town, CO 80444. Tel. 303/569-2665.**
**$ Rates:** Average $120 double, plus damage deposit. AE, MC, V.
This central booking agency will place you in a historic home—often an *entire* historic house—for the length of your stay in Georgetown. Facilities vary widely with properties.

**GEORGETOWN MOTOR INN, 1100 Rose St., Georgetown, CO 80444. Tel. 303/569-3201.** 31 units, 1 suite (all with bath). TV TEL
**$ Rates:** $42 single; $45 double. AE, CB, DC, DISC, MC, V.
Located just a couple blocks off I-70 but within easy walking distance of downtown shops, restaurants, and historic properties, this motel has large sunny rooms with king-size beds. One kitchenette is available. A swimming pool is open in summer.

**THE PECK HOUSE, 83 Sunny Ave. (P.O. Box 428), Empire, CO 80438. Tel. 303/569-9870.** 11 rms (9 with bath).
**$ Rates:** $35–$60 double. AE, MC, V.
Colorado's oldest hotel is in the small community of Empire, 5 miles from Georgetown on U.S. 40, just off I-70 toward Denver. Established in 1862, it was originally a stagecoach house. Today the guest rooms are furnished in oak, walnut, and maple. A wide porch makes a fine place for viewing the Empire Valley. The dining room has lithographs of scenes out of the mining era and is open to the public daily, year round, with Sunday brunch a local tradition. There is a lounge with a Franklin stove and good conversation.

## WHERE TO DINE

**HAPPY COOKER, 412 Sixth St., Georgetown. Tel. 569-3166.**
**Cuisine:** SOUP AND BAKED GOODS.
**$ Prices:** $3–$6. MC, V.
**Open:** Summer, daily 8am–6pm; winter, daily 8am–4pm.
Crêpes, waffles, original soups, and home-baked bread are offered at this restaurant, which also offers cheesecakes and quiches.

**MARTI'S CRAZY HORSE, 1211 Argentine St., Georgetown. Tel. 569-2475.**
**Cuisine:** INTERNATIONAL.
**$ Prices:** Appetizers $2–$7; lunch $4–$8; dinner $10–$19. AE, DISC, MC, V.
**Open:** Daily 11am–10pm. Cocktails until 1:30am.
A pleasant garden-style restaurant/saloon at the north end of town, Marti's circles the globe with recipes like tempura shrimp, lasagne, chiles rellenos, and buffalo burgers. The surf and turf—an 8-ounce ribeye steak with scampi—is a dinnertime favorite.

**THE RAM, 606 Sixth St., Georgetown. Tel. 569-3263.**
**Cuisine:** AMERICAN/CONTINENTAL. **Reservations:** Recommended at dinner.
**$ Prices:** Lunch $4–$8; dinner $11–$22. AE, CB, DC, DISC, MC, V.
**Open:** Wed–Mon 11am–midnight.
A Georgetown institution, the Ram offers a casual and historic atmosphere. Lunches include burgers, fish and chips, deli sandwiches, quiches, and salads. Dinners are more gourmet: roast duck, prime rib, veal marsala, trout amandine. Wednesday night is spaghetti night: all you can eat for $5.95 (kids $3.95).

# CHAPTER 6

# COLORADO SPRINGS

**N**early two centuries ago, in 1806, army Lt. Zebulon Pike led a company of soldiers on a trek of exploration around the base of an enormous mountain toward which they had been marching for over 100 miles. He called it "Grand Peak," declared it unconquerable, and moved on.

Today, the 14,110-foot mountain we now know as Pikes Peak has been conquered so often that an auto highway and a cog railway ascend it. And where previously there was naught but sagebrush-speckled prairie, today a thriving city sprawls.

Neither mineral wealth nor ranching was the cornerstone of the city; instead, 19th-century tourism was responsible. In fact, when founded in 1871, Colorado Springs was the first genuine resort community west of Chicago.

General William J. Palmer, builder of the Denver & Rio Grande Railroad, established the resort on his rail line at 6,035 feet elevation, at the confluence of two creeks. The state's growing reputation as a health center, with its high mountains and mineral springs, convinced him to build at the foot of Pikes Peak. It would lure affluent easterners, he said—so he named the resort Colorado Springs, because most of the fashionable resorts back east were "springs." The mineral waters at Manitou were only 5 miles distant, and soon Palmer exploited them—installing as resident physician one Dr. Samuel Solly, who exuberantly trumpeted the benefits of Manitou's springs in print and word of mouth.

The gold strikes of the 1890s at Cripple Creek, on the southwestern slope of Pikes Peak, added a new dimension to Colorado Springs life—that of a commercial center. Among those who cashed in on the boom was Spencer Penrose, a middle-aged Philadelphian and Harvard graduate who came to the Springs in 1892, made some astute investments, and became very rich. Penrose, like Palmer a man ahead of his time, believed that the automobile would revolutionize life in the United States. He promoted the creation of new highways, and to show the effectiveness of motor cars in the mountains, built (in 1913–15) the Pikes Peak road with more than $250,000 of his own money. During World War I, at a cost of over $2 million, he built the Broadmoor, Colorado's most luxurious hotel, at the foot of Cheyenne Mountain.

World War II brought the defense industry. Camp Carson and Ent Air Force Base were built in 1942. On the north side of Colorado Springs, the $200-million U.S. Air

# WHAT'S SPECIAL ABOUT COLORADO SPRINGS

## Natural Spectacles

☐ Pikes Peak summit, reached by cog railway, road, or trail, for its unparalleled view.

☐ Garden of the Gods, a tract of red sandstone pinnacles 300 million years old, home to a remarkable variety of fauna and flora.

☐ Cave of the Winds, a geological wonderland 10 minutes from downtown.

## Architectural Highlights

☐ The Broadmoor (1918), built in the style of grand foreign hotels by Warren and Wetmore, architects of New York's Grand Central Terminal.

☐ Colorado Springs Fine Art Center (1936), a community arts center of monolithic concrete design, built by John Gaw Meem of Santa Fe.

☐ Cadet Chapel (1958) with its 17 soaring spires on the Air Force Academy campus.

## Museums

☐ Western Museum of Mining and Industry, where the history and practice of mining come to life.

☐ The Pro Rodeo Hall of Fame and American Cowboy Museum, immortalizing the most "western" of sports.

☐ The May Natural History Museum, featuring a world-famous collection of 7,000 tropical insects and other invertebrates.

☐ Colorado Springs Pioneers Museum, including a remarkable collection of 121 traditional quilts.

## American Heritage

☐ The U.S. Air Force Academy (4,400 cadets), with a museum and other public areas.

☐ The U.S. Olympic Training Center.

## Events/Festivals

☐ Pikes Peak Auto Hill Climb, an international July 4 "race to the clouds" since 1916.

☐ Pikes Peak or Bust Rodeo in August, now in its sixth decade.

☐ Territory Days (May) and Springspree (June), street festivals with food and live entertainment.

## For the Kids

☐ Cheyenne Mountain Zoo, with 500 animals on the side of Cheyenne Mountain.

☐ Ghost Town, where youngsters can relive the rough-and-tumble days of the Old West.

☐ North Pole, where Santa Claus shares the magic of Christmas even in the heat of summer.

---

Force Academy opened to cadets in 1958. With this military presence, it's no surprise that numerous high-technology corporations have chosen to locate in Colorado Springs as well.

Modern Colorado Springs is a rapidly growing city of 281,000 people. Its population has more than doubled since 1970. Pikes Peak, Manitou Springs, and the Air Force Academy remain major tourist draws, along with the startling rock pinnacles of the Garden of the Gods and the U.S. Olympic Training Center.

# 1. ORIENTATION

## ARRIVING

**BY PLANE** The **Colorado Springs Airport,** 5750 East Fountain Boulevard (tel. 719/596-0188), is not a commuter satellite of Denver. But over 150 direct, major-carrier flights arrive at and depart from the Springs daily from Chicago, St. Louis, Dallas/Fort Worth, Phoenix, Las Vegas, Salt Lake City, and Albuquerque. And the airport is just a short drive from major hotels, in the southeastern part of the city.

Plans are currently underway for a $113-million airport expansion, which would include a new terminal for up to 160 new flight gates.

**Major airlines** serving Colorado Springs include American (tel. 632-7760, or 800/433-7300), America West (tel. 630-0737, or 800/247-5692), Continental (tel. 473-7580, or 800/525-0280), Delta (tel. 599-5333, or 800/221-1212), Trans World (tel. 599-4400, or 800/221-2000), and United (tel. 635-0570, or 800/428-4322).

**Regional and commuter airlines** connect Colorado Springs with Denver and other points in the state; they include Mesa (tel. 591-6211, or 800/637-2247); and United Express (tel. 635-0570, or 800/727-7077).

The **Airport Express** limo bus service (tel. 719/599-0505) operates direct ground service between Colorado Springs and Denver Stapleton airports. The cost is $25 airport-to-airport, and an extra $10 for hotel dropoff or pickup.

City **bus fare** from the airport to downtown is 75¢. **Taxi** service to hotels runs $6 to $8.

**BY BUS**    **Greyhound/Trailways,** 327 South Weber Street (tel. 719/635-1505), has regular daily arrivals and departures to towns, cities, and resort communities throughout the state. Call for route, fare, and schedule information.

**BY CAR**    The principal artery to and from the north (Denver: 70 miles) and south (Pueblo: 42 miles), **Interstate 25** bisects Colorado Springs. **U.S. 24** is the principal east-west route through the city.

Visitors traveling via I-70 from the east can take Exit 359 at Limon and follow U.S. 24 into the Springs. Traveling via I-70 from the west, the most direct route is Exit 201 at Frisco, then Colo. 9 (via Breckenridge) 53 miles to Hartsel Junction, and then U.S. 24 east 66 miles to the Springs.

# TOURIST INFORMATION

Offices of the **Colorado Springs Convention and Visitors Bureau** are at 104 South Cascade Avenue, Colorado Springs, CO 80903 (tel. 719/635-7506, or 800/DO-VISIT; fax 719/635-4968). Ask for the "Official Visitors Guide to Colorado Springs and the Pikes Peak Region," a 56-page compendium with a comprehensive listing of accommodations, restaurants, and all other visitor services in the area.

The **Visitor Information Center,** located in the same Sun Plaza Building at the corner of Cascade Avenue and Colorado Avenue, is open in summer, daily from 8:30am to 5pm; in winter Monday through Friday from 8:30am to 5pm. The bureau also operates a weekly **events line** with a 24-hour recording (tel. 635-1723).

Additional information on regional attractions can be obtained from the **Pikes Peak Country Attractions Association,** a division of the Manitou Springs Chamber of Commerce, 354 Manitou Avenue, Manitou Springs, CO 80829 (tel. 719/685-5089, or 800/642-2567).

# CITY LAYOUT

It's easy to get around central Colorado Springs, laid out as it is on a classic grid pattern.

If the I-25/U.S. 24 interchange is the center of the city, downtown Colorado Springs lies in the northeast quadrant—bounded on the west by I-25 and on the south by U.S. 24 **(Cimarron Street). Boulder Street** to the north and **Wahsatch Avenue** to the east complete the downtown frame. **Nevada Avenue** (U.S. 85)

## IMPRESSIONS

*Could one live in constant view of these grand mountains without being elevated by them into a lofty plane of thought and purpose?*
—GEN. WILLIAM J. PALMER, FOUNDER OF COLORADO SPRINGS, 1871

parallels the freeway for 15 miles through the city, intersecting it twice; **Tejon Street** and **Cascades Avenue** also run north-south through downtown between Nevada and the freeway. **Colorado Avenue** and **Bijou Avenue** are the busiest east-west downtown cross streets.

West of downtown, Colorado Avenue extends through the historic **Old Colorado City** district and the quaint foothill community of **Manitou Springs,** rejoining U.S. 24—itself a busy but less interesting artery—as it enters Pike National Forest.

South of downtown, Nevada Avenue intersects **Lake Avenue,** the principal boulevard into the Broadmoor, and proceeds south as Colo. 115 past Fort Carson.

North and east of downtown, **Academy Boulevard** (Colo. 83) is the street name to remember. From the south gate of the Air Force Academy north of the Springs, it winds through residential hills, crosses **Austin Bluff Parkway,** then runs without a curve 10 miles due south, finally curving west to intersect I-25 and Colo. 115 at Fort Carson. U.S. 24, which exits downtown as **Platte Avenue,** and **Fountain Boulevard,** which leads to the airport, are among its cross streets. Austin Bluff Parkway extends west of I-25 as **Garden of the Gods Road,** affording access to that natural wonder.

City street addresses are divided by Pikes Peak Avenue into "north" and "south"; by Nevada Avenue into "east" and "west."

A basic but efficient Colorado Springs map can be found in the center of the city's "Official Visitors Guide." Inquire at the visitor information center or local bookstores for more detailed maps.

# 2. GETTING AROUND

**BY BUS** The city bus service is provided by **Colorado Springs Transit Management** (tel. 475-9733 or 471-POOL). Buses operate on a limited schedule—6:15am to 6:15pm Monday through Saturday only—so taxis or private vehicles are the only alternatives on evenings and weekends. Fares on in-city routes are 60¢ for adults; 40¢ for children 12 to 18; 25¢ for children 6 to 11, seniors, and disabled persons; free for children under 6. Routes outside the city limits cost 75¢ for adults, 50¢ for children.

A tourist vehicle, the **Jolly Trolley,** runs from Memorial Day to Labor Day between downtown and the Pikes Peak Cog Railway. Traveling back and forth down Colorado Avenue, it makes frequent stops in Manitou Springs and Old Colorado City. An all-day pass is $3.

**BY TAXI** Call **Yellow Cab** (tel. 634-5000). Fares are $2.50 for the first mile, $1.10 for each additional mile. Taxis are not normally hailed on the streets. A few stands are at the major hotels.

**BY CAR** For regulations and advice on driving in Colorado, see "Getting Around" in Chapter 2. The **American Automobile Association (AAA)** maintains an office in Colorado Springs at 3850 Village Seven Road (tel. 719/591-2222), open Monday through Friday from 9am to 5pm and on Saturday from 9am to noon.

**Parking** Most downtown streets have parking meters, with rates of about 25¢ an hour—have your change ready. Downtown parking lots and hotel garages get about $1 an hour for short-term parking. Outside of downtown, free parking is generally available on sidestreets.

**Rental Cars**  Car-rental agencies in Colorado Springs—some of which have offices in or near downtown as well as at the municipal airport—include: **Avis** (tel. 596-2751, or 800/331-1212); **Budget,** 303 West Bijou Street (tel. 473-6535, or 800/222-6772); **Dollar,** 5750 East Fountain Boulevard (tel. 591-6464, or 800/421-6868); **Enterprise,** 803 West Colorado Avenue (tel. 636-3900); **General,** 1565 Vapor Trail (tel. 574-0442, or 800/327-7607); **Hertz,** 5750 East Fountain Boulevard (tel. 596-1863, or 800/327-7607); **National** (tel. 596-1519, or 800/227-7368); **Payless,** 1645 Newport Drive (tel. 597-4444, or 800/423-9515); or **Thrifty,** 4180 Center Park Drive (tel. 574-2472, or 800/FOR-CARS).

For the traveler seeking true luxury, consider **California Limousine,** 324 Swope Avenue (tel. 630-1048).

**ON FOOT**  Each of the main sections of town can be easily explored without a vehicle. It's fun, for instance, to wander the winding streets through Manitou Springs or explore the Old Colorado City "strip." Between neighborhoods, however, distances are considerable. Unless you're particularly fit, it's wise to take a bus or a taxi.

## _FAST_ FACTS  COLORADO SPRINGS

**American Express**  To report a lost card, call 800/528-4800; to report lost traveler's checks, 800/221-7282.

**Area Code**  719.

**Baby-sitters**  Front desks or concierges at major hotels often can make arrangements on your behalf. Otherwise, try **A-Able Sitter Service** (tel. 633-9009) or **ABC Baby Sitting Agency** (tel. 635-4229).

**Banks**  Leading banks, all with downtown branches, include **Colorado National Bank** (tel. 633-5542), **First National Bank of Colorado Springs** (tel. 471-5000), and **United Bank** (tel. 636-1361). Most banks are open Monday through Thursday from 9am to 4pm and on Friday from 9am to 6pm.

**Plus System**  (tel. 800/THE-PLUS) cash machines can be found at strategic locations throughout the city.

**Dentist**  For 24-hour referrals, call the **Colorado Springs Dental Society Emergency and Referral Service** (tel. 597-8538; if no answer, 473-3168).

**Doctor**  For referrals, call **Memorial Hospital Physicians Referral** (tel. 475-5226) or the **Colorado Springs Doctors Exchange** (tel. 632-1512). Minor illnesses and injuries are treated outpatient, and emergencies are tended 24 hours, at the **Colorado Springs Medical Center,** 5209 South Nevada Avenue (tel. 475-7700) and four other locations.

**Drugstores**  Reliable prescription services are available at **Walgreen's Drug Stores,** one of which you'll find at 28 South Tejon Street (tel. 634-3742). If it's 3 in the morning and you can't get your prescription, call a hospital.

**Emergencies**  For police, fire, or medical emergencies, call **911.** For Colorado State Patrol emergencies, call 303/635-3581.

**Eyeglasses**  Outside of downtown, you can get 1-hour replacement of lost or broken glasses at **Pearl Vision Center** stores in major shopping malls. More convenient may be **Charlotte's,** 2501 West Colorado Avenue (tel. 473-8066), in Old Colorado City.

**Hairdressers & Barbers**  Most full-service salons are outside downtown. Try the **Middleton Salon,** 5747 North Academy Boulevard, at Vickers Street (tel. 548-1543), or the **Viva Salon,** 3645 Star Ranch Road (tel. 579-8482) near Broadmoor. Both cater to men and women. **Fantastic Sams** has a half-dozen salons in the metropolitan area, offering haircuts for under $10.

**Hospitals**  Full medical services, including 24-hour emergency treatment, are offered by **Memorial Hospital,** 1400 East Boulder Street (tel. 475-5000, or 475-5221 for emergency); and **St. Francis Hospital,** 825 East Pikes Peak Avenue (tel. 636-8800, or 636-8850 for emergencies). Both are just east of downtown. **Penrose Hospital,** 2215 North Cascade Avenue (tel. 630-5333), and **Penrose Community Hospital,** 3205 North Academy Boulevard (tel. 591-3216), are on the north side.

**Information**   See "Orientation," above.

**Laundry/Dry Cleaning**   Nearly every major hotel offers valet drop-off and pickup service, but the charge can be steep. Few have guest laundries. Your hotel can direct you to the nearest coin laundrette. For dry cleaning, **One Hour Cleaners** has four locations in the city, including 1859 South Nevada Avenue (tel. 473-1597).

**Libraries**   The **Colorado Springs Public Library,** 20 North Cascade Avenue (tel. 473-2080), has its main library (the Penrose Public Library) in the heart of downtown. There are branches throughout the metropolitan area. A local library card is required to check out material. Open Monday through Wednesday from 10am to 9pm, Thursday through Saturday from 10am to 5:30pm, and on Sunday from 1 to 5pm.

**Liquor Laws**   See "Fast Facts: Colorado" in Chapter 2.

**Lost Property**   Consult the city police (tel. 632-6611).

**Newspapers/Magazines**   The *Gazette Telegraph* is published daily in Colorado Springs, and is by far the city's most widely read newspaper. Both Denver dailies—the *Denver Post* and *Rocky Mountain News*—are also sold at newsstands throughout the city. *Springs* magazine and *Steppin' Out* are free monthly arts-and-entertainment tabloids. *USA Today* and the *Wall Street Journal* can be purchased on the streets and at major hotels.

**Photographic Needs**   Try **50-Minute Photo,** downtown at 115 East Kiowa Street (tel. 630-1991) and in the north end at 6902 North Academy Boulevard (tel. 598-6412). Also reliable is **Gerard's Photo Lab of Colorado,** 891 Elkton Drive (tel. 594-0848).

**Police**   In an emergency, dial **911.** For standard business, call 632-6611.

**Post Office**   The **Main Post Office** is downtown at 201 East Pikes Place Avenue (tel. 570-5339), open Monday through Friday from 9am to 5pm. There are many other branches. For late-night pickup, you'll have to visit the **Airport Branch,** 3655 East Fountain Boulevard (tel. 570-5377).

**Radio/TV**   More than a dozen AM and FM **radio stations** in the Colorado Springs area cater to all musical, news, sports, and entertainment tastes. Among them are KCME (88.7 FM) and KRDO (95.5 FM) for classical, KILO (94.1 FM) and KKFM (96.1 FM) for hard rock, KKCS (101.9 FM and 1460 AM) for country, KKLI (106.3 FM) for light rock, KSPZ (93.1 FM) and KVUU (99.9 FM) for contemporary rock, and KVOR (1300 AM) for all news. Major **television stations** include Channel 5 (NBC), 8 (PBS), 11 (CBS), 13 (ABC), and 21 (independent). Cable or satellite service is available at most hotels.

**Religious Services**   Most major religious denominations, and many minor ones, are represented in Colorado Springs. Check the *Yellow Pages* for a complete listing of houses of worship.

**Safety**   Colorado Springs is a very safe city, but use common sense when you visit. Stay alert. Be aware of your immediate surroundings, and keep a close eye on your possessions. Be especially careful with cameras, purses, and wallets, all favorite targets of thieves and pickpockets.

**Shoe Repairs**   Shoes and boots are quickly repaired, often while you wait, at **Rocky Mountain Boot and Shoe Repair,** 110 East Cheyenne Road (tel. 630-8459), behind Safeway.

**Taxes**   Colorado state **sales tax** is 3.7%. Each county tacks an additional local tax on top of that. In El Paso County (Colorado Springs), it's 4%—a total of 7.7%. The **hotel tax** in Colorado Springs, added to room charges, is 9.2%.

**Telephone/Fax**   Local calls are normally 25¢. Facsimiles can be transmitted by most major hotels at a nominal cost to guests. For **directory assistance,** dial 1-555-1212.

**Useful Telephone Numbers**   Poison control center (tel. 630-5333),

**rape assistance** (tel. 303/430-5656), **road conditions** (tel. 635-7623 for a recording), **ski reports** (tel. 303/837-9907 for a recording), **time** (tel. 630-1111), **weather** (tel. 596-1116).

# 3. ACCOMMODATIONS

The rates listed here are the officially quoted off-the-street prices, or "rack rates," and don't take into account any individual or group discounts. (See "Accommodations" in Chapter 4 for suggestions on how to save money.)

In these listings, the following categories define price ranges: "Expensive," more than $110 per night double; "Moderate," $75 to $110; "Inexpensive," $40 to $75; "Budget," less than $40 per night double. An additional 9.2% **city bed tax** is levied onto all bills, and is not included in the rates.

## EXPENSIVE

**THE BROADMOOR, Lake Circle at Lake Ave. (P.O. Box 1439), Colorado Springs, CO 80901. Tel. 719/634-7711,** or 800/634-7711. Fax 719/577-5779. 532 rms, 18 suites. A/C TV TEL

**$ Rates:** Mid-May to mid-Oct, $210–$240 single or double; $310–$1,590 suite. Mid-Oct to mid-May, $120–$160 single or double; $240–$1,200 suite. Winter packages may cost as little as $49.50 per person per night. CB, DC, MC, V. **Parking:** Free.

A Colorado Springs institution and a tourist attraction in its own right, the Broadmoor is a sprawling resort complex of pink Mediterranean-style buildings and modern additions at the foot of Cheyenne Mountain. It began in 1885 as the dream of a German count, who envisioned a sort of American Monte Carlo. James de Pourtales constructed a Georgian casino on a small lake and laid trolley lines from downtown Colorado Springs, 5 miles away. But the casino burned in 1897 and a planned grand hotel was never built. It was up to Spencer Penrose, 2 decades later, to take up where Count de Pourtales had left off. Built in the Italian Renaissance style, the Broadmoor opened in 1918. Its marble staircase, brass chandeliers, della Robbia tile, hand-painted beams and ceilings, and carved marble fountain remain spectacles today, along with a priceless art collection featuring original work by Toulouse-Lautrec and Ming Dynasty ceramicists. The first names entered on the guest register were those of John D. Rockefeller, Jr., and his party.

Today there are guest rooms in three separate buildings—Broadmoor Main, adjacent Broadmoor South, and Broadmoor West, on the site of the original casino across Broadmoor Lake—on the 3,000-acre grounds. Guest rooms are spacious and luxurious, as might be expected. Recently refurbished, all contain early 20th-century antiques and original works of art. Rooms typically have two queen-size or one king-size bed, desks and tables, plush seating, secluded luggage areas, and excellent lighting. Service is impeccable: The hotel staffs two employees for every room.

**Dining/Entertainment:** Charles Court (see "Dining," below) is the Broadmoor's finest restaurant. The Tavern (see "Dining," below) focuses on steak and seafood and offers an option of dining in a tropical Garden Room or being serenaded by chamber musicians. The Lake Terrace Dining Room is especially popular for Sunday brunch ($6.50 to $11.50). The elegant Penrose Room, on the ninth floor of Broadmoor South, serves wild game, new American cuisine, and to-die-for desserts; open for dinner only, its main dishes run $17.50 to $29.50. More casual are the Broadmoor Golf Club (members and hotel guests only), with luncheon soups, salads, and sandwiches ($5.50 to $12.75) and light dinner dishes ($10.50 to $19.50); the

Golden Bee (see "Evening Entertainment," below) pub fare ($5.50 to $9); and Julie's, a sidewalk café and ice-cream shop. There are four lounges, one in each building. Across Lake Circle is the Broadmoor International Theatre.

**Services:** 24-hour room service, full concierge service, valet laundry, no-smoking rooms, facilities for the disabled, shuttle bus between buildings.

**Facilities:** Sports facilities include three golf courses, three swimming pools, 16 tennis courts (4 indoor), squash court, trap and skeet-shooting grounds, bicycle rental, exercise room, aerobics classes, saunas, Jacuzzi, Broadmoor World Arena (ice skating and hockey), and Spencer Penrose Stadium (rodeo and equestrian). There are 19 shops (boutiques, galleries, jeweler, florist, druggist, hair salon, travel agent, and gift shop), a cinema, a car-rental agency, a post office, and a service station. Up to 1,600 at a sitting can be accommodated for meetings; there are 30 meeting rooms and a conference center. The hotel owns El Pomar Carriage House Museum, the Broadmoor International Theatre, Cheyenne Mountain Zoo, and Will Rogers Shrine of the Sun.

**CHEYENNE MOUNTAIN CONFERENCE RESORT, 3225 Broadmoor Valley Rd., Colorado Springs, CO 80906. Tel. 719/576-4600,** or 800/428-8886. Fax 719/576-4711. 254 rms, 14 suites. A/C TV TEL
**$ Rates:** Late Apr to mid-Oct, $175 single; $230 double; $300–$410 suite. End of Mar to late Apr and mid-Oct to Thanksgiving, $125 single; $170 double; $255–$365 suite. Thanksgiving to the end of Mar and other major hols, $95 single; $120 double; $225–$330 suite. 30-day advance booking is requested. AE, CB, DC, DISC, MC, V. **Parking:** Free.

Designed specifically to attract conferences, this fine resort in southern Colorado Springs hosts independent travelers as space permits. Eight satellite lodges surround a large main lodge, all of them built of rough-hewn cedar with massive beams and native moss rock. A skylit cathedral ceiling gives the central lobby a majestic feel.

Every guest room has a private deck or balcony, most of them with an impressive view toward the southern Rockies. Because of the business orientation, all have comfortable work areas with computer outlets and modem capability. Most rooms have two double beds, dressers and easy chairs, a vanity and separate dressing table, and built-in hairdryers. The "executive king" also features a large private Jacuzzi. Local phone calls are 50¢.

**Dining/Entertainment:** Remington's (see "Dining," below) has been voted Colorado Springs's "most romantic" restaurant. The Mountain View Dining Room wins raves for its buffet: all-you-can-eat breakfast ($7.75) and lunch ($12.25) spreads. A limited but changing choice of dinner dishes ($15 to $23) always includes beef, seafood, poultry, and another meat in new American preparations. The Will Rogers Lounge features a piano bar, and bands playing light contemporary music during the summer season.

**Services:** Room service most hours, concierge, valet laundry, no-smoking rooms, facilities for the disabled.

**Facilities:** A 35-acre lake with a swimming beach, boat and sailboard rentals, and trout fishing; golf course, 18 tennis courts (6 indoors), four swimming pools (one indoor), fitness center with weight equipment and racquet courts, bicycle path and rentals, adult games room (billiards, cards, other table games); state-of-the-art conference facilities include 24 meeting rooms that handle up to 420 for banquets.

# MODERATE

**THE ANTLERS DOUBLETREE HOTEL, 4 S. Cascade Ave., Colorado Springs, CO 80903. Tel. 719/473-5600,** or 800/528-0444. Fax 719/444-0417. 284 rms, 6 suites (all with bath). A/C TV TEL
**$ Rates:** Apr–Oct, $95 single; $105 double. Nov–Mar, $75 single; $85 double. Year round, $150–$750 suite. AE, CB, DC, DISC, ER, JCB, MC, V. **Parking:** $4 per day self-parking, $6 per day valet parking.

The Antlers has been a Colorado Springs landmark for more than a century— although there have been three different Antlers on the same site. The first two were built by city founder Gen. William Palmer. A turreted Victorian showcase, built in 1883, was named for the general's collection of deer and elk trophies. After it was destroyed by fire in 1898, Palmer built an extravagant Italian Renaissance–style building that survived until 1964, when it was leveled to make room for the new Antlers Plaza. That in turn was closed for over a year after it was purchased by Doubletree Hotels—and reopened only in October 1990 after a dramatic facelift.

Antique black-walnut nightstands from the old Antlers provide a touch of historic continuity in every guest room. The rooms, appointed in brown and beige shades, feature king-size, queen-size, or double beds, armoires with televisions, clock radios, two telephones (50¢ for local calls), and ample closet space. Corner rooms are larger, with desks. The 13th-floor concierge level has a hospitality room and additional amenities.

The hotel offers a full range of services and dining and other facilities.

**COLORADO SPRINGS MARRIOTT, 5580 Tech Center Dr., Colorado Springs, CO 80919. Tel. 719/260-1800,** or 800/962-6982. Fax 719/260-1492. 302 rms, 8 suites (all with bath). A/C TV TEL
**$ Rates:** Late May to mid-Oct, $65–$102 single or double; mid-Oct to late May, $49–$102 single or double. Year round $230 suites. AE, CB, DC, DISC, MC, V. **Parking:** Free.
Set atop a low hill overlooking the businesses of the Colorado Springs Technological Center, the red-brick Marriott dominates the surrounding scenery. The interior was designed to incorporate the red sandstone colors of the natural landscape. In the lobby, a large fireplace set against tall picture windows gives warmth to cool nights.

Guest rooms have mauve or lime color schemes and handsome wood furnishings. All have a king-size or two double beds, a large desk with telephone (75¢ local calls) and computer modem jack, easy chair with ottoman, full-length mirrors, vanities, in-room movies, and AM/FM radio alarm clocks. "Executive kings," some of them reserved for women travelers, have a sitting room separate from the bedroom. The concierge level offers complimentary breakfasts, an honor bar, and upgraded amenities.

The hotel offers a full range of services and dining and other facilities.

**EMBASSY SUITES, 7290 Commerce Center Dr., Colorado Springs, CO 80919. Tel. 719/599-9100,** or 800/EMBASSY. Fax 719/599-4644. 207 suites (all with bath). A/C TV TEL
**$ Rates** (including full breakfast): $99 single; $109 double. AE, CB, DC, DISC, MC, V. **Parking:** Free.
Entering this hotel, with its central atrium, is like walking into a South American garden. Waterfalls feed a recycling stream that runs through jungle vegetation, in the midst of the red tile and decorative ironwork of a Spanish colonial hacienda.

Standard suites have a kitchen separated from the living area, and a separate bedroom. Cooking facilities include a microwave, refrigerator, wet bar, and coffee maker. There's a table with seating for four and a sleeper sofa in the living area. The bedroom has a king-size bed, private deck or balcony, wardrobe closet, armoire with remote-control cable TV, clock radio, telephone (50¢ local calls), and vanity adjoining the modern bathroom.

The hotel offers a full range of services and dining and other facilities.

**HEARTHSTONE INN, 506 N. Cascade Ave., Colorado Springs, CO 80903. Tel. 719/473-4413,** or 800/521-1885. 24 rms (22 with bath), 1 suite. A/C
**$ Rates** (including full breakfast): $25–$85 single without bath, $45–$105 single with bath; $35–$95 double without bath, $55–$115 double with bath. AE, MC, V. **Parking:** Free.
This elegant small downtown hotel is actually two historic homes (one built in 1885, the other in 1900) connected by a carriage house. Listed on the National Register of Historic Places, and the winner of numerous preservation awards, the inn is filled with

fascinating old photographs and antiques, as well as reproduction king- and queen-size brass beds.

Each room has a personality of its own. The Study, for instance, is a parlor-style room with built-in bookcases and a fireplace. The Solarium has an open-air latticed porch. The Sewing Room has an antique treadle sewing machine that functions as a nightstand. The third-floor Loft has three dormer windows, a queen-size brass bed, and a tiny child's bed with a child-size rocking chair. No pets permitted.

The hotel offers a full range of services and dining and other facilities.

**RED LION HOTEL–COLORADO SPRINGS, 1775 E. Cheyenne Mountain Blvd. (I-25 at Circle Dr.), Colorado Springs, CO 80906. Tel. 719/576-8900,** or 800/547-8010. Fax 719/576-4450. 293 rms, 6 suites (all with bath). A/C TV TEL
**$ Rates** (including continental breakfast): $75–$105 single; $85–$115 double; $300–$400 suite. AE, CB, DC, DISC, ER, MC, V. **Parking:** Free.

The most impressive features of this hotel are its two courtyards. One, sporting a fountain and sun deck, provides a pleasant view for inward-looking rooms in this five-story property. The second offers a sunny recess for coffee-shop diners.

The spacious guest rooms have two queen-size beds (no doubles) or a king-size, a desk/dresser, table and chairs, and two vanities. All but 50 of the rooms have a private balcony. The appointments are dark desert rose or cypress green. Business travelers appreciate the two-line phones (local calls 50¢), modern hookups, and separate sitting area in the "king" rooms.

The hotel offers a full range of services and dining and other facilities.

**SHERATON COLORADO SPRINGS HOTEL, 2886 S. Circle Dr. (I-25 Exit 138), Colorado Springs, CO 80906. Tel. 719/576-5900,** or 800/325-3535 worldwide, 800/635-3304 direct. Fax 719/576-5900 ext. 1717. 486 rms, 16 suites (all with bath). A/C TV TEL
**$ Rates:** $65–$100 single; $75–$110 double; inquire for suites. AE, CB, DC, DISC, MC, V. **Parking:** Free.

Eleven acres of landscaped grounds and a beautiful skylit indoor garden set this Sheraton apart from others. The grounds feature trees, waterfalls, and three plaza-style courtyards. The indoor garden offers a pool, Jacuzzi, and patio dining among palms and other tropical plants.

The rooms are equally inviting. Double rooms have private balconies, views of the indoor or outdoor pool, and desks, along with standard features such as clock radios, full-size mirrors, and vanities. North wing rooms lack the private deck, but offer refrigerators and built-in hairdryers. A half-dozen bilevel suites have a king-size bed in a loft and a sleeper sofa downstairs.

The hotel offers a full range of services and dining and other facilities.

---

 **FROMMER'S COOL FOR KIDS:**
## HOTELS

**Hearthstone Inn** (see p. 114) Well-behaved children who respect antique furnishings will be delighted by the toddler-size bed and rocking chair in the Loft.

**McLaughlin Family Lodge** (see p. 116) Well away from busy streets, this one delights parents as well as kids with its playground and pool.

**Sheraton Colorado Springs Hotel** (see p. 115) Two swimming pools, a separate children's pool, shuffleboard, and a putting green will keep the kids happy.

# INEXPENSIVE

**HOLDEN HOUSE 1902 BED & BREAKFAST INN, 1102 W. Pikes Peak Ave., Colorado Springs, CO 80904. Tel. 719/471-3980.** 5 rms (all with bath).

**$ Rates** (including full breakfast): $57–$85 single or double; $52–$80 for stays of 2 nights or longer. AE, DISC, MC, V. **Parking:** Free.

Innkeepers Sallie and Welling Clark restored this storybook Colonial Revival–style Victorian, and its adjacent 1906 carriage house, and filled the rooms with antiques and family heirlooms. Located near Old Colorado City, it has a living room with a tile fireplace, a front parlor with a television, and verandas where a gourmet breakfast is served on warm summer mornings.

The guest rooms are named after Colorado mining areas, and each contains some memorabilia of that district. All have queen-size beds. Largest is the turreted Aspen Room, with a romantic "tub for two." The Cripple Creek and Leadville rooms are smaller. In the Carriage House, the gabled Goldfield Room features a skylight above the bed; the two-room Silverton Room has a "sleigh bed" and clawfoot tub.

Not permitted are smoking, children, or pets.

**MCLAUGHLIN FAMILY LODGE, 183 Crystal Park Rd., Manitou Springs, CO 80829. Tel. 719/685-5278.** 25 cabins (16 with kitchen, all with bath). A/C

**$ Rates:** $30–$45 without kitchen, $45–$80 with kitchen. Sixth night free. MC, V.

Spread across 15 acres away from busy streets, at the foot of Pikes Peak, these rustic cabins attract families with a heated swimming pool and children's playground. The cabins vary in size and facilities, from four units with a simple double bed to a three-bedroom unit, with a fireplace, that sleeps 12. Most of the cabins have kitchens fully stocked with pots and utensils. TVs can be installed on request. A percentage of all room payments supports Cheyenne Village, a community program for developmentally disabled adults.

**SHERATON INN NORTH ACADEMY, 8110 N. Academy Blvd. (at I-25), Colorado Springs, CO 80920. Tel. 719/598-5770,** or 800/333-3535. Fax 719/598-5770 ext. 586. 193 rms, 7 suites (all with bath). A/C TV TEL

**$ Rates:** Mid-May to Sept, $70 single; $80 double. Oct to mid-May, $50 single; $60 double. Year round, $180–$225 suite. AE, CB, DC, DISC, ER, MC, V. **Parking:** Free.

The nearest full-service hotel to the Air Force Academy has a large and beautiful atrium, with fountains spurting beneath a skylight. Guest rooms have king-size or double beds, light-wood furnishings, dressing tables, and remote-control TV with in-house movies. There are also three large Jacuzzi suites.

The Garden Terrace restaurant serves three meals daily beneath the atrium skylight. Shadows lounge hops on weekends with disc jockeys playing music of the '50s, '60s, and '70s. The hotel has a 24-hour indoor pool, hot tub, sauna, guest laundry, gift shop, complimentary airport shuttle, and other amenities.

**TWO SISTERS INN, 10 Otoe Place, Manitou Springs, CO 80829. Tel. 719/685-9684.** 4 rms (2 with bath), 1 cottage.

**$ Rates** (including full breakfast): $52 without bath, $65 with bath; $80 cottage. MC, V. **Parking:** Free.

Originally built in 1919 as a boarding house by two sisters, this bed and breakfast, not far from the Pikes Peak Cog Railway, is still owned and operated by two women—sisters in spirit if not actually in blood. East Coast refugees Wendy Goldstein and Sharon Smith have furnished the four bedrooms and separate honeymoon cottage with family heirlooms and photographs.

The four cozy rooms in the main house feature Victorian frills and furnishings, such as quilts and clawfoot bathtubs. The cottage has a feather bed, a wood stove, and an old-fashioned kitchen . . . though cooking is not encouraged. Every guest gets his or her daily quotient of fresh Manitou Springs mineral water.

Well-supervised children are permitted; smoking and pets are not.

**VILLA MOTEL, 481 Manitou Ave., Manitou Springs, CO 80829. Tel. 719/685-5492,** or 800/341-8000. 47 rms (all with bath, 7 with kitchen). A/C TV TEL
**$ Rates:** Memorial Day–Labor Day, $62–$68 single or double. Early Oct to early May, $26 single; $32–$40 double. Shoulder periods, $36–$44 single; $44–$50 double. AE, CB, DC, DISC, MC, V.

A two-story chalet-style motel opposite a streamside city park, the Villa has numerous facilities that make it a popular place for families. All rooms have ceramic tile baths, cable TV, radios, free local phone calls, and courtesy coffee and tea service. The motel has a heated pool and whirlpool, as well as a coin-op laundry. Seven units have kitchenettes. Kids are welcome; pets are not.

## BUDGET

**AMERICAN YOUTH HOSTEL–COLORADO SPRINGS, 3704 W. Colorado Ave., Colorado Springs, CO 80904. Tel. 719/635-8910.** 48 dormitory beds.
**$ Rates:** $10 for AYH members, $12 for nonmembers. No credit cards. **Closed:** Mid-Sept to mid-May.

Located in the Garden of the Gods campground, this hostel—comprised of a series of streamside cabins—is blessed with a remarkably beautiful location. As with all hostels, toilets and showers are shared, and there's a common kitchen, laundry, TV room, and telephone. This hostel also has a huge swimming pool and hot tub. Located on a city bus line, it's open mid-May to mid-September only.

**ECONOLODGE DOWNTOWN, 714 N. Nevada Ave., Colorado Springs, CO 80903. Tel. 719/636-3385.** 37 rms (3 with kitchen, all with bath). A/C TV TEL
**$ Rates:** Mid-May to mid-Sept, $30–$36 single; $34–$38 double. Mid-Sept to mid-May, $24–$26 single; $26–$34 double. Kitchen units $5 extra. AE, CB, DC, DISC, MC, V.

A convenient and comfortable hotel near Colorado College, the Econolodge has rooms with double beds and standard furnishings. Pets are permitted. There's also a heated outdoor swimming pool and complimentary coffee for guests.

**RED WING MOTEL, 56 El Paso Blvd. (at Beckers Lane), Manitou Springs, CO 80829. Tel. 719/685-9547.** 27 rms (10 with kitchen, all with bath). A/C TV TEL
**$ Rates:** Mid-May to mid-Sept, $39 single; $39–$45 double. Mid-Sept to mid-May, $26 single; $26–$30 double. AE, CB, DC, DISC, MC, V.

Set back a block off busy Manitou Avenue, this motel faces a fenced-in swimming pool with a kids' slide and sundeck. Nearby is a covered patio for picnicking. The spacious rooms have basic furnishings, with in-room coffee and hot-water heating. Ten have kitchenettes.

## CAMPING

**CRYSTAL KANGAROO CAMPGROUND, 625 Crystal Park Rd. (P.O. Box 71), Manitou Springs, CO 80829. Tel. 719/685-5010.**
**$ Rates:** $11.50 tent, $14.50 full RV hookup, $1 each person after two. MC, V.

There are 14 acres of open and shaded sites on this hillside plot overlooking Manitou Springs from the south. Fireplaces and picnic tables, two bath houses, a grocery, laundry, recreation room, and other facilities assist campers.

**GARDEN OF THE GODS CAMPGROUND, 3704 W. Colorado Ave., Colorado Springs, CO 80904. Tel. 719/475-9450.** or 800/345-8197.

**$ Rates:** $15–$20 for two people. Extra person $2. AE, MC, V. **Closed:** Mid-Oct to mid-Apr.

Near the park, this large campground offers 250 full RV hookups and additional tent sites. It has tables, a barbecue pit, bath houses, a grocery, laundry, heated swimming pool, Jacuzzi, and games room.

# 4. DINING

The categories below define a "Very Expensive" restaurant as one in which most dinner main courses are priced above $20; "Expensive," $15 to $20 for main courses; "Moderate," $10 to $15; "Inexpensive," $6 to $10; and "Budget," less than $6.

## VERY EXPENSIVE

**BRIARHURST MANOR, 404 Manitou Ave., Manitou Springs. Tel. 685-1864.**
   **Cuisine:** CONTINENTAL/AMERICAN. **Reservations:** Required.
**$ Prices:** Appetizers $3.95–$15; main courses $15–$35. Seniors' and children's portions and prices. 20% service charge added to bill. AE, CB, DC, DISC, MC, V.
   **Open:** Dinner only, Mon–Sat 6–10:30pm.
The original 1876 stone home of Manitou Springs founder Dr. William Bell, this magnificent Tudor mansion has all the style of an English country house. Its pink sandstone walls are accented by the emerald green of surrounding grounds. Designated for demolition in 1975, the restaurant was purchased by chef Sigi Krauss, an East German who came to Colorado Springs after 10 years in Vail. Krauss restored its rich wood interior, including a Gothic oak staircase, and turned it into a world-renowned restaurant. (Look for it next to the Buffalo Bill Wax Museum.)
   The Briarhurst features a different continental menu each month. During my visit, it was Provençal: bouillabaisse, lapin aux herbes (rabbit), cuisses de grenouille (frogs' legs), and cailles farcies (quail stuffed with sour cherries and served on goose-liver toast). Always available as starters are steak tartare and pâté de maison, and main dishes like entrecôte, rack of lamb, and fresh rainbow trout.

**CHARLES COURT, Broadmoor West, in the Broadmoor, Lake Circle. Tel. 634-7711.**
   **Cuisine:** INTERNATIONAL. **Reservations:** Required.
**$ Prices:** Appetizers $5.50–$12; main courses $7.75–$15.50 at lunch, $20–$28.50 at dinner. CB, DC, MC, V.
   **Open:** Breakfast Mon–Sat 7–10am, Sun 7–10:30am; lunch Mon–Sat 11:30am–2pm, Sun noon–2pm; dinner Sun–Fri 6:30–9:30pm, Sat 6–9:30pm.
The English country-manor atmosphere of this outstanding restaurant, with picture windows looking across Broadmoor Lake to the Italianate original hotel, lends itself to a fine dining experience. Attentive tableside service adds to the experience.
   Diners can start with Brie in a sweet red-pepper sauce; sea scallops, sautéed with Pernod, artichokes, and raddichio; or escargots with forest mushrooms and a Boursin cheese demi-glâce. There's also a delicious apple-and-lobster bisque, or a warm legume-and-partridge salad. Main dishes might include grilled tuna in an orange-tarragon butter, veal Zweiglehoffer (with shrimp, Pernod, and béarnaise sauce), or medallions of beef madeira. And there's always a fantasy of dessert selections.

**REMINGTON'S, in the Cheyenne Mountain Conference Resort, 3225 Broadmoor Valley Rd. Tel. 719/576-4600.**
   **Cuisine:** CONTINENTAL. **Reservations:** Required.
**$ Prices:** Appetizers $3.75–$6.95; main courses $18.50–$24. A 15% service charge is added to all bills. AE, CB, DC, DISC, MC, V.
   **Open:** Dinner seatings from 6–9pm.

Colorado Springs's "most romantic" restaurant, according to readers of the daily *Gazette Times*, is an intimate 18-table gem in a spacious foothill resort lodge. Contemporary art adorns the walls, but the view outside attracts more attention.

Diners can begin with oyster Padua (in beluga caviar) or a crab-and-asparagus terrine. Classic Caesar and wilted-spinach salads are prepared tableside. Main dishes range from Remington's trio (beef, lamb, and veal with charcutière sauce), and duckling Aberdeen (in a cider sauce), to lobster tail saffron beurre blanc. A creative fixed-price menu ($31.50) changes every 2 months.

## EXPENSIVE

**LA PETITE MAISON, 1015 W. Colorado Ave. Tel. 632-4887.**
   **Cuisine:** CONTINENTAL. **Reservations:** Recommended.
$ **Prices:** Appetizers $2.75–$5.50; main courses $6.50–$8.50 at lunch, $10.95–$18.50 at dinner. AE, CB, DC, DISC, MC, V.
   **Open:** Lunch Tues–Fri 11:30am–2pm; dinner Tues–Sat 5:30–10pm.
An unimposing blue house on the south side of the main road between downtown and Old Colorado City, this friendly restaurant has a simple French country interior decor, with strains of Mozart and Verdi operas wafting through the air.

Chef Holly Mervis has gained local fame for imaginative variations on classic recipes. Featured appetizers include duck liver and hazelnut pâté, and a goat cheese–stuffed chile with black beans. For dinner, the provincial plat du jour is always wonderful; otherwise, consider the lamb chops dijonnaise or the fresh fish special. Mediterranean fish stew makes a marvelous lunch.

**THE MARGARITA AT PINE CREEK, 7350 Pine Creek Rd. Tel. 598-8667.**
   **Cuisine:** INTERNATIONAL. **Reservations:** Recommended.
$ **Prices:** Fixed-price meal $6.50 at lunch, $16 at dinner Tues–Fri, $22 Sat. AE, CB, DC, MC, V.
   **Open:** Lunch Tues–Fri 11:30am–2pm; dinner Tues–Sat 6–9pm.
Local newspaper readers say this restaurant has the "best ambience" in Colorado Springs. Located at the north end of the city, near the Woodmen Road exit from I-25, the Margarita occupies a modified southwestern structure with tile floors and stuccoed walls. A tree-shaded outdoor patio is open in summer.

All meals are a set price. Lunches feature a choice of soup (usually a beef barley and a seafood or mushroom bisque), salad, and homemade bread. Six-course Mexican dinners are served Tuesday through Friday; Call ahead if you're a vegetarian or have other dietary requirements. Saturday night there's a special baroque dinner, with continental cuisine accompanied by a harpsichordist and flutist.

**THE TAVERN, Broadmoor Main, at the Broadmoor, Lake Circle. Tel. 634-7711.**
   **Cuisine:** STEAK/SEAFOOD. **Reservations:** Recommended.
$ **Prices:** Appetizers $5–$9.50; main courses $6.50–$16 at lunch, $14–$25 at dinner. Children's menu $3.25–$4.25. CB, DC, MC, V.
   **Open:** Lunch Mon–Sat 11am–2pm; dinner Mon–Sat 5–10pm.
Original Toulouse-Lautrec lithographs on the walls mark the Tavern as a place with unusual class . . . and a few unexpected surprises. The main restaurant features chamber music or light jazz on stage, both at noon and at night. Adjoining is the Garden Room, richly planted with tropical foliage. In either room, service is impeccable—and this is the Broadmoor's informal dining spot!

Lunch specials include a London broil *au jus,* seafood crêpes Louise, Welsh rarebit, or a variety of sandwiches and salads. Dinners are more elaborate: Choose from prime rib, filet mignon, chateaubriand for two, blackened or broiled salmon or swordfish, or half a roast duck or chicken.

## MODERATE

**ANTHONY'S, 1919 E. Boulder St. Tel. 471-3654.**
   **Cuisine:** ITALIAN. **Reservations:** Recommended.

COLORADO
★ Denver
Colorado Springs

## ACCOMMODATIONS:
American Youth Hostel-
Colorado Springs **1**
Antlers Doubletree Hotel **2**
Broadmoor, The **3**
Cheyenne Mountain
Conference Resort **4**
Colorado Springs Marriott **5**
Econolodge Downtown **6**
Embassy Suites **7**
Hearthstone Inn **8**
Holden House 1902 Bed &
Breakfast Inn **9**
McLaughlin Family Lodge **10**
Red Lion Hotel-
Colorado Springs **11**
Red Wings Motel **12**
Sheraton Colorado Springs **13**
Sheraton Inn North
Academy **14**
Two Sisters Inn **15**
Villa Motel **16**

## DINING:
Adams Mountain Cafe **1**
Anthony's **2**
Beckett's **3**
Briarhurst Manor **4**
Charles Court **5**
Craftwood Inn **6**
Edelweiss Restaurant **7**
Giuseppe's Old Depot
Restaurant **8**
Henri's **9**
Jelly's **10**
Juniper Valley Ranch **11**
La Petit Maison **12**
Le Peep **13**
Manitou Pancake &
Steak House **14**
Margarita at Pine Creek **15**
Mason Jar, The **16**
Mayfield's Cafe, Wine Bar
and Grill **17**
Old Chicago **18**
Remington's **19**
Stagecoach Inn, The **20**
Tavern, The **21**

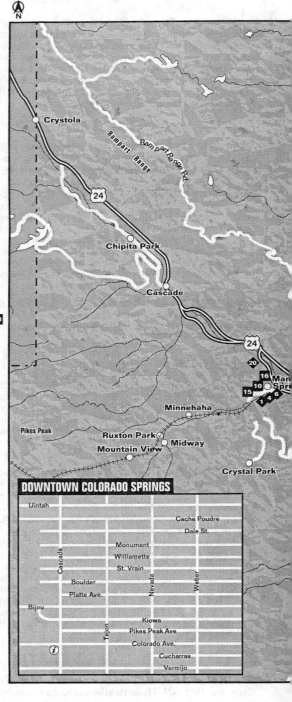

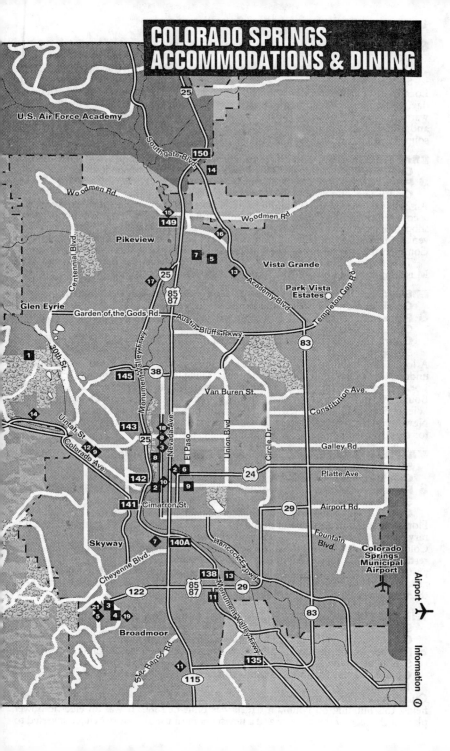

**$ Prices:** Appetizers $3.50–$5.95; lunch $5.95–$9.95; dinner $6.95–$14.95. AE, MC, V.

**Open:** Lunch Mon–Fri 11am–2pm; dinner Tues–Thurs and Sun 5–10pm, Fri–Sat 5–11pm.

Located in a quiet eastside neighborhood, Anthony's is a tranquil escape from a hectic day. In summer, it has an outdoor patio for dining; in winter, a blazing fire keeps you warm. All pastas, from manicotti to mostaccioli, are homemade. Chicken Parmigiana and saltimbocca alla romana are favorite dishes of regulars. All dinners come with soup, salad, and garlic bread, and a plate of linguine accompanies meat dishes.

**CRAFTWOOD INN, 404 El Paso Blvd., Manitou Springs. Tel. 685-9000.**
**Cuisine:** ROCKY MOUNTAIN. **Reservations:** Recommended.
**$ Prices:** Appetizers $3.50–$7; main courses $9.50–$22.50. MC, V.
**Open:** Dinner daily 5–10pm; brunch Sun 10am–2pm.

An English Country Tudor building with beamed ceilings, stained-glass windows, and a copper hooded fireplace, the Craftwood Inn was built in 1912 as a coppersmith shop. Today it specializes in game and other regional cuisine—dishes like juniper venison bourguignon, grilled piñon trout, and roast pheasant with Zinfandel sauce. Consider, too, pumpkin soup as a starter, and prickly pear sorbet for dessert.

To reach the Craftwood Inn, turn off Manitou Avenue at the Buffalo Bill Wax Museum; go uphill one block, and turn left on El Paso Boulevard.

**EDELWEISS RESTAURANT, 34 E. Ramona Ave. Tel. 633-2220.**
**Cuisine:** GERMAN. **Reservations:** Recommended.
**$ Prices:** Appetizers $3.10–$4.95; lunch $3.25–$6.50; dinner $7.75–$14.75. AE, CB, DC, DISC, MC, V.
**Open:** Lunch Mon–Fri 11:30am–1:30pm; dinner Sun–Thurs 5–9:30pm, Fri–Sat 5–10pm.

A lovely stone building with a big inside fireplace and outside patio, the Edelweiss underscores its Bavarian atmosphere with strolling folk musicians on weekend nights. Located south of I-25 near the intersection of South Tejon Street and Cheyenne Boulevard, just west of Nevada Avenue, it offers a hearty menu of Jagerschnitzel, Wiener Schnitzel, Sauerbraten, Bratwurst, and other old-country specials—as well as New York strip steak and fresh fish and chicken dishes. Don't miss the fruit strudels for dessert!

**MAYFIELD'S CAFE, WINE BAR AND GRILL, 802 Village Center Dr. Tel. 528-8400.**
**Cuisine:** NEW AMERICAN. **Reservations:** Recommended.
**$ Prices:** Appetizers $3.75–$4.25; main courses $4.75–$5.95 at lunch, $11.95–$14.50 at dinner. AE, MC, V.
**Open:** Lunch Tues–Fri 11am–2:30pm; dinner Tues–Sat 5–9pm.

Floral wreaths and garlands of peach and mauve haphazardly adorn this contemporary restaurant, located in the Rockrimmon neighborhood in the northwestern part of Colorado Springs. Recipes tend to be invented here more frequently than at other restaurants—but they rarely if ever fail. Tried and true are a variety of salads and pastas for lunch. Feeling adventurous? Come for dinner. Start with a red chili steak tartare, go on to fresh grilled mahi mahi with papaya salsa or curried roast game hen, then finish with a cappuccino and chocolate-hazelnut cheesecake.

**THE STAGECOACH INN, 702 Manitou Ave., Manitou Springs. Tel. 685-9335.**
**Cuisine:** STEAK/SEAFOOD. **Reservations:** Recommended.
**$ Prices:** Appetizers $3.25–$5.95; main courses $4.95–$6.75 at lunch, $10.50–$16.95 at dinner. DISC, MC, V.
**Open:** Lunch Mon–Sat 11am–3pm; dinner daily 5–9:30pm; brunch Sun 10:30am–2:30pm.

Once a stop on the stage route between Colorado Springs and the Cripple Creek gold fields, this building on Fountain Creek was built in 1880. It was an electric power plant at the turn of the century and a newspaper print shop before being converted to this restaurant. It offers, as its slogan says, "affordably elegant fine dining." Soups, salads, and sandwiches like the buffalo barbecue are luncheon fare; dinner main courses vary from tenderloin of beef Elizabeth to grilled garlic shrimp and chicken Stagecoach, a preparation that varies from day to day.

## INEXPENSIVE

**BECKETT'S, 128 S. Tejon St. Tel. 633-3230.**
 **Cuisine:** AMERICAN.
 **$ Prices:** Lunch $4.65–$8.45; dinner $7.45–$14.95. AE, MC, V.
 **Open:** Lunch Mon–Sat 11am–2pm; dinner daily 5–10pm.
Located downtown in the 1890s Alamo Building, Beckett's has a classic brewhouse atmosphere of stonework and dark-wood accents. Four handcrafted ales and one stout are brewed and served here: Try a taster and sample them all. The kitchen prepares such dishes as rotisserie chicken, alder-smoked salmon, baby back ribs, and pasta and grilled shrimp.

**GIUSEPPE'S OLD DEPOT RESTAURANT, 10 S. Sierra Madre St. Tel. 635-3111.**
 **Cuisine:** ITALIAN/AMERICAN.
 **$ Prices:** Lunch $3.60–$9.75; dinner $5.75–$13.95. AE, CB, DC, DISC, MC, V.
 **Open:** Daily 11am–11pm.
Old Engine 168 occupies a place of honor in front of this restaurant, lodged in a restored Denver & Rio Grande train station downtown. Spaghetti, lasagne, and stone-baked pizza are house specialties. On the American side of the ledger, you can get a full slab of baby back ribs, an engineer's cut of prime rib, a pepper steak flamed with cognac, fried chicken, or Louisiana shrimp Créole.

**HENRI'S, 2427 W. Colorado Ave. Tel. 634-9031.**
 **Cuisine:** MEXICAN.
 **$ Prices:** Lunch or dinner $4.50–$10.25. AE, CB, DC, MC, V.
 **Open:** Tues–Sat 11:30am–10pm, Sun noon–8pm (shorter midweek hours in winter).
Four-foot-tall tin masks and Emilio Velasco murals decorate the walls of this Colorado City establishment, which has remained in the Ruiz family since grandfather Henri opened it in 1947. The family atmosphere persists in the warmth of the service and the authenticity of the food. Try the chili rellenos, the chicken fajitas, or the tacos al carbon. The margaritas may be the best in the city.

**JUNIPER VALLEY RANCH, Colo. 115 Colorado Springs. Tel. 576-0741.**
 **Cuisine:** AMERICAN. **Reservations:** Recommended.
 **$ Prices:** Full family-style dinner $9.95–$10.50.

---

 **FROMMER'S COOL FOR KIDS:**
### RESTAURANTS

**Edelweiss Restaurant** (see p. 122) Kids will enjoy the strolling musicians playing German folk music on weekends, and they'll love the apple and cherry strudels.

**Giuseppe's Old Depot Restaurant** (see p. 123) An original locomotive stands outside this old Denver & Rio Grande Railroad station. Spaghetti and pizza are always great kids' food.

**The Mason Jar** (see p. 124) The friendly staff gives children crayons and coloring pages to keep them busy as they wait for their meal, ordered off a kids' menu.

**Open:** Dinner only, Wed–Sat 5–9pm, Sun 1–8pm. **Closed:** Dec–Apr.

This little red mud house on the Parker Homestead, bordering Fort Carson, is almost hidden by juniper and skunk brush. It hasn't changed its menu since opening in 1951. But four generations of the Parker family make it work. There are just two choices for dinner: skillet-fried chicken or baked ham. It must be good, for the crowds keep coming back.

**THE MASON JAR, 5050 N. Academy Blvd. Tel. 598-1101.**
  **Cuisine:** AMERICAN.
**$ Prices:** Lunch or dinner $4.50–$12. Children's meals $2.40. DISC, MC, V.
  **Open:** Daily 11am–10pm.

The Mason Jar caters to every member of the family. Children, for instance, get crayons and coloring pages, as well as a more manageable menu selection. This is basic American country cuisine: fried chicken, pork chops, prime rib, Boston bluefish filets. And there's a special health-conscious menu for those wary of fried foods and fatty meats. There's a second Mason Jar in Old Colorado City at 2925 West Colorado Avenue (tel. 632-4820).

**OLD CHICAGO, 118 N. Tejon St. Tel. 634-8812.**
  **Cuisine:** PASTA/PIZZA.
**$ Prices:** Lunch $4.50–$7.50; dinner $5.50–$9.50. AE, MC, V.
  **Open:** Lunch Mon–Sat 11am–3pm; dinner Mon–Thurs 5–10pm, Fri–Sat 5–11pm, Sun 11am–10pm.

The door handles are made of Chicago Cubs bats. Etched-glass dividers in the restaurant depict the Chicago skyline as seen from Lake Michigan. This is Colorado, not Illinois, but everybody loves the Cubs. A special feature is the pasta bar—6 sauces daily (from a list of 18) to cloak your spaghetti, linguine, or fettuccine. Old Chicago boasts 25 draft and 85 bottled beers; drink them all and you'll be a "Hall of Foam" member.

There are Old Chicagos throughout the Front Range, including another restaurant on the north side at 7115 Commerce Center Drive (tel. 593-7678).

# BUDGET

**ADAMS MOUNTAIN CAFE, 733 Manitou Ave., Manitou Springs. Tel. 685-1430.**
  **Cuisine:** INTERNATIONAL/NATURAL FOODS.
**$ Prices:** Breakfast $1.85–$5.25; lunch $2.50–$5.95; dinner $5.95–$9.95. No credit cards.
  **Open:** Breakfast/lunch daily 8am–3:30pm; dinner Tues–Thurs and Sun 5:30–8pm, Fri–Sat 5:30–9:30pm.

Downstairs is a Victorian dining room offering live acoustic guitar on Thursday and harp music on Sunday. Upstairs, a cozy coffeehouse has a balcony overlooking bustling Manitou Avenue. In either room, the fare is healthy. About half the delicious meals are vegetarian, the remainder chicken or shrimp. Try apple-blueberry granola for breakfast, an Indonesian tempeh sandwich for lunch, spinach lasagne or a chicken burrito for dinner.

**JELLY'S, 1887 S. Nevada Ave. Tel. 520-1588.**
  **Cuisine:** AMERICAN.
**$ Prices:** Breakfast $1.95–$6.25; lunch $1.95–$4.95; dinner $3.60–$7.95. MC, V.
  **Open:** Daily 6am–9pm.

This country-style café likes to do things as they used to be done, especially when it comes to making fruit jelly! Everything from rhubarb to plum is in a jar here, and served (if you like) with your omelet or your PB&J sandwich. Deli-style sandwiches are big at lunch, home-style chicken, steak, and catfish at dinner. Ask about the Home-style Dinner Special.

**LE PEEP, 6385 N. Academy Blvd. Tel. 590-1771.**
  **Cuisine:** INTERNATIONAL.
**$ Prices:** Breakfast $1.75–$6.25; lunch/dinner $3.95–$7.95. MC, V.

**Open:** Mon–Fri 6:30am–9pm, Sat–Sun 7am–9pm.

Best known for its crêpes, Le Peep is not French at all, but tongue-in-cheek American . . . as well as Cajun (blackened chicken), Italian (fettuccine with meat sauce), Mexican (huevos que bueno), and perhaps even Philadelphian (cheese steak). Those mile-high skillet crêpes include southwestern crêpes (with chorizo sausage and diced chiles), chicken crêpes Benedict (in a hollandaise sauce), and Aspen fruit crêpes (topped with whipped cream and cinnamon).

**MANITOU PANCAKE AND STEAK HOUSE, 26 Manitou Ave. Tel. 685-9225.**
   **Cuisine:** AMERICAN.
**$ Prices:** Breakfast $1.95–$6.45; lunch $1.69–$5.65; dinner $3.50–$7.95. MC, V.
   **Open:** Mon–Sat 6am–10pm, Sun 6am–2pm.

Perhaps the best bargain in town, this popular restaurant serves an 8-ounce top sirloin with two vegetables and bread for just $5.95! There are a variety of home-cooked plate specials for lunch and dinner, including pot roast, grilled ham, and chicken and dumplings. There's also an all-you-can-eat soup-and-salad bar. The breakfast menu features a variety of omelets.

# 5. ATTRACTIONS

Pikes Peak region attractions can be placed in three broad categories: natural (Pikes Peak, Garden of the Gods, Cave of the Winds), educational (the Air Force Academy, Olympic Training Center, local museums), and commercial (including the overdone string of Manitou Springs tourist lures). There's room in a well-rounded itinerary for all of them.

## SUGGESTED ITINERARIES

**IF YOU HAVE 1 DAY**   Start your morning by taking the **cog railway** to the top of **Pikes Peak** for the spectacular view. Have lunch at one of the charming restaurants in Manitou Springs, then drive north to spend the afternoon exploring the **Air Force Academy.**

**IF YOU HAVE 2 DAYS**   Spend your first day as suggested above.
   There's something magical about the **Garden of the Gods** with the early-morning light glancing off the red sandstone spires. Afterward, tour **Cave of the Winds** and the nearby **Manitou Cliff Dwellings.** Pass the afternoon visiting the U.S. **Olympic Training Center.** If your budget allows, enjoy dinner at one of the fine restaurants in the **Broadmoor hotel;** at the very least, have a drink and explore this magnificent property.

**IF YOU HAVE 3 DAYS**   Spend your first 2 days as suggested above.
   On Day 3, head west via U.S. 24 and Colo. 67 to the fascinating 1890s gold bonanza town of **Cripple Creek,** for the morning, lunch, and perhaps into the afternoon. If it's not too late, circle back to **Colorado Springs** via the **Florissant Fossil Beds National Monument.**

**IF YOU HAVE 5 DAYS OR MORE**   Spend Days 1–3 as suggested above.
   On Day 4, give yourself at least one more day in **Colorado Springs** to catch some of the sights you've missed, like **Miramont Castle,** the **Pioneer Museum,** and the **Pro Rodeo Hall of Fame.**
   For your fifth day, use the Springs as a base for exploring the southeastern part of the state, including **Pueblo,** the **Royal Gorge** near Cañon City, and **Bent's Old Fort** near La Junta.

## ❓ DID YOU KNOW . . . ?

- Katherine Lee Bates wrote the words to "America the Beautiful" after seeing the view from the top of Pikes Peak in 1893.
- The Pikes Peak Auto Hillclimb is the second-oldest car race in America, after the Indianapolis 500.
- The U.S. Air Force Academy is Colorado's foremost tourist attraction, drawing 1.4 million visitors per year.
- The North American Air Defense Command (NORAD) in Colorado Springs is the continent's first warning system of a nuclear-missile strike.
- Nikola Tesla, inventor of the first alternating-current electrical system, created artificial lightning above his Colorado Springs home at the turn of the 20th century.

# THE TOP ATTRACTIONS

## UNITED STATES AIR FORCE ACADEMY, off I-25. Tel. 472-2555.

Colorado Springs's pride and joy got its start in 1954, when Congress authorized the establishment of a U.S. Air Force Academy and selected this 18,000-acre site—on a broad mesa buffered on the west by the Rockies, 12 miles north of downtown—from among 400 other locations. The first class of cadets enrolled in 1958. Each year since, about 4,500 cadets have begun the 4 years of rigorous training required to become air force officers. Today the academy draws more visitors than any other single attraction in the Rocky Mountains.

Approach the academy through the North Gate, off I-25 Exit 156B. Soon after entering the grounds, at the intersection of North Gate Boulevard and Stadium Boulevard, you'll see an impressive outdoor **B-52 display.** Where North Gate Boulevard becomes Academy Drive, another mile or so farther, look to your left to see the **Cadet Field House,** where basketball and ice hockey games are played (see "Sports & Recreation," below), and the **Parade Ground,** where cadets can be spotted marching some Saturday mornings and on special occasions.

Academy Drive soon curves to the left. Six miles from the North Gate, signs mark the turnoff to the **Barry Goldwater Air Force Visitor Center.** Open daily year round, it has a variety of exhibits and films on academy history and cadet life, extensive literature and self-guided tour maps, and the latest information and schedules on academy activities. There's also a large gift shop, coffee shop, public telephones, and rest rooms.

A short trail from the Visitor Center leads to the **Cadet Chapel.** Its 17 gleaming aluminum spires soar 150 feet skyward, and within are separate chapels for the major Western faiths. The public can visit Monday through Saturday from 9am to 5pm and on Sunday from 1 to 5pm. The chapel is closed for 5 days around graduation and during special events.

Also within easy walking distance of the Visitor Center are the **Academy Planetarium** (tel. 472-2778), a classroom for astronomy, physics, and navigation classes that offers periodic free public programs; **Arnold Hall** (tel. 472-4499), the social center (open daily from 9am to 5pm), which offers historical exhibits, a cafeteria, and a theater featuring a variety of public shows and lectures throughout the year; and **Harmon Hall** (tel. 472-2520), the administration building, where potential cadets can obtain admission information.

After leaving the Visitor Center, continue south, then east, on Academy Boulevard to Stadium Boulevard, where you can't miss **Falcon Stadium** on your left. If you're in town in the fall, try to attend a football game.

Turn right on Stadium Boulevard and follow it out to South Gate Boulevard, which leaves the academy grounds at I-25 Exit 150B. En route, you'll pass the **Thunderbird Airmanship Overlook,** where you might be lucky enough to watch cadets parachuting, soaring, and practicing their takeoffs and landings in U.S. Air Force Thunderbirds.

For specific information about the academy, write Visitor Services Division, Directorate of Public Affairs, U.S. Air Force Academy, Colorado Springs, CO 80840.

**Admission:** Free.

**Open:** Daily 9am–5pm; additional hours for special events.

**PIKES PEAK COG RAILWAY,** 515 Ruxton Ave., Manitou Springs. Tel. 685-5401.

A century old in 1991, the train to the summit of the Front Range's most imposing mountain is more popular than ever. The first passenger train climbed 14,110-foot Pikes Peak on June 30, 1891. Steam power was slowly replaced by diesel between 1939 and 1957. Four custom-built Swiss twin-unit rail cars, each seating 216 passengers, were put into service in 1989. It takes 75 minutes to ascend and to descend the 9-mile line, with grades up to 25°; including a stay of 40 minutes on top of the mountain, a round-trip requires 3¼ hours.

The journey is exciting from the start, but passengers begin to "ooh" and "ah" when the track leaves the aspen and pine forests and creeps above the timberline at about 11,500 feet. The view from the summit takes in Denver, 75 miles north; New Mexico's Sangre de Cristo range, 100 miles south; the Cripple Creek mining district, on the mountain's western flank, and wave after wave of Rocky Mountain subranges to the west; and the seemingly endless sea of Great Plains to the east. The Summit House at the top of Pikes Peak has a restaurant and gift shop.

Take a jacket or sweater, because it can be very cold and/or windy at the top. If you've got cardiac or respiratory restrictions, give this trip a miss.

**Admission:** $20 adults, $10 children 5–11, $9 children under 5 (but those held on lap are free).

**Open:** June–Aug, eight departures daily; in May and Sept–Oct, two to six departures daily. Definite May–Oct departures from Manitou Springs at 9:20am and 1:20pm. Reservations recommended.

**GARDEN OF THE GODS,** 1400 Glen Ave. Tel. 578-6933.

One of the West's most unique geological sites, the Garden of the Gods was a wintering place of Ute tribespeople until a century ago. The Native Americans were no doubt impressed by the spectacular red sandstone pillars, sculpted by rain and wind, freezing and thawing, over 300 million years. The 1,300-acre park was deeded to the city in 1907.

Located where several life zones and ecosystems converge—Great Plains grasslands, Southwest piñon and juniper, Rocky Mountain pine forests—the park harbors a variety of plant and animal communities. Oldest survivors in the park are the ancient, twisted junipers, some 1,000 years old. The strangest animals are honey ants, which gorge themselves with honey in the summer and fall to become living honey pots to feed their colonies during winter hibernation.

Hiking maps are available at the **visitor center,** which also offers displays on the history, geology, plants, and wildlife of the park. Twice a day in summer, park naturalists host 45-minute walks through the park and afternoon interpretive programs. You may spot technical rock climbers on some of the park spires (they must first register at the visitor center).

In the center of the park is the Garden of the Gods Trading Post, built in 1900 in pueblo style and decorated with Navajo sand paintings. A wide choice of southwestern native arts and crafts are sold here. Its Patio Café specializes in buffalo burgers.

For a unique look at the Garden of the Gods, step into the **Camera Obscura** on the southeastern side of the park. A 13-foot-focal-length lens, mounted in a tower above the room, revolves and projects a 360° magnified view of the surrounding landscape on a 60-inch-wide circular disk.

Also in the park is the **White House Ranch Historic Site** (see "More Attractions," below).

**Admission:** Free.

**Open:** Park, May–Oct, daily 5am–11pm; Nov–Apr, daily 5am–9pm. Visitor center, early June to Labor Day, daily 9am–5pm; Labor Day to early June, daily 10am–4pm. Trading Post, early June to Labor Day, daily 8am–8pm; Labor Day to early June, daily 9am–4:30pm. **Closed:** Thanksgiving and Dec 25–Jan 1. **Directions:** Take Garden of the Gods Road west off I-25 (Exit 146) and turn south on 30th Street, or follow Ridge Road north off U.S. 24 or Colorado Avenue.

**UNITED STATES OLYMPIC TRAINING CENTER, 1750 E. Boulder St., at Union Blvd. Tel. 632-5551.**

When NORAD and the Air Defense Command moved their operations into Cheyenne Mountain in 1978, this 36-acre site in the middle of Colorado Springs became home to the U.S. Olympic Committee. Today the complex provides a sophisticated training center for more than half of the 41 U.S. Olympic sports, including such high-profile sports as track and field, swimming, basketball, and gymnastics. Other centers are in Lake Placid, New York, and San Diego, California. Some 14,000 athletes of all ages train or attend the developmental programs each year.

Visitors are encouraged to stop first at the **visitor center** for a guided tour. These start every 30 minutes and begin with a film on the U.S. Olympic effort. Tours take in the **Sports Center,** with five gymnasiums and a weight-training room; the **Sports Science Center,** where new training techniques involving biomechanics, physiology, psychology, and computer engineering are pioneered; the **Indoor Shooting Center,** featuring two 50-meter ranges; and an all-weather 400-meter track. One mile south of the OTC, in Memorial Park off Union Boulevard, is the **7-Eleven Velodrome** for bicycle and roller speed skating.

A gift shop next to the visitor center sells Olympic-logo merchandise. Proceeds support OTC training programs.

**Admission:** Free.

**Open:** Summer, 1-hour tours Mon–Sat 9am–4pm, Sun 10am–3pm; less frequently in winter. Gift shop, Mon–Sat 10am–6pm, Sun noon–5pm.

# MORE ATTRACTIONS
## ARCHITECTURAL HIGHLIGHTS

**THE BROADMOOR, Lake Circle at Lake Ave. Tel. 719/634-7711.**

This famous Italian Renaissance-style resort hotel has been a Colorado Springs landmark since it was built by Spencer Penrose in 1918. (See "Accommodations," above.)

**Admission:** Free.

**Open:** Daily year round.

**GLEN EYRIE, 30th St. off Garden of the Gods Rd. Tel. 598-1212** ext. 269.

The private Tudor-style castle of Gen. William Palmer, founder of Colorado Springs, is now a retreat center overlooking the Garden of the Gods. Palmer furnished it with 24 fireplaces, many removed from medieval cathedrals and castles during his travels in Europe: One of them was carved by Benedictine monks between the 12th and 14th centuries. Guided 1¼-hour tours are offered weekdays in summer, Sunday in winter; reservations are advised. Sunday brunch tours are offered sporadically.

**Admission:** $5 adults, $4 seniors, $3 students 13–17, free for children 12 and under.

**Open:** Guided tours, June–Aug, Mon–Fri at 1:30 and 3:30pm; Sept–May, Sun at 1:30 and 3:30pm.

**MIRAMONT CASTLE MUSEUM, 9 Capitol Hill Ave., Manitou Springs. Tel. 685-1011.**

Built into a hillside by a wealthy French priest as a private home in 1895, and converted by the Sisters of Mercy into a sanitorium in 1907, this unique Victorian mansion has always inspired curiosity. At least nine identifiable architectural styles are incorporated into the structure, among them Gothic, Romanesque, Tudor, and Byzantine. The "castle" has four stories, 28 rooms, 14,000 square feet of floor space, and 2-foot-thick stone walls. One room is a miniature museum, another a model railroad museum. Light meals and tea are served from 11am to 4pm in the Queen's Parlour. The mansion is just off Ruxton Avenue, en route from Manitou Avenue to the Pike's Peak Cog Railway.

**Admission:** $2.50 adults, $1 children 6–12, free for children under 6.

**Open:** June–Aug, daily 10am–5pm; Sept–May, daily 1–3pm; Victorian Christmas, four weekends preceding Christmas Eve, Fri–Sun noon–4pm.

## HISTORIC BUILDINGS

**MCALLISTER HOUSE, 423 N. Cascade Ave., at St. Vrain St. Tel. 635-7925.**

This Gothic cottage, listed in the National Register of Historic Places, was built of brick in 1873 when the builder, an army major named Henry McAllister, learned that the local wind was of such force as to have blown a train off the tracks nearby! It contains many original furnishings, including three marble fireplaces. The house was ahead of its time with the installation of running water. Today it is a property of the Colonial Dames of America, who lead guided tours.

**Admission:** $2 adults, $1 seniors and students, 75¢ children 6–13, free for children under 6.

**Open:** Summer, Wed–Sat 10am–4pm, Sun noon–4pm; winter, Thurs–Sat 10am–4pm, Sun noon–4pm.

**WHITE HOUSE RANCH HISTORIC SITE, Gateway Rd., Garden of the Gods. Tel. 578-6777.**

History of three different pioneer eras comes to life at this working ranch at the east entrance to Garden of the Gods park. Visitors can see how Coloradans lived during the homestead era (1868), the ranch era (1895), and the estate period (1907). Besides the original homestead, general store, and ranch, there's an arboretum and a nature trail for the blind.

**Admission:** $3 adults, $2.75 seniors, $1.50 children 6–12, free for children under 6.

**Open:** Memorial Day–Labor Day, Wed–Sun 10am–4pm; Labor Day–Dec 23, Sat 10am–4pm, Sun noon–4pm; Jan–May, open only selected weekends for special events.

## MUSEUMS & GALLERIES

**COLORADO SPRINGS FINE ARTS CENTER, 30 W. Dale St., west of N. Cascade Ave. Tel. 634-5581.**

Georgia O'Keeffe, John James Audubon, John Singer Sargent, Charles Russell, Albert Bierstadt, Nicolai Fechin, and other famed painters and sculptors are represented in the permanent collection of the **Fine Arts Museum** here, one of several facilities that call the center home. When it opened in 1936, the center was the first facility in the U.S. built for the purpose of combining performing arts and visual arts; there's also a theater, concert hall, and the **Taylor Museum** of southwestern Hispanic and Native American art. The Alice Bemis Taylor Collection of Spanish colonial folk art is one of the largest such collections in the world. There's also a special gallery for the blind. Famed Santa Fe architect John Gaw Meem designed the building, a sort of monolithic concrete structure.

**Admission:** Galleries, $2.50 adults, $1.50 seniors and students 13–21, $1 children 6–12, free for children under 6. Free for everyone Sat 10am–noon. Separate admission for performing-arts events.

**Open:** Galleries, Tues–Sat 10am–5pm, Sun 1–5pm.

**COLORADO SPRINGS PIONEERS MUSEUM, 215 S. Tejon St. Tel. 578-6650.**

Housed in the former El Paso County Courthouse, built in 1903 and listed on the National Register of Historic Places, this excellent museum tells the story of Colorado Springs in a variety of exhibits. Ranching, mining, railroads, and medicine all have their memorabilia. The original courtroom has been preserved and used in old *Perry Mason* episodes. There are also displays of fine arts, decorative arts, and ceramics. Perhaps the high point of a visit is the 120-piece Lula Evans quilt collection, so large only a few quilts can be shown at a time.

**Admission:** Free.

**Open:** Mon–Sat 10am–5pm, Sun 1–5pm.

**HALL OF PRESIDENTS LIVING WAX STUDIO, 1050 S. 21st St., Old Colorado City. Tel. 635-3553.**

COLORADO

Black Forest Observatory ❶
Cave of the Winds ❷
Garden of the Gods ❸
Glen Erie ❹
McCallister House ❺
Miramont Castle
    Museum ❻
Pike's Peak Cog Railway ❼
Seven Falls ❽
The Broadmoor ❾
United States
    Air Force Academy ❿
United States Olympic
    Training Center ⓫
White House Ranch
    Historic Site ⓬

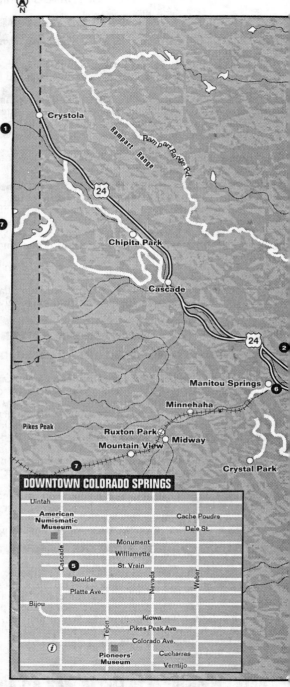

## DOWNTOWN COLORADO SPRINGS

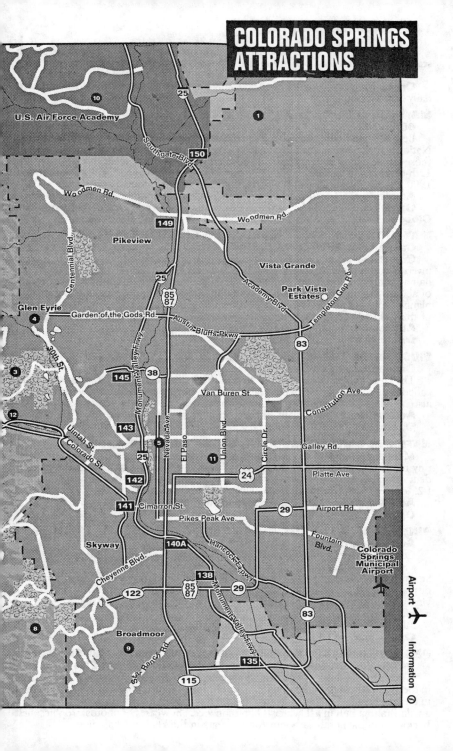

More than 100 life-size wax figures, all crafted at Madame Tussaud's London studios, are assembled in 26 room-size chapters of American history.

**Admission:** $3.50 adults, $1.75 children 6–11, free for children under 6.

**Open:** Memorial Day–Labor Day, daily 9am–9pm; Labor Day–Memorial Day, daily 10am–5pm.

## MANITOU CLIFF DWELLINGS MUSEUM, U.S. 24, Manitou Springs. Tel. 685-5242.

Before Mesa Verde and other archeological treasure troves were protected by the National Park Service, zealous scientists horded many of the finest artifacts. Some of those artifacts have been reacquired and are displayed in this excellent re-creation of a 12th-century cliff village, built by archeologists in Phantom Cliff Canyon around 1900. Native American dancers perform during the high tourist season.

**Admission:** $3 adults, $1.50 children 7–11, free for children under 7.

**Open:** June–Aug, daily 9am–6pm; May and Sept to mid-Oct, daily 10am–5pm. **Closed:** Mid-Oct to Apr.

## MAY NATURAL HISTORY MUSEUM OF THE TROPICS, 710 Rock Creek Canyon Rd. Tel. 576-0450.

One of the world's outstanding collections of giant insects and other tropical invertebrates is presented at this museum. James F. May (1884–1956) spent more than half a century exploring the world's jungles while compiling this illustrious collection of about 7,000 arthropods. Museums of photography and space exploration are also planned adjacent to the Golden Eagle Ranch RV park and campground, 4 miles south of the Colorado Springs city limits, a mile west of Colo. 115 opposite Fort Carson.

**Admission:** $3 adults, $1.50 children.

**Open:** May–Sept, daily 9am–5pm. **Closed:** Oct–Apr.

## MUSEUM OF THE AMERICAN NUMISMATIC ASSOCIATION, 818 N. Cascade Ave., at Dale St. Tel. 632-2646.

The largest collection of its kind west of the Smithsonian Institute consists of eight galleries of coins, tokens, medals, and paper money from around the world. There's also a collectors' library at this downtown locale.

**Admission:** $1 adults, 50¢ children 10–17, free for children under 10.

**Open:** Tues–Sat 8:30am–4pm.

## NATIONAL CARVERS MUSEUM, Baptist Rd. Tel. 481-2656.

More than 14,000 wood carvings of all sizes and subjects are on display here, from tiny miniatures to individual portraits to life-size dioramas. A carver is on hand to demonstrate the art, and there's a fine little gift shop. The museum is a mile west of I-25 off Exit 158, just north of the U.S. Air Force Academy.

**Admission:** $3 adults, $2 seniors and children under 13.

**Open:** Daily 9am–5pm.

## PIKES PEAK AUTO HILL CLIMB RACE CAR MUSEUM, 135 Manitou Ave., Manitou Springs. Tel. 689-5996.

Commemorating the nation's second-oldest auto race (after the Indianapolis 500), this museum displays nearly a century of memorabilia, including a 1900 Stanley Steamer that was the first car to climb Pikes Peak. Even presidential limousines are displayed. Such racing legends as Mario Andretti, Parnelli Jones, and Al and Bobby Unser have competed in the annual July race—156 turns on a gravel highway, ending at 14,110 feet above sea level.

**Admission:** $2 adults, $1 children under 12.

**Open:** June–Oct 1, daily 9am–5pm. **Closed:** Oct 2–May.

## PRO RODEO HALL OF FAME AND AMERICAN COWBOY MUSEUM, 101 Pro Rodeo Dr. (off Rockrimmon Blvd. West). Tel. 593-8847.

A multimedia theatrical presentation sketches the history of cowboys and rodeos in the West. Displays on the development of ropes, saddles, chaps, and boots are seen in Heritage Hall. A special video technique gives viewers a realistic, jouncing ride atop a wild Brahma bull in a Theater II film sequence. Showcases of photos, trophies, belt buckles, and memorabilia honor rodeo greats in the Hall of Champions.

**Admission:** $4 adults, $3.75 seniors, $1.25 children 5–12, free for children under 5.

**Open:** Memorial Day–Labor Day, daily 9am–5pm; Labor Day–Memorial Day, Tues–Sat 9am–4:30pm, Sun noon–4pm. **Closed:** New Year's Day, Easter, Thanksgiving, and Christmas.

## WESTERN MUSEUM OF MINING AND INDUSTRY, 1025 North Gate Rd. Tel. 598-8850.

Historical mining artifacts from the early days of hard-rock mining, restored to operating condition, are what makes this 15,000-square-foot museum hum. Summer and fall tours take in a 10-stamp gold and silver ore mill, a working hoist house, and a blacksmith shop. Visitors may pan for gold in a trough. An operating Corliss steam engine with a 17-ton flywheel is a special attraction. The museum is located across I-25 from the North Gate of the Air Force Academy.

**Admission:** $3 adults, $1 children 5–17, free for children under 5.

**Open:** Daily 9am–4pm. **Closed:** New Year's Day, Easter, Thanksgiving, and Christmas.

## WORLD FIGURE SKATING HALL OF FAME, Broadmoor World Arena, 20 First St. Tel. 635-5200.

Ice skates, costumes, medals, and other memorabilia of skating greats who have trained here are displayed in a special exhibit area off the ice arena. A highlight is the historic Eddie H. Shipstad skate collection. There's also a library of books and documents about skating, and a gift shop. The arena is on the Broadmoor hotel grounds.

**Admission:** Free.

**Open:** June–Aug, Tues–Sat 10am–4pm; Sept–May, Mon–Fri 10am–4pm.

## NATURAL ATTRACTIONS

## BLACK FOREST OBSERVATORY, 12815 Porcupine Lane. Tel. 495-3828.

The observatory may not be "natural," but the heavens it studies are as pure as exist! The largest public observatory in Colorado offers public viewing by reservation. It's located off Colo. 83 east of the Air Force Academy and north of Research Parkway.

**Admission:** $5 adults, $2.50 for children under 12.

**Open:** By reservation.

## CAVE OF THE WINDS, U.S. 24, Manitou Springs. Tel. 685-5444.

Discovered by two boys on a church outing in 1881, this impressive underground cavern has offered public tours for well over a century. The 40-minute Discovery Tour takes visitors along a well-lit three-quarter-mile trail through 20 subterranean chambers, complete with classic stalagmites, stalactites, crystal flowers, and limestone canopies. In the Adventure Room, modern lighting techniques return visitors to an era when spelunking was done by candle and lantern. There's also a physically demanding, 2½-hour Wild Tour that's guaranteed to get participants dirty: Armed only with flashlights and helmets, adventurers slither and scramble through remote tunnels of the Manitou Grand Caverns system.

**Admission:** $7 adults, $4 children 6–15, free for children under 6.

**Open:** Memorial Day–Labor Day, daily 9am–9pm; Labor Day–Memorial Day, daily 10am–5pm. Adventure Tours depart every 15 minutes. Wild Tours are conducted three times daily in summer, other times by reservation.

## SEVEN FALLS, South Cheyenne Canyon, Cheyenne Blvd. Tel. 632-0752.

A spectacular 1-mile drive through a box canyon, including a transit of the Pillars of Hercules where the canyon narrows to just 42 feet, climaxes at these cascading falls. Seven separate waterfalls dance down a granite cliff, illuminated during the summer months by colored lights. A 265-foot stairway beside the falls leads to the Eagle Nest viewing platform. A mile-long trail atop the plateau passes the grave of 19th-century author Helen Hunt Jackson (*Ramona*) and ends at a panoramic overlook of Colorado Springs.

**Admission:** $4.50 adults, $2 children 6–12, free for children under 6.

**Open:** Memorial Day–Labor Day, daily 8am–11pm; other months, reduced hours.

## NEIGHBORHOODS

**MANITOU SPRINGS, Manitou Ave. off U.S. 24 West.**

Manitou (Ute for "Great Spirit") might seem to be a tourist-trap town, but the souvenir selling and tourist catching is all done with cheerful humor—great spirit, if you would—and the Rockies all around you are real. There are numerous charming restaurants, shops, and galleries between the kitsch pitchers.

Manitou was called the Saratoga of the West a century ago when long trips to "take the waters" at the mineral springs were more the style in Victorian vacationing. Even President Ulysses S. Grant visited with his wife. Famous back then was Manitou Ginger Champagne, made with the local naturally active mineral water and a secret recipe including ginger. But a fire burned down the bottling plant and the recipe was lost—ending this era in soft-drink history. There is word, however, that the brand may reappear in stores before long.

**OLD COLORADO CITY, Colorado Ave. between 21st and 31st Sts.**

Founded in 1859, before Colorado Springs itself, Colorado City boomed in the 1880s after General Palmer's railroad came through. Tunnels led from the respectable side of town to the saloon and red-light district so that city fathers could carouse without being seen going or coming back—or so the legend goes. Today this historic district has an interesting assortment of shops, galleries, and restaurants.

## PANORAMAS

**PIKES PEAK HIGHWAY, off U.S. 24 at Cascade.**

There is perhaps no view in Colorado to equal the 360° panorama from the 14,110-foot summit of Pikes Peak. Whether by cog railway (see "The Top Attractions," above) or private vehicle, the ascent—though not for the faint of heart—is one that no able-bodied visitor should miss. This 19-mile toll highway (paved for 7 miles, all-weather gravel thereafter) starts at 7,400 feet, some 4 miles west of Manitou Springs. There are numerous photo stops en route up the mountain, and restaurant/gift shops at 11 miles and at the summit. Deer, mountain sheep, and other animals can often be seen on the slopes, especially above the timberline (around 11,500 feet).

This 156-curve toll road is the site of the annual July 4 Pikes Peak Auto Hill Climb, the Pikes Peak Marathon foot race in August, and the New Year's Eve climb and fireworks show.

**Admission:** $5 adults, $2 children 6–11, free for children under 6.

**Open:** June 10–Labor Day, daily 7am–6:30pm; Apr–June 9 and Labor Day to the first major snowfall (late Oct), 9am–3pm. **Closed:** Late Oct to Mar.

## PARKS & GARDENS

**MONUMENT VALLEY PARK, Monument Creek from Bijou St. north to Fontanero St. Tel. 578-6640.**

This long, slender park follows Monument Creek through downtown Colorado Springs beside the I-25 freeway. At its south end are formal zinnia, begonia, and rose gardens. In the middle are demonstration gardens of the Horticultural Art Society. There are softball/baseball fields, a swimming pool, volleyball and tennis courts, children's playgrounds, picnic shelters, and two trails—the 4¼-mile Monument Creek Trail for walkers, runners, and cyclists, and the 1-mile Monument Valley Fitness Trail at the north end of the park, beside Bodington Field.

**Admission:** Free.

**Open:** Daily year round.

**NORTH CHEYENNE CAÑON PARK, Cheyenne Blvd. west of 21st St. Tel. 634-9320.**

This small piece of the Rocky Mountains is entirely within the Colorado Springs city limits. North Cheyenne Creek races across pinkish-red Pikes Peak granite formations, dropping 1,800 feet in 5 miles in a series of cascades and waterfalls. The elevation range supports a variety of native grasses and wildflowers, including numerous rare orchids, as well as a White Fir Botanical Preserve. There are six picnic areas in the park and several hiking trails, the longest of which is the 3-mile Columbine Springs Trail. Exhibits on history, geology, flora, and fauna can be found at the **visitor center** at the foot of Helen Hunt Falls; nature walks and interpretive programs leave from here at 11am and 3pm daily in summer. A back road from the upper end of the park leads through Pike National Forest to Cripple Creek.

**Admission:** Free.

**Open:** Visitor center, early June to Labor Day, daily 9am–5pm; Sept–Oct, Sat–Sun 10am–4pm. **Closed:** Nov to early June.

**PALMER PARK, Maizeland Rd. off Academy Blvd. Tel. 578-6640.**

Deeded to the city in 1899 by its founder, Gen. William Jackson Palmer, this 722-acre preserve features hiking, biking, and equestrian activities spread across a low mesa in central Colorado Springs. It boasts a variety of minerals (including quartz, topaz, jasper, and tourmaline), a rich vegetation (including a yucca preservation area), and considerable wildlife. The **Edna Mae Bennet Nature Trail** is a self-guided excursion; there are numerous other trails, including those shared with riders from the adjoining **Mark Reyner Stables.** The park also includes 12 separate picnic areas, softball/baseball fields, and volleyball courts.

**Admission:** Free.

**Open:** Daily year round.

## COOL FOR KIDS

In addition to the listings below, children will also enjoy the following attractions described in "More Attractions" above: Hall of Presidents Living Wax Studio, May Natural History Museum of the Tropics, and Miramont Castle Museum.

**THE BOARDWALK, Pioneer Plaza Mall, N. Circle Dr. and Galley Rd. Tel. 520-FUNN.**

This entertainment center has video arcades, kiddie rides, bumper cars, Skeeball, and other activities.

**Admission:** $3 for 1 hour, $5 for 3 hours, $8 all day; 50¢ more for a game card.

**Open:** Mon–Thurs 11am–midnight, Fri–Sat 11am–1am, Sun 9am–midnight.

**BUFFALO BILL WAX MUSEUM, 404 W. Manitou Ave., Manitou Springs. Tel. 685-5900.**

The legends of the Old West—Kit Carson and Davy Crockett, Jesse James and his gang, Wyatt Earp's gunfight at the OK Corral—are depicted by 107 life-size wax figures in 32 realistic displays.

**Admission:** $2.50 adults, $2 children 12–16, $1 children 6–11, free for children under 6.

**Open:** Apr 15–30, daily 9am–6pm; May–Aug, daily 8am–6pm; Sept, daily 9am–5pm. **Closed:** Oct–Apr 14.

**CHEYENNE MOUNTAIN ZOO, Zoo Rd. off Mirada Rd. Tel. 475-9555.**

Located south of the Broadmoor hotel on the cool lower slopes of Cheyenne Mountain, 6,800 feet above sea level, this menagerie claims to be America's only mountain zoo. Not large by big-city standards, it nevertheless boasts some 600 animals from the familiar to the exotic—tigers, lions, elephants, hippopotamuses, monkeys, giraffes, and many more. New exhibits include rocky cliffs for mountain goats, a pebbled beach for penguins, and an animal-contact area where children can pet certain creatures. There's even an antique carousel.

Admission to the zoo includes road access to the **Will Rogers Shrine of the Sun,** a tall wooden structure built without nails in 1937 as a memorial to the beloved humorist. Inside is a pictorial biography of Rogers; outside, an impressive view of the surrounding countryside.

**Admission:** $5 adults, $4 seniors, $2.50 children 3–11, free for children under 3.

**Open:** Summer, daily 9am–5pm; winter, daily 9am–4pm.

**GHOST TOWN, 400 S. 21st St., Old Colorado City. Tel. 634-0696.**
Comprised of authentic 19th-century buildings relocated from other parts of Colorado, this "town" is out of the elements and under cover in Old Colorado City. There's a sheriff's office, jail, saloon, general store, livery stable, blacksmith shop, rooming house, assayer's office, and more. Animated frontier characters tell stories of the Old West, while a shooting gallery, antique arcade machines, and nickelodeons provide additional entertainment.
**Admission:** $3 adults, $1.50 children under 12.
**Open:** Summer, Mon–Sat 9am–6pm, Sun 1–6pm; winter, Wed–Sat 10am–4pm, Sun 1–4pm.

**MANITOU WATER SLIDE, 324 Manitou Ave., Manitou Springs. Tel. 685-5867.**
This water park has more than the thrilling slides. It includes a miniature golf course and the Miracle House, where gravity isn't what you thought it was.
**Admission:** $4 for 1 hour, $8 for all day; slide, $2.50 for 5 rides, $3.50 for 10 rides.
**Open:** Memorial Day weekend–Labor Day, daily 10am–8pm (golf until 11pm).

**NORTH POLE, foot of Pikes Peak Hwy. off U.S. 24, 5 miles west of Manitou Springs. Tel. 684-9432.**
Santa's workshop is busy from mid-May right up until Christmas Eve. Not only can kids visit shops where elves have some early Christmas gifts for sale, but they can also see Santa himself and whisper their requests into his ear. This 25-acre storybook village features numerous rides, including a miniature train and the *Enterprise* space shuttle, as well as magic shows and musical entertainment, snack shops, and an ice-cream parlor.
**Admission:** $7 ages 2–59, $3 seniors 60 and over, free for children under 24 months.
**Open:** May 15–31, daily 9am–5pm; June–Aug, daily 9am–6:30pm; Sept–Dec 24, Fri–Tues 9am–5pm. **Closed:** Christmas–May 14.

## ORGANIZED TOURS

Half- and full-day bus tours of Colorado Springs, Pikes Peak, Cripple Creek, the Air Force Academy, and other nearby attractions are offered by Gray Line Tours, doing business as **Pikes Peak Tours,** 3704 West Colorado Avenue (tel. 719/633-1181, or 800/345-8197). A variety of tours are offered May through October, including an evening visit to the Cave of the Winds and Seven Falls. Prices range from $15 to $50 per person.

Customized tours can be arranged through **Tailored Tours of Colorado Springs,** 3014 Brenner Place (tel. 574-7176), sponsored by the American Association of University Women; or **Talk of the Town,** 1313 Sunset Road (tel. 633-2724).

The leading local adventure-tour operator is **Gentle Earth Tours,** 2301 West Vermijo Street (tel. 633-2301). Trips may have a geology or natural-history orientation, and often involve hiking, rafting, or some other physical activity.

---

# 6. SPORTS & RECREATION

## SPECTATOR SPORTS

**AUTO RACING** The annual **Pikes Peak Auto Hill Climb** (tel. 685-4400), known as "the Race to the Clouds," is held annually on July 4. An international field of drivers negotiate the winding, hairpin turns of the final 12.4 miles of the Pikes Peak Highway, to the top of the 14,110-foot mountain.

**BASEBALL** The **Colorado Springs Sky Sox** of the Pacific Coast League, a

Cleveland Indians AAA farm team, play a full 140-game season, with 70 home games at Sky Sox Stadium, 4385 Tutt Avenue (tel. 597-3000). The season begins the second week of April and runs through Labor Day. Games normally begin at 7:05pm weekdays and 1:35pm weekends, though times are subject to change. Tickets are $4.50 for reserved seating, $3 for general admission. Call the stadium or check the newspaper sports pages for schedule information.

The **Air Force Academy** plays a spring schedule (Feb–May) against major college competition.

**BASKETBALL**   The **Air Force Academy** plays a full major-college schedule against NCAA Division 1 competition, primarily against Western Athletic Conference foes. The 30-game season begins in late November and continues until about mid-March. Home contests are played in Cadet Field House (tel. 472-1895).

**FOOTBALL**   Those same **Air Force Academy Falcons,** winners of the 1990 Liberty Bowl and members of the Western Athletic Conference, play an 11-game season from September to November. Falcon Stadium (tel. 472-1895 for ticket information) seats 52,153 fans. Call for schedules and ticket information.

**GREYHOUND RACING**   The **Rocky Mountain Greyhound Park,** 3701 North Nevada Avenue (tel. 719/632-1391 or 303/571-1775) has parimutuel dog races from September to November, Tuesday through Saturday at 8:15pm and Monday, Wednesday, and Saturday at 1:30pm. Admission is $1; reserved clubhouse seats are $3.

During Denver's June-to-August greyhound-racing season, there's off-track betting at this park.

**ICE HOCKEY**   There are not one, but two outstanding college ice-hockey teams in Colorado Springs. The **Air Force Academy,** of course, plays its home games during the winter season at the Cadet Field House (tel. 472-1895). **Colorado College,** a small but highly acclaimed 4-year institution in downtown Colorado Springs, plays its home hockey matches at the Broadmoor World Arena, 20 First Street (tel. 635-5200). Call for schedules and ticket information.

**RODEO**   The **Pikes Peak or Bust Rodeo,** held annually (since 1941) the second week of August, is a major stop on the Professional Rodeo Cowboys Association circuit. Its purse of over $135,000 makes it the second-largest rodeo in Colorado (after Denver's National Western Stock Show), 15th in North America. Events are held at 2pm and 8pm at 10,000-seat Penrose Stadium, 1045 West Rio Grande Avenue off Fountain Creek Boulevard (tel. 635-3547 or 520-6710). Various events around the city, including a parade, observe rodeo week.

**SOCCER**   A new community stadium in **Sand Creek Community Park,** on Tutt Avenue, opened in 1990. Used by teams from the Air Force Academy, Colorado College, and the University of Colorado–Colorado Springs, it seats 2,000 (there are plans to expand the seating capacity).

Not only does the Air Force Academy have one of the nation's premier collegiate soccer teams, but it also hosts the annual **Pikes Peak Invitational Soccer Tournament** (tel. 590-9977). Youth teams from 22 states compete in June on the academy athletic fields. The 1992 tournament will be the 17th annual.

# RECREATION

Most of the state and federal agencies that deal with aspects of outdoor recreation are headquartered in Denver. There are branch offices in Colorado Springs for the **Colorado Division of Parks and Outdoor Recreation,** 2126 North Weber Street (tel. 471-0900); the **Colorado Division of Wildlife,** also at 2126 North Weber Street (tel. 473-2945); and the **U.S. Forest Service,** Pike National Forest Ranger District, 601 South Weber Street (tel. 636-1602).

Leading sporting-goods dealers in the city include **Grand West Outfitters,** 1330 North Academy Boulevard (tel. 596-3031), and **Mountain Chalet,** 226 North Tejon Street (tel. 633-0732).

**AERIAL SPORTS**   Novices can get lessons in hang-gliding from the **Eagle's Nest School of Hang Gliding,** P.O. Box 25985, Colorado Springs, CO 80936 (tel. 719/594-0498). Classes are conducted year round by reservation, at a site 15 miles south of the city.

The **Black Forest Soaring Society,** 24566 David Johnson Loop, Elbert, CO 80106 (tel. 303/648-3623), some 30 miles northeast of the Springs, offers glider rides, rentals, and instruction. On Labor Day weekend, the **Colorado Springs Balloon Classic** sees more than 100 hot-air balloons launched from the city's Memorial Park. Admission is free.

**BICYCLING**   Aside from the 4-mile loop trail around Monument Valley Park (see "Parks & Gardens" in "Attractions," above), there are numerous other urban trails for bikers. Inquire at the city's Visitor Information Center, 104 South Cascade Avenue (tel. 635-1632), for the **Colorado Springs Area Bicycle Access Map.**

Off-road mountain biking has become "the thing to do" in Colorado in recent years. **Challenge Unlimited,** 1519 North Tejon Street (tel. 633-6399), hosts fully equipped, guided rides for every level of experience. Full-day trips in the Pikes Peak area include gourmet lunches.

**FISHING**   Most Colorado Springs anglers drive south 40 miles to the **Arkansas River,** or west to the Rocky Mountain streams and lakes, like **Eleven Mile Canyon Reservoir** and **Spinney Mountain Reservoir** on the South Platte River west of Florissant. Bass, catfish, walleye pike, and panfish are found in the streams of eastern Colorado; trout is the preferred sport fish of the mountain regions.

**Angler's Covey,** 917 West Colorado Avenue (tel. 471-2984), is a specialty fly-fishing shop and a good source of general fishing information for southern Colorado. It offers guided half- and full-day trips, as well as licenses, rentals, flies, tackle, and so forth.

**GOLF**   There are four municipal courses: **Cimarron Hills Golf Club,** 1850 Tuskegee Place (tel. 597-2637); **Patty Jewett Golf Course,** 900 East Española Street (tel. 578-6827); **Pinecreek at Briargate,** 7710 North Union Boulevard (tel. 594-9260); and **Valley Hi Municipal Golf Course,** 610 South Chelton Road (tel. 578-6351). Call for current greens fees and to reserve tee times.

The Springs's finest golf clubs are private. The 54-hole **Broadmoor Golf Club** (tel. 634-7711, ext. 5628) at the Broadmoor hotel has courses designed by Robert Trent Jones and Arnold Palmer, two driving ranges, and two pro shops. Its resident pro, Dow Finsterwald, is a former PGA champion. Greens fees are $40; mandatory carts, $22. Stay at the Broadmoor and you can play its courses. Ditto the **Cheyenne Mountain Conference Resort,** 3225 Broadmoor Valley Road (tel. 576-4600).

**HIKING**   Opportunities abound in municipal parks (see "Parks & Gardens" in "Attractions," above) and Pike National Forest, which bounds Colorado Springs to the west. The U.S. Forest Service district office can provide maps and general information.

Especially popular are the 7.5-mile **Waldo Canyon Trail,** with its trailhead just east of Cascade off U.S. 24; the 10-mile **Mount Manitou Trail,** starting in Ruxton Canyon above the hydroelectric plant; and the 12-mile **Barr Trail** to the summit of Pikes Peak. The new **Mueller State Park** (tel. 303/687-2366), 7½ miles south of Divide en route to Cripple Creek, has 25 miles of hiking and backpacking paths.

Backpackers into something a little different might consult **Pikes Peak Llama Treks,** 418 Pleasant Street (tel. 473-1468), about day hikes and extended trips, including fishing expeditions.

**HORSEBACK RIDING**   The **Mark Reyner Stables,** 3524 Paseo Road, at Palmer Park (tel. 634-4173), and the **Academy Riding Stables,** 4 El Paso

Boulevard, near the Garden of the Gods (tel. 633-5667), offer guided trail rides and lessons for children and adults by reservation.

**HUNTING** Opportunities for hunters abound in the plains east of Colorado Springs (especially for waterfowl) and in the Rockies west of the city (for deer, bear, even cougars). For information and license requirements, consult the Colorado Division of Wildlife or the U.S. Forest Service, Pike National Forest.

**ICE SKATING** The **Plaza Ice Chalet,** 111 South Tejon Street (tel. 633-2423), is open for public ice skating daily, with year-round instruction and rentals. **Broadmoor World Arena,** 30 First Street (tel. 635-5200 or 634-7711 ext. 5795), offers instruction and skate rental at times not already reserved for technical figure skaters or hockey teams. The arena has hosted four world figure-skating championships, and it's the site of the Broadmoor Ice Revue. Call for prices and schedules.

**RIVER RAFTING** Colorado Springs is only 40 miles from the Arkansas River near Cañon City. Among the licensed white-water outfitters who tackle the Royal Gorge is **Echo Canyon River Expeditions,** P.O. Box 1002, Colorado Springs, CO 80901 (tel. 719/275-3154, or 800/748-2953 Apr–Sept). Trips last 3 hours to 5 days, and range in price from about $40 to $400.

**SKIING** A small, family-oriented area, **Ski Broadmoor,** 4550 Cheyenne Mountain Zoo Road (tel. 635-3200), is primarily for beginning skiers. Owned by the Broadmoor hotel and operated by Vail Associates, it closed prior to the 1991–92 winter season, but many hope it will reopen soon.

The nearest major ski areas are **Breckenridge,** 105 miles northwest, and **Monarch,** 120 miles west near Garfield.

**SWIMMING** If your accommodation doesn't have a pool of its own, visit **Municipool,** 270 Union Boulevard (tel. 578-6634). There are also water slides and other wet-and-wild activities at **Colorado Springs Waterslide,** 501 West Garden of the Gods Road (tel. 597-6490), and **Manitou Water Park,** 327 Manitou Avenue, Manitou Springs (tel. 685-5867).

**TENNIS** Many city parks have tennis courts, including **Monument Valley Park,** just above Bijou Street north of downtown. Call the city Park and Recreation Department (tel. 578-6640) for information.

# 7. SAVVY SHOPPING

Five principal areas attract shoppers in Colorado Springs. The Manitou Springs and Old Colorado City neighborhoods are best for souvenir hunting and arts and crafts galleries. The Citadel and Chapel Hills malls combine major department stores with a variety of fashionable boutiques. Downtown Colorado Springs, of course, also has numerous fine shops.

**Shopping hours** vary from store to store and from shopping center to shopping center. In general, it's safe to say that shops will be open Monday through Friday from 10am to 9pm, on Saturday from 10am to 6pm, and on Sunday from noon to 5pm. Stores that cater to tourists have longer hours in summer, shorter hours in winter. Some may close their doors entirely between October and April.

## SHOPPING A TO Z
### ANTIQUES

**THE ANTIQUE EMPORIUM AT MANITOU SPRINGS, 719 Manitou Ave., Manitou Springs. Tel. 685-9195.**

A variety of furniture, books, clothing, glassware, household items, and other antiques can be found here.

**THE VILLAGERS, 2426 W. Colorado Ave., Old Colorado City. Tel. 632-1400.**
A diverse array of quality antiques and collectibles are sold. All proceeds go to Cheyenne Village, a community of adults with developmental disabilities.

## ART

**BUSINESS OF ART CENTER, 513 Manitou Ave., Manitou Springs. Tel. 685-1861.**
This renovated historic building is home to numerous artists' studios and a resource library, as well as a contemporary gallery and retail shop. Fine paintings and limited-edition prints, ceramics, textiles, sculpture, jewelry, and other works are displayed and sold. There's also an art-activities area for children. Open Monday through Saturday from 10am to 5pm.

**COLORADO SPRINGS ART GUILD/GALLERY, 731 N. Cascade Ave. Tel. 389-0303.**
A showcase for local artists, the guild has promoted fine arts in the Colorado Springs area since the late 1940s. It sponsors quarterly and annual juried shows and classes. Open Tuesday through Saturday from 10am to 5pm.

**COMMONWEAL ARTISTS CO-OP, 102 Cañon St., Manitou Springs. Tel. 685-1008.**
Local artists and craftspeople share responsibilities for this cooperative gallery.

**EL DORADO FINE ARTS GALLERY, 2504 W. Colorado Ave., Old Colorado City. Tel. 634-4075.**
Paintings in all media, sculpture, pottery, prints, and art cards are exhibited.

**MICHAEL GARMAN GALLERIES, 2418 W. Colorado Ave., Old Colorado City. Tel. 471-1600.**
Garman's lifelike sculpted miniatures delight everyone. His Old West dioramas are noteworthy, but slices of urban life and traditional Americana are equally wonderful.

## CRAFTS

**VAN BRIGGLE ART POTTERY, 600 S. 21st St., Old Colorado City. Tel. 633-7729.**
Founded in 1900 by Artus Van Briggle, who applied Chinese matte glaze to Rocky Mountain clays and imaginative art nouveau shapes, this is one of the oldest active art potteries in the United States. Today artisans demonstrate their craft, from "throwing on the wheel" to glazing and firing. Finished works are sold in a showroom.

## FASHIONS

**M.J. CREATIONS, 130 N. Tejon St. Tel. 632-4133.**
Classic and innovative women's fashions for moderate prices, with an emphasis on active wear.

**MILLER STOCKMAN, Citadel Mall, 750 Citadel Dr. E. Tel. 574-1520.**
In business since 1918, this purveyor of western wear stocks such brands as Abilene, Justin, and Stetson.

**WESTERN WAREHOUSE, 5506 N. Academy Blvd. Tel. 590-9711.**
This full-service western-wear outlet boasts more than 5,000 pairs of boots in stock, as well as a Native American jewelry counter.

## FOOD

**PATSY'S CANDY KITCHEN, 1540 S. 21st St. Tel. 633-7215.**
A popular chocolate and confection manufacturer, Patsy's offers factory tours. There's also a retail outlet here.

## GIFTS & SOUVENIRS

**COMPASSION INTERNATIONAL, 3955 Cragwood Dr. (Union Blvd. and Austin Bluffs Pkwy.). Tel. 594-9900.**
Third World gifts and other unusual items are sold at this store, which benefits a group that helps 130,000 children around the world. A video, photographs, and personal letters tell their story. Open Monday through Friday from 9am to 5pm.

**MUSHROOM MONDAY T-SHIRTS, 941 Manitou Ave., Manitou Springs. Tel. 685-1142.**
This large, well-established souvenir shirt shop has more than 100 shirt styles and colors, in all sizes. Thousands of designs can be applied with custom screen-printing.

**SIMPICH CHARACTER DOLLS, 2413 W. Colorado Ave., Old Colorado City. Tel. 636-3272.**
Exquisite handmade dolls are the creation of this specialty shop, which also stages classical string marionette productions. The shop is open Monday through Saturday from 10am to 5pm; call for puppet show times and reservations.

**SWISS MISS SHOP, 8455 U.S. 24 West, Cascade. Tel. 684-9679.**
Seemingly transplanted from the Alps, this 18-room gallery sells European-style gifts such as music boxes, cuckoo clocks, beer steins, Hummel figurines, and Tom Clark gnomes. One mile west of the Pikes Peak turnoff; open Monday through Saturday from 10am to 5pm.

## JEWELRY

**MANITOU JACK'S TRADING CO., 742 Manitou Ave., Manitou Springs. Tel. 685-5004.**
Black Hills gold, 10- and 14-karat, is the specialty here. There's also an extensive collection of Native American jewelry, pottery, sand paintings, and other art. The shop will create custom jewelry and perform repairs.

**OSBURN'S GIFT SHOP, 951 Manitou Ave., Manitou Springs. Tel. 685-9614.**
Colorado gold and silver, gold nuggets, Black Hills gold jewelry, Navajo silver jewelry, and other gem creations are available.

## MALLS & SHOPPING CENTERS

**CHAPEL HILLS MALL, 1710 Briargate Blvd. (N. Academy Blvd. at I-25). Tel. 594-0111.**
Joslins, Sears, Mervyn's, and K-Mart are among the 130-plus shops here. There's also a Gart Bros. sporting goods, a Fashion Bar, a cinema complex, and a dozen food outlets from Greek to Chinese. Open Monday through Saturday from 10am to 9pm and on Sunday from 11am to 6pm.

**THE CITADEL, 750 Citadel Dr. E. (N. Academy Blvd. at E. Platte Ave.). Tel. 591-2900.**
Southern Colorado's largest mall has 175 shops, including May D & F, J. C. Penney's, and Sears. Picnic-on-the-Terrace has 17 food outlets. Open Monday through Saturday from 10am to 9pm and on Sunday from 11am to 6pm.

## WINE

**PIKES PEAK VINEYARDS, 3901 Janitell Rd. Tel. 576-0075.**
Southern Colorado isn't renowned for its wine, but these vineyards are worth a

visit. Tours and wine tastings are offered in summer daily from 11am to 5pm; in winter, on Saturday from 11am to 5pm or by appointment.

# 8. EVENING ENTERTAINMENT

The Colorado Springs entertainment scene is spread throughout the metropolitan area. Pikes Peak Center, the Colorado Springs Fine Arts Center, the Broadmoor International Theatre, Colorado College, and the various facilities at the U.S. Air Force Academy are all outstanding venues for the performing arts. The city also supports dozens of cinemas, nightclubs, bars, and other after-dark attractions.

Current weekly entertainment schedules can be found in the Friday *Gazette Telegraph.* Consult also the listings in *Springs* magazine and *Steppin' Out,* free monthly tabloids.

Tickets for nearly all major entertainment and sporting events can be obtained from **TicketMaster** (tel. 303/290-TIXS) or its outlets, including Gart Bros. sporting goods (tel. 719/531-0606). Credit-card orders can be placed on American Express, MasterCard, or VISA. The agency adds a $3 charge to every ticket.

## THE PERFORMING ARTS
### MAJOR PERFORMING ARTS COMPANIES
### Classical Music & Opera

**COLORADO OPERA FESTIVAL, 27 S. Tejon St. Tel. 473-0073.**
Three performances of a classical opera are presented every year in late July at the Pikes Peak Center. In 1991 Mozart's *The Magic Flute* drew capacity crowds. English-language productions feature nationally known opera singers.
**Admission:** Tickets, $11–$45.

**COLORADO SPRINGS SYMPHONY ORCHESTRA, 1014 N. Weber St. Tel. 633-0333.**
This fine professional orchestra annually performs two dozen classical concerts, as well as youth and pops concerts, chamber concerts, a summer series, and two Christmastime institutions—*The Nutcracker* ballet and "Christmas Pops on Ice" at the Broadmoor World Arena. Most performances are at the Pikes Peak Center.
**Admission:** Tickets, $5–$22.

### Theater Companies

**BLUEBARDS, Arnold Hall Theatre, U.S. Air Force Academy. Tel. 472-4499.**
The Air Force Academy's cadet theater group performs to appreciative townspeople as well as fellow cadets.

**STAR BAR PLAYERS, Lon Chaney Theatre, City Auditorium, 221 E. Kiowa St. Tel. 578-6855.**
This resident theater company presents four full-length plays a year, two studio productions, and a children's Christmas show.

### Dance Companies

**COLORADO SPRINGS DANCE THEATRE, Pikes Peak Center, 190 S. Cascade Ave. Tel. 630-7434.**
The company presents several annual productions, including *The Nutcracker* ballet at Christmas, and supports leading national choreographers and dance companies on visits to Colorado Springs.
**Admission:** Tickets, $12 and $14.

**ROCKY MOUNTAIN CLOGGERS, P.O. Box 16706, Colorado Springs, CO 80901. Tel. 392-4791.**

This national exhibition clog-dance team does its best to start its audiences toe-tapping and hand-clapping. Dates vary.

## MAJOR CONCERT HALLS & ALL-PURPOSE AUDITORIUMS

**ARNOLD HALL THEATRE, Cadet Social Center, U.S. Air Force Academy. Tel. 472-4499.**
Everything from stage plays to lectures to concerts by top-name national performers takes place at this campus auditorium. Call for a current schedule.

**BROADMOOR INTERNATIONAL THEATRE, Lake Circle. Tel. 634-7711.**
Such entertainers as Liberace, Harry Belafonte, Jack Benny, and Bob Hope have performed here. The hall has a hydraulic-lift orchestra pit and 16,000 square feet of unobstructed, column-free seating.

**CITY AUDITORIUM, 221 E. Kiowa St. Tel. 578-6652.**
Conventions, trade shows, and concerts are regularly scheduled in the main hall. The Lon Chaney Theatre, with its resident Star Bar Players, is active with stage productions. There's also a small restaurant, the Curtain Call Café.

**COLORADO SPRINGS FINE ARTS CENTER, 30 W. Dale St. Tel. 634-5581.**
The performing-arts schedule at this civic facility (see "Museums & Galleries" in "Attractions," above) includes the Young Actors Theater, a repertory theater company, dance programs and concerts, and several film series.

**PIKES PEAK CENTER, 109 S. Cascade Ave. Tel. 520-7459.**
The primary performing-arts facility in Colorado Springs, this 2,000-seat concert hall in the heart of downtown has been acclaimed for its outstanding acoustics. The city's symphony orchestra and dance theater call it home. Top-flight touring entertainers usually make their concert appearances here as well.

## THEATERS

**FRONT RANGE COMMUNITY THEATRE, Monument. Tel. 488-2992.**
A fine small theater group based in a community 5 miles north of the Air Force Academy, just off I-25, the Front Range Theatre presents about four productions a year, including a summer musical with show tunes or contemporary pop music.

**OPEN EGG GALLERY & THEATRE, 318 N. Tejon St. Tel. 635-9240.**
There's always room for an avant-garde theater company, and this is Colorado Springs's. A recent favorite was an adaptation of Franz Kafka's *The Trial*.

**SIMPICH MARIONETTE THEATER, 2413 W. Colorado Ave., Old Colorado City. Tel. 636-3272** or 636-3539.
Classical string puppet productions are offered by this exclusive doll shop on an irregular basis. Call for show times and reservations.

## DINNER THEATER

**ABOUT TOWN DINNER THEATRE, 1837 S. Nevada Ave., Suite 171. Tel. 576-4845.**
Comedies, musical revues, and weekend melodramas like *The Legacy of Cuervo Gold, or, Chili Today, Hot Tamale* are the fare dished up by this tongue-in-cheek troupe. Many performances are at the Club House Restaurant, 130 East Kiowa Street (tel. 633-0590). Dinner is at 6:30pm, the show at 8pm.
**Admission:** Tickets, $17.50 dinner and show, $9 show only; reduced rates for children.

**FLYING W RANCH, 3330 Chuckwagon Rd. Tel. 598-4000,** or 800/748-3999.
This working cattle and horse ranch just north of the Garden of the Gods treats visitors to a western village of a dozen restored buildings and a mine train. The western stage show features bunkhouse comedy, cowboy balladry, and foot-stompin'

fiddle, banjo, and guitar music. Steak dinners are served ranch style at 5 and 8pm nightly, mid-May through September. The Winter Steak House is open October to December and March to May on Friday and Saturday evenings.

**Admission:** Tickets, $10 dinner and show.

**IRON SPRINGS CHATEAU, 444 Ruxton Ave., Manitou Springs. Tel. 685-5104** or 685-5572.

Located near the foot of the Pikes Peak Cog Railway, this popular comedy/melodrama dinner theater urges patrons to boo the villain and cheer the hero. Past productions have included *Gunsmoke Bonanza* and *The Promontory Point Predicament, or, She'll Be Comin' Round the Mountain When She Comes*—the latter starring Poker Pearl and Manly Darling. A family-style dinner, served Wednesday through Sunday from 6 to 7:15pm, offers all you can eat of fried chicken or barbecued ribs. You'll need reservations. Showtime is mid-May through September 8:30pm, with a late-night curtain-call revue at 10:50pm.

**Admission:** Tickets, dinner and show, $17 adults, $16 seniors, $9 children; show only, $9 adults, $8 seniors, $4.50 children.

**MCKENNA'S PUB AND RESTAURANT, 3725 Austin Bluffs Pkwy. Tel. 599-3020.**

The dinner show here is anything but melodramatic. Instead, a lively cast presents musical revues featuring Broadway and popular music from years past, often the '50s and '60s. Shows start at 6:30pm on Friday and Saturday.

**Admission:** Tickets, $15.75.

# THE CLUB & MUSIC SCENE
## NIGHTCLUBS, CABARETS & COMEDY CLUBS

**CAHOOTS, in the Colorado Springs Marriott, 5580 Tech Center Dr. Tel. 260-1800.**

There's live Top-40 music for dancing every night except Monday at this lively hotel nightclub, perhaps the most elegant in Colorado Springs. Cahoots is open from 5pm to 2am Tuesday to Thursday, from 4pm to 2am on Friday, and from 7pm to 2am on Saturday.

**Admission:** Free Tues–Thurs, $3 Sat–Sun.

**JEFF VALDEZ' COMEDY CORNER, 1305 N. Academy Blvd. Tel. 591-0707.**

A regionally syndicated television show, "Almost Live," makes its home at this club, which features local and touring stand-up comedians Wednesday through Sunday. Doors open at 7pm; shows are at 8:30pm Wednesday through Friday, and at 8pm and 10:30pm Saturday and Sunday.

**Admission:** $4–$20, depending on performer.

## COUNTRY & ROCK MUSIC

**COWBOYS, 3900 Palmer Park Blvd. Tel. 596-1212.**

Two-steppers and country-and-western music lovers flock to this east-side club, open daily from 4pm to 2am.

**Admission:** Sun–Tues $1; Wed $3 women, $4 men; Thurs $1 women, $2 men; Fri–Sat $2 women, $3 men.

**THE CLUB HOUSE RESTAURANT AND UNDERGROUND PUB, 130 E. Kiowa St. Tel. 633-0590.**

This popular hangout for college students and other young people offers progressive rock on its basement stage. Open daily from 11am to 2am.

**Admission:** Free Mon–Wed, $2–$4 Thurs–Sun.

## JAZZ, BLUES & FOLK MUSIC

**DUBLIN DOWNS, Dublin House Restaurant, 1850 Dominion Way. Tel. 528-1704.**

Leading regional jazz combos and solo musicians hold forth at this club. Hours are

from 4pm to 1am Monday through Friday, and from 10:30am to 1am Saturday and Sunday.
**Admission:** $3 Fri–Sat (for basement club).

### POOR RICHARD'S RESTAURANT, 324 N. Tejon St. Tel. 632-7721.

An eclectic variety of performers appear here, presenting everything from acoustic folk to Celtic melodies, jazz to Broadway revues. There are even open-mike nights when anything goes. Open daily till 10pm.
**Admission:** Free or $2–$5, depending on performer.

## DANCE CLUBS & DISCOS

### MAXI'S LOUNGE, in the Red Lion Hotel, 1775 E. Cheyenne Mountain Blvd., at I-25. Tel. 576-8900.

A disc jockey plays rock classics of the '60s through the '80s for dancing most nights. Open daily.
**Admission:** Free.

### SHADOWS, in the Sheraton Inn North Academy, 8110 N. Academy Blvd., at I-25. Tel. 598-5770.

Shadows draws an older crowd on weekends, when DJs spin the discs of the '50s, '60s, and '70s. Open daily till 2am.
**Admission:** Free.

## THE BAR SCENE

### BECKETT'S RESTAURANT AND BREWPUB, 128 S. Tejon St. Tel. 635-3535.

Five different handcrafted ales and stouts, including Harvest Wheat, Red Dog Ale, and Grizzly Brown, highlight the drink menu at this casually elegant spot. Steak, seafood, and pasta dishes dominate the meal menu.

### THE GOLDEN BEE, rear basement entrance of the Broadmoor International Theatre, Lake Circle. Tel. 634-7111.

An opulent English pub was disassembled, shipped from Great Britain, and reassembled piece by piece to create this delightful drinking establishment. You can drink imported Bass Ale by the yard if you choose, while enjoying a beef-and-kidney pie or other such pub fare.

### JUDGE BALDWIN'S BREWING COMPANY, in the Antlers Doubletree Hotel, 4 S. Cascade Ave. Tel. 473-5600.

If you don't like the home concoction at this fine brewpub, you've got a choice of 20 other "designer beers" from around the United States—such as Pete's Wicked Ale from Palo Alto, California, or Simpatico Amber from Dubuque, Iowa. There's a fine light meal menu and a sinful dessert selection.

### THE RITZ GRILL, 15 S. Tejon St. Tel. 635-8484.

Especially popular with young professionals after work and the chic clique later in the evening, this restaurant-lounge, with a large central bar, brings an art deco feel to downtown Colorado Springs.

## LASER LIGHT SHOW

### LASER CANYON, Cave of the Winds, U.S. 24, Manitou Springs. Tel. 685-5446.

Laser light-show enthusiasts won't want to miss this one. Effects 15 stories high and half a mile long are projected within a canyon adjacent to Cave of the Winds, enhanced by a concert sound system. There's one show nightly at 9pm, May 1 through September 15.

**Admission:** Tickets, $3 adults, $1 children 6–15, free for children under 6.

---

# 9. EASY EXCURSIONS FROM COLORADO SPRINGS

---

## CRIPPLE CREEK

This famous old mining town on Pikes Peak's southwestern flank was known as the world's greatest gold camp after the precious mineral was first discovered here in 1890. By the time mining ceased in 1961, over $800 million worth of ore had been taken from the surrounding hills. Today, with the beginning of limited-stakes casino gambling in late 1991, residents of this picturesque mountain village—45 miles west of Colorado Springs via U.S. 24 west and Colo. 67 south—await a different kind of gold rush.

At the turn of the 20th century, Cripple Creek (elevation 9,396 ft.) had a population of 25,000, making it the fourth-largest city in Colorado. (Today, there are about 700.) It had a stock exchange, two opera houses, five daily newspapers, 16 churches, 19 schools, and 73 saloons, plus an elaborate streetcar system, and a railroad depot that saw 18 arrivals and departures a day. The neighboring community of **Victor** (elevation 9,729 ft.), 6 miles south, had 18,000 residents (now 300). It is said that the streets of Victor really were paved with gold—poorer grades of ore not fit for the mills. And there were 11 other towns in the district, most of them now ghost towns with names like Altman, Anaconda, Cameron, Elkton, Gillett, Goldfield, and Independence.

The Cripple Creek area has known some famous folk over the years. Lowell Thomas was a newspaper reporter in Victor, where Jack Dempsey fought his first professional fight in the Gold Coin Club. Bernard Baruch was a telegrapher at the Midland terminal depot. Texas Guinan, the New York burlesque queen, started in show biz as a church organist in Anaconda. Groucho Marx, stranded without money for a cigar, drove a grocery wagon in Cripple Creek for a time.

One of the town's unique attractions is a herd of wild donkeys—descendants of the miners' runaways—that roam freely through the hills and into the streets during the summer months. The year's biggest celebration, Donkey Derby Days in late June, is climaxed by a donkey race from Victor to Cripple Creek.

For travel information on the area, contact the **Cripple Creek Chamber of Commerce,** P.O. Box 650, Cripple Creek, CO 80813 (tel. 719/689-3041); the **Victor Chamber of Commerce,** P.O. Box 123, Victor, CO 80860 (tel. 719/689-3211); or the **Cripple Creek Two Mile High Club,** 347 East Bennett Avenue, Cripple Creek, CO 80813 (tel. 719/689-2594).

### WHAT TO SEE & DO

**CRIPPLE CREEK DISTRICT MUSEUM, east end of Bennett Ave. Tel. 689-2634.**

Located in the old Midland Terminal Depot, this outstanding small museum is packed with turn-of-the-century relics. There is a floor of Victorian rooms, a floor of transportation and mining artifacts, an adjacent assay office where fire-testing of local ores persists, and a heritage gallery with a natural-history display, old photographs, and paintings. Of special interest are multilevel glass models of district mines.
    **Admission:** $2 adults, $1 children 5 to 12, free for children under 5.
    **Open:** Mid May–mid Sept, 10am–5pm daily; rest of year, 10am–5pm Sat–Sun.

**CRIPPLE CREEK & VICTOR NARROW GAUGE RAILROAD CO., Midland Terminal Depot, east end of Bennett Ave. Tel. 689-2640.**

Before or after a museum tour, many visitors board this old train for a 4-mile trip past abandoned mines to the ghost town of Anaconda. A 15-ton "iron horse" steam

locomotive pulls the train out of the station approximately every 45 minutes beginning at 10am, Memorial Day weekend through the first weekend of October.
**Admission:** $5 adults, $2.50 children 12 and under.
**Open:** Memorial Day weekend–first weekend of Oct; first run 10am, last run 4pm.

### MOLLIE KATHLEEN GOLD MINE, Colo. 67 North. Tel. 689-2465.

Rated by the National Geographic Society as the single most outstanding tour in Colorado, this is a rare chance to spend time inside an actual gold mine. Experienced hard-rock miners join visitors on a 1,000-foot underground descent to explain and demonstrate the mining process. Gold production ceased at the Mollie Kathleen in 1961 because of the high costs of hard-rock mining, but the equipment remains in place. Guides point out gold veins and give visitors a free ore specimen.
**Admission:** $8 adults, $5 children 5 to 12, children under 5 free.
**Open:** Memorial Day–Oct, 9am–5pm daily.

### MOUNT PISGAH SCENIC DRIVE, 1 mile west on Teller Co. Rd. 1. Tel. 689-2304 or 689-2127.

A private road leads to the top of a knob providing a 360° view, including almost half of Colorado. The proprietors claim to offer the longest view of the Continental Divide in the United States.
**Admission:** $2 adults, $1 teenagers, free for children under 12.
**Open:** May–Dec, daily 9am–sunset, weather permitting. **Closed:** Jan–Apr.

### OLD HOMESTEAD PARLOUR HOUSE, 353 E. Myers Ave. Tel. 689-3090.

The last and most elegant of Cripple Creek's infamous brothels stands alone on an otherwise deserted street, one block south of Bennett Avenue. Now a museum, the house has such original fixtures as velvet drapes, Persian carpets, and a 17th-century liquor cabinet. The tour includes music and entertainment rooms, a dining area, and the five second-floor bedrooms.
**Admission:** $2.
**Open:** May–Oct, daily 11am–4pm.

### VICTOR/LOWELL THOMAS MUSEUM, City Hall, Third and Victor Sts., Victor. Tel. 689-2766.

Memorabilia from the days when Victor was known as "the city of mines," and a family collection memorializing hometown boy Lowell Thomas, are the focuses of this small museum.
**Admission:** $1 adults, free for children under 12.
**Open:** May 1–Oct 15, daily 9am–5pm.

## Scenic Drives

Three separate drives of particular beauty offer alternatives to Colo. 67 out of Cripple Creek and Victor. None is paved, all are narrow and winding, but all are passable to everyday vehicles under normal road and weather conditions. All are roughly 30 miles in length, but require some 90 minutes to negotiate.

The **Gold Camp Road** leads east from Victor to Colorado Springs via the North Cheyenne Cañon. Teddy Roosevelt said that this trip up the old Short Line Railroad bed had "scenery that bankrupts the English language."

The **Phantom Canyon Road** leads south from Victor to Florence, following another old narrow-gauge railroad bed known as the Gold Belt Line. Ghost towns and fossil areas mark this route.

The **Shelf Road** leads south from Cripple Creek to Cañon City on an old toll stage route blasted out of the sidewall of Fourmile Canyon. This route is not recommended to anyone afraid of heights, and should definitely be avoided when the road is wet, unless you have a four-wheel-drive vehicle.

## WHERE TO STAY

**IMPERIAL HOTEL, 123 N. Third St., Cripple Creek, CO 80813. Tel.**

**719/689-2922,** or 719/471-8878 in Colorado Springs. 31 rms, 2 suites (19 with bath). A/C TV
**$ Rates:** $28–$38 single; $35–$45 double. AE, MC, V.

Built in 1896 following a disastrous fire that razed most of the city, the fully renovated Imperial is the only original Cripple Creek hotel still standing. Except for a few years during World War II, it has been in continuous operation. Every room is a little different, and many share baths, but all are furnished with Victorian antiques.

The hotel has two terrific dining rooms and four bars, the best known of which is the Red Rooster—so called because of its international collection of roosters. The Imperial Players, the longest-running melodrama company in the United States, perform two shows daily (except Monday) in the Gold Bar Room Theatre, mid-June through Labor Day; times are 2 and 8:30pm Tuesday through Saturday, and 1 and 4:30pm on Sunday. Tickets are $6 to $8 for adults, $3.50 for children under 12.

**PORTLAND INN, 412 W. Portland Ave. (P.O. Box 32), Victor, CO 80860. Tel. 719/689-2102.** 4 rms (1 with bath).
**$ Rates** (including continental breakfast): $35–$75 single or double. AE, DISC, MC, V.

This restored turn-of-the-century home has a private living room and kitchen for guests, a sun deck, and an outdoor hot tub. Hot, homemade breads are served with a large continental breakfast. Children are very welcome.

## WHERE TO DINE

**THE BRANCH, Melody's Mall, 236 E. Bennett Ave. Tel. 689-3127.**
**Cuisine:** DELI.
**$ Prices:** $4–$10. MC, V.
**Open:** Daily 11am–8pm.

Homemade soups, salads, sandwiches, quiche, and nightly dinner specials are the healthy fare here. Musicians play while you dine.

**RED LANTERN INN, 353 Myers Ave. Tel. 689-2519.**
**Cuisine:** STEAK/SEAFOOD. **Reservations:** Suggested.
**$ Prices:** Main courses $6–$16. AE, DISC, MC, V.
**Open:** May–Sept, Sun–Thurs 6–9pm, Fri–Sat 6–10pm.

The dining room of the Old Homestead Parlour House becomes a fine, fully licensed restaurant in the evening, boasting prime rib, barbecued ribs, chicken, seafood, Rocky Mountain oysters, and 24-ounce Porterhouse steaks.

# FLORISSANT

A small village 35 miles west of Colorado Springs on U.S. 24, Florissant was given the French name for "flowering" because its hillsides are ablaze with wildflowers in spring.

There's superb **fishing** at lakes and streams in this area, particularly for German browns and cutthroats at Spinney Mountain Reservoir west of here. And the 7,000-acre **Dome Rock State Wildlife Area** to the east attracts nature-loving hikers with its elk, bighorn sheep, eagles, and other creatures. Half a mile south on Teller County Road No. 1 is the Florissant Fossil Beds National Monument.

**FLORISSANT FOSSIL BEDS NATIONAL MONUMENT, P.O. Box 185, Florissant, CO 80816. Tel. 748-3253.**

The fossils in this 6,000-acre National Park Service property are preserved in rocks of ancient Lake Florissant, which existed in the Oligacene Epoch, 26 to 38 million years ago. Volcanic eruptions over half a million years trapped plants and animals under layers of ash and dust; the creatures were fossilized as the sediment settled and became shale.

The detailed impressions, first discovered in 1874, offer the most extensive record of this kind in the world today. Some 80,000 specimens have been removed by scientists, including 11,000 separate species of insects! Dragonflies, beetles, ants; every known species of fossil butterfly in the New World; plus spiders, fish, some mammals and birds—all are perfectly preserved from as long ago as 35 million years. Leaves from birches, willows, maples, beeches, and hickories, and needles from fir trees and sequoias, are plentiful. Palm trees show how the climate has changed.

Mud flows also buried forests during this long period of time, petrifying the trees where they stood. Nature trails pass petrified sequoia stumps, one 10 feet in diameter and 11 feet high. All told, the national monument has some 12 miles of hiking trails.

There's a display of fossil impressions at the **visitor center,** which also offers interpretive programs.

An added attraction within the national monument is the homestead of Adaline Hornbek, who pioneered the land here with her three sons in 1878. Still containing period furnishings, it's open to visitors.

A 16-mile all-weather gravel road connects Florissant directly with Cripple Creek. **Admission:** $3.

**Open:** Mid-May to mid-Sept, daily 8am–7pm; the rest of the year, daily 8am–4:30pm. **Closed:** New Year's Day, Thanksgiving, and Christmas.

# BOULDER

**K**nown primarily as a young people's town, Boulder (pop. 84,000) is a sophisticated university community, a center for high-technology industries, and one of America's outdoor-sports capitals. The University of Colorado has been here since 1877, but it is only in the decades since World War II that the city has blossomed.

Set at the foot of the Flatiron Range of the Rockies, just 30 miles northwest of downtown Denver and only 74 feet higher than the "Mile High City," Boulder was settled by hopeful miners in 1858 and named for the large rocks in the area. Welcomed by Chief Niwot and the resident southern Arapahoe tribespeople, the miners struck gold in the nearby hills the following year. By the 1870s Boulder had become a regional rail and trade center for mining and farming. The university, founded later that decade, became the economic mainstay after the bottom fell out of mining around the turn of the century.

Since the 1950s Boulder has grown as a center for scientific and environmental research. The National Center for Atmospheric Research, the National Bureau of Standards, the Solar Forecast Center, and other modern governmental institutions located here. IBM, Storage Tek, Ball Aerospace, and other forward-looking private firms followed. (To some folks, Boulder is "Silicon Mountain.")

## 1. ORIENTATION

### ARRIVING

**BY AIR**  Boulder doesn't have its own commercial airport. Air travelers must fly into Denver's Stapleton International Airport, then make ground connections to Boulder.

The **Boulder Airporter** limo van (tel. 303/321-3222) leaves Stapleton hourly from 8am to 10pm, and Boulder hourly from 6am to 8pm; weekends and holidays have a more restricted schedule. Passengers should check in at the Airport Counter, Baggage Level, Door 6, at Stapleton. Pickups in Boulder are scheduled from certain hotels, on call from others, and from the University of Colorado campus. One-way fare is $8 per person for the 40-minute drive from the airport, or $11.50 for door-to-door pickup service.

**Boulder Limousine Airport Express** (tel. 449-5466) charges $32 to take two people from Boulder to Stapleton Airport in a formal limousine; $38 for up to six people in a stretch limousine.

By **Boulder Yellow Cab** (tel. 442-2277), the airport fare is $36 one way, for one to five passengers.

**Regional Transportation District (RTD) buses** (tel. 299-6000) make

# WHAT'S SPECIAL ABOUT BOULDER

### People-Watching

☐ The Pearl Street Mall, once the haunt of "Mork and Mindy," still frequented by a fascinating cross section of people.

☐ The University of Colorado, the leading institute of higher learning in the Rockies.

### Natural Attractions

☐ The Flatirons, a dramatic geologic uplift that creates a jagged wall behind Boulder.

☐ Boulder Creek Path, a 5½-mile park through the middle of the city.

### Industrial Tours

☐ The National Center for Atmospheric Research, which studies global warming, acid rain, and other world problems.

☐ Celestial Seasonings, the company that made herbal teas fashionable, imports 100 ingredients from 35 countries.

☐ Boulder Brewing Co., the nation's first microbrewery (in 1979).

### The Arts

☐ The Colorado Music Festival, with top classical artists from all over the world.

☐ Leanin' Tree Museum of Western Art, one of the finest contemporary western art displays.

☐ The Colorado Shakespeare Festival, rated one of the top three in the U.S.

### Events/Festivals

☐ The Kinetic Conveyance Challenge, with the most creative and bizarre human-powered land vehicles and sea vessels imaginable.

☐ The CU Trivia Bowl, featuring trivia buffs of all ages.

☐ The Great American Beer Festival attracts more than 60 small breweries to the nation's largest beer-tasting exhibit.

### Sports

☐ The University of Colorado football team, national collegiate champion in 1990, attracting tens of thousands of fans to home games.

☐ The Number One sports town in America according to *Outside* magazine.

---

one-way airport runs for $2.50 (exact change required). Trips start from or end at the main terminal at 14th Street and Walnut Street hourly, daily from 6am to 11pm.

**BY BUS   Greyhound/Trailways** buses (tel. 292-6111) have regular daily arrivals and departures from the RTD Terminal at 14th Street and Walnut Street. Call for route, fare, and schedule information.

**BY CAR**   The **Boulder Turnpike (U.S. 36)** departs I-25 north of Denver, almost opposite the I-76 interchange, and passes through the suburbs of Westminster, Broomfield, and Louisville before reaching Boulder some 25 minutes later.

If you're coming in from the north, take the Longmont exit from I-25 and follow **Colo. 119** all the way. Longmont is 7 miles due west of the freeway; Boulder is another 15 miles southwest via the Longmont Diagonal.

**Other routes** leading into and out of Boulder are U.S. 36 north to Lyons and Rocky Mountain National Park; Colo. 119 west to Nederland and Central City; Colo. 93 south to Golden; and Colo. 7 east to Brighton.

## TOURIST INFORMATION

The **Boulder Bureau of Conference Services and Cultural Affairs,** 2440 Pearl Street (at Folsom Street), Boulder, CO 80302 (tel. 303/442-1044, or 800/444-

0447), is open Monday through Friday from 9am to 5pm with excellent maps, brochures, and general information on the city.

From Memorial Day to Labor Day, there are additional **visitor information centers** at the Davidson Mesa overlook, a couple of miles southeast of Boulder on U.S. 36 from Denver; and on the Pearl Street Mall at 14th Street.

## CITY LAYOUT

From the mountains on Boulder's west, numbered north-south streets run east, beginning with 3rd Street. (The eastern city limits are at 61st Street, although the numbers run all the way to the Boulder County line at 124th Street in Broomfield.) U.S. 36, where it does a 45° turn to the north upon entering Boulder, becomes **28th Street,** a major commercial artery. The **Longmont Diagonal** (Colo. 119 east), coming in from the northeast, intersects 28th at the north end of the city.

To reach downtown Boulder from the highway, turn west on **Canyon Boulevard** (Colo. 119 west) and north on **Broadway,** which would be 12th Street if it had a number. It's two blocks to the **Pearl Street Mall,** a four-block pedestrians-only strip from 11th Street to 15th Street that constitutes the city center. Boulder's few one-way streets circle the Mall: 15th Street is one way north, 11th and 14th one way south, **Walnut Street** (a block south of the Mall) one way east, and **Spruce Street** (a block north) one way west.

Broadway continues across the Mall, eventually joining U.S. 36 north of the city. South of Arapahoe Avenue, Broadway turns to the southeast, skirting the University of Colorado campus and becoming Colo. 93 (the **Foothills Highway** to Golden) after crossing **Baseline Road.** Baseline follows a straight line from east Boulder, across U.S. 36 and Broadway, past Chautauqua park and up the mountain slopes. To its south, **Table Mesa Drive** pursues a similar course.

The **Foothills Parkway** (not to be confused with the Foothills Highway) is the principal north-south route on the east side of Boulder, extending from U.S. 36 at Table Mesa Drive to the Longmont Diagonal; **Arapahoe Avenue,** a block south of Canyon Boulevard, continues across 28th Street as Colo. 7, the main east-west route.

# 2. GETTING AROUND

**BY BUS** The **Regional Transportation District (RTD),** 14th Street and Walnut Street (tel. 299-6000), operates Monday through Friday from 5am to midnight and on Saturday and Sunday from 6am to midnight. Fares within the city are 60¢, (15¢ for seniors). A 10-ride book costs $4.75. There are schedules at the depot and other locations around the city.

**BY TAXI** **Boulder Yellow Cab** (tel. 442-2777) offers 24-hour service. Rates are $1.20 at flagfall and $1.20 per mile. It's almost always necessary to call for a taxi.

**BY CAR** For regulations and advice on driving in Colorado, see "Getting Around" in Chapter 2. There's a local office of the **American Automobile Association (AAA)** at 1933 28th Street (tel. 442-0383).

**Parking** Most downtown streets have parking meters, with rates of about 25¢ an hour. Downtown parking lots get about $1 an hour for short-term parking. Outside downtown, free parking is generally available on side streets.

**Car Rentals** Car-rental agencies in Boulder include: **Avis,** 4700 Baseline Road (tel. 499-1136, or 800/331-1212); **Budget,** 1345 28th Street (tel. 444-9054, or 800/222-6772); **Hertz,** 1760 14th Street (tel. 443-3520, or 800/327-7607); and **National,** 2960 Center Green Court (tel. 442-5110, or 800/227-7368).

**BY BICYCLE** Boulder is a wonderful place for bicycling, with bike paths throughout the city and an extensive trail system leading for miles beyond (see "Sports & Recreation," below).

Among several places that rent mountain and touring bikes are **Doc's Ski and Sports,** 629 South Broadway (tel. 499-0963), and **Full Cycle,** 1205 13th Street, near campus (tel. 440-7771). Rates are typically $5 an hour, $20 a day.

If the shop is out of the "Boulder Bicycling Map" ($3), check with the visitor center or the **City of Boulder Bicycle Program** (tel. 441-3216).

**ON FOOT**   Many of Boulder's attractions can best be seen by pure footpower, especially around the Pearl Street Mall and University of Colorado campus.

# FAST FACTS     BOULDER

**Area Code**   The telephone area code for the Boulder region is 303.

**Baby-sitters**   Front desks at major hotels often can make arrangements on your behalf. The city **Child Care Referral Service** (tel. 441-3180), open Monday through Friday from 1 to 5pm, can also help.

**Banks**   Most banks are open Monday through Thursday from 9am to 4pm and on Friday from 9am to 6pm. Major banks include **1stBank,** 6500 Lookout Road (tel. 530-1000); **Arapahoe National Bank,** 2500 Arapahoe Avenue (tel. 443-4933); and **Colorado National Bank,** Crossroads Mall, 28th Street and Arapahoe Avenue (tel. 444-1234). **Plus System** (tel. 800/THE-PLUS) cash machines can be found at strategic locations throughout the city.

**Drugstores**   Reliable prescription services are available at the **Medical Center Pharmacy** in the Boulder Medical Center, 2750 North Broadway (tel. 440-3111), and **Jones Drug and Camera Center,** 1370 College Avenue (tel. 443-4420). If it's 3 in the morning and you can't get your prescription, call a hospital.

**Emergencies**   For police, fire, or medical emergencies, call **911.** For **Colorado State Patrol** emergencies, call 303/239-4501.

**Eyeglasses**   You can get fast repairs or replacement of lost or broken glasses at **Boulder Optical,** 1928 14th Street (tel. 442-4521), just off the Pearl Street Mall.

**Hairdressers/Barbers**   A couple of good bets on the Mall are **Barbara the Barber,** 1035 Pearl Street (tel. 449-3061), and **Pompadours,** 1320 Pearl Street, Suite 200 (tel. 938-8015). For budget cuts, try **Supercuts,** 1310 College Avenue (tel. 444-8922).

**Hospitals**   Full medical services, including 24-hour emergency treatment, are available at **Boulder Community Hospital,** 1100 Balsam Avenue, at North Broadway (tel. 440-2037).

**Information**   See "Orientation," above.

**Laundry/Dry Cleaning**   Most major hotels offer valet drop-off and pickup service. Some motels may have guest laundries. A popular student Laundromat is **Duds 'n Suds,** in the Crossroad Commons, 2317 30th Street (tel. 440-WASH), so named because the washing machines share turf with a tavern! For dry cleaning, try **Dependable Cleaners,** Village Shopping Center, Folsom Avenue south of Canyon Boulevard (tel. 443-0290).

**Libraries**   The main branch of the **Boulder Public Library** is at 9th Street and Canyon Boulevard (tel. 441-3100). It's open Monday through Thursday from 9am to 9pm, on Friday and Saturday from 9am to 6pm, and on Sunday from noon to 6pm. A local library card is required to check out material. Visitors are also welcome to use the University of Colorado's **Norlin Library.**

**Liquor Laws**   See "Fast Facts: Colorado" in Chapter 2.

**Lost Property**   Consult the **Boulder Police** (tel. 441-4444).

**Newspapers/Magazines**   The *Boulder Daily Camera* is an award-winning daily newspaper. Many townspeople also read the campus paper, the *Colorado Daily,* available all over town. Both Denver dailies—the *Denver Post* and *Rocky Mountain News*—are also sold at newsstands throughout the city. The free *Boulder* magazine, published three times a year, lists seasonal events and other information on restaurants and the arts.

**Photographic Needs**   For standard processing requirements (including

2-hour slide processing) as well as custom lab work, see **Photo Craft Laboratories,** downtown at 1881 Ninth Street (tel. 447-2157) and at 3550 Arapahoe Avenue (tel. 442-6410). For equipment and repairs, see **Jones Drug and Camera Center,** 1370 College Avenue (tel. 443-4320).

**Police**   In an emergency, dial **911.** For standard business, call 441-4444.

**Post Office**   The **Main Post Office** is downtown at 15th Street and Walnut Street (tel. 938-1100), open Monday through Friday from 9am to 5pm.

**Radio/TV**   Boulder radio stations include KBCO (1190 AM and 97.3 FM) for album-oriented rock; KBOL (1490 AM) for news, sports, and contemporary rock; KGNU (88.5 FM), public radio; KPOF (910 AM) for Christian news and music; and KVOD (99.5 FM) for classical music. Boulder also is within reception range of most Denver stations. The local cable TV channel is 28. For other stations, see "Fast Facts: Denver" in Chapter 4.

**Religious Services**   Not only are most major religious denominations represented in Boulder, but the city is a major center for followers of New Age and Eastern belief systems. Check the *Yellow Pages* for a complete listing.

**Safety**   See "Fast Facts: Denver" in Chapter 4.

**Shoe Repairs**   Shoes and boots are quickly repaired, often while you wait, at **Quik-Step** in the Crossroads Mall (tel. 444-5519).

**Taxes**   Colorado state **sales tax** is 3.7%. Boulder County tax is 5.7%—a total of 9.4%. This also applies to hotel rooms.

**Telephone/Fax**   Local calls are normally 25¢. Facsimiles can be transmitted by most major hotels at a nominal cost to guests, or 24 hours a day from **Kinko's,** 1717 Walnut Street (tel. 442-4521). For **directory assistance,** dial 1-555-1212.

**Useful Telephone Numbers**   The **poison control center** (tel. 629-1123), **rape assistance** (tel. 443-7300), **road conditions** (tel. 639-1111 for a recording, or 639-1234 statewide), **ski reports** (tel. 837-9907 for a recording), **weather** (tel. 398-3964).

# 3. ACCOMMODATIONS

These categories define price ranges: "Expensive," more than $100 per night double; "Moderate," $70 to $100; "Inexpensive," $40 to $70; "Budget," less than $40 per night double. An additional 9.4% sales tax is levied onto all bills, and is not included in the rates.

## EXPENSIVE

**CLARION HARVEST HOUSE, 1345 28th St., Boulder, CO 80302. Tel. 303/443-3850,** or 800/CLARION. Fax 303/443-1480. 265 rms, 5 suites. A/C TV TEL

**$ Rates:** Nov–May 15, $89–$110 single; $109–$130 double. May 16–Aug, $95–$115 single; $115–$135 double. Sept–Oct, $93–$113 single; $113–$133 double. Year-round suites $150–$395. AE, CB, DC, DISC, JCB, MC, V.
   **Parking:** Free.

Few downtown hotels anywhere could have grounds as spacious and lovely as the Harvest House, dubbed the Clarion chain's "hotel of the year" for 1990. Located on the mountain side of U.S. 36 as it enters Boulder from Denver, the Harvest House looks like almost any other four-story hotel from the front. But the hotel's backyard melds into a park surrounding the east end of the 4.8-mile Boulder Creek Path, a worthy object of city pride (see "Attractions," below). Guests can swim, ride bicycles, play tennis or volleyball, and pretend they're at a country resort.

No guest room has less than a "deluxe" designation. All rooms (appointed in dark mauves or peaches) have one king-size or two double beds, a lounge chair and ottoman, remote-control TV, and direct-dial phone (50¢ local calls). Spacious VIP Tower accommodations have upgraded amenities such as hairdryers and bathrobes, daily newspapers, and an extra phone jack for a computer modem; they also include a continental breakfast and cocktail hour in the wing's Club Room.

**Dining/Entertainment:** The Bistro serves three American-style meals daily. Steak and seafood specials run $12.25 to $16.95 at dinner; lunch sandwiches and light dishes are in the $3.50 to $7.50 range. The Bistro is open Monday through Saturday from 6:30am to 10pm and on Sunday from 6:30am to 2pm and 5 to 10pm. Champ's, a popular sports bar with a big fireplace for winter gatherings, is also open daily.

**Services:** Room service, valet laundry, no-smoking rooms, facilities for the disabled.

**Facilities:** 15 tennis courts (5 indoors), indoor lap pool and hot tub, outdoor swimming pool and hot tub, baby pool, exercise room, bicycle rentals at Boulder Creek path, playground, volleyball and basketball courts; meeting space for up to 700.

## MODERATE

**THE BRIAR ROSE, 2151 Arapahoe Ave., Boulder, CO 80302. Tel. 303/442-3007.** 9 rms (7 with bath). A/C TEL

**$ Rates** (including continental breakfast): May–Sept, $53 single without bath, $73–$85 single with bath; $73 double without bath, $93–$105 double with bath. Oct–Apr, $49 single without bath, $68–$78 single with bath; $68 double without bath, $88–$98 double with bath. AE, DC, MC, V.

A country-style brick home set amid a lovely garden, this mid-city bed and breakfast might remind you of Grandma's. Every room is furnished with period antiques, from the bedrooms to the parlor to the back sun porch. Each guest room has handmade feather comforters, fresh fruit and flowers; tea and coffee (and a decanter of sherry) are always on in the dining room. You even get a chocolate at bedtime.

Five rooms are in the main house, four in a separate "cottage." Of the first five, two deluxe rooms have their own fireplaces and big queen-size featherbeds. Three others share two baths—but bathrooms are designed to assist with issues of modesty. All four cottage rooms have private baths and either patios (downstairs) or balconies (upstairs). Breakfast may be continental, but it's gourmet: croissants, granola, fresh nut breads, yogurt with fruit, and much more.

**HOTEL BOULDERADO, 2115 13th St. (at Spruce St.), Boulder, CO 80302. Tel. 303/442-4344,** or 800/433-4344. Fax 303/442-4378. 133 rms, 27 suites (all with bath). A/C TV TEL

**$ Rates:** $82–$92 single; $94–$104 double; $124–$136 suite. Extra person $12. AE, CB, DC, DISC, MC, V. **Parking:** Free.

Opened on January 1, 1909, this elegant and historic hotel still has the same Otis elevator that wowed visiting dignitaries on opening day. The colorful leaded-glass ceiling and cantilevered cherrywood staircase are other reminders of days past, along with the rich woodwork of the balusters around the mezzanine and the handsome armchairs and settees in the main-floor lobby.

The original five-story hotel, just a block off the Pearl Street Mall, has 42 bright and cozy guest rooms, every one a little bit different. All have been recently renovated down to the wiring and plumbing, but they retain a Victorian flavor with their antique furnishings (including desks), floral wallpaper, and other touches. The construction a few years ago of a spacious North Wing almost quadrupled the number of rooms, while perpetuating the turn-of-the-century feel in the wallpaper and reproduction antiques. Every room has a clock radio and hairdryer; deluxe units also have vanities and refrigerators.

The hotel offers a full range of services and dining and other facilities.

**HOLIDAY INN BOULDER, 800 28th St., Boulder, CO 80303. Tel. 303/ 443-3322,** or 800/456-4329. Fax 303/443-0397. 165 rms (all with bath). A/C TV TEL
$ **Rates:** May 15–Aug, $69–$89 single; $79–$99 double. Sept–May 14, $49–$69 single; $59–$79 double. AE, CB, DC, DISC, JCB, MC, V. **Parking:** Free.
Located at the south end of Boulder on the U.S. 36 Frontage Road near the Baseline Road exit, this hotel has one of the nicer "Holidomes" around. The central garden atrium features an indoor swimming pool fed by a fountain, a large adjacent whirlpool, and comfortable café seating.

Standard rooms have a king-size or two double beds, southwestern-theme decor (in peach or blue), watercolors of the city, and all the usual furnishings. Executive rooms are a little larger, with desks and clock radios. Local phone calls are 50¢. Most rooms face the atrium, though some have outside entrances.

The hotel offers a full range of services and dining and other facilities.

**PEARL STREET INN, 1820 Pearl St., Boulder, CO 80302. Tel. 303/444- 5584,** or 800/232-5949. 6 rms, 1 suite (all with bath). A/C TV TEL
$ **Rates** (including continental breakfast): Apr–Sept, $78–$98 single; $88–$108 double. Oct–Mar, $58–$78 single; $68–$88 double. AE, MC, V. **Parking:** Free.
Yossi Shem-Avi's wonderful guest house, three blocks south of the Pearl Street Mall, is a restored turn-of-the-century Victorian with a contemporary wing added in 1985. It offers the best of both worlds: a bed-and-breakfast with private entrances, the intimacy of a B&B with some of the luxury touches of a large hotel.

Rooms, all of which face a central courtyard, feature a crisp, bright decor with antique furnishings—a sort of meeting of the old and the new. Every room has a private bath and fireplace. Breakfast, and afternoon tea or wine, are served in the courtyard or a quiet dining room.

## INEXPENSIVE

**GOLDEN BUFF LODGE, 1725 28th St., Boulder, CO 80301. Tel. 303/ 442-7450,** or 800/999-BUFF. Fax 303/442-8788. 104 rms, 8 suites (all with bath). A/C TV TEL
$ **Rates:** May–Sept, $62–$70 single; $67–$75 double; $70–$80 suite. Oct–Apr, $52–$60 single; $57–$65 double; $60–$80 suite. 20%–25% less for stays of 2 weeks or longer. AE, CB, DC, DISC, MC, V. **Parking:** Free.
This one- and two-story motel takes up a full city block. Rooms are spacious, with queen-size beds, small working desks with phones (25¢ local calls), refrigerators, clock radios, and hairdryers. A few kitchen units are available. Half of the rooms are no-smoking, and air-filtration units are available on request.

The Golden Buff Restaurant, open Sunday through Thursday from 6:30am to 9pm and on Friday and Saturday from 6:30am to 10pm, is a popular family restaurant with a garden feel and a "natural" emphasis in its cooking. Beef, chicken, vegetarian, and Mexican dishes run $5 to $12.50. The motel offers room service. Other facilities include an outdoor swimming pool (seasonal), whirlpool, saunas, exercise room, mountain-bike rentals, and a guest laundry. Up to 50 people can be accommodated for meetings.

**HIGHLANDER INN, 970 28th St., Boulder, CO 80303. Tel. 303/443- 7800,** or 800/525-2149. Fax 303/443-7800, ext. 155. 48 rms, 24 suites (all with bath). A/C TV TEL
$ **Rates:** May 15–Oct 15, $56–$63 single; $59–$65 double; $65–$74 suite. Oct 16–May 14, $40–$46 single; $40–$49 double; $49–$60 suite. AE, CB, DC, DISC, MC, V. **Parking:** Free.
The comfortable lobby of this motel features a volume of menus of Boulder restaurants, a nice touch for visitors. Standard guest rooms are in the rear of the motel, shielded from traffic noise by solid brick walls. Units have queen-size or double beds, teal or mauve color schemes, coffee makers, and direct-dial phones (35¢ local calls). The motel also has 12 two-bedroom suites (one room with a king-size bed and a

refrigerator, the second room with two double beds) and 12 apartments for long-term rentals, with fully equipped kitchenettes and microwaves. No-smoking rooms are available.

Free coffee, tea, and hot chocolate are always on in the lobby. There's a 24-hour desk (with sundry sales), a guest laundry, outdoor swimming pool, and meeting rooms.

**UNIVERSITY INN, 1632 Broadway (near Arapahoe Ave.), Boulder, CO 80302. Tel. 303/442-3830,** or 800/258-7917. 39 rms (all with bath). A/C TV TEL

**$ Rates:** $43–$62 single; $48–$67 double. AE, CB, DC, DISC, MC, V. **Parking:** Free.

Conveniently located between campus and the Pearl Street Mall, and within walking distance of both, this two-story motel has distinctive sky-blue trim on white brick. The simple, cozy rooms have king-size, queen-size, or double beds, light-wood furnishings, refrigerators, and direct-dial phones (25¢ local calls). Most have showers only; if you need a room with a bathtub, ask. Family rooms and no-smoking rooms are available. There's a guest laundry and outdoor swimming pool.

## BUDGET

**FOOT OF THE MOUNTAIN MOTEL, 200 W. Arapahoe Ave., Boulder, CO 80303. Tel. 303/442-5688.** 18 rms (all with bath). TV TEL

**$ Rates:** $35–$40 double. AE, DISC, MC, V.

A series of rustic log cabins (with bright-red trim) near the east gate of Boulder Canyon, this motel dates to 1930, but has been fully modernized. Across the street is Eben Fine Park, at the top end of the Boulder Creek Path. Behind the cabins is an acre of park and picnic land. Despite their age, the cabins are very nice, with pine walls, queen-size or double beds, refrigerators, and private hot-water heaters. There's complimentary coffee in the office every morning.

**BOULDER YOUTH HOSTEL, 1127 College Ave., Boulder, CO 80302. Tel. 303/442-0522** or 442-9304.

**$ Rates:** $12–$15 per person for dorm beds. No credit cards.

As at most youth hostels, guests come here expecting to share—and they do. Toilets, showers, kitchen, TV room, telephone, laundry, and other facilities are on a community basis. Just off the University of Colorado campus, the hostel is open for registration daily from 7:30 to 10am and 5pm to midnight.

# 4. DINING

Dining in this university town tends to be more casual than in Denver (with a few notable exceptions), at least as wide-ranging in terms of ethnic variety, but no less expensive. In this listing, I consider a "Very Expensive" restaurant to be one in which most dinner main courses are priced above $20; "Expensive," $15 to $20; "Moderate," $10 to $15; "Inexpensive," $6 to $10; and "Budget," less than $6. Several restaurants offer discounted meals before 6:30pm.

There are over 200 restaurants in this city of 80,000-plus, fully one-third of them in a 12-square-block chunk of downtown—between 9th Street and 15th Street on the Pearl Street Mall or its flanking streets, Walnut and Spruce. Nevertheless, especially in summer and on weekends, dinner reservations are advised. A few restaurants may expect gentlemen to wear a coat and tie. It's appropriate to tip 15% to 20% of your tab.

## VERY EXPENSIVE

**FLAGSTAFF HOUSE RESTAURANT, 1138 Flagstaff Rd. (west up Baseline Rd.). Tel. 442-4640.**

**ACCOMMODATIONS:**
Boulderado, Hotel **1**
Briar Rose, The **4**
Clarion Harvest House **3**
Foot of the Mountain Motel **9**
Golden Buff Lodge **6**
Highlander Inn **7**
Holiday Inn Boulder **5**
Pearl Street Inn **2**
University Inn **8**

**DINING:**
European Cafe, The **12**
Flagstaff House Restaurant **7**
14th Street Bar & Grill **2**
John's Restaurant **11**
La Estrellita **9**
New York Delicatessen, The **4**
Original Indo-Ceylon Restaurant, The **8**
Pasta Jay's **3**
Pour La France **5**
Tom's Tavern **6**
Walnut Brewery **10**
Winston's **1**

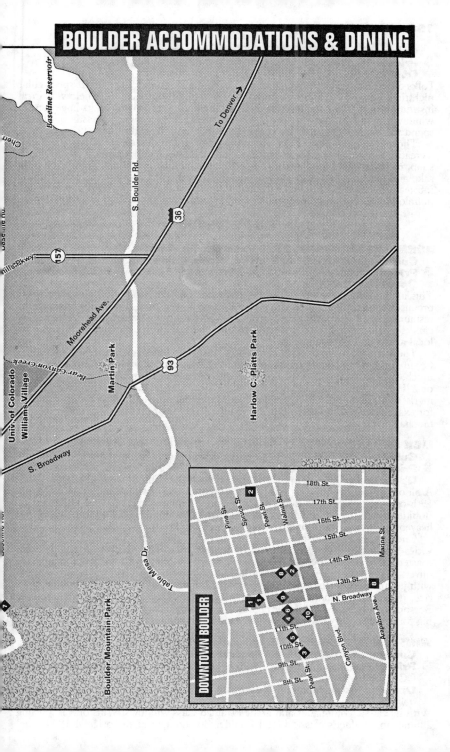

# BOULDER ACCOMMODATIONS & DINING

**Cuisine:** NEW AMERICAN/REGIONAL. **Reservations:** Required.
$ **Prices:** Appetizers $8–$16; main courses $22–$37. AE, CB, DC, MC, V.
**Open:** Dinner only, Sun–Fri 6–10pm, Sat 5–10pm.

Folks drive all the way from Denver to dine at the Flagstaff House for its spectacular nighttime view of the lights of Boulder, spread out about 1,000 feet below. A local institution since 1953, the restaurant is simple but elegant, relying on its huge picture windows for atmosphere. Service is very attentive but exceedingly measured: Plan to spend the entire evening if you come for dinner, and dress the part.

The menu is heavy on Rocky Mountain game and fresh seafood, all prepared with a creative touch. Starters, for instance, include salads of quail or skate, a chilled peach soup, mesquite-smoked alligator and rattlesnake, and baby scallops in the shell with sake and ginger. Main dishes might include a fresh John Dory with black truffles, lobster and shrimp with shiitake cannelloni, breast of duck with wild rice, and grilled buffalo filet with roasted peppers.

# EXPENSIVE

**JOHN'S RESTAURANT, 2328 Pearl St. Tel. 444-5232.**
**Cuisine:** CREATIVE CONTINENTAL. **Reservations:** Highly recommended.
$ **Prices:** Appetizers $2.50–$10; main courses $13–$20. AE, DISC, MC, V.
**Open:** Daily 6–10pm.

This unimposing beige house on the south side of Pearl Street occupies the former premises of an antique store. Chef John Bizzarro—yes, that's his name—opened his restaurant in 1974, drawing raves from all who have eaten here. Meals are served by candlelight in several interconnected rooms; the walls are decorated with work by local artists and photographers.

The menu is an olio of classic French, Spanish, and Italian dishes, tossed with some Cajun and Santa Fe–style creations, and liberally seasoned with Bizzarro's own deft touch. You can start with duck-liver pâté with pistachios, oysters in brandy and cream, or a Hopi squash with green chiles and cilantro, then move to the main dishes: mariscos Catalan, chicken Agrigento, filet mignon au poivre, or sweetbreads madeira, for example. Finish up with John's Chocolate Intensity (a trademarked dessert) or a mocha soufflé glaze.

**LICK SKILLET CAFE, 471 Boulder St., Gold Hill. Tel. 449-7775.**
**Cuisine:** NEW AMERICAN. **Reservations:** Highly recommended.
$ **Prices:** Appetizers $4–$6; main courses $14.75–$22.50. MC, V.
**Open:** Dinner Tues–Sun 5:30–10pm; brunch Sat–Sun 8:30am–2:30pm.

A bit out of the way but well worth the 20-minute drive, the Lick Skillet is lodged in a 19th-century prospector's office in the historic mining village of Gold Hill, west of Boulder. From the patio there's a superb view of mountains (and a clear shot of the heavens on warm, starry nights); inside, a fireplace keeps chilly diners warm.

Chef-owner Eric Burson opened the café in 1986, when he was 21. His menu varies seasonally, but features such appetizers as a wild-mushroom tamale with roasted garlic and red-pepper cream, and a ragoût of clams with spinach, tomato, and olives. Main dishes might include grilled swordfish on angel-hair pasta, elk sautéed with juniper and blueberries, or a vegetarian Johnny cake of white-bean purée, wild rice, mushrooms, onions, corn, and zucchini. The Lick Skillet is so popular that Burson no longer laments that he couldn't get into medical school: "My hands are too big for brain surgery." There's no smoking in his restaurant.

**WINSTON'S, in the Hotel Boulderado, 2115 13th St. Tel. 442-4344.**
**Cuisine:** SEAFOOD/STEAK. **Reservations:** Recommended.
$ **Prices:** Main courses $4.50–$7.95 at lunch, $11.95–$17.95 at dinner. AE, CB, DC, DISC, MC, V.
**Open:** Breakfast Mon–Fri 7–10:30am; lunch Mon–Fri 11am–2:30pm; dinner daily 5–10pm; brunch Sat–Sun 7am–2:30pm.

With its classic colonnades and arched stained-glass windows, Winston's is a fitting adjunct to Boulder's classic Hotel Boulderado. Lodged in the original 1909 hotel dining room, it features fresh fish and shellfish flown in daily from the Pacific, Atlantic, and Gulf coasts.

Fine prime rib and chicken dishes are on the menu as well, but here you should focus on the fresh "catch of the day" list. On a recent visit, that included seared yellowfin tuna with lemon-rosemary cream, mako shark with a teriyaki-and-macadamia topping, and jumbo sea scallops sautéed with shiitake mushrooms and sun-dried tomatoes in chardonnay. Always on the menu is baked salmon Winston, served on a bed of spinach and wild mushrooms, wrapped in pastry, baked and served with béarnaise sauce. Oysters and smoked Colorado trout are popular starters.

# MODERATE

**THE EUROPEAN CAFE, in the Arapahoe Village Shopping Center, 2460 Arapahoe Ave. Tel. 938-8250.**
**Cuisine:** CONTINENTAL. **Reservations:** Recommended.
**$ Prices:** Appetizers $5.95–$6.95; main courses $5.95–$7.95 at lunch, $11.95–$16.95 at dinner. AE, MC, V.
**Open:** Lunch daily 11am–2pm; dinner Mon–Sat 5:30–10pm, Sun 5:30–9:30pm.

Simple and elegant, this restaurant belies its location in a shopping center with fine presentation and cuisine. The decor features glass-top tables, large mirrors, strong flower arrangements, and a soft burgundy color scheme.

The luncheon menu features salads (such as the asparagus salad with avocadoes and enoki mushrooms), pastas, and light dishes. Dinners typically start with an appetizer such as pâté, escargots, or smoked salmon with caviar; and continue with a continental delight such as cuisses de grenouille piquante (spicy frogs' legs), suprême de volaille Comte d'Armagnac, and a variety of filets and tournedos. The wine list is superb, the dessert menu scrumptious.

**14TH STREET BAR & GRILL, 1400 Pearl St. Tel. 444-5854.**
**Cuisine:** COUNTRY EUROPEAN. **Reservations:** Recommended.
**$ Prices:** Appetizers $2.50–$6.95; main courses $4.95–$10.95 at lunch, $9.95–$14.95 at dinner. MC, V.
**Open:** Mon–Thurs 11:30am–10pm, Fri–Sat 11:30am–midnight, Sun 5–10pm.

An open, airy restaurant with big windows facing the corner of 14th and Pearl, this is as good a place for people-watching as it is for dining—and it's great for dining! The open wood grill and pizza oven, abstract modern art on the walls, and long (and crowded) bar let you know that this is a place where creative people like to have fun.

The lunch menu offers spinach, pasta, and southwestern chicken salads; deli-style sandwiches; pastas; and unusual homemade pizzas, such as one with chorizo sausage, garlic, and roasted green chiles, another with shrimp, spinach, olives, and feta cheese. The dinner menu changes nightly, but could feature bouillabaisse served with a side of angel-hair pasta, roasted chicken in a proscuitto-mushroom sauce, or beef tenderloin stuffed with cheese and cilantro.

**THE ORIGINAL INDO-CEYLON RESTAURANT, 2010 14th St. (downstairs). Tel. 449-5636.**
**Cuisine:** SOUTH ASIAN. **Reservations:** Recommended.
**$ Prices:** Appetizers $2.25–$2.75; main courses $7–$14. MC, V.
**Open:** Dinner only, Tues–Sat 5–9:30pm, Sun 5–9pm.

Now, here's a place for adventuresome palates. Owned and operated by Mike Ford, a former Peace Corps volunteer in the island nation of Sri Lanka, the Indo-Ceylon offers excellent food and attentive service together with a low-key ambience of posters and banners. Smoking is not permitted.

The menu runs the gamut of South Asian cuisines, from the spicy-hot curries of Sri Lanka and southern India to the oven-baked tandooris of northern India. Curries dominate—but as connoisseurs know, a curry can be any of dozens of blends of spices, not simply a cumin-heavy powder sifted from a store-bought can. There's crab curry with coconut milk, chicken korma in a ginger-and-yogurt marinade, red beef curry with chiles, and straw-mushroom curry in a tomato-and-green-onion preparation. The first Wednesday of every month is reserved for a gourmet Ceylonese dinner with rice, eight curries, and condiments for $15.75 per person; reservations are required at least 24 hours in advance.

# INEXPENSIVE

**LA ESTRELLITA, 2037 13th St. Tel. 939-8822.**
  **Cuisine:** MEXICAN.
  **$ Prices:** Appetizers $1.25–$4.50; meals $4.50–$8.95.
  **Open:** Mon–Thurs 11am–10pm, Fri–Sat 11am–11pm (bar open Fri–Sat until 2am).

Drawing on recipes developed by his parents at the original La Estrellita in Fort Lupton in the 1950s and '60s, John Montoya established this restaurant in 1986—and it's still growing in popularity. You'll get all the standard tacos, tostadas, enchiladas, tamales, and chile relleños here, in generous portions, as well as a few surprises: costillas adobadas (Mexican-style ribs), Indian tacos, stuffed sopaipillas, and more. Fajitas are a big seller.

**PASTA JAY'S, 925 Pearl St. Tel. 444-5800.**
  **Cuisine:** ITALIAN. **Reservations:** Not accepted.
  **$ Prices:** Appetizers $2.25–$4.25; meals $4.50–$9.95. MC, V.
  **Open:** Mon–Sat 11am–10:30pm.

Expect a long line when you arrive at this Mediterranean bistro, with its red-checked tablecloths indoors and its huge outdoor patio facing Pearl Street. Pasta Jay's is on a first-name basis with many of its customers, and they keep coming back—prepared to wait an hour or two, unless they come before 6pm. Good food, generous portions, and low prices are the attractions here: manicotti, gnocchi, tortellini, rigatoni, eggplant or chicken parmigiana, and other Italian classics. Jay's also has great pizza, and sandwiches before 5pm. No smoking is permitted; beer and wine are served.

**WALNUT BREWERY, 1123 Walnut St. (near Broadway). Tel. 447-1345.**
  **Cuisine:** AMERICAN.
  **$ Prices:** Appetizers $3.45–$5.95; lunch $4.95–$7.75; dinner $6.95–$13.95. MC, V.
  **Open:** Mon–Sat 11am–1am, Sun 5pm–midnight.

This looks as a brewery should. Brick walls, prominent brew tanks, warehouselike decor, big beer-label signs against one wall. Order an appetizing taster of the brewery's six handcrafted beers, but don't ignore the food. Lunches feature the brew burger and the brewer's club, as well as duck enchiladas and superb, beer-battered fish-and-chips. The Mexican treats remain on the dinner menu, along with pastas (chicken in red ale, served on linguine, for instance) and gourmet dishes: alder-smoked salmon, tenderloin of beef with roasted garlic, Danish baby back ribs.

# BUDGET

**THE NEW YORK DELICATESSEN, 1117 Pearl St. Tel. 449-5161.**
  **Cuisine:** DELI.
  **$ Prices:** $2–$8.95. AE, MC, V.
  **Open:** Summer, daily 8am–9pm, winter, daily 8am–8pm.

Remember television's *Mork and Mindy?* Back in the '70s, Robin Williams and Pam Dawber made their home-away-from-home at this authentic New York–style deli on the Pearl Street Mall. Enjoy matzoh brei or blintzes, Coney Island hot dogs or Reuben sandwiches. Soups, salads, and pastries are prepared fresh daily. There's booth seating or a great outside deck for dining in, and take-out service is welcomed. Nanu, nanu.

**POUR LA FRANCE, 1001 Pearl St. Tel. 449-3929.**
  **Cuisine:** FRENCH.
  **$ Prices:** $3.95–$8.95. MC, V.
  **Open:** Mon–Sat 7am–midnight, Sun 8am–10pm.

A café and bistro on the mall, Pour La France is like a Paris brasserie—a casual sidewalk café with an awning shading outdoor diners and big windows giving the same view to those eating inside. You can start your day with a double espresso and

Grand Marnier French toast or eggs Benedict, and a few hours later return for a croissant sandwich or a pissaladière (a Gruyère pizza). Dinners feature pastas, crêpes, and beef bourguignon, and the desserts are everything French pastries should be.

**TOM'S TAVERN, 11th and Pearl Sts. Tel. 443-3893.**
   **Cuisine:** AMERICAN.
**$  Prices:** $3.95–$6.60. MC, V.
   **Open:** Mon–Sat 11am–midnight, Sun 1–9:30pm.
Boulder's most popular place for a good hamburger, Tom's has been a neighborhood institution for three decades. Located in a turn-of-the-century building that once housed an undertaker, the tavern offers vinyl-upholstered booths indoors, a row of patio seating outdoors. Besides the one-third-pound burgers and other sandwiches, Tom's serves dinner anytime: a 10-ounce steak, fried chicken, or a vegetarian casserole, all in the $6 range.

# 5. ATTRACTIONS

Boulder is more a place to explore for its "feel," its atmosphere, than for any one or two particular attractions. Besides, the University of Colorado, the Pearl Street Mall, and the Boulder Creek Path are most typically "Boulder." But there's plenty more.

## THE TOP ATTRACTIONS

**BOULDER CREEK PATH, 55th St. and Pearl Pkwy. to Arapahoe Ave. and Canyon Blvd. Tel. 441-3400.**
   This nature corridor cuts a 5½-mile swath through Boulder, from east to west along the rushing waters of Boulder Creek, but it doesn't even require so much as a street crossing. The peaceful, wooded path deals with traffic by a series of bridges and underpasses, linking several of the city's parks with the University of Colorado campus, government buildings, and other points of interest. It's a special favorite of walkers, runners, and bicyclists.
   The eastern access to the path is from 55th Street at Pearl Parkway, just south of Valmont Road. Look for prairie-dog colonies and wetlands, where up to 150 species of birds have been identified. At 30th Street south of Arapahoe Road, it cuts through **Scott Carpenter Park** (named for Colorado's native-son astronaut), popular for swimming in summer, sledding in winter. Between 28th Street and Folsom Road, it skirts the grounds of the Clarion Harvest House (see "Accommodations," above), with its extensive recreational facilities (including bicycle rentals) and its **underground fish observatory.** The university's Folsom Stadium is just a few steps up the hill to the south.
   A historic train and bandstand mark **Central Park** at Broadway and Canyon Boulevard. Here, the trail is just 2½ blocks south of the Pearl Street Mall. In short order, you'll pass the Boulder Municipal Building, the **City of Boulder Sculpture Park,** fishing ponds where kids under 12 can angle for free and keep their catch, and the Boulder Justice Center, a merging of courts and jail facilities. Near 3rd and Canyon, look for the **Xeriscape Garden,** where drought-tolerant plants are used to test reduced water usage.
   At the west end of the Boulder Creek Path is **Eben G. Fine Park,** named for the discoverer of Arapahoe Glacier, a major source of municipal water. There are plans to extend the path up Boulder Canyon to connect with other byways, thus creating a regional bicycle-pedestrian trail system.

**PEARL STREET MALL, Pearl St. from 11th to 15th Sts.**
   This four-block-long pedestrian mall marks at once Boulder's downtown core and its center for dining, shopping, strolling, and (especially) people-watching. Musicians, mimes, jugglers, and other buskers hold forth on the landscaped mall day and night, winter and summer; and you'll find everyone from starched-shirted lawyers to

dreadlocked Rastafarians watching the shows. Locally owned businesses and galleries share the mall with trendy boutiques, sidewalk cafés, and major chains including Laura Ashley, Banana Republic, and Pendleton. Don't miss the bronze statue of Chief Niwot, king of the southern Arapahoe, in front of the **Boulder County Court-house** between 13th and 14th. Niwot, who welcomed the first Boulder settlers, was killed in southeastern Colorado in the Sand Creek Massacre of 1864.

## UNIVERSITY OF COLORADO, east side of Broadway between Arapahoe Ave. and Baseline Rd. Tel. 492-6301.

The largest university in the state, with 22,000 students (including 4,000 graduate students) and 1,600 acres, the University of Colorado dominates all else in Boulder. Its student population, its cultural and sports events, and its intellectual atmosphere have shaped Boulder into the city it is today.

**Old Main,** on the Norlin Quadrangle, was the first building erected after the university was established in 1876. At first it housed the entire school. Later, pink sandstone buildings of Italian Renaissance style came to predominate on campus. Of special interest are the **U.C. Heritage Center,** on the third floor of Old Main; the **Henderson Museum** (see "More Attractions," below), a natural-history museum in the Henderson Building on Broadway; the **Mary Rippon Outdoor Theatre,** behind the Henderson Museum, site of the annual Colorado Shakespeare Festival; the **Fiske Planetarium and Science Center,** between Kittredge Loop Drive and Regent Drive on the south side of campus; and the **Norlin Library,** on the Norlin Quadrangle, the largest research library in the state, with extensive holdings of American and English literature. Free **campus tours** start at the Admissions Office in the Regent Administrative Center, Regent Drive off Broadway.

**Admission:** Free.
**Open:** Tours Mon–Fri at 10:30am and 2:30pm, Sat at 10:30am.

## NATIONAL CENTER FOR ATMOSPHERIC RESEARCH, 1850 Table Mesa Dr. Tel. 497-1174.

I. M. Pei designed this striking pink sandstone building overlooking Boulder from high atop Table Mesa in the southwestern foothills. Scientists here study such phenomena as the greenhouse effect, acid rain, wind shear, sunspots, tides, even the behavior of insects, to gain a better understanding of the earth's atmosphere. Satellites, weather balloons, robots, and super-computers that can simulate the world's climate are among the technological tools on display.

**Admission:** Free.
**Open:** Self-guided tours, Mon–Fri 8am–5pm, Sat–Sun and hols 9am–3pm; guided tours, June–Sept, daily at noon and by appointment.

# MORE ATTRACTIONS

## INDUSTRIAL TOURS

## BOULDER BREWERY, 2880 Wilderness Place, near Valmont Rd. Tel. 444-8448.

From the grinding of the grain to the bottling of the beer, the 25-minute tour of this microbrewery—America's original, trendsetting "designer" brewery—ends as all brewery tours should: in the tasting room. Tours lead past glistening copper vats that turn out 100 kegs of beer a day. (The mammoth Coors brewery in Golden produces 300,000 kegs an hour!) The tasting room is actually a deli-style restaurant that overlooks the bottling area. The menu, which changes weekly, features such choices as beer-cheese soup, brewery stew with bratwurst, fresh salads, and sandwiches. Lunches run $4.50 to $5.50.

**Admission:** Free.
**Open:** Mon–Fri 11am–5pm, Sat 11am–3pm and 5pm–sunset; lunch, Mon–Sat 11am–2pm; tours, Mon–Sat 11am and 1pm.

## CELESTIAL SEASONINGS, 4600 Sleepytime Dr. (off Spine Rd. and Longmont Diagonal). Tel. 530-5300.

The nation's leading manufacturer of herbal teas moved into a modern new building in northeastern Boulder in late 1990. The tour is an experience for the senses. The company, which began in a Boulder garage in the 1970s, now produces 40 teas (24 of them without caffeine) from over 100 different herbs and spices, which it imports from 35 foreign countries. Here at the plant, you'll observe everything from the importation bays to the blending process to packaging, from the production of tea bags to boxing for shipment. The visitor center includes a retail outlet.
**Admission:** Free.
**Open:** Daily for tours; call ahead for schedule.

## MUSEUMS & GALLERIES

### BOULDER HISTORICAL SOCIETY MUSEUM, 1206 Euclid Ave. Tel. 449-3464.

Ensconced on University Hill in the 1899 Harbeck House, a French château-style sandstone mansion with a Dutch-style front door and Italian tile fireplaces, this museum has an impressive collection of over 35,000 objects and photographs. Built by a New York stockbroker who maintained a direct line to Wall Street, it features a Tiffany window on the stairway landing, a built-in buffet with leaded-glass doors, and hand-carved mantels throughout. Stuffed mannequins are busy cooking in the authentic old-fashioned kitchen. The wardrobes in the upstairs bedrooms contain an extensive collection of Victorian and Edwardian clothing, and there are exquisite quilts on the beds.
**Admission:** $1 suggested donation.
**Open:** Tues–Fri 10am–4pm, Sat noon–4pm; in summer only, also Sun 1–4pm.

### HENDERSON MUSEUM, University of Colorado, Henderson Bldg., Broadway between 15th and 16th Sts. Tel. 492-6892 or 492-6165.

The natural history and anthropology of the Rocky Mountains and Southwest are the focus of this campus museum, founded in 1902. Anasazi pottery and antique Pueblo, Navajo, and Spanish colonial textiles are featured exhibits, along with collections in geology, paleontology, botany, entomology, zoology, and the arts. The main gallery has special displays that change throughout the year.
**Admission:** Free.
**Open:** Mon–Fri 9am–5pm, Sat 9am–4pm, Sun 10am–4pm.

### LEANIN' TREE MUSEUM OF WESTERN ART, 6055 Longbow Dr. (off Spine Rd. and Longmont Diagonal). Tel. 530-1442.

You may know Leanin' Tree as the world's largest publisher of western-art greeting cards. What's not so well known is that here, upstairs in the corporate headquarters, is an outstanding collection of 140 original paintings and 60 bronze sculptures by contemporary artists—all depicting scenes from the Old or New West. Represented are award-winning pieces from the National Academy of Western Art and Cowboy Artists of America. Many of the works have been reproduced on the company's greeting cards, for sale in the downstairs shop.
**Admission:** Free.
**Open:** Mon–Fri 8am–4:30pm, Sat on a limited basis.

## PARKS & GARDENS

### CHAUTAUQUA PARK, 9th St. and Baseline Rd. Tel. 442-3282 or 440-3776 (restaurant).

During the late 19th and early 20th centuries, more than 400 Chautauquas—adult education and cultural entertainment centers—sprang up around the United States. This 26-acre city park, on a hillside above downtown, is one of the few remaining Chautauqua parks in the country. In summer, it still hosts a wide-ranging program of music, dance, theater, and film, including the Colorado Music Festival. There are playgrounds, picnic grounds, tennis courts, and hiking trailheads. The historic Chautauqua Dining Hall, which first opened on July 4, 1898, serves three meals daily at moderate prices, Memorial Day through Labor Day, and there is some lodging available in cottages of varying sizes.

N

**COLORADO**

★ Denver

Boulder

Boulder Brewery ➐
Boulder Creek Path ➊
Boulder Historical
  Society Museum ➒
Celestial Seasonings ➑
Henderson Museum ➍
Leanin' Tree Museum
  of Western Art ➎
National Center
  for Atmospheric Research ➏
Pearl Street Mall ➋
University of Colorado ➌

Wonderland Lake

Sumac Ave.

Iris Ave.

19th St.

Balsam Ave.

Edgewood Dr.

Folsom Ave.

28th St.

30th St.

47th St.

51st St.

57th St.

Jay Rd.

Independence Rd.

Longmont Diagonal

To Longmont

To Rocky Mountain National Park

Hayden Lake

Valmont Dr.

Valmont Dr.

Boulder Creek

Farmer's Ditch

Leggett
Reservoir

Valley View Rd.

55th St.

Arapahoe Ave.

Pearl St.

Folsom Ave.

Canyon Blvd.

Arapahoe Ave.

University of Colorado

U.C.B. East Campus

Sunshine Dr.

4th St.

Mapleton Ave.

Pine St.

Pearl St.

Walnut St.

Boulder Historical
Society & Museum

Boulder Art Center

Flagstaff

36

119

7

7

7

7

3

3

4

2

1

# BOULDER ATTRACTIONS

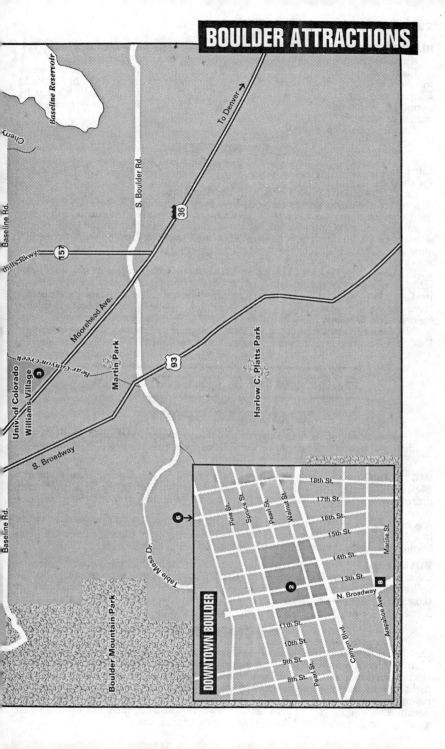

Baseline Reservoir

Chew Creek

Baseline Rd.

To Denver →

S. Boulder Rd.

36

Foothills Pkwy.

157

Moorehead Ave.

Bear Canyon Creek

93

Univ. of Colorado
Williams Village ❸

Martin Park

Harlow C. Platts Park

S. Broadway

Baseline Rd.

Table Mesa Dr.

Boulder Mountain Park

❻→

### DOWNTOWN BOULDER

18th St.
17th St.
16th St.
15th St.
14th St.
13th St.

Pine St.
Spruce St.
Pearl St.
Walnut St.

Marine St.

❷

N. Broadway

❽

Arapahoe Ave.

Canyon Blvd.

11th St.
10th St.
9th St.
8th St.

Pearl St.

**ELDORADO CANYON STATE PARK, Colo. 170, Eldorado Springs. Tel. 494-3943.**
Eight miles southwest of Boulder, this 272-acre park is known around the world for the technical rock climbing offered by the sheer sandstone walls of Eldorado Canyon, reaching heights of 850 feet. If you're not a climber yourself, it's equally exciting to watch others scale the walls. There is also picnicking, hiking, and fishing, but no camping.
**Admission:** $3 per vehicle.

## COOL FOR KIDS

City parks and the University of Colorado's Fiske Planetarium offer the best diversions for children.
On the **Boulder Creek Path** (see "The Top Attractions," above), youngsters are charmed by the **underwater fish observatory** behind the Clarion Harvest House. They can feed the huge trout (25¢ machines cough up handfuls of fish food) swimming behind a special glass barrier on the creek. Farther up the path, on the south bank around Sixth Street, **Kids' Fishing Ponds** stocked by the Boulder Fish and Game Club are open to children under the age of 12. There's no charge for either activity.
In summer, the **Boulder Parks and Recreation Department** (tel. 441-3400) schedules a variety of music, dance, and theater performances for children in some of its 56 parks. Two year-round sports centers have public pools: **South Boulder Recreation Center,** 1360 Gillaspie Drive (tel. 441-3448), and **North Boulder Recreation Center,** 3170 Broadway (tel. 441-3444). Call for schedules and times.
The **Fiske Planetarium** (tel. 492-5002) has an after-school and summer Science Discovery Program and Saturday "Stories Under the Stars."

# 6. SPORTS & RECREATION

## SPECTATOR SPORTS

The major attraction is University of Colorado college baseball, basketball, and football. For tickets write or phone the Ticket Office, Campus Box 372, Boulder, CO 80309 (tel. 303/49-BUFFS).

**BICYCLING** The highlight of the racing year is the **Coors International Bicycle Classic,** held over 2 weeks in mid-August. One of the most important professional races in the world, it follows a different course through the mountains from year to year, but always concludes with the climactic stage in Boulder. For spectator guides and other information, see the **Bike Race Store,** 1737 Pearl Street (tel. 440-7326). To find out about other bicycle-racing events, call the hotline for the **Bicycle Racing Association of Colorado** (tel. 303/820-2453).

**VOLLEYBALL** It may seem out of place here in the mountains, but each June sees the **Jose Cuervo Doubles Volleyball Tournament,** a professional beach-volleyball tournament that attracts the best two-person teams in the nation. There's a separate division for amateurs in this tournament, played at the South Boulder Recreation Center, 1360 Gillaspie Drive (tel. 441-3410).

## RECREATION

*Outside* magazine has designated Boulder as the leading outdoor-sports town in North America—and who am I to argue? The city itself owns 6,000 acres of park lands, including more than 200 miles of hiking trails and long stretches of bicycle paths. Several canyons lead down from the Rockies directly into Boulder, attracting mountaineers and rock climbers. Families enjoy picnicking and camping in the beautiful surroundings. It seems that everywhere you look, men and women of all ages are running, walking, biking, skiing, or otherwise active.

Well-established sporting-goods stores in the city include **Chivers Sports,** 2000 30th Street (tel. 442-2493), which focuses on skiing, tennis, swimming, and soccer; and **Doc's Ski and Sport,** 629 South Broadway (tel. 499-0963), which sells, rents, and repairs skis, mountain bikes, and rollerblades.

Visitors interested in joining a group outdoor adventure can start by contacting **Colorado Adventure Network,** 3585 Arthur Court, Boulder, CO 80302 (tel. 303/444-0952).

**BICYCLING**   Some days, you may see more bikes than cars in Boulder. Paths run along many of the city's major arteries, local racing and touring events are scheduled year round, and there's a proliferation of local bike stores, including **University Bicycles,** 839 Pearl Street (tel. 444-4196), for rentals and repairs, and the **Bike Race Store,** 1737 Pearl Street (tel. 440-7326), for event information.

For maps of the city's 50 miles of bike paths, check the **City of Boulder Bicycle Program,** Division of Transportation, P.O. Box 791, Boulder, CO 80306 (tel. 303/441-3216); or **Boulder County Bikeways,** P.O. Box 471, Boulder, CO 80306 (tel. 303/441-3900). Every year in July, the city, county, and university co-sponsor the **Boulder Bike Week,** including races, a kids' bike rodeo, safety forums, and maintenance clinics.

Visitors can join the Bike Group of the **Colorado Mountain Club** (tel. 449-1135) on Saturday and Sunday bike tours, November through April. Bikers leave the parking lot at Coco's, 28th Street and Iris Street, at 10am each weekend day. Meanwhile, **Boulder Velo Club** members meet the first Tuesday of every month at the Bike Race Store. Rides, meetings, and other events are published in the *Daily Camera* community calendar.

**CLIMBING**   If you're interested in tackling the nearby mountains and cliffs with ropes and pitons, contact **The Boulder Mountaineer,** 1335 Broadway (tel. 442-8355), or the **International Alpine School** (tel. 494-4904).

The **Flatiron Range,** easily visible from downtown Boulder, and nearby **Eldorado Canyon** are two favorites among expert rock scalers.

**FISHING**   Favored fishing areas near Boulder include **Boulder Reservoir,** North 51st Street, 1½ miles north of Jay Road, northeast of the city off the Longmont Diagonal; **Lagerman Reservoir,** west of North 73rd Street off Pike Road, about 15 miles northeast of the city, where nonmotorized boats can be used; **Barker Reservoir,** just east of Nederland on the Boulder Canyon Drive (Colo. 119), for bank fishing; and **Walden Ponds Wildlife Habitat,** about 6 miles east of downtown on North 75th Street. Don't forget to get a license and check local laws (see "Sports & Recreation" in Chapter 1 for details).

**GOLF**   Local courses are the **Coal Creek Golf Course,** 585 West Dillon Road, Louisville (tel. 666-PUTT); the **Flatiron Golf Course,** 5706 Arapahoe Avenue (tel. 441-7851); and the **Lake Valley Golf Course,** Neva Road off U.S. 36 north (tel. 444-2114).

**HEALTH CLUBS**   Among private clubs with wide-ranging facilities are the **Boulder Athletic Club,** 1715 15th Street (tel. 442-9790); the **Flatiron Athletic Club,** 505 Thunderbird Drive (tel. 499-6590); and the **Rallysport Health and Fitness Club,** 2727 29th Street (tel. 449-4800).

The city operates the **North Boulder Recreation Center,** 3170 Broadway (tel. 441-3444), and the **South Boulder Recreation Center,** 1360 Gillaspie Drive (tel. 441-3448).

**HIKING & BACKPACKING**   From Chautauqua Park, Ninth Street and Baseline Road (tel. 441-3408), rangers lead hikes and offer advice on trips into **Boulder Mountain Parks.** These include 4,625 acres bordering the Boulder city limits to the west and south, including the Flatirons and Flagstaff Mountain. You can pick up a "Boulder Mountain Park Trail Map" from the city Chamber of Commerce, 2440 Pearl Street (tel. 442-1044). A very popular hike is the Enchanted Mesa Trail, which leaves from Chautauqua Park, joins the longer Mesa Trail, and follows the ridge of the Flatirons about 6 miles to Eldorado Springs.

Boulder County Parks offer nice day hikes into the **Betasso Preserve,** 6 miles west of Boulder off Sugarloaf Road; **Boulder Falls,** 8 miles west of the city on Boulder Canyon Drive; and **Walker Ranch,** 8½ miles southwest via Flagstaff Road.

Numerous **Roosevelt National Forest** trailheads leave the Peak to Peak Highway (Colo. 72) west of Boulder. Check with the U.S. Forest Service, Boulder Ranger District, 2995 Baseline Road (tel. 444-6001). West of Boulder, on the Continental Divide, is the **Indian Peaks Wilderness Area** (tel. 444-6003). More than half of the area is fragile alpine tundra; permits are required from June 1 to September 15. North of Boulder, via Estes Park, is **Rocky Mountain National Park** (tel. 586-2371), covered in Chapter 9.

**HORSEBACK RIDING** Several area ranches offer day rides and pack trips, including **Broken Arrow Ranch,** Sunshine Drive, 15 miles west of Boulder via Mapleton Avenue (tel. 459-3460); **Heil Valley Ranch,** Lefthand Canyon Drive, northwest of Boulder (tel. 444-0238); and **Peaceful Valley Ranch,** near Lyons, north of Boulder (tel. 440-9632).

**RUNNING** The best place to get information about running or walking is the **Runners Roost,** 1129 Pearl Street (tel. 443-9868), which sells shoes and apparel and acts as headquarters for the many race events the city hosts. Most of these are "fun runs," varying in distance from 5km to a half-marathon (13 miles), over the year.

The **Bolder Boulder** (tel. 444-RACE), held every Memorial Day, attracts 20,000 runners who circle the 10km course. The **Boulder Roadrunners** (tel. 443-9615) sponsor fun runs of variable pace, time, and distance every Sunday morning.

**SKIING** Friendly **Eldora Mountain Resort** (tel. 440-8700 in Boulder, or 1-258-7082) is just 21 miles (about a 40-minute drive) west of downtown Boulder via Hwy. 119 through Nederland. RTD buses leave Boulder for Eldora daily at 8:10am during ski season. Vail Associates, the principal owners, recently built a large new ski-school building and expanded the area's snowmaking capacity for a longer season.

For downhill skiers and snowboarders, Eldora has 32 trails geared primarily to the novice and intermediate, but with some expert terrain among its 210 acres. Fifteen runs are lighted for night skiing Wednesday through Saturday. The area has five double-chair lifts, one rope tow, and a vertical of 1,400 feet. Adult tickets are $23 for a full day, $18 for a half day, $14 at night. Seniors 65 to 69 pay $15; those 70 and over ski free. Children 6 to 12 pay $11, or $8 for a half day or at night; those 5 and under ski free. The season extends from mid-November to early April, snow permitting.

For cross-country skiers, Eldora has 18km (11 miles) of track skiing loops, and an overnight hut available by reservation. Rates are $5 for a full day of track skiing, $3 for a half day.

Nordic skiers have more to choose from at **Peaceful Valley Ski Ranch,** Star Route, Lyons, CO 80540 (tel. 303/440-9632), north of Boulder en route to Estes Park. The ranch has 75km (45 miles) of backcountry trails, plus snowshoeing, sleigh rides, and 66 lodge rooms for overnights.

You can get equipment rentals at **Crystal Ski Shop,** 3216 Arapahoe Avenue (tel. 449-7669). **Mountain Sports,** 821 Pearl Street (tel. 443-6770), specializes in equipment for backcountry trips: cross-country, telemark, and touring skis, plus snowshoes.

**HANG-GLIDING** The atmospheric conditions generated by the peaks of the Front Range are ideal for year-round hang-gliding. **The Cloud Base,** 5534 Independence Road (tel. 530-2208), offers rides and lessons from the Boulder Municipal Airport, 2 miles northeast of downtown. Introductory scenic flights start at $40 an hour.

**SWIMMING** There are four public pools within the city. Indoor pools, both open daily year round, are at the **North Boulder Recreation Center,** 3170 Broadway (tel. 441-3444), and the **South Boulder Recreation Center,** 1360 Gillaspie Drive (tel. 441-3448). Outdoor pools, both open daily from Memorial Day to Labor Day, are **Scott Carpenter Pool,** 30th Street and Arapahoe Avenue (tel. 441-3440), and **Spruce Pool,** 21st Street and Spruce Street.

**TENNIS** There are more than 30 public courts in the city. The **North and South**

**Boulder Recreation Centers** (see "Swimming," above) each have four lighted courts, and accept reservations. Others are at **Arapahoe Ridge Park,** Eisenhower Drive south of Arapahoe Street; **Bucknell Park,** 31st Street and Bucknell Street; **Chautauqua Park,** 9th Street and Baseline Road; **Columbine Park,** 20th Street and Glenwood Street; and **Martin Park,** 36th Street and Eastman Street.

**WATER SPORTS**    For boat or canoe rentals, sailboard instruction, or swimming (and tanning) at a sandy beach, head for **Boulder Reservoir** (tel. 441-3456), on North 51st Street off the Longmont Diagonal northeast of the city.

# 7. SAVVY SHOPPING

## SHOPPING A TO Z

### ANTIQUES

**ART SOURCE INTERNATIONAL, 1237 Pearl St. Tel. 444-4080.**
 Natural-history prints, maps, and rare books on western Americana—all from the 18th and 19th centuries—are the specialty here, along with a collection of one-of-a-kind, turn-of-the-century Colorado photographs. Open Monday through Friday from 9am to 5pm, on Saturday from 10am to 5pm, and on summer Sundays.

### ARTS & CRAFTS

**ART MART, 1222 Pearl St. Tel. 443-8248.**
 More than 120 local artisans are represented in this gallery, which presents their watercolors, pastels, ceramics, hand-blown glass, and Native American jewelry and textile art. Open daily from 10am to 7pm, with extended hours in summer.

**BOULDER CENTER FOR THE VISUAL ARTS, 1750 13th St. (between Arapahoe Ave. and Canyon Blvd.). Tel. 443-2122.**
 Two exhibition galleries display the works of local, state, and contemporary national artists. There are also frequent live performances of music, dance, and poetry readings in the center. Open Tuesday through Saturday from 11am to 5pm and on Sunday from 1 to 5pm.

**COYOTE GALLERY, 1401 Pearl St. Tel. 444-3323.**
 Leading contemporary southwestern artists display their paintings, pottery, wood carvings, jewelry, textiles, and other crafts. Open Monday through Wednesday from 9:30am to 6:30pm and Thursday through Saturday from 9:30am to 9pm, and in summer also on Sunday from noon to 5pm.

**HANDMADE IN COLORADO, 1426 Pearl St. Tel. 938-8394.**
 A small cooperative of local artists make everything right here—including weavings, quilts, stained glass, jewelry, and ceramics. Open Monday through Saturday from 10am to 6pm and on Sunday from noon to 5pm (until 9pm in summer and on holidays).

**LYONS GALLERY, 2012 10th St. Tel. 443-1803.**
 Primarily a gallery of photographic art, Lyons also showcases wearable art by Susan Noe, fashioned from titanium and niobium. Open Tuesday through Saturday from 11am to 7pm.

**MACLAREN/MARKOWITZ GALLERY, 1011 Pearl St. Tel. 449-6807.**
 Works by nationally known artists in a variety of mediums and styles are presented here, including R. C. Gorman, Doug West, and David Grojean. Open Monday through Saturday from 10am to 5:30pm and on Sunday from noon to 5pm.

## FASHIONS

**KALAHARI, 2015 10th St. Tel. 449-0770.**

This designer boutique specializes in practical and elegant women's clothing. The Kalahari line is manufactured here in Boulder; other fashion lines and accessories are also sold. Open Monday through Saturday from 10am to 6pm, with extended hours in summer.

**TRADERS OF THE LOST ART, 1429 Pearl St. Tel. 440-4058.**

This import shop carries colorful clothing and accessories from Asia, Africa, South America, and other locations around the world.

**ZIPPETY DOO-DA, 2425 Canyon Blvd. Tel. 449-2522.**

It's all for the kids here—children's clothing and accessories, including such lines as Flapdoodles, Gotcha, and Monkeywear, from newborn to size 14. There's a play area for kids while parents shop. Open Monday through Friday from 10am to 6pm, on Saturday from 10am to 5:30pm, and on Sunday from noon to 5pm.

## FOOD

**ALFALFA'S, 1651 Broadway. Tel. 442-0997.**

The original Alfalfa's—a natural-foods supermarket that has since expanded to two locations in greater Denver—is here in Boulder. Even if you're not cooking for yourself, stop for a drink at the juice bar.

## GIFTS & SOUVENIRS

**BOULDER HOLDING COMPANY, 1107 Pearl St. Tel. 443-4430.**

Perhaps the most remarkable feature of this unusual store is its kaleidoscope collection: 200 different styles by more than 30 different artists. But there's a little of everything else delightful in the store, too. Open Monday through Thursday from 10am to 6pm, on Friday and Saturday from 10am to 10pm, and on Sunday from 11am to 5pm, with extended hours in summer.

**ECOLOGY HOUSE, 1441 Pearl St. Tel. 444-7023.**

Every gift in the shop, from T-shirts to jewelry, sculpture to stained glass, has an environmental theme. Part of the proceeds from every sale go to environmental causes. Open daily from 10am to 8pm.

## JEWELRY

**BLUE STAR GEMS, 1035 Pearl St. Tel. 443-9629.**

Amethyst, lapis, tourmaline, opal, blue topaz—these and many other stones are available here, rough cut or in fine settings. There are polished crystals, sculpted figurines, and distinctive gold and silver jewelry. Open on Monday from 10am to 4pm, Tuesday and Wednesday from 10am to 6pm, Thursday through Saturday from 10am to 8pm, and on Sunday from noon to 7pm.

**FLORENCE BEAR JEWELRY & ANTIQUES, 2014 Broadway. Tel. 443-6311.**

Native American jewelry, including many hard-to-find pieces, highlight this shop, in business for two decades. Gold and silver work is also presented. Open Monday through Saturday from 10:30am to 5:30pm and on Sunday from 1 to 5pm, with extended hours in summer.

## MALLS & SHOPPING CENTERS

**ARAPAHOE VILLAGE SHOPPING CENTER, 2640 Arapahoe Ave., at Folsom Ave.**

This is one of several mid-size shopping centers near the junction of Arapahoe and 28th Street.

**CROSSROADS MALL, 28th St. between Pearl St. and Arapahoe Ave.**

This 175-store shopping center is anchored by Sears, J. C. Penney's, May D&F,

Mervyn's, and Montgomery Ward. There are also a wide variety of clothiers, jewelers, and stationers, at least half a dozen restaurants, and various other shops. A marked "Walkers Track" attracts locals on rainy days.

**PEARL STREET MALL, Pearl St. from 11th to 15th Sts.**
The core of downtown Boulder, the mall contains a wide choice of shops, galleries, and restaurants. See "The Top Attractions" in "Attractions," above.

---

# 8. EVENING ENTERTAINMENT

Boulder is a highly cultured community, especially noted for its summer music, dance, and Shakespeare festivals. But major entertainment events take place here year round, both downtown and on the University of Colorado campus.

There's also a wide choice of nightclubs and bars—but it hasn't always been so here. Boulder was dry for 60 years, from 1907 (13 years before national Prohibition) until 1967! The first new bar in the city, the Catacombs in the Hotel Boulderado, finally opened in 1969.

Current entertainment schedules can be found in the *Daily Camera*'s weekly *Friday Magazine;* in either of the Denver dailies, the *Denver Post* or the *Rocky Mountain News;* or in *Westword,* the Denver weekly. Tickets for nearly all major entertainment and sporting events can be obtained from **TicketMaster** (tel. 290-TIXS) or its outlets, including Gart Bros. Sporting Goods (tel. 449-9021). Credit-card orders can be placed on American Express, MasterCard, or VISA. The agency adds a $3 charge to every ticket.

## THE PERFORMING ARTS

### MAJOR PERFORMING ARTS COMPANIES & EVENTS

#### Classical Music & Opera

**ARTIST SERIES, Macky Auditorium Concert Hall, University of Colorado. Tel. 492-8008.**
Such famed and varied international artists as Isaac Stern, Dave Brubeck, Dance Brasil, and the Royal Philharmonic Orchestra of London have appeared in Boulder through this annual subscription series. Emerging and regional artists also perform on and off campus.

**BOULDER BACH FESTIVAL, 2010 14th St. Tel. 442-4222.**
First presented in 1981, this celebration of the music of Johann Sebastian Bach includes four performances during the first week of April. Normally, guest conductors lead three orchestra presentations on campus, and there's an organ recital at a nearby church. The festival also includes preconcert lectures and a children's concert.

**BOULDER INTERNATIONAL CHAMBER PLAYERS. Tel. 447-8364.**
Artists present an eclectic mix of music, from Beethoven sonatas to the classical sarod-and-tabla of North India. Performances, typically the second Thursday of the month, are scheduled at various locales around the city.

**BOULDER PHILHARMONIC ORCHESTRA. Tel. 449-1343.**
This acclaimed community orchestra performs an annual fall-to-spring season at Macky Auditorium, bringing in world-famous artists including violinist Nadia Sonnenberg, guitarist Carlos Montoya, and pianist Pinchus Zukerman. Conductor Oswald Lehnert also presents *The Nutcracker* ballet with the Boulder Ballet Ensemble, Thanksgiving weekend. Tickets are $8 to $23.

## Dance Companies

**BOULDER BALLET ENSEMBLE. Tel. 447-1968.**
This community group, established in 1984, is best known for its production of
*The Nutcracker* with the Boulder Philharmonic on Thanksgiving weekend.

## FESTIVALS

**COLORADO DANCE FESTIVAL, Dept. B, P.O. Box 356, Boulder, CO
80306. Tel. 303/442-7666.**
Dancers from all over the world flock to Boulder for this 8½-week event, from
early June to early August. Diverse performances are interspersed with classes,
workshops, lectures, film and video screenings, and panel discussions.

**COLORADO MUSIC FESTIVAL, 1035 Pearl St, Suite 302, Boulder, CO
80302. Tel. 303/449-1397.**
The single biggest arts event of every year in Boulder lasts 7 weeks, from mid-June
to early August. Principal musicians from the world's leading orchestras comprise the
Colorado Festival Orchestra, under the direction of Giora Bernstein, and present four
performances a week at the acoustically revered Chautauqua Auditorium. Visiting
artists and conductors add to the high standard of classical and contemporary
performances. The festival has been held since 1976. There's a children's concert in
late June and an outdoor pops concert on the Fourth of July.

**COLORADO SHAKESPEARE FESTIVAL, Campus Box 261, University of
Colorado, Boulder, CO 80309. Tel. 303/492-8181.**
Considered one of the top three Shakespearean festivals in the United States, this
7½-week event annually attracts more than 40,000 theatergoers between late June and
mid-August. Held since 1958 in the University of Colorado's Mary Rippon Outdoor
Theatre, it offers 14 performances of each of three of the great bard's plays—typically
a comedy, a history, and a tragedy. Actors, directors, designers, and everyone
associated with the productions are fully schooled Shakespearean professionals. A
fourth non-Shakespearean production, usually a contemporary classic, is presented
indoors in the nearby University Theatre.
Performances are Tuesday through Sunday at 8:30pm (8pm for the indoor play),
with 2pm matinees about twice a week. Tickets run $11 to $26 for a single
performance, $33 to $78 for a four-play package.
During the festival, company members conduct 75-minute backstage tours at 6pm
before each show. The tour reveals actors and technicians preparing for that evening's
performance, and includes a visit to the company's costume exhibit. Adults pay $3;
children 5 to 11, $2.

## MAJOR CONCERT HALLS, THEATERS & ALL-PURPOSE
## AUDITORIUMS

**BOULDER THEATER, 2030 14th St., at Pearl St. Tel. 444-3600.**
Built in 1935 in art deco style, this fully restored, two-level cabaret-style theater
seats 840. With full bar service and a proscenium stage, it is well suited to concerts by
touring rock and jazz musicians. Of special note are the theater's frescoed ceilings and
surrealistic murals of Joshua trees on opposite walls.

**CHAUTAUQUA AUDITORIUM, 900 Baseline Rd. Tel. 422-3282.**
First opened on July 4, 1898, this National Historic Landmark in Chautauqua
Park is an all-wood building notable for the clarity of its acoustics. That's why the
Colorado Music Festival is held here every summer, and why dance, theater, and
various concert performances are staged in the auditorium and adjacent Community
House throughout the year. A trolley shuttle takes Chautauqua patrons from a free
parking lot at Baseline Junior High School, 20th Street and Baseline Road, to the
auditorium for concerts on summer weekends.

**THE GUILD THEATER, 4840 Sterling Dr. Tel. 442-1415.**
The Upstart Crow community theater group offers a four-play season of

20th-century plays at the Guild Theatre in the early autumn, late autumn, winter, and spring. Tennessee Williams and Sean O'Casey were among playwrights presented in the 1990–91 season. The Boulder Acting Conservatory Theatre, for children 5 to 18, also makes its home here.

**MACKY AUDITORIUM CONCERT HALL, University of Colorado, University Ave. and Macky Dr. Tel. 492-6352.**
The campus concert hall is home to the Boulder Philharmonic Orchestra and to major touring concert acts throughout the year.

**MARY RIPPON OUTDOOR THEATRE, University of Colorado, Hellems Bldg., Broadway between 15th and 16th Sts. Tel. 492-8181.**
Home of summer Shakespeare since 1944, and the official birthplace of the Colorado Shakespeare Festival in 1958, this beautiful garden theater was built by the Works Progress Administration in 1936 and named for the university's first woman professor. Nestled in the courtyard between the Hellems and Henderson buildings, it seats 1,004.

**THE NOMAD PLAYHOUSE, 1410 Quince St. Tel. 443-7510.**
The Nomad Players stage five productions a year, September to June, including musicals, comedies, and dramas.

**SPACE FOR DANCE, 3404 Walnut St. Tel. 444-1357.**
A variety of local dance troupes use this space for productions, frequently two or more weekends a month.

### DINNER THEATER

**BOULDER DINNER THEATER, 5501 Arapahoe Ave. Tel. 449-6000.**
Servers pull double duty here: First they bring you dinner in this cabaret-style theater; then they perform popular Broadway musicals without missing a beat. Dinner is served Tuesday through Sunday at 6:15pm, with showtime at 8pm. There's also a 12:15pm Sunday matinee (showtime 2pm).
**Admission:** $21–$27 for dinner and show.

# THE CLUB & MUSIC SCENE
## CABARET

**BOULDER THEATER, 2030 14th St., at Pearl St. Tel. 444-3600.**
This downtown art deco–style cabaret theater presents a continuing schedule of concerts by touring rock, country, jazz, and blues musicians. In the same week, they've presented performers as diverse as instrumentalist Wynton Marsalis, country singer Rosanne Cash, original Doors guitarist Robby Krieger, the hard-rock Psychedelic Zombies, and feminist activist Starhawk. There's full bar service.
**Tickets:** $6–$20.

## COUNTRY & ROCK MUSIC

**BOULDER CITY LIMITS, 47th St. and Longmont Diagonal. Tel. 444-6666.**
Boulder's only country-and-western nightclub offers live swing and two-step music Thursday through Saturday night. Country dance lessons are offered on Wednesday and before the band starts on Saturday, and there are jitterbug lessons on Tuesday. After 7pm Tuesday, you can play pool for free. Open daily.
**Admission:** Free or $2–$5, depending on night.

**J. J. McCABE'S CAFE, 945 Walnut St. Tel. 449-4130.**
There's live rock music Tuesday through Sunday, and a blues jam session Monday night, at this casual downtown café-bar. Mexican food and hamburgers, big-screen sports television, and a set of pool tables keep everyone happy.
**Admission:** $1–$4.

**TULAGI, 1129 13th St. Tel. 442-1369.**

An informal college bar on the Hill off campus, Tulagi features live rock music most nights.

## JAZZ, BLUES & FOLK MUSIC

**BRILLIG CAFE AND GALLERY, 1322 College Ave. Tel. 443-7461.**
This artsy throwback to past decades hosts the Boulder Folkhouse every Thursday evening.
**Admission:** Free.

**MEZZANINE LOUNGE, in the Hotel Boulderado, 13th and Spruce Sts. Tel. 442-4344.**
Light jazz combos or soloists perform nightly in Victorian surroundings. This is a great place to have a conversation with friends without being overwhelmed by loud music.
**Admission:** Free.

## DANCE CLUBS & DISCOS

**BENTLEY'S, in the Broker Inn, 30th St. and Baseline Rd. Tel. 449-1752.**
Disc jockeys play dance music nightly at this flashy singles bar that tends to attract young professionals rather than a college crowd. Free hors d'oeuvres are served Monday through Friday from 4 to 7pm (on Wednesday until 9pm, with $1.50 cocktails).
**Admission:** Free.

**BOULDER EXPRESS, 2075 30th St. Tel. 443-8162.**
The college students' favorite disco is an upscale club with frenetic sounds lasting into the wee hours nightly. Expect a line after 9pm on Friday and Saturday.

**POTTER'S, 1207 Pearl St. Tel. 444-3100.**
The Pearl Street Mall's most popular dance club has live music on Tuesday, disco sounds other nights. There are nightly "special events," a big-screen TV for major sports, and seven dart boards for competitive types. Open daily.
**Admission:** Free.

# THE BAR SCENE
## PUBS & WINE BARS

**THE JAMES PUB, 1922 13th St. Tel. 449-1922.**
Every important city has an Irish pub, and this is Boulder's. You'll find Harp Lager and a dozen other beers on tap, Irish coffee, and such pub grub as corned beef and cabbage. Irish musicians even perform on occasion. Come for lunch or dinner, or for happy hour after 10pm.

**OUTBACK SALOON, 3141 28th St. Tel. 444-0081.**
This Australian pub—the owners invite "blokes" and "sheilas" to their "Aussie boozer"—serves meat pies, sausage rolls, and even beetroot burgers. Live rock and blues groups play dance music Wednesday through Saturday night.

**WALNUT BREWERY, 1123 Walnut St., near Broadway. Tel. 447-1345.**
The second-largest microbrewery in the United States (in terms of beer production) has its restaurant/bar/brewery in a historic brick warehouse off the Pearl Street Mall. Six beers are regularly brewed on the premises—Big Horn Bitter, Swiss Trail Wheat Ale, Buffalo Gold Premium Ale, Old Elk Brown Ale, The James Irish Red Ale, and Devil's Thumb Stout—plus seasonal specials like Spiranthes Ale, made from a white orchid grown locally.

**THE CORNER BAR, in the Hotel Boulderado, 13th and Spruce Sts. Tel. 442-4344.**

Probably the best bar in Boulder for people-watching, this Hotel Boulderado institution features a fresh-oyster bar and an extensive list of wines by the glass.

## OLD CHICAGO, 1102 Pearl St. Tel. 443-5031.

A pizza-and-pasta chain found throughout the Front Range, Old Chicago has two trademarks: its list of 110 beers from around the world (ask for a passport), and its sports-bar focus on Chicago teams (Cubs, White Sox, Bears, Bulls, Black Hawks).

## THE SINK, 1165 13th St. Tel. 444-SINK.

The spacey wall murals are straight out of the '60s, but this off-campus establishment has actually been open since 1949. Talk to students in the "Ratroom," or dine on burgers or ragged-edge pizza. Open daily from 11am to 10pm.

## THE WALRUS, 11th and Walnut Sts. Tel. 443-9902.

This is where local university students come to play games—pool, darts, foosball, shuffleboard, and more—or to down $1 draft beers while circulating from table to table to see friends.

## WEST END TAVERN, Pearl St. between 9th and 10th Sts. Tel. 444-3535.

The West End seems to have a lock on the annual "best neighborhood bar" balloting conducted by the *Daily Camera*. Sunny afternoons find dozens of Boulderites perched on the tavern's roof garden, and evenings see them tuned in to a wide-ranging selection of jazz, blues, or other live music in the trendy bar. Fare includes hot chili, pizza, and char-broiled sandwiches.

# CHAPTER 8
# NORTHEASTERN COLORADO

It would be hard to describe northeastern Colorado more perfectly or succinctly than with the now-famous words of "America the Beautiful" penned by Katherine Lee Bates after her ascent of Pikes Peak in 1893.

Here indeed are the spacious skies, stretching without obstacle or interruption hundreds of miles eastward from the foot of the Rocky Mountains.

Here are the golden, rolling, irrigated fields of wheat and corn, spreading along the valleys of the South Platte and Republican rivers and their tributaries, such as the Cache la Poudre and Big Thompson.

The western edge of this magnificent country is defined by the regal Rockies themselves. Impressive geological features mark the foothills, where the mountains meet the Great Plains at Fort Collins and Loveland.

A different Colorado exists on the sparsely populated plains, one that inspired James Michener's novel *Centennial*. Alive are memories of the Comanche buffalo hunters who first inhabited the region; trailblazers and railroad crews who opened up the area to white settlement; hardy pioneer farmers who endured drought, economic ruin, and so many other hardships; and ranchers like John W. Iliff, who carved a feudal empire built on longhorn cattle. Pioneer museums, frontier forts, old battlefields, and preserved downtown districts won't let history die. Vast open stretches—wetlands swollen with migrating waterfowl, the starkly beautiful Pawnee National Grassland—remain to remind us that Colorado wilderness is not the sole domain of the Rockies.

## 1. FORT COLLINS

65 miles N of Denver, 34 miles S of Cheyenne, Wyo.

**GETTING THERE    By Plane**    Most visitors to Fort Collins fly into Denver's Stapleton International Airport (see Chapter 4). The **Airport Express** (tel. 482-0505) leaves Stapleton for Fort Collins hourly on the half hour, daily 8:30am to 9:30pm; and leaves Fort Collins daily, with departures every 30 to 90 minutes from 4:45am to 6pm. Call for reservations, specific schedules, and pickup locations. Fare is $13 one way to or from major hotels; only cash is accepted.

The small **Fort Collins–Loveland Municipal Airport** (tel. 221-1300), off I-25 Exit 259, 10 miles south of Fort Collins, is served by **Continental Express** from Denver (tel. 800/525-0280) and also handles charters. Private planes land at the **Fort Collins Valley Airpark,** County Road 9E off Mulberry Street (tel. 484-4186).

**By Bus**    Greyhound/Trailways, 338 East Mountain Avenue, at Riverside

# WHAT'S SPECIAL ABOUT NORTHEASTERN COLORADO

## Natural Attractions

☐ Poudre Canyon, containing the Cache la Poudre River, the first Colorado river designated a national Wild and Scenic River.

☐ Pawnee National Grassland, where the federal government and ranchers work to enhance wildlife habitat and reduce soil erosion.

☐ Bonny State Recreation Area, with boating, fishing, and swimming on the only sizable reservoir for 100 miles around.

## The Arts

☐ Benson Park Sculpture Garden in Loveland, site every August of the largest outdoor sculpture show and sale in the U.S.

☐ Kit Carson County Carousel in Burlington, a National Historic Landmark and a menagerie of carved wooden animals.

☐ The Living Trees of Sterling, artist Brad Rhea's whimsical wood sculptures, making poetic statements at locations throughout the city.

## Museums

☐ Fort Morgan Museum, tracing Native American history back 13,000 years to Clovis points.

☐ Overland Trail Museum in Sterling, recalling the westward migration and holding unusual collections of branding irons and barbed wire.

☐ Meeker Home Museum in Greeley, the original home of Union Colony founder Nathan Cook Meeker.

## Industrial Tour

☐ Anheuser-Busch Brewery in Fort Collins, home of the company's famous Clydesdales.

## Special Events

☐ Valentine's Day in Loveland, with its annual remailing of cards and love letters with a Cupid cachet and postmark.

☐ Julesburg's Pony Express Reride in June, retracing the mail carriers' route from their only Colorado station.

☐ The Brush Rodeo, held over the Fourth of July weekend, the world's largest amateur rodeo.

## Historic Villages

☐ Greeley's Centennial Village, with 22 buildings recalling life from the 1860 agricultural colony era to the 1920s.

☐ Burlington's Old Town, offering 24 buildings of living history, plus can-can shows, gunfights, and hayloft melodramas.

---

Avenue (tel. 221-1327), provides intercity service, with major connections from Denver and Cheyenne.

**By Car**  Coming from south or north, take I-25 Exit 269 (Mulberry Street, for downtown Fort Collins), Exit 268 (Prospect Road, for Colorado State University), or Exit 265 (Harmony Road, for south Fort Collins). From Rocky Mountain National Park, follow U.S. 34 to Loveland, then turn north on U.S. 287. The drive takes about 1¼ hours from Denver or Estes Park, about 40 minutes from Cheyenne.

**SPECIAL EVENTS**  The first weekend in May, **Cinco de Mayo** is celebrated in Old Town; the third weekend in August, **New West Fest** takes place in Old Town and Library Park; the third week in September is **Balloon Fest,** on Mulberry Street near I-25; and in mid-October, go to Old Town for **Oktoberfest.**

---

A trading post was established here in 1862 on the Cache la Poudre River, named for a powder cache left by French fur trappers. A stage station and army camp, commanded by Col. William O. Collins, followed. The fort was abandoned in 1867, but the settlement prospered, first as a quarrying and farming center, and by 1910 in sugar-beet processing.

Today Fort Collins is regarded as one of the fastest-growing cities in the United States, with an average annual growth rate of 3.5%. Population leaped from 43,000 in 1970 to 65,000 in 1980 to 87,800 in the 1990 census, not including the many Colorado State University students. CSU was established in 1879; today it is nationally known for its forestry and veterinary medicine schools, and its research advances in space engineering and bone cancer. Major employers in the city are the Anheuser-Busch Brewery and Hewlett-Packard computer systems. The National Institute of Standards and Technology, which coordinates the precise universal time and frequency, transmitting it to radios all over the world, is also located here.

# ORIENTATION

## INFORMATION

The **Fort Collins Convention & Visitors Bureau** has a visitor information center at 420 South Howes Street (P.O. Box 1998), Fort Collins, CO 80522 (tel. 303/482-5821, or 800/274-FORT). That's two blocks west of the intersection of College Avenue and Mulberry Street.

## CITY LAYOUT

Fort Collins is located at the foot of the Rockies on the Cache la Poudre River, a major tributary of the South Platte. Downtown "Fort" is 4 miles due west of I-25. **College Avenue** (U.S. 287) is the main north-south artery and the city's primary commercial strip; **Mulberry Street** (Colo. 14), which crosses I-25 at Exit 269, the major Fort Collins interchange, is the main east-west thoroughfare.

**Downtown Fort Collins** extends north of Mulberry on College to Jefferson Street; **Old Town** is contained in a triangle bounded by College, Jefferson, and Mountain Avenue, which parallels Mulberry four blocks to its north. The main **Colorado State University campus** is in the mile-square sector bounded by Mulberry Street on the north, Prospect Road on the south, College Avenue on the east, and Shields Street on the west. Drake Road, Horsetooth Road, and Harmony Road cross College Avenue at 1-mile intervals south of Prospect. Taft Hill Road and Overland Trail parallel College at 1-mile intervals west of Shields; Lemay Avenue and Timberline Road are at 1-mile intervals east.

# GETTING AROUND

**BY BUS**   The city bus system, known as **Transfort** (tel. 221-6620), operates seven routes throughout Fort Collins Monday through Saturday from 6:30am to 6:30pm, except major holidays. (From late May through late August service starts at 7:30am.) Route 1 operates from downtown, 6 miles straight down College Avenue, and is accessible to the disabled; call for information on other routes. Fares are 55¢ for adults, 25¢ for seniors and the disabled, 30¢ for youths 6 to 17, children under 6 ride free; exact change is required. A 10-ride ticket is $4.50.

**BY STREETCAR**   More for fun than for practical urban transport, a restored 1919 Birney streetcar—the **Fort Collins Municipal Railway** (tel. 224-5372)—runs on its original track from City Park, 1½ miles east down Mountain Avenue to Sherwood Street, four blocks west of College Avenue. Service is May to September, on weekends and holidays only, from noon to 5pm; fare is $1 for adults, 50¢ for children 12 and under.

**BY TAXI**   Taxi service is provided 24 hours a day by **Yellow Cab** (tel. 493-8200) and **Shamrock Taxi** (tel. 224-2222).

**BY BICYCLE** There are more than 56 miles of designated **bikeways** in Fort Collins, including the 5-mile Spring Creek Trail and the 6-mile Poudre River Trail. Rent bikes from **Lee's Cyclery,** 202 West Laurel Street (tel. 482-6006), and ask for the "Tour de Fort" bicycle route map from the visitor information center or city offices. Bicycles are not allowed on College Avenue.

## FAST FACTS

The **area code** is 303. In case of **emergency,** call **911;** for standard business, call police at 484-4220 or the Larimer County sheriff at 482-6442. The **Poudre Valley Hospital** is at 1024 Lemay Avenue (tel. 482-4111), between Prospect Road and Riverside Avenue just east of downtown. *The Coloradoan,* a Gannett **newspaper,** is published daily. The main **post office** is in the Federal Building, 301 South Howes Street (tel. 482-2837). State and county **tax** adds 8.95% to hotel bills.

## WHAT TO SEE & DO

**OLD TOWN, between College and Mountain Aves. and Jefferson St.**
A red-brick pedestrian walkway, flanked by street lamps and surrounding a bubbling fountain, is the focus of this restored historic district. The main plaza extends diagonally northeastward from the intersection of College Avenue and Mountain Avenue; on either side are shops and galleries, restaurants and nightspots. Band concerts and a string of special events keep the plaza lively, especially from mid-spring to mid-fall. Walking-tour maps are usually available from individual merchants and city offices.

**COLORADO STATE UNIVERSITY, University and College Aves. Tel. 491-6444.**
Fort Collins revolves around the university, with its 20,000 students and 4,500 more faculty and staff. Founded in 1879 as Colorado Agricultural College, and later renamed Colorado A&M University, its athletic teams are still affectionately called the "Aggies," though they've been the Rams for decades. The A on the hillside behind Hughes Stadium helps keep the name alive.
Campus visits usually start at the Administration Building, on **The Oval** where the school began, or **Lory Student Center,** University Avenue and Center Avenue (tel. 491-6444), which houses a cafeteria, bar, bookstore, activities center, ballroom, and other facilities. Appointments can be made to visit the renowned **Veterinary Teaching Hospital,** 300 West Drake Road (tel. 221-4535), and the **Equine Teaching Center** at the Foothills Campus off West Laporte Avenue (tel. 491-8373). The **CSU Art Department,** on Pitkin Street (tel. 491-6774), has five different galleries with revolving exhibits; and the **University Theatre** in Johnson Hall, on East Drive (tel. 491-5116), presents student productions year round.

**ANHEUSER-BUSCH BREWERY, 2351 Busch Dr. (I-25, Exit 271). Tel. 490-4691.**
Opened in mid-1988, the brewery has become one of Fort Collins's leading employers—and its top tourist attraction. Six million gallons of beer are produced here each year, and distributed to 10 western states. Tours of the brewing facility leave from the visitors center, which includes exhibits on the Anheuser-Busch company, a gift shop and tasting room/restaurant. You needn't join a tour to visit the elegant barn that's home to the giant Clydesdale draft horses, used to promote Budweiser and other Busch beers since 1933.
**Admission:** Free.
**Open:** May–Oct, daily 10am–5pm; Nov–Apr, Wed–Sun 9am–4pm. **Closed:** Major hols.

**AVERY HOUSE, 328 W. Mountain Ave. Tel. 221-0533.**
Custom-built in 1879 for banker-surveyor Franklin Avery and his wife, Sara, this Victorian home at the corner of Mountain Avenue and Meldrum Street was constructed of red and buff sandstone from the quarries west of Fort Collins. The city purchased the house in 1974, and is continuing to restore it to its original Victorian

splendor—from furniture to wallpaper to frescoed ceilings. The grounds, with their gazebo and fountain, are popular for weddings and receptions.

**Admission:** By donation.

**Open:** Second and fourth Wed of every month, 1–3pm, and Apr–Oct, also Sun 1–3pm.

### FORT COLLINS MUSEUM, 200 Mathews St. Tel. 221-6738.

In the turn-of-the-century Carnegie Library building at the southeast corner of Oak Street and Mathews Street, a block south of Old Town, the museum has a collection that ranges from mammoth molars to Folsom points, pioneer artifacts to high-tech glimpses of Fort Collins's future. An outdoor courtyard has an 1844 trapper's cabin, an 1864 army cabin, and an 1884 one-room schoolhouse. Major summer events are **Rendezvous**, a re-enactment of the fur-trading era, in early June, and **Skookum Day,** with demonstrations of blacksmithing, quilting, weaving, and other pioneer-era skills, the third Saturday of July.

**Admission:** Free.

**Open:** Tues–Sat 10am–5pm, Sun noon–5pm. **Closed:** Major hols.

### THE FARM AT LEE MARTINEZ PARK, 600 N. Sherwood St. Tel. 221-6665.

City slickers—adults as well as children—can try their hands at such farm chores as feeding goats, milking cows, and grinding flour. Early 20th-century farm machinery is on display; country crafts are sold in the Silo Store. Special programs are scheduled year round, and there are weekend pony rides for the kids in spring and summer.

**Admission:** Free; pony rides $2.

**Open:** Wed–Sat 10am–6pm, Sun noon–6pm; hours change seasonally.

### SWETSVILLE ZOO, 4801 E. Harmony Rd. Tel. 484-9509.

Don't come to Bill Swets's zoo expecting to find animals—not live ones, that is. The Sculpture Park is a menagerie of six dozen dinosaurs and other real and imaginary animals, flowers, and windmills—all constructed from car parts, farm machinery, and other scrap metal. There's also a miniature three-quarter-mile steam train and an outdoor exhibit of old farm equipment and a 10-seat bicycle. The zoo is southeast of Fort Collins, on the east side of I-25.

**Admission:** By donation.

**Open:** Daily dawn–dusk, year round.

## WHERE TO STAY

### MODERATE

### FORT COLLINS MARRIOTT, 350 E. Horsetooth Rd., Fort Collins, CO 80525. Tel. 303/226-5200, or 800/548-2635. Fax 303/226-5200, request fax. 215 rms (all with bath), 13 suites. A/C TV TEL

**$ Rates:** $79–$109 single Mon–Fri, $69–$89 Sat–Sun; $89–$119 double Mon–Fri, $79–$99 Sat–Sun; $96–$400 suite. AE, CB, DC, DISC, ER, MC, V.

**Parking:** Free.

Located in south Fort Collins, the Marriott boasts a direct walkway to the city's largest shopping center, Foothills Fashion Mall, as well as other shops and banks. The spacious lobby, which makes nice use of pink marble, is built around a central gas fireplace. Patrons are soothed by piped classical music.

Most rooms have light-pastel decor, a king-size or two double beds, and standard hotel furnishings. Vanities are outside the bathroom. Some suites have canopy beds. TVs offer in-room movies; local phone calls are 75¢.

The hotel offers a full range of services and dining and other facilities.

### HOLIDAY INN UNIVERSITY PARK, 425 W. Prospect Rd., Fort Collins, CO 80524. Tel. 303/482-2626, or 800/HOLIDAY. Fax 303/493-6265. 208 rms (all with bath), 51 suites. A/C TV TEL

**$ Rates:** $68.50–$78.50 single; $73.50–$83.50 double; $95–$195 suite; $49 double with 7-day advance reservation. AE, CB, DC, DISC, JCB, MC, V.

**Parking:** Free.

Conveniently located across the street from the Colorado State University main campus and adjacent to the Spring Creek trail for bikers and runners, this is the city's largest hotel. It's built around a beautiful central atrium with a three-story waterfall, trees, and standing plants.

Standard rooms have one king-size or two oversize double beds, and all standard hotel furnishings, including a credenza with remote-control television, direct-dial phone (local calls 45¢), and attractive serigraphs on the walls. Appointments are light blue and beige. Many of the suites have minibars.

The hotel offers a full range of services and dining and other facilities.

## INEXPENSIVE

**ELIZABETH STREET GUEST HOUSE, 202 E. Elizabeth St., Fort Collins, CO 80524. Tel. 303/493-BEDS.** 3 rms (1 with bath).
**$ Rates** (including full breakfast): $35–$41 single or double without bath, $45–$55 single or double with bath. AE, MC, V.

This 1905 American Foursquare brick home, just a block off College Avenue, at Elizabeth Street and Remington Street, is a little like grandma's house. There's a three-story dollhouse at the entrance and various dolls and other miniatures on shelves throughout, as well as impressive leaded windows and oak woodwork. Guest rooms are individually decorated with antiques and country crafts. The Alaska Room has a private bath; other rooms share 1½ baths. No smoking is permitted in the rooms. Guests have access to a TV, phone, and refrigerator. Coffee, tea, and fruit are always available.

**HELMSHIRE INN HOTEL, 1204 S. College Ave., Fort Collins, CO 80524. Tel. 303/493-4683.** Request fax. 25 rms (all with bath). A/C TV TEL
**$ Rates** (including full breakfast): $53 single; $59 double. Discounts for stays over 5 days. AE, CB, DC, MC, V.

A three-story custom-built inn across College Avenue from the CSU campus at Edwards Street, the Helmshire has a lobby like a living room and a lovely adjoining dining room, where buffet breakfasts and catered dinners are served. Each guest room is a little different, but every one has a private bath and kitchenette (with refrigerator, microwave oven, wet bar, and utensils for two), and is furnished with antiques and re-creations. Ask for a back room—they're quieter. Local phone calls are 30¢. Children are welcome. The building has an elevator and facilities for the disabled. Hot drinks are available around the clock, and there's complimentary wine in the lobby from 6 to 9:30pm.

## BUDGET

**MULBERRY INN—ECONOLODGE, 4333 E. Mulberry St., Fort Collins, CO 80524. Tel. 303/493-9000,** or 800/234-5548. 116 rms (all with bath), 4 suites. A/C TV TEL
**$ Rates:** May–Sept, $35 single; $39–$42 double. Oct–Apr, $32 single; $35–$37 double. Suites $75–$95; Jacuzzi units $49 Mon–Fri, $62 Sat–Sun. AE, CB, DC, DISC, MC, V.

All guest rooms at this large motel have inside entrances. Most rooms have queen-size beds, a desk with a phone (local calls free), a television with in-room movies, and other standard furnishings. There are double Jacuzzis in 32 rooms; the four suites have Jacuzzis, wet bars, and large private decks. The motel restaurant serves dinner Tuesday through Sunday and breakfast Friday through Sunday; there's also a lounge, an outdoor swimming pool, no-smoking rooms, and facilities for the disabled.

**TOWN & COUNTRY MOTEL, 1513 N. College Ave., Fort Collins, CO 80524. Tel. 303/484-0870,** or 800/825-4678. 29 rms (all with bath), 1 suite. A/C TV TEL
**$ Rates:** Mid-May to Sept, $32–$42 single or double; Oct to mid-May, $28–$32 single or double. AE, CB, DC, DISC, ER, MC, V.

A Budget Host property at the north end of town, on U.S. 287 near Willox Lane, this pleasant Ma-and-Pa motel has been owned and operated by Tom and Karen

Weitkunat since 1975. Kids enjoy its playground equipment. Rooms are of wood-panel and concrete-block construction, with orange shag carpeting. Ten units have full kitchens; all have coffee makers. Most rooms have a shower but no bath, so if you need a tub, request it.

# WHERE TO DINE
## EXPENSIVE

**NICO'S CATACOMBS, 115 S. College Ave. Tel. 482-6426.**
   **Cuisine:** CONTINENTAL. **Reservations:** Recommended.
   **$ Prices:** Appetizers $4.25–$7.50; main courses $10.95–$23.50. AE, CB, DC, MC, V.
   **Open:** Dinner only, Mon–Sat 5–10pm.
If Frank Sinatra hung out in northern Colorado, you'd probably find him at Nico's. A classic, dimly lit cellar restaurant, with a richly decorated lounge separated from the main dining room by a stained-glass partition, Nico's features tableside service and daily specials (including fresh seafood) announced on blackboards.
   You can start with a shellfish dish such as mussels Marseille, or perhaps the pâté maison, then move on to rack of lamb paloise, steak Diane flambé, or chateaubriand bouquetière for two. The lounge also serves a pre- and posttheater menu that features a "macho platter" of fried alligator, juliennes of rattlesnake, and Rocky Mountain oysters.

**THE WINE CELLAR, 3400 S. College Ave. Tel. 226-4413.**
   **Cuisine:** CONTINENTAL. **Reservations:** Highly recommended.
   **$ Prices:** Appetizers $6.95–$7.95; main courses $4.95–$7.95 at lunch, $11.95–$23.95 at dinner. AE, CB, DC, DISC, MC, V.
   **Open:** Lunch Mon–Fri 11am–2pm; dinner Sun–Thurs 5–9pm, Fri–Sat 5–10pm.
Perhaps the city's most elegant restaurant, the Wine Cellar is not a cellar at all. It maintains an Old World look, with burgundy-colored tablecloths, small wine casks atop room dividers, lush plants and dimly lit lamps suspended from the ceilings, and a double-sided fireplace separating the dining area from the spacious lounge. An outdoor deck is especially popular on summer weekends, and there's live jazz in the lounge Wednesday through Saturday nights.
   Lunches feature light dishes, but dinner is the big occasion. You might start with a Caesar salad or steak tartare, and follow with a brochette of shrimp pancetta, veal Sirbu, baked pheasant, prime rib . . . or vegetarian Wellington. A dessert favorite is baklava cheesecake. The Wine Cellar, appropriately, has Fort Collins's best wine list—130 vintages, many of them by the glass.

## MODERATE

**JAY'S AMERICAN BISTRO, 151 S. College Ave. Tel. 482-1876.**
   **Cuisine:** CREATIVE CONTINENTAL. **Reservations:** Recommended.
   **$ Prices:** Appetizers $4.50–$5.95; main courses $8.95–$15.95; breakfast $2.25–$5.75; lunch $1.95–$5.75. AE, MC, V.
   **Open:** Breakfast/lunch Mon–Sat 6:30am–2pm, Sun 7am–2pm; dinner Tues–Sat 5–9pm.
This pleasant café near the CSU campus offers pastel decor, the work of local artists on the walls, and evening candlelight. The menu changes every couple of months; appetizers might include smoked shrimp Indonesian or barbecued duck spring rolls. There are always six to eight French dishes, such as veal sweetbreads and chicken tarragon, plus fresh seafoods, pastas (try the angel-hair), stir-frys, and Southwest-influenced dishes. A pianist performs Friday and Saturday nights.

**CUISINE! CUISINE!, 130 S. Mason St. Tel. 221-0399.**
   **Cuisine:** NEW AMERICAN. **Reservations:** Recommended.
   **$ Prices:** Appetizers $4.75–$6.75; main courses $9–$18. MC, V.

**Open:** Lunch, Fri only, 11am–2pm; brunch Sun 11am–2pm; dinner Mon–Sat 5:30–9pm; dessert Sat 9–10pm.

Creativity emanates from every corner of Cuisine! Cuisine!, abstract paintings and prints cover the walls of three small rooms, and modern jazz wafts from the sound system. Tulips and oil candles help contribute to the serene atmosphere. The cuisine is most creative of all. The menu changes daily, often with international influences. I started with an appetizer of Cajun prawns in shiitake mushroom sauce, followed by a queso flameado—a baked white Cheddar flamed with brandy and a side of homemade raspberry peach chutney. The "turf and surf" dish of lamb chops and scallops was perfectly spiced. Other choices were seared tuna steak with a roasted red-pepper crab sauce, and pork tenderloin pressed in macadamia-nut flour and sautéed. There's always something on the menu for vegetarians.

**MARSANNE'S CAFE, 400 S. Meldrum St. Tel. 484-6744.**
   **Cuisine:** INTERNATIONAL. **Reservations:** Recommended for dinner.
$ **Prices:** Appetizers $4.25–$5.50; main courses $9–$14.50; breakfast $2.50–$6.75; lunch $3–$6.95. MC, V.
   **Open:** Mon–Thurs 8am–9:30pm, Fri 8am–10pm, Sat 9am–10pm, Sun 9am–2pm.

Local artisans are at home in this slate-colored 1904 house with gingerbread trim, at the corner of West Magnolia Street opposite Lincoln Center. The center coordinates occasional dinner-theater performances, and there are changing art exhibits on the walls. There's a healthy menu here—omelets and whole-grain pancakes for breakfast; deli sandwiches, pastas, soups, and salads for lunch. Dinners range from ginger salmon to blackened chicken breast, fettuccine Alfredo to a New York pepper steak. Between-meal specialties are chocolate truffle torte and French vanilla coffee. The café has a cozy outdoor patio, a sun room, and a full bar.

## INEXPENSIVE

**BISETTI'S, 120 S. College Ave. Tel. 493-0086.**
   **Cuisine:** ITALIAN. **Reservations:** Not accepted.
$ **Prices:** Appetizers $3.95–$5.65; main courses $3.95–$6.95 at lunch, $6.50–$12.95 at dinner. AE, CB, DC, DISC, MC, V.
   **Open:** Lunch Mon–Fri 11am–2pm; dinner Sun–Thurs 5–9pm, Fri–Sat 5–10pm.

The first thing you'll notice, upon entering this long-standing family business, is the ceiling: From one end to the other dangle empty chianti bottles signed by over a decade of consumers. This is a dark, candlelit room; two adjoining rooms are brighter and more modern. The menu features a variety of pastas, from spaghetti and lasagne to rigatoni and manicotti. Full main courses include veal saltimbocca, basil fettuccine with chicken, and smoked salmon Alfredo. Come before 6:30pm Monday through Saturday for early-bird dinner specials as low as $5.25.

**NATE'S STEAK & SEAFOOD PLACE, Cottonwood Corners, S. College Ave. at Horsetooth Rd. Tel. 223-9200.**
   **Cuisine:** STEAK/SEAFOOD. **Reservations:** Accepted.
$ **Prices:** Appetizers $1.95–$4.25; main courses $3.95–$5.95 at lunch, $6.95–$12.95 at dinner. AE, CB, DC, MC, V.
   **Open:** Sun–Thurs 11am–10pm, Fri–Sat 11am–11pm.

There's a vaguely Cape Cod feel to this casual south-end establishment, with its blue-and-white decor, seascapes, and yachting pictures. A daily list of fresh seafood catches—prepared as you like them—highlights the menu. There's also a variety of steaks, ribs, and barbecued chicken at dinnertime; soups, salads, and sandwiches for lunch. An outdoor patio draws crowds on summer afternoons.

**NOVAK'S LITTLE BUDAPEST, 146 N. College Ave. Tel. 482-7771.**
   **Cuisine:** HUNGARIAN. **Reservations:** Accepted.
$ **Prices:** Lunch $4.85–$7.75; dinner $6.85–$13.95. CB, DC, MC, V.
   **Open:** Mon–Thurs 11am–9pm, Fri 11am–10pm, Sat noon–10pm, Sun noon–8pm.

Simple eastern European decor marks this downtown restaurant, from woven tablecloths to dolls and other folk crafts on mantels around the walls. A baker's dozen of main-dish choices include the shepherd's combo of chicken paprikás, beef pörkölt (in a mushroom sauce), székely töltött káposzta (stuffed cabbage), and kolbász (homemade pork sausage) on pearl noodles. Vegetarians are also catered to. Desserts include dobos torta, a six-layered pastry filled with milk-chocolate cream, coated with almonds and frosting, and topped with a burnt-sugar toffee.

## BUDGET

**AVOGADRO'S NUMBER, 605 S. Mason St. Tel. 493-5555.**
   **Cuisine:** DELI.
$ **Prices:** Breakfast $1.50–$4.25; lunch or dinner $2.95–$4.45. MC, V.
   **Open:** Mon–Thurs 7am–11pm, Fri 7am–midnight, Sat 8am–midnight, Sun 8am–11pm.
A college hangout just north of campus, Avogadro's is a throwback to the '60s with its macramé room dividers and jungle-theme wall mural: Among the faces peeking through the tropical foliage are Albert Einstein and Timothy Leary. The menu runs the gamut from steaks and hamburgers to tempeh burgers, omelets to granola. There's live bluegrass music Friday and Saturday nights.

**COOPER SMITH'S PUB & BREWING, 5 Old Town Sq. Tel. 498-0483.**
   **Cuisine:** ENGLISH/AMERICAN. **Reservations:** Accepted for parties of eight or more.
$ **Prices:** $3.95–$7.25. AE, MC, V.
   **Open:** Mon–Sat 11am–1:30am, Sun 11am–midnight.
This modern brewpub isn't just a place for beer drinking. Within its brick walls is an open kitchen that prepares such traditional pub specialties as fish and chips, bangers and mash, and highland cottage pie. You can also get local treats like catfish Delacroix and Pojoaque Valley green chile stew, as well as hamburgers, other sandwiches, salads, and soups. A late-night menu is served Monday through Saturday until 1am and on Sunday until 11pm. There's also a children's menu.

**EL BURRITO, 404 Linden St. Tel. 484-1102.**
   **Cuisine:** MEXICAN.
$ **Prices:** $2.95–$6.95. AE, CB, DC, MC, V.
   **Open:** Sun–Thurs 11am–9pm, Fri–Sat 11am–10pm.
Mama Godíñez has been concocting her authentic Mexican specialties at this tiny north-of-downtown restaurant. Year-in, year-out, Fort Collins residents have voted it the spot with the best burritos in town. It's also got great tacos, enchiladas, and chiles relleños.

**SILVER GRILL CAFE, 218 Walnut St., Old Town. Tel. 484-4656.**
   **Cuisine:** AMERICAN.
$ **Prices:** Breakfast 60¢–$4.35; lunch $1.25–$5.25. MC, V.
   **Open:** Mon–Sat 6am–2pm, Sun 7am–1pm.
Continually operated since 1933, this working man's café attracts blue- *and* white-collar types, as well as seniors, students, and families. When there's a line outside, as there often is on weekends, coffee is served to those waiting! Come for the giant cinnamon rolls, or standard American fare: eggs and pancakes, biscuits 'n' gravy for breakfast; burgers and other sandwiches for lunch; "noontime dinners" like chicken-fried steak, roast beef, and fried chicken.

# SPORTS & RECREATION

## SPECTATOR SPORTS

The **Colorado State University Rams,** which play in the Western Athletic Conference, provide the main attraction for fans of spectator sports. **Football** games are at CSU Hughes Stadium, Overland Trail near County Road 42C; **basketball** is played at Moby Gym, North Drive near Washington Street on the main campus; and the **baseball** field is on South Drive near Washington. For tickets, call 491-7267.

## RECREATION

**HORSETOOTH RESERVOIR**   The city's most popular area for outdoor recreation is Horsetooth Reservoir, only about 15 minutes west of downtown, just over the first ridge of the Rocky Mountain foothills. The 7-mile-long, man-made lake—on the site of the 19th-century Stout Quarry and community—is named for the distinctive tooth-shaped rock that has long been an area landmark. It's reached via County Road 44E or 42C, both off Overland Trail, or County Road 38E off Taft Hill Road.

There are boat rentals for waterskiing and fishing at the **North Inlet Bay Marina,** 4314 Shoreline Road, and a campground and swimming beach in the South Bay area. Sailboarding and even scuba diving are also popular. The **Foothills Trail** for hikers and mountain bikers runs along the east side of the reservoir from Dixon Dam north to Michaud Lane. **Horsetooth Mountain Park,** on the reservoir's southwestern shore, has 25 miles of hiking and cross-country skiing trails. Near the north end of the lake is a **Sports Cycle Park** for motorcycles and all-terrain vehicles, as well as snowmobiles in winter.

On the northwestern shore of the lake is **Lory State Park** (tel. 226-4517), reached through Laporte. It has hiking and horse trails, and plenty of opportunities for rock climbing. The top of **Arthur's Rock**—a hike of 2 miles—offers a marvelous view across Fort Collins and the northeastern Colorado plains. In the park are the **Double Diamond Stables** (tel. 224-4200), where horse rentals, guided rides, and chuckwagon dinners are arranged.

**OTHER PARKS**   Major Fort Collins parks include: **City Park,** 1500 West Mulberry Street (tel. 484-6686), with boat rentals, miniature train rides, a nine-hole golf course, and an outdoor swimming pool; **Edora Park,** 1420 East Stuart Street (tel. 221-6679), whose Edora Pool and Ice Center (EPIC) is considered one of the finest indoor swimming pools and ice rinks in the United States; **Lee Martiñez Park,** 600 North Sherwood Street (tel. 221-6665), notable not only for its farm (see "What to See & Do" above) but for its fishing and horseback riding opportunities; and **Rolland Moore Park,** 2201 South Shields Street (tel. 221-6667), which features a complex for racquetball and handball players. You'll find picnic grounds, tennis courts, and softball fields at all four parks.

**PARTICIPATORY SPORTS**   Fort Collins offers a number of possibilities. (See also "Other Parks" above.)

**Biking**   Bicyclists (see "Getting Around," above) and joggers use two asphalted trails through the city: **Poudre River Trail,** southeast from North Taft Hill Road to East Prospect Road; **Spring Creek Trail,** west from East Prospect Road to West Drake Road.

**Fishing & Hunting**   Fishing and hunting opportunities abound in the nearby **Roosevelt National Forest.** For further information, contact the **U.S. Forest Service,** Estes-Poudre Ranger District, 148 Remington Street (tel. 482-3822), or Redfeather Ranger District, 1635 Blue Spruce Drive (tel. 498-1375); and the **Colorado Division of Wildlife,** 317 West Prospect Road (tel. 484-2836).

**Golf**   For golfers, Fort Collins has four public courses, including **Collindale Golf Course,** 1441 East Horsetooth Road (tel. 221-6651), and **Southridge Greens,** 5750 South Lemay Avenue (tel. 226-2828); plus two private courses and a driving range.

**River Rafting**   River-rafting enthusiasts can get half-day trips on the Cache la Poudre and full-day rides down the North Platte with **Adrift Adventures,** 1816 Orchard Place (tel. 493-4005), or **Wanderlust Adventures,** 3500 Bingham Hill Road (tel. 484-1219)

**Skiing**   Cross-country skiers can take stay overnight in a backcountry yurt system owned by **Never Summer Nordic** (tel. 484-3903). The yurts are located near Cameron Pass, west of Fort Collins off Colo. 14 in Roosevelt National Forest.

**Swimming**   The **Community Pool,** 424 South Sherwood Street (tel. 221-6675), also has a coin-operated spa.

# SHOPPING

Visitors enjoy shopping in **Old Town Square,** at Mountain Avenue and College Avenue. Shops of note here include the **Walnut Street Gallery,** Building 21, Old Town Square (tel. 221-2383), which displays the work of nationally and regionally known artists; and **Trimble Court Artisans,** 114 Trimble Court (tel. 493-9579), an arts-and-crafts co-op just off the main plaza.

Also downtown is the **One West Contemporary Art Center,** 500 North College Avenue at Oak Plaza (tel. 482-ARTS), housed in a 1911 Italian Renaissance–style building that for six decades was the Fort Collins post office. The visual-arts complex now has six galleries, an art school, library, and gift shops. It's open Tuesday through Saturday from 10am to 5pm.

Northern Colorado's largest shopping mall is the **Foothills Fashion Mall,** 215 East Foothills Parkway, at College Avenue and Horsetooth Road (tel. 226-5555). Anchored by four department stores—May D&F, J.C. Penney's, Sears, and Mervyn's—it has more than 100 specialty stores and a food court, and is open Monday through Friday from 10am to 9pm, on Saturday from 10am to 6pm, and on Sunday from noon to 5pm (closed major holidays).

# EVENING ENTERTAINMENT

**THE PERFORMING ARTS**   Fort Collins's principal venue for the performing arts is **Lincoln Center,** 417 West Magnolia Street, at Meldrum Street (tel. 221-6730). Built in 1978, the center includes the 1,180-seat Performance Hall and the 220-seat Mini-Theatre, as well as an art gallery and an outdoor sculpture garden. It is home to the Fort Collins Symphony, the Canyon Concert Ballet, the Larimer Chorale, the OpenStage Theater, and the Children's Theater. Annual concert, dance, children's, and travel film series are presented.

The **Fort Collins Symphony** (tel. 482-4823), established in 1949, performs a regular season and special events—such as *The Nutcracker* (with the **Canyon Concert Ballet**) during the Christmas season, and a collaboration with the **Larimer Chorale** in the spring. On summer nights, the orchestra plays frequent outdoor concerts at various locations.

The **OpenStage Theatre** (tel. 221-5805) is the leading professional stage group. It offers five contemporary adult productions annually, as well as various popular, classical, operatic, and musical pieces through the season.

Notable summer concert series are the **Lincoln Center Brown-Bag Lunches** (tel. 221-6730), the **Old Town Evening Concerts** (tel. 484-6500), and the **CSU–Lory Student Center Lagoon Concert Series** (tel. 491-1101), all offering a range of jazz, contemporary, and classical music. Also on the CSU campus, the **Theatre Under the Stars** (tel. 482-4823) features three plays on alternating nights late June through July.

**NIGHTCLUBS**   The college crowd does its drinking and mingling at **Fort Ram,** a large dance club near the railroad tracks at 450 North Linden Street (tel. 482-5026). There's live music a few blocks away in Old Town at **Linden's,** 214 Linden Street (tel. 484-1780), the spot for blues and reggae, and the **Old Town Ale House,** 25 Old Town Square (tel. 493-2213), for jazz and rock. Or try **The Wine Cellar,** 3400 South College Avenue (tel. 226-4413), for jazz at 9pm Wednesday through Saturday. A regular is Mark Sloniker, a Fort Collins resident who's developing a national following. Country-and-western dancers head for the **Sundance,** 2716 East Mulberry Street (tel. 484-1600).

Many Fort Collins folk head 24 miles up the Poudre River to the **Mishawaka Inn,** 13714 Poudre Canyon, Colo. 14 (tel. 482-4420), where top regional bands—and occasional national acts—perform. Keep an ear open for the Subdudes, a Fort Collins rock band with a growing national following.

Comedy fans will enjoy live stand-up acts nightly except Tuesday at **Comedy Works,** 7 Old Town Square (tel. 221-5481).

**THE BAR SCENE  Cooper Smith's Pub & Brewing,** 5 Old Town Square (tel. 498-0483), attracts everyone from students to business executives with its pub menu and custom beers, including Poudre Pale Ale and Horsetooth Stout. Nearby, **Old Chicago,** 147 South College Avenue (tel. 482-8599), features an international list of 125 beers. There's a dance floor downstairs at **Washington's,** 132 Laporte Avenue (tel. 493-1603), a lively bar with eclectic decor. The **County Cork Pub,** 2439 South College Avenue (tel. 493-7213), is a popular Irish-style bar. **Boomers Sports Bar,** 1500 East Mulberry Street (tel. 484-2739), attracts a sports-oriented crowd.

**MOVIES**  There are well over a dozen cinemas, including the **Mann University Mall** complex, 2273 South College Avenue (tel. 221-4375). The off-campus favorite, the **Aggie Theatre,** 204 South College Avenue (tel. 224-3772), still offers $1.50 admission.

# EASY EXCURSIONS FROM FORT COLLINS

**POUDRE CANYON**  Running about 70 miles up Colo. 114 west of Fort Collins, this beautiful canyon follows the Cache la Poudre River to its source near the Continental Divide at 10,276-foot Cameron Pass. The first Colorado river with a national Wild and Scenic River designation, the Cache la Poudre offers outstanding trout fishing and white-water rafting, as well as picnicking, camping, hiking, and wildlife watching (deer and bighorn sheep) near its banks.

The upper canyon was the site for the first episode of the TV miniseries *Centennial.* Near the top of the canyon, the Rawah Wilderness encompasses the alpine lakes of the Medicine Bow Mountains, much loved by backpackers and horse packers. The Cameron Pass area is used by snowmobilers and cross-country skiers in winter.

The scenic drive begins 10 miles northwest of Fort Collins, where Colo. 14 turns west off U.S. 287.

**RED FEATHER LAKES**  Located about 45 miles northwest of Fort Collins, this cluster of small lakes attracts fishermen as well as campers, hikers, and cross-country skiers. The high-plateau village, which offers lodging and basic amenities, is reached by turning left at Livermore, about 21 miles north of Fort Collins on U.S. 287.

A short distance from the Livermore turnoff, on the North Fork of the Cache la Poudre, is a historic 1880s guest ranch, the **Cherokee Park Ranch,** P.O. Box 97, Livermore, CO 80536 (tel. 800/628-0949). Open mid-May to early October, it offers an all-inclusive 1-week package—including lodging, meals, and a variety of outdoor sports—at a price of $750 for adults, $350 to $500 for children.

Both the Poudre Canyon and Red Feather Lakes are in **Roosevelt National Forest.** For further information, contact the Fort Collins offices of the **U.S. Forest Service:** Estes-Poudre Ranger District, 148 Remington Street (tel. 482-3822), or Redfeather Ranger District, 1635 Blue Spruce Drive (tel. 498-1375).

---

# 2. LOVELAND

52 miles N of Denver, 13 miles S of Fort Collins

**GETTING THERE  By Plane**  Visitors who fly into **Denver's Stapleton International Airport** can reach Loveland aboard the **Front Range Airporter** (tel. 669-5466).

The small **Fort Collins–Loveland Municipal Airport,** 4824 Earhart Road, Loveland (tel. 669-7182), off I-25 Exit 259, 7 miles northeast of downtown Loveland, is served by **Continental Express** from Denver (tel. 800/525-0280) and also handles charters.

**By Bus   Greyhound/Trailways,** 1630 North Lincoln Avenue (tel. 669-8579), provides intercity service.

**By Car**   Loveland is at the junction of U.S. 287 and U.S. 34. Coming from south or north, take I-25 Exit 257. From the west (Rocky Mountain National Park) or east (Greeley), follow U.S. 34 directly to Loveland. The drive takes about 1 hour from Denver or Estes Park.

**ESSENTIALS   Orientation**   Loveland is on the banks of the Big Thompson River, at the foot of the Rockies. The city is notable for more than a dozen lakes within or just outside the city limits—including Lake Loveland, just west of city center. U.S. 34, known as **Eisenhower Boulevard,** the main east-west thorough-fare, does a slight jog around the lake. **Lincoln Avenue** (one way northbound) and **Cleveland Avenue** (one way southbound) comprise U.S. 287 through the city. The main downtown district is along Lincoln and Cleveland south of Seventh Street, seven blocks south of Eisenhower.

**Information**   Contact the **Loveland Chamber of Commerce,** 114 East Fifth Street (at Cleveland Avenue), Loveland, CO 80537 (tel. 303/667-6311).

**Getting Around**   Taxi service is provided 24 hours a day by **Yellow Cab** (tel. 669-8522) and **Shamrock Taxi** (tel. 667-6767).

**Fast Facts**   The **area code** is 303. In case of **emergency,** call **911;** for standard business, call the police at 667-2151. The **hospital** is McKee Medical Center, 2000 North Boise Avenue (tel. 669-4640) in the northeastern part of the city. The *Reporter-Herald* **newspaper** is published daily. The main **post office** is at 446 East 29th Street (tel. 667-0344), just off Lincoln. State and county **tax** adds 8.95% to hotel bills.

**SPECIAL EVENTS**   Loveland features the **Valentine Kiss-Off** and **Sweet-heart Balloon Rally** in February, the **Loveland Arts Festival** in May, and the **Corn Roast Festival,** the **Larimer County Fair and Rodeo,** and the **Rocky Mountain Bluegrass Festival** in August.

　　To get your **Valentine's Day cards remailed** from Loveland before February 14, you must address and stamp them, leaving room on the lower left of the envelopes for the special Loveland cachet, and mail them in a large envelope to Postmaster, Attn.: Valentines, Loveland, CO 80538. Mark SPECIAL HANDLING on the outer envelope.

------------

**T**he earliest settlements in the Big Thompson Valley were a trading post in the late 1850s and a community that grew around a flour mill in the late 1860s. Loveland was founded in the early 1870s as a station for the new Colorado Central Railroad, and was named for railroad president William Loveland. That "lovestruck" moniker later proved fortuitous, for today Loveland has gained fame as the "Sweetheart City": Some 250,000 Valentine's Day cards are remailed from here every February with a Loveland postmark and cachet. At other times of the year the city is an agricultural center, especially for sugar-beet production. The population is around 37,000.

# WHAT TO SEE & DO
## ATTRACTIONS
### In-Town Attractions

**BENSON PARK SCULPTURE GARDEN, 29th St. between Aspen and Beech Sts. Tel. 663-2940.**
　　A large number of sculptures are permanently displayed among the trees and plants at this city park. More significantly, this is the site of "Sculpture in the Park," the largest outdoor sculpture show and sale in the United States. Held annually the

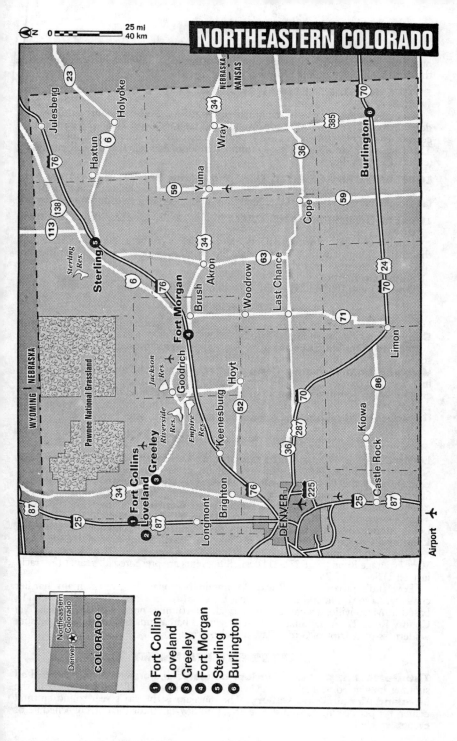

# NORTHEASTERN COLORADO

0 ⸺ 25 mi
⸺ 40 km

Julesburg
Holyoke
Haxtun
Sterling
Sterling Res.
Fort Morgan
Brush
Akron
Woodrow
Wray
Yuma
Cope
Last Chance
Goodrich
Jackson Res.
Riverside Res.
Empire Res.
Greeley
Fort Collins
Loveland
Keenesburg
Hoyt
Longmont
Brighton
Limon
Kiowa
Castle Rock
Burlington
DENVER

Pawnee National Grassland

WYOMING
NEBRASKA
KANSAS

Airport ✈

## COLORADO

Northeastern Colorado
Denver ★

1 Fort Collins
2 Loveland
3 Greeley
4 Fort Morgan
5 Sterling
6 Burlington

second weekend of August, it features work by more than 160 artists. There are numerous studios and two casting foundries near the park, which is located opposite the northwest shore of Lake Loveland.

**BOYD LAKE STATE RECREATION AREA, 3720 N. County Rd. 11C. Tel. 669-1739.**

One of the largest lakes in the northern Front Range is located just a mile east of downtown Loveland via Madison Avenue and County Road 24E. The park here is geared to water sports, including yachting regattas and annual hydroplane races. There are white sand beaches for swimming, modern campsites, and excellent fishing (especially for walleyes).

**LOVELAND CIVIC CENTER, Third and Adams Sts. Tel. 667-6130.**

City offices are located in a beautiful modern complex surrounded by 17 landscaped acres, a 1½-acre lake, fountains, and a 400-seat outdoor amphitheater.

**LOVELAND MUSEUM AND GALLERY, 503 N. Lincoln Ave. Tel. 667-6070.**

Exhibits of local historical artifacts and the work of regional and national artists fill this fine small museum. A "Life on Main Street" display depicts Loveland at the turn of the 20th century. Art exhibits change monthly.

**Admission:** Free.

**Open:** Tues–Wed and Fri 9am–5pm, Thurs 9am–9pm, Sat 10am–4pm.

## Nearby Attractions

U.S. 34 west of Loveland follows the Big Thompson River through **Big Thompson Canyon** for 30 miles to Estes Park, the gateway to Rocky Mountain National Park. After passing **Devil's Backbone,** an unusual geological formation, this marvelously scenic route enters the canyon about 9 miles from Loveland. You can stop at **Viestenz-Smith Mountain Park,** 4 miles farther, with hiking trailheads, picnicking, and playground areas. The one small community along this route, **Drake,** another 4 miles past the mountain park, has cabins, food, and other facilities. A side route from Drake follows the North Fork of the Big Thompson through tiny **Glen Haven,** beside the **Comanche Peak Wilderness,** to Estes Park.

## SPORTS & RECREATION

Loveland has over 670 acres in 24 parks. **North Lake Park,** at 29th Street and Taft Street, has paddle boats and a miniature, narrow-gauge train, the Buckhorn Northern. Golfers enjoy the 18-hole **Loveland Municipal Golf Course,** 2115 West 29th Street. For year-round indoor recreation—including swimming, gymnasium, and racquet sports—try the **Chilson Recreation Center,** 700 East Fourth Street. There's even a small zoo, the **Thompson Valley Wild Life Park,** at 1016 South St. Louis Avenue. For full information on these and other recreation sites, contact **Loveland Parks and Recreation,** 700 East Fourth Street (tel. 667-1634).

Greyhounds run from March through May at **Cloverleaf Dog Racing,** 2527 West Frontage Road (tel. 667-6211). Satellite events are presented all year at the track, just off U.S. 34 at I-25.

Loveland's proximity to Rocky Mountain National Park offers many hardier challenges. One outfit taking advantage is the **Buckhorn Llama Co.** (tel. 667-7411), based in Masonville, a small community about 10 miles northwest of Loveland via County Road 27. A day hike and lunch with a llama runs $35 to $50 per person; wilderness pack trips of 3 to 5 days are also arranged.

## EVENING ENTERTAINMENT

**The Performing Arts   Outdoor concerts** and presentations are staged all summer long at Foote Lagoon, in Civic Center Park, and at Peters Park, next to the **Loveland Museum and Gallery.** The museum is the city's year-round cultural center, for performing as well as fine arts. Call 667-6070 for the current schedule of events.

**The Club & Bar Scene**   Several Loveland lounges offer live music on weekends. Among the most popular bars are **Cyrus McGee's Pub & Grill,** 142 Barberry Place (tel. 663-7100) off Hwy. 402 (14th Street S.E.); **Rear of the Steer,** in the Black Steer, 436 North Lincoln Avenue (tel. 667-6679); and **Springfield's,** 281A East 29th Street (tel. 663-1550).

# WHERE TO STAY

**BEST WESTERN COACH HOUSE RESORT, 5542 E. U.S. 34, Loveland, CO 80537. Tel. 303/667-7810,** or 800/528-1234. 88 units (all with bath). A/C TV TEL
**$ Rates:** Oct–Apr, $26–$46 single; $33–$51 double. May–June and Sept (after Labor Day), $31–$51 single; $38–$56 double. July–Labor Day, $36–$56 single; $41–$61 double. AE, CB, DC, DISC, MC, V.
Nestled beside U.S. 34 as it enters Loveland from the east, this expansive, modern motel features indoor and outdoor swimming pools, a tennis court, whirlpool bath, games room, barbecue area, moderately priced restaurant (serving three meals daily), and lounge. Rooms have king-size or queen-size beds, cable TV with in-room movies, and direct-dial phones. Pets are accepted.

**BUDGET HOST EXIT 254 INN, 2716 S. East Frontage Rd., I-25, Loveland, CO 80537. Tel. 303/667-5202,** or 800/825-4254. 40 units (all with bath). A/C TV TEL
**$ Rates:** $28–$31 single; $38–$42 double. AE, CB, DC, DISC, MC, V.
An inexpensive alternative beside the freeway, this motel has individually heated rooms with king-size or queen-size beds, satellite TV, and direct-dial phones. A few rooms have hot tubs. There's a coin-operated laundry, a playground for the kids, and a restaurant nearby. Small pets are permitted. The motel is accessible to the disabled.

**LOVELANDER BED AND BREAKFAST INN, 217 W. Fourth St., Loveland, CO 80537. Tel. 303/669-0798.** 9 rms, 1 suite (all with bath).
**$ Rates** (including full breakfast): $44–$88 single; $54–$98 double. AE, DC, MC, V.
Bob and Marilyn Wiltgen's rambling 1902 Victorian, just west of downtown, is undoubtedly Loveland's most charming accommodation. Every room has period antiques, including vintage iron or hardwood beds, writing tables, and clawfoot bathtubs. All rooms have private baths, and one has a whirlpool. Breakfast is served in the dining room or on a flagstone terrace, and afternoon tea or wine is offered in front of the parlor fireplace or amid the collection in the plush library. Outside, guests can enjoy rose and herb gardens and fruit trees. Neither pets nor smoking are permitted; children over 10 are welcome.

**SYLVAN DALE GUEST RANCH, 2939 N. County Rd. 31D, Loveland, CO 80538. Tel. 303/667-3915.** 24 units (all with bath).
**$ Rates:** Mid-June to Aug, $325 per person for 3 nights with full board; Sept to mid-June, $55–$85 double for bed and breakfast. No credit cards (personal and traveler's checks accepted).
A working cattle and horse ranch on the banks of the Big Thompson 7½ miles west of Loveland, the Sylvan Dale urges guests to join in with daily ranch chores and roundups. There's horseback riding, a heart-shaped outdoor pool (popular for weddings), tennis and volleyball courts, lakes stocked with rainbow trout, an indoor recreation room, and a kids' play area. The ranch has 14 rooms in its Wagon Wheel Lodge, four duplex cabins, and two large individual cabins. Summer guests must schedule 3- or 6-day full-board stays; the rest of the year, overnight guests are welcomed. The ranch offers complimentary van service from Loveland.

# WHERE TO DINE

**THE PEAKS CAFE, 425 E. Fourth St. Tel. 669-6158.**
   **Cuisine:** NATURAL FOODS.
   **$ Prices:** Breakfast $1.25–$2.50; lunch $1.15–$4.25. MC, V.

**Open:** Mon–Fri 7am–6pm, Sat 8am–5pm.

Come in the morning for breakfast burritos, porridge, yogurt parfait, or the weekly Wednesday "pancake fest." Lunch offers salads, soups, a healthy spinach lasagne, "build-your-own" deli sandwiches, and other health-conscious foods. The café also serves home-baked goods, ice cream, and espressos.

**THE SUMMIT, 3208 W. Eisenhower Blvd. (U.S. 34). Tel. 669-6648.**
   **Cuisine:** STEAK/SEAFOOD. **Reservations:** Recommended.
$ **Prices:** Appetizers $2.95–$6.95; main courses $5.50–$7.50 at lunch, $8.95–$18.95 at dinner. AE, CB, DC, MC, V.
   **Open:** Lunch Mon–Fri 11:30am–2pm; dinner Sun–Thurs 5–9:30pm, Fri–Sat 5–10:30pm; brunch Sun 10am–2pm.

Arguably Loveland's finest restaurant, the Summit offers magnificent views of the Rockies from its location off U.S. 34, as it heads west toward Estes Park. The menu features three cuts of prime rib, New York and sirloin steaks, tenderloin of elk, chicken piccata or marsala, fresh fish, shrimp Diane, Alaskan snow crab, and much more. There are wines by the glass, espresso drinks, and homemade pies.

# 3. GREELEY

54 miles N of Denver, 30 miles SE of Fort Collins

**GETTING THERE  By Plane**   Visitors who fly into **Denver's Stapleton International Airport** can travel on to Greeley with the **Greeley Commuter System,** 609 Eighth Avenue (tel. 353-4557).
   The **Greeley–Weld County Airport,** 600 Crosier Avenue (tel. 356-9141), east of the city, serves private planes and charters.

**By Bus**  Greyhound/Trailways, 107 18th Street (tel. 353-5050), provides intercity service.

**By Car**   Greeley is located at the intersection of U.S. 34 (east-west) and U.S. 85 (north-south). The city is exactly midway between Denver and Cheyenne, Wyoming—both of which are more directly reached by U.S. 85 than by I-25. U.S. 34 heads west 17 miles to I-25, beyond which are Loveland and Rocky Mountain National Park. To the east, U.S. 34 ties Greeley to Fort Morgan via I-76, 37 miles away.

**ESSENTIALS  Orientation**   Greeley is located on the Cache la Poudre River just west of the point where it joins the South Platte. Laid out on a standard grid, it's an easy city in which to find your way around—provided you don't get confused by the numbered streets (which run east-west) and numbered avenues (which run north-south). It helps to know which is which when you're standing at the corner of 10th Street and 10th Avenue. **Eighth Avenue** (U.S. 85 north) and **11th Avenue** (U.S. 85 south) are the main north-south streets through downtown. **Ninth Street** is U.S. 34 Business, jogging into **10th Street** west of 23rd Avenue. The **U.S. 34 Bypass** joins U.S. 85 in a cloverleaf just south of town.

**Information**   Contact the **Greeley Convention & Visitors Bureau,** 1407 Eighth Avenue, Greeley, CO 80631 (tel. 303/352-3566).

**Getting Around**   The city bus system, with the highly imaginative name of **The Bus,** provides in-town transportation. Its main terminal is at 1200 A Street (tel. 353-2812). Taxi service is provided 24 hours a day by **Yellow Cab** (tel. 352-7660) or **Greeley Commuter** (tel. 353-TAXI). There's also a service for the elderly and handicapped called **Medicab** (tel. 353-2111).

**Fast Facts**   The **area code** is 303. In case of **emergency,** call **911;** for standard business, call the police (tel. 353-6123) or the Weld County Sheriff (tel. 356-4000). The **hospital,** North Colorado Medical Center, is at 1801 16th Street (tel. 351-4121), just west of downtown. The *Greeley Tribune* **newspaper**—named, of course, for the *New York Tribune* that contributed to the city's founding—is published daily. The main **post office** is at 925 11th Avenue (tel. 353-0398). State and county **tax** adds 6.7% to hotel bills.

**SPECIAL EVENTS**   The **UNC Jazz Festival** is held on the last weekend of April at the University of Northern Colorado (tel. 351-2200). The first week of July the **Independence Stampede** is held in Island Grove Park, 14th Avenue and A Street (tel. 356-2855). The **Weld County Fair,** in August, is also at Island Grove Park (tel. 356-4000).

---

**G**reeley is one of the few cities in the world that owes its existence to a newspaper. It was founded in 1870 as a sort of prairie Utopia by Nathan C. Meeker, farm columnist for the *New York Tribune*. Meeker named the settlement—first known as Union Colony—in honor of his patron, *Tribune* publisher Horace Greeley. Through his widely read column, Meeker recruited more than 100 pioneers from all walks of life and purchased a tract on the Cache la Poudre from the Denver Pacific Railroad.

City lots were laid out surrounded by farms, and each colonist contributed a membership fee, giving the right to a farm parcel and an option on a town lot. Lots had to be improved within 1 year for the claim to continue valid. Proceeds from the sale of town lots went for projects for "the common good." Within a year, the colony's population was at 1,000. Greeley himself, an unsuccessful 1872 presidential candidate, visited the city in late 1870.

The population has been growing steadily ever since: At the 1990 census, it was nearly 60,000. Greeley's economy is supported almost exclusively by agriculture, with more than 96% of Weld County's 2.5 million acres devoted to either farming or raising livestock. A combination of irrigated and dry-land farms produce grains (including oats, corn, and wheat) and root vegetables (especially sugar beets, onions, potatoes, and carrots).

# WHAT TO SEE & DO
## ATTRACTIONS
### In-Town Attractions

**CENTENNIAL VILLAGE, Island Grove Park, 1475 A St., at N. 14th Ave. Tel. 350-9224.**

This collection of buildings, depicting life in Greeley between 1860 and 1920, was established as a 1976 Bicentennial project. Visitors enter the 5½-acre site through an old railroad depot; inside are 16 historic buildings and six reproductions, among them homestead houses, a one-room school, newspaper office, log-cabin courthouse, and rural church. Selma's Store sells crafts and regional history books.

**Admission:** $2.50 adults, $1 seniors and children 6–16, children under 6 are free.

**Open:** Memorial Day–Labor Day, Mon–Fri 10am–6pm, Sat–Sun 1–5pm; mid-Apr to Memorial Day and Labor Day to mid-Oct, Tues–Sat 10am–3pm. Guided tours are given hourly.

**MEEKER HOME MUSEUM, 1324 Ninth Ave. Tel. 353-9221.**

This two-story adobe brick residence, built in 1870 for Greeley founder Nathan Cook Meeker, is on the National Register of Historic Places. The Union Colony era (1870–85) is interpreted through guided tours of the home, which is furnished with Meeker family belongings and 19th-century antiques.

**Admission:** Free.

**Open:** Memorial Day–Labor Day, Tues–Sat 10am–5pm, Sun 1–5pm; Labor Day–Memorial Day, Tues–Sat 10am–3pm, Sun 1–5pm.

**GREELEY MUNICIPAL MUSEUM, 919 Seventh St. Tel. 350-9220.**

Housed in the east wing of the Civic Center, the museum contains an archives with the original Union Colony records, a Colorado Collection with many rare and out-of-print books about the state, and a gallery of changing exhibits pertaining to Greeley and Weld County history.

**Admission:** Free.
**Open:** Tues–Sat 9am–5pm.

## Nearby Attractions

**NORTH OF GREELEY**   The **Pawnee National Grasslands** (tel. 353-5004) begins about 25 miles northeast of Greeley and extends for about 60 miles east, to the boundary of Weld County. Nomadic Native American tribes lived in this desertlike area until the late 19th century; farmers subsequently had little success in cultivating the grasslands. Today the region is administered by the U.S. Forest Service, which works with ranchers to enhance the wildlife habitat, reduce soil erosion, and provide clean water. Activities on public land include hiking, horseback riding, hunting, camping, and picnicking. Antelope, coyotes, and prairie dogs are among the prolific wildlife.

There are many ways to the grasslands; one is to follow U.S. 85 north 11 miles to Ault, then east on Colo. 14 toward Briggsdale, 23 miles away.

On the south side of the grasslands, west of Briggsdale, are the two **Pawnee Buttes,** part of a steep, curving escarpment that cuts down from Wyoming. These sedimentary rock formations, once native lookout posts, stand half a mile apart and rise 350 feet above the plains.

**SOUTH OF GREELEY**   South from Greeley, U.S. 85 travels south-southeast to Denver. There are interesting stops en route in **Platteville,** 16 miles from Greeley; **Fort Lupton,** 25 miles; and **Brighton,** 32 miles.

Just south of Platteville is **Fort Vasquez,** 13412 U.S. 85 (tel. 785-2832). A historical adobe reconstruction of a fur trader's fort of the 1830s, it has exhibits on trapping and trading, on the indigenous Plains tribe, and displays of artifacts excavated at the fort. It's open Memorial Day weekend to Labor Day, Monday through Saturday from 10am to 5pm and on Sunday from 1–5pm, with limited hours through September.

The **Fort Lupton Museum,** at First Street and McKinley Street (Hwy. 52), Fort Lupton (tel. 857-6694), is a one-room museum with south Weld County artifacts; it's open business hours Monday through Friday.

Brighton's **Front Wheel Drive Auto Museum,** 250 North Main Street (tel. 659-6536 evenings), is open by appointment only. The technical and historical exhibits show designs used in front-wheel-drive automobiles from the 1890s to 1980s. The **Adams County Museum,** 9601 Henderson Road, Brighton (tel. 659-7103), presents the county's various cultures Monday through Friday from 10am to 4:30pm and on Saturday from 1–5pm.

## SPORTS & RECREATION

The sports highlight of the year comes for 6 weeks in July and August when the **Denver Broncos** of the National Football League hold their preseason training camp at the University of Northern Colorado. Free tickets to Bronco scrimmages can often be obtained: call 352-3566.

## EVENING ENTERTAINMENT

**THE PERFORMING ARTS**   Greeley's cultural focus is the **Union Colony Civic Center,** 10th Avenue at Seventh Street (tel. 356-5555, or 356-5000 for the box office). Opened in late 1988, the center hosts national touring artists and companies in the 1,700-seat Monfort Concert Hall or the 220-seat Hensel Phelps Theatre. The **Greeley Civic Theater** (tel. 330-3261) stages four to six plays a year in the Phelps Theatre.

The **Greeley Philharmonic Orchestra,** the oldest orchestra west of the Mississippi River, has an October-to-May season with about 10 performances at the University of Northern Colorado's Foundation Hall. The **Little Theatre of the Rockies** offers five summer-stock productions with a company of professionals and drama students. The University Garden Theater is the scene of **Concerts Under the Stars** in July and August, presented by the Colorado Philharmonic, the Greeley

Summer Symphonic Band and Festival Choir, and others. For information or tickets to any of these events, call 351-2200.

A 3-day **jazz festival** (tel. 351-2200) is held on the UNC campus in late April or early May. Cultural programs scheduled by the university are also open to the public (tel. 351-2265). The third week in July, an **Arts Picnic** (tel. 353-6123, ext. 390) is held in Lincoln Park, Ninth Street and 10th Avenue. Programs are given by the Greeley Philharmonic Symphonette, the Greeley Chorale, the Greeley Chamber Orchestra, popular and country music groups, and dance groups.

Among Greeley's more popular nightspots are **Potato Brumbaugh's Restaurant & Saloon,** 2400 17th Street (tel. 356-6340), and the **Smiling Moose Bar & Grill,** 2501 11th Avenue (tel. 356-7010).

# WHERE TO STAY

**BEST WESTERN RAMKOTA INN & CONFERENCE CENTER, 701 Eighth Ave., Greeley, CO 80631. Tel. 303/353-8444,** or 800/528-1234. 146 rms (all with bath), 4 suites. A/C TV TEL
**$ Rates:** $49–$54 single; $57–$62 double. AE, CB, DC, DISC, MC, V.
This former Radisson property is located downtown on Business Route 85. It offers a heated indoor swimming pool, in-room movies, and two restaurants: Legends and Stetson's. The hotel has no-smoking rooms, facilities for the disabled, and a gift shop.

**HOLIDAY INN OF GREELEY, 609 Eighth Ave., Greeley, CO 80631. Tel. 303/356-3000,** or 800/HOLIDAY. 100 rms (all with bath). A/C TV TEL
**$ Rates:** Mid-June to late Aug, $42–$47 single; $46–$51 double. Late Aug to mid-June, $38–$44 single; $44–$49 double. AE, CB, DC, DISC, MC, V.
A newly renovated downtown motel, this Holiday Inn offers guests a heated swimming pool, in-room movies, free local phone calls, and a coin-operated laundry. Camfield's restaurant serves three moderately priced meals daily, and the lounge is a popular evening oasis. Pets are accepted.

**WINTERSET INN OF GREELEY, 800 31st St., Evans, CO 80620. Tel. 303/339-2492,** or 800/777-5088. 47 rms (all with bath), 2 suites. A/C TV TEL
**$ Rates:** June to early Sept, $29 single; $32–$37 double. Early Sept to May, $25 single; $29–$33 double. Suites $46. AE, CB, DC, DISC, MC, V.
A lower-cost alternative to the downtown hotels, the Winterset is located two blocks south of the U.S. 34 bypass in the neighboring community of Evans. All rooms have satellite TV with in-room movies, and access to the heated swimming pool. Pets are accepted with payment of a $10 deposit. There's live entertainment most nights in the cocktail lounge.

# WHERE TO DINE

**THE ARMADILLO, 111 S. First St., La Salle. Tel. 284-6560.**
   **Cuisine:** MEXICAN.
**$ Prices:** $5.95–$11.95. AE, MC, V.
   **Open:** Daily 11am–10pm.
Occupying a large brick building beside the Union Pacific tracks in La Salle, 5 miles south of Greeley, this Mexican establishment offers an extensive and varied menu. You'll get all the usual meals here—enchiladas, tamales, and the like—and a few dishes you may not have heard of. Try gorditas, chicken or pork with a cilantro dressing, served between two corncakes. Every meal comes with rice, salad, and black beans.

**CABLE'S END, 3780 W. 10th St. Tel. 356-4847.**
   **Cuisine:** ITALIAN.
**$ Prices:** Dinner $6.95–$13.95. MC, V.
   **Open:** Mon–Sat 11am–1am, Sun 11am–11pm.
Locally famous for its homemade pastas, including spaghetti and ravioli, Cable's End also offers fresh seafood, prime rib, steaks, chicken . . . and pizza. There's a seafood-and-pasta special on Friday night, a prime rib–and–pasta special on Saturday.

Kids eat for $1 from the children's menu on Sunday, and on Monday night, it's all the spaghetti you can eat for $2.95. Don't miss the homemade cheesecake. Soup, salads, and sandwiches are the lunch fare. There's live music on Friday and Saturday nights.

**POTATO BRUMBAUGH'S RESTAURANT & SALOON, 2400 17th St. Tel. 356-6340.**
   **Cuisine:** AMERICAN. **Reservations:** Suggested.
**$ Prices:** $8.95–$15.95. AE, CB, DC, MC, V.
   **Open:** Lunch Mon–Fri 11am–2pm; dinner Mon–Sat 5–10pm. **Closed:** New Year's and Christmas days.

Named for a character in James Michener's *Centennial,* this casually elegant restaurant in the Cottonwood Square shopping center follows the novel's theme in its western decor. The menu features steaks, prime rib, poultry, fresh seafood, and a variety of light dishes.

---

# 4. FORT MORGAN

### 81 miles NE of Denver, 45 miles SW of Sterling

**GETTING THERE   By Plane   Denver's Stapleton International Airport** is less than 90 minutes away. There are small municipal airfields for private planes and charters in Fort Morgan and Brush, 10 miles east.

**By Train   Amtrak** trains make daily stops on the Denver–Chicago route at the Fort Morgan depot, located on Ensign Street south of Railroad Avenue (tel. 800/872-7245).

**By Bus   Greyhound/Trailways** provides intercity service. The bus station is on West Platte Avenue between Euclid Street and West Street (tel. 876-8072).

**By Car   Fort Morgan** is located on U.S. 34 at I-76, the main east-west route between Denver and Omaha, Nebraska. U.S. 34 proceeds west to Greeley and Estes Park, east to Wray and southern Nebraska. Colorado 71 is the principal north-south route through Fort Morgan.

**ESSENTIALS   Orientation** Situated in the South Platte River valley, Fort Morgan, appropriately named its principal east-west thoroughfare **Platte Avenue.** The north-south artery, **Main Street,** divides it and other streets into east and west designations. I-76 exits onto Main Street north of downtown.

**Information** Contact the **Fort Morgan Area Chamber of Commerce,** 300 Main Street (P.O. Box 971), Fort Morgan, CO 80701 (tel. 303/867-6702).

**Fast Facts** The **area code** is 303. In case of **emergency,** call **911.** The **Fort Morgan Community Hospital,** 1000 Lincoln, Fort Morgan (tel. 303/867-3391) has 40 beds. The main **post office** is on State Street between Kiowa Avenue and Beaver Avenue, a block east of Main. State and county **tax** adds 6.7% to hotel bills.

**SPECIAL EVENTS** The Fort Morgan area offers the following: the **Brush Spring Festival,** in May in Brush; **Huck Finn & Becky Thatcher Days,** in June in Fort Morgan; the **Tin Man Triathlon,** in June in Fort Morgan; the **Morgan County Fair,** in August in Brush; and the **Spanish Fiesta,** in September in Fort Morgan.

---

**E**stablished as a military outpost in 1864, the original Fort Morgan housed about 200 troops who protected stagecoaches and pioneers traveling the Overland Trail from marauding Cheyenne and Arapahoe warriors. The threat had passed by 1870 and the fort was dismantled. But the name stuck when the city was founded in 1884 by an irrigation engineer from Greeley.

   The town grew in the 20th century with the establishment of the Great Western Sugar Company for sugar-beet processing and a pair of oil discoveries in the 1920s and

1950s. Cattle ranching has always been important. Today Fort Morgan has a population of about 9,000.

The city's most famous citizen was big-band leader Glenn Miller, who graduated from Fort Morgan High School in 1921 and formed his first band, the Mick-Miller Five, in the city.

# WHAT TO SEE & DO
## ATTRACTIONS

**FORT MORGAN MUSEUM, City Park, 414 Main St. Tel. 867-6331.**

An impressive collection of northeastern Colorado Native American artifacts, beginning with Clovis points 13,000 years old, is the highlight of this museum—the smallest one in Colorado to be accredited by the American Association of Museums. Other permanent exhibits focus on farming, ranching, and the railroad history of Morgan County, including old Fort Morgan, and a display on the life of native son Glenn Miller. The 1920s Hillrose Drugstore soda fountain, a town social center, has been fully restored.

**Admission:** Free.

**Open:** Mon and Fri 10am–5pm, Tues–Thurs 10am–5pm and 6–8pm, Sat 11am–5pm; also Sun 1–5pm in summer.

**FORT MORGAN HISTORICAL DRIVING TOUR. Tel. 867-6331.**

Obtain a brochure from the museum or chamber of commerce for a self-guided tour to 13 sites around Morgan County. Included are a monument marking the site of **Old Fort Morgan** on Riverview Avenue at Lake Street, three blocks east of Main off I-76; **Rainbow Bridge,** a 1923 engineering marvel and National Historic Site on Colo. 52 at Riverside Park; remains of the **Overland Trail,** which parallels I-76 on its north side for 4 miles west from the Fort Morgan exit; and **Orchard,** a community 22 miles west of Fort Morgan on Colo. 144, where part of the TV miniseries *Centennial* was filmed. Many sets are still standing, including the Railroad Arms Hotel.

**OASIS ON THE PLAINS MUSEUM, 18881 Morgan County Rd. 1. Tel. 867-3191.**

This working ranch museum displays artifacts of early homesteading in the northeastern Colorado plains.

**Admission:** Free.

**Open:** Sun noon–4pm, or by appointment.

**SHERMAN STREET NATIONAL HISTORIC DISTRICT, 400 and 500 blocks of Sherman St. Tel. 867-6331.**

Four Victorian mansions built between 1886 and 1926 are of special interest. Located on either side of East Platte Avenue, six blocks east of Main Street, they include a 19th-century Queen Anne home; a home with decorative spindlework porches, a barn, carriage house, and water tower; an American Foursquare home; and a brick Georgian Revival–style house. Each is associated with a prominent city pioneer.

The Fort Morgan Museum publishes a walking-tour brochure both for Sherman Street and for the nine-block downtown district, the latter noting 44 buildings that made up the early town.

## SPORTS & RECREATION

Impressive **Riverside Park,** off Main Street between I-76 and the South Platte River, offers facilities for swimming and tennis, an archery range, a nature trail, a handful of campsites, and ice skating in winter. Best of all, it's free.

Some 25 miles northwest of Fort Morgan is **Jackson Lake State Recreation Area,** 26363 Morgan County Rd. 3 (tel. 645-2551), off Colo. 144, 2½ miles north of Goodrich. The park offers a variety of water sports on a 2,700-acre reservoir. There are more than 200 campsites, sandy beaches for swimming, boating, and waterskiing. Anglers fish year round for walleye, bass, catfish, and panfish. Hunters pursue waterfowl, game birds, and rabbits in a tightly controlled Labor Day–to–Memorial Day season. Skaters and cross-country skiers enjoy the lake in winter. There's a fee for overnight use.

The **Brush Rodeo,** the world's largest amateur rodeo, is held in the town of Brush, 10 miles east, over the Fourth of July weekend.

## EVENING ENTERTAINMENT

On Friday night, hundreds of townsfolk head for the **Country Steak Out,** 19592 East Eighth Avenue (tel. 867-7887), for an evening of dancing to live country-and-western music.

## WHERE TO STAY

**BEST WESTERN PARK TERRACE MOTOR HOTEL, 725 Main St., Fort Morgan, CO 80701. Tel. 303/867-8256,** or 800/528-1234. 24 rms (all with bath). A/C TV TEL
**$ Rates:** $32 single; $36.50–$40.50 double. AE, CB, DC, DISC, MC, V.
A pleasant property four blocks south of I-76, the Park Terrace has rooms with queen-size beds, individual heating, full baths, direct-dial phones, and cable TV with in-room movies. There's a swimming pool and restaurant, serving three meals daily. Pets are accepted.

**CENTRAL MOTEL, 201 W. Platte Ave., Fort Morgan, CO 80701. Tel. 303/867-2401.** 13 rms (all with bath), 4 suites. A/C TV TEL
**$ Rates:** Mid-May to mid-Sept, $32 single; $36–$41 double. Mid-Sept to mid-May, $30 single; $34–$36 double. AE, CB, DC, DISC, MC, V.
If you're staying more than a day or two, consider the Central: Refrigerators and microwaves are installed at no extra charge, and six two-bedroom units include four with full kitchens. Every room has queen-size beds, individual hot-water heating, cable TV with HBO, and direct-dial phones. There are no-smoking rooms and facilities for the disabled; pets require advance approval.

## WHERE TO DINE

**COLONIAL RESTAURANT, 300 E. Platte Ave. Tel. 867-7633.**
 **Cuisine:** AMERICAN/MEXICAN.
**$ Prices:** $6.95–$13.95. MC, V.
 **Open:** Mon–Sat 6am–9pm, Sun 7am–8pm.
You'll get three hearty meals a day at this long-established restaurant, two blocks east of Main Street. There's an ample salad bar at lunch and dinner. Seniors' discounts and a children's menu are available.

## EASY EXCURSIONS FROM FORT MORGAN

**BRUSH** Brush, 10 miles east of Fort Morgan on I-76 and U.S. 34, is an attractive town in its own right. With a population of 4,200, it is the second-largest community in Morgan County. The **Brush Area Chamber of Commerce,** 301 Edison Street, Brush, CO 80723 (tel. 303/842-2666), has information.

The **All Saints Church of Eben Ezer,** 122 Hospital Road (tel. 842-2861), is on the National Register of Historic Places. Founded as a tuberculosis sanitorium in 1903, it was dedicated as a church in 1918. Its pointed Gothic arches, pitched beamwork ceiling, and art-glass windows are reminiscent of a 12th- or 13th-century Danish structure; in fact, the Crown Prince and Princess of Denmark visited in 1918, and there's a Danish Pioneer Museum on site. Open Monday through Friday from 8am to 5pm; free admission.

**WRAY** Wray (pop. 2,300), about 10 miles from the Nebraska state line, is the Yuma County seat. The **Wray Museum,** 205 East Third Street (tel. 332-5063), open Tuesday through Saturday from 10am to 5pm and on Sunday from 1 to 5pm (free admission), displays native artifacts, pioneer memorabilia and photographs, and replicas from Smithsonian-sponsored digs in the area. **Flirtation Point,** the oddly named first Masonic Temple in eastern Colorado, was built with stones from all 48 contiguous states. Just east of town, the human-made **Lions Amphitheater** on Fourth Street provides a stage for concerts, sunrise services, and graduation ceremonies in a beautiful sandstone canyon.

   **Beecher Island Battleground,** a National Historic Site 17 miles south on U.S. 385, commemorates one of the last skirmishes between white pioneers and Native Americans in Colorado, in September 1868. Today the site offers camping, picnicking, and hiking. There's hiking, fishing, and hunting as well in the **Sandsage and Stalker Lake State Wildlife Areas,** both west of Wray on U.S. 34 (tel. 332-5382).

   You can learn more about the Wray area from the **Yuma County Tourism Information Center,** 330 East Third Street, Wray, CO 80758 (tel. 303/332-4828). For information about all of eastern Colorado, consult **Colorado Plains, Inc.,** P.O. Box 324, Wray, CO 80758 (tel. 303/332-4364).

# 5. STERLING

125 miles NE of Denver, 407 miles W of Omaha, Neb.

**GETTING THERE   By Plane   Denver's Stapleton International Airport** is 2 hours away. There's a **municipal airport** for private planes and charters off Colo. 14 west of town.

**By Train   Amtrak** trains on the Denver-Chicago route make daily stops in Sterling (tel. 800/872-7245).

**By Bus   Greyhound/Trailways,** 730 N. Third St., Sterling (tel. 303/522-5522), provides intercity service.

**By Car**   Sterling is located at the junction of I-76, U.S. 6, and Colo. 14. I-76, of course, links the city with Denver and Omaha, Nebraska. U.S. 6 branches east from Sterling to Holyoke and southern Nebraska. Colorado 14 runs almost due west to Fort Collins, 100 miles away.

**ESSENTIALS   Orientation**   Exit I-76 at Sterling, turn west over the South Platte River, and you'll be in the center of town. **Main Street** runs east-west; **Division Street** runs north-south.

**Information**   Contact the **Logan County Chamber of Commerce** and the **Northeast Colorado Travel Planning Region** at P.O. Box 1683, Sterling, CO 80751 (tel. 303/522-5070, or 800/544-8609).

**Fast Facts**   The **area code** is 303.

**SPECIAL EVENTS**   Area events include the **National Junior College Rodeo,** in Sterling; the **Pony Express Re-Ride,** in June in Julesburg; **Beef Expo** and **Hay Days,** both in June in Sterling; the **Logan County Fair,** in August in Sterling; the **Phillips County Fair,** in August in Holyoke; the **Sedgwick County Fair,** in August in Julesburg; **Sugar Beet Days,** in September in Sterling; and the **Corn Festival,** in October in Haxtun.

**C**heyenne and Arapahoe tribes hunted buffalo on these prairies for centuries. After the Civil War, the tall grasses drew herds of longhorn cattle—and with them John Wesley Iliff, a millionaire rancher who owned and operated 650,000 acres of land across northeastern Colorado. Iliff's empire was short-lived, as the longhorn boom petered out soon after the invention of barbed wire in 1874. Corn, wheat, and sugar beets became the economic mainstays of the South Platte River valley, along with livestock ranching and oil and natural gas production.

   Sterling was founded in 1874 by settlers from Mississippi and Tennessee, disgruntled with the Reconstruction of the post–Civil War South. The population grew more rapidly after the Union Pacific Railroad came through in 1881, and today the city has about 11,000 inhabitants.

# WHAT TO SEE & DO

## ATTRACTIONS

### LIVING TREES OF STERLING.

The often-whimsical sculptures of artist Brad Rhea, a Logan County resident since 1978, have given the city a unique cultural attraction. Rhea's work—people and animals carved from tree trunks—can be found all over Sterling. A quintet of giraffes, *Skygrazers,* nibble on sky in Columbine Park. A Revolutionary War minuteman stands guard before the National Guard Armory. A thespian raises the masks of comedy and tragedy high above his head at the entrance to the Oak Street Theatre. A golfer raises his club beside the first tee at the Sterling Country Club. And so forth. City merchants have free maps of sculpture sites.

### OVERLAND TRAIL MUSEUM, Centennial Sq., U.S. 6 at I-76. Tel. 522-3895.

The history of the Overland Trail, which followed this stretch of the South Platte River on its way to the Far West, is told in this fine museum, a 1936 stone replica of old Fort Sedgwick. Artifacts from the Plains tribespeople, pioneers who made the 1862–68 migration west, and later 19th-century settlers fill indoor display cases. Look for unique collections of ranch branding irons and barbed wire, antique furniture, and medical supplies. On the grounds are a pioneer schoolhouse and prairie church.

**Admission:** Free.

**Open:** Apr–Oct, Mon–Sat 9am–5pm, Sun and hols 10am–5pm.

### TENNANT ART GALLERY, Northeastern Junior College, 100 College Dr. Tel. 522-6600.

Located in the Hayes Student Center, this gallery displays outstanding paintings of the Old West by nationally known artists. Nearby E. S. French Hall houses two visual-arts galleries: an upstairs presentation of William Sanderson's art, and a downstairs showcase of work by regionally and nationally recognized artists.

**Admission:** Free.

**Open:** Mon–Wed and Fri 8am–4pm, Thurs 8am–4pm and 6:30–8:30pm.

## EVENING ENTERTAINMENT

**The Prairie Players,** a local theater company, presents several productions each year at the **Oak Street Theatre** (tel. 522-7026).

Popular bars in Sterling are **Fergie's West Inn Pub,** 324 West Main Street (tel. 522-4220), and the **Silver Dollar Steakhouse & Lounge,** 110 Popular Street (tel. 522-9834).

# WHERE TO STAY

### BEST WESTERN SUNDOWNER, Overland Trail St., Sterling, CO 80751. Tel. 303/522-6265, or 800/528-1234. 29 rms (all with bath). A/C TV TEL

**$ Rates:** May–Oct, $49 single; $56–$60 double. Nov–Apr, $43 single, $49–$54 double. AE, CB, DC, DISC, MC, V.

Set in pleasant garden surroundings across the street from the Overland Trail Museum, this outstanding property is two blocks off I-76 via U.S. 6. Facilities include a swimming pool, Jacuzzi, fitness center, and guest laundry. Rooms have king-size or queen-size beds. No-smoking rooms and family units are available. Guests get fresh homemade cookies and complimentary coffee every morning.

### PARK INN INTERNATIONAL, East U.S. 6 at I-76, Sterling, CO 80751. Tel. 303/522-2625, or 800/835-PARK. Fax 303/522-1321. 101 rms (all with bath). A/C TV TEL

**$ Rates:** May–Oct, $36–$42 single; $38–$52 double. Nov–Apr, $26–$36 single; $32–$46 double. Children stay free in parents' room. AE, CB, DC, DISC, MC, V.

There's a little of everything at this motel—from the tropical Parkdome courtyard with its indoor pool, whirlpool, sauna, exercise area, and video arcade, to the family restaurant serving three meals daily. Guests stay in queen-size beds, watch in-room movies on remote-control TVs, and have a coin-operated laundry at their disposal. No-smoking rooms are available, and pets are permitted. The motel offers room service and a courtesy van, and there are meeting facilities as well.

## WHERE TO DINE

**T. J. BUMMER'S, 203 Broadway. Tel. 522-8397.**
   **Cuisine:** AMERICAN.
**$ Prices:** $3.95–$11.95. MC, V.
   **Open:** Daily 24 hours.
This Sterling institution is best known for its "Brahma Bull burgers," but you'll also get steaks, chicken, deep-fried prawns, and other all-American favorites. If you've got a craving for a stack of pancakes at 4 in the morning, this is the place to come. Families are especially welcome.

## EASY EXCURSIONS FROM STERLING

**HEADING NORTH** U.S. 138 parallels I-76, following the north shore of the South Platte, en route to Julesburg, 60 miles northeast of Sterling.

**Iliff,** 12 miles from Sterling, was the headquarters for John Iliff's late 19th-century cattle empire. Today, only 200 people live in the village.

**Crook,** 15 miles farther, has several interesting historical sites, including two **Overland Trail stage stations:** Lillian Springs and Spring Hills. Ask directions at the **Crook Museum,** Fourth Avenue and Fourth Street (tel. 886-2451), open in summer on Sunday from 2 to 4pm, or the Town of Crook offices, P.O. Box 158, Crook, CO 80726 (tel. 303/886-2222, or 800/544-8609).

Near **Sedgwick,** 15 miles northeast of Crook, look for the buffalo grazing at the **Price Ranch.**

**Julesburg** (pop. 1,600), in Colorado's northeasternmost corner, was once called by Mark Twain "the wickedest city in the West." Some of that century-old history is recounted at the **Fort Sedgwick Depot Museum,** 202 West First Street (tel. 474-3504 or 474-2264). The museum preserves artifacts from the Pony Express, Overland Trail, Oregon Trail, and Fort Sedgwick. Open Memorial Day to Labor Day, Monday through Saturday from 9am to 5pm and on Sunday from 11am to 5pm, and other times by appointment.

The 14-year-old "Buffalo Bill" Cody signed on with the Pony Express here in Julesburg, the only place the Express stopped in Colorado. (It veered north through the lower mountains of Wyoming.) A reride of the original route is a major event here each June.

You can get further information on the town from the **Julesburg Chamber of Commerce,** 122 West First Street, Julesburg, CO 80737 (tel. 303/474-3504).

**HEADING EAST** U.S. 6 runs 60 miles east from Sterling to the Nebraska border. **Fleming,** 19 miles from Sterling, originally settled by homesteaders in the 1880s, has several sights. They include the **Fleming Heritage Museum Park,** U.S. 6 on the west end of town, which features an old schoolhouse-turned-museum and a railroad depot–turned–craft shop, open Memorial Day to Labor Day, Monday through Saturday from 10am to 6pm and on Sunday from 1 to 6pm; and **Al's Country Western Museum,** 2 miles west on U.S. 6, with various antique wagons, cars, and other early forms of transportation, open daily from 8am to 4pm.

**Haxtun** (pop. 1,000), 30 miles from Sterling, has numerous late 19th-century sites; obtain a walking-tour brochure from local merchants.

**Holyoke** (pop. 2,200), 47 miles east of Sterling, boasts the **W. E. Heginbotham Library,** 539 South Baxter Avenue, an impressive 1919 Craftsman Bungalow listed on the National Register of Historic Places, open on Monday from 9am to 5pm and Tuesday through Saturday from 1 to 5pm. The **Holyoke Chamber of Commerce,** P.O. Box 134, Holyoke, CO 80734 (tel. 303/854-3517), has Phillips County information.

**HEADING SOUTH** Sixteen miles south of Sterling via Colo. 63 is the **Summit Springs Battlefield**——the site of the last conflict in Colorado between the

Cheyennes and the U.S. Cavalry, on July 11, 1869. Today it's open for hiking and picnicking.

# 6. BURLINGTON

163 miles E of Denver, 385 miles W of Topeka, Kans.

**GETTING THERE   By Plane**   The **Burlington–Kit Carson County Airport** is 4 miles south of the city on U.S. 385. A municipal airport, it handles private planes and charters.

**By Bus   Greyhound/Trailways** provides intercity service, with four arrivals and departures daily from the Coastal Convenience Store, 440 South Lincoln Street, at I-70 (tel. 346-8155).

**By Car**   Burlington is located on east-west I-70, 14 miles from the Kansas border. U.S. 385, which runs the length of Colorado's eastern frontier, makes a north-south pass through the town.

**ESSENTIALS   Orientation**   The town lies on the north side of I-70. **Rose Avenue** (U.S. 24) runs east-west through the center of Burlington. Main north-south streets are **Eighth Street** (U.S. 385 north), on the east side of town; **Main Street** (14th Street); and **Lincoln Street** (U.S. 385 south), on the west side of town.

**Information**   The **Colorado Welcome Center** is on I-70 beside Burlington Old Town (P.O. Box 157), Burlington, CO 80807 (tel. 719/346-5554). For information specifically on Burlington, contact the **Burlington Chamber of Commerce,** 480 15th Street, Burlington, CO 80807 (tel. 719/346-8070).

**Fast Facts**   The **area code** is 719. In case of **emergency, call 911.** The **Kit Carson County Memorial Hospital** is at 186 16th Street (tel. 719/346-5311). The main **post office** is on Donelan Avenue at Main Street.

**SPECIAL EVENTS**   In early June there's the **Longhorn Cattle Drive** in Burlington; in July, the **Harvest Festival** in Limon and the **Tumblewood Festival** in Cheyenne Wells; in August the **Kit Carson County Fair** in Burlington, the **Lincoln County Fair** in Hugo, and **Kit Carson Day** in Kit Carson; in September, **Colorado's Outback Festival** in Burlington; and in December, **Old Town Christmas** in Burlington.

---

**D**ry-land farmers established Burlington and other "Outback" communities along the Kansas City–Denver rail line in the 1880s. Today the largest community in east-central Colorado, Burlington (pop. 3,100) has preserved its turn-of-the-century heritage with its impressive Old Town and famous carousel. Wheat is very much the dominant crop, though you'll also find corn and dry beans.

## WHAT TO SEE & DO

### ATTRACTIONS

**KIT CARSON COUNTY CAROUSEL, County Fairgrounds, 15th St. at Colorado Ave. Tel. 719/346-8070.**
    This is the town's pride and joy, the only National Historic Landmark in eastern Colorado. Carved in 1905 by the Philadelphia Toboggan Company, it is fully restored and operational, and is one of the few wooden carousels left in America that still wears its original coat of paint. The 46 stationary animals—mostly horses, but also including giraffes, zebras, camels, a seahorse, a lion, a tiger, and others—march counterclockwise around three tiers of oil paintings, representing the life-styles and

interests of the American Victorian middle class. A Wurlitzer Monster Military Band Organ, one of only two of that size and vintage in operation today, provides the music.
**Admission:** 25¢ a ride.
**Open:** Memorial Day–Labor Day, daily 1–5pm and 7–8:30pm. Private tours given at other times: Write P.O. Box 28, Stratton, CO 80836, with 2 weeks' advance notice.

**OLD TOWN, 420 S. 14th St. Tel. 719/346-7382,** or 800/288-1334.
Two dozen turn-of-the-century buildings make up this living-history museum. The structures and their period furnishings and artifacts depict the heritage of early plains settlers. Visit the blacksmith, carpenter, grocer, newspaper editor, saloon keeper, barber, jailer, druggist, schoolteacher, parson, and other pioneers. There are cancan shows, gunfights, hayloft melodramas, and other special events throughout the summer and on weekends. Belgian draft horses pull the "Old Town Express" wagon around the re-created village. There's also a large emporium for souvenir hunters.
**Admission:** $3 adults, $2 children 12–18, $1 children 3–11.
**Open:** Memorial Day–Labor Day, daily 8am–9pm; Labor Day–Memorial Day, daily 9am–6pm.

## WHERE TO STAY

**ECONOLODGE, 450 S. Lincoln St., Burlington, CO 80807. Tel. 719/346-5555,** or 800/446-6900. 108 rms (all with bath), 4 suites. A/C TV TEL
**$ Rates:** $22.50–$31.50 single; $27.50–$40.50 double; $43.90 suite. AE, CB, DC, DISC, MC, V.
Conveniently located next to Old Town, this standard motel offers spacious units with in-room movies and direct-dial phones. There's a swimming pool for summer visitors, carburetor plug-ins for winter travelers, and a dining room and lounge serving three meals daily.

**SLOAN'S MOTEL, 1901 Rose Ave., Burlington, CO 80807. Tel. 719/346-5333,** or 800/524-9999. 27 rms (all with bath). A/C TV TEL
**$ Rates:** Memorial Day–Labor Day, $30 single; $34 double. Labor Day–Memorial Day, $25 single; $30 double. AE, CB, DC, DISC, MC, V.
A children's playground and indoor swimming pool keep the youngsters happy at this east Burlington property. All rooms have queen-size or double beds, cable TV, and clock radios. Facilities for the disabled are available.

## WHERE TO DINE

**HOOF AND HORN, 46281 U.S. 24, 2 miles west of Burlington. Tel. 719/346-7107.**
**Cuisine:** STEAK/SEAFOOD.
**$ Prices:** $7.95–$15.95. AE, CB, DC, MC, V.
**Open:** Breakfast/lunch Mon–Fri 7am–2pm; dinner Mon–Sat 5–10pm.
This casual and popular restaurant serves three meals daily, including a luncheon buffet for noontime visitors. Steaks, prime rib, and seafood are the fare in the evening.

**PRAIRIE PINES RESTAURANT, 48678 Snead Dr., off U.S. 385 2 miles north of Burlington. Tel. 719/346-8698.**
**Cuisine:** STEAK/SEAFOOD.
**$ Prices:** $8.95–$18.95. AE, CB, DC, MC, V.
**Open:** Lunch Tues–Sun 11am–2pm; dinner Tues–Sun 5–10pm.
The golf course outside the big picture windows may have only nine holes, but that's enough to keep diners fascinated watching the duffers chipping onto the final green. Enjoy soup, salad, or sandwich for lunch; fine steaks, poultry, and seafood in the evening.

## EASY EXCURSIONS FROM BURLINGTON

I-70 west from Burlington passes numerous interesting communities en route to Denver. **Stratton, Seibert,** and **Flagler,** all in Kit Carson County about 15 miles from one another, are farming centers. At **Arriba,** 52 miles west of Burlington, take Exit 383 from I-70 to see the **Tarada Mansion** (tel. 719/768-3468). This private home, looking like a miniature White House on the plains, offers tours of its various rooms, furnished with beautiful antiques and ancient Roman artifacts. A restaurant serves lunch daily, and dinner on Friday and Saturday by reservation.

Tiny **Genoa,** another 12 miles west, is notable for the **Genoa Tower Museum,** otherwise called the "World's Wonder View Tower." It's on the I-70 Frontage Road at Exit 371 (tel. 719/763-2309). Billed as "the highest point between the Rocky Mountains and the Mississippi River," the tower does offer great views of the surrounding plains, as well as an eclectic collection of artifacts ranging from fossils and arrowheads to Elvis Presley memorabilia. It's open Memorial Day to Labor Day, daily from 8am to 8pm.

**Limon** (pop. 1,800) is the largest community between Burlington (74 miles distant), Denver (89 miles), and Colorado Springs (71 miles). U.S. 24 branches southwest off I-70 here for Colorado Springs. As a major junction, this is a good place for a bite to eat—try the **Limon Livestock Exchange Café,** 1255 Dairy Lane (tel. 719/775-2307)—or a sleep. A recommended motel is the **Preferred Motor Inn,** I-70 Exit 361 (P.O. Box 220), Limon, CO 80828 (tel. 719/775-2385, or 800/341-8000).

Limon's main attraction is the *Limon Twilight Limited,* an old train refurbished to offer dinner shows at 7pm on Saturday, June to September. The depot is at E Avenue and First Street (tel. 719/495-2223). Limon's **Schoolhouse Museum,** 517 D Avenue (tel. 719/775-2350), is open by appointment only.

U.S. 287 southeast from Limon follows the old **Smoky Hill Trail,** known by many travelers as the Starvation Trail because of the dearth of food and water en route. The principal communities along the way are **Hugo,** 14 miles from Limon; **Kit Carson,** 61 miles; and **Cheyenne Wells,** 86 miles southeast of Limon and 38 miles almost due south of Burlington.

Each town has an interesting historical museum. The **Lincoln County Museum,** 617 Third Avenue, Hugo (tel. 719/743-2209), is housed in a restored family home; it contains 19th-century antiques and a fascinating "costume room" of old clothing. The **Kit Carson Museum,** on U.S. 287, Kit Carson (tel. 719/962-3262), displays frontiersman Kit Carson's six-shooter as part of its exhibits on town history. The **Cheyenne Wells Museum,** 91 East First Street, Cheyenne Wells (tel. 719/767-5773), is located in the cells and living quarters of the old town jail, and is on the National Register of Historic Places. Within are Native American artifacts, antiques, and other historical items. Open daily in summer, or by appointment.

# CHAPTER 9

# THE NORTHERN ROCKIES

The northern half of the Colorado Rockies is truly the climax of United States mountain wilderness, the crown on the head of the great range that dominates the American West.

This is rugged beauty at its best, extending on either side of the meandering Continental Divide down sawtooth ridgelines, through precipitous river canyons, and across broad alpine plains. Here, snowfall is measured in feet, not inches; when spring's golden sun finally melts away the frost, amazing arrays of alpine wildflowers greet the new beginning.

These Rockies are known as America's winter playground, and that's as it should be. Names of the region's resorts roll off the tongues of skiing households throughout the world, and are a part of the lore and legend of the sport: Aspen, Vail, Steamboat Springs, Breckenridge.

But this is also wonderful summer recreation territory. No one knows that better than Coloradans themselves, who flock here in every season to feel a oneness with the wilderness. Although out-of-state tourists predominate in July and August, locals opt for May and September as their favorite months: The temperature is only slightly lower, and there's more room to spread their wings.

One resort town that thrives on summer business is Estes Park, the gateway to Rocky Mountain National Park. To the northwest is Steamboat Springs, first and foremost a ranching town. Real cowboys—not urban imitations—share the streets with skiers and other vacationers.

Winter Park—remarkably, a mountain park owned by the City of Denver—may not get as much publicity as other Rockies resorts, but it soon may. Though it's now a relatively laid-back community, somewhat off the beaten track, it's miles closer to the Front Range than other leading resorts, and has extraordinary expansion plans.

Summit County, perhaps, has more major ski areas within a half hour's drive of one another than anywhere else in the country. Breckenridge, Copper Mountain, Keystone, Arapahoe Basin, and (just across the Continental Divide) Loveland Basin make this a winter sportsman's dream. Dillon Reservoir at Frisco is a major summer destination for boaters.

Year after year, Vail is voted America's single favorite ski resort. Why? For one, accessibility: The community is right on I-70. The mountain offers seemingly endless terrain for all abilities of skier. The town, only three decades old, has evolved into a high-class European-style enclave where traffic is restricted but the "beautiful people" are not. It's a charmer, though not a cheap one.

Aspen, too, is synonymous with Colorado and the Rocky Mountains. The town has kept its Victorian mining-town atmosphere while becoming, since the 1940s, the quintessential ski-resort community. It's as popular with the mink-stole set as with the blue-jeans-and-flannel-shirt generation. But, like Vail, prices in Aspen are very high.

# 1. ESTES PARK

71 miles NW of Denver, 42 miles SW of Fort Collins

**GETTING THERE    By Plane**    Visitors fly into **Denver's Stapleton International Airport,** and continue to Estes Park with the **Estes Park Bus Company** or **Charles Limousine** (see below).

**By Bus**    The **Estes Park Bus Company, 205** Park Lane (tel. 303/586-8108, or 800/824-1104), and **Charles Limousine** (tel. 303/586-5151, or 800/950-DASH) connect the town with Boulder and Denver.

**By Car**    The most direct route is U.S. 36 from Denver and Boulder. At Estes Park, that highway joins U.S. 34, which runs up the Big Thompson River Valley from I-25 and Loveland, and continues through Rocky Mountain National Park to Granby. An alternative scenic route to Estes Park is Colo. 7, the "Peak-to-Peak Highway" that transits Central City (Colo. 119), Nederland (Colo. 72), and Allenspark (Colo. 7) under different designations.

**SPECIAL EVENTS**    Area events include: the **Great Spring Run Off and Stanley Steamer Tour,** in May in Estes Park; the **Rooftop Fair and Rodeo,** in the third week of July in Estes Park; **Western Days,** in the third week of July in Grand Lake; the **Estes Park Music Festival,** during July and August in Estes Park; the **Grand Lake Yacht Club Regatta,** the second week of August in Grand Lake; the **Americade of the Rockies Motorcycle Rally,** during Labor Day week in Estes Park; the **Scottish-Irish Highland Festival,** in the second weekend of September in Estes Park; and the **Elk Festival,** in late September in Estes Park.

---

**U**nlike other Colorado mountain communities, most of which got their starts in mining, Estes Park has always been a resort town. Long known by Utes and Arapahoes, the high plain (7,522 ft.) was discovered in 1859 by rancher Joel Estes. He soon sold his homestead to Griff Evans, who built it into a dude ranch. One of Evans's guests, the British Earl of Dunraven, was so taken by the region, he purchased most of the valley and operated it as his private game reserve until thwarted by such settlers as W. E. James, who built Elkhorn Lodge as a "fish ranch" to supply Denver restaurants.

But the growth of Estes Park is inextricably linked with two individuals: Freelan Stanley and Enos Mills. Stanley, a Bostonian who with his brother, Francis, had invented the kerosene-powered Stanley Steamer automobile in 1899, settled in Estes Park in 1907, launched a Stanley Steamer shuttle service to and from Denver, and in 1909 built the landmark Stanley Hotel on a hilltop overlooking the village. Mills, an innkeeper-turned-conservationist author and lecturer, was the prime advocate for the creation of Rocky Mountain National Park. President Woodrow Wilson signed the bill creating the 400-square-mile park in 1915; today it attracts over 2.8 million visitors annually.

## ORIENTATION

**INFORMATION**    The **Estes Park Area Chamber of Commerce,** P.O. Box 3050, Estes Park, CO 80517 (tel. 303/586-4431, or 800/44-ESTES), has a visitor center off U.S. 34, just east of its junction with U.S. 36. For information on the national park, write or phone Park Headquarters, **Rocky Mountain National Park,** Estes Park, CO 80517 (tel. 303/586-2371).

**CITY LAYOUT**    U.S. 34 and U.S. 36 enter Estes Park from the east, on either side of Lake Estes. The highways proceed together through downtown Estes Park as **Elkhorn Avenue;** U.S. 34 Bypass branches to the north and west as **Wonderview Avenue,** rejoining Elkhorn on the west side of town and paralleling the Fall River as it climbs into Rocky Mountain National Park. U.S. 36, now known as **Moraine Avenue,** turns south and west off Elkhorn at a town-center intersection; it follows Glacier Creek to the junction of Bear Creek Road, then ascends to the national park headquarters and visitor center.

# GETTING AROUND

During the summer, the **Estes Park Trolley** (tel. 586-8866) operates on four routes daily from 8am to 10pm, for a fare of $1, including one reboarding. All trolleys meet on the hour and half hour at the Estes Park Transit Center, at Elkhorn Avenue and McGregor Avenue. They serve nearly all motels, hotels, and campgrounds in and around the town.

Also in summer, a free national-park **shuttle bus** runs from the Glacier Basin parking area to Bear Lake. Departures are every 12 to 30 minutes between 8am and 5:30pm daily, from Memorial Day to mid-August, weekends only from mid-August to mid-September.

There's year-round taxi service with **Estes Park Tour and Taxi** (tel. 586-8440).

Road tours into Rocky Mountain National Park and other area points of interest are conducted throughout the summer season by **Charles Limousine** (tel. 303/586-5151, or 800/950-DASH), **Estes Park Bus Co.** (tel. 303/586-8108, or 800/824-1104), and **Rocky Mountain National Park Tours Ltd.** (tel. 586-TOUR). Rates start as low as $10 and go up to $45 for full-day tours. Four-wheel-drive backcountry tours are conducted by **American Wilderness Tours,** 481 West Elkhorn Avenue (tel. 586-4237), with rates starting at $15.

# FAST FACTS

In case of **emergency,** call **911;** for regular business, contact the Estes Park Police, 170 MacGregor Avenue (tel. 586-4465), or the Larimer County Sheriff, 205 Park Lane (tel. 586-9511). In the national park, call 586-2371 for emergencies. The **hospital,** Estes Park Medical Center is at 555 Prospect Avenue (tel. 586-2317). The **post office** is at 215 West Riverside Drive (tel. 586-8177). For **road information,** call 586-4000. State and local **tax** add 8.2% to hotel bills.

# WHAT TO SEE & DO

## ATTRACTIONS

### ROCKY MOUNTAIN NATIONAL PARK, Estes Park, CO 80517-8397. Tel. 303/586-2371.

Stopping along the Trail Ridge Road to make snowballs in the middle of August is one of the many delights of a visit to Rocky Mountain National Park, one of the largest and most popular national parks in the United States.

Snow-covered peaks stand over lush valleys and shimmering alpine lakes. Certainly, this sort of beauty is not unusual in the Colorado Rockies—but the variety in ecological zones, which change with elevation, is. At lower elevations, about 7,500 to 9,000 feet, ponderosa pine and juniper cloak the sunny southern slopes, with Douglas fir on the cooler northern slopes. Blue spruce and lodgepole pine cling to streamsides, with occasional groves of aspen. Elk and mule deer thrive here. On higher slopes, forests of Englemann spruce and subalpine fir take over, interspersed with wide meadows alive with wildflowers in the spring and summer. This is also bighorn sheep country. Above about 10,500 feet the trees become increasingly gnarled and stunted, until they finally disappear and alpine tundra takes over. Fully one-third of the park is in this bleak world, many of its plants identical to those found in the Arctic.

Within the 414 square miles (265,113 acres) protected by the national park are 17 mountains above 13,000 feet. Longs Peak, at 14,255 feet, is the highest.

✪ **Trail Ridge Road,** which cuts west through the middle of the park from Estes

Park, then south down its western boundary to Grand Lake, is one of America's great alpine highways. Climbing to 12,183 feet near **Fall River Pass,** it's the highest continuous auto highway in the United States. Depending on snowfall, the road is open from Memorial Day to mid-October. The 48-mile scenic drive from Estes Park to Grand Lake takes about 3 hours, including stops at numerous scenic outlooks. Exhibits at the **Alpine Visitor Center** (open in summer daily from 9am to 5pm) at Fall River Pass, 11,796 feet above sea level, explain life on the alpine tundra.

**Fall River Road,** the original park road, leads to the pass from Estes Park via Horseshoe Park Junction. West of the **Endovalley** picnic area, the road is one way uphill. As you negotiate its gravelly switchbacks, you get a clear idea of what early auto travel was like in the West. This road, too, is closed in winter.

One of the few paved roads in the Rockies that leads into a high mountain basin is **Bear Lake Road.** As a result, it's one of the most crowded. Numerous trails converge at Bear Lake, southwest of park headquarters via Moraine Park.

Wise visitors to the national park avoid crowds by putting on a backpack or climbing onto a horse. Rocky Mountain has 355 miles of trails leading into all corners of the park (see "Sports & Recreation," below). Backcountry permits are required for overnight hikes; they're obtained free at park headquarters and ranger stations. Backcountry camping is limited to 1 week from June to September. The park also offers fishing and mountaineering, plus cross-country and downhill skiing in winter.

Entering the park from Estes Park, it's wise to make your first stop at **Park Headquarters,** U.S. 36 west of Colo. 66 (tel. 586-2371). There's a good interpretive exhibit here, a wide choice of books and maps for sale, and general park information. It's open in summer, daily from 8am to 9pm; in winter, daily from 8am to 5pm. The new **Kawuneeche Visitor Center** (open in summer daily from 7am to 7pm; winter, daily from 8am to 4:30pm) is located at the Grand Lake end of the Trail Ridge Road (tel. 303/887-3331 or 627-3471). Besides the Alpine Visitor Center, the **Moraine Park Museum** (open mid-June to mid-September, from 9am to 5pm), on Bear Lake Road (tel. 586-3777), also has full visitor facilities, in addition to its excellent natural-history exhibits. Campfire talks and interpretive ranger programs are offered at each visitor center between June and September. Consult the biweekly "High Country Headlines" newsletter for scheduled activities, which vary from photo walks to fly fishing and orienteering.

The park has five **campgrounds** with a total of 589 sites. Nearly half (247) are at Moraine Park; another 150 are at Glacier Basin. Moraine Park, Timber Creek (100 sites), and Longs Peak Trailhead (26 tent sites) are open year round; Glacier Basin and Aspenglen (54 sites) are seasonal. Camping is limited to 3 days at Longs Peak and 7 days at the other sites. Arrive early in summer if you hope to snare one of these first-come/first-served campsites.

**Admission:** $5 per week per vehicle; camping, summer $9 per campsite, off-season $7 per campsite.

**Open:** Park, daily year round; high country, summer only, as snow conditions permit.

### ENOS MILLS CABIN, Colo. 7 opposite Longs Peak Inn. Tel. 586-4706.

The early 20th-century conservationist's cabin and 200-acre homstead have been preserved as a museum and nature center, 8 miles south of Estes Park. Memorabilia in the cabin include original copies of his 15 books and the cameras that took 17,000 photographs.

**Admission:** Free.

**Open:** Daily 9am–6pm.

### ESTES PARK AREA HISTORICAL MUSEUM, 200 Fourth St. at Elkhorn Ave. Tel. 586-6256.

Pioneer artifacts from the earliest Estes Park settlers—homesteaders who came to ranch cattle in the 1870s—are displayed here. Of particular interest is the story behind a book: *A Lady's Life in the Rocky Mountains,* written during that era by an intrepid Englishwoman named Isabella Bird. The museum also organizes historical

**walking tours** through downtown Estes Park, taking in such sights as the old Josephine Hotel and the 1877 Elkhorn Lodge (one of Colorado's earliest resorts).
**Admission:** Free.
**Open:** Mid-May to Sept, Mon–Sat 10am–5pm, Sun 1–5pm; Oct to mid-May, Tues–Sat 10am–5pm.

## MACGREGOR RANCH MUSEUM, Devil's Gulch Rd. Tel. 586-3749.

Founded in 1873 by A. Q. MacGregor, the ranch displays diaries of early settlers, 19th-century ranching implements, and antique furnishings. This is still a working ranch, but things are done the old-fashioned way: Hay, for instance, is harvested by horse-drawn reapers. It's located north of Estes Park, off the U.S. 34 Bypass.
**Admission:** Free.
**Open:** Memorial Day–Labor Day, Tues–Sat 11am–5pm.

## PROSPECT MOUNTAIN AERIAL TRAMWAY, 420 E. Riverside Dr. Tel. 586-3675.

Panoramic views of Longs Peak and the Continental Divide, plus Estes Park village itself, are afforded by this lift. Its lower terminal is one block south of the post office. Its upper terminal has a gift shop and snack bar. Numerous trails converge atop the mountain.
**Admission:** $4 adults, $2 children under 12.
**Open:** Mid-May to Mid-Sept, daily 10am–5pm.

## SPORTS & RECREATION

Estes Park is a major center for outdoor recreation. Aside from the Rocky Mountain National Park (see "Attractions," above), many activities take place in the 1,240-square-mile **Roosevelt National Forest**. Obtain information on hiking, horseback riding, fishing, and other sports from the Estes-Poudre Ranger District Office, 161 Second Street (P.O. Box 2747), Estes Park, CO 80517 (tel. 303/856-3440).

Within the city, the **Estes Park Recreation & Park District**, 690 Big Thompson Highway (tel. 586-8191, or 800/345-2361 in Colorado), is in charge of a marina, two golf courses, a swimming pool, tennis courts, and other facilities.

**BALLOONING**   Hot-air-balloon rides are offered by **Estes Park Adventures,** 401 East Elkhorn Avenue (tel. 586-2303).

**BICYCLING**   Bicyclists pay only $2 to enter Rocky Mountain National Park. A park brochure describes various suggested routes. Rentals and repairs are available at **Colorado Bicycling,** 184 East Elkhorn Avenue (tel. 586-4241).

**BOATING**   The **Lake Estes Marina,** 1770 Big Thompson Highway (tel. 586-2011), offers rentals of motorboats, sailboats, paddle boats, canoes, kayaks, and sailboards. Kayaking and windsurfing lessons are available by appointment. The marina is open Memorial Day to mid-September.

**FISHING**   Four species of trout are fished in national park and national forest streams and lakes: brown, rainbow, brook, and cutthroat. A state fishing license is required ($18.25 for a 5-day nonresident license, if you're 15 or older); live bait is not permitted. Bear Lake is closed to fishing, as are some lakes and streams at the east side of the park, where the greenback cutthroat is being reintroduced to its native habitat. Get a license and be schooled in regulations at **Scot's Sport Shop,** 870 Moraine Avenue (tel. 586-2877). Or make it easy and fish without a license at **Trout Haven,** 810 Moraine Avenue (tel. 586-2944).

**GOLF**   There are two courses: **Estes Park Golf Course** (18 holes), 1080 South St. Vrain Street (tel. 586-8146); and **Lake Estes Executive Golf Course** (9 holes), 690 Big Thompson Highway (tel. 586-8176). Working on your putting? Try **Tiny Town Miniature Golf** (19 holes), 830 Moraine Avenue (tel. 586-6333).

**HIKING & BACKPACKING**   The national park visitor center has U.S. Geological Survey topographic maps and guidebooks for sale, and rangers will be happy to suggest trails that are lightly used. One trail that is decidedly *not* lightly used is the **Deer Ridge Trail**, with a trailhead in downtown Estes Park!

Easy trails include the **Sprague Lake Nature Trail** (0.5 mile), the **Alberta Falls Trail** from the Glacier Gorge Parking Area (0.6 mile), and the **Bierstadt Lake Trail** from the Bear Lake Parking Area (1.6 miles). Moderately difficult trails include the **Emerald Lake Trail** from the Bear Lake Parking Area (1.8 miles), the **Fern Lake Trail** from Moraine Park (3.8 miles), and the **Lulu City Trail** from the Colorado River Trailhead (3.1 miles). Strenuous trails include the **Finch Lake Trail** from the Wild Basin Ranger Station (4.5 miles), the **Lawn Lake Trail** from Horseshoe Park (6.2 miles), and the **Timber Lake Trail** from near Never Summer Ranch (4.8 miles).

Remember that overnight camping in backcountry areas requires a park permit.

**HORSEBACK RIDING**   Stables where horses can be hired for guided rides are found at several locations in and outside the national park. **Sombrero Ranch Stables,** opposite the Lake Estes dam on the Big Thompson Highway (U.S. 34) (tel. 586-4577), has liveries in the park at Moraine Park (tel. 586-2327) and Glacier Basin (tel. 586-3244). The **National Park Village Stables** are at National Park Village North on U.S. 34 west, Fall River Road (tel. 586-5269); the **Cowpoke Corner Corral** is at Glacier Lodge on the YMCA road (tel. 586-5890). You can also try **Elkhorn Stables,** 650 West Elkhorn Avenue (tel. 586-3291).

Day hikes with llamas are offered by **Walkabout Llama Hikes** (tel. 586-5940) and **Keno's Llama & Guest Ranch** (tel. 586-2827).

**MOUNTAINEERING**   The **Colorado Mountain School,** P.O. Box 2062, Estes Park, CO 80517 (tel. 303/586-5758), is a national park–sanctioned technical climbing school and summer-winter guide service. Maps and equipment can be obtained from **Colorado Wilderness Sports,** 358 East Elkhorn Avenue (tel. 586-6548). The most popular climb is Longs Peak; the highest mountain in the park. It can be ascended by those without experience via the "Keyhole," but its north and east faces are for experts only. Longs Peak information is available from the ranger station at the trailhead (tel. 586-4975).

**RIVER RAFTING**   Raft trips down the Cache la Poudre, Colorado, and Arkansas rivers—priced from $42 for 1 day, $115 for 2 days—can be organized by **Colorado Wilderness Sports,** 358 East Elkhorn Avenue (tel. 586-6548), or **Rapid Transit Rafting,** P.O. Box 4095, Estes Park, CO 80517 (tel. 303/586-8852, or 800/367-8523). Longer trips are offered on the Green, Yampa, and Dolores rivers, as well as kayak lessons for eventual runs down the Big Thompson River.

**SKIING**   **Estes Park Skiing Centers** have two full-service shops: 875 Moraine Avenue (tel. 586-2468) for downhill sales and repairs, and 156 East Elkhorn Avenue (tel. 586-2114) for cross-country rentals. If you're headed into the backcountry for nordic skiing, stop by the national park headquarters for a permit and a brochure titled "Ski Touring in Rocky Mountain National Park." Some backcountry areas are closed because of avalanche danger.

**SNOWMOBILING**   Snowmobiling is permitted on the west side of the park only. Register at the **Kawuneeche Visitor Center,** at the Grand Lake end of Trail Ridge Road (tel. 303/887-3331).

**SWIMMING**   The **Estes Park Aquatic Center,** 660 Community Drive (tel. 586-2340), is open for public and lap swims. Call for current schedules. Admission is $2 for adults, $1.50 for children and seniors.

## SHOPPING

The **Fine Arts Guild of the Rockies,** P.O. Box 1165, Estes Park, CO 80517, publishes a directory of 19 village art galleries. Of special note is the **Art Center of Estes Park** in the Stanley Village Shopping Center, Wonderview Avenue at U.S. 34 (tel. 586-5882). One of its galleries represents local artists; the other offers changing exhibits of a wide range of media. Open Memorial Day to September, daily from 11am to 5pm; October to December, Thursday through Saturday from 11am to 4pm.

Interesting collections of galleries and gift shops include the **Old Church Shops,** 157 West Elkhorn Avenue, and **Sundance Center for the Arts,** 150 East Riverside Drive. Also look for **Glassworks Studio & Gallery,** 456 Moraine Avenue (tel. 586-8619), with sales and demonstrations of hand-blown glass and ceramics; and **Serendipity,** 117 East Elkhorn Avenue, traders in Native American arts and crafts. And if you're a serious antique collector, check out the antiquities available at the **Stanley Hotel.**

Ten miles south of Estes Park via Colo. 7 is the  **Charles Eagle Plume Indian Store & Museum** (tel. 586-4710). A University of Colorado graduate now in his 70s, Eagle Plume is one-fourth Native American (Blackfoot), and a true entertainer and entrepreneur. His fascinating collection of museum-quality artifacts is not for sale, but the trading post has much more that is: crafts, pottery, jewelry, baskets, rugs, and more. It's open mid-May to mid-September, daily from 9am to 5pm.

Just for fun, check out **Estes Surf & Sport,** 443 West Elkhorn Avenue (tel. 586-9094), which sells and trades new and used sporting goods. Here, hundreds of miles from any breakers, is the Rockies' largest display of surfboards and surfing memorabilia, plus continuously playing surf movies.

## EVENING ENTERTAINMENT

The **Stanley Hotel** (see "Where to Stay," below), 333 Wonderview Avenue (tel. 303/586-3371, or 800/ROCKIES), is the focus for the performing arts in Estes Park. Summer and fall **theater** seasons are offered in Stanley Hall Thursday through Sunday nights, with optional dinner reservations preceding the show; and a **Fine Arts Concert Series** offers symphony and chamber music in the Music Room at 2pm every Sunday throughout the year. In summer, the **Estes Park Music Festival** also presents free classical concerts at 8pm on Monday and Wednesday.

Nine miles south of Estes Park off Colo. 7, the **Rocky Ridge Music Center,** 465 Longs Peak Road (tel. 586-4031), offers a series of 20 concerts over 6 weeks beginning in late June.

The **Centennial Playhouse** at National Park Village South, 3450 Fall River Road (tel. 586-2885), presents melodramatic dinner shows on summer evenings. Chuckwagon dinner country-and-western shows are offered Monday through Saturday night, Memorial Day through Labor Day, by the **Barleen Family Country Music Dinner Theatre,** Woodstock Drive at Colo. 7 (tel. 586-5749 or 586-5741), and the **Lazy B. Ranch,** 1915 Dry Gulch Road (tel. 586-5371).

For live music and dancing, check out **Lonigan's Saloon,** 110 West Elkhorn Avenue (tel. 586-4346), or the **Gaslight Pub,** 246 Moraine Avenue (tel. 586-5978).

# WHERE TO STAY

Over 120 lodging establishments have more than 3,000 rooms. You can get help finding accommodations from the **Estes Park Area Chamber of Commerce Lodging Referral Service** (tel. 303/586-4431, or 800/44-ESTES).

## EXPENSIVE

**CASTLE MOUNTAIN LODGE, 1520 Fall River Rd., Moraine Route, Estes Park, CO 80517. Tel. 303/586-3664.** 28 cabins. TV
**$ Rates:** Mid-June to August, $65–$125 single or double; $139–$230 two- and three-bedroom cabins. $5 per person extra for three or more in a cabin. Discounts of about 15% for stays of 3 nights; special weekly rates. Fall and spring rates 27%–37% less; winter rates, 37%–50% less. AE, DISC, MC, V.

These modern rustic cabins on Fall River, in a wooded tract facing Castle Mountain, offer guests a wide choice of options. No two cabins are alike, ranging in size from studio cottages to three-bedroom units. All except a pair of studios have full kitchens with refrigerators. Most cabins have fireplaces, hideabed sofas, barbecues, and outdoor furniture.

There is a playground for children, and a "peripatetic pet policy" allows critters for $5 a day by advance arrangement.

**RIVERSONG, Lower Broadview Dr. off Mary's Lake Rd. (P.O. Box 1910), Estes Park, CO 80517. Tel. 303/586-4666.** 9 rms (all with bath). **$ Rates** (including breakfast): $85–$125 single or double. MC, V.

A 1920 Craftsman mansion on the Big Thompson River, this elegant bed-and-breakfast has 27 forested acres with hiking trails and a trout pond, as well as prolific wildlife. It's at the end of a country lane, the first right off Mary's Lake Road after it branches off U.S. 36 south.

The cozy bedrooms, all named after wildflowers, are decorated with a blend of antique and modern country furniture. Various rooms have ornate brass beds, skylit whirlpools, clawfoot tubs, and/or woodstoves. All have private bathrooms, but none has phones or TVs—it's designed that way. Smoking is not permitted.

**Dining/Entertainment:** Hosts Sue and Gary Mansfield will prepare gourmet candlelight dinners by advance arrangement, but you must supply your own alcoholic beverage.

**STANLEY HOTEL, 333 Wonderview Ave. (P.O. Box 1767), Estes Park, CO 80517. Tel. 303/586-3371,** or 800/ROCKIES. 92 rms (all with bath), 8 condo suites. TV TEL **$ Rates:** $65–$125 single; $70–$130 double; $150 condo suite. Many special off-season packages. AE, DISC, JCB, MC, V.

Freelan Stanley, co-inventor of the Stanley Steamer automobile, built this magnificent white-pillared edifice in 1909 on 1,400 acres and an initial investment of $500,000. The equal of European resorts of the time in services and amenities, it was built into solid rock on a hilltop. Today the hotel is a registered National Historic District—an unusual honor for a single property. A Stanley Steamer remains on display, of course.

As is often the case in older hotels, every room is different, though each is brightly carpeted and decorated with gold wallpaper and some antiques. They have queen-size beds and ceiling fans, and most have mirrors. If the corridors look familiar, it's because Stephen King used the hotel as the model for his novel *The Shining*.

**Dining/Entertainment:** Continental cuisine is served most of the year in the MacGregor Room; in summer, fine dining is moved into the Dunraven Room, which otherwise serves as a bistro-lounge. Concerts on Stanley's own Steinway are offered in the Music Room. There's dinner theater June to December in Stanley Hall.

**Services:** Room service.

**Facilities:** Outdoor swimming pool, Jacuzzi, tennis, croquet, exercise room, gift shop; gallery with the largest collection of antiquities for sale in the western United States—ancient Roman, Greek, and Egyptian pieces, some valued up to $36,000.

**STREAMSIDE CABINS, 1260 Fall River Rd., Moraine Route (P.O. Box 2930), Estes Park, CO 80517. Tel. 303/586-6464.** 19 suites (all with bath). TV **$ Rates:** June–Sept, $105–$170 single or double; Oct–May, $50–$75 single or double. AE, DISC, MC, V.

The first time I drove in here, nearly three dozen mule deer were milling around Jan and Bob Van Horn's chalet home office. That's not unusual: The deer, as well as some elk and occasional bighorn sheep, are such regular visitors that they've been given names. Indeed, these 16 acres on the Fall River, less than a mile west of Estes Park via U.S. 34, are surrounded by woods and meadows rife with wildflowers. They are a lure to wildlife.

Everything is top drawer in these solid-wood cabins. In fact, the semiweekly

*Trail-Gazette* newspaper has rated them the "Best Lodging in Estes" for several years. Most have beamed cathedral ceilings, skylights, and southwestern country decor. Furnished like condominiums, they have wall-to-wall carpeting, king- and queen-size beds, Jacuzzi tubs or steam baths, full fireplaces, cable television, decks or patios with gas grills, and (with only two exceptions) full electric kitchens equipped for gourmet chefs. Romantic suites pamper couples through an "Affairs of the Heart" package.

**WIND RIVER RANCH, Colo. 7 (P.O. Box 3410), Estes Park, CO 80517.** Tel. 303/586-4212, or 800/523-4212. 15 rms, 10 cabins (all with bath).
**$ Rates** (including full board): $130 single; $210–$250 double. Discounts for children. MC, V. **Closed:** Mid-Sept to early June.

Owned and operated by the Irvin family since 1973, this 120-year-old guest ranch is located 7¼ miles south of Estes Park on the Peak-to-Peak Highway, at the 9,000-foot level in the Tahosa Valley. Guests stay in the ranch house, with five rooms surrounding a huge central living area, or any of 10 cabins. Six cabins are spacious two-bedroom units; the rest have one bedroom. All guests share the ranch house's big living room, huge fireplace, library, and games area.

**Dining/Entertainment:** Prices include all meals, but you must supply your own alcoholic beverages. A varied entertainment program (6 nights a week, in season) may have a musician one night, a naturalist's lecture the second, a Bingo game the third, and a movie the fourth.

**Facilities:** Heated swimming pool, hot tub, trout-stocked fish pond. Day camp program for children 4–12, Monday through Friday. The stables have 40 horses for riding: 1-hour lessons are $10, all-day rides are $40, and 1-week use of a horse is $140.

## MODERATE

**BALDPATE INN, 4900 S. Colo. 7 (P.O. Box 4445), Estes Park, CO 80517. Tel. 303/586-6151.** 13 rms (4 with bath), 2 cabins.
**$ Rates** (including full breakfast): $60 single or double without bath, $75 single or double with bath; $100–$125 cabin. MC, V. **Closed:** Nov–Apr.

This inn claims that its display of keys—more than 20,000 of them—is the world's largest. Built in 1917, the inn was named for the novel *Seven Keys to Baldpate,* in which each of seven hotel guests believes he or she possesses the only key to the place. Guests here are encouraged to add their own key to the collection.

The rooms have views of Longs Peak from a 9,000-foot-high site on the side of Twin Sisters Mountain. Seven miles from Estes Park township, the lodge also offers lunches and dinner. Guests can fish for trout in Lily Lake adjoining the property. Board games and books from a selection in the inn's library draw guests around a stone fireplace on cool evenings.

**BEST WESTERN LAKE ESTES RESORT, 1650 Big Thompson Hwy. (U.S. 34) (P.O. Box 1466), Estes Park, CO 80517. Tel. 303/586-3386,** or 800/292-VIEW. 60 rms (all with bath), 4 suites. TV TEL
**$ Rates:** June 21–Sept 7, $60–$80 single; $60–$90 double; $89–$100 suite. May 25–June 20 and Sept 8–28, $50–$64 single; $50–$75 double; $73–$80 suite. Sept 29–May 24, $40–$54 single; $40–$65 double; $63–$70 suite. AE, CB, DC, DISC, JCB, MC, V.

Perhaps the distinguishing feature of this motel is the 5,000-gallon Jacuzzi tub (it seats 30) that's housed inside a solarium-greenhouse, adjacent to the outdoor swimming pool. There's also a sports court, children's playground, sauna, and guest laundry.

Rooms, in two buildings, have fine cherrywood furnishings and other special touches, like hairdryers and phones in every bathroom. A dozen rooms with king-size beds have views across Lake Estes. Fireplace suites have desks, two TVs, and three phones. Family units sleep six to eight. No-smoking rooms are available.

**GLACIER LODGE, Hwy. 66 (P.O. Box 2656), Estes Park, CO 80517. Tel. 303/586-4401.** 3 rms (all with bath), 25 suites. TV

**$ Rates:** Early June to mid-Sept, $48–$75 rooms; $90–$112 suites, single or double. Late May to early June and mid- to end of Sept, $38–$65 rooms; $80–$102 suites, single or double. Oct to late May, $32–$38 rooms; $58–$92 suites, single or double. MC, V.

Deer and elk frequently visit these lovely cabins, spread across a woodland by the Big Thompson River. You've even got to cross a rustic bridge to get to them. Poolside chalets are 1½-bedroom cabins with a loft, full kitchen, and fireplace. Cozy, homey river duplexes have outside decks overlooking the stream. River triplexes are similar, ranging from earthy to country quaint in decor. The lodge has a swimming pool, sports court, playground, fishing, lending library, and its own stables. Every Tuesday evening in summer there's a western steak fry at Campfire Corral; on Friday nights, a "buckaroo roundup" for kids.

**HOLIDAY INN OF ESTES PARK, U.S. 36 and Colo. 7 (P.O. Box 1468), Estes Park, CO 80517. Tel. 303/586-2332,** or 800/HOLIDAY. Fax 303/586-2332, ext. 299. 154 rms (all with bath). A/C TV TEL

**$ Rates:** Late June to early Sept, $65–$92 single or double; $139–$155 suite. Early to the end of Sept, $55–$75 single or double; $95–$105 suite. Oct to mid-May, $39–$65 single or double; $89–$105 suite. Children under 18 free in same room with adult. AE, CB, DC, DISC, JCB, MC, V.

The modern lodge at first appearance leads you to believe that this may not be a typical Holiday Inn—but the cavernous HoliDome, with its indoor swimming pool, reaffirms your faith in the chain. Most rooms have two double beds; a handful have balconies overlooking the indoor pool. All have standard furnishings, in-room movies (free) and direct-dial phones (local calls 45¢).

The Aspens restaurant and lounge serves three meals daily, including Sunday champagne brunch; no smoking is permitted in the restaurant. The motel offers no-smoking rooms, room service, valet or guest laundry, a fitness room, games room, and gift shop, and will accept pets. Facilities for the disabled are available. A new conference center handles 1,000, theater style.

**THE SAPPHIRE ROSE INN, 215 Virginia St. (P.O. Box 3663), Estes Park, CO 80517. Tel. 303/586-6607.** 16 units (11 with bath) TV

**$ Rates** (including breakfast): $60 room, single or double; $85 cabin; $90 cottage; $90–$120 apartment. No credit cards.

Victorian antiques, crystal, and china adorn this renovated bed-and-breakfast house, just uphill from downtown Estes Park. Four oddly shaped rooms in the main house share two baths. The property also boasts a turn-of-the-century farm cabin moved from Rocky Mountain National Park, a two-bedroom cottage with a stone fireplace, five outer units with gas stoves and tape decks, and a large contemporary apartment building (across Virginia Street) with five modern, upscale rooms, complete with Jacuzzi tubs, stereo systems, and jungle decor.

When award-winning chef Harry Marsden, an Englishman by way of Au Relais in Sonoma, Calif., opened the Sapphire Rose in 1988, it was inevitable that he'd be back in the kitchen in no time. Indeed, Marsden's creative continental cuisine is served Monday through Saturday at 7:30pm, by reservation. It's $30 well spent.

## INEXPENSIVE

**ALLENSPARK LODGE, Colo. 7 Business Loop (P.O. Box 247), Allenspark, CO 80510. Tel. 303/747-2552.** 10 rms (4 with bath).

**$ Rates** (including continental breakfast): Mid-May to October, $31–$70 single or double; Nov to mid-May, $29–$60 single or double. MC, V.

There's a historic ambience to this three-story lodge, built in 1933 of native stone and hand-hewn ponderosa pine logs. Located 16 miles south of Estes Park, in a tiny village at the southeast corner of the national park, the lodge has four bedrooms with private baths and six others which share. Every room has mountain views and original handmade 1930s pine furniture. At the top end is the Hideaway Room, with a brass bed, bear-claw tub, and fine linens; the lowest-priced room is the Bear Cub Room, with a single twin bed. Guests share the stone fireplace in the Great Room, Ping-Pong and pool in the Game Room, books in the Library, and breakfast, afternoon wine, and hors d'oeuvres in the Wilderquest Room.

**COLORADO COTTAGES, 1241 High Dr., Moraine Route, Estes Park, CO 80517. Tel. 303/586-4637,** or 800/468-1236. 10 rms, 1 suite (all with bath). TV

**$ Rates:** Mid-June to Labor Day, $51–$71 single or double; $86 suite. Labor Day to mid-June, $41–$56 single or double; $70 suite. Winter hols, $46–$63 single or double; $78 suite. AE, DISC, MC, V.

These tiny blue-slate, shingled cabins have fully equipped kitchenettes with refrigerators, a fireplace (with wood provided), heater, queen-size or double beds, tiny three-quarter baths, barbecues, and picnic tables. Furnishings are basic. Three units are modernized, with a microwave in place of a stove, and a full bath. Some rooms sleep as many as eight. There's a playground for kids.

## BUDGET

**H-BAR-G RANCH HOSTEL, 3500 H-Bar-G Rd., off Dry Gulch Rd. (P.O. Box 1260), Estes Park, CO 80517. Tel. 303/586-3688.** 130 beds.

**$ Rates:** $7.25 per bed. Youth hostel association memberships required: $25 for adults (18–54), $15 for seniors (55+), $10 for youth (under 18), $35 for families.

Bring your own bedding (sleeping bag or sheet sack) to throw on your dormitory bunk, and be prepared to pitch in with daily chores. That's the hosteler's way. There are separate bunkhouses for men and women, and family cabins by advance reservation, but everyone shares the kitchen, games room, and bath facilities. Hiking trails lead into the national forest and national park from the hostel; you'll also find tennis and volleyball courts, barbecues and fireplace. Check in between 5:15 and 9pm, or wait for daily pickups at 5pm at the Estes Park Tourist Information Center. The hostel is 5½ miles north of Lake Estes.

## CAMPGROUNDS

Aside from the Rocky Mountain National Park campgrounds, discussed above, these are among the commercial sites in the Estes Park area.

**MARY'S LAKE CAMPGROUND, 2120 Mary's Lake Rd. (P.O. Box 2514), Estes Park, CO 80517. Tel. 303/586-4411.** 130 sites.

**$ Rates:** $13.50–$16.50 per campsite for two people. Extra person $1.75.

Forty of the campsites are reserved for tenters; the remainder are for recreational vehicles. Most RV spaces have sewer hookups, as well as water and electricity. The campground has bathhouses, a laundry, swimming pool, and games room; firewood is available, and pets are allowed.

**NATIONAL PARK RESORT, 3501 Fall River Rd., Moraine Route, Estes Park, CO 80517. Tel. 303/586-4563.** 100 sites.

**$ Rates:** $14.50–$16.50 per campsite for two people. Extra person $1.50.

All but 10 of the sites here have water and electric hookups; they're best suited for tenters. Facilities include bathhouses and a laundry; firewood is supplied and pets are permitted.

# WHERE TO DINE

## EXPENSIVE

**THE FAWN BROOK INN, Colo. 7 Business Loop, Allenspark. Tel. 747-2556.**
**Cuisine:** CONTINENTAL. **Reservations:** Recommended.

**$ Prices:** Appetizers $9.85–$12.85; main courses $19.85–$32.25.
**Open:** Memorial Day–Labor Day, dinner Tues–Sat 5–9pm, Sun 4–8:30pm; brunch Sun noon–2pm. Mar–May and Oct–Dec, dinner only, Thurs–Sat 5–9pm. **Closed:** Jan–Feb.

Very "olde countrye" in appearance, this establishment, 16 miles south of Estes Park, belies its rustic atmosphere by serving up what many consider the finest gourmet cuisine and intimate service in the Rocky Mountain National Park area. The menu focuses on continental dishes with a German flair.

Start with a wild-game pâté, langoustino remoulade, or Caesar salad prepared tableside. Then move on to a wide choice of main dishes, from sweetbreads Monte Carlo to sauerbraten, chateaubriand Escoffier to sole meunière, fondue bourguignonne to seafood maltaise. Leave room for the superb desserts.

## LA CHAUMIERE, U.S. 36, Pinewood Springs. Tel. 823-6521.

**Cuisine:** FRENCH. **Reservations:** Recommended.
**$ Prices:** Appetizers $2.50–$5.75; main courses $12.50–$17.50. MC, V.
**Open:** Dinner only, Mon–Sat 5:30–8:30pm, Sun noon–8pm. **Closed:** Mon Oct–May.

A father-and-son team, Heinz and Andy Fricker are at the helm at this small restaurant, 12 miles southeast of Estes Park en route to Lyons. Heinz, who regards French cuisine as an art form, delights diners with an array of masterpieces such as roast duckling with wild rice and corn pancakes, poached salmon with herbed hollandaise, and roast lamb with rosemary sauce. The menu changes weekly.

## MODERATE

## THE DUNRAVEN INN, 2470 Hwy. 66. Tel. 586-6409.

**Cuisine:** ITALIAN. **Reservations:** Highly recommended.
**$ Prices:** Appetizers $3.95–$5.95; main courses $6.95–$13.50. AE, CB, DC, MC, V.
**Open:** Summer, dinner only, Mon–Sat 5–11pm, Sun 5–10pm; winter, dinner only, Mon–Sat 5–10pm, Sun 5–9pm.

The *Mona Lisa* is everywhere in this self-proclaimed "Rome of the Rockies." Every possible design of the *Mona*, from a mustachioed lady to opera posters, has found its way onto the walls—as well as autographed dollar bills, posted by their former owners. The provincial charm extends to the cuisine. House specialties are lasagne, veal parmigiana, chicken cacciatore, and Dunraven italiano: a char-broiled sirloin steak in a sauce of green peppers, black olives, mushrooms, and tomatoes. There's a wide choice of pastas, seafoods, and coffee and dessert specials.

## GAZEBO RESTAURANT & TAVERN, 205 Virginia Dr. Tel. 586-9564.

**Cuisine:** INTERNATIONAL. **Reservations:** Recommended.
**$ Prices:** Appetizers $2.50–$6.50; lunch $4.25–$10.95; Sun brunch $5.50–$10.50; dinner $8.50–$15.95. 20% discount for seniors. AE, MC, V.
**Open:** Summer, daily 11:30am–9pm; winter, daily 11:30am–8pm.

The Courtyard Shops are one of Estes Park's architectural showpieces, with their terraces, waterfalls, and other landscaping. The Gazebo has taken full advantage of its location by spreading through three levels. The tavern is at ground level, dining room in the middle, and gazebo on top. You can get standard beef, veal, poultry, seafood, and vegetarian dishes here, but for something different try spuntini, a hollowed-out *boule* of homemade bread, filled with chili, beef stew, or a seafood or chicken casserole, and served with a salad. For dinner, try Khyber chicken or cubed beef, marinated overnight in yogurt and spices, broiled, and served with a chutney relish.

## OLD PLANTATION, 128 E. Elkhorn Ave. Tel. 586-2800.

**Cuisine:** AMERICAN. **Reservations:** Highly recommended.
**$ Prices:** Lunch $5.75–$11.95; dinner $11.95–$16.25. MC, V.
**Open:** Memorial Day–Oct, daily 11:30am–9pm.

Serving hearty, traditional American fare, this restaurant has been run by members of the Burgess family for over six decades. The dining room is dotted with antiques, and the walls show off works of early western artists. The place is known for its Yankee pot roast and roast duckling. Steak, veal, and fresh trout are served too, and the soups and fruit pies are homemade. Also here is a pleasant lounge, the Coat of Arms Tavern.

## INEXPENSIVE

### LA CASA, 222 E. Elkhorn Ave. Tel. 586-2807.
**Cuisine:** MEXICAN/CAJUN. **Reservations:** Recommended for large parties.
**$ Prices:** $6.95–$13.95. AE, CB, DC, DISC, MC, V.
**Open:** Daily 11am–10pm.
One thing that the Mexican and Cajun cuisines have in common, besides the Gulf of Mexico, is a high level of spiciness. You'll get that at the Estorito family's fun restaurant on Estes Park's main street. In summer, there's seating in a lovely outdoor garden. Try blackened shrimp, voodoo chicken, or a spicy beef burrito. Margaritas are on tap, and there's live entertainment nightly.

### MOUNTAINEER RESTAURANT, 540 S. St. Vrain St. Tel. 586-9001.
**Cuisine:** AMERICAN. **Reservations:** Not necessary.
**$ Prices:** Breakfast $1.95–$5.95; lunch $2.45–$5.75; dinner $5.25–$6.95. MC, V.
**Open:** Daily 6am–8:30pm.
Candy Edward's bargain eatery is a family favorite, just outside downtown. Have an omelet or steak and eggs for breakfast, a chili dog or a shrimp basket for lunch, southern fried chicken or liver and onions for dinner. As if the prices weren't already great, there's a children's menu with nothing over $1.50.

### P.S. FLOWERS, 247 W. Elkhorn Ave. Tel. 586-5735.
**Cuisine:** INTERNATIONAL.
**$ Prices:** $5.25–$13.75. AE, MC, V.
**Open:** Lunch daily 11am–4:30pm; dinner daily 5:30–10pm.
The motto at this pub-style restaurant is, If it's not going to be good, and fun, one should stay home and eat oatmeal. There's a fresh trout sandwich for lunch, deep-fried with lettuce and tomato, fries, and coleslaw; fish and chips, bratwurst, and Mexican specialties are also served. For dinner, try the beef Stroganoff, rack of lamb, crab legs, barbecued ribs, or fettuccine Alfredo. The specialty at the outdoor beer garden is ale—by the yard.

# AN EASY EXCURSION FROM ESTES PARK

## GRAND LAKE

The west gateway to Rocky Mountain National Park is at ✪ **Grand Lake,** a village with board sidewalks and still a few horses being ridden along the main drag. Located in the shadow of Shadow Mountain at the park's southwestern corner, the community—at 8,370 feet elevation—is actually within **Arapahoe National Recreation Area,** which encompasses Grand Lake and two other larger bodies of water: Shadow Mountain Reservoir and Lake Granby.

In summer, it's easy to get to Grand Lake, 48 miles from Estes Park via the Trail Ridge Road (U.S. 34). In winter, when Grand Lake is a ski-touring and snowmobiling mecca, it's a bit trickier. From Denver, it's 101 miles: Travel west on I-70 42 miles to the Empire exit; follow U.S. 40 through Winter Park, 47 miles to Granby; then turn north on U.S. 34 another 14 miles to Grand Lake.

**WHAT TO SEE & DO**   The Grand Lake Yacht Club, the world's highest-altitude yacht club, hosts the **Lipton Cup Regatta** in mid-August. The club was organized in 1902, when sails were added to rowboats; it began the regatta 10 years later. Grand Lake, which reaches a depth of 400 feet, is the largest natural lake in the state; it is linked by channels to the other two large lakes, both of them dammed portions of the

Colorado River. Water from the three is pumped under the mountains via the Alva Adams Tunnel to the Big Thompson River and Lake Estes, where it is channeled to the plains for irrigation. The national recreation area that encompasses the lakes offers boating, fishing, hiking, horseback riding, cross-country skiing, snowmobiling, picnicking, and camping. There's also an 18-hole golf course in Grand Lake, and marinas on each of the lakes.

Tours are offered at the **Holzwarth Ranch,** an early homestead, and at the **Granby Pumping Plant.** The **Kaufman House,** on Pitkin Avenue, an early log structure, serves as the museum of the Grand Lake Historical Society, and is open to the public. A summer repertory company stages **theater productions.** For information on these and other attractions and activities, contact the **Grand Lake Chamber of Commerce,** P.O. Box 57, Grand Lake, CO 80447 (tel. 303/627-3402).

**WHERE TO STAY**   There are about three dozen motels, guest ranches, and lodges with cabins in the Grand Lake area. Among the nicest are **The Rapids Lodge,** 201 Rapid Lane (P.O. Box 1400), Grand Lake, CO 80447 (tel. 303/627-3707), with 19 elegant units on the Tonahutu River priced at $40 to $75 for double occupancy, and fine dining in a historic log cabin; and the **Bighorn Lodge,** 613 Grand Avenue (P.O. Box 1260), Grand Lake, CO 80447 (tel. 303/627-8101, or 800/621-5923), a main-street hotel with 20 rooms at $42 to $75 double. The **Grand Lake Central Reservation Service** (tel. 303/443-5391, or 800/462-LAKE) can help with arrangements.

**WHERE TO DINE**   The **Corner Cupboard Inn,** 1028 Grand Avenue (tel. 627-3813), offers aged prime meats and family dining in a building dating to 1881. Other likely dining establishments are the **Mountain Inn,** 612 Grand Avenue (tel. 627-3385), and (for breakfast and lunch only) the **Chuck Hole Café,** 1119 Grand Avenue (tel. 627-3509).

---

# 2. STEAMBOAT SPRINGS

158 miles NW of Denver, 335 miles E of Salt Lake City, Utah

**GETTING THERE   By Plane**   The **Steamboat Springs Airport** (known as the "STOLPort"), 4 miles west of town on Elk River Road (tel. 879-9042), is served by **Continental Express** (tel. 303/879-2648, or 800/525-0280), with connections to and from **Denver's Stapleton International Airport** several times daily, year round.

From mid-December through March, the **Yampa Valley Regional Airport,** 22 miles west of Steamboat near Hayden (tel. 276-3669), greets Boeing 727s, 737s, and 767s. **American Airlines** (tel. 800/443-7300) offers daily nonstop service from Chicago, Dallas/Fort Worth, and Los Angeles, and Saturday nonstops from Newark and San Jose; **Continental Airlines** (tel. 800/525-0280) has daily nonstops from Denver and Saturday nonstops from Cleveland and Houston; **Northwest Airlines** (tel. 800/225-2525) has daily nonstops to and from Minneapolis/St. Paul; and **America West Airlines** (tel. 800/247-5692) has three flights a week to and from Phoenix.

For transportation between Steamboat and the airports, call **Steamboat Express** (tel. 879-3400) or **Trailhead Transit** (tel. 468-2438).

**By Bus   Greyhound/Trailways,** 30670 Moffat Avenue (tel. 879-0866), offers daily intercity service. **Steamboat Express,** 1401 Lincoln Avenue (tel. 303/879-6050, or 800/525-BOAT), a service of Panorama Coaches, travels daily in ski season between Denver's Stapleton International Airport and Steamboat Springs.

**By Car**   The most direct route to Steamboat Springs from Denver is to take I-70 west 68 miles to Silverthorne, Colo. 9 north 38 miles to Kremmling, and U.S. 40 west 52 miles to Steamboat. (*Note:* Rabbit Ears Pass, 25 miles east of Steamboat, can be treacherous in winter.) If you're traveling east on I-70, exit at Rifle, proceed 88 miles north on Colo. 13 to Craig, then take U.S. 40 east 42 miles to Steamboat. From Fort Collins, take Colo. 14 west 147 miles via Walden. From Salt Lake City or the Pacific Northwest, you have two choices: Either follow U.S. 40 east through Vernal; or take I-80 east through Rock Springs, Wyoming, exit at Creston (82 miles east of Rock Springs), take Wy. 789/Colo. 13 south 91 miles to Craig, then turn east on U.S. 40.

**Car Rentals:** Car rentals are available at the airports. **At Steamboat Springs Airport,** try Advantage (tel. 879-5737), Budget (tel. 879-3103), Dollar (tel. 879-5969), Hertz (tel. 870-0880), or National (tel. 879-0800). **At Yampa Valley Airport,** look for Budget (tel. 276-3612), Hertz (tel. 276-3304), and National (tel. 276-3596).

**SPECIAL EVENTS** Area events include the **Cowboy Downhill,** the second week of January; the **Winter Carnival,** the first full week of February; the **Cardboard Classic and Ski Area Closure,** over the second weekend of April; the **Yampa River Festival,** over the first weekend of June; **Cowboy Roundup Days,** over the Fourth of July weekend; **Rainbow Weekend,** on the third weekend of July; the **Vintage Auto Race and Aircraft Fly-in,** over the Labor Day weekend; the **Ski Area Opening,** on Thanksgiving weekend; and the **Torchlight Parade,** on New Year's Eve.

---

**N**umerous mineral springs and abundant wild game made this a summer playground for Ute tribespeople for centuries before the arrival of the white man. Mid-19th-century trappers swore they heard the chugging sound of "a steamboat comin' 'round the bend" until investigation revealed a bubbling mineral spring. Prospectors never thrived here, as they did elsewhere in the Rockies, though coal mining has proven profitable. Ranching and farming—cattle and sheep, hay, wheat, oats, and barley—were the economic mainstays until tourism became paramount, and agriculture remains of key importance to the community.

Skiing has been synonymous with Steamboat ever since Carl Howelsen, a Norwegian ski-jumping and cross-country champion, moved to the town in 1914. He lived in Steamboat for 7 years, during which time he built the ski area that bears his name (Howelsen Hill) and organized the first Winter Carnival. Development of Storm Mountain began in 1958; the mountain officially opened in 1963, and was renamed Mount Werner after the 1964 avalanche death in Europe of Olympic skier Buddy Werner, a Steamboat native and prime backer of the resort. The Steamboat Ski Company, established in 1970, has put tens of millions of dollars into resort improvements in the past two decades. Continuing expansion is planned.

Today Steamboat Springs, at an elevation of 6,700 feet, has a year-round population of about 7,000.

# ORIENTATION

**INFORMATION** The **Steamboat Springs Chamber Resort Association,** 625 South Lincoln Street (P.O. Box 774408), Steamboat Springs, CO 80477 (tel. 303/879-0740 or 879-0880), provides visitor information. There's a second office on the third floor of Gondola Square (tel. 879-0882).

**CITY LAYOUT** There are really two Steamboats. The ski resort, known here as Steamboat Village, is about 2 miles southeast of the town itself, a division that seems to work well for everyone. If you're coming in from Denver, U.S. 40 approaches Steamboat from the south and parallels the Yampa River through town. **Mount Werner Road,** which turns east off U.S. 40, leads directly to the resort community, centered around **Mount Werner Circle** and **Ski Time Square.** U.S. 40 is known as **Lincoln Avenue** through the town of Steamboat, where it is crossed by 3rd Street through 13th Street. You'll cross the Yampa to Howelsen Hill and River Street if you turn left on **5th Street;** wind uphill to the Strawberry Park Hot Springs if you turn right on **7th Street,** and find your way to the Steamboat Springs Airport and Steamboat Lake if you turn right on **Elk River Road** (County Road 129), half a mile beyond 13th.

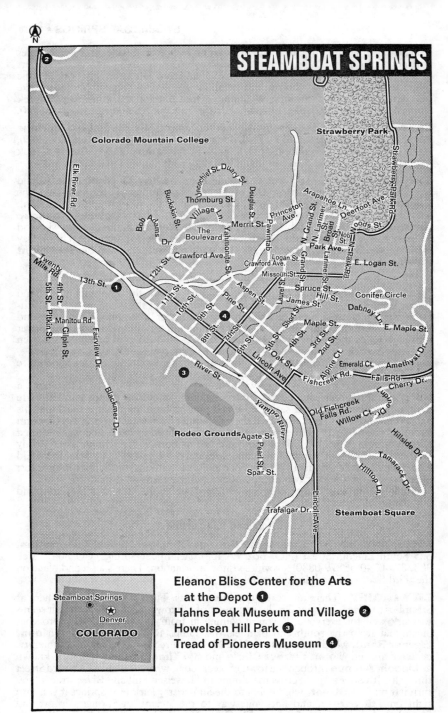

N

STEAMBOAT SPRINGS

Strawberry Park

Colorado Mountain College

Strawberry Park Rd.

Elk River Rd.

Uneochief St. Duany St.
Douglas St.
Thornburg St.
Buckskin St.
Village Ln.
Bob Adams Dr.
The Boulevard
Merrit St.
Pawintab
Princeton Ave.
Arapahoe Ln.
Deerfoot Ave.
Woods St.

Twenty Mile Rd.
13th St.
12th St.
Crawford Ave.
Yahmonite St.
Crawford Ave.
Logan St.
N. Grand St.
N. Larimer St.
Broad St.
Noble St.
N. Park Rd.
Park Ave.
Larimer St.
E. Logan St.

4th St.
5th St.
Pitkin St.
Gilpin St.
Manitou Rd.
Fairview Dr.
Blackmer Dr.

11th St.
10th St.
9th St.
8th St.
7th St.
6th St.
5th St.

Aspen St.
Pine St.
Missouri St.
Laurel St.
Hill St.
Spruce St.
James St.
Conifer Circle
Dabney Ln.
E. Maple St.
Maple St.
Short St.
4th St.
3rd St.
2nd St.
Alpine Ct.
Emerald Ct.
Amethyst Dr.

Oak St.
Lincoln Ave.
Fishcreek Rd.
Falls Rd.
Cherry Dr.
Lupine Dr.

River St.

Yampa River

Old Fishcreek Falls Rd.
Willow Ct.

Hillside Dr.

Rodeo Grounds
Agate St.
Pearl St.
Spar St.

Tamarack Dr.
Hilltop Ln.

Trafalgar Dr.
Lincoln Ave.
Steamboat Square

Steamboat Springs
★ Denver
COLORADO

Eleanor Bliss Center for the Arts
   at the Depot ❶
Hahns Peak Museum and Village ❷
Howelsen Hill Park ❸
Tread of Pioneers Museum ❹

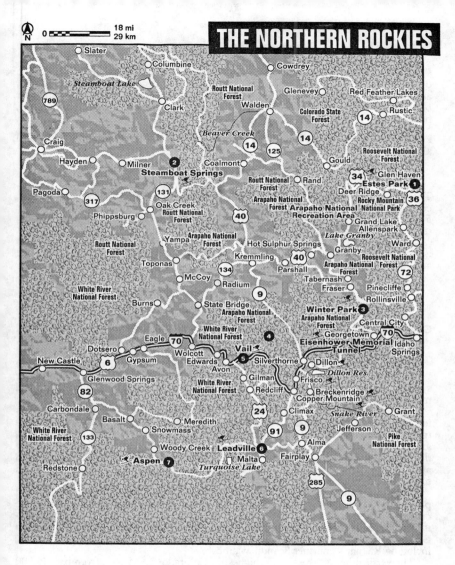

# THE NORTHERN ROCKIES

0 ——— 18 mi
——— 29 km

Slater
Columbine
Cowdrey
Steamboat Lake
Glenevey
Red Feather Lakes
789
Clark
Walden
Rustic
Craig
Hayden
Milner
Coalmont
Colorado State
Forest
14
Routt National
Forest
Beaver Creek
14
125
14
Gould
Roosevelt National
Forest
Pagoda
317
131
Steamboat Springs
Routt National
Forest
Rand
34
Glen Haven
Estes Park
Oak Creek
Routt National
Forest
Arapaho National
Forest
Deer Ridge
Rocky Mountain
National Park
36
Phippsburg
40
Arapaho National
Recreation Area
Grand Lake
Allenspark
Yampa
Arapaho National
Forest
Hot Sulphur Springs
Lake Granby
Ward
Routt National
Forest
Toponas
Kremmling
40
Granby
Roosevelt National
Forest
72
McCoy
134
Parshall
Tabernash
Radium
9
Fraser
Pinecliffe
White River
National Forest
Burns
State Bridge
Winter Park
Rollinsville
Arapaho National
Forest
Arapaho National
Forest
Central City
Eagle
70
White River
National Forest
4
Georgetown
70
Dotsero
Wolcott
Vail
Eisenhower Memorial
Tunnel
Idaho
Springs
New Castle
6
Gypsum
Edwards
5
Silverthorne
Dillon
Glenwood Springs
Avon
Gilman
Frisco
Dillon Res.
82
White River
National Forest
Redcliff
Breckenridge
Copper Mountain
Carbondale
Basalt
Meredith
24
Climax
Snake River
Grant
Snowmass
91
9
Jefferson
White River
National Forest
133
Woody Creek
Leadville
Alma
Pike
National Forest
Redstone
Aspen
Malta
Fairplay
Turquoise Lake
285
9

The
Northern
Rockies
Denver
COLORADO

1 Estes Park
2 Steamboat Springs
3 Winter Park
4 Summit County
5 Vail
6 Leadville
7 Aspen

# GETTING AROUND

**BY BUS** **Steamboat Springs Transit** (tel. 879-3717) has a "Red Line" in the downtown area, a "Green Line" serving the resort and its condominium community, and a "Blue Line" connecting the two. Blue Line buses run three times an hour between 6:30am and 11:30pm and require exact fares of 50¢. During ski season, buses run every 10 minutes during peak-use periods.

**BY TAXI** **Steamboat Taxi** (tel. 879-3335) and **Alpine Taxi-Limo** (tel. 879-2800) also serve the community.

# FAST FACTS

The **area code** is 303. In case of **emergency,** call **911;** for regular business, contact the police at 840 Yampa Avenue (tel. 879-1144) or the Routt County Sheriff at 522 Lincoln Avenue (tel. 879-1090). **Routt Memorial Hospital,** 80 Park Avenue, off Seventh Street (tel. 879-1322), provides 24-hour medical service. A 24-hour **pharmacy** is City Market, 1825 Central Park Plaza (tel. 879-7317). The **post office** is at 300 Lincoln Avenue (tel. 879-0363). For **road information,** call 879-1260. State and local **tax** add 9.2% to hotel bills.

# WHAT TO SEE & DO

## ATTRACTIONS

**STEAMBOAT SKI AREA, Steamboat Ski & Resort Corporation, 2305 Mt. Werner Circle, Steamboat Springs, CO 80487. Tel. 303/879-6111,** or 879-7300 for daily ski reports.

When devoted skiers think of Steamboat, the first things that come to mind are "champagne powder" and aspen glades. Because of a unique localized weather system, an average of 27 feet (325 inches) of light, dry snow is dumped on the mountain each winter.

Four peaks comprise Mount Werner. **Christie Peak,** the lower mountain area, is ideal for beginners. **Thunderhead Peak,** served by the "Silver Bullet" gondola, is mainly intermediate. Three separate restaurants, not counting the ski-school cafeteria, are located at the gondola terminal, and Billy Kidd, the 1970 world ski champion and director of skiing at Steamboat for two decades, makes a ski run from here with anyone who cares to join him, Monday through Saturday at 1pm, whenever he's in town—which is most of the winter.

**Storm Peak** accesses the extreme "Chutes" area, advanced mogul runs and powder bowls, as well as "Buddy's Run," one of the Rockies' great intermediate cruisers. The most famous tree runs—"Shadows" and "Twilight"—are on **Sunshine Peak,** along with more bump runs and cruising slopes. In **Rendezvous Saddle,** mid-mountain at the foot of "High Noon," are two more restaurants, including Ragnar's gourmet Scandinavian café.

The vertical here is the second highest in Colorado: 3,665 feet, from base (6,900 feet) to summit (10,565 feet). Skiable terrain of 2,500 acres (61% groomable) includes 103 named runs, served by 21 lifts—the eight-passenger gondola, a quad chair, seven triple chairs, nine double chairs, a ski-school chair, and two surface lifts. That gives Steamboat an hourly uphill capacity of over 29,000 skiers.

**Admission:** Tickets, $35 per day adults, $33 per day if a multiday ticket is purchased; $20 per day youth on a multiday basis. Full rental packages average $14; 2-hour lessons are $27. Kids under 12 ski free with parents who purchase a 5-or-more-day lift ticket and stay in a Chamber Resort Association member accommodation.

**Open:** Thanksgiving–Easter, daily 9am–4pm.

**ELEANOR BLISS CENTER FOR THE ARTS AT THE DEPOT, 13th St. at Twenty Mile Rd. Tel. 879-4434** or 879-9008.

The historic Steamboat Springs train depot is now the home of the Steamboat Arts

Council, which coordinates music, dance, theater, and visual-arts activities in the upper Yampa Valley. The Golub Gallery here has exhibits and shows year round.
**Admission:** Free.
**Open:** Mon–Fri 9am–5pm and some weekends.

## FISH CREEK FALLS, Fish Creek Falls Rd. Tel. 879-1870.

A footpath leads to a historic bridge at the base of this breathtaking 283-foot waterfall. There's a special overlook with a trail and ramp designed for the disabled, as well as a picnic area and hiking trails. The falls are just 4 miles from downtown Steamboat in Routt National Forest. Turn right off Lincoln Avenue onto Third Street, go one block, and turn right again onto Fish Creek Falls Road.

## FORD/MICHELIN ICE DRIVING SCHOOL, Mount Werner Rd. (P.O. Box 774167), Steamboat Springs, CO 80477. Tel. 879-6104.

America's first school of ice driving is a terrific way to learn safe winter driving, the hands-on way. Director Jean-Paul Luc, a former world-class rally driver from France, instructs courses on a 1-mile circuit—packed with frozen water and snow, and guarded by high snow banks—at the foot of Mount Werner. Classes combine personal and videotape instruction with on-track practice.
**Price:** $80 for a 3-hour course, up to $290 for a 2-day course.
**Open:** Mid-Dec to mid-Mar, daily 9am–5pm. Course admission by appointment only. **Closed:** Mid-Mar to mid-Dec.

## HAHNS PEAK MUSEUM AND VILLAGE, Routt County Rd. 129. Tel. 879-6781.

This historic gold-mining town, while not exactly thriving, still clings to life 24 miles north of Steamboat Springs, near Steamboat Lake. Established in 1860, it was the scene in 1898 of a famous jailbreak by members of the Butch Cassidy gang, and its 1911 schoolhouse is listed in the National Register. The small museum contains interesting memorabilia. Pyramid-shaped Hahns Peak, elevation 10,389 feet, may be ascended by Jeep trail. En route to Hahns Peak, stop at the **Clark Store,** 54175 Routt County Road 129 (tel. 879-3849), an old-fashioned country store with everything from a post office and library to fishing equipment, ski rentals, and huge ice-cream cones.

## HOWELSEN HILL PARK, River St. Tel. 879-4300.

The community's pride and joy is this beautiful park and recreation complex on the south side of the Yampa River, opposite downtown via Fifth Street. Howelsen Hill (see "Sports & Recreation," below) was Steamboat's original ski area, and is still nationally important as a nordic site. The Lodge at Howelsen Hill offers an exhibit on the history of local skiing. The park also is the location of the **Romick Rodeo Arena,** where the Professional Rodeo Cowboy Association holds a weekly series from mid-June to Labor Day, as well as facilities for tennis, softball, soccer, volleyball, skateboarding, horseback riding, and hiking. There are picnic areas and playgrounds.
**Admission:** Free.
**Open:** Daily 8am–10pm.

## TREAD OF PIONEERS MUSEUM, 800 Oak St., at Eighth St. Tel. 879-2214.

This beautifully restored Victorian house features exhibits on Routt County pioneer ranch life—including work implements and home furnishings—as well as a new display highlighting the history of skiing in Steamboat Springs. Ask for a brochure describing a historic walking tour of Steamboat Springs, incorporating 10 sites dating as far back as 1872.
**Admission:** $2.50 adults, $1 children 6–12.
**Open:** Memorial Day to mid-Sept, daily noon–8pm; Dec–Easter, Tues–Sat 1–5pm; the rest of the year, by appointment.

## BUD WERNER MEMORIAL LIBRARY, 1289 Lincoln Ave. Tel. 879-0240.

A collection of skiing memorabilia, focusing on Steamboat's Werner family, long considered the "first family" of ski racing in the Colorado Rockies, is the highlight of a visit. The library is a full-service facility with books and current periodicals.

**Admission:** Free.
**Open:** Mon–Thurs 9am–8pm, Fri 9am–6pm, Sat 9am–5pm, Sun noon–5pm.

## SPORTS & RECREATION

Most outdoor recreation pursuits are enjoyed in 1.1-million-acre **Routt National Forest,** which virtually surrounds Steamboat Springs. With elevations ranging from about 7,000 to 13,000 feet, the national forest offers opportunities for camping, hiking, backpacking, mountain biking, horseback riding, fishing, hunting, snowmobiling, snowshoeing, cross-country skiing, and more. Less than 25 miles east of Steamboat is the 9,426-foot **Rabbit Ears Pass** area, which takes its name from a unique summit rock formation said to resemble rabbit ears. For Routt National Forest information, check with the Hahns Peak District office, 57 10th Street (tel. 879-1870).

Two wilderness areas in the forest are easily reached from Steamboat. Immediately north of town is the **Mount Zirkel Wilderness Area,** a region of rugged peaks approached through 10,800-foot Buffalo Pass, on Forest Road 60 off Strawberry Park Road via Seventh Street. Southwest of Stillwater Reservoir, some 40 miles south of Steamboat via Colo. 131 through Yampa, is the **Flat Tops Wilderness Area,** notable for its alpine meadows and sheer volcanic cliffs. No motorized vehicles or mountain bikes are allowed in wilderness areas.

Some 27 miles north of Steamboat Springs on Routt County Road 129 is the **Steamboat Lake State Recreation Area** (tel. 879-3922), encompassing 1,550-acre Steamboat Lake and 190-acre Pearl Lake. Activities at the two lakes include summer camping (there are 222 campsites), picnicking, fishing, hunting, boating (with rentals), waterskiing (on Steamboat Lake only), swimming, canoeing, and nature walks. In winter, there's ice fishing, cross-country skiing, snowmobiling, and snowshoeing. Admission is $3 per vehicle.

Information on most activities can be obtained from the **Steamboat Springs Parks and Recreation Department** (tel. 879-2060). Agencies that will arrange activities for visitors, both summer and winter, include the **Steamboat Activity Center,** 720 Lincoln Avenue or Gondola Square, Steamboat Village (tel. 303/879-2062, or 800/748-2062) and **Windwalker Tours** (tel. 879-8065).

**BALLOONING**  Get a bird's-eye view of Steamboat and the Yampa River Valley, summer or winter, while floating quietly aloft in a colorful hot-air balloon. Operators include **Aero Sports** (tel. 879-7433), **Balloons Over Steamboat** (tel. 879-3298), **Eagle Balloon Tours** (tel. 879-8687), and **Pegasus Balloon Tours** (tel. 879-9191). A 30-minute ride runs about $65; a full hour, about $110.

**BICYCLING**  The new 5-mile, dual-surface **Yampa River Trail** connects downtown Steamboat Springs with Steamboat Village, and links area parks and national forest trails. The **Mount Werner Trail** links the river to the ski area, which itself has numerous slopes open to mountain bikers in summer. **Spring Creek Trail** climbs from Yampa River Park into the Routt National Forest. Touring enthusiasts can try the 110-mile loop over Rabbit Ears and Gore passes, rated one of the 10 most scenic rides in America by *Bicycling* magazine.

Bicycle racers are lured to Steamboat for the **Steamboat Stage Race** in early June, the **Steamboat Mountain Bike Classic Stage Race** in late June, the **Steamboat Road and Mountain Bike Challenge** in mid-July, and the **Rabbit Ears Hillclimb Bike Race** in August.

You can rent bikes from **Sore Saddle Cyclery,** Central Park Plaza and three other locations (tel. 879-1675); **Steamboat Trading Company,** 1850 Ski Time Square Drive (tel. 879-0083); and **Ski Haus International,** 1450 South Lincoln Avenue (tel. 879-0385). Typical rates are $10 for a half day, $15 for a full day.

Free tours of **Moots Cycles Bicycle Factory,** 1136 Yampa Street (tel. 879-1675), a custom bicycle frame builder, are offered by appointment.

**BOATING**  At **Steamboat Lake** (tel. 879-7019 for the marina) and at **Stage-**

coach Lake, a newly developed reservoir 17 miles southeast of Steamboat Springs off County Road 14 (tel. 736-8342), there are ample opportunities for water lovers. Canoes, paddleboats, and sailboards can be rented for $12 an hour; Hobie Cats and Laser sailboats run $22 an hour; motorboats for fishing start at $25 for 2½ hours.

**DOG SLEDDING**   Dog sledding is offered by the **Steamboat Sled Dog Express** (tel. 879-4662 or 879-2062).

**FISHING**   There are nearly 100 lakes and reservoirs, and almost 600 miles of streams, in Routt County. Trout—rainbow, brown, brook, and cutthroat—are prolific. **Buggywhip's Fish & Float Service** (tel. 303/879-8033, or 800/759-0343) leads half- and full-day stream-wading and float-fishing trips on the Yampa, Elk, North Platte, and Green rivers for rates starting at $90. **Creative Sports,** 431 Pine Street (tel. 879-1568), and **Straightline,** 744 Lincoln Avenue (tel. 879-7568), offer fly-fishing and fly-tying classes throughout the winter, and guided fishing trips beginning in March. **Steamboat Lake Outfitters** (tel. 303/879-4404, or 800/342-1889) also offers guide service.

You can get equipment, licenses, and information from **Bear Paw Sporting Goods,** 1106 Lincoln Avenue (tel. 879-8154), or **Steamboat Springs Sporting Goods,** 908 Lincoln Avenue (tel. 879-7774). Visitors are welcome at the **Finger Rock Fish Rearing Unit** of the Colorado Department of Wildlife, 5 miles south of Yampa on Colo. 131.

**GOLF**   The **Sheraton Steamboat Golf Club,** Clubhouse Drive (tel. 879-2220), designed by Robert Trent Jones, Jr., in 1972, is considered one of the Rockies' finest courses. The 18-hole, 6,906-yard course offers spectacular scenery and challenging fairways. Greens fees from mid-May through September are $43 for Sheraton guests, $58 for the public; from April to mid-May and October until the snow falls, it's $28 for Sheraton guests, $33 for the public. There are considerable discounts for late-afternoon tee times. Call for information on lessons, clinics, and packages.

**Steamboat Golf Club,** U.S. 40 west of town (tel. 879-4295), is a 9-hole municipal course; greens fees Monday through Friday are $13 for 9 holes, $18.50 for 18 holes; on Saturday and Sunday, $14.50 for 9 holes, $21 for 18 holes. **Inner Links,** 1855 Ski Time Square Drive (tel. 879-2916), is an ideal winter remedy for the snowbound golfer. A life-size video simulation that puts you on some of the world's finest courses, it's almost like an indoor driving range!

**HIKING & BACKPACKING**   Visit the **Routt National Forest** district office, 57 10th Street (tel. 879-1870), for detailed area maps and trail information. There are many, many opportunities in the **Mount Zirkel Wilderness Area,** immediately north of Steamboat, and the **Flat Tops Wilderness Area,** 48 miles southwest. An especially fascinating 4-hour day hike in the Flat Tops area takes you from Stillwater Reservoir to the Devil's Causeway, with unforgettable views. Backpacking and camping rentals are offered by **Ski Haus International,** 1450 South Lincoln Avenue at Pine Grove Road (tel. 879-0385).

**HORSEBACK RIDING**   Several area ranches offer trail rides by the hour, the half day, or overnight. They include **Del's Triangle 3 Ranch,** 218 River Road (tel. 879-4109); **Dutch Creek Guest Ranch,** 61565 County Road 62, Clark (tel. 879-8519); **Elk River Guest Ranch,** 29840 County Road 64 (tel. 879-3843); **Glen Eden Stables,** 61276 County Road 129 (tel. 879-3864 or 879-5736), **Steamboat Lake Outfitters,** Steamboat Lake (tel. 879-4404 or 879-5590); and **Taylor Creek Ranch,** 51440 Elk River Road (tel. 879-9072). Typical adult rates are $15 for a 1-hour ride, $50 for a half day, $150 for an overnight.

There's also a summer equestrian program at the **Steamboat Resort** (tel. 879-6111), with guided rides leaving half hourly, 10:30am to 2:30pm, from the Thunderhead gondola terminal.

**HOT SPRINGS**   More than 100 mineral springs are located in and around the

Steamboat Springs area. Black, Heart, Iron, Lithia, Soda, Sulphur, and Steamboat—the springs for which the town was named—are located in parks of Steamboat Springs. Their healing and restorative qualities were recognized for centuries by Utes. James Crawford, the first white settler in this town, in 1875, regularly bathed in Heart Spring and helped build the first log bathhouse over it in 1884.

Today Heart Spring is part of the **Steamboat Springs Health & Recreation complex,** 136 Lincoln Avenue (tel. 879-1828), in downtown Steamboat Springs. Besides the human-made pools into which the spring's waters flow, there's a lap pool, a water slide, a weight room, tennis courts, fitness classes, and massage therapy. Suits and towels can be rented for $1.50; pool admission is $4.50 for adults, $2.50 for youths 13 to 17, and $1 for children under 13 and seniors. It's open daily from 7am to 9pm.

The **Hot Springs at Strawberry Park** (tel. 879-0342) are 7 miles north of downtown. There are no suit rentals here, and the water is a bit on the hot side at 105°, but it's a wonderful experience to spend a moonlit evening in a sandy-bottomed, rock-lined soaking pool with snow piled high around you. Follow Strawberry Park Road, off Park Avenue via Seventh Street. Open Sunday through Thursday from 10am to 10pm and Friday and Saturday from 10am to midnight; admission is $5.

A free city parks department brochure, **"The Springs of Steamboat: A Walking Tour,"** will acquaint you with other mineral springs in the town area.

**HUNTING**  There's big-game hunting in Routt National Forest for deer, elk, antelope, moose, black bear, and mountain lion, and in adjacent areas for waterfowl, ground birds, and small mammals. The **Steamboat Springs Chamber Resort Association** (tel. 879-0880) has Division of Wildlife hunting information and regulations, and a list of guides and outfitters.

**ICE SKATING**  The **Howelsen Ice Skating Rink,** 243 River Road (tel. 879-0341), rents skates, offers lessons and free skating, and organizes ice hockey and broomball competitions. Admission is $3.50 for adults, $2 for children 13 and under; skate rentals are $3 for adults, $2 for children.

**KAYAKING**  There are kayak gates on the Yampa River, with major competitions the second weekend of June every year during the Yampa River Festival. If you have an interest in this exciting water sport, talk to the **Mountain Sports Kayak School,** 1835 Central Park Drive (tel. 879-6910 or 879-8794).

**MOUNTAINEERING**  Mountain climbing in the summer becomes ice climbing in the winter, and there's plenty of both in the Steamboat area. Consult **Backdoor Sport of Steamboat,** 24 Fifth Street (tel. 879-6249), or **Rocky Mountain Ventures,** 208 Ninth Street (tel. 879-4857).

**RIVER RAFTING**  White-water trips on numerous Colorado rivers are offered by **Buggywhip's Fish & Float Service** (tel. 303/879-8033, or 800/759-0343), and **Adventures Wild Rafting** (tel. 303/879-8747, or 800/8325-3989). The Yampa, Cross Mountain Fork, North Platte, Eagle, Roaring Fork, Green, Colorado, and Arkansas rivers are tackled by these companies, which charge from $22 for a half day on the Yampa through town to $115 for a full day or $595 for an extended trip on expert (Class IV and V) rapids.

**RODEO**  The **Romick Rodeo Arena** at Howelsen Hill Park (tel. 879-4300) is the site each year, from mid-June to Labor Day, of the 13-week Summer of ProRodeo Series of the Professional Rodeo Cowboy Association. Some of the world's best compete in Brahma bull riding, bareback and saddle bronc riding, steer wrestling, calf roping, team roping, and barrel racing. In the Wrangler Ram Scramble, children are invited to try to pluck a ribbon from the tail of a ram for a special prize. Rodeo tickets are $6 for adults, $1 for children.

**SKIING**  Besides the **Steamboat Ski Area** (see "Attractions," above), there's **Howelsen Hill** (tel. 879-2170 or 879-2043), which opened in 1915 and has remained open every winter since. The first accredited public-school ski classes in North

America were taught on this slope. The hill, which offers day and night skiing, has 30 acres of terrain served by a double-chair and a poma lift. Vertical rise is 440 feet, to a 7,136-foot summit elevation. Tickets are $10 Monday through Friday (9am to 4pm), $12 on Saturday and Sunday (9am to 10pm), and $8 for night skiing only (Tuesday through Sunday from 4 to 10pm). The bobsled run costs $5 per trip.

Howelsen Hill has bred more North American skiers for international competition than any other—primarily because of its ski-jumping complex. The U.S. ski-jumping team trains each year on the 20-, 30-, 50-, 70-, and 90-meter jumps.

A new ski area, **Lake Catamount,** has been proposed for construction 7 miles south of Steamboat. In the meantime, adventurous skiers can get backcountry thrills with **Peak Experience Snowcat Tours** (tel. 879-8125) and **Steamboat Powder Cats** (tel. 303/879-5188, or 800/288-0543), both of which lead tours into untracked wilderness.

Cross-country skiers usually make their first stop at the **Steamboat Ski Touring Center** at the Sheraton Steamboat Resort Golf Club, Clubhouse Road (tel. 879-8180). Some 25km (15 miles) of groomed cross-country trails are set across the fairways beside Fish Creek, near the foot of the mountain. The daily trail fee is $7.50; rental packages run $9. There are also lessons, equipment rentals, and citizens' races. Swede Sven Wiik is the director of skiing here.

There are many other touring areas throughout Routt National Forest. Obtain trail maps and information from the national forest district office, 57 10th Street (tel. 879-1870). Popular areas include Rabbit Ears Pass, 25 miles east of Steamboat on U.S. 40, and Dunkley Pass, 25 miles south on Colo. 131. Guided backcountry ski tours are offered by **Rocky Mountain Ventures,** 208 Ninth Street (tel. 879-4857).

The cross-country trails and rustic resort atmosphere of the **Home Ranch,** 54880 County Road 29 (tel. 879-9044), in the Elk River Valley 18 miles north of Steamboat, have been widely praised.

Ski and snowboard rental, sales, and repairs are offered by a variety of Steamboat-area shops, among them **Inside Edge Sports** (tel. 879-1250), **Powder Pursuits** (tel. 879-9086), **Ski Haus International** (tel. 879-0385), **Sport Stalker** at the Gondola (tel. 879-0371) and Ski Time Square (tel. 879-2445), and **Terry Sports** (tel. 879-8414 or 879-3237).

**SLEIGH RIDES**   Take a sleigh ride to dinner with **Double Runner Sleigh Rides** (tel. 879-8877) or **Franni's Sleigh and Dinner Rides** (tel. 879-1312). Several local guest ranches also offer horse-drawn sleigh trips.

**SNOWMOBILING**   Snowmobilers consider the Continental Divide Trail, running over 50 miles from Buffalo Pass, north of Steamboat, to Gore Pass, west of Kremmling, to be one of the finest maintained trails in the Rockies. For information, check with Routt National Forest or with the **Routt Powder Riders** snowmobile club, P.O. Box 43, Steamboat Springs, CO 80477 (tel. 303/879-2355). Many guest ranches and other agencies offer winter tours, including **Emerald Mountain Snowmobile Tours** (tel. 879-8065), **High Mountain Snowmobile Tours** (tel. 879-9073), and **Steamboat Snowmobile Tours** (tel. 879-1551 or 879-6500).

**SWIMMING**   Many hotel and condominium properties have their own swimming pools. You'll also find pools at the **Glen Eden Resort,** 54737 County Road 29, Clark (tel. 879-3907); the **Steamboat Athletic Club,** 33250 Storm Meadows Drive (tel. 879-1036); and the **Steamboat Health & Recreation Association,** 136 Lincoln Avenue (tel. 879-1828).

## SHOPPING

Pick up a free brochure, "Gallery Guide," when you visit the Eleanor Bliss Center for the Arts at the Depot (see "Attractions," above). There are 13 major galleries in town, including the **Artisans' Market,** 626 Lincoln Avenue (tel. 879-7512), a nonprofit cooperative of local artists who create a very wide range of arts and crafts; and the **Steamboat Art Company,** 903 Lincoln Avenue (tel. 879-3383), focusing on western art and American handcrafts.

## EVENING ENTERTAINMENT

**THE PERFORMING ARTS** Summer is a busy time for the performing arts in Steamboat. The **Strings in the Mountains Chamber Music Festival,** P.O. Box 774627, Steamboat Springs, CO 80477 (tel. 303/879-5056), offers six performances a week, Tuesday through Saturday, for 5 weeks, mid-July to mid-August, featuring members of major national symphony orchestras. Tickets are $4 to $6 on Tuesday and Wednesday, free for Thursday student performances, $8 for Friday celebrity recitals, free for Saturday matinees in Gondola Square, and $12 for Saturday-night concerts.

"Strings" overlaps with the **Perry-Mansfield Performing Arts Camp,** at 40755 County Road 36 (tel. 879-7125), whose alumni include actors Dustin Hoffman and Lee Remick, and dancer José Limon. The camp has operated continually since 1913. Youth 10 and older are taught theater, music, dance, and riding from the third week of June to the first week of August. One dance and three theater productions are staged to sell-out audiences in the camp's Julie Harris Theater.

The **Steamboat Community Players** produce several stage plays over the course of the year, including a couple in the summer. The troupe performs at the **Seventh Street Playhouse,** Seventh Street and Aspen Street (tel. 879-3254).

**Music in the Square** brings a wide variety of performers to Gondola Square at the ski area, at noon every Saturday and Sunday in summer. A visual artist offers an exhibit and demonstration before, during, and after the concert.

**THE CLUB & BAR SCENE** The nightlife scene, while never dull, comes especially alive in winter as *après-ski.* At Steamboat Village, **The Inferno,** Gondola Square (tel. 879-5111), is a hot dance club for the 20s set, with live music; the rustic **Tugboat Saloon & Eatery,** Ski Time Square (tel. 879-7070), attracts more of a local crowd for rock music and dancing; and **Buddy's Run,** in the Sheraton Steamboat Resort (tel. 879-2220), does a quick-change from a foot-of-the-slopes bar to an evening comedy club at 8 and 10pm Tuesday through Friday nights. Other lively bars at the mountain include the **Clock Tower Saloon,** Ski Time Square (tel. 879-1111), favored by hard rockers; and **Dos Amigos,** at 1910 Mount Werner Road (tel. 879-4270), a friendly neighborhood Mexican restaurant and bar.

In downtown Steamboat, the **Old Town Pub & Restaurant,** Sixth Street and Lincoln Avenue (tel. 879-2101), serves up live blues or rock most nights, along with big-screen ski movies; and **Buffalo Wild Wings and Weck** ("BW-3"), 729 Lincoln Avenue (tel. 879-2431), has live music Friday through Sunday. Sundance Plaza, midway between the resort and downtown, offers the **Steamboat Saloon** (tel. 879-7797), northwestern Colorado's biggest country-and-western nightclub.

# WHERE TO STAY

Most accommodations charge according to three or four different ski seasons. Rates are highest during the Christmas holiday season: mid-December through New Year's Day. Next highest is the "regular" February to March season. "Value" season is usually January, and "low" seasons run from the beginning of ski season (Thanksgiving) to mid-December and April until the area closes. Rates are normally much lower during the summer season, Memorial Day to mid-October. Because vacancy rates are so high during shoulder seasons—April to May and October to November—many accommodations close and give their staffs vacation at these times.

**Steamboat Reservation Services** (tel. 800/922-2722) can make all lodging bookings and any other travel arrangements for visitors to Steamboat Springs.

## VERY EXPENSIVE

**CHATEAU CHAMONIX, 2349 Apres Ski Way, Steamboat Springs, CO 80477. Tel. 303/879-7511,** or 800/833-9877. Fax 303/879-9321. 27 units (all with bath). A/C TV TEL

**$ Rates:** Two-bedrooms, $112–$127 summer (Easter–Thanksgiving), $220–$235 low season, $300–$370 regular and value seasons, $465–$480 Christmas season; three-bedrooms, $162 summer, $270 low season, $370–$425 regular and value seasons, $580 Christmas season. MC, V. **Parking:** Free covered lot.

Located a few steps from the base of the Silver Bullet gondola, this is one of the most convenient accommodations at Steamboat Village. Two buildings have condominium units with private decks facing the slopes. All have fireplaces and fully equipped kitchens with refrigerators, and have furnishings of pine, walnut, or oak. Most of the units are two-bedroom suites, with twin beds in one room, a king-size bed in the master bedroom, and a Jacuzzi tub in the adjoining private bathroom. There's a 45¢ charge for local phone calls.

**Facilities:** Swimming pool, outdoor hot tub, sauna, ski lockers, conference room.

**THE HOME RANCH, 54880 Routt County Rd. 129 (P.O. Box 822), Clark, CO 80428. Tel. 303/879-1780,** or 800/223-7094. Fax 303/879-1795. 13 units (all with bath). TV TEL

**$ Rates** (including full board): Summer, $300–$350 lodge room; $325–$410 cabin; $700 two-bedroom cabin; children $90–$125 extra. Winter, $270–$345 lodge room; $315–$400 cabin; $685 two-bedroom cabin; children $75–$120 extra. AE, MC, V.

Acclaimed by publications from *Travel & Leisure* magazine to the *Los Angeles Times,* Ken Jones's Home Ranch injects a large dose of luxury into the Elk River Valley, 19 miles north of Steamboat. By summer a guest ranch that draws horse lovers and fly fishers, it becomes in winter a refuge for cross-country skiers. The Main House has a particularly welcoming ambience with its soft leather couches, huge stone fireplace, grand piano, displays of paintings and crafts by local artisans, and library (on a loft above the living room).

Lodge rooms, with king-size beds, are furnished with antiques and reproductions. Two rooms have charming children's lofts. Special touches include humidifiers, hairdryers, bathrobes, and coffee makers. Each of the "modern rustic" guest cabins, 5 to 10 minutes' walk from the lodge, has a Jacuzzi tub on its porch; they also boast antique furnishings, native crafts, original artwork, hairdryers, coffeemakers . . . and boot jacks, to avoid tracking the stable mud into the house. On your bed at night, you'll get a "Far Side" cartoon instead of a chocolate: "It's better for your teeth," Jones explains.

**Dining/Entertainment:** Three gourmet meals a day are served family style in the Main House. There are no menu choices, so the staff must be advised in advance of special dietary requirements.

**Services:** Airport transfers, weekly laundry, children's counselor, masseuse on call; 1:1 staff-to-guest ratio.

**Facilities:** Heated swimming pool, sauna, Jacuzzis; stable with horseback riding and lessons; fly-fishing lessons and 2 miles of private river; guided hiking trips into the Mount Zirkel Wilderness; cross-country skiing equipment, lessons, and 40km (25 miles) of set tracks.

**TORIAN PLUM AT STEAMBOAT, 1855 Ski Time Square Dr., Steamboat Springs, CO 80487. Tel. 303/879-8811,** or 800/228-2458, 800/824-5161 in Colorado. Fax 303/879-7374. 47 units (all with bath). A/C TV TEL

**$ Rates:** One-bedroom, $99 mid-Apr to mid-Nov, $180 low ski season, $395 Christmas week, $265 value season, $295 regular and pre-Christmas week; two-bedroom, $109 summer, $215 low ski season, $545 Christmas week, $345 value season, $425 regular and pre-Christmas week; three-bedroom, $270 low ski season, $555 regular and pre-Christmas week, $720 Christmas week, $500 value season. AE, CB, DC, DISC, MC, V. **Parking:** Free underground lot.

This slopeside condominium development has one-, two-, and three-bedroom units with handsome light-wood furnishings. Each unit has a fully equipped and tiled kitchen (with microwave and dishwasher), washer/dryer, whirlpool tub, private balcony, and cable TV with HBO. Two plush couches face the fireplace.

The manager is Steamboat Premier Properties, Ltd., which also operates the neighboring Bronze Tree and Trappeur's Crossing condominium developments. All have equivalent facilities and summer rates; regular ski-season rates for a two-bedroom condo start at $360 at the Bronze Tree, $265 at Trappeur's.

**Services:** Concierge, shuttle van, ski lockers.

**Facilities:** Outdoor heated swimming pool, outdoor and indoor hot tubs, sauna, tennis courts.

## EXPENSIVE

**THE RANCH AT STEAMBOAT, 1 Ranch Rd. (off Clubhouse Dr.), Steamboat Springs, CO 80487. Tel. 303/879-3000,** or 800/525-2002, 800/237-2624 in Colorado. Fax 303/879-5409. 88 units (all with bath). TV TEL
**$ Rates:** $109–$130 one- and two-bedrooms in summer, $210–$275 during the regular ski season, $400 during the Christmas season; three- and four-bedroom units are higher. AE, MC, V. **Parking:** Free private garages.

Spread across a 36-acre hillside on Burgess Creek, not far from Ski Time Square, these one- to four-bedroom condominiums offer a peaceful, quiet location. They're especially popular for company getaways.

The two-story condo units are furnished in deluxe style, with full kitchens (including microwaves), large fireplaces, private barbecue decks, and washer/dryer facilities. There's a direct entrance from the private garage into the kitchen. The only real drawback is the price of local phone calls: $1!

**Dining/Entertainment:** Continental breakfast is served weekend mornings only in the Executive Meeting Room.

**Services:** Full front-desk services, shuttle vans.

**Facilities:** Swimming pool, hot tubs, saunas, recreation center, weight room, tennis courts; meeting facilities for 175.

**SHERATON STEAMBOAT RESORT, Base Village (P.O. Box 774808), Steamboat Springs, CO 80477. Tel. 303/879-2220,** or 800/848-8878. Fax 303/879-7686. 270 rms (all with bath), 29 suites and condos. A/C TV TEL
**$ Rates:** Late May to mid-Oct, $59–$89 midweek, $69–$99 weekends; winter, low season $109–$119, value season $159–$169, Christmas and regular season $229–$239. Children under 17 stay free in parents' room. AE, CB, DC, MC, V. **Parking:** Free underground lot. **Closed:** 1 month in spring and 1 month in fall.

Steamboat Springs's premier hotel property is located in the heart of Ski Time Square, at the foot of the "Silver Bullet" gondola. The Sheraton opens directly onto the ski slopes, and every room has a view of the mountain, valley, or slopes. In summer, sports lovers enjoy its golf club, one of the finest in the Rockies.

Opened in the mid-1970s, the hotel was fully renovated in 1991. A typical room has two queen-size beds or an executive king-size and a hideabed sofa, a private balcony, and a large closet with full mirror doors. Rooms in the newer West Wing are slightly larger and more modern.

**Dining/Entertainment:** Remington's fine dining establishment has a view straight up the Headwall chair lift. Breakfast (7 to 11am), Sunday brunch, and dinner (5:30 to 10pm) are served daily. The restaurant has Steamboat's largest soup-and-salad bar; steak, seafood, and poultry dishes run $11.75 to $17.95. Buddy's Run, open winters only, serves skiers' breakfasts and lunches from 7am to 5pm; in the evening, it's a comedy club, with shows Tuesday through Friday at 8 and 10pm. The hotel also has H. B. Longbaugh's sports bar and Cinnamon's pastry shop.

**Services:** Room service (7am to 10pm), concierge (8am to 6pm), valet and guest laundry, children's summer day-camp program, no-smoking rooms, facilities for the disabled.

**Facilities:** Golf club and cross-country ski course (see "What to See & Do," above), year-round heated swimming pool, hot tubs, saunas, massage, games room, gift and sundry shop, ski storage and rental; meeting facilities for 800.

## MODERATE

**THE HARBOR AT STEAMBOAT, 703 Lincoln Ave. (P.O. Box 774109), Steamboat Springs, CO 80477. Tel. 303/879-1522,** or 800/543-8888, 800/334-1012 in Colorado. Fax 303/879-1737. 52 rms (all with bath), 10 suites. TV TEL
**$ Rates** (including continental breakfast): $43–$65 single or double in summer

(Easter–Thanksgiving), $50–$65 in low season, $95–$115 in value and regular season, $130–$160 in Christmas season; $75 suite in summer and low season, $115–$130 in value and regular seasons, $180 at Christmas. AE, CB, DC, DISC, JCB, MC, V. **Parking:** Free (covered).

A European-style hotel that dates to 1940, the Harbor has expanded in recent years with an adjoining motel and condominium complex. Guests still enter the hotel through polished bronze doors from a turn-of-the-century London bank, and register in a small, antique-filled lobby. This isn't a Victorian showcase, but the decor is simple and homey.

Each of the 15 hotel guest rooms has a different design. All offer period furnishings and huge walk-in closets, but sometimes-lackluster maintenance. Motel units (23), which face Howelsen Hill, are economical rooms with brass beds. Downtown Steamboat's only condos (24) have fully supplied kitchens with stoves and refrigerators. Local phone calls cost 50¢.

Services and facilities include free bus pass, hot beverages, Wednesday après-ski party, ski storage, Jacuzzis, sauna, steam room, gift shop, and boutique.

**SKY VALLEY LODGE, 31490 E. U.S. 40 (P.O. Box 3132), Steamboat Springs, CO 80477. Tel. 303/879-7749,** or 800/538-7519. Fax 303/879-6044. 24 rms (all with bath or shower). TV TEL
**$ Rates** (including continental breakfast): Late May to Thanksgiving, $50 single; $60 double. Winter, $75–$105 single or double in low season, $155–$195 in Christmas season, $90–$130 in value season, $125–$155, in regular season. Extra person $8. AE, CB, DC, DISC, MC, V. **Parking:** Free. **Closed:** Mid-Apr to late May.

Located below Rabbit Ears Pass with a spectacular view of the upper Yampa River Valley, this lodge—actually two rustic lodges, 8½ miles east of Steamboat Springs—offers country-manor charm in a woodsy setting. Guests get to know each other while sitting around a big fireplace in the main living-room area.

Each cozy room is a bit different, but all have an alpine pension atmosphere. Only four units have full baths; others have showers only, and sinks are in the bedroom. There are king-size and queen-size brass beds and wood beds, and several day beds; floral decor predominates. Local calls cost 50¢.

Gourmet family-style dinners are served Wednesday through Monday, with a choice of three main courses each night (8.25–$15.25). A full bar opens at 3pm daily. Services and facilities include a shuttle to the Ptarmigan Inn at the foot of the ski slopes, where equipment can be stored; outdoor hot tub, coed saunas, games room.

## INEXPENSIVE

**THE INN AT STEAMBOAT, 3070 Columbine Dr. (P.O. Box 771797), Steamboat Springs, CO 80477. Tel. 303/879-2600,** or 800/872-2601. Fax 303/879-9270. 31 rms, 1 suite (all with bath). TV TEL
**$ Rates** (including full breakfast): Easter–Thanksgiving, $35 single; $46 double; additional person $3. Thanksgiving–Easter, $45 single; $55 double; additional person $10. AE, MC, V. **Parking:** Free.

A large ranch-style bed and breakfast, the inn is one of the least expensive accommodations in the Steamboat Village area, surrounded by upscale condominiums. Etched-pine decor and a large stone fireplace add flair. The inn has an outdoor swimming pool, sauna, and games room, and offers ski-tuning services and a shuttle to the mountain and downtown.

Rooms are like spacious motel units with queen-size, double, or bunk beds. Sliding glass doors lead to private decks. The TV rests on a long credenza. Local phone calls are free.

**STEAMBOAT BED & BREAKFAST, 442 Pine St. (P.O. Box 772058), Steamboat Springs, CO 80477. Tel. 303/879-5724.** 6 rms (all with bath).
**$ Rates** (including full breakfast): Mid-Apr to mid-Nov, $40 single; $50–$60 double. Mid-Nov to mid-Apr, $50 single; $65–$75 double. MC, V. **Parking:** On street.

Steamboat Springs's first house of worship, an 1891 Congregational church that lost its steeple and top floor to a lightning strike, is now a fine bed and breakfast. Owner Steve Evans, a mountain-biking and hiking guide, won a civic beautification award for his gardens after he bought the church in 1987, and spent 2½ years remodeling it. Today there are antiques in every room, reproduction antique beds, and hardwood floors. Guests share a huge living/dining room with a stone fireplace and complimentary sherry, an upstairs library, and a music conservatory with a piano . . . and a television.

## WHERE TO DINE
### EXPENSIVE

**HAZIE'S, Thunderhead Terminal, Silver Bullet Gondola. Tel. 879-8770.**
   **Cuisine:** CREATIVE CONTINENTAL. **Reservations:** Recommended for lunch, required for dinner.
**$ Prices:** Lunch appetizers $3.75–$6.25, main courses $6.95–$10.95; four-course fixed-price dinner $41, including round-trip gondola ride. AE, MC, V.
   **Open:** Lunch daily 11:30am–2:30pm; dinner Tues–Sat 6:30–8:30pm.
Steamboat's most exciting dining experience can be found at the top of the gondola, midway up Mount Werner. The views of the upper Yampa River valley are spectacular by day, romantic by night, as the lights of Steamboat Springs spread out at the foot of the mountain. Lunch features a chicken Durango salad, Hazie's buffalo burger, veal Yorkshire, and fettuccine Alfredo. But it's at dinner that Hazie's really struts its stuff. This is a package deal: round-trip gondola transportation and four courses—an appetizer, soup or salad, main course, and dessert—for $41. You can start with smoked Norwegian salmon or escargots bourguignons à la fromage, then select from a choice of eight main dishes, such as shrimp cilantro, pheasant aux pêches, and beef Wellington. Desserts are made fresh daily. Service is impeccable, and there's an extensive wine selection.
   Don't feel that you must wear a coat and tie, incidentally. A neat ski sweater and slacks will do just fine. Evening child care is available: call 879-6111, ext. 218.

**RAGNAR'S, Rendezvous Saddle, Sunshine Peak. Tel. 879-6111, ext. 575 (lunch) or 465 (dinner).**
   **Cuisine:** SCANDINAVIAN/CONTINENTAL. **Reservations:** Recommended for lunch, required for dinner.
**$ Prices:** Lunch appetizers $4.50–$6.95, main courses $6.75–$11.95; fixed-price four-course dinner $55 (children 12 and under $42), including gondola and sleigh rides. AE, DISC, MC, V.
   **Open:** Ski season only, lunch daily 11:30am–2:15pm; dinner Thurs–Sat at 6pm.
   **Closed:** Off-season.
And now for something completely different: Travel by moonlight, across the mid-mountain slopes, to a Scandinavian-style dinner at this charming restaurant. Named for Norwegian ski jumper Ragnar Omtvedt, who set the first national jumping distance record on Howelsen Hill in 1916, Ragnar's has skis, snowshoes, and various bric-a-brac on its walls, and lacy window curtains facing the High Noon slopes.
   Dinner includes such hors d'oeuvres as pickled herring in wine sauce; a main-course choice of oven-baked salmon with puff pastry and white asparagus, roast chicken stuffed with juniper berries and garnished with a chestnut sauce, or mesquite-broiled filet mignon; and delectable homemade desserts. For midday lunch, consider fyldt pandekager (seafood crêpes), stekt lammekølle (leg of lamb), or a smørrebrød platter (an assortment of open-face sandwiches).

### MODERATE

**CAFE BLUE BAYOU, 701 Yampa St. Tel. 879-8282.**
   **Cuisine:** CREOLE/CAJUN. **Reservations:** Recommended.
**$ Prices:** Appetizers $4.95–$13.95; main courses $8.95–$21.95. AE, MC, V.
   **Open:** Daily 5:30pm–midnight (bar open later).

A large outside deck overlooks the Yampa River opposite Howelsen Hill. Pictures of New Orleans mansions adorn the walls, and an antebellum staircase ascends to intimate upstairs dining rooms. This is Steamboat's answer to Cajun elegance.

Start with a plateful of shrimp—in coconut batter, Cajun-grilled, or sautéed in beer—or oysters Bayou, poached with champagne and cream. Don't overlook the alligator (really!) stew. As a main dish, consider chicken Dauphine, veal La Louisianne, stuffed flounder, or smoked blackened prime rib. For dessert, try apricot bread pudding or Cointreau cake.

**DOS AMIGOS, 1910 Mount Werner Rd., Ski Time Square. Tel. 879-4270.**
**Cuisine:** MEXICAN. **Reservations:** Accepted.
**$ Prices:** Appetizers $2.95–$6.25; main courses $5.95–$14.95. AE, MC, V.
**Open:** Winter, bar menu 2:30pm–midnight; dinner 5–10pm daily. Summer, daily 3:30pm–midnight; dinner Tues–Sun 5:30–10pm.

The mountain's oldest Mexican café, established in 1975, is a casual place dominated by its large and popular bar. Pictures cover the stuccoed walls, and green plants add a homey ambience. Start with a margarita or two, then try some of the authentic cuisine—such as Yucatán sopa de lima (a savory chicken, lime, and tortilla soup), fajitas pescado (shrimp and red snapper fajitas), Indian stone-roast steak, or spinach and mushroom enchiladas, popular with vegetarians.

**LA MONTAÑA, Village Center Shopping Plaza, 2500 Village Dr. at Apres Ski Way. Tel. 879-5800.**
**Cuisine:** MEXICAN. **Reservations:** Recommended.
**$ Prices:** Appetizers $3.50–$8.25; main courses $9.95–$17.50. DISC, MC, V.
**Open:** Dinner only, daily 5:30–10pm (bar daily 3:30pm–midnight in winter, 4:30pm–midnight in summer).

This isn't your everyday Mexican restaurant: It's a gourmet experience. The festive decor sets the mood, with greenhouse dining and handsome photos by owner Tom Garrett decorating the stuccoed walls elsewhere.

Start with the restaurant's award-winning grilled braided sausage, a mesquite-grilled combination of elk, lamb, and chorizo sausage. Then choose between sizzling fajitas (with chicken, pork, shrimp, beef, or elk); traditional southwestern dishes such as red chile pasta; or such Tex-Mex favorites as enchiladas and chiles rellenos. Perhaps the epicure's choice would be the elk tenderloin with a pecan-nut crust and bourbon-cream sauce, served with roasted sweet-pepper relish.

**ORE HOUSE AT THE PINE GROVE, 1465 Pine Grove Rd. at U.S. 40. Tel. 879-1190.**
**Cuisine:** GAME/STEAK/SEAFOOD. **Reservations:** Recommended.
**$ Prices:** Appetizers $3.95–$6.75; main courses $7.95–$25.50. AE, DISC, JCB, MC, V.
**Open:** Dinner only, daily 5–10pm (bar open to 2am, to midnight Sun).

The century-old barn of the late, lamented Pine Grove Ranch was converted into this restaurant in 1971. Longtime Steamboat residents and visitors alike appreciate the rustic atmosphere. Artifacts such as wagon wheels, old stoves, and a sleigh were found on the ranch and live on in the restaurant; other memorabilia and photographs came from throughout the state.

Many folks come to the Pine Grove (as it's commonly known) for the ranch-raised game, including buffalo and elk steaks, skewered venison, cherry-smoked pheasant, and braised duck with orange sauce. Various cuts of steak and prime rib, Rocky Mountain rainbow trout and fresh seafood, and mesquite-smoked chicken are also offered. There's a kids' menu, too.

## INEXPENSIVE

**BUFFALO WILD WINGS AND WECK (BW-3), 729 Lincoln Ave. Tel. 879-2431.**
**Cuisine:** AMERICAN. **Reservations:** Not necessary.
**$ Prices:** $1.80–$6.70. AE, MC, V.

**Open:** Mon–Sat 11am–2am, Sun 11am–midnight.

Locals love "BW-3," downtown Steamboat's only late-night dining establishment. "Weck" is a German-style Kimmelweck roll, on which buffalo and beef burgers, char-grilled steaks, and barbecues are served. As the name implies, spicy chicken wings are another house specialty. There's dancing here too, to a compact-disc jukebox.

**INNER-LINKS, Torian Plum Plaza, Base Village. Tel. 879-2916.**
> **Cuisine:** DELI. **Reservations:** Not accepted.
> **$ Prices:** Lunch $3.95–$6.95; dinner $8.95–$11.95. AE, DISC, MC, V.
> **Open:** Mon–Sat 10am–2am, Sun 10am–midnight.

If you've never seen an indoor country club, here's your chance. The indoor courtyard atmosphere of this sports bar and grill caters to winter-weary duffers with six championship golf courses on video—and you get to practice your swing by swatting the ball into the simulated fairway. Lunch specials will give you a discount on an hour of golf with your sandwich or salad. But even nongolfers enjoy the partylike atmosphere, along with tasty soups, salads, sandwiches, desserts, and daily specials like Hog Island crab cakes and Moroccan lamb stew. There's also a children's menu.

**THE TUGBOAT SALOON & EATERY, Ski Time Square. Tel. 879-7070.**
> **Cuisine:** AMERICAN. **Reservations:** Not accepted.
> **$ Prices:** Breakfast/lunch $2.95–$6.50; dinner $4.50–$6.95. AE, MC, V.
> **Open:** Winter, daily 7:30am–10pm; summer, daily 11am–10pm (bar open Mon–Sat to 2am, Sun to midnight). **Closed:** Easter–Memorial Day.

Oak floors and rough barn-wood walls cloaked with game and fishing trophies, sports memorabilia, and celebrity photographs are the trademark of this foot-of-the-slopes establishment. The hand-carved cherrywood bar, circa 1850, came from the Log Cabin Saloon in Baggs, Wyoming, a Butch Cassidy hangout; look for the bullet hole in one of the columns. Budget fare includes omelets and *huevos* (Mexican egg dishes) for breakfast, a variety of burgers and deli sandwiches for lunch, and pasta specials for dinner. Many folks sup on nachos, teriyaki wings, and other generous appetizer plates. Live music starts nightly at 9pm.

# EASY EXCURSIONS FROM STEAMBOAT SPRINGS

U.S. 40 west from Steamboat Springs leads 25 miles to **Hayden,** a ranching center of about 2,000 people that has preserved a strong Old West flavor. Points of interest include the **Hayden Heritage Center,** 300 West Pearl Street (tel. 276-4380), open Wednesday, Friday, and Saturday from 11am to 3pm; and the **Old Hayden Trading Company,** 108 Walnut Street (tel. 276-4247), an authentic trading post with a jewelry and leather workshop.

South and east from Steamboat, U.S. 40 passes through Rabbit Ears Pass and Muddy Pass en route to **Kremmling** (pop. 1,300), 52 miles away. Located on the Amtrak rail line, Kremmling is a center for rafting. (Check with the **Colorado Whitewater Yacht Club,** 309 Park Avenue; tel. 724-9333.) The **Kremmling Museum,** in the Old Jail on Town Square (tel. 724-3396), offers displays of area history daily from 9am to 5pm in summer, Thursday through Saturday in winter.

Colorado 131 follows the Yampa River south from Steamboat, branching off U.S. 40 just south of Steamboat Village. It's 74 winding miles from Steamboat to I-70 at Wolcott, through the villages of **Oak Creek, Phippsburg, Yampa,** and **Toponas,** old ranching and coal-mining towns. Locals in Oak Creek, 22 miles from Steamboat, swear by the Chinese food at **Chelsea's** on Main Street (tel. 736-8538), open nightly from 5 to 11pm. Landmark buttes, glaciated valleys, and fossil deposits add to the scenic beauty of this route. **State Bridge,** 15 miles from I-70, is where the highway crosses the Colorado River and rail line; it's a rafting center.

Just past Rabbit Ears Pass, Colo. 14 turns east off U.S. 40 for a 122-mile passage to

Fort Collins. The highlight of this drive is the **North Park** area, a broad, high basin surrounded by various Rocky Mountain ranges, and a paradise for ranchers—as well as hunters and anglers. The population center is **Walden** (pop. 950); get outdoor recreation information here from the North Park District office of **Routt National Forest,** 612 Fifth Street (tel. 723-4707). Worth a visit is the **North Park Pioneer Museum,** 460 McKinley Street (tel. 723-4711), open in summer, Tuesday through Sunday from noon to 6pm, or by appointment.

# 3. WINTER PARK

67 miles W of Denver

**GETTING THERE   By Plane**   Visitors fly into **Denver's Stapleton International Airport,** and may continue to Winter Park aboard **Home James** (tel. 303/726-5060, or 800/451-4844) buses, which leave Denver 10 times daily during ski season, less frequently in summer. Fare is $21 per person one way, $40 round-trip.

**By Train**   Winter Park Resort claims to be the only ski area in the United States to have rail service directly to the slopes. The dramatically scenic   ✪ **Rio Grande Ski Train** between Denver and Winter Park has been making regular runs over the same route since 1940, stopping just 50 yards from the foot of the lifts. On its 2-hour run, the train climbs almost 4,000 feet and passes through 29 tunnels (including the 6.2-mile Moffat Tunnel). The train, which operates weekends from Christmas to Easter (but not including those holidays), leaves Denver promptly at 7:15am and Winter Park at 4:15pm. Same-day round-trip fare is $25 coach or $40 first-class. For ticket information, call 303/296-I-SKI.

The **Amtrak** *California Zephyr* stops daily in Fraser, 2 miles north of Winter Park, on its Chicago–Denver–San Francisco–Los Angeles route. The rail line's "Snowball Express" package brings thousands of skiers to Winter Park each year. Call 800/USA-RAIL for schedules and fares from your city.

**By Bus   Greyhound/Trailways,** U.S. 40 at Vasquez Road (tel. 292-6111), offers regular service on the main route between Denver and Steamboat Springs.

**By Car**   From Denver or any other points east and west, exit I-70 at Empire and climb 24 miles over Berthoud Pass on U.S. 40 to Winter Park. U.S. 40 links Winter Park directly to Steamboat Springs, 101 miles northwest, and, via U.S. 34 (at Granby) and Rocky Mountain National Park, to Estes Park, 84 miles north. A precipitous, winding gravel road over Rollins Pass (11,671 ft.) from Rollinsville, near Boulder, is open in summer only.

**SPECIAL EVENTS**   Winter Park area events include the **Denver University Winter Carnival,** in late January; the **Spring Splash (Ski Area Closing Day),** in mid-April; the **Reggae Sunsplash,** on the second Sunday of June; the **American Music Festival,** on the second Saturday of July; the **Jazz Festival,** on the third weekend in July; **Alpine ArtAffair,** on the last weekend in July; the **Mountain Bike Festival,** on the first weekend of August; the **Rocky Mountain Wine and Food Festival,** on the third weekend in August; and the **Torchlight Parade,** on Christmas Eve.

**O**riginally a Ute and Arapahoe hunting ground, the Fraser Valley was first settled by whites in the 1850s. The laying of a rail track over Rollins Pass in 1905, and the completion of the 6.2-mile Moffat Tunnel in 1928, opened the forests of Grand County to logging, which long supported the local economy while providing Denver with raw materials for its growth.

The opening of the Winter Park ski area in January 1940, at the west portal of the

Moffat Tunnel, helped induce the Colorado ski boom. Owned by the city of Denver and operated by a private corporation, it is today the fourth-largest ski resort in the state (after Aspen, Vail, and Steamboat). The longterm masterplan for the resort includes construction of a 4.1-mile highway tunnel for more rapid road access from Denver and Boulder, and development of a major base village.

Winter Park's elevation is about 9,000 feet. The year-round population is about 500 in Winter Park and 500 more in neighboring Fraser, plus about 3,000 overnight guests in peak summer or winter seasons.

## ORIENTATION

**INFORMATION** Main sources of visitor information are the **Winter Park/ Fraser Valley Chamber of Commerce,** P.O. Box 3236, Winter Park, CO 80442 (tel. 303/726-4118), and the **Winter Park Resort,** P.O. Box 36, Winter Park, CO 80442 (tel. 303/726-5514, or 800/453-2525 for central reservations). The chamber of commerce **Visitor Center,** off U.S. 40 at Vasquez Road, is open daily from 8am to 5pm year round.

**CITY LAYOUT** U.S. 40, or **Winter Park Drive** runs almost directly north-south through the community. Coming from Denver, you first cross Berthoud Pass, and 15 miles later see the **Winter Park Resort** on your left. About 1 mile farther is downtown Winter Park; **Vasquez Road,** one of the few side roads with accommodations, is the first major left turn as you arrive. Two miles farther on U.S. 40 is **Fraser,** site of the Amtrak terminal and several condominium developments.

## GETTING AROUND

The **Ski Lift** (tel. 390-LIFT), a free local shuttle service, runs to/from most accommodations and the Winter Park Resort base area in winter. **Winter Park Taxi Service** (tel. 726-5060) does the yeoman's share of taxi work. "Skierized" **car rentals** are available from Hertz (tel. 303/726-8993, or 800/654-3131) and National (tel. 303/726-4879, or 800/328-4567).

## FAST FACTS

The **area code** is 303. In case of **emergency,** call **911;** for regular business, contact the Grand County Sheriff (tel. 726-5666). The **hospital,** Winter Park Medical Center, U.S. 40 in downtown Winter Park (tel. 726-9616), and 7 Mile Medical Clinic, at the Winter Park Ski Area (tel. 726-8066), can handle most medical emergencies. The **post office** is at Winter Park Center on U.S. 40 in the heart of town. For **road information,** call 586-4000. State, county, and city **taxes** add 8.2% to hotel bills.

## WHAT TO SEE & DO
### ATTRACTIONS

**WINTER PARK RESORT, Winter Park Recreational Association, P.O. Box 36, Winter Park, CO 80482. Tel. 303/726-5514** or 303/892-0961 in Denver, or 800/453-2525 outside Colorado or 800/621-SNOW for daily ski reports.

Winter Park is one of those rare resorts that seem to have something for everyone. Experts drool over the chutes and steep mogul runs on Mary Jane mountain, but intermediates and beginners are well served on other slopes. Moreover, Winter Park is noted for wide-ranging programs for children and the disabled.

The resort comprises three interconnected mountain areas. **Winter Park** mountain has 12 chairs that serve intermediate and novice slopes. **Mary Jane,** famous for its expert terrain and "Backside" glade skiing, in 1992 added an above-timberline area called Parsenn Bowl; it has seven chairs and a separate base area. **Vasquez Ridge,** served by a single high-speed quad chair, is heavily intermediate.

The vertical is 3,000 feet, from the 9,000-foot base to the 12,000-foot summit of North Cone, atop Parsenn Bowl. Skiable terrain of 1,340 acres includes 110 trails, served by 20 lifts—four high-speed quads, four triple chairs, and 12 double chairs—giving the resort an uphill capacity of over 30,000 skiers per hour.

Annual snowfall averages 368 inches, nearly 31 feet—the most of any major destination resort in Colorado. (Wolf Creek Pass, a day area near Pagosa Springs, does better.) Nine restaurants and three bars are on the mountain or at the base, including The Club Car at the Mary Jane base and a new (for the 1992–93 season) mountaintop restaurant on Winter Park mountain.

Winter Park's $3-million, 32,000-square-foot **Children's Center,** the first of its kind at a ski resort, includes its own rest rooms and kitchen, play area and rental shop, with a walkway to the children's instruction hill. The **National Sports Center for the Disabled,** founded in 1970, is the largest of its kind in the world. More than 23,000 ski lessons are given each year to disabled children and adults, who pay a discounted rate of just $20 per day for lessons, adaptive equipment, and lift tickets. The World Disabled Ski Championships were held here in 1990.

**Admission:** Tickets, $34 per day adults, $22 half day, $28 per day for multiday tickets; $15 per day children 6–13 and seniors 62–69; free for those under 6 and over 69. Special beginner's lift rates. Full rental packages are available; 4½-hour class lessons run $15–$40. Snowboard lessons also available.

**Open:** Third week of Nov to third week of Apr, Mon–Fri 9am–4pm, Sat–Sun and hols 8:30am–4pm. **Closed:** Late Apr to late Nov.

## COZENS RANCH HOUSE RESTORATION MUSEUM, U.S. 40 between Winter Park and Fraser. Tel. 726-5488.

A series of 1870s ranch buildings, including a family residence, a small hotel, a stage stop, and the original Fraser Valley post office, have been restored by the Grand County Historical Association. They give a glimpse of life in Colorado's pioneer era.

**Admission:** $2 adults, $1 children.

**Open:** Memorial Day–Oct 1, daily 10am–5pm; Oct 2–Dec 14 and Apr 16–Memorial Day, Wed–Sun 10am–5pm; Dec 15–Apr 15, Sun–Wed and Fri 10am–5pm, Thurs and Sat 10am–9pm.

## RIO GRANDE CABOOSE MUSEUM, Ski Train Terminal, Winter Park Resort. Tel. 726-4118.

A vintage 1945 caboose has been converted to a ski museum, with a display of ski memorabilia and historical photos showing the half-century development of the Winter Park ski area. It doubles as a visitor information center. Around the base of the mountain are exhibits on ski patrol, ski lifts, and snowmaking technology.

**Admission:** Free.

**Open:** Daily 9am–5pm.

## SPORTS & RECREATION

A majority of recreational pursuits in the Fraser Valley area are undertaken in **Arapahoe National Forest** (tel. 887-3331).

**ALPINE SLIDE**   Colorado's longest alpine slide thrills summer visitors to Winter Park Resort (tel. 726-5514).

**BICYCLING**   As a mountain-biking center, Winter Park has won national recognition for its expansive trail system and established race program. Many of the off-road bike trails connect to 500 miles of backcountry roads and trails in the adjacent national forest. The **King of the Rockies Off-Road Stage Race,** held each year in August, is one of the top professional mountain-bike races in America; part of it is run on the 30-mile **Tipperary Creek Trail,** generally considered Colorado's best mountain-bike trail.

Bike rentals and repairs are available at numerous locations, including **Winter Park Sports Shop,** Kings Crossing Shopping Center, Winter Park Drive at Kings Crossing Road (tel. 303/726-5554, or 800/222-7547), and **Europa Sports,** Gasthaus Eichler, Winter Park Drive at Vasquez Creek (tel. 303/726-5133, or 800/543-3899). For specific information on trails and races, call the **Winter Park Fat Tire Society** (tel. 800/521-BIKE).

**BOATING**   The **Arapahoe National Recreation Area,** 30 miles north via U.S. 34, has marinas on three large lakes—Lake Granby, Shadow Mountain Reservoir, and Grand Lake. See "An Easy Excursion from Estes Park," above, for details.

**FISHING**   During his presidency (1953–61), Dwight Eisenhower enjoyed fishing the **Fraser River** and its tributary at Fraser, **St. Louis Creek.** Both streams remain rich in trout—rainbow, cutthroat, brown, and brook. Area lakes, including **Meadow Creek Reservoir** and **Williams Fork Reservoir,** also have mackinaw (lake trout) and landlocked kokanee salmon.

**GOLF**   The **Pole Creek Golf Club,** Grand County Road 5 (tel. 726-8847), tabbed by *Golf Digest* magazine as one of the 75 best public golf courses in the United States, is located near Tabernash, about 10 miles northwest of Winter Park. A 7,000-yard, 18-hole championship course, it was designed by Ron Kirby and Gary Player. There are miniature golf courses at **Winter Park Resort** (tel. 726-5514) and **A'Maze Labyrinth 'n' Grill,** Safeway Center, U.S. 40 (tel. 726-9555).

**HIKING & BACKPACKING**   Check with **Arapahoe National Forest** (tel. 887-3331) for trail maps and other information. Beautiful **Rocky Mountain National Park** (see "Estes Park," above) is less than an hour's drive north.

**HORSEBACK RIDING**   Several stables offer rides into **Arapahoe National Forest** (tel. 887-3331). Check with **Sumerlin Horses** (tel. 726-8035).

**ICE SKATING**   There's ice skating on outdoor rinks at **Meadowridge Resort** (tel. 726-4253) and **Fraser Valley Elementary School** (tel. 726-4708), both in Fraser. Rentals are available; call for hours. Another rink is open to the public at **Snow Mountain Ranch–YMCA of the Rockies,** Tabernash (tel. 726-4628).

**RIVER RAFTING**   Half-day, full-day, and multiday trips on the Colorado, Arkansas, Eagle, North Platte, and other rivers are offered by numerous local outfitters, including **Mad Adventures** (tel. 303/726-5290, or 800/451-4844), **Raven Adventure Trips** (tel. 303/887-2141, or 800/332-3381), and **Timber Rafting** (tel. 303/887-2141, or 800/332-3381). Adult rates start around $45 for a full day.

**RODEO**   Every Saturday night for 8 weeks, beginning the Fourth of July weekend, the **High Country Stampede Rodeos** hold forth at Fraser's John Work Arena (tel. 726-4118). Professional and top amateur cowboys compete in bronco riding, calf roping, and other events. A barbecue precedes the rodeo.

**ROLLER SKATING**   There's public roller skating at the **Snow Mountain Ranch–YMCA of the Rockies** (tel. 726-4628).

**SKIING (ALPINE)**   The **Winter Park Resort** (see "Attractions," above) isn't the only mecca for winter-sports enthusiasts. Alpine skiers, for instance, have two other small resorts within a short drive of Winter Park.

   **Berthoud Pass Ski Area,** U.S. 40, Berthoud Pass (tel. 303/670-1666), is designed for skiers who enjoy the challenge and adventure of ungroomed slopes. With a base elevation of 10,817 feet, it's Colorado's highest ski resort and one of its oldest, dating from 1937. From the summit, at 11,963 feet, it's possible to ski for miles downhill, on either side of the pass, to be returned to base facilities by shuttle buses. There are only three lifts—a double, a triple, and a quad chair. Snowboard and monoski lessons are available. Full-day tickets are $20 for adults, $15 for students, $10 for children (13 and under) and seniors. Equipment rentals start at $10.

   **Silver Creek Ski Area,** U.S. 40, Granby (tel. 303/887-3384, or 800/448-9458), is a small family-oriented area mainly known for its beginner's area and intermediate slopes. With a 1,000-foot vertical drop to a base elevation of 8,200 feet, it is served by three double chairs and a triple chair. Full-day tickets are $22 for adults, $12 for juniors (6 to 12) and seniors (60 to 69). Under 6 and over 69 ski free. Equipment rentals start at $11 for adults, $7 for juniors. Special beginner lesson/lift/rental packages run $33.

See "Skiing (Nordic)," below for additional sources of equipment rentals.

**SKIING [NORDIC]**  The outstanding cross-country skiing in the Fraser Valley area is highlighted by what the *Denver Post* calls "the best touring center in Colorado." The **Devil's Thumb—Idlewild Cross-Country Centers** have more than 90km (56 miles) of groomed trails linking **Ski Idlewild,** in the town of Winter Park (tel. 726-5564), with the **Devil's Thumb Ranch,** on Grand County Road 83, 6½ miles north of Fraser (tel. 726-8231). Full rentals and instruction are available at both centers, along with guided 6-hour backcountry tours and a telemark hill at Devil's Thumb.

Trail fees for adults are $8 for a full day, $5 for a half day; children 6 to 12 and seniors, $5 for a full day, $3 for a half day; under 6, free. Full-day rentals are $14 for adults, $10 for children and seniors, $7 for children under 6. Group lessons are $14 for adults, $10 for children and seniors, including the trail fee. There's also a shuttle service between the two centers.

**Snow Mountain Ranch—YMCA Nordic Center,** on U.S. 40 between Tabernash and Granby (tel. 887-2152), features 65km (40 miles) of groomed trails for all abilities, including 3km (2 miles) of lighted track for night skiing. The trail fee is $6 for adults ($4 for Y members), $2 for children 6 to 12. Rentals are $10 for adults, $5 for children.

For other nordic opportunities, talk to local ski shops or Arapahoe National Forest (tel. 887-3331).

Rental equipment for downhill or cross-country skiing can be obtained from more than a dozen outlets in the Winter Park area, including **Alpine Sun Ski & Sport,** U.S. 40, Winter Park (tel. 303/726-5107, or 800/752-3424); **Le Ski Lab,** U.S. 40, Winter Park (tel. 303/726-9841, or 800/322-8567); and the **Winter Park Sports Shop,** Kings Crossing, U.S. 40, Winter Park (tel. 303/726-5554, or 800/222-SKIS).

**SLEIGH RIDES**  Old-fashioned sleigh rides to elaborate dinners are offered by **Dashing Thru the Snow Sleigh Rides** (tel. 726-5376), at $32 for adults, $22 for children; and **Dinner at the Barn** (tel. 726-4923), at $33.50 for adults, $21 for children. For shorter afternoon and evening rides, including hot chocolate around a bonfire, check with **Jim's Sleigh Rides** (tel. 726-5527), **Ray's Sleighs,** Devil's Thumb Ranch (tel. 726-5632), or **Summerlin Horses** (tel. 726-4311 or 726-4532). Many of the sleigh riders offer summer hayrides.

Jim's Sleigh Rides (tel. 726-5527), offers 1-hour, 5-mile winter **dog-sled runs.** Jim's nine canines leave five times a day, from 9am to 3:30pm, at rates of $75 per couple, $60 for a single, $10 extra per child. The kennel is half a mile north of Hernando's Pizza on U.S. 40 in Winter Park.

**SNOWMOBILING**  Snowmobile rentals and guided tours are offered by **Sporting Country Guide Service,** Beaver Village Lodge (tel. 726-9247), and **Trailblazer Snowmobile Tours,** Fraser Valley Tubing Hill (tel. 303/726-8452, or 800/669-0134). Boots and helmets are provided. Rates are $30 an hour, $45 for 2 hours.

**SWIMMING**  There are public pools at the **Snowblaze Athletic Club,** Winter Park (tel. 726-9342), with a $10 daily walk-in fee; and the **Snow Mountain Ranch—YMCA of the Rockies,** Tabernash (tel. 726-4628), which charges $2 for a non-YMCA-member day pass.

**TENNIS**  Public tennis courts can be found at the **Fraser Community Center,** Fraser (tel. 726-4708), and **Idlewild Lodge,** Winter Park (tel. 726-5562).

**TUBING [SNOW]**  The **Fraser Valley Tubing Hill,** Fraser (tel. 726-5954), offers a return to childhood for many adults. For $8 an hour by day, $9 an hour by night (additional hours $1), you can slide down a steep hill in a big inner tube. Open Monday through Friday from 4 to 10pm and on Saturday, Sunday, and holidays from 10am to 10pm.

**MISCELLANEOUS** Children and adults alike enjoy getting lost and found at the full-size **A'Maze Labyrinth 'n' Grill,** Safeway Center, U.S. 40, Winter Park (tel. 726-9555).

## EVENING ENTERTAINMENT

Several outstanding music events are hosted in summer at Winter Park Resort. The **Reggae Sunsplash at Winter Park** (the second Sunday of June), the **American Music Festival** (the second Saturday of July), and the **Winter Park Jazz Festival** (the third weekend of July) all draw nationally known performing artists, including Bonnie Raitt, Lyle Lovett, Wynton Marsalis, David Sanborn, and Harry Connick, Jr.

Broadway plays and musicals are presented throughout the year by the Grand County Theatre Association at the **Balcony Dinner Theatre,** Cooper Creek Square, Cooper Way at Winter Park Drive (tel. 726-4037).

There's live music and dancing at **The Slope,** on U.S. 40 half a mile from the ski resort (tel. 726-5727); rock disco with occasional country-and-western bands at **The Stampede,** Cooper Creek Square (tel. 726-9433); and live rock music Wednesday through Saturday nights at the **Crooked Creek Saloon** in downtown Fraser (tel. 726-9250).

First-run movies are presented nightly at the **Silver Screen Cinema** (tel. 726-5390).

# WHERE TO STAY

There are more than 100 accommodation properties in the Fraser Valley, including hotels, condominiums, family-style mountain inns (serving breakfast and dinner daily), European Plan lodges, and motels. Bookings can be made by **Winter Park Central Reservations,** P.O. Box 36, Winter Park, CO 80482 (tel. 303/726-5587, 303/447-0588 in Denver, or 800/452-2525). The agency can also book air and rail tickets, rental cars, airport transfers, lift tickets, ski-school lessons, ski rentals, and many other activities.

Ski-season rates vary according to skier traffic. Although there are slight differences in seasonal definitions among accommodations, most have their highest rates during the 2-week Christmas–New Year's period (referred to here as "Christmas"). Next busiest is "peak" season (February and March), followed by "value" season (most of January) and "low" season (mid-November to mid-December and early to mid-April, when the area closes). "Summer" season runs from mid-April to mid-November, though many accommodations close their doors during the April–May "mud season" and again mid-October to mid-November. There's some gray area from lodge to lodge about where one "season" ends and another "begins," so confirm rates before booking.

## EXPENSIVE

**C LAZY U RANCH, Colo. 125 (P.O. Box 378), Granby, CO 80446. Tel. 303/887-3344.** 18 rms, 21 cottages (all with bath).
**$ Rates** (including full board): Early June–late Sept (weekly), $1,250–$1,600 single, $2,000–$2,250 double. Christmas (daily), $155–$210 single; $300–$375 double. Jan–Mar (daily), $120–$140 single; $175–$275 double. **Closed:** Late Sept to Dec 21 and Apr 1–May 30.

Regarded by some as the finest guest ranch in the United States, the C Lazy U offers a little of everything for summer and winter visitors. Located 7½ miles northwest of Granby on Willow Creek, a rich trout-fishing stream, it's a great place for riding enthusiasts: You get your own horse for a week! Included in the rates are riding instruction and trail rides with a real western wrangler.

Ranch accommodations include 18 lodge rooms, 20 two-bedroom cottages or duplexes, and a three-bedroom cottage. All have full or three-quarter baths; some have fireplaces. No pets are permitted.

**Dining/Entertainment:** Full gourmet meals are served in the dining room to guests only, and there's a cocktail lounge. Country-and-western bands, square dancing, staff shows, and cookouts are occasional features.

**Services:** Children's and teenagers' program; nature program.

**Facilities:** Heated swimming pool, Jacuzzi, sauna, tennis and racquetball courts, skeet-shooting range, ice skating, cross-country ski trails, children's playground; guest laundry.

## MODERATE

**THE INN AT SILVER CREEK, U.S. 40 (P.O. Box 4222), Silver Creek, CO 80446. Tel. 303/887-2131,** or 800/526-0590. 223 rms, 119 suites (all with bath). A/C TV TEL

**$ Rates:** Summer and peak season, $53 single or double; $85 suite. Christmas, $66 single or double; $98 suite. Low and value seasons, $43 single or double; $75 suite. AE, CB, DC, DISC, MC, V.

This outstanding year-round resort is located 15 miles north of Winter Park and 2 miles southeast of Granby. It's becoming a popular conference location with its meeting area, fine restaurants, all-seasons athletic facilities, and a full range of services.

Every room is luxurious, with a whirlpool and steam cabinet in the bath. Each unit has a full deck or balcony, and cable TV with in-room movies. Third-floor rooms and suites have vaulted ceilings, skylights, and lofts. Suites and efficiencies have a fireplace, wet bar (with refrigerator and microwave), and dining and living areas.

**IRON HORSE RESORT RETREAT, 257 Winter Park Dr. (P.O. Box 1286), Winter Park, CO 80482. Tel. 303/726-8851,** or 800/621-8190. 76 rms, 44 suites (all with bath). A/C TV TEL

**$ Rates** (single or double): Peak season, $95 lodge room; $130 studio; $195–$250 one-bedroom; $260–$340 two-bedroom. Christmas, $130 lodge room; $170 studio; $260–$330 one-bedroom; $320–$415 two-bedroom. Value season, $85 lodge room; $99 studio; $145–$200 one-bedroom; $215–$270 two-bedroom. Low season, $69 lodge room; $79 studio; $120–$165 one-bedroom; $175–$220 two-bedroom. Summer, $55 lodge room; $65 studio; $90–$110 one-bedroom; $115–$135 two-bedroom. AE, CB, DC, DISC, MC, V. **Parking:** Free, underground.

Billing itself as Winter Park's only ski-in/ski-out lodging, the Iron Horse—so named for its proximity to the Rio Grande Railroad that serves the resort—can be reached via a bridge off the ski (or summer bike) trail from Mary Jane mountain to the Winter Park base. Most folks, however, make their first visit to this fine condominium hotel by road.

Every unit has a kitchen with microwave, a private deck or balcony, a fireplace (with wood provided daily), and cable color television. The light southwestern decor and handsome wood furnishings feel right at home in the pine forests. There are one- and two-bedroom suites, as well as 16 Premium Suites with wet bars, washer/dryers, jetted tubs, skylights, and a 10-person dining area.

The resort offers a full range of services as well as dining, athletic, and meeting-room facilities.

**SNOWBLAZE, U.S. 40 (P.O. Box 66), Winter Park, CO 80482. Tel. 303/726-5701,** or 800/525-2466. 73 units.

**$ Rates** (single or double): Low season, $72 studio; $146 two-bedroom; $197 three-bedroom. Value season, $85 studio; $170 two-bedroom; $227 three-bedroom. Pre-Christmas and Feb, $94 studio; $188 two-bedroom; $251 three-bedroom. Christmas and Mar, $115 studio; $230 two-bedroom; $307 three-bedroom. Summer, $66 studio; $94 two-bedroom; $125 three-bedroom. AE, CB, DC, MC, V.

One of Winter Park's more prestigious condominium developments, Snowblaze

244 • THE NORTHERN ROCKIES

features the Fraser Valley's leading athletic club on site. The units are in downtown Winter Park, 1½ miles from the ski area by shuttle. All rooms have full baths (one per bedroom), fully equipped kitchens, electric stoves and/or microwaves, and color TVs. Two- and three-bedroom units also have fireplaces (with wood provided) and private dry saunas. All have simple but handsome decor, with big picture windows and rich wood furnishings.

Winter Park Adventures, the property management firm for Snowblaze, has 14 other area properties and a variety of packages.

**THE VINTAGE, 100 Winter Park Dr. (P.O. Box 1369), Winter Park, CO 80482. Tel. 303/726-8801,** or 800/472-7017, 800/325-4082 in Colorado. Fax 303/726-9230. 101 rms, 20 suites (all with bath). A/C TV TEL

**$ Rates:** Jan–Feb, $79 hotel room; $99–$120 studio; $200 one-bedroom; $260 two-bedroom. Peak season (Christmas and Mar), $95 hotel room; $110–$140 studio; $240 one-bedroom; $300 two-bedroom. Low season, $49 hotel room; $60–$70 studio; $90 one-bedroom; $120 two-bedroom. Summer, $55 hotel room; $70–$80 studio; $110 one-bedroom; $140 two-bedroom. AE, CB, DC, DISC, MC, V.

Châteaulike, the Vintage rises five stories above the foot of Winter Park's ski slopes, not far from the Mary Jane base facilities. A full-service resort hotel, it offers convenient access, excellent dining and atmosphere, and luxury accommodations. Every room in the hotel has a view of either the Winter Park slopes or the Continental Divide. Even the studio efficiencies have fireplaces and kitchens, as well as cable television. Birch furnishings accent light-pastel appointments to yield a modern mountain atmosphere.

The hotel offers a full range of services as well as athletic and meeting facilities.

## INEXPENSIVE

**DEVIL'S THUMB RANCH RESORT, Grand County Rd. 83 (P.O. Box 640), Tabernash, CO 80478. Tel. 303/726-5632.** 21 rms (all with bath), 2 cabins, 2 dormitories.

**$ Rates:** Winter, $45–$90 single; $60–$90 double; $100–$120 cabin single or double; $20 dorm bed. Summer, $35–$80 single; $40–$80 double; $80–$100 cabin single or double; $15 dorm bed. JCB, MC, V.

This is the sort of place that attracts outdoor sports lovers by droves. Established in 1937, the ranch—8 miles north of Winter Park—is as famous today for its cross-country skiing in winter (see "Sports & Recreation" in "What to See & Do," above) as for its horseback riding and mountain biking in summer. Accommodations are available for all pocketbooks, from a honeymoon cabin with a four-poster lodgepole pine bed to eight-bed dormitory rooms in the Bunkhouse. Most guests stay in the elegant log Elk Lodge, where they have cozy rooms with private baths, and access to a spa, sauna, TV, and billiards room. The Ranch House Restaurant and Saloon lure Winter Park residents for regional cuisine at moderate prices.

**ENGELMANN PINES, 1035 Cranmer Ave. (P.O. Box 1305), Winter Park, CO 80482. Tel. 303/726-4632.** 6 rms (2 with bath).

**$ Rates** (including breakfast): Winter, $55 single without bath, $75 single with bath; $65 double without bath, $85 double with bath. Summer, $35 single without bath, $55 single with bath; $45 double without bath, $65 double with bath. AE, MC, V.

Antique furnishings add a country touch to this contemporary home in residential Winter Park. Heinz and Margaret Engel serve Swiss confections and other treats around their large fireplace in winter, and invite guests to use the Jacuzzi and catch the free shuttle to the ski resort or from the Amtrak station. In summer, mountain bikers and hikers appreciate the same trailhead across the street that cross-country skiers use in winter. Guests have limited use of the kitchen. No smoking or pets are allowed, and there are restrictions on children.

**GÄSTHAUS EICHLER, Winter Park Dr. at Vasquez Creek (P.O. Box 430), Winter Park, CO 80482. Tel. 303/726-5133,** or 800/543-3899. 15 rms (all with bath). TV TEL

$ **Rates:** Peak season, $65 single; $90 double. Christmas, $70 single; $100 double. Value and low seasons, $55 single; $70 double. Summer, $39 single; $59 double. Add $20 per person, per day, for European Plan (breakfast and dinner). Half price for children 2–10 staying in parents' room. CB, DC, MC, V. **Closed:** Mid-Apr to May.

When Hans and Hannelore Eichler moved to Colorado from their hometown of Duisburg, Germany, they brought with them their concept of what an alpine *Gästhaus* ought to be like. The charm of this small inn is exactly what you'd expect to find at a European resort. Lace curtains and down comforters grace each room, and private whirlpool baths are available. The Eichlers' daughter, Anke, and her husband, Kurt, manage Europa Sports on the premises, and the Gästhaus Eichler Restaurant is an unforgettable experience.

**SOMETHING SPECIAL, 1848 Grand County Rd. 83 (P.O. Box 800), Winter Park, CO 80482. Tel. 303/726-5360.** 3 rms (1 with bath).
$ **Rates** (including breakfast): Summer $40–$60; winter $50–$80. AE.
Located on 14 wooded acres near Devil's Thumb Ranch, 8 miles north of Winter Park, this quaint bed-and-breakfast is the home of Noel Wilson, widow of former Winter Park Ski School director Bill Wilson. Noel has three cozy rooms, one with a private bath, available year round; she offers down comforters, an outdoor cookout area, and complimentary evening refreshments. Guests may use the kitchen, but no smoking is permitted.

**WOODSPUR, Van Anderson Rd. (P.O. Box 249), Winter Park, CO 80482. Tel. 303/726-8417,** or 800/626-6562. 32 rms (all with bath).
$ **Rates:** Nov–Apr (including breakfast and dinner), $67 single; $114 double; $30 children 5–11 in room with parents. May–Oct (including continental breakfast), $35 single; $50 double; $20 children 5–11 in room with parents. Special rates for three or more in room. MC, V.
A rustic mountain lodge off Vasquez Road, en route to the proposed site of a third ski-area base development, the Woodspur has all the earmarks of a classic ski lodge. Most rooms have queen-size or double beds and either two or four single bunks, encouraging sharing by groups of young people. They've all got private baths, but only a dozen rooms (those without bunk beds) have tubs; most have showers only. Winter rates include home-cooked dinners as well as breakfasts. Guests share a large fireplace, library, recreation room, outdoor Jacuzzi, sauna, and frontier-style bar.

## BUDGET

**SNOW MOUNTAIN RANCH–YMCA OF THE ROCKIES, U.S. 40 near Tabernash (P.O. Box 169), Winter Park, CO 80482. Tel. 303/887-2152** or 303/443-4743 in Denver. 260 units.
$ **Rates:** $24–$45 lodge room; $79–$145 cabin (sleeping 5–12). Camping $10–$14. Weekly rates. No credit cards.
This YMCA ranch, and a sister property outside Estes Park, are enormously popular among Denverites and other Rocky Mountain–area residents. The ranch offers both bunk beds in lodge rooms—some with full baths, others with central showers—and housekeeping cabins of two to five bedrooms with fireplaces. YMCA membership is required, and will be sold by the ranch for a nominal additional charge. Facilities here include two restaurants, a gift shop, coin-op laundry, indoor swimming pool, tennis court, ice-skating rink, cross-country skiing/jogging trails, horse stables, and a playground.

**WINTER PARK YOUTH HOSTEL, opposite Cooper Creek Square, U.S. 40 (P.O. Box 3323), Winter Park, CO 80482. Tel. 726-5356.** 6 rms (none with bath).
$ **Rates:** Winter, $9 for Youth Hostel Association members, $13 for nonmembers; summer, $7 for members, $10 for nonmembers. No credit cards.
Six large mobile homes contain rooms with two to four bunk beds each, as well as

two rooms with double beds for couples. Everyone shares the kitchen and bath. There's no curfew or age restrictions, but you'll have to reserve ahead in winter.

# WHERE TO DINE

## EXPENSIVE

**GÄSTHAUS EICHLER, U.S. 40 at Vasquez Creek. Tel. 726-5133.**
    **Cuisine:** GERMAN. **Reservations:** Recommended.
**$ Prices:** Dinner, appetizers $5.95–$9.50; main courses $12.95–$20.95. CB, DC, MC, V.
    **Open:** Breakfast daily 7:30–10am; dinner daily 5–9pm. **Closed:** Mid-Apr to May.
A delightful Teutonic atmosphere dominates this outstanding restaurant, located on the bottom floor of a European-style pension. Start your gourmet dinner with baked Camembert or traditional potato pancakes. Then contemplate which of the house specialties you'll try: Rindsrouladen (stuffed rolled beef with red cabbage); Jägerschnitzel (pork in a mushroom-and-onion sauce), or Huhner ragoût (chicken simmered in chardonnay). Be sure to leave room for a strudel!

**RESTAURANT ON THE RIDGE, Meadow Ridge Resort Clubhouse, Fraser. Tel. 726-4000.**
    **Cuisine:** STEAK/SEAFOOD. **Reservations:** Recommended.
**$ Prices:** Appetizers $3.50–$5.95; main courses $2.95–$5.95 at lunch, $9.95–$18.95 at dinner. AE, MC, V.
    **Open:** Mon–Sat 11:30am–10pm, Sun 9:30am–1pm and 5–10pm.
Spacious but intimate, casual but elegant, this restaurant occupies the glass-enclosed dining room and outdoor deck of a condominium-complex clubhouse in Fraser. The cuisine is an interesting blend of new American (to wit, appetizers like duck ravioli and tempura artichokes), continental (chicken Oscar, fettuccine Alfredo), steaks (T-bone, New York strip), and seafood (Alaskan king crab, fresh fish). In winter, you get a view of a lighted ice-skating rink as you dine.

**SOUFFLES, Park Place Shopping Center, U.S. 40. Tel. 726-9494.**
    **Cuisine:** CREATIVE CONTINENTAL. **Reservations:** Recommended.
**$ Prices:** Appetizers $3.50–$25; main courses $14.50–$27.50. AE, MC, V.
    **Open:** Nov 15–Apr 15, dinner only, daily 5–10pm. **Closed:** Apr 16–Nov 14.
It's a shame this restaurant is open only 5 months a year, because nonskiers never get a chance to experience it. Oil candles cast their glow through intimate dining rooms, and impressionist paintings of ski slopes adorn the walls. Light jazz is piped through the dining area, while '60s music livens the adjacent lounge. Chef David Lazarus's nightly fixed-price menu is always a good bet. Otherwise, you might start with a lobster bisque or spinach salad, then move on to medallions of venison or a trout amandine. Dessert? Order a hot soufflé, of course.

## MODERATE

**THE LAST WALTZ, King's Cross Shopping Center, U.S. 40. Tel. 726-4877.**
    **Cuisine:** AMERICAN/MEXICAN.
**$ Prices:** Breakfast $2.75–$6.75; lunch $2.50–$6.95; dinner appetizers $3.25–$6.75, main courses $5.95–$14.95. AE, CB, DC, DISC, MC, V.
    **Open:** Daily 7am–9:30pm.
A favorite place for locals who enjoy good home-cooking, this café treads the line between cultures at every meal: flapjacks, lox and bagels, or migas (a south-of-the-border egg scramble) for breakfast; Cajun-blackened ham, Rocky Mountain Reuben, or quesadilla (Mexican cheese) sandwiches for lunch. In the evening, you'll have to

decide between crabmeat enchiladas and the like, or swear your allegiance to a honey-and-pecan fried chicken or a 12-ounce ribeye steak.

**DENO'S SWISS HOUSE, U.S. 40, downtown Winter Park. Tel. 726-5332.**
   **Cuisine:** BISTRO.
**$ Prices:** Appetizers $2.25–$6.95; main courses $3.95–$17.95. AE, MC, V.
   **Open:** Daily 11am–11pm.
Locals frequent and visitors always seem to find this self-proclaimed "mountain bistro" on Winter Park's main drag. With its casual atmosphere and impressive bar scroll—75 international beers, over 300 varietal wines—it might be written off as a pub. But the cuisine is indeed gourmet: pasta dishes such as angel hair with wild mushrooms and duck, a New York steak with Gorgonzola-brandy sauce, rack of lamb roasted Greek style, fresh fish, and chicken or veal marsala. There's a good choice of sandwiches, pizzas, and appetizers.

**AL DENTE, in the Raintree Inn, U.S. 40. Tel. 726-4217.**
   **Cuisine:** ITALIAN. **Reservations:** Recommended.
**$ Prices:** Appetizers $4.25–$5.95; main courses $5.95–$13.95. MC, V.
   **Open:** Dinner only, daily 5–9:30pm.
Where is Al Denté? "Just pas-ta ski area," of course! Pasta is the calling card for this establishment about 1½ miles south of downtown Winter Park: For $5.95, you can fill your plate at the nightly pasta bar, and seconds are only 75¢ more. Southern Italian veal, beef, chicken, seafood, and vegetarian dishes, served with soup or salad, appeal to gourmets; a favorite is scampi saltimbocca, wrapped in prosciutto, topped with mozzarella, and served with pasta and vegetables.

### INEXPENSIVE

**BEV'S BUNNERY, Park Place Center. U.S. 40. Tel. 726-5774.**
   **Cuisine:** DELI.
**$ Prices:** Breakfast $1.75–$4.95; lunch $1.25–$4.95. MC, V.
   **Open:** Daily 7am–5pm.
You can't come to Bev's without trying the home-baked breads—such as Bavarian farmers rye, oat Komplet, or wheat-and-honey Müsli. Eat it as French toast, on the side with an omelet, with a bowl of hot soup, or on either side of a thick deli-style sandwich.

**CROOKED CREEK SALOON & EATERY, U.S. 40, Fraser. Tel. 726-9250.**
   **Cuisine:** AMERICAN/MEXICAN.
**$ Prices:** Breakfast $1.95–$5.95; lunch $2.95–$7.95; dinner appetizers $1.50–$5.95, main courses $3.95–$14.95. MC, V.
   **Open:** Daily 7am–10pm (bar, Mon–Sat 7am–2am, Sun 7am–midnight).
The Fraser Valley's favorite drinking spot, the Crooked Creek is opening eyes with biscuits and gravy, and steak and eggs, while its late-night crowd is still in dreamland. You can get an Awesome Fatboy Burger most anytime, a hearty bowl of green chili, or a rack of barbecued baby back ribs after 5pm. If you're especially hungry, 14 ounces of Kansas City steak will probably do the trick.

# 4. SUMMIT COUNTY
67 miles W of Denver, 114 miles NW of Colorado Springs,
23 miles E of Vail

**GETTING THERE   By Plane**   Visitors fly into **Denver's Stapleton International Airport,** and continue to Frisco, Breckenridge, Keystone, and/or Copper

Mountain via shuttle. **Resort Express** (tel. 303/468-7600, or 800/334-7433), **Schuss Transportation** (tel. 303/668-0500, or 800/999-1967), and **The Skiers' Connection** (tel. 303/668-0200, or 800/824-1104) have shuttle buses (rates about $26 one way); **Summit Limousine Service** (tel. 303/468-0117), based at Keystone Village, offers luxury transport to Summit County resorts.

**By Bus**   **Greyhound/Trailways** (tel. 303/668-5703) makes stops in Frisco, Copper Mountain, and Keystone.

**By Car**   I-70 runs through the middle of Summit County. For Keystone, exit on U.S. 6 at Dillon; the resort is 6 miles east of the interchange. For Breckenridge, exit on Colo. 9 at the county seat of Frisco; the resort town is 10 miles south. Copper Mountain is right on I-70 at the Colo. 91 interchange.

**SPECIAL EVENTS**   Summit County offers the following events: the **Ullr Fest,** on the third week of January, in Breckenridge; the **Ski Fiesta,** on the fourth Saturday of February, in Keystone; the **John Elway Celebrity Ski Race and Eenie Weenie Bikini Contest,** over the first weekend of April, in Copper Mountain; the **Beachin' at the Basin Spring Skiing Blowout,** over the Memorial Day weekend, in Arapahoe Basin; the **Keystone Music Festival,** from late June to mid-August, in Keystone; **Bach, Beethoven, and Breckenridge,** during all of July, in Breckenridge; **Michael Martin Murphey's West Fest,** over Labor Day weekend, in Copper Mountain; the **Breckenridge Festival of Film,** in the third week of September, in Breckenridge; **Frisco Founders Day,** on the third weekend of September, in Frisco; and the **Colorado Snow Sculpting Championships,** during the first full week of January, in Breckenridge.

---

**S**ummit County boomed during the late 19th-century silver and gold rushes. The single largest gold nugget ever found in Colorado—13 pounds, 7 ounces—was uncovered in 1887 by Breckenridge miner Tom Groves. Copper Mountain gained a reputation for the copper ore it produced around the same time, and Frisco was home to 3,500 miners, 19 dance halls, and 20 saloons. Dillon, relocated from its original townsite (flooded by the construction of Dillon Reservoir), once boasted the world's longest and highest ski jump. Historical sites throughout the county are readily shown by the Summit County and Frisco historical societies.

The economy of modern Summit County is tied to the growth in recreational sports—skiing in the winter; fishing, hiking, and biking in the summer—and to the real-estate boom that has accompanied it. Though skiers began coming to Arapahoe Basin in 1945 and to Loveland, just outside the county, in 1955, the winter-sports boom truly began with the opening of Breckenridge resort in 1961. Keystone opened in 1969 and Copper Mountain in 1972, putting five ski resorts within a 10-mile radius of Dillon Reservoir. Resort expansion and community growth continues today.

# ORIENTATION

Summit County's elevation at Dillon Reservoir is 9,015 feet; Keystone is at 9,300 feet, Breckenridge at 9,600 feet, and Copper Mountain Village at 9,700 feet. Full-time population of the county is about 5,000, some 25% of whom live in the county seat of Frisco.

**INFORMATION**   The main source of visitor information for the entire region is the **Summit County Chamber of Commerce,** P.O. Box 214, Frisco, CO 80443 (tel. 303/668-0376 or 468-6205, or 800/365-6365 for central reservations). The chamber has an information center at the junction of Colo. 9 and U.S. 6 (Summit Boulevard at Main Street), en route from I-70 to Breckenridge.

For additional information on the resort communities, contact the **Breckenridge**

**Resort Chamber,** 309 North Main Street (P.O. Box 1909), Breckenridge, CO 80424 (tel. 303/453-6018, or 800/221-1091); the **Copper Mountain Resort Association,** P.O. Box 3003, Copper Mountain, CO 80443 (tel. 303/968-6477, or 800/525-3891); **Keystone Resort,** P.O. Box 38, Keystone, CO 80435 (tel. 303/468-4126, or 800/222-0188); or the **Lake Dillon Resort Association,** P.O. Box 446, Dillon, CO 80435 (tel. 303/468-6222, or 800/365-6365).

**COUNTY LAYOUT**   The heart of Summit County is **Dillon Reservoir,** its arms reaching like an octopus to the southwest, where the county seat, **Frisco,** is located; to the south, pointing directly up the Blue River toward **Breckenridge;** to the north, site of the town of **Dillon;** and to the east, up U.S. 6, the artery to **Keystone, Arapahoe Basin,** and **Loveland Pass.** I-70 follows the western shore of the lake, separating Dillon from **Silverthorne** at the top end and swinging past **Copper Mountain** (6 miles south of Frisco) before climbing over Vail Pass.

## GETTING AROUND

**Summit Stage** (tel. 453-1241 or 453-1339) provides *free* year-round service between Frisco, Dillon, Silverthorne, Keystone, Breckenridge, and Copper Mountain, daily from 6:30am to 11:30pm. Expresses serve all destinations but Silverthorne during peak travel hours.

Taxi service is provided by **Around Town Taxi** (tel. 453-TAXI) in Breckenridge and **Summit Taxi** (tel. 468-8294) in Dillon/Silverthorne. You can get around Breckenridge on the free **Town Trolley** (tel. 453-2368, ext. 7272), and there's also free shuttle service within the Keystone Resort (tel. 468-2316).

## FAST FACTS

The **area code** for all of Summit County is 303. In case of **emergency,** call **911;** for regular business, call the Summit County Sheriff (tel. 453-2232). **Hospitals** include the Summit Medical Center, 0038 County Road 103, Frisco (tel. 668-3300), and the Breckenridge Medical Center, 410 South French Street, Breckenridge (tel. 453-6934). **Post offices** are at 400 Granite Street, Frisco (tel. 668-5505), and 300 South Ridge Street, Breckenridge (tel. 453-2310). State and county **taxes** add 9.45% to hotel bills. For **weather and road** conditions, call 453-1090.

## WHAT TO SEE & DO

### ATTRACTIONS

**BRECKENRIDGE SKI AREA, Breckenridge Ski Corporation, P.O. Box 1058, Breckenridge, CO 80424. Tel. 303/453-5000** or 303/453-6118 for snow reports.

Spread across three large mountains on the west side of the town of Breckenridge, this area ranks fourth in size among Colorado's ski resorts. Once known for its wealth of open, groomed beginner and intermediate slopes, Breckenridge in recent years has expanded its acreage for expert skiers as well.

**Peak 8,** the original ski mountain, is highest of the three at 12,998 feet and has the greatest variety. **Peak 9,** heavily geared to novices and intermediates, rises above the principal base area. **Peak 10,** served by a single quad chair, is predominantly expert territory. The vast back bowls of Peak 8, and the North Face of Peak 9, are likewise advanced terrain. There are restaurants high on Peaks 8 and 9, and three cafeterias at the base of the slopes.

All told, the resort has 1,600 skiable acres, with 112 trails served by 16 lifts—four quad chairs, one triple chair, eight double chairs, and three surface lifts for beginners—for an uphill capacity of 24,430 skiers per hour. Available vertical is 3,398 feet; average annual snowfall is 255 inches (over 21 feet).

Among Breckenridge's more interesting programs are its **Women's Ski Seminars,** taught exclusively by women for women skiers of all abilities. Four such seminars are offered during the year, over 3-day weekends in December, January, February, and March. "Women only" ski-school classes are available throughout the ski year.

**Admission:** Tickets, $36 a day adults, to as low as $29 a day for multiday tickets; $15 a day children 6–12 and seniors 60–69; free for children under 6 and seniors over 69. Full-day class lessons $36.

**Open:** Third Sat of Nov to the third Sun of Apr, daily 9am–3:45pm. **Closed** (for skiing): Last week of Apr to third week of Nov.

**COPPER MOUNTAIN RESORT, P.O. Box 3001, Copper Mountain, CO 80443. Tel. 303/968-2318,** or 800/458-8386; or 303/968-2100, or 800/457-5429 for snow report.

From Copper Mountain village, the avalanche chutes on the west face of Ten Mile Mountain seem to spell out the word *SKI*. Though this is a natural coincidence, Arapaho National Forest officials like to say that Copper has "terrain created for skiing."

What makes Copper special is its topography, naturally dividing the mountain into beginner, intermediate, and expert areas. The "American Flyer" lift serves the gentle novice runs on the lower slopes of 12,313-foot **Union Peak,** up to the right of the main day lodge, while the "American Eagle" climbs to the intermediate trails on the western flank of 12,360-foot **Copper Peak.** The eastern flank of Copper Peak drops off more sharply, and it is here, and in the high-altitude Spaulding and Resolution bowls, that most of the expert terrain lies.

The area has a vertical drop of 2,760 feet and 1,200 patrolled acres of skiing, with an additional 350 acres open to guided "extreme" skiing. The 76 trails are served by 20 lifts—two high-speed quad chairs, six triple chairs, eight double chairs, and four beginners' surface lifts—for an uphill capacity of 28,250 skiers per hour. The average annual snowfall is 255 inches (21 feet, 3 inches).

There are two restaurants on the mountain, and several more in the base village. Also at the base are 25km (15 miles) of cross-country track, an ice-skating pond, a full-service racquet and athletic club, and other amenities of a totally self-contained resort village.

**Admission:** Tickets, $68 adults for 2 days out of 3, to as low as $30 a day for 4- to 6-day tickets; $16 a day children 12 and under, for tickets of 3 or more days; $16 a day beginners; $24 a day seniors 60–69; free for seniors over 70. Equipment rentals average $19 a day; full-day class lessons start at $40.

**Open:** Mid-Nov to late Apr, Mon–Fri 9am–4pm, Sat–Sun 8:30am–4pm. **Closed:** Late Apr to mid-Nov.

**KEYSTONE RESORT, P.O. Box 38, Keystone, CO 80435. Tel. 303/468-4126,** or 800/451-5930; or 303/468-4111 for snow report.

Keystone is not only a superb mountain for intermediate skiers, it's also the single largest night-skiing mountain in America. It's possible to take the gondola to dinner in the Summit House atop 11,640-foot Keystone Mountain, then spend several hours working off your meal on 13 cruising trails, some as long as 3 miles.

The resort here (see "Where to Stay," below) was built from the ground up, and ski-area development has proceeded in much the same fashion. Spacious **Keystone Mountain** offers 500 acres of intermediate terrain and ample beginner slopes. Over its back side are **North Peak** and the new (in 1991–92) **Outback** region, both with advanced intermediate and expert runs. A second gondola now connects the Summit House with the Outpost, a new restaurant atop 11,660-foot North Peak. Keystone also manages **Arapahoe Basin** (see "Sports & Recreation," below), 5 miles distant.

Keystone's vertical drop is 2,340 feet; the North Peak/Outback complex has 1,920 of its own. Together, they offer nearly 1,100 acres of skiing, 71 trails, and 18 lifts—including two connecting high-speed gondolas, four quad chairs, three triple chairs, six double chairs, and three surface lifts. Total uphill capacity is almost 30,000 skiers per hour. Average annual snowfall is 230 inches (about 19 feet).

**Admission:** Tickets, $37 a day adults, to as low as $29 a day for multiday tickets;

$16 a day children 12 and under, or $14 a day for multiday tickets. Ticket prices include Arapahoe Basin. Equipment rentals average $15 a day; full-day class lessons start at $28.
**Open:** Late Oct to mid-Apr, daily 8:30am–10pm. **Closed:** mid-Apr to late Oct.

## AMAZE 'N BRECKENRIDGE, 710 S. Main St., Breckenridge. Tel. 453-7262.

Colorado's largest human maze, this a two-level labyrinth of twists and turns offers prizes to participants who can "beat the clock." There's also a grill-style restaurant, an indoor miniature golf course, and a video arcade.
**Admission:** $4 adults, $3 children 5–12, free for children under 5. Additional maze runs $2.
**Open:** Dec 21 to Jan 15 11am–7pm. Call for summer hours. **Closed:** Fall to mid-Dec.

## BRECKENRIDGE NATIONAL HISTORIC DISTRICT, Breckenridge. Tel. 453-9022.

The entire Victorian core of this 19th-century mining town has been carefully preserved. Colorfully painted shops and restaurants occupy the old businesses and homes, most of them dating from the 1880s and 1890s. The Summit Historical Society conducts guided 90-minute walking tours beginning from the Breckenridge Resort Chamber **Information Center** at 309 North Main Street. The main historic district focuses on Main Street, and extends east for two blocks on either side of Lincoln Avenue, for four blocks to High Street. Among the 254 buildings in the district are the 1909 **Summit County Courthouse,** 200 East Lincoln Avenue; and the **William Harrison Briggle House,** 104 North Harris Street, which houses the historical society's decorative-arts museum. The society also leads tours to the outskirts of town to visit the underground shaft of the hardrock **Washington Gold Mine** and the gold-panning operation at **Lomax Placer Gulch.**
**Admission:** Tours, $3–$5 adults, $2 ages 4–12.
**Open:** June–Aug, Wed–Sun 10am–4pm by appointment.

## DILLON SCHOOLHOUSE MUSEUM, Summit Historical Society, 403 E. LaBonte St., Dillon. Tel. 468-6079.

A one-room country school—filled with such artifacts of early Colorado education as desks with inkwells, McGuffey readers, and scientific teaching apparatus—is the highlight of Dillon's "historic park." Also on the site are the 1885 Lula Myers ranchhouse and the Depression-era Honeymoon Cabin. All buildings were moved from Old Dillon (now beneath the waters of the reservoir) or Keystone. Tours are conducted to the 1884 Montezuma Schoolhouse, located at 10,200 feet elevation in the 1860s mining camp of Montezuma.
**Admission:** By donation.
**Open:** Dillon Museum, Memorial Day–Labor Day, Wed–Sun 11am–4pm; or by appointment. Montezuma Schoolhouse, July 4 to mid-Aug, Sat only.

## FRISCO HISTORICAL SOCIETY MUSEUM AND HISTORIC PARK, 120 Main St., Frisco. Tel. 668-3428.

Located in the turn-of-the-century Staley House, this museum presents an interpretive exhibit of life-styles on the Continental Divide during the early part of the 20th century.
**Admission:** Free.
**Open:** Summer, Tues–Sun 11am–4pm; winter, Tues–Sat 11am–4pm.

## SPORTS & RECREATION

Two national forests—**Arapaho National Forest** and **White River National Forest**—overlap the boundaries of Summit County. These recreational playgrounds offer opportunities not only for downhill and cross-country skiing, but also for hiking and backpacking, horseback riding, boating, fishing, hunting, and bicycling in summer, and for snowmobiling and other cold-weather pursuits in winter. White

River National Forest encompasses the **Eagles Nest Wilderness Area** and Arapaho National Forest includes **Green Mountain Reservoir,** both in the northern part of the county.

The U.S. Forest Service's Dillon Ranger District (tel. 468-5400) has maps and guides to hiking trails, bike paths, campsites, and two- and four-wheel-drive tours. The USFS's *"Recreation Opportunity Guide"* is available at visitors centers.

**ALPINE SLIDE**   Peak 8 at Breckenridge has a dual-track alpine slide during the summer months. Call 453-2368 for schedules and ticket information.

**BICYCLING**   Whether you're a touring bicyclist or a mountain biker, Summit County can accommodate you. There are more than 40 miles of paved **bicycle paths** in the county, including a 35-mile path from Breckenridge (with a spur from Keystone) to Frisco and Copper Mountain, continuing across Vail Pass to Vail. This spectacularly beautiful two-lane path is off-limits to motorized vehicles of any kind.

More energetic cyclists can try the **Devil's Triangle,** a difficult 80-mile loop that begins and ends in Frisco after climbing four mountain passes (including 11,318-ft. Fremont Pass) and visiting five towns.

Numerous trails beckon mountain bikers into the wilderness. Some of them retrace 19th-century mining roads and burro trails, often ending in ghost towns.

Summit County's premier race event for mountain bikers is the annual **Fall Classic,** a 2-day, three-stage race organized by the Breckenridge Fat Tire Society (tel. 453-1872). Several **Summit Mountain Challenges** are organized as recreational races for beginners as well as experts. Other annual events include **Women on Wheels,** a weekend of mountain biking, maintenance training, and seminars designed exclusively for women; and the **Day of the Bicycle,** celebrating bicycling with a postride party and prizes.

Rentals, repairs, and general information can be obtained from **Cycopath Skis & Bikes,** 116 North Main Street, Breckenridge (tel. 453-9231); **Kodi Rafting & Bikes,** Bell Tower Mall, Breckenridge (tel. 303/453-2194, or 800/525-9624); and **Wilderness Sports,** Summit Place Center, Colo. 9 at I-70, Silverthorne (tel. 468-8519).

**BOATING**   Summit County is graced by two beautiful mountain lakes for watersports enthusiasts: **Dillon Reservoir,** often called Lake Dillon, on I-70 between Dillon and Frisco; and **Green Mountain Reservoir,** about 25 miles northwest of Silverthorne on Colo. 9.

At 9,000 feet elevation, Dillon Reservoir claims to be the home of America's highest yacht club. Colorful regattas are scheduled most weekends throughout the summer. The **Dillon Marina,** Marine Drive, Dillon (tel. 468-5100), offers hourly rentals of powerboats, sailboats, fishing boats, and pontoon boats in summer daily between 8am and 7pm. Lake tours and canoe rentals are available from **Osprey Adventures,** 810 Main Street, Frisco (tel. 668-5573).

The **marina at Green Mountain Reservoir** in Heeney (tel. 369-4632) also rents boats. Sailing, waterskiing, and board sailing are popular activities.

**DOG SLEDDING**   You can get pulled behind a team of nine huskies with **Snow Cap's Dog Sled Rides,** Breckenridge (tel. 453-0276). Five different trips leave daily in winter between 9:30am and 1:30pm.

**FISHING**   There are great trout streams throughout the county. Popular for brook, brown, cutthroat, lake, and rainbow trout, as well as kokanee salmon, are the Blue River, Ten Mile River, Snake River, and Straight Creek. For lake fishing, try Dillon River, Green Mountain Reservoir, and Pass Lake. The **Blue River,** from Lake Dillon Dam to its confluence with the Colorado River at Kremmling, is rated a Gold Medal–category fishing stream.

**Mountain Angler,** 311 South Main Street, Breckenridge (tel. 453-4665), offers year-round guide service, fly-fishing instruction, and tackle and license sales.

**GOLF**   The county has four golf courses. The **Breckenridge Golf Club,** 200 Clubhouse Drive, Breckenridge (tel. 453-9104), is a public course designed by Jack

Nicklaus. The **Copper Creek Golf Club,** Wheeler Circle, Copper Mountain Resort (tel. 968-2339), at 9,650 feet is the highest 18-hole course in North America. The **Keystone Ranch Golf Course,** Keystone Ranch Road, Keystone (tel. 468-4250), designed by Robert Trent Jones, Jr., is rated by *Golf Digest* as the leading resort course in Colorado, and one of the top 50 in the United States. The **Eagles Nest Golf Club,** Colo. 9, 3 miles north of Silverthorne (tel. 468-0681), is another 18-hole course.

**HIKING & BACKPACKING** The **Colorado Trail** cuts a swath through Summit County. It enters from the east across Kenosha Pass, follows the Swan River to its confluence with the Blue River, then climbs over Ten Mile Mountain to Copper Mountain. The trail then turns southerly toward the Tennessee Pass, north of Leadville.

There are myriad hiking opportunities in the national forests and the Eagles Nest Wilderness Area. Consult the U.S. Forest Service office or a visitor information center for maps and details.

**HORSEBACK RIDING** One of the most popular rides in Summit County is the breakfast ride offered by **Breckenridge Stables** at Breckenridge Mountain Lodge, 600 South Ridge Street, Breckenridge (tel. 453-4438). Call for reservations for this and other rides. The **Eagles Nest Equestrian Center,** Colo. 9, 3 miles north of Silverthorne (tel. 468-0677), offers trail rides in summer, sleigh rides in winter.

**ICE SKATING** All three major resort communities boast groomed ponds for ice skating. Rentals and lessons are available at all. **Keystone Lake** is the largest outdoor rink in the United States; it's open in winter, daily from 10am to 5pm and 6 to 10pm. **Maggie Pond,** at the base of Peak 9 at Breckenridge, is open daily from 9am to 9pm. Copper Mountain's **West Lake** offers free skating for resort guests daily from noon to 10pm.

**RIVER RAFTING** Trips through the white water of the Blue River—which runs through Breckenridge to Frisco—as well as longer journeys on the Colorado and Arkansas rivers are offered by various companies. They include the **Adventure Company,** 101 Ski Hill Road, Breckenridge (tel. 453-0747); **Kodi Rafting & Bikes,** Bell Tower Mall, Breckenridge (tel. 303/453-2194, or 800/525-9624); and **Performance Tours,** 110 Ski Hill Road, Breckenridge (tel. 303/453-0661, or 800/328-RAFT).

**SKIING (ALPINE)** One of the highlights of skiing in Summit County is the **Ski the Summit Pass,** an interchangeable multiday ticket that allows purchasers to ski at Breckenridge, Copper Mountain, Keystone, and Arapahoe Basin for one price. It can be bought at any of the resorts; the cost is $33 per day for adults, $17 per day for children 6 to 12, for 4 days or 6 days.

The three larger resorts are discussed in "Attractions" above. The fourth, **Arapahoe Basin,** on U.S. 6, between Keystone and Loveland Pass, is one of Colorado's oldest, having opened in 1945. It is now operated by Keystone Resort, P.O. Box 38, Keystone, CO 80435 (tel. 303/468-4126, or 800/451-5930). Several features make Arapahoe exceptional. Most of its acreage is intermediate and expert terrain, much of it above timberline, and it is traditionally the last Colorado ski area to close for the season—often not until early June. Arapahoe offers a 1,670-foot vertical, from its summit at 12,450 feet to its base at 10,780 feet. It is served by one triple and four double chairs. Full-day tickets are $33 for adults, $20 for seniors 60 to 69, $16 for children 6 to 12; children under 6 and seniors over 69 ski free.

Just across the county line, on the east side of I-70's Eisenhower Memorial Tunnel through the Continental Divide, is the **Loveland ski area,** P.O. Box 899, Georgetown, CO 80444 (tel. 303/569-3203). Comprised of Loveland Basin and Loveland Valley, it was created in the late 1930s by a Denver ski club because of its heavy annual snowfall (375 inches, or more than 31 feet). You can still see the original rope-tow cabins from 1942, when all-day tickets cost $2. (Tickets are now $28 for adults, $15 for seniors 60 to 69, $12 for children 6 to 12; children under 6 and seniors over 69 ski free.) There's good beginner-intermediate terrain here, with a vertical of

1,430 feet and a base elevation of 10,800 feet. Lifts include one quad chair, two triples, and five doubles. The resort is Colorado's first to open, in mid-October, and it generally remains open until mid-May.

Skiers who want a backcountry experience on untracked wilderness peaks can call **Colorado Heli Ski** in Frisco (tel. 303/668-5600, or 800/TRY-HELI-SKI). Helicopters serve 150 square miles of the White River National Forest, at a cost of $80 to $425 for scenic charters and guided runs.

There are literally dozens of shops throughout Summit County from which to rent or buy ski equipment and clothing. They include **Blue River Sports,** 600 South Park Street, Breckenridge (tel. 303/453-1110, or 800/525-9823), across the street from the Peak 9 Quicksilver lift; **Mountain View Sports,** Mountain View Plaza, U.S. 6, Keystone (tel. 468-0396); **Rebel Sports,** 100 West Ski Hill Road, Breckenridge (tel. 453-2565) and 154 Wheeler Place, Copper Mountain (tel. 303/968-6644, or 800/228-4757); and **Virgin Islands Ski Rental,** Summit Place Shopping Center, U.S. 6 off I-70 Exit 205, Silverthorne (tel. 303/468-6655, or 800/525-9186).

**SKIING (NORDIC)** The **Frisco Nordic Center,** on Colo. 9 east of Frisco (tel. 668-0866), sits on the shore of Dillon Reservoir. Its trail network includes 35km (21 miles) of set tracks and access to backcountry trails. The lodge has a cafeteria and a shop with rentals and retail sales; cross-country instruction is also offered. The masterplan for the Nordic Center was developed by Olympic silver medalist Bill Koch, probably America's greatest nordic skier of the last 50 years. Open November to April, daily from 9am to 4pm, it charges $8 a day for adult tickets.

Peak's Trail connects the Frisco Nordic Center to the **Breckenridge Nordic Ski Center,** on Willow Lane near the foot of Peak 8 (tel. 453-6855), and the **Whatley Ranch,** 2 miles north of Breckenridge (tel. 453-2600). Trail tickets are interchangeable among the three centers. Copper Mountain has its own **Trak Cross-Country Center** at Union Creek (tel. 968-2318, ext. 6342), at the west end of the resort village. See "Skiing (Alpine)" for more equipment rental information.

**SLEIGH RIDES** Sleigh rides are offered by **Alpine Adventures,** Breckenridge (tel. 453-0111); **Eagles Nest Sleigh Rides,** Colo. 9, Silverthorne (tel. 468-0677); **Nordic Sleigh Rides,** Ski Hill Road, Breckenridge (tel. 453-2005); and **Two Below Zero Sleighrides,** Frisco Nordic Center (tel. 453-1520).

**SNOWBOARDING** Snowboard enthusiasts can get equipment and lessons from **First Tracks Snowboarding Ltd.,** 311 South Main Street, Breckenridge (tel. 453-4049).

**SNOWMOBILING** Snowmobilers can join guided tours or rent machines from **Back Country Adventures,** Dillon (tel. 468-1040); **Good Time Rentals,** 402 Main Street, Frisco (tel. 668-0930); or **Tiger Run Tours,** 128 South Main Street, Breckenridge (tel. 453-2231). The latter company leads tours to old ghost towns and mining camps, including an excursion to the Dry Gulch gold camp for dinner.

**WINTER ADVENTURE PARK** At **Summit Adventure Park,** 16197 Colo. 9 at Swan Mountain Road, east of Frisco (tel. 303/453-0353, or 800/253-0723), you can take a guided snowmobile trip, ride an inner tube down a 45° slope, race around the Yamaha Snoscoot track, or enjoy a sleigh ride. There are fees for each activity. Open in winter, daily from 8am to 10pm.

## SHOPPING

**IN BRECKENRIDGE** A variety of shops and galleries occupy the historic buildings along Breckenridge's Main Street.

Of particular interest in the realm of art are the work of R. C. Gorman, Star York, and other New Mexico artisans in the **Meerdink Gallery,** Plaza Building 1 in the Village at Breckenridge Resort, 655 South Park Street (tel. 453-9688); Bev Doolittle's striking camouflage oils at the **Silver Shadows Gallery** in the Four Seasons Mall, 411 South Main Street (tel. 453-4938); and the unique handcrafted jewelry in the **Skilled Hands Gallery,** 110 South Main Street (tel. 453-7818).

## EVENING ENTERTAINMENT

Summer festivals are the big cultural events of the year in Summit County. Breckenridge hosts two music festivals and a film festival, Keystone has a summer-long music festival, and Copper Mountain has a major end-of-summer event.

**SPECIAL EVENTS** The Breckenridge Music Institute's Festival of Music at the Summit, more commonly known as ✪ **Bach, Beethoven and Breckenridge,** runs for a full month from late June to late July. Musicians from leading orchestras and universities across the United States perform choral, pops, and jazz concerts, string and vocal quartets, woodwind and brass quintets, with guest conductors. Concerts are at 8pm most nights in the Event Tent in the center of Breckenridge; tickets are $8 to $20, with discounts for students and seniors. Contact the Breckenridge Music Institute, P.O. Box 1254, Breckenridge, CO 80424 (tel. 303/453-9142).

**Genuine Jazz in July,** the second weekend of the month, showcases Colorado jazz ensembles with styles ranging from Dixieland to bebop to New Age. Breckenridge bars and nightclubs host Friday- and Saturday-night performances; a weekend pass to all participating clubs costs $25, or $15 for 1 night. Free Saturday- and Sunday-afternoon concerts are outdoors at Maggie Pond, at the base of Peak 9.

The **Breckenridge Festival of Film,** held the third full weekend of September, attracts Hollywood directors and actors to town to judge and discuss over 20 films in all genres. The casual interaction between stars and attendees makes this festival unique. Past guests have included Alan Arkin, Angie Dickinson, Elliot Gould, James Earl Jones, Malcolm McDowell, Mary Steenburgen, Rod Steiger, Donald Sutherland, and Jon Voight. Contact the Breckenridge Festival of Film office for information (tel. 453-6200).

The ✪ **Keystone Music Festival** includes performances by the 90-piece National Repertory Orchestra and the Summit Brass throughout the summer, from late June to mid-August. Concerts are held most Wednesdays and Saturdays at 7pm in the 1,000-seat Keystone Pavilion (at the end of Mountain House Road), with occasional other presentations. Music ranges from pops to classical and chamber. Conductors typically discuss works with concertgoers before each performance. Tickets for most concerts are $12 or $14. For information, contact Keystone Resort (tel. 468-2316).

Every Labor Day weekend, Copper Mountain is the scene for country singer **Michael Martin Murphey's West Fest.** The 3-day event focuses on the art, culture, and music of the American West with a full slate of guest appearances. For information, contact Copper Mountain Resort (tel. 968-2882).

**BARS & CLUBS** Breckenridge is the nightlife capital of Summit County, but every community has its watering holes and dance spots.

Popular bars in Breckenridge include the **Breckenridge Brewery & Pub,** 600 South Main Street (tel. 453-1550), whose microbrews include Avalanche, a full-bodied amber ale called "the one you can't get away from"; **Colt's Downunder Sports Bar,** 401 South Main Street (tel. 453-6060), where the sounds of a live "oldies" band called 24 Karat Gold often drown out the sounds of Australian rules football shown on 13 big-screen satellite TVs; the **Gold Pan Saloon,** 105 North Main Street (tel. 453-5499), which claims to be the oldest continuously operated bar west of the Mississippi River; and **JohSha's,** 500 South Park Street (tel. 453-4146), currently the most popular live-music dance club in town.

In Frisco, **Moose Jaw Food & Spirits,** 208 Old Main Street (tel. 668-3931), is a burgers, pool, and darts hangout. Silverthorne's **Old Dillon Inn,** 321 Blue River Parkway (tel. 468-2791), serves terrific margaritas across an 1875 Old West bar. Copper Mountain offers live music for dancing at **O'Shea's Copper Bar** in the Copper Junction Building (tel. 968-2318, ext. 6504). In Keystone, the **Snake River Saloon,** 23074 U.S. 6 (tel. 468-2788), has live rock music nightly all winter, weekends in summer, and has been called one of America's great ski bars by *Playboy*.

**THEATER** The **Backstage Theatre,** Bell Tower Mall, in the Village at Breckenridge, 605 South Park Street (tel. 453-0199), has presented lighthearted stage productions during the winter season since 1975.

# WHERE TO STAY

Thousands of rooms are available at the various Summit County resorts at any given time. Even so, during peak seasons, finding accommodation may be difficult. **Summit County Central Reservations** (tel. 800/365-6365) can assist, as can **Breckenridge Central Reservations** (tel. 303/453-2918, or 800/221-1091).

Seasons vary somewhat from hotel to hotel, condo to condo, but some generalizations can be made. Rates will be highest during the holiday season—mid-December through the New Year's holidays—and next highest during the peak ski season, January through March. (Some establishments discount January and even early February, focusing higher rates on school vacation periods.) Early ski season (until mid-December) and late season (the first few weeks of April) are almost as low-priced as summer. The spring "mud season" (the end of ski season until the end of public school in June), and fall (usually mid-September to mid-November), are the least expensive times.

## BRECKENRIDGE

### Expensive

**BEAVER RUN RESORT AND CONFERENCE CENTER, 620 Village Rd. (P.O. Box 2115), Breckenridge, CO 80424. Tel. 303/453-6000,** or 800/288-1282. Fax 303/453-4284. 224 rms, 326 suites. TV TEL

**$ Rates:** Mid-Apr to mid-Nov, $75–$80 single or double; $90–$95 studio; $95–$125 one-bedroom; $135–$180 two-bedroom. Mid-Nov to mid-Dec, $100 single or double; $125 studio; $150–$175 one-bedroom; $240–$295 two-bedroom. Holiday periods, $190 single or double; $235 studio; $270–$325 one-bedroom; $460–$535 two-bedroom. Jan to mid-Apr, $125–$145 single or double; $150–$180 studio; $185–$235 one-bedroom; $295–$410 two-bedroom. Three- and four-bedroom units also available. AE, CB, DC, DISC, JCB, MC, V.
**Parking:** Free underground lot.

Over 800 staff serve guests at this spacious conference hotel, which consists of four separate buildings connected by covered walkways. Located at the foot of the Peak 10 slopes, with superb year-round athletic facilities, this is a favorite of corporate visitors.

Room styles vary from standard hotel rooms to four-bedroom premium suites. Hotel rooms are simple but nice, with southwestern motifs; they have two queen-size beds and the usual furnishings. Deluxe studios have intimate double spa tubs, efficiency kitchenettes, and soft contemporary pastel decor. One-bedroom units all have fireplaces and balconies, plus full kitchens with refrigerators. Two-bedroom town homes have two queen-size beds in one room, one in the other, and two bathrooms; including the hideaway sofa, they can sleep eight.

**Dining/Entertainment:** Spencer's is one of Breckenridge's outstanding restaurants, serving three meals daily in a casual contemporary setting. Steak and seafood choices dominate the dinner menu, priced $15.95 to $24.95. Meals are also served in the Copper Top Bar and Restaurant and G. B. Watson's Mercantile deli/pizzeria. Tiffany's Night Club dominates the evening lounge action; three other bars include one poolside, open in summer.

**Services:** Concierge, valet laundry, free shuttle, ski storage, day-care program, no-smoking rooms, facilities for the disabled.

**Facilities:** Outdoor and indoor/outdoor swimming pools, seven hot tubs, saunas, massage therapy, weight and exercise room, three tennis courts, miniature golf, games room, four guest laundries, ski shop, gift shop, meeting space for 650.

**BRECKENRIDGE SPA, 112 Edwards Dr. (P.O. Box 391), Breckenridge, CO 80424. Tel. 303/453-9300** or 800/736-1607. Fax 303/453-0625. 30 rms, 15 suites. TV TEL

**$ Rates:** Mid-Nov to mid-Apr (except holidays), $115 single; $135–$150 double; $165 suite. Christmas and spring vacation (Feb) weeks, $130 single; $155–$165 double; $175 suite. Mid-Apr to mid-June and late Sept to mid-Nov, $60 single;

$75–$85 double; $95 suite. Mid-June to late Sept, $75 single; $90–$110 double; $120 suite. **Closed:** May. AE, DISC, MC, V.

From below, this refurbished log building—a European-style spa with a Rocky Mountain atmosphere—looks like a mountaintop Tibetan monastery. Once you've entered through the landscaped garden, you'll find a superb view. Stone fireplaces and deer-antler chandeliers add a regional touch.

Each room has a different theme, but all feature country elegance in a rustic setting. They typically have hardwood floors, Southwest decor and artwork, balconies (or views), and two queen-size beds. The Longs Peak Room has colorful floral prints in a rustic setting, pedestal sinks, and other antique touches. The Mount Lincoln Room has a Native American theme; the Crestone Peak Room, quilts. Suites have sitting areas and kitchens with refrigerators and microwaves.

**Dining/Entertainment:** Three meals daily are served in the western ambience of the Summit. Dinners ($13.95 to $19.95) feature international dishes, steaks, and seafood. Summer buffets are presented on an outdoor deck with an 18-foot canopied river-rock grill and mining cars full of salads, pastas, and drinks.

**Services:** Room service, concierge, complimentary shuttle for skiers and dinner guests.

**Facilities:** Full spa services (massage, wraps, skin treatments, fitness consulations), three-story athletic club (with weight/exercise facilities and racquetball courts), outdoor swimming pool, hot tub, sauna; meeting space for 100.

**RIVER MOUNTAIN LODGE, 100 S. Park St. (P.O. Box 7188), Breckenridge, CO 80424. Tel. 303/453-4711,** or 800/325-2342, 800/553-4456 in Colorado. Fax 303/453-4711, ext. 7012. 55 suites. TV TEL

**$ Rates** (including breakfast): Early/late season, $90 studio; $120–$135 one-bedroom. Holiday periods, $185 studio; $220–$235 one-bedroom. Jan to mid-Feb, $125 studio; $150 one-bedroom. Mid-Feb to Mar, $165 studio; $195–$205 one-bedroom. Mid-Apr to mid-Nov, $60–$70 studio; $70–$95 one-bedroom. Studio lofts and penthouses (both sleep four) also available. Children 12 and under stay free in parents' room. AE, DISC, MC, V. **Parking:** Free underground lot.

Cross a covered bridge over the Blue River to reach this pleasant accommodation at the foot of Peak 9. Very popular with vacationing British skiers, it has an English-pub-style Fireside Lounge at the entry. You can ski in from the slopes on the Four o'Clock Run, but you must hop a shuttle to the lifts.

One of the truly nice features is that every guest room has a private washer/dryer! Studios have a queen-size Murphy bed and sofa sleeper, a full kitchen, and a balcony or walkout patio. The one-bedroom units have queen-size beds, fireplaces, and walk-through baths. Studio lofts have an additional queen with a sky-lit three-quarter bath at the top of a circular staircase.

**Dining/Entertainment:** There's live music Thursday through Saturday in winter. A lounge is open daily in winter, weekends the rest of the year.

**Services:** Facilities for the disabled.

**Facilities:** Small health club with weights, steam room, sauna, aerobics studio, tanning; ski shop; three hot tubs (two outdoors); meeting space for 100.

**THE VILLAGE AT BRECKENRIDGE, 655 S. Park St. (P.O. Box 8329), Breckenridge, CO 80424. Tel. 303/453-2000,** or 800/800-7829. Fax 303/453-3116. 60 rms, 395 suites. TV TEL

**$ Rates:** Mid-Apr to mid-Dec, $85 single or double; $90–$105 studio; $125 one-bedroom; $175–$235 two-bedroom. Holiday season, $140 single or double; $155–$175 studio; $235 one-bedroom; $345–$535 two-bedroom. Regular season, hotel $115–$135 single or double; $125–$160 studio; $170–$195 one-bedroom; $225–$475 two-bedroom. Three-bedroom units also available. AE, DISC, MC, V. **Parking:** Free underground lot.

As the name implies, this really is a village. Eleven buildings, spread across 18½ acres of grounds, include guest rooms, restaurants, lounges, ski and sports shops, clothing stores, recreation centers, and everything else a visitor might need. The lower terminal of Peak 9's Quicksilver Chair is within the Village, so you could enjoy a Breckenridge ski vacation without seeing anything else of Breckenridge!

Accommodations run the gamut from hotel rooms and studios with kitchenettes to three-bedroom condominium suites. Standard hotel rooms are in the Village Hotel, studio suites in the Liftside Inn, deluxe hotel suites in the Hotel Breckenridge, condominium units in Plaza Condominiums, and deluxe condo units in the Châteaux. All are tastefully appointed; hotel rooms, though lacking the cooking facilities of other units, still feature coffee makers for early-morning get-up-and-go.

**Dining/Entertainment:** Ten restaurants and lounges are part of the complex. Serving steak, pasta, Mexican, Chinese, and other foods, they include the Breckenridge Cattle Co. in Plaza I, the Café Breck in Plaza III, Jake T. Pounder's in the Village Hotel, the Village Pasta Company, and Bamboo Gardens in the Bell Tower Mall. The Gold Strike Saloon at the base of Peak 9 is a town watering hole.

**Services:** Ski storage, concierge, baby-sitting, valet laundry, no-smoking rooms, facilities for the disabled.

**Facilities:** Two health clubs, with 12 indoor/outdoor hot tubs, steam room, saunas, two swimming pools, racquetball, weight and exercise equipment, massage therapy, chiropractor, and paddleboats in summer; meeting space for 600; 26 guest laundries, hair salon, video arcade.

## Moderate to Inexpensive

**RIDGE STREET INN BED & BREAKFAST, 212 N. Ridge St. (P.O. Box 2854), Breckenridge, CO 80424. Tel. 303/453-4680.** 4 rms (2 with bath), plus dormitory beds.

**$ Rates** (including full breakfast): Early and late season, $65 single or double without bath, $75 single or double with bath; $25 dorm bed. Holiday season, $85 single or double without bath, $95 single or double with bath; $30 dorm bed. Regular season, $78 single or double without bath, $88 single or double with bath; $30 dorm bed. Summer, $40 single or double without bath, $45 single or double with bath; $15 dorm bed. **Closed:** Mid-Apr to late May. MC, V.

Carol Brownson's 1890 Victorian, once the home of merchant John Roby and his family, serves different clienteles. Downstairs off the kitchen are two large bedrooms, both with private baths and their own entrances. Upstairs off the library nook are two more bedrooms, which share one bathroom. At the top of the stairs are dormitory rooms: one with six bunks (usually saved for men), another with four bunks (for women), and a loft with two bunks. Two bathrooms serve the dorms. Everyone gets the same gourmet breakfast; no one is permitted to smoke in the house.

**SWISS INN BED AND BREAKFAST, 205 S. French St. (P.O. Box 556), Breckenridge, CO 80424. Tel. 303/453-6489.** Fax 303/453-4915. 4 rms (all with bath), 2 dorms (shared bath).

**$ Rates** (including full breakfast): Winter, $65–$85 single or double; $25–$30 dorm bed. Summer, $35–$45 single or double; $10–$15 dorm bed. No credit cards.

Swiss chef Dan Gnos and his wife, Sandy, own this classic Victorian, located on the shuttle-bus line two blocks off Main Street. Gnos's culinary skills grace the breakfast table every morning. As at the Ridge Street Inn, there are dormitory bunks for frugal travelers, rooms with private or shared baths for others more well-heeled. All guests converge on two cozy lounges with Franklin-style fireplaces—one with cable TV, the other a reading room—or the hot tub, especially popular in winter.

**WILLIAMS HOUSE 1885 BED & BREAKFAST, 303 N. Main St. (P.O. Box 2454), Breckenridge, CO 80424. Tel. 303/453-2975.** 4 rms (all with bath).

**$ Rates** (including full breakfast): Winter, $89–$106 single or double. Holiday periods, $125 single or double. Summer, $55–$65 single or double. **Closed:** May and Oct. AE

Late 19th-century antiques grace every room of this charming historic home, originally the home of Emma Asmintas Williams. Diane Jaynes and Fred Kinat now own the B&B, which has a sun room, a parlor with a fireplace, and a living room with a television and high-tech sound system. All rooms have private baths; marble-top vanities and bathrobes are special touches. Baked egg dishes are the breakfast favorite. Smoking, children, and pets are all taboo.

## COPPER MOUNTAIN

**CLUB MED–COPPER MOUNTAIN, 50 Beeler Place, Copper Mountain, CO 80443. Tel. 303/968-2161,** or 800/CLUB-MED. Fax 303/968-2166.

**$ Rates** (per person, double occupancy): Early or late season, $135; holiday periods, $190–$205; regular season, $140–$180. Reduced rates for weekly stays and for children 3–11. **Closed:** Late Apr to early Nov. AE, MC, V.

One of only two American entries in this famed international chain of "jet-set" resorts (the other is in Florida), Club Med occupies a modern seven-story lodge near the west end of Copper Mountain village. The main doors open to a central cocktail lounge beside a cozy fireplace, creating an immediate atmosphere of leisure.

Guest rooms are simple but adequate. All have twin beds, full bathrooms, and attractive appointments. Many have mountain views.

One of the main draws is the 40-instructor Club Med ski school, the only one in the United States that uses the French method of training. Adult and children's lessons, as well as snowboarding instruction, are offered.

**Dining/Entertainment:** The main dining room serves three buffet-style meals daily. On the lower level are a more intimate restaurant for private dining, and a nightclub featuring live entertainment and dancing.

**Services:** Transportation from Denver airport (fee).

**Facilities:** Outdoor Jacuzzi, sauna, exercise and aerobics classes, big-screen TV, theater, boutique, ski-rental shop, guest laundry.

**COPPER MOUNTAIN RESORT, I-70 Exit 195 (P.O. Box 3001), Copper Mountain, CO 80443. Tel. 303/968-2882,** or 800/458-8386. Fax 303/968-2308. 600 units (all with bath). A/C TV TEL

**$ Rates:** Early and late season, $80–$120 single or double; $135–$170 one-bedroom; $195–$265 two-bedroom. Regular season, $135–$160 single or double; $190–$230 one-bedroom; $315–$390 two-bedroom. Holiday season, $120–$170 single or double; $170–$255 one-bedroom; $250–$425 two-bedroom. Summer, $70 single or double; $125 one-bedroom; $200 two-bedroom. Higher rates for three- and four-bedroom suites and penthouse suites. AE, CB, DC, DISC, JCB, MC, V.

The vast majority of rooms in Copper Mountain village are condominium units, managed by the resort's Copper Mountain Lodging Services division or five other private management firms. The Copper Mountain Resort Association provides central reservation services for all. Ranging from simple hotel rooms and efficiency studios to luxurious town homes of one to four bedrooms along the golf course, they are all within walking distance of ski lifts.

All guests register at the Village Square, at the end of Ten Mile Circle; rooms here have kitchens, fireplaces, and a sort of whitewashed Santa Fe appearance. The five-story Telemark Inn, on Beeler Place, features one-bedroom lofts and Murphy-bed studios with full kitchens and fireplaces. At the other end of the spectrum, The Woods and The Greens at Copper Creek are elegant homes away from home.

**Dining/Entertainment:** Resort restaurants include the Clubhouse (tel. 968-2882, ext. 6514), serving breakfast and lunch year round, winter fondues, and summer barbecues Wednesday through Sunday evenings. Farley's Tavern and Steakhouse, in the Snowflake Building (tel. 968-2577), features steaks, seafood, and nightly light rock. Jacques' Loft, on the third floor of the Center (ext. 6515), with pizza and sandwiches daily, big-screen TV for sports, and live rock music Thursday through Saturday nights. Others are O'Shea's Copper Bar, in the Copper Junction Building (see "Where to Dine," below); Pesce Fresco, on the second floor of the Mountain Plaza Building (ext. 6505), with seafood and pasta specialties and a seasonal jazz piano bar; and Rackets Restaurant, in the athletic club (see "Where to Dine," below). There are several other restaurants in the village, and four more on the mountain. The Copper Commons lounge in the day lodge also offers après-ski entertainment.

**Services:** Concierge, shuttle service, valet laundry, ski storage, no-smoking rooms, facilities for the disabled.

**Facilities:** Guests have free use of the $3-million Copper Mountain Racquet and Athletic Club, which has a swimming pool, hot tubs, saunas, steam rooms, weight and exercise room, tanning beds, racquetball and indoor tennis courts, a nursery, and a pro shop. Individual properties may also have a pool, sauna, and/or Jacuzzi. Most have guest laundries. Other resort facilities include a medical center, fire station, travel agency, post office, service station, chapel, grocery and many other shops. There's meeting space for 700.

## DILLON/SILVERTHORNE

**ALPEN HUTTE, 471 Rainbow Dr. (P.O. Box 919), Silverthorne, CO 80498. Tel. 303/468-6336.** 66 dormitory beds (shared bath).
**$ Rates:** Winter, $20–$25 dorm bed; summer, $12–$15 dorm bed. Lower prices for Youth Hostel Association members. DISC, MC, V.

Summit County's response to European skiers' hostels, the Alpen Hutte has much in common with its youth-hostel cousins: midday closure (9:30am to 3:30pm), a midnight curfew, and a handful of in-house regulations. But it remains one of the best deals around for hard-core skiers. There are four to eight bunks per room, and two large bathrooms per floor. One bedroom is handicapped-equipped. Guests share a TV room and a living room with a stone fireplace and overstuffed sofas. Owner Fran Colson and her son, Dave, add a small charge for breakfast and dinner, if desired.

**BLUE VALLEY GUEST HOUSE, Blue River Route 9, Dillon, CO 80435. Tel. 303/468-5731,** or 800/530-3866. 3 rms (2 with bath).
**$ Rates** (including continental breakfast): Winter, $70 single or double without bath, $80 single or double with bath; summer, $50 single or double without bath, $60 single or double with bath. MC, V.

This contemporary stone-and-cedar inn is located 2½ miles north of Silverthorne on the east bank of the Blue River as it flows out of Dillon Reservoir. Guests are encouraged to fish the Gold Medal trout river from private frontage. There's a large outdoor hot tub near the riverbank, and breakfast is served on a roomy deck overlooking the stream. Inside, guests can enjoy the fireplace and television, as well as down comforters on their beds. Neither smoking nor pets are permitted. A full suite (with living/dining room and kitchen) is available for $150.

## FRISCO

**HOLIDAY INN—SUMMIT COUNTY, I-70 Exit 203 (P.O. Box 10), Frisco, CO 80443. Tel. 303/668-5000,** or 800/782-7669. Fax 303/668-0718. 213 rms, 5 suites (all with bath). A/C TV TEL
**$ Rates** (single or double): Early and late season and Jan, $69–$99; holiday season, $155–$175; Feb, $95–$115 Mon–Fri, $119–$135 Sat–Sun; Mar, $125–$145; spring and fall, $49–$69; July–Labor Day, $59–$89. Suites $160–$225. Children 19 and under stay free in parents' room. AE, CB, DC, DISC, JCB, MC, V.

Located beside the shoreline wetlands of Dillon Reservoir, this Holiday Inn—centrally located to all of Summit County's ski resorts—maintains the feel of a ski lodge with its warm fireplace seating. During the winter season this is a milieu for ski-movie parties with hot-chocolate and spiced-wine parties.

Many second-floor rooms have balconies with views across the lake. All have standard hotel furnishings; most feature two double beds or a queen-size bed and sleeper sofa. Decor is light pastel with rich blue carpeting. Local phone calls are 50¢.

The County Fare restaurant specializes in salads and sandwiches for lunch, steaks and seafood for dinner. The hotel lounge offers free hors d'oeuvres during its 4 to 6pm happy hour.

Services and facilities include room service, valet laundry, no-smoking rooms, facilities for the handicapped; HoliDome with indoor swimming pool, Jacuzzi, steam room, tanning booth, exercise and weight room, games area with pool tables, and a video arcade; ski rentals and repairs; guest laundry; gift shop; meeting space for 250.

**TWILIGHT INN, 308 Main St. (P.O. Box 397), Frisco, CO 80443. Tel. 303/668-5009.** 12 rms (8 with bath).
**$ Rates** (including continental breakfast): Winter, $60–$70 double without bath,

$73–$105 double with bath; summer, $40–$50 double without bath, $47–$73 double with bath. AE, DISC, MC, V.

Most rooms in this contemporary bed-and-breakfast inn, located in downtown Frisco, have private decks or balconies and antique furnishings. Guests can relax around the fireplace in the large living room or in front of the television in the cozy library. Amenities include a hot tub, steam room, laundry room, and locked storage area. Children are catered to with cribs and highchairs, and some pets may be accepted.

## KEYSTONE

**KEYSTONE RESORT, U.S. 6 (P.O. Box 38), Keystone, CO 80435. Tel. 303/468-2316,** or 800/541-0346 for Keystone Lodge, 800/222-0188 for condominium lodging. Fax 303/468-1126. 1,127 units (all with bath). TV TEL
**$ Rates** (single or double): May–Oct, $119–$150 Keystone Lodge; $85–$100 Mountain Inn; $100–$130 studio; $115–$160 one-bedroom. Nov–Apr, Lodge and Inn, $160–$210 low season; $180–$220 high season; $125–$230 studio; $150–$280 one-bedroom. Higher rates for deluxe units and two- to four-bedroom condos. Children under 18 stay free in parents' room. AE, CB, DC, DISC, MC, V.

Spacious Keystone Resort has two main centers of activity. One is Keystone Lake, and the second is Keystone Mountain House Village, a mile east at the foot of the ski lifts. River Run Plaza, by the gondola terminal east of the Mountain House Village, and Old Keystone Village, west of the lodge en route to Keystone Ranch, are other areas of development.

All 152 rooms in the Keystone Lodge, a member of the Preferred Hotels Worldwide group, are oriented for mountain views. The pleasant rooms, spacious and without frills, all have cable TV with in-room movies, radios, phones, and refrigerators. The Keystone Mountain Inn, with 103 ski-in, ski-out rooms, is mainly efficiency studios with kitchens, along with a few one-bedroom suites (some with private spas). Keystone Condominiums comprise 850 condo units and private homes, ranging in size from one to four bedrooms. There's access to Jacuzzis, saunas, and swimming pools at all of them, along with daily housekeeping, kitchens, and fireplaces.

**Dining/Entertainment:** All told, there are 26 places to eat in Keystone Village. There's fine dining at the Keystone Ranch (see "Where to Dine," below); the Garden Room for continental cuisine and the Bighorn Room for steaks, both in the Keystone Lodge; RazzBerry's in the Keystone Mountain Inn; and the SkiTip Lodge (see below). Families can find three meals a day at the Edgewater Café (in the Lodge), enjoy seafood meals at the Commodore Restaurant, relax with burgers and Mexican food in the mining decor of Ida Belle's Bar and Grille, put away pizza at the Last Chance Saloon, grab a sandwich at the Tip Top Deli, or attend a Thursday-night barbecue and barn dance at Keystone Stables (summer only). Atop Keystone Mountain, reached via gondola, is the Outpost, whose elegant centerpiece—the Alpenglow Stube—serves elegant wild game and other regional dishes, at a price to match the view.

**Services:** Room service, concierge, valet parking, valet laundry, free shuttle-bus system (operates three times hourly between the Lodge, Mountain Village, and other developments).

**Facilities:** 11 swimming pools, saunas, Jacuzzis, fitness center with weight room, indoor/outdoor tennis center (14 courts), golf, bicycle paths, stables, boating, llama trekking, ice-skating; children's center, science school, day-camp program, petting farm, "Family Fun Park" (with volleyball, horseshoes, playground, and a tepee); guest laundries, boutiques, ski shops, many other stores; the University of Denver's Institute for Lifelong Learning (tel. 800/322-8598) operates May to September; the $10-million Keystone Conference Center with meeting space for 1,800.

**SKI TIP LODGE, 764 Montezuma Rd. (P.O. Box 38), Keystone, CO 80435. Tel. 303/468-4202,** or 800/222-0188. 22 rms (17 with bath).
**$ Rates** (including continental breakfast in summer, full breakfast and dinner in winter): Summer, $45–$55 single; $70–$90 double. Winter, low season, $69–$104 single, $114–$150 double; high season, $89–$114 single, $134–$160 double. AE, CB, DC, MC, V.

In stark contrast to Keystone's modern core, the historic SkiTip offers a serene, rustic setting. Nestled in a pine forest by the Snake River, about 2 miles east of the lodge and a brisk walk from the River Run Plaza gondola terminal, the lodge dates back to the 1880s, when it was a stagecoach stop on the way to the Montezuma gold mines. Arapahoe Basin developer Max Dercum bought it in the 1940s and turned it into the first skiers' guest lodge in Colorado. He sold the property to Keystone Resort in 1983, but its rough-hewn log construction has been maintained.

Seventeen rooms are appointed with antiques, quilts, and lace curtains. Five other rooms share baths. There's no TV or phone, so guests are forced to fraternize with other visitors around the fireplace or in the Rathskeller bar.

**Dining/Entertainment:** Four-course dinners are served nightly in a country-inn atmosphere (see "Where to Dine," below).

**Facilities:** Hot tub, swimming pool, two tennis courts, nature trails; all Keystone Resort facilities are open to SkiTip Lodge guests.

## CAMPGROUNDS

Many of the **Arapaho National Forest** campgrounds (tel. 303/468-5400) in Summit County are found around the shores of Dillon Reservoir. **Heaton Bay** (72 sites), **Peak One** (79 sites), **Pine Cove** (50 sites), and **Prospector** (108 sites)—all on Dam Road north of Frisco or on Colo. 9 south toward Breckenridge—have water, bathhouses, and other facilities.

Numerous other campgrounds are around Green Mountain Reservoir, 25 miles north of Silverthorne on Colo. 9. They include **Cataract Creek** (4 primitive sites), **Elliot Creek** (64 sites), **McDonald Flats** (44 sites), and **Prairie Point** (39 sites).

All campgrounds charge an $8 overnight fee per vehicle, except Cataract Creek, which is free.

# WHERE TO DINE

## BRECKENRIDGE

### Expensive

**BRIAR ROSE RESTAURANT, 109 E. Lincoln St. Tel. 453-9948.**
   **Cuisine:** REGIONAL/STEAK/SEAFOOD. **Reservations:** Highly recommended.
   **$ Prices:** Appetizers $6; main courses $13–$26. AE, CB, DC, MC, V.
   **Open:** Dinner only, daily 5–10pm.
Located uphill from Breckenridge's only traffic light (on Main Street), the Briar Rose is arguably the town's most elegant restaurant. Classical oil paintings, fine music, and white-linen service underscore the sophistication. The adjoining lounge is somewhat less refined: Its decor includes nude paintings and big-game heads.

You can start with escargots or frogs' legs in garlic butter. Dinners feature game when available—elk, moose, buffalo, and caribou. Other popular choices include slow-cooked prime rib, veal medallions sautéed in lemon butter, beef tips in wine with mushrooms and green peppers, shrimp Venetian (sautéed with mushrooms, green peppers, and tomatoes in a butter-and-wine sauce), and Briar Rose chicken (in a light tomato sauce with carrots, almonds, and cloves).

### Moderate

**ADAMS STREET GRILL, Main and Adams Sts. Tel. 453-4700.**
   **Cuisine:** INTERNATIONAL. **Reservations:** Recommended.
   **$ Prices:** Appetizers $2.95–$6.50; main courses $3.95–$6.95 at lunch, $8.95–$16.95 at dinner. MC, V.
   **Open:** Summer, Mon–Thurs 11am–10pm, Fri 11am–11pm, Sat 10am–11pm, Sun 10am–10pm; winter, 11am–10pm. Earlier closing in spring and fall.
There are five different seating levels at this popular restaurant, which has two outdoor decks—one overlooking Main Street, a second facing Ten Mile Mountain.

The interior offers understated Southwest decor, with a tile floor and a rose-and-dark-aquamarine color scheme.

The menu has a little of everything, starting with an oyster bar and a pasta sheet. You can also get French, Mexican, or Cajun dishes here, or opt for something home-spun such as shrimp Adams Street—sautéed with green peppers, tomatoes, and mushrooms, and served on linguine with a cream sauce. There are regional game specials; American standards such as barbecued pork spareribs, steak teriyaki, and honey-almond chicken; and vegetarian dishes such as zucchini Rockefeller, stuffed with spinach, onions, and mushrooms, and baked.

**BRECKENRIDGE CATTLE CO., Plaza I Bldg., The Village at Breckenridge Resort, 655 S. Park St. Tel. 453-3111.**
**Cuisine:** STEAKS/SEAFOOD. **Reservations:** Recommended.
**$ Prices:** Appetizers $4–$10.75; main courses $10.95–$20.95. AE, MC, V.
**Open:** Dinner only, daily 5–10pm.

The large windows of this classic steakhouse overlook Maggie Pond, site of year-round activity. Inside, the ambience is that of a garden. Flagstones add a finished touch. The menu ranges from pasta stir-fries to a 16-ounce T-bone. Between are roast chicken with honey-mustard sauce, lamb chops with mint sauce, pan-fried catfish, calves' liver with bacon and onions, and steak Del Monaco. Early diners (5 to 6pm) save 20% on their tabs. There's also a children's menu. An acoustic guitarist plays Wednesday through Sunday nights in the lounge.

**HEARTHSTONE CASUAL DINING, 130 S. Ridge St. Tel. 453-1148.**
**Cuisine:** NEW AMERICAN/STEAKS. **Reservations:** Recommended.
**$ Prices:** Appetizers $2.95–$6.95; main courses $3.95–$6.95 at lunch, $9.95–$17.95 at dinner. AE, MC, V.
**Open:** Lunch Mon–Sat 11am–3pm; dinner Sun–Thurs 4:30–9:30pm, Fri–Sat 4:30–10:30pm; brunch Sun 10am–3pm.

This wonderful restaurant in the 1886 Kaiser House is among Breckenridge's favorites. Blue on the outside, with white trim and wrought iron, it has a rustic yet elegant interior decor. There are fine views across the Ten Mile Range from the upstairs lounge.

You can get great lunches here—jalapeño-wrapped shrimp, turkey-and-avocado sandwiches, half-pound burgers—but dinner is the meal "to die for." Start with baked Brie or steamed mussels. Then mull over your main dish: fresh seafood, such as Hearthstone shrimp (with garlic and ginger) or yellowfin tuna (grilled with a tarragon-Dijon sauce); Hearthstone chicken (breaded with macadamia nuts and coconut, topped with a cream sauce of pineapple, rum, and brandy); a variety of steaks and slow-roasted prime rib. Vegetarians choices are also offered. An early-diners' menu, offered from 4:30 to 5:30pm, cuts a couple of dollars off dinner prices.

**POIRRIER'S CAJUN CAFE, 224 S. Main St. Tel. 453-1877.**
**Cuisine:** CAJUN/CREOLE. **Reservations:** Recommended.
**$ Prices:** Appetizers $4.95–$8.95; main courses $5.95–$9.95 at lunch, $12.95–$19.95 at dinner. AE, MC, V.
**Open:** Lunch daily 11:30am–2pm; dinner daily 5:30–10pm.

This Reliance Place brownstone is straight out of New Orleans, with sidewalk café seating behind a wrought-iron railing. Two rooms inside display harlequin masks and photos of Louisiana. Indeed, owners Bobby and Connie Poirrier are native Cajuns from Lafayette, La., "the heart of Acadiana."

For lunch, order yourself a "po-boy," New Orleans–style red beans and rice, or Bayou gumbo. At dinnertime, take a close look at the house specialties. There's poisson Hymel (a catfish filet surrounded with crayfish étoufée, served with steamed rice and gumbo), blackened catch of the day, chicken à la Poirrier (with a mushroom-and-sweet-pepper sauce), and ribeye steak. Finish your meal with Lafayette bread pudding. A children's menu is available.

**TILLIE'S, 215 S. Ridge St. Tel. 453-0669.**
**Cuisine:** AMERICAN. **Reservations:** Recommended at dinner.

**$ Prices:** Appetizers $2.75–$4.95; main courses $5.75–$6 at lunch, $10.95–$15.95 at dinner. MC, V.

**Open:** Lunch daily 11am–4pm; dinner daily 5–11pm (bar, Mon–Sat 11am–2am, Sun 11am–midnight).

A chainsaw-carved eagle doing duty as a flagstaff greets visitors to this backstreet Victorian bar and grill. Once inside, the tin ceiling, leaded-glass windows, and marble-top bar lend a late 19th-century ambience. Gourmet hamburgers—8 ounces of grilled beef on a French roll—and homemade soups are the rage at lunchtime. Dinner features barbecued country-style pork ribs, New York strip steak, and teriyaki kebabs. Don't miss the "morning after" breakfast special on Sunday: 50¢ for eggs, sausage, home-fries, and toast when you buy a bloody Mary or any other cocktail.

## Inexpensive

### THE BLUE MOOSE, 540 S. Main St. Tel. 453-4859.

**Cuisine:** INTERNATIONAL. **Reservations:** Not necessary.

**$ Prices:** Breakfast $2.95–$4.50; lunch/dinner $4.25–$14.95. MC, V.

**Open:** Breakfast daily 7am–1pm; lunch daily 11:30am–2pm; dinner daily 5–10pm. **Closed:** Dinner in spring and fall.

This small café with nondescript decor has a huge local following, perhaps because it caters to vegetarians as much as to meat eaters. For every beef burger there's a falafel burger, for every drunken chicken (marinated in tequila and lime) there's a stir-fry wok dish, and for every steak au poivre there's a pasta Alfredo. Fresh seafood is available nightly. Local artists jam here on Wednesday evenings, and Mondays are "mad martini nights" for ladies.

### HORSESHOE II RESTAURANT, 115 S. Main St. Tel. 453-7463.

**Cuisine:** AMERICAN. **Reservations:** Not accepted.

**$ Prices:** Breakfast $2.75–$5.95; lunch $3.95–$6.50; dinner $8.95–$15.95. MC, V.

**Open:** Daily 7:30am–10pm.

A classy family-style restaurant in a historic 19th-century building, the Horseshoe II (yes, there was once a I) is set in the heart of downtown Breckenridge. It has two outdoor patios, ornate walls and ceilings, lace curtains, and mounted horseshoes (of course). The bar is equally popular for espressos and alcoholic beverages.

You can get three meals a day here, starting with breakfasts, including the Breck-Mex Express and the H.A.B. (high-altitude breakfast) consisting of two eggs, two pancakes, breakfast meat, and juice. Lunch offers salads and sandwiches, including the TACT: turkey, avocado, cream cheese, and tomato. Dinners are more elaborate, and feature the likes of linguine with smoked trout, pecan-and-chicken stir-fry, lamb chops, prime rib, and fresh salmon.

### MI CASA, 600 Park Ave. Tel. 453-2071.

**Cuisine:** MEXICAN. **Reservations:** Recommended.

**$ Prices:** Appetizers $3.95–$5.95; main courses $6.25–$13.95. AE, MC, V.

**Open:** Dinner only, daily 4–10pm (bar open at 3pm).

A large room with stuccoed walls, tile floor, wooden furniture, and baskets of silk flowers hanging from a beamed ceiling, Mi Casa is arguably Breckenridge's best Mexican restaurant. Its adjoining cantina is among the most popular, with margaritas by the liter and tequila (pronounced "ta-*kill*-ya") shooters.

House specialties include Cancun and Yucatán chicken, snapper al ajillo (with garlic), Acapulco scallops, and carne asada a la tampiqueña. Standard burritos, tostadas, and enchiladas are also on the menu, along with fajitas and fresh seafood dishes. There's a children's menu, as well as a few non-Mexican steaks and burgers.

### PASTA JAY'S, 326 S. Main St. Tel. 453-5800.

**Cuisine:** ITALIAN. **Reservations:** Not accepted.

**$ Prices:** Appetizers $2.25–$4.25; meals $4.50–$9.95. MC, V.

**Open:** Mon–Sat 11am–10:30pm.

This casual Mediterranean-style bistro occupies a modern log cabin in the Centennial Square plaza on Jefferson Avenue. Like its namesake in Boulder, it has a crowded outdoor deck, low prices, and generous portions of good food. Pastas, eggplant or chicken Parmigiana, and pizza are especially good. Cheesesteak and other sandwiches are available before 5pm. Smoking isn't allowed.

## COPPER MOUNTAIN

**O'SHEA'S COPPER BAR, Copper Junction Bldg. opposite Mountain Plaza. Tel. 968-2882, ext. 6504.**
**Cuisine:** AMERICAN/MEXICAN. **Reservations:** Not necessary.
**$ Prices:** Breakfast $2.95–$4.95; appetizers $1.95–$4.95; main courses $5.95–$12.95. AE, CB, DC, DISC, JCB, MC, V.
**Open:** Winter, daily 7am–10pm; summer, daily 11am–9pm.
There are two floors to this restaurant—a casual, mountain-style café on the top level, and a Basement Bar with live rock music. You'll eat well upstairs before joining the party. There are buffets for all meals, including Mexican dishes at lunch and prime rib at dinner. Or order off the menu: huevos rancheros in the morning, a bad-boy salad or motherlode burger at midday, mesquite chicken or buffalo shrimp at night. There's a kids' menu, but here's good news: Kids' items are free with an adult dinner main dish!

**RACKETS, in the Copper Mountain Racquet and Athletic Club, Copper Road at Ten Mile Circle. Tel. 968-2882, ext. 6386.**
**Cuisine:** SOUTHWESTERN. **Reservations:** Recommended.
**$ Prices:** Appetizers $4.95–$8.95; main courses $13.95–$26.95. AE, CB, DC, DISC, MC, V.
**Open:** Dinner only, daily 4–10pm.
The second floor of an athletic club may seem an unlikely location for a fine restaurant, but it works. Guests enter through a fireside seating area. Handsome wood decor is an earmark of the main restaurant, and there's outdoor patio seating as well. You can start your meal with the likes of a smoked-duck quesadilla, help yourself to what may be the best salad bar in the Rockies, then decide on a main course: spicy grilled shrimp? baked stuffed chicken piñon? a coho salmon and prime rib combination? You can't go wrong.

## DILLON/SILVERTHORNE

**THE HISTORIC MINT, 341 Blue River Pkwy., Silverthorne. Tel. 468-5247.**
**Cuisine:** STEAK/SEAFOOD. **Reservations:** Recommended.
**$ Prices:** Appetizers $3.95–$6.95; main courses $7.95–$15.95. AE, MC, V.
**Open:** Dinner only, daily 5–10pm (bar opens at 4pm).
Cook your own dinner on a charcoal grill amid rough-hewn plank walls in a historic 1862 building. Steaks, chicken, and fresh seafood—including tuna, mahimahi, snapper, salmon, and swordfish, depending on availability—are available. There are daily Cajun specials. All dinners include the 23-item salad bar.

**PUG RYAN'S, 101 Dillon Mall, Dillon. Tel. 468-2145.**
**Cuisine:** STEAK/SEAFOOD. **Reservations:** Recommended.
**$ Prices:** Appetizers $4.95–$7.95; main courses $10.95–$18.95. AE, MC, V.
**Open:** Dinner only, daily 5–10pm.
From the deck of Dillon's oldest steakhouse you can gaze across Marina Park to the waters of Dillon Reservoir. Diners enjoy fresh oysters on the half shell while watching the sun set, then cut into slow-roasted prime rib or the daily seafood special. Children are welcome everywhere but the Fireside Lounge, a community gathering place for a quarter-century.

## FRISCO

**CHARITY'S, 307 Main St., Frisco. Tel. 668-3644.**
**Cuisine:** INTERNATIONAL. **Reservations:** Recommended.
**$ Prices:** Appetizers $2.95–$5.95; main courses $5.95–$9.95 at lunch, $6.95–$14.95 at dinner. AE, MC, V.

**Open:** Lunch daily 11:30am–5pm; dinner daily 5–10pm; bar, Mon–Sat 11:30am–2am, Sun 11:30am–midnight.

Named for one of the women said to have resided in this building—then a popular brothel—during the heyday of mining, Charity's offers a wide selection of Mexican foods and grill items. South-of-the-border items include chimichangas, enchiladas, chile relleños, chile verde, Navajo tacos, and snapper Veracruz. There's plenty of fresh seafood: grilled mahimahi, trout Grand Marnier, and sea scallops au gratin, for instance. Southwestern lime chicken, charcoal-broiled steaks, pasta, pizza, burgers, and miner's stew fill out the varied menu.

**GOLDEN ANNIE'S, 603 Main St., Frisco. Tel. 668-0345.**
 **Cuisine:** STEAK/SEAFOOD. **Reservations:** Recommended.
 **$ Prices:** Appetizers $2.95–$5.95; main courses $5.95–$9.95 at lunch, $8.95–$17.95 at dinner. AE, MC, V.
 **Open:** May–Oct lunch daily 11:30am–3pm; dinner daily 5–10pm. Nov–Apr, dinner daily 5–10pm (bar, Mon–Sat 11:30am–2pm; Sun 11:30am–midnight).

Golden Annie's was a late 19th-century claim at the mining camp of Masontown, overlooking Frisco from Mountain Royal. Local legend says that the mine, along with Masontown, was destroyed by an avalanche on New Year's Eve 1912. But fortuitously, no one was home: They were all celebrating in Frisco. Today this mesquite grill and bar serves steaks (New York, ribeye, T-bone, filet mignon), seafood (snapper, swordfish, salmon, shrimp, fresh catch), fajitas, barbecues, and "finger food."

## KEYSTONE

**KEYSTONE RANCH, Keystone Ranch Rd. Tel. 468-4161.**
 **Cuisine:** CREATIVE REGIONAL. **Reservations:** Required.
 **$ Prices:** Six-course dinner $38, $22 for children 12 and under. AE, MC, V.
 **Open:** May–Oct, lunch daily 11:30am–2pm; dinner daily 5:45–9pm. Nov–Apr, dinner only, daily 5:45–9pm.

A working cattle ranch for over three decades until 1972, the Keystone Ranch now boasts riding stables, a fine golf course, and this outstanding gourmet restaurant built of pine logs from the forest that surrounds it. Utes and Arapahoes made their summer camps in the 19th century where the golf course now lies, at the foot of Keystone Mountain; it doesn't take much imagination here to visualize the smoke of their campfires in the twilight.

The food here is as imaginative as the setting. The six-course menu offers a choice of appetizer, including knödel of pheasant, served warm with sautéed spinach and forest mushrooms over a sauce of sweet red peppers, or lamb sauté Montezuma, tossed with chiles, pine nuts, and cilantro. That's followed by a soup, a salad, and a fruit sorbet to cleanse the palate. Main dishes, which vary seasonally, follow: Peru Creek veal (rolled with a pemmican of wild game and fruits, served with crab and corn cooked in the husk), Willow Creek muscovy duck (boneless breast with a pear polenta and brandy sauce, and a julienne of leeks), and Soda Ridge beef (marinated with horseradish, served with a watercress sauce over potato cakes). Local game and fresh seafood dishes are prepared with whim and inspiration, depending on what's available. Desserts include Gorgonzola apple tart and hazelnut logs with dried cherries.

There's no smoking in the restaurant. You won't need a tie, gentlemen, but wear slacks and your best ski sweater.

**SKI TIP LODGE, 764 Montezuma Rd. Tel. 468-4202.**
 **Cuisine:** REGIONAL. **Reservations:** Required.
 **$ Prices:** Four-course dinner $27. AE, CB, DC, MC, V.
 **Open:** Winter, lunch Mon–Sat 11:30am–2pm; dinner daily 5:45–9pm. Summer, dinner daily 5:45–9pm; brunch Sun 8am–1pm.

Some say the food at this casual country inn, an 1880s stagecoach stop, is the best in Summit County. A nightly choice of meat, poultry, and seafood dishes is offered, which might include roast loin of pork, trout sautéed with pecans and lemon butter, apple-smoked Cornish hens with wild rice, braised pheasant breast with port wine and shallots, or peppered smoked beef tenderloin with balsamic vinegar sauce. Soup, salad, home-baked bread, and delectable desserts are included. Lunches offer all the soup and bread you can eat. There's a full lounge. Smoking is not permitted.

# 5. VAIL

109 miles W of Denver, 150 miles E of Grand Junction

**GETTING THERE   By Plane**   From mid-December to early April, visitors can fly directly into **Eagle County Airport,** 35 miles west of Vail near the town of Eagle, at I-70 Exit 140 or 147 (tel. 303/524-7700 or 949-5480). **American Airlines** (tel. toll free 800/433-7300) has daily nonstops from Chicago and Dallas/Fort Worth, and on Saturday from New York (LaGuardia). **America West Airlines** (tel. 800/225-5692) offers nonstop service Thursday through Monday from Phoenix, and on Saturday from Los Angeles and San Francisco.

Most visitors fly into **Denver's Stapleton International Airport,** and continue to Vail aboard any of four shuttle services: **Airport Transportation Service** (tel. 303/476-7576, or 800/247-7074); **Colorado Mountain Express** (tel. 303/949-4227, or 800/525-6363); **Vail Valley Transportation** (tel. 303/476-8008, or 800/882-8872); or **Vans to Vail** (tel. 303/476-4467, or 800/222-2112). Vans or buses leave the Denver airport daily, every half hour, from 8am to 11pm.

**By Bus**   Coaches of **Greyhound/Trailways** (tel. 303/476-5137) stop in Vail at the Vail Transportation Center, South Frontage Road at East Meadow Drive. For Beaver Creek, they stop in the village of Avon.

**By Car**   Vail is right on the I-70 corridor, so it's exceedingly easy to find your way there. Just take Exit 176, whether you're coming from the east (Denver) or the west (Grand Junction). A more direct route from the south may be U.S. 24 through Leadville; this Tennessee Pass road joins I-70 5 miles west of Vail.

**SPECIAL EVENTS**   The Vail area holds the following annual events: the **Mountain Man Winter Triathlon,** on the first weekend of February, in Beaver Creek; **Taste of Vail,** over the first weekend of April, in Vail; **Kick-off to Summer,** over Memorial Day weekend, in Vail/Lionshead; the **Salute to the USA,** on July 4, in Avon; the **Bravo! Colorado Festival,** from early July to early August, in Vail and Beaver Creek; the **Vail Arts Festival,** in mid-July, in Vail/Lionshead; **Eurofest,** on the last weekends of July and August, in Beaver Creek; the **Eagle County Fair and Rodeo,** on the second weekend of August, in Eagle; the **Beaver Creek Arts Festival,** over the third weekend of August, in Beaver Creek; and **VailFest,** in mid-September, in Lionshead.

**N**ative American Ute tribespeople didn't take kindly to the first incursions into this valley by white gold-seekers in the 1850s and 1860s. They set the forests alight in "spite fires"—burnings that created the wide-open ridges and back bowls that have made Vail Mountain famous as a ski resort today.

But no substantial amount of gold was found in the Gore Valley, as it was then known, and until U.S. 6 was built through Vail Pass (named for a highway engineer) in 1939, the only inhabitants were a handful of sheep ranchers. Veterans of the 10th Mountain Division, who trained during World War II at Camp Hale, 23 miles south of the valley, returned in the 1950s to ski the Rockies. One of them, Peter Seibert, urged development of this mountain land in the White River National Forest. His investment company began construction in 1962, and the entire ski resort— immediately among the three largest ski areas in the United States—was completed and ready to open in December 1963. Additional ski-lift capacity made Vail America's largest ski resort by 1964.

A Tyrolean-style pedestrian village grew around the base, attracting many rich and famous citizens—among them former President Gerald Ford. Readers of *Ski* and *Snow Country* magazines annually vote the resort the country's most popular.

Vail Associates opened the luxurious new Beaver Creek resort, 11 miles west near Avon, in 1981; it had originally been plotted as the site of the 1976 Winter Olympics, until Colorado voters turned thumbs down on that extravaganza.

## ORIENTATION

The town of Vail is located at an elevation of 8,150 feet. The year-round population is around 4,000.

**INFORMATION**    For information on Vail and surrounding areas, contact the **Vail Resort Association,** 241 East Meadow Drive, Vail, CO 81657 (tel. 303/476-1000, or 800/525-3875); **Vail Associates, Inc.,** P.O. Box 7, Vail, CO 81658 (tel. 303/476-5601, or 800/525-2257); or the **Eagle Valley Chamber of Commerce,** P.O. Box 964, Eagle, CO 81631 (tel. 303/328-5220).

The resort association's **visitor information office** is near the Vail Transportation Center at 111 South Frontage Road, open daily.

**CITY LAYOUT**    There's no getting around the fact that narrow Vail Valley, hemmed in on the south and north by steep mountains, is in a long strip along Gore Creek. In fact, as you come in from the east across Vail Pass, you'll find a whole strip of separate communities: East Vail (Exit 180), Vail (Exit 176), West Vail (Exit 173), Minturn and Eagle-Vail (Exit 171), Avon and Beaver Creek (Exit 167), and Edwards (Exit 163).

The town of Vail is mostly on the south side of the interstate, which you exit on Vail Road. The two main skiing areas are **Vail Village,** slightly to the east, and **Lionshead,** to the west. Because much of Vail is open to pedestrians only, it's wise to park in one of the major garages off South Frontage Road, then get hold of one of several available tourist maps to find your way through the network of lanes.

## GETTING AROUND

The Town of Vail runs a **free shuttle-bus service** between 7am and 1am daily. Shuttles in the Vail Village–Lionshead area run every 3 to 5 minutes, and there are regularly scheduled trips to West Vail and East Vail. There's also free transportation between Beaver Creek Resort and the village of Avon (tel. 949-1938). Buses between Vail and Beaver Creek, an 11-mile trip, run daily from 8am to midnight; the charge is $2 each way.

**Vail Valley Taxi** (tel. 476-TAXI) operates throughout the area, as does **Admiral Limousines** (tel. 303/741-6464, or 800/828-8680).

For **auto rentals,** try **Hertz** (tel. 303/476-7707, or 800/654-3131) or **Thrifty** (tel. 303/949-7787, or 800/367-2277); both are at the Eagle County Airport.

## FAST FACTS

The **area code** is 303. In case of an **emergency,** call **911;** for regular business, contact the Vail Police (tel. 479-2100). The **hospital,** Vail Valley Medical Center, is on West Meadow Drive between Vail Road and East Lionshead Circle (tel. 476-2451). The **post office** is on North Frontage Road West, opposite Donovan Park (tel. 476-5217). For **road information,** call 479-2229. State, county, and city **taxes** add 8.2% to hotel bills in Vail, 9.4% in Beaver Creek. TV8 offers local cable **television** programs.

## WHAT TO SEE & DO
### ATTRACTIONS

**VAIL MOUNTAIN, Vail Associates, Inc., P.O. Box 7, Vail, CO 81658. Tel. 303/476-5601,** or 800/525-2257; or 303/476-4888 for daily snow reports. Fax 303/949-2315.

In his *Skiing America* guide, author Charles Leocha writes, "Vail comes closest of any resort in America to epitomizing what many skiers would call perfection." I agree. You can arrive at the base village, unload and park your car once, and never have to drive again until it's time to go. You'll find all the shops, restaurants, and nightlife you could ever want within a short walk from your hotel or condominium. And the skiing is unparalleled.

The area boundaries stretch 7 miles from east to west along the ridgetop, from **Outer Mongolia** to **Game Creek Bowl**, and the skiable terrain is measured at 3,834 acres. Virtually every lift on the front (north-facing) side of the mountain has runs for every level of skier, with a predominance of novice and intermediate terrain. (The longest run, 4½-mile **Riva Ridge,** is mainly intermediate.) The world-famous Back Bowls are decidedly *not* for beginners, and there are few options for intermediates. The seven bowls—from west to east, Sun Down, Sun Up, Tea Cup, China, Siberia, Inner Mongolia, and Outer Mongolia—are strictly for advanced and experts; snow and weather conditions determine just *how* expert you ought to be. They are served by only three lifts, one of them a short surface lift to access the Mongolias. One trip down the Slot or Rasputin's Revenge will give you a fair idea of just how good you are.

From Mongolia Summit, at 11,450 feet, Vail has a vertical drop on the front side of 3,250 feet; on the back side, 1,850 feet. Average annual snowfall is 334 inches (nearly 28 feet). All told, there are 120 named trails served by 20 lifts—a gondola, nine quad chairs, two triple chairs, six double chairs, and two surface lifts—with a skier capacity of 35,820 per hour. Meet the Mountain tours begin at Wildwood Shelter, atop Lift 3 (Hunky Dory), Sunday through Tuesday at 1pm; and former U.S. Olympic medalist Cindy Nelson, the director of skiing here, invites advanced and intermediate skiers to join her on a run on Friday at 1pm.

Ten **mountain restaurants** include two that ask for reservations: the **Cook Shack** (tel. 479-2030), with creative American cuisine at the Summit, and the **Wine Stube** (tel. 479-2034) at Eagle's Nest, with international cuisine atop the Lionshead Gondola. The Native American–themed **Two Elk Restaurant** on the Far East summit has southwestern cuisine and pasta, baked potato, and salad bars. **Wok 'n' Roll,** in China Bowl, is a ski-by pagoda with Asian fast food; the **Dog Haus** offers ski-by hot dogs at the foot of the Avanti Express; **Wildwood Shelter** has Italian food; **Eagle's Nest** has taco and yogurt bars. And **Mid-Vail** has two levels of cafeterias: **Golden Peak** and **Trail's End** serve breakfast, lunch, and après-ski drinks.

Vail has an outstanding children's program. The **Golden Peak Children's Skiing Center** (tel. 479-2040) and the **Adventure Company** (tel. 479-9090) are under the aegis of the Ski School. Call 479-2048 for recorded information on a wide range of day and night family activities. There are daily **NASTAR** races, and a **Marlboro pay-to-race** self-timing course (50¢ a run) on the Swingsville run, off the Mountaintop Express.

**Admission: Tickets,** $40 per day adults, $37 per day for multiday tickets, $35 for a half day; $27 per day children 12 and under, $22 for a half day; $30 per day seniors 65–69; free for seniors 70 and older. Multiday tickets are interchangeable between Vail and Beaver Creek. Single-ride tickets, $14 adults, $8 children. Full rental packages average $14.

**Open:** Thanksgiving to the third week of Apr, daily 8:30am–3:30pm.

**BEAVER CREEK RESORT, Vail Associates, Inc., P.O. Box 7, Vail, CO 81658. Tel. 303/949-5750,** or 800/525-2257; or 303/476-4889 for daily snow report. Fax 303/949-2315.

Vail's "other" mountain is an outstanding resort in its own right, one with a more secluded atmosphere than its better-known neighbor. Located up a valley 1½ miles off the I-70 corridor, Beaver Creek combines European château–style elegance in its base village with expansive slopes for novice and intermediate skiers. The **Grouse Mountain** lift, opened for the 1991–92 season, reaches previously inaccessible expert terrain.

From the village, the Centennial Express lift to **Spruce Saddle** reaches wide-open northwest-facing midmountain slopes and the **Stump Park** beginners' area. Opposite, the **Strawberry Park** lift accesses **Larkspur Bowl** and the **McCoy Park** cross-country area at 9,840 feet. Three other lifts—Larkspur, Grouse Mountain, and Westfall (serving the expert Birds of Prey area)—leave from **Red-Tail Camp** at midmountain.

Beaver Creek's vertical is 3,340 feet, from the 8,100-foot base to the 11,400-foot summit. There are 940 developed acres, though Vail Associates are licensed to develop up to 5,600: plans are on the drawing board. Currently, 11 lifts (two quad chairs, five triples, and four doubles) serve 59 trails with a capacity of 19,075 skiers per hour. Average annual snowfall is 330 inches.

There are five **mountain restaurants,** including the widely praised **Beano's Cabin.** Others include **Rafters,** at Spruce Saddle (tel. 949-6050 for reservations), the **Spruce Saddle Cafeteria,** the **Red-Tail Camp** fast-food stop, and **McCoy's,** offering breakfast, lunch, and après-ski entertainment at the base.

**Admission: Tickets,** $40 per day adults, $37 per day for multiday tickets, $35 for a half day; $27 per day children 12 and under, $22 for a half day; $30 per day seniors 65–69; free for seniors 70 and older. Multiday tickets are interchangeable between Beaver Creek and Vail. Single-ride tickets $14 adults, $8 children. Full rental packages average $14.

**Open:** Daily 8:30am–3:30pm.

## COLORADO SKI MUSEUM, Vail Transportation Center, Vail. Tel. 476-1876.

The history of more than a century of Colorado skiing—from the boards that mountain miners first strapped on their feet, to the post–World War II resort boom, to Coloradans' success in international racing—is depicted in this popular showcase. Also included are the evolution of ski equipment and fashions, and the role of the U.S. Forest Service. A theater presents historical and current ski videos. The museum incorporates the **Colorado Ski Hall of Fame,** with plaques and photographs honoring Vail founder Peter Seibert, filmmaker Lowell Thomas, Olympic skier Buddy Werner, and others.

**Admission:** $1 adults, 50¢ children 12–18, free for children under 12.

**Open:** Tues–Sun 10am–6pm. **Closed:** May and Oct, except by appointment.

## EAGLE COUNTY HISTORICAL SOCIETY MUSEUM, Chambers Park, Fairgrounds Rd., Eagle. Tel. 328-6464.

Located in a large early 20th-century barn on the Eagle River, this museum presents exhibits that document the history of the valley from prehistoric Native Americans to modern day. Displays in a nearby caboose describe the importance of rail traffic. The society also operates the **Gore Creek Schoolhouse Museum** at Ford Park in Vail and the **Red Cliff Museum** in the 19th-century town hall at Red Cliff, 12 miles south of I-70 off U.S. 24.

**Admission:** Free.

**Open:** Memorial Day–Labor Day, daily 10am–4pm.

## BETTY FORD ALPINE GARDENS, Ford Park, South Frontage Rd. east of Vail Village, Vail. Tel. 476-7471.

Billed as "the highest public gardens in the world," this peaceful tract features more than 1,500 hardy perennials from around the world, along with an experimental rock garden and a meditation garden, employing elements of Chinese Zen and Japanese moss gardens.

**Admission:** Free.

**Open:** Snow-melt to snowfall, daily dawn–dusk.

## SPORTS & RECREATION

**BALLOONING** **Camelot Balloons** (tel. 476-4743) and **Colorado Balloon Adventures** (tel. 845-9907) fly year-round, including champagne breakfast flights.

**BICYCLING** Casual summer visitors can take the Lionshead Gondola to Eagle's

Nest on Vail Mountain, rent mountain bikes (and helmets) there, and cruise downhill on what *had* been ski runs to return their bikes at the base of the gondola.

But there are many other choices for avid bikers, both on backcountry trails and road tours. The 13½-mile **Vail Pass Bikeway** connects the mountain village to Copper Mountain, from which additional bike paths lead to Breckenridge and Keystone. Another popular trip is the 15-mile **Red Sandstone Road** to Piney Lake, beginning from North Frontage Road West a mile west of the Vail exit from I-70.

**Christy Sports,** 293 Bridge Street, Vail (tel. 476-2244), is among many sporting-goods companies that rent mountain and touring bicycles.

There are numerous competitive events throughout the summer season at Vail. Among them is the early-June **Ride of Your Life,** a 1-hour, 16-mile mountain-bike race that includes ski-gate slaloms on Vail Mountain.

**BOBSLEDDING** The ✪ **Vail Bobsled** runs a 3,200-foot course beginning just below Mid-Vail near the Short Cut run. The ride lasts about 1 minute and costs $11 per ride per person. Helmets are provided.

**FISHING** The streams and mountain lakes surrounding Vail are rich with rainbow, brook, brown, and cutthroat trout, and mountain whitefish. **Gore Creek** through the town of Vail is one popular anglers' venue, especially toward evening from its banks in the Vail Golf Course. Also good are the **Eagle River,** joined by Gore Creek 5 miles downstream near Minturn; the **Black Lakes** near the summit of Vail Pass; and 60-acre **Piney Lake** (see directions under "Bicycling," above). At the latter site, the **Piney River Ranch,** 884 Spruce Court, Vail, CO 81657 (tel. 303/476-3941), will rent canoes and small boats for fishing, and also will supply fly rods and waders.

**Nova Guides,** P.O. Box 2018, Vail, CO 81658 (tel. 303/949-4232), lead fishing trips on the Colorado, Arkansas, Eagle, and Roaring Fork rivers, as well as many lakes and streams in the White River National Forest. Float fishing or shore fishing runs $75 per person for a half day (4 hours). All equipment is furnished; licenses are extra.

Vail's longest-established sporting-goods store for fishermen is **American Angler,** 225 Wall Street (tel. 476-1477).

**GOLF** There are four 18-hole public courses and one private club in the Vail valley. Play dates depend on snow conditions, but usually are mid-May to mid-October.

Generally considered the outstanding area course is the **Beaver Creek Resort Golf Club,** 75 Offerson Road, Beaver Creek (tel. 949-7123), designed by Robert Trent Jones, Jr. The **Vail Golf Club,** 1778 Vail Valley Drive, Vail (tel. 479-2260), and the private, Jack Nicklaus–designed **Country Club of the Rockies** at Arrowhead resort, 2 miles west of Beaver Creek on U.S. 6 (tel. 926-3029), co-host the annual Gerald R. Ford Invitational Golf Tournament in August.

Other courses include the **Eagle-Vail Golf Course,** 0431 Eagle Drive, Avon (tel. 949-5267), a challenging course with the lowest greens fees and rentals in the valley; and the **Singletree Golf Course,** 1265 Berrycreek Road, Edwards (tel. 926-3533), 7 miles west of Beaver Creek off I-70 Exit 163, which opens earlier than the other courses (Apr 1) because of its lower elevation.

**HIKING & BACKPACKING** The surrounding White River National Forest has a plethora of trails leading to pristine lakes and spectacular panoramic views. The **Holy Cross Wilderness Area** to the southwest of Vail, encompassing 14,005-foot Mount of the Holy Cross, has more than 100 miles of trails; so awesome is this region that it was nearly awarded national monument status in the 1950s, rejected only because of its relative inaccessibility and short recreational season. Nearly as impressive is the **Eagle's Nest Wilderness Area** to the north. For information on these and other hiking areas, consult the **Holy Cross Ranger District Office,** 401 Main Street (P.O. Box 190), Minturn, CO 81645 (tel. 303/827-5715).

Among the less strenuous walks in the immediate Vail area is the 11-mile **Two Elk Trail,** a National Scenic Trail. It starts in East Vail, just south of the Gore Circle Campground on old U.S. 6, and ends in Minturn.

For supplies and more information, visit **Vail Mountaineering,** 500 Lionshead Mall, Vail (tel. 476-4223).

**HORSEBACK RIDING**  The **Spraddle Creek Ranch,** 100 North Frontage Road East, Vail (tel. 476-6941), is geared for family day outings. Located across I-70 from the Vail interchange, it features a pony ring for children.

For more serious pack trips, visit **Beaver Creek Stables** at the Beaver Creek Resort (tel. 845-7770) or **Piney River Ranch,** 15 miles north of Vail via Red Sandstone Road (tel. 476-3941).

**ICE SKATING**  There's public skating at the **John A. Dobson Ice Arena,** East Lionshead Circle (tel. 479-2270); admission is $4 for adults, $3.25 for children 17 and under. **Nottingham Lake** in Avon (tel. 949-4280) has afternoon and evening skating, as well as a hockey rink and speed-skating lane. The **Vail Golf Club,** 1778 Vail Valley Drive (tel. 476-8366), has a small outdoor rink.

**RIVER RAFTING**  The Eagle River, just a few miles west of Vail, offers excellent white water during the summer, especially during the May-June thaw. Families can enjoy the relatively gentle (Class II–IV) lower Eagle, west of Minturn; the upper Eagle, above Minturn, is significantly rougher (Class IV–V rapids). The Colorado and Arkansas rivers are also readily accessible—the former at State Bridge, 35 miles northwest via Colo. 131, and the latter at Buena Vista, 73 miles south via U.S. 24.

Rafting companies include **Nova Guides,** P.O. Box 2018, Vail, CO 81658 (tel. 303/949-4232), and **Colorado River Runs,** Star Route, Box 32, Bond, CO 80423 (tel. 303/653-4292, or 800/826-1081). Rates typically run $60 to $75 for a full-day journey, including lunch; $45 to $50 for a half-day trip.

**SKIING (ALPINE)**  There's another ski resort in Eagle County: **Arrowhead at Vail,** P.O. Box 3418, Vail, CO 81658 (tel. 303/926-3029, or 800/332-3029). Located 2 miles west of Beaver Creek on U.S. 6, it's a small family-oriented area, with one high-speed quad-chair lift and a beginners' surface lift serving 11 runs, nearly all of them for intermediates or novices. The mountain has a 1,700-foot vertical, from a base elevation of 7,400 feet to the summit of 9,100. With annual snowfall of just 115 inches (not quite 10 feet), it doesn't open until Christmas week, but then stays open until early April, daily from 9am to 3:30pm. Full-day tickets are $22 for adults, $14 for children 16 and under and seniors 65 to 69; family rates are available.

Adventurous downhillers who want to get away from the crowded slopes can try helicopter skiing with **Colorado Heli-Ski U.S.A.** (tel. 303/668-5600, or 800/TRY-HELI-SKI); or snow-cat tours with **Nova Guides** (tel. 949-4232), **Piney River Ranch** (tel. 476-3941), or **Resolution Snotours** (tel. 476-2556).

For rentals or sales of ski equipment, there are many, many options. Try **American Ski Exchange,** 225 Wall Street, Vail (tel. 303/476-1477, or 800/327-1137); **Christy Sports,** 182 Avon Road, Avon (tel. 949-0241); or **Kenny's Double Diamond Ski Shop,** 520 Lionshead Mall, Vail (tel. 476-5500). You can outfit the children, meanwhile, at **KidSport,** 122 East Meadow Drive, Vail (tel. 303/476-1666, or 800/833-1729).

**SKIING (NORDIC)**  Cross-country skiers needn't feel left out by the emphasis on downhill skiing here. Each of the resorts has ample nordic terrain set aside, and there's a tremendous system of winter trails through the surrounding mountains.

Vail's **Golden Peak Cross-Country Skiing Center** (tel. 476-5601, ext. 4390), located at the bases of Chairs 6 and 12 at Vail Village, has 20km (12 miles) of trails, part of them on the Vail Golf Course. In addition, an 8-mile (13km) track extends to the **Vail Nordic Center,** 75 South Frontage Road East (tel. 476-8366); in summer, this is the Vail Nature Center.

Beaver Creek Resort has a nordic skiing center on its golf course, and a 30km (18-mile) mountaintop track system in 9,840-foot **McCoy Park** (tel. 949-5750, ext. 4313), atop the Strawberry Park Chair (Lift 12). Most of the high-altitude terrain here is intermediate, though there's some for both beginners and advanced cross-country skiers; telemarking lessons are available.

All these areas are open for lessons and touring daily from 10am to 4pm, with rentals of cross-country equipment, snowshoes, and sleds.

For general information on the wonderful network of backcountry trails in the Vail area, consult the **Holy Cross Ranger District Office,** White River National

Forest, P.O. Box 190, Minturn, CO 81645 (tel. 303/827-5715). Of particular note is the system of trails known as the **Tenth Mountain Trail Association Hut System.** Generally following the World War II training network of the Camp Hale militia, the trails cover 261 miles and link Vail with Leadville and Aspen with Arrowhead; eventually, the two sections will connect. There are 14 overnight cabins, and more are being built. Hikers and mountain bikers also use this trail. For reservations and other information, contact the association at 1280 Ute Avenue, Aspen, CO 81611 (tel. 303/925-5775).

For more information on equipment rentals, see "Skiing (Alpine)," above.

**SLEIGH RIDES**   At the Vail Golf Club, **Steve Jones' Sleigh Rides** (tel. 476-8057 or 479-2260) offers afternoon rides and dinner packages. **The Bristol** (tel. 476-0200 or 926-2111) has similar offerings at Arrowhead resort near Avon.

**SNOWMOBILING**   Three tours daily—lunch, afternoon, and dinner—are conducted at the **Piney River Ranch,** Red Sandstone Road (tel. 476-3941). You can also go snowmobiling with **Nova Guides** (tel. 949-4232) or **Timberline Tours** (tel. 476-1414).

**SWIMMING**   Call for free-swim hours at the public **Eagle-Vail Swim Club,** 0099 Eagle Drive, Avon (tel. 949-4257). Numerous private clubs in Vail offer swimming for a fee; they include the **Vail Athletic Club,** 352 East Meadow Drive (tel. 476-0700), and the **Vail Run Resort,** 1000 Lionsridge Loop (tel. 476-1500).

**TENNIS**   There are 40 public courts in the Vail valley, including nine at **Golden Peak,** at the foot of Lift 6, and six at **Ford Park,** on South Frontage Road east of Vail Village. Lofty guest and court fees are charged by resort condominiums with indoor/outdoor courts, including the **Vail Racquet Club,** 4690 Racquet Club Drive (tel. 476-4840).

## SHOPPING

Vail is noted for its fine-art galleries. Among the many of note are **Driscol Galleries,** 100 East Meadow Drive (tel. 476-5171), with life-size sculpture gardens and impressionist paintings; **Lone Mountain Gallery,** 450 East Lionshead Circle (tel. 476-8513), focusing on fine Native American arts and crafts; and **Vail Fine Art Gallery,** 141 East Meadow Drive (tel. 476-2900), specializing in American and international masters. For a full gallery listing, write the **Vail Valley Arts Council,** P.O. Box 1153, Vail, CO 81658.

Vail and Beaver Creek also have a large number of fine clothiers and jewelers, along with every other kind of shop.

## EVENING ENTERTAINMENT

**THE PERFORMING ARTS**   The summer season's big cultural event is the ✪ **Bravo! Colorado Music Festival,** from July 4 through the first week of August. Established in 1988, the festival features everything from classical orchestral and chamber music to vocal and pops, from baroque to modern jazz, foreign ethnic performances to youth concerts. Performance days and times vary, but there are typically chamber-music concerts on Tuesday at 8pm at the **Chapel at Beaver Creek** (tickets: $15), major concerts on Saturday and Sunday at 6pm at the **Gerald Ford Amphitheatre** in Ford Park, Vail (tickets: $12.50), and more intimate presentations in **The Lodge at Vail** (tickets: $15). For tickets or more information, contact the festival office at 953 South Frontage Road, Suite 104, Vail, CO 81657 (tel. 303/476-0206).

The **Bolshoi Ballet Academy at Vail,** a satellite school to the famous Bolshoi of Moscow, teaches the Russian style of artistic expression to about 50 young dancers from the United States, Canada, and Mexico. In 1991 the parent Bolshoi Ballet

Academy of Moscow performed in Vail, and may do so again; for information, contact the Vail Valley Foundation, P.O. Box 309, Vail, CO 81658 (tel. 303/476-9500).

Vail's Ford Amphitheatre hosts **Hot Summer Nights** concerts of contemporary rock or jazz every Friday evening of July and August. Beaver Creek Resort's **Jazz on the Green,** which runs late June through Labor Day weekend, features regional jazz sounds from across America on Sunday at noon on the resort's south lawn.

**DINNER THEATER**   So far as Vail's nightlife scene goes, ✪ **Club Majiks,** at the Crossroads Shopping Center, West Meadow Drive at Willow Bridge Road (tel. 476-2626), heads the list. Former Tony Award–winning Broadway producer Mark Schwartz (*La Cage aux Folles, My One and Only*) operates this dinner club/cabaret, where the staff perform hits from such musicals as *Cabaret, West Side Story,* and *A Chorus Line.* The food at Majiks is truly gourmet: a four-course meal with such dishes as mesquite-grilled swordfish, loin of venison, and duck confit. Open Tuesday through Saturday night during the winter and summer seasons; closed spring and fall.

**DANCE CLUBS**   Vail's greatest concentration of nightclubs can be found in a 1½-block stretch of Bridge Street from Hanson Ranch Road north to the covered bridge over Gore Creek. From mountainside to creek, they include **Cyrano's** (tel. 476-5551), **The Club** (tel. 479-0556), the **Red Lion** (tel. 476-7676), **Vendetta's** (tel. 476-5070), and **Nick's** (tel. 476-6700). All have music for dancing: either live rock, rhythm-and-blues, or disco.

Just off Bridge Drive on Gore Creek Drive is **Sheika's,** a lively disco at Gasthof Gramshammer (tel. 476-5626). There are dance clubs in the Evergreen Lodge (the **Altitude Club**), 250 South Frontage Road West (tel. 476-7810), and Marriott Mark Resort (**Bogie's**), 715 West Lionshead Circle (tel. 476-4444).

Country music enthusiasts find swing and two-step on the dance floor at the **Sundance Saloon,** Sunbird Lodge, Lionshead Gondola (tel. 476-3453); or **The Jackalope,** West Vail Mall (tel. 476-4314).

**BARS & PUBS**   Piano bars draw quieter types to **Babau's Café** at L'Ostello, 705 West Lionshead Circle (tel. 476-2050); **Mickey's** in the Lodge at Vail, 174 East Gore Creek Drive (tel. 476-5011); and **Ludwig's** in the Sonnenalp Hotel, 20 Vail Road (tel. 476-5656). Acoustic guitarists soothe nerves at the **Hong Kong Café,** Wall Street (tel. 476-1818), and **C. J. Capers,** 2211 North Frontage Road West (tel. 476-5306).

In Beaver Creek, the place to go is the **Beaver Trap Tavern,** St. James Place (tel. 845-8930); in Avon, try **Rug's Pub,** Benchmark Plaza, 48 East Beaver Creek Boulevard (tel. 949-7099).

One of Vail's newest establishments is the **Hubcap Brewery and Kitchen,** at the Crossroads Shopping Center, West Meadow Drive at Willow Bridge Road (tel. 476-5757). Vail's first brewpub, the Hubcap invites beer connoisseurs to its huge beer garden, where they can sip such homemade delights as White River Wheat Ale and Rainbow Trout Stout.

# WHERE TO STAY

In general, winter season is mid-November to mid-April; summer is the opposite, mid-April to mid-November. Prices are lowest in summer, highest during the Christmas holiday period, and they remain relatively high through the prime January-to-March ski season. Early and late winter seasons (mid-November to mid-December and April until area closing) are moderately priced.

## VAIL

### Expensive

**THE LODGE AT VAIL, 174 E. Gore Creek Dr., Vail, CO 81657. Tel. 303/476-5011,** or 800/231-0136. Fax 303/476-7425. 138 rms, 84 suites. TV TEL

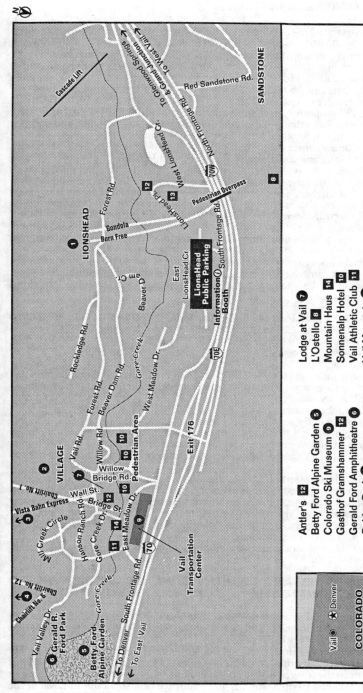

# VAIL

Antler's **12**
Betty Ford Alpine Garden **5**
Colorado Ski Museum **9**
Gasthof Gramshammer **12**
Gerald Ford Amphitheatre **6**
Golden Peak **4**
LionsHead **1**
Lions Square Lodge **13**

Lodge at Vail **7**
L'Ostello **8**
Mountain Haus **14**
Sonnenalp Hotel **10**
Vail Athletic Club **11**
Vail Mountain **3**
Vail Village **2**

COLORADO

Vail ● ★ Denver

Information ⓘ

**$ Rates:** Winter, $275–$400 single; $330–$455 double; $500–$1,300 suite. Summer, $140–$160 single; $195–$215 double; $175–$450 suite. 2-week minimum stay over Christmas holidays. AE, DC, MC, V. **Parking:** Free.

Vail's original deluxe hotel—owned by Venice Simplon Orient Express, and a member of the Leading Hotels of the World—sits at the base of the Vista Bahn Express in the heart of Vail Village. (Follow Vail Road south from the main Vail interchange, through two lights and around a curve to the left, to the end of the road.) As with most Vail properties, once you've parked, you needn't use your car again until you return home. Everything you need is within a few steps: winter and summer recreation, restaurants, lounges, boutiques, galleries—and stunning views.

The Lodge offers deluxe hotel rooms and one-, two-, and three-bedroom suites. All have private balconies, mahogany furnishings and paneling, mini-refrigerators, full-view mirrors, and floral-pattern appointments. The bathrooms, finished with marble, feature hairdryers, phones, and heated towel racks. Suites, each with a fireplace and full kitchen, are individually owned and decorated by their personal owners, with touches that vary from French provincial to Colorado western.

**Dining/Entertainment:** The five-star Wildflower Inn (see "Where to Dine," below) serves creative American cuisine in a garden atmosphere. The Café Arlberg offers a deluxe breakfast buffet, lunch, and country Italian cuisine on winter evenings. Mickey's piano bar has featured Mickey Poage at the ivories for 17 years.

**Services:** 24-hour room service, concierge, valet laundry, international currency exchange, business center, baby-sitting, ski storage, no-smoking rooms.

**Facilities:** Heated swimming pool, Jacuzzis, sauna, exercise room, six tennis courts, gift shop, meeting space for 175.

### L'OSTELLO, 705 W. Lionshead Circle, Vail, CO 81657. Tel. 303/476-2050, or 800/283-VAIL. Fax 303/476-9265. 49 rms, 3 suites. TV TEL

**$ Rates:** Winter, early/mid/late season, $170–$245 double; holiday and peak season (Feb–Mar), $240–$295 double. Summer, $95–$135 double. AE, MC, V. **Parking:** Free.

A European-style mountain inn just 100 yards from the Lionshead Gondola terminal, L'Ostello lives up to its claim of being "long on sophistication but short on formality." "The Refuge," as its Italian name translates, has a big central fireplace completely surrounded by sunken seating, and one of the Vail Valley's outstanding restaurants.

Guest rooms are fairly simple. Older rooms have a double Murphy bed, a double sofa sleeper, light-wood furnishings, and a wet bar. Renovated rooms are more special: They have a rich contemporary appearance and feature individual home-entertainment centers. A compact-disc and video-cassette library is complimentary to guests.

**Dining/Entertainment:** L'Ostello restaurant has won national acclaim for its northern Italian cuisine (see "Where to Dine," below). Babau's Café offers light meals daily from 4:30pm, and major jazz piano entertainment Tuesday through Sunday nights. Breakfast is served daily from 7 to 10am in the L'Ostello dining room.

**Services:** Room service, concierge, valet laundry, complimentary *USA Today* (delivered to your room each morning).

**Facilities:** Heated outdoor swimming pool, fitness center, massage room, meeting space for 100.

### SONNENALP HOTEL AND COUNTRY CLUB, 20 Vail Rd., Vail, CO 81657. Tel. 303/476-5656, or 800/654-8312. Fax 303/476-1639. 80 rms, 100 suites. TV TEL

**$ Rates** (including full breakfast): Winter, $155–$270 single; $165–$280 double; $295–$660 suite. Summer, $95–$125 single; $105–$135 double; $170–$265 suite. DC, MC, V. **Parking:** Free.

This is one of Vail's more unusual hotels, encompassing three separate buildings that extend—interrupted by other properties—for two blocks along the south side of Gore Creek, from the covered bridge across Willow Bridge Road to the Vail Interfaith Chapel. Each building has the warmth and ambience of a small inn in Bavaria, the original home of owners Rosana and Johannes Fässler. Yet the hotel is able to offer the amenities of a large resort complex complete with golfing at the Singletree Golf Course (see "Sports & Recreation" in "What to See & Do," above), 18 miles east near Edwards.

Creekside, garden-level, and Village View hotel rooms, and a wide variety of suites, are furnished with loving detail. From carved pine armoires to down comforters and pillows, all furniture and appointments are imported from the German Alps—right down to staff uniforms.

**Dining/Entertainment:** Ludwig's (see "Where to Dine," below) is an intimate creekside dining room serving continental and new American cuisines. The casual Bully Pub features soup and salad bar, pastas, pizzas, and sandwiches. The Swiss Chalet offers traditional Swiss foods: raclette and cheese and beef fondues.

**Services:** Room service, concierge, valet laundry.

**Facilities:** Full European health spa and cosmetic boutique, two heated outdoor swimming pools, hot tubs, four tennis courts, golf course (with Swing Dynamics Institute); kindergarten program for children; meeting space for 150.

**VAIL ATHLETIC CLUB, 352 E. Meadow Dr. (at Vail Valley Dr.), Vail, CO 81657. Tel. 303/476-0700,** or 800/822-4754. Fax 303/476-6451. 31 rms, 7 suites. TV TEL

**$ Rates:** Winter, $215–$365 single or double; $385–$750 suite. Summer, $110 single or double; $225 suite. AE, MC, V. **Parking:** Free.

The town's leading athletic club, including a Human Performance Center with two doctors and a nutritionist on staff, is the centerpiece of this friendly hotel. A cozy, pine-paneled lobby and lounge area with several comfortable couches immediately give guests a feeling of relaxation.

Located on the highway side of Gore Creek, just off South Frontage Road, the VAC has rooms with balconies and mountain views overlooking Vail Village or the creek. Guest rooms have two queen-size beds or one king-size bed and a full bath. Suites have a kitchen, living room with fireplace, one bedroom, and two full baths. Rooms are appointed in pastel shades of mauve, peach, and green; each has a humidifier and terry-cloth robes.

**Dining/Entertainment:** Breakfast and dinner are served at the club's restaurant, 352 East. The lounge has live grand-piano entertainment.

**Services:** Room service, concierge, complimentary shuttle van, valet laundry, baby-sitting, secretarial service, complimentary newspaper, ski storage, no-smoking rooms, facilities for the disabled.

**Facilities:** Athletic club and spa (with a swimming pool, handball and squash courts, Jacuzzi, sauna, and other facilities), gift shop, guest laundry, barbershop, beauty salon; meeting space for 50.

## Moderate

**ANTLERS AT VAIL, 680 W. Lionshead Place, Vail, CO 81657. Tel. 303/456-2471,** or 800/843-VAIL. Fax 303/476-4146. 69 suites (all with bath). TV TEL

**$ Rates:** Winter, $170–$270; summer, $85–$120. AE, DC, DISC, MC, V. **Parking:** Free.

These luxurious condominium units near the foot of the Lionshead Gondola have a long reputation for friendly service and unobstructed views up Vail Mountain. Units range in size from studios to three-bedroom suites; each has a full-size, fully equipped kitchen, a fireplace, a private view balcony, and satellite TV (with HBO and free video-cassette recorder). Facilities include a heated outdoor swimming pool, Jacuzzi, sun deck, two saunas, guest laundry, and ski storage. There's meeting space for 150.

**GASTHOF GRAMSHAMMER, 231 E. Gore Creek Dr., Vail, CO 81657. Tel. 303/476-5626.** 24 rms, 4 suites (all with bath). Fax 303/476-8816. TV TEL

**$ Rates:** Winter, $190–$220 single or double; $275–$485 suite. Summer, $75 single; $80–$95 double; $150–$245 suite. AE, DC, MC, V. **Parking:** Free.

Austria natives Pepi and Sheika Gramshammer built this Tyrolean lodge three decades ago and watched Vail Village grow up around it. The Gramshammers still greet guests personally at their lodge, which maintains a deluxe European-style ambience all the way to the goose-down comforters. There's a wide choice of room types: standard (two double beds), deluxe (two queen-size or one king-size), deluxe with kitchenette, studio apartment, studio suites with connecting bedroom, one-bedroom apartment, two-bedroom suite, and family suite.

Pepi's Restaurant serves continental cuisine for lunch and dinner; the Antlers Room specializes in wild game and veal. Pepi's Bar frequently has live music, and Sheika's Night Club is popular for disco dancing. The lodge also has a sports equipment and fashion shop.

**LION SQUARE LODGE, 660 W. Lionshead Place, Vail, CO 81657. Tel. 303/457-2281,** or 800/525-5788. Fax 303/476-7423. 28 rms, 75 suites (all with bath). TV TEL
**$ Rates:** Winter, $195 lodge; $310 one-bedroom; $455 two-bedroom. Summer, $85 lodge; $105 one-bedroom; $175 two-bedroom. AE, CB, DC, DISC, JCB, MC, V. **Parking:** Free.

A ski-in, ski-out property on Gore Creek at the base of the Lionshead Gondola, the Lion Square offers deluxe lodge rooms or one-, two-, and three-bedroom condominiums. All condo units have mountain views, spacious living rooms with balconies and wood-burning fireplaces, and fully equipped kitchens.

There are complimentary coffee, cookies, and newspapers in the lobby each morning, and the K.B. Ranch Co. serves steak and seafood dinners. The lodge offers concierge, valet laundry, and a free local shuttle van. Facilities include a heated outdoor swimming pool, hot tubs, sauna, ski and bicycle storage, and meeting space for 400.

**MOUNTAIN HAUS AT VAIL, 292 E. Meadow Dr. (P.O. Box 1748), Vail, CO 81658. Tel. 303/476-2434,** or 800/237-0922. Fax 303/476-3007. 24 rms, 51 suites (all with bath). TV TEL
**$ Rates:** Winter, $120–$330 single; $120–$495 double; $325–$830 suite. Summer, $85–$155 single; $85–$205 double; $190–$330 suite. AE, MC, V.

Located in Vail Village on East Meadow Drive at Bridge Street, at the covered bridge across Gore Creek, these privately owned condominiums have been individually decorated by their owners. Guests can choose between handsome, spacious hotel rooms and one- to four-bedroom condo units. All have fireplaces (wood is provided), private balconies, and fully equipped kitchens. Two-bedroom units sleep six: There's a sleeper sofa in the living room, two bathrooms, and a ski room at the entrance.

The Mountain Haus has a heated outdoor swimming pool, indoor and outdoor Jacuzzis, men's and women's steam rooms and saunas, a guest laundry, and valet laundry service. The desk is staffed 24 hours.

## Inexpensive

**PARK MEADOWS LODGE, 1472 Matterhorn Circle, Vail, CO 81657. Tel. 303/476-5598.** 12 rms, 15 suites (all with bath). TV TEL
**$ Rates:** Winter, $55–$105; summer, $35–$65. Weekly rates available; children 12 and under stay free in parents' room. MC, V.

Located in West Vail, a 10-minute walk from the Cascade Village Lift and the terminus of the free Vail shuttle, the Park Meadows is one of the few family-style economy lodges left in the Vail valley. All rooms—efficiency studios, one-bedroom and two-bedroom suites—have kitchenettes and hideaway sofas. There's a central sitting area with a large fireplace and board games, a recreation room with a pool table, a hot tub in an outdoor courtyard, and a coin laundry.

**THE ROOST LODGE, 1783 N. Frontage Rd. W., Vail, CO 81657. Tel. 303/476-5451,** or 800/873-3065. 72 rms (all with bath). TV TEL
**$ Rates** (including continental breakfast): Winter, $58–$114; summer, $39–$59. MC, V.

Personal attention in a country-inn atmosphere is the boast of the Roost, a family-run ski lodge on the north side of I-70 in West Vail. Rooms are cozy, with pleasing appointments. The lodge has an enclosed outdoor swimming pool, Jacuzzi, and sauna, and is accessible to the disabled. A free lodge shuttle runs to Vail Village on the hour, daily from 8am to midnight.

## WEST OF VAIL

### Expensive

**BEAVER CREEK LODGE, 24 Avondale Lane (P.O. Box 2578), Beaver Creek, CO 81620. Tel.** 303/845-9800, **or** 800/732-6777. Fax 303/845-8242. 86 suites. A/C TV TEL
**$ Rates** (including breakfast): $275–$325 suites; condo units to $475. AE, CB, DC, MC, V. **Parking:** Free underground valet parking.
The phrase "casually elegant" can be overworked, but it fits this brand-new (in 1990) all-suite property. Located in the heart of Beaver Creek at the foot of the Centennial Express Lift, it's built around an interior atrium, but it avoids the institutional appearance of many other atrium hotels.

The hotel's 70 efficiency suites have handsome oak furnishings and paneling throughout. All have queen-size beds and sleeper sofas, fully equipped kitchenettes with microwave ovens and wet bars, gas-light fireplaces, humidifiers, two TVs (one with a video-cassette recorder), and two phones. Another 16 condominium units are ideal for families and groups.

**Dining/Entertainment:** The Black Diamond Bar and Grill serves a breakfast buffet, lunch, and dinners of gourmet continental and new American cuisine. Dining indoors is bistro style; outside, there's a viewing deck. Many folks gravitate to the Atrium Lobby Bar for après-ski.

**Services:** Room service, 24-hour concierge, individual ski lockers.

**Facilities:** Indoor/outdoor swimming pool, Jacuzzi, steam room, sauna, exercise equipment, ski-rental shop, retail shops and boutiques; meeting space for 300.

**CAMBERLEY CLUB HOTEL, Scott Hill Rd. (P.O. Box 18450), Beaver Creek, CO 81620. Tel.** 303/845-7900, **or** 800/866-7666. Fax 303/845-7809. 60 rms. TV TEL
**$ Rates:** Winter, $250–$400 single or double; $650–$975 suite. Summer, $95–$175 single or double; $270–$405 suite. MC, V. **Parking:** Covered valet parking.
Pine and aspen groves camouflage this handsome lodge, situated on a hillside overlooking Beaver Creek Resort from the west. Skiers can easily come and go from the Strawberry Park Lift to the hotel, which has a stately, almost Tudor-style elegance.

Rooms are furnished in Bavarian charm, with a southwestern ambience. They've got adobe walls and natural-pine furniture, as well as a panoramic view of the resort village. Each room has a king-size or two double beds with goose-down comforters. Amenities include hairdryers and terry-cloth robes, and every room has a video-cassette recorder with its television; the hotel maintains a free video library for guests.

**Dining/Entertainment:** Colours Restaurant serves three meals daily, including gourmet continental dinners. Tea is offered in the library each afternoon, and there are complimentary hors d'oeuvres in the lounge.

**Services:** 24-hour room service, ski valet, business center.

**Facilities:** Heated outdoor swimming pool, Jacuzzi, steam rooms, fitness center, games room, recreation programs; meeting space for 150.

**HYATT REGENCY BEAVER CREEK, P.O. Box 1595, Avon, CO 81620. Tel.** 303/949-1234, **or** 800/233-1234. Fax 303/949-4164. 298 rms. MINIBAR TV TEL
**$ Rates:** Winter, $330–$415 single or double; $490–$2,000 suite. Summer, $159–$185 single or double; $325–$940 suite. Seasonal packages. Children 18 and under stay free in parents' room. Singles matched with same-sex roommate on request. AE, CB, DC, DISC, JCB, MC, V. **Parking:** Free.
An architecturally unique hotel at the foot of the Beaver Creek lifts, the Hyatt blends features of medieval European alpine monasteries with Rocky Mountain styles and materials. The exterior is native stone, offset with stucco and rough timbers; a domed cupola, peaked roofs, and copper flashing are singular touches. The interior is

of rough-hewn pine and sandstone; wall-size fireplaces enhance numerous cozy alcoves furnished with overstuffed chairs and sofas. Elk-antler chandeliers and works by contemporary artisans lend a western ambience. Guest rooms have a European country elegance, knotty-pine furnishings, and a stenciled border to the ceiling and walls. The raised beds have dust ruffles, pillow shams, and quilted comforters. The TV and minibar are in an armoire. Most rooms have private balconies. The bathroom features a marble-top vanity, hairdryer, heated towel rack, and coffee maker.

**Dining/Entertainment:** The Patina Grill, open for three meals daily, has an open fireplace for cold days and an outdoor terrace for warm ones. The menu offers everything from gourmet American cuisine to light snacks. The Crooked Hearth lounge and eatery serves fondues and pizzas around another large fireplace, and offers live entertainment most nights. The Double Diamond Deli has all manner of snacks, and even prepares picnic baskets for mountain hikes and rides. The Lobby Lounge has a piano bar for evening cocktails, and the Skiers' Cafeteria offers quick meals and a daily après-ski party. The Hyatt has a cozy library with books and chessboards.

**Services:** Room service, concierge, complimentary ski valet, Camp Hyatt children's day program.

**Facilities:** Full-service health spa (with indoor/outdoor swimming pool, six open-air Jacuzzis, saunas, weight and exercise room, aerobics and water aerobics classes, facials, massages, and herbal wraps), five tennis courts; retail boutiques, jewelry, and sportswear; meeting space for 750.

**THE LODGE AT CORDILLERA, 2205 Cordillera Way (P.O. Box 1110), Edwards, CO 81632. Tel. 303/926-2200,** or 800/548-2721. 28 rms and suites. A/C TV TEL
**$ Rates** (including breakfast): Winter, $145–$325; summer, $125–$225. AE, CB, DC, DISC, JCB, MC, V. **Parking:** Free valet parking.

Like a mountain château in the Pyrenees of southwestern France, this luxurious hideaway nestles in 2,000 acres of private forest 13 miles west of Vail, and about 3 miles from Beaver Creek. Chinese slate roofs crown the sophisticated edifice of native woods, stone, and stucco.

The same Rocky Mountain timber and stone, along with elegant wrought iron, are used in the handsome, residential-style guest rooms. Hand-worked Spanish and French furnishings lend an Old World touch. More than half the rooms feature wood-burning fireplaces; all have king- or queen-size beds with down comforters, remote-control cable television, and private balconies or decks with views of the New York Range of the Rockies.

**Dining/Entertainment:** The Restaurant Picasso is one of the Vail Valley's finest dining establishments (see "Where to Dine," below). A European buffet breakfast, included with the room bill, is also served here. The Lobby Lounge presents piano music Wednesday through Sunday in season.

**Services:** Room service, concierge, valet laundry.

**Facilities:** European spa and salon (outdoor swimming pool and 25m/82-ft. indoor lap pool, indoor and outdoor Jacuzzis, steam room and sauna in men's and women's locker rooms, weight and exercise room, aerobics, massage, hydrotherapy, body treatments), 15 miles of mountain-biking or cross-country skiing trails, two tennis courts; meeting space for 125.

## Moderate

**EAGLE RIVER INN, 145 N. Main St. (P.O. Box 100), Minturn, CO 81645. Tel. 303/827-5761,** or 800/344-1750. 12 rms (all with three-quarter bath). TV
**$ Rates** (including breakfast): Winter, single or double, $89–$99 early and late season, $129–$155 regular season, $175 holiday periods; summer, $79 single or double. MC, V. **Closed:** Late Apr to June 1.

Built in 1894 when the Denver & Rio Grande Railroad first made the village of Minturn a stop on its route, the picturesque Eagle River Inn has had many incarnations. Its latest makeover, in 1986, turned it into one of the finest bed and breakfasts in the Rocky Mountain region. It feels like Santa Fe throughout, from the *sala*-style lobby (complete with *kiva* fireplace, *bancos*, and other southwestern-style furnishings) to the bright and breezy second- and third-story guest rooms. The rooms feature tiled three-quarter baths and down comforters.

Breakfast is "gourmet continental," including homemade granola, fresh fruit, and baked goods. In the evening, the inn hosts a wine-and-cheese hour; and the hot tub on a deck overlooking the Eagle River is always available.

## Inexpensive

**COMFORT INN, 0161 W. Beaver Creek Blvd. (P.O. Box 5510), Avon, CO 81620. Tel. 303/949-5511,** or 800/423-4374. Fax 303/949-7762. 143 rms, 4 suites (all with bath). A/C TV TEL

**$ Rates** (including continental breakfast): Winter, $79–$195 single or double. Summer, $49–$75 single or double; $59–$84 suite. AE, DC, DISC, ER, JCB, MC, V. **Parking:** Free.

A four-story hotel just off the I-70 Avon/Beaver Creek interchange, this comfortable franchise establishment has a big fireplace in its lobby lounge and modified southwestern decor. Most of the spacious rooms have two queen-size beds; a few boast king-size beds. All rooms have remote-control cable television. No-smoking rooms are available. There's indoor ski storage and a free shuttle to Beaver Creek Resort, a heated outdoor pool, a Jacuzzi, and a guest laundry.

## CAMPING

**SYLVAN LAKE STATE PARK, Brush Creek Rd., 16 miles south of Eagle. Tel. 303/625-1607.** 50 sites.

**$ Rates:** $6 per site, plus state parks pass. No credit cards.

Two separate campgrounds on this beautiful 40-acre trout-fishing lake in the White River National Forest accommodate tents and recreational vehicles. There are bathhouses, fire pits, water, and other facilities.

# WHERE TO DINE

## VERY EXPENSIVE

**BEANO'S CABIN, foot of Larkspur Lift, Beaver Creek Resort. Tel. 949-9090.**

**Cuisine:** REGIONAL. **Reservations:** Required.

**$ Prices:** Fixed-price, $69 adults, $46 children under 12. MC, V.

**Open:** Lunch daily 11:30am–2:30pm; dinner Thurs–Fri 5:30–9:30pm (departures every 50 minutes, 4:45–8:55pm, from Rendezvous Cabin).

One splurge that every Beaver Creek visitor should make is the sleigh-ride dinner trip (or in summer, the horse-drawn wagon ride) to Beano's. This isn't the log homestead that Chicago lettuce farmer Frank "Beano" Bienkowski built on Beaver Creek Mountain in 1919—it's far more elegant. Diners board the 42-passenger, snowcat-driven sleighs at the base of the Centennial Lift, arriving 15 minutes later for a candlelit dinner around a crackling fire with musical entertainment.

The four-course menu includes fresh bread, homemade soup, salad, and a choice of four dishes: rib-eye steak, roast leg of lamb, applewood-roasted chicken with blue-corn stuffing, or fresh fish. Desserts are included; try the chocolate bread pudding with bourbon whipped cream.

**L'OSTELLO, 705 W. Lionshead Circle. Tel. 476-2050.**

**Cuisine:** NORTHERN ITALIAN. **Reservations:** Recommended.

**$ Prices:** Appetizers $9–$12; main courses $28–$36. AE, MC, V.

**Open:** Dinner only, daily 5:30–10:30pm.

Under the same ownership as New York's *nuova cuccina* Andiamo, L'Ostello ("The Refuge") is an ultra-contemporary dining room in a small European-style hotel. Tiny hanging halogen light fixtures, unusual metal chairs with embroidered cushions, and a tile floor provide the atmosphere: The restaurant is otherwise devoid of decoration, which allows diners to focus on the food.

You can start with such appetizers as deep-fried spinach gnocchi or a salad of grilled wild mushrooms. The fine choice of dishes changes on a regular basis, but may include crabmeat ravioli with carrot-butter sauce, roast rack of lamb with goat cheese in phyllo, roast halibut with braised artichokes, or grilled sirloin with sesame risotto. Vegetables are grilled and served with three different accompaniments: tapenade, pesto, and a sun-dried-tomato pesto.

**RESTAURANT PICASSO, in the Lodge at Cordillera, 2205 Cordillera Way, Edwards. Tel. 926-2200.**
   **Cuisine:** MODERN FRENCH. **Reservations:** Recommended.
**$ Prices:** Fixed-price dinners $40–$50. AE, MC, V.
   **Open:** Dinner only, daily 5:30–9:30pm.
Original works by Pablo Picasso actually hang on the walls of this sophisticated restaurant, which combines European elegance with Rocky Mountain splendor. Belgian chef Philippe van Cappellen is as much an artist in the kitchen as was Picasso in his studio. His menu changes nightly, but is invariably memorable.

You can start with asparagus parfait with caviar, buffalo carpaccio, or duck ballotine with truffles and pistachio. Main dishes might include filet of beef bordelaise, boneless quail with oyster mushrooms baked in puff pastry, escalope of salmon on a sauce of sweet red peppers, roast breast of duck with beaujolais and candied garlic—you get the idea. Leave room for dessert: walnut mousse with nougatine and chocolate sauce, mango tart with almond ice cream, puff pastry brioche with rhubarb, apples, and peaches. . . .

### EXPENSIVE

**THE BRISTOL AT ARROWHEAD, Country Club of the Rockies, 0676 Sawatche Dr., Edwards. Tel. 926-2111.**
   **Cuisine:** CREATIVE AMERICAN. **Reservations:** Recommended.
**$ Prices:** Appetizers $6.95–$8.95; main courses $15.95–$25.50; lunch $3.75–$7.50. AE, MC, V.
   **Open:** Lunch daily 11:30am–3pm; dinner daily 6–10pm.
You can enjoy a sleigh ride for dinner, but unlike Beano's, that's a fringe benefit here, not the means to the end. The dining room at this popular golf-and-ski resort center, 3 miles east of Beaver Creek off I-70 Exit 163, is decidedly not far off the beaten path.

The menu is inspired by imagination and international culinary knowledge. Appetizers include four-mushroom croustade, lobster quesadilla, and—in a bow to Japan and Mexico—*takoshimi,* or *sashimi* (raw fish) tacos. There are fresh cooked seafood specials daily, as well as Mandarin vermicelli, topped with sliced grilled duck breast, in orange-sesame dressing; filet mignon stuffed with Anaheim chile, grilled, and topped with ancho chile butter; blackened salmon Cajun style with peach-and-mint chutney; peppered pheasant breast; and porcini mushroom pasta.

**CHANTICLER, 710 W. Lionshead Circle. Tel. 476-1441.**
   **Cuisine:** CONTINENTAL. **Reservations:** Recommended.
**$ Prices:** Appetizers $6.25–$9.95; main courses $13.50–$24.95. AE, DISC, MC, V.
   **Open:** Dinner only, daily 5–10pm.
Victorian surroundings greet you in this intimate French-country restaurant in the Vail Spa. Pewter antiques and fine artwork grace the shelves and walls, and beautiful brass chandeliers hang over the candlelit tables. Service is attentive but not intrusive.

Wild game and fish grace the menu. You can start with a carpaccio of venison or escargots with artichoke hearts, then move on to continental favorites: tournedos aux champignons, médaillons de veau à l'estragon, sole avec mousseline de saumon et coquille St-Jacques, poulette Normandie, or a light seafood pasta.

**THE GOLDEN EAGLE INN, Village Hall, Beaver Creek Mall. Tel. 949-1940.**
   **Cuisine:** CREATIVE REGIONAL.
**$ Prices:** Appetizers $5.95–$8.95; main courses $14.95–$27.95; lunch $8.50–$12.95. AE, MC, V.
   **Open:** Daily 11:30am–midnight.

Sidewalk tables on the Beaver Creek promenade are the outstanding feature of this restaurant, owned by Austrian Pepi Langeggar of Vail's Tyrolean Inn. Appetizers include a baked almond-coated Brie and venison in phyllo with mushroom cream. Main courses feature loin of elk in a hazelnut-and-burgundy sauce, rack of lamb with plum chutney, grilled pheasant breast with a red-currant and amaretto sauce, pastas, and fresh seafood.

## IMPERIAL FEZ, 1000 Lions Ridge Loop. Tel. 476-1948.

**Cuisine:** MOROCCAN. **Reservations:** Recommended.
**$ Prices:** Fixed-price dinner $25 for five courses, $30 for six courses. MC, V.
**Open:** Dinner only, daily 5–10pm.

Remember the old cartoons, where the Bedouin's tent looks tiny from the outside but cavernous inside? That's not unlike the Imperial Fez, where you find yourself in a giant Moroccan tent when you walk through the door. Owner Rafih Benjelloun will seat you on cushions at a low, round table, then spread white towels across your laps to keep you from being too messy while you eat with your fingers. (Finger bowls are provided.) Belly dancers and sword dancers add to the entrancing atmosphere.

The equally exotic meals start with harrira (lamb-and-lentil soup) or sharbat (vegetarian soup), shlada (salad), and b'stella (pastry filled with Cornish hen, spiced eggs, fruits, almonds, and spices). Main courses cover a wide range of foods and preparations, like apricot lamb, fish in paprika sauce, Moroccan baked beef tajine, or spicy quail M'shui. There are also poultry, prawns, and vegetarian offerings. For dessert, have a cup of mint tea and a chocolate b'stella.

## SWEET BASIL, 193 E. Gore Creek Dr. Tel. 476-0125.

**Cuisine:** CREATIVE AMERICAN. **Reservations:** Recommended.
**$ Prices:** Appetizers $6–$9.50; main courses $4–$8.95 at lunch, $18–$25 at dinner. AE, MC, V.
**Open:** Lunch daily 11:30am–2:30pm; dinner daily 5:30–10pm.

Simple modern decor, with contemporary art on the peach-colored walls and tasteful use of mirrors and large windows, is the earmark of this pleasant restaurant. A deck looks out on the Lodge Promenade in the center of Vail Village. Diners can sit at private tables or be served at the wine bar, the only part of the restaurant where smoking is permitted.

Luncheon favorites here include smoked-duck salad with wild rice, dried apples, and maple-mustard dressing; and spicy lamb-sausage pizza with barbecue sauce. For dinner, you can start with a butternut-squash-and-chive soup with crab fritters, or grilled rabbit and Gorgonzola risotto. Popular choices include roast pheasant with grilled gnocchi and vegetable ragoût, grilled swordfish filet with Chinese black-bean sauce, and roast veal chop with Gorgonzola cream.

## TYROLEAN INN, 400 E. Meadow Dr. Tel. 476-2204.

**Cuisine:** REGIONAL/CONTINENTAL. **Reservations:** Recommended.
**$ Prices:** Appetizers $5.75–$8.95; main courses $14.95–$29.95. AE, DC, MC, V.
**Open:** Dinner only, daily 5:30–10pm.

The Langeggar family—Austrian-born Pepi and Ann, sons Siegmund and Peter—are proud of their Old World roots. Pepi established this Vail landmark more than two decades ago, and the ambience today remains decidedly alpine, with gracious, friendly service and authentic Tyrolean decor. In the summer, there's dining on an outdoor patio beside gurgling Gore Creek.

Wild game, when available, is the house specialty: venison sauerbraten, pheasant Kroatzbeere—or for the total experience, the wild-game medley of wild boar Budapest, elk forestière, and caribou Midnight Sun. You'll always find such items as pepper steak Madagascar, wienerschnitzel, Muscovy duck, scampi papriche, and cioppino Mediterranean.

## WILDFLOWER INN, in the Lodge at Vail, 174 E. Gore Creek Dr. Tel. 476-8111.

**Cuisine:** CREATIVE AMERICAN. **Reservations:** Recommended.
**$ Prices:** Appetizers $6–$21; main courses $19–$32. AE, DC, MC, V.
**Open:** Dinner only, Wed–Mon 6–10pm.

Fine china, silver, and crystal grace the Lodge's upscale dining room, a garden affair on the second floor, with a broad outdoor deck facing Vail Mountain. Chef Jim Cohen, whom Julia Child said is one of the nation's top 13 chefs, jokingly classified his cuisine as "post-modern Hebrew," and there may be a grain of truth there. Tuna-and-truffle tartare, fois-gras terrine, and salt-cod ravioli are among the appetizers offered. Then come the delightful main dishes: grilled duck breast on spinach pancakes with a red-pepper sauce, sautéed anglerfish with fried shallots, braised Sephardic short ribs, and roast veal breast with matzoh stuffing.

## MODERATE

**BLU'S, 193 E. Gore Creek Dr. Tel. 476-3113.**
   **Cuisine:** INTERNATIONAL. **Reservations:** Recommended at dinner.
**$ Prices:** Appetizers $5.25–$6.25; main courses $8.95–$15.95; breakfast/lunch $4.50–$6.95. MC, V.
   **Open:** Daily 9:30am–11pm.
This eatery, located down the stairs from the Children's Fountain by Gore Creek, off Willow Bridge Road, is a local favorite—in no small part because it offers breakfasts daily until 5pm for late risers.
   Omelets and crêpes are specialties, notably the baked seafood Florentine crêpe and the chicken pesto omelet. Midday, you can opt for a deli sandwich, pasta dishes (including Japanese yaki soba), and salmon hash O'Brien. Dinner is somewhat more upscale, with such starters as pâté maison and Mazatlán shrimp, and main dishes including pistachio schnitzel, mustard pepper steak, and pan-fried red trout.

**CYRANO'S, 298 Hanson Ranch Rd. Tel. 476-5551.**
   **Cuisine:** PACIFIC RIM. **Reservations:** Recommended.
**$ Prices:** Appetizers $3.75–$8.50; main courses $9.50–$19.50; lunch $5.25–$9.50. AE, MC, V.
   **Open:** Lunch Mon–Fri 11am–3pm; dinner daily 5–10pm; brunch Sat–Sun 8am–3pm.
Flavors of the Orient, the South Pacific, and Latin America spice up the menu at Cyrano's, which has dubbed itself a "Pacific bar and grill." The bar (see "Evening Entertainment" in "What to See & Do," above) is downstairs, the restaurant upstairs—surrounded by foliage, contemporary paintings, and light jazz music.
   You can get a truly international meal here. Start with chicken satay (Indonesian), crab spring rolls (Vietnamese), or seafood tamales (Mexican). Then consider mahimahi with macadamia nuts and wasabi lime butter (Hawaiian), Szechuan pepper steak (Chinese), or garlic shrimp with sweet chile sauce (Thai).

**LUDWIG'S, in the Sonnenalp Hotel, 20 Vail Rd. Tel. 476-5656.**
   **Cuisine:** CREATIVE CONTINENTAL. **Reservations:** Recommended.
**$ Prices:** Appetizers $5.25–$7.50; main courses $12.25–$19.50; breakfast buffet $12; Sun brunch $11.50–$22. MC, V.
   **Open:** Breakfast Mon–Sat 7–11am; dinner only, Thurs–Tues 5:30–10:30pm; Sun brunch 7am–noon.
Chef Mark Spitzer is the only "master chef" designated by Les Chaînes des Rôtissieures in the state of Colorado, and that's reason enough to visit this classical European dining room. Named after Bavaria's King Ludwig, it has an intimate creekside location and frequent "opera dinners," featuring resident musician Cindy Saunders at the piano. You may have seen the televised VISA advertisements ("They don't take American Express") showing off Spitzer's Bavarian cream pie.
   Your meal here might start with a gravlax of smoked salmon, a lobster bisque, or a wilted-spinach salad. For a main course, consider grilled venison sausage with polenta cakes, sautéed Gulf shrimp in a citrus beurre blanc, tenderloin of beef stuffed with cabbage and chardonnay sauce, or tortellini with prosciutto.

**MONTAUK FRESH SEAFOOD, 549 Lionshead Mall. Tel. 476-2601.**
   **Cuisine:** SEAFOOD. **Reservations:** Recommended.
**$ Prices:** Appetizers $4.95–$6.95; main courses $14.95–$18.95; lunch $5.95–$8.95. AE, MC, V.

**Open:** Daily 11:30am–10pm.

Gary Boris, the managing partner of this seafood grill, grew up around the harbors of Montauk Point, New York. Now that he's landlocked, he flies in fresh fish daily from both coasts, as well as the water of Hawaii and the Gulf of Mexico. The area's only raw bar is stocked not only with oysters, but with clams, shrimp, and crab as well.

Lunch—chowders (including shellfish gazpacho) and sandwiches—is often served on the outdoor patio. A blackboard menu, featuring 8 to 10 grilled fresh catches, complements the dinner menu. Try sautéed softshell crab, roast swordfish provençal, Japanese barbecued shrimp, pan-fried trout in a cornmeal crust . . . or if you're not in a fish mood, New York steak or chicken Paillard. A children's menu is available.

**THE RED LION, 304 Bridge St. Tel. 476-7676.**
   **Cuisine:** STEAK/SEAFOOD. **Reservations:** Recommended at dinner.
**$  Prices:** $6–$17. MC, V.
   **Open:** Sun–Thurs 11am–11pm, Fri–Sat 11am–midnight.
Established soon after the village of Vail, the Red Lion has been a popular spot for people-watching for nearly three decades. Crowds may spill out into the streets at dinnertime; look up at the porch and you'll see folks staring back down at you. Food here is traditional but good and filling: hickory-smoked barbecued swordfish, baby back ribs, and spareribs; gourmet hamburgers and chicken sandwiches; soups and salads; and Mexican dishes. Bar-goers are drawn by the Around the World Beer Club (over 50 varieties), live entertainment nightly, and 12 TVs for sporting events.

**VENDETTA'S, 291 Bridge St. Tel. 476-5070.**
   **Cuisine:** NORTHERN ITALIAN. **Reservations:** Recommended.
**$  Prices:** Main courses $12.95–$26.95; lunch $5–$8. AE, MC, V.
   **Open:** Lunch daily 11am–3pm; dinner daily 5–11pm.
Located on busy Bridge Street in the heart of Vail Village, Vendetta's is a casual, friendly spot as famous for its après-ski (on a sunny deck) and nightly entertainment as it is for its outstanding Italian cuisine. Pasta lovers enjoy such dishes as cannelloni Ferrara (stuffed with veal, chicken, and beef), manicotti Veneziana (baked with four cheeses), and lasagne pasticciate verdi (baked with beef and sausage). osso buco (baked veal shank), bistecca alla Florentine (an Italian pepper steak), and pollo Valle d'Aostana (a sautéed, batter-dipped chicken) are meat favorites, and seafood specials range from scampi Sambuca to cioppino to fettuccine frutti di mare.

**INEXPENSIVE**

**BAD ATTITUDE CAFE, 536 Lionshead Mall. Tel. 476-8025.**
   **Cuisine:** AMERICAN/MEXICAN.
**$  Prices:** $5–$12. MC, V.
   **Open:** Lunch daily 11am–3pm; dinner 5–10pm.
The largest and sunniest deck in Vail seats 150 people beside the Lionshead Gondola terminal. Year round, diners enjoy steaks, burgers, and enchiladas. There's live après-ski entertainment daily from 3:30 to 7pm in winter.

**D. J. McCADAMS, 616 W. Lionshead Circle. Tel. 476-2336.**
   **Cuisine:** AMERICAN.
**$  Prices:** $4–$7. MC, V.
   **Open:** Daily 24 hours.
Got an uncontrollable urge to munch at 2am? This small, modern-day diner in Concert Hall Plaza is the place to come for a breakfast burrito, chili-cheese omelet, or perhaps a calorie-rich dessert crêpe. Be prepared to crowd in: There's not much room.

**MINTURN COUNTRY CLUB, 131 Main St., Minturn. Tel. 827-4114.**
   **Cuisine:** STEAK/SEAFOOD. **Reservations:** Recommended.
**$  Prices:** Main courses $7.95–$14.95. MC, V.
   **Open:** Dinner only, daily 5:30–10pm.
You won't need your putter at this spot in the old Minturn post office. Instead, be ready to have fun cooking your own dinner. Toss a steak, chicken, fish, or lobster on the large open grill, then share cooking tips with your neighbors while season-

ing your meal with teriyaki sauce, garlic powder, butter, and spices scattered around the grill's perimeter. Main-dish prices include a salad bar.

# 6. LEADVILLE

113 miles W of Denver, 59 miles E of Aspen

**GETTING THERE  By Plane**  The **Lake County Airport,** Road 23 off U.S. 24 South (tel. 719/486-2627), 2 miles south of downtown, at 9,927 feet elevation is said to be America's highest commercial airport. Service here is strictly air-taxi and charter, however, so most visitors must fly into **Denver's Stapleton International Airport** and rent a vehicle there. There's no regularly scheduled shuttle service to Leadville from Denver.

**By Bus**  Bus and van shuttles to and from Vail, Breckenridge, and other nearby communities are operated by **Dee Hive Tours,** 506 Harrison Avenue (tel. 486-2339), and the **Leadville Transit Department,** 800 Harrison Avenue (tel. 486-1040).

**By Car**  Coming from Denver, leave I-70 at Exit 195 (Copper Mountain) and proceed south 24 miles on Colo. 91. From Grand Junction, depart I-70 at Exit 171 (Minturn) and continue south 33 miles on U.S. 24. From Aspen, take Colo. 82 east 44 miles over Independence Pass, then turn north on U.S. 24 for another 15 miles. There's also easy access from the south via U.S. 24 from Colorado Springs (139 miles), Pueblo (156 miles), Alamosa (135 miles), and Gunnison (118 miles).

**SPECIAL EVENTS**  Leadville hosts the following annual events: the **Two Mile High Mushers' Sled Dog Races,** in February; the **Great Peaks Quadrathlon Race,** on the third weekend of May; the **Leadville Music Festival,** in mid- to late July; the **Boom Days Celebration,** over the first weekend of August; the **International Pack Burro Race,** on the first Sunday of August; and the **Victorian Christmas Homes Tour,** in December.

There was a time, not much more than a century ago, when Leadville was the most important city between St. Louis and San Francisco. Founded in 1860 on the gold that glimmered in prospectors' pans, the Oro City site quickly attracted 10,000 miners who worked $5 million in gold out of a 3-mile stretch of the California Gulch by 1865. When the riches were gone, the town was deserted. A smaller lode of gold-bearing quartz kept Oro City alive for the next decade.

In 1875 prospectors Bill Stevens and Al Wood discovered that the carbonates of lead ores in the valley's heavy black soil were laden with "15 ounces of silver to the ton." They located the California Gulch's first paying silver lode. Over the next two decades, until the silver crash of 1893, "Leadville" (as it had been designated by the Post Office Department) grew to have an estimated 30,000 residents—among them Horace Tabor, who parlayed his mercantile and mining investments into unimaginable wealth; and "the Unsinkable" Molly Brown, whose husband made his fortune here before moving to Denver, where the family lived at the time of Molly's *Titanic* heroism. Many buildings of the silver boom (which produced $136 million between 1879 and 1889) have been preserved in what may be Colorado's most complete National Historic District.

Today, though Leadville's population has dwindled, mining remains a key industry. Some 90% of the world's molybdenum, an element used to strengthen steel, is produced atop Fremont Pass at Climax, 12 miles north of Leadville en route to Copper Mountain. Gold, silver, lead, and zinc are mined at four other large deposits around Lake County.

## ORIENTATION

Leadville has the highest elevation of any incorporated city in the United States: 10,152 feet, nearly 2 miles high. The population is around 3,500.

**INFORMATION**   You'll get the information you need from the **Leadville/Lake County Chamber of Commerce,** 809 Harrison Avenue (P.O. Box 861), Leadville, CO 80461 (tel. 719/486-3900).

**CITY LAYOUT**   U.S. 24 is Leadville's one main street. Entering from the north, the highway is known as **Poplar Street;** it staggers west one block at **Ninth Street.** Turn left at the traffic light (one of two in town) and you stay on U.S. 24, now **Harrison Avenue.** The next seven blocks south, to **Second Street,** are the heart of this historic town. Leadville's other stop light is at the intersection of Harrison Avenue and **Sixth Street,** which proceeds west to civic and recreational complexes. A block north, **Fifth Street** climbs east to the old train depot and 13,186-foot Mosquito Pass, America's highest, open to four-wheel-drive vehicles in summer.

## GETTING AROUND

Check with the **Leadville Transit Department,** 800 Harrison Avenue (tel. 486-1040), or **Dee Hive Tours,** 506 Harrison Avenue (tel. 486-2339), for local information.

Auto rentals are available through **Leadville Leasing** at the airport (tel. 486-2627).

A seven-passenger **horse-drawn surrey** tours Leadville daily, June to Labor Day, daily 10am to 4pm, from the chamber of commerce office.

**Leadville Air Tours** (tel. 486-2627) conducts tours of the city and surrounding Rockies for $20 per person (minimum of 2).

## FAST FACTS

The **area code** is 719. In case of **emergency,** call **911;** for regular business, call the Leadville Police (tel. 486-1365) or the Lake County Sheriff (tel. 486-1249). The sheriff's office also provides road reports. For medical assistance, visit 37-bed **St. Vincent General Hospital,** West Fourth Street and Washington Street (tel. 486-0230), or **Lake County Medical Associates,** 825 West Sixth Street (tel. 486-1264). The **post office** is at West Fifth Street and Pine Street, a block west of Harrison Avenue (tel. 486-1667).

## WHAT TO SEE & DO
### ATTRACTIONS

**THE EARTH RUNS SILVER: EARLY LEADVILLE, 809 Harrison Ave. Tel. 486-3900.**

This 30-minute multi-image production uses six slide projectors, music, and narration to tell the story of Leadville and many of its famous and infamous personalities. It's presented in the Old Church Arts and Humanities Center, next door to the chamber of commerce, where tickets are sold.

**Admission:** $3 adults, $2 children 6–16.

**Open:** Continuous showings in May, daily 11am–5pm; June–Oct 15, daily 10am–5pm; inquire for winter hours; Oct 16–Apr, Sun–Fri every 2 hours 10am–4pm, Sat 10am, noon, and 2pm.

**HEALY HOUSE AND DEXTER CABIN, 912 Harrison Ave. Tel. 486-0487.**

The refined Victorian social and cultural life of the privileged classes of the late 19th century is reflected in these two adjacent houses, which are a state historical museum. The three-story, wood-frame Healy House was built in 1878 by mining engineer August Meyer, who made it a center of social activity. Daniel Healy leased it as a boarding house from 1897 to 1902; this atmosphere is re-enacted today, as costumed guides assume the roles of schoolteacher boarders. The adjacent Dexter Cabin was built of logs in 1879 by philanthropist James Dexter, who used the building as a gentlemen's poker club.

**Admission:** $2.50 adults, $1.25 children 6–16 and seniors over 62, free for children under 6.

**Open:** Memorial Day weekend–Labor Day, Mon–Sat 10am–4:20pm; Sun 1–4:20pm; Sept, Sat–Sun 10am–4:30pm; the rest of the year, by appointment.

## HERALD DEMOCRAT NEWSPAPER MUSEUM, 717 Harrison Ave. Tel. 486-0641.

Until it went offset and weekly in 1986, the *Herald Democrat*—once published by Simon Guggenheim—was Colorado's last operating daily letterpress newspaper. That hot-lead equipment has been preserved as a museum, along with the 1900-era newsroom, historic issues of the paper, and various displays. Souvenir newspapers are printed for visitors during the tour.

**Admission:** $2 adults, $1 children 13–18, free for children under 13.

**Open:** Memorial Day–Labor Day, Mon–Thurs 8am–4pm, Fri–Sat 10am–6pm, Sun noon–6pm; other seasons, Mon–Tues and Thurs–Fri 10am–4pm or by appointment. **Closed:** Wed and Sat–Sun, Labor Day–Memorial Day.

## HERITAGE MUSEUM, 102 Ninth St., at Harrison Ave. Tel. 486-1878.

Thirty miniature dioramas, along with displays of mining artifacts, depict various episodes of Leadville history. An art gallery with rotating exhibits gives a taste of the cultural present.

**Admission:** $2.50 adults, $1.50 seniors 60 and over, $1 children 6–16, free for children under 6.

**Open:** July–Aug, daily 9am–5pm; June and Sept, daily 10am–4pm; Oct–May, Fri–Sun 11am–4pm.

## LEADVILLE, COLORADO & SOUTHERN RAILROAD, 326 E. Seventh St., at Hazel St. Tel. 486-3936.

The scenic train ride departs the 1884 C&S Depot, three blocks east of U.S. 24, and follows the old "high line" to the headwaters of the Arkansas River. The train turns around near the molybdenum mining camp of Climax, with a spectacular view of Fremont Pass, and returns past the old Round House Water Tower at French Gulch. From here, there's a dramatic look at Mount Elbert, Colorado's tallest mountain, at 14,433 feet.

**Admission:** $16.50 adults, $9.75 children 4–12, free for children 3 and under.

**Open:** 2¾-hour tours, mid-June to Labor Day, daily at 9:30am and 2pm; Sept, Sat–Sun at 9:30am and 2pm. **Closed:** Oct to mid-June.

## LEADVILLE NATIONAL HISTORIC DISTRICT. Tel. 486-3900.

A great many buildings—especially brick and masonry structures, but also some wood-frame houses—have survived from Leadville's heyday. Most of them line seven blocks of Harrison Avenue, the main drag, or Chestnut Street, which intersects it at the south end of downtown. The chamber of commerce can provide self-guided walking-tour maps ($1.50), walking-tour tapes ($3), or self-guided driving-tour maps of the district ($1.50).

## MATCHLESS MINE MUSEUM, 2 miles east up Seventh St. Tel. 486-0371.

Visitors can get a surface view of Horace Tabor's Matchless Mine, then take a guided tour of the cabin where Tabor's widow, Baby Doe, spent the final 36 years of her life waiting to strike it rich once more before freezing to death in 1935.

**Admission:** $1 adults, free for children under 12.

**Open:** Memorial Day–Labor Day, daily 9am–5pm; or by appointment.

## NATIONAL MINING HALL OF FAME AND MUSEUM, 120 W. Ninth St. Tel. 486-1229.

This fascinating museum presents the finest survey of geology and the American mining industry to be found in the Rocky Mountain region. You'll find descriptions of the mining of various ores, from silver and gold to copper, zinc, lead, and coal; working models of mining machinery; and 22 sequential dioramas giving an episode-by-episode history of Colorado gold mining. There are dioramas of individual mines, including the Climax molybdenum mine, and displays of crystals and luminescent minerals. Recently opened is a life-size model of a hard-rock mine. The Mining Hall of Fame honors dozens of pioneering mining engineers and other industry leaders with biographical plaques. The museum store offers interesting gifts and publications.

**Admission:** $2 adults and children over 12, $1 seniors and ages 12 and under.
**Open:** Mar–Oct, daily 9am–5pm; Nov–Feb, Mon–Fri 9am–3pm, Sat–Sun 10am–2pm; and by appointment.

### TABOR HOME MUSEUM, 116 E. Fifth St. Tel. 486-0551.

The home of millionaire merchant Horace Tabor and his first wife, Augusta, from 1877 to 1881, is filled with period furnishings and Tabor family memorabilia. Tours include a taped narration of the era. After the Tabors' divorce, the house remained in the family with Augusta's sister and brother-in-law, the Melvin Clarks.

**Admission:** $2 adults, 50¢ children.
**Open:** Memorial Day–Labor Day, daily 9am–5:30pm; the rest of the year, Wed–Sat 10am–4pm.

### TABOR OPERA HOUSE, 308 Harrison Ave. Tel. 486-1147.

Horace Tabor financed the construction of this wonderful Victorian opera house in 1879. Over the next 75 years the acoustically outstanding theater hosted the great performers of the era, from the Ziegfeld Follies to the New York Metropolitan Opera, and from prizefighter Jack Dempsey (a Colorado native) to magician Harry Houdini (whose "vanishing" square is still evident on the stage floor). Autographed photographs of many of the entertainment greats line the walls of the foyer. Guided and self-guided tours of the 880-seat theater are available; you're encouraged to wander the aisles, visit the original dressing rooms, and study many of the original sets and scenery. The Crystal Comedy Company still performs melodramas here 3 nights a week in summer, helping to re-enact the great days of theater in Leadville.

**Admission:** Tours, $3 adults, $1.50 children 6–11, free for children under 6; melodrama, mid-June to mid-Aug, $6 adults, $3 children.
**Open:** Memorial Day–Oct 1, Sun–Fri 9am–5pm; the rest of the year, in favorable weather or by appointment.

## SPORTS & RECREATION

**BICYCLING** Mountain-bike rentals ($4 per hour, $15 per day) and organized tours (about $10 an hour) are offered by **10th Mountain Sports,** 112 East Seventh Street (tel. 486-2202). The **Mosquito Pass Challenge** on a late August weekend taxes mountain bikers with steep climbs at high elevation. Biking, along with running, kayaking, and cross-country skiing, is a key component of the annual mid-May **Great Peaks Quadrathlon,** which starts at Quail Mountain Ranch near Twin Lakes.

**FISHING** There's good trout and kokanee fishing at **Turquoise Lake, Twin Lakes,** and other small high-mountain lakes, as well as at beaver ponds located on side streams of the **Arkansas River.** There's also limited stream fishing.

Licenses and information can be obtained from **Leadville Surplus & Sporting Goods,** 1001 Poplar Street (tel. 486-1888), and other local stores. **Huck Finn Pond** at City Park, West Fifth Street at Leiter Street, is open for children's fishing in July.

**GOLF** The **Mount Massive Golf Course,** 3½ miles west of Leadville at 259 County Road 5 (tel. 486-2176), claims to be the world's highest nine-hole golf course. But in fact, it will have to settle for being the highest in North America at 9,700 feet; the Gulmarg course in Kashmir, India, has an elevation edge.

**HIKING & MOUNTAINEERING** The **U.S. Forest Service,** San Isabel National Forest office, 2015 North Poplar Street (tel. 486-0749), has detailed maps for hikers and backpackers. The more adventurous can attempt an ascent of **Mount Elbert** (14,433 ft.) or **Mount Massive** (14,421 ft.); either can be climbed in a day without technical equipment, though altitude and abruptly changing weather conditions are factors that must be weighed.

**HORSEBACK RIDING** There are stables at **Pa and Ma's Guest Ranch,** 4 miles west of Leadville on U.S. 24 at East Tennessee Road (tel. 486-3900).

**RIVER RAFTING** Expeditions on the Arkansas River, including thrilling Brown's Canyon, are organized by **10th Mountain Sports,** 112 East Seventh Street (tel. 719/486-2202, or 800/748-2044), or by **Twin Lakes Expeditions,** Colo. 82, Twin Lakes (tel. 486-3928).

**RUNNING** The **Leadville 20K Road & Trail Run** is held on June 1, beginning and ending at the Matchless Boat Ramp, at the southeast corner of Turquoise Lake; and the **Leadville Trail 100 Mile Ultra Race** is held the third weekend of August, leading south from Leadville on trails and backroads to the abandoned mining camp of Winfield and returning along the same route.

**SKIING   Ski Cooper,** P.O. Box 896, Leadville, CO 80461 (tel. 719/486-3684, or 486-2277 for snow reports), began in 1942 as a training center for 10th Mountain Division troopers from Camp Hale during World War II. Located 10 miles north of Leadville on U.S. 24 near Tennessee Pass, it offers numerous intermediate and novice runs, and hosts backcountry **Chicago Ridge Snowcat Tours** for experts. The lifts—a triple chair, double chair, T-bar, and beginners' poma—serve 21 runs on a 1,200-foot vertical. Full-day tickets are $18 for adults, $11 for children 6 to 12, $9 for seniors 60 to 69, and free for others; lessons start at $15, full rental packages at $10. There's also a cross-country track laid out at the foot of the mountain.

**SWIMMING** The **Lake County Intermediate School Recreation Complex,** West Sixth Street and McWethy Drive (tel. 486-2564), offers an Olympic-size pool, a 160-yard indoor track, a gymnasium, a 22-person whirlpool spa, weight training, a racquetball court, and roller skating.

## EVENING ENTERTAINMENT

From mid-June to mid-August, the **Crystal Comedy Company** presents melodramatic revues on Wednesday, Thursday, and Saturday at 8pm at the Tabor Opera House. Titles change, but stories remain much the same, such as past hits *The Sour Stone Medicine Mine* and *Where There's a Mine There's the EPA.* Tickets are $6.

Music, storytelling, and period-attired artisans help relive the spirit of an 1860s mining camp in **Oro City: The Rebirth of a Miner's Camp,** on U.S. 24 a mile south of downtown Leadville, the last weekend of June and first two weekends of August.

For 2 weeks in July each year, the **Leadville Music Festival** brings fine classical and contemporary music to the high Rockies with visiting artists from Loyola University and other major colleges.

Nightlife in Leadville is on the quiet side. If it's lively somewhere, it will be the **Pastime Saloon,** 120 West Second Street (tel. 486-9986), with an original Chinese bar from Oro City; or the **Silver Dollar Saloon,** 315 Harrison Avenue (tel. 486-9914), an Irish-style bar decorated with pictures of "Baby Doe" Tabor.

# WHERE TO STAY

**CLUB LEAD, 500 E. Seventh St., Leadville, CO 80461. Tel. 719/486-2202,** or 800/748-2044. 10 rms (4 with bath).
**$ Rates** (including breakfast): $16 adults, $8 children 4–6, children under 4 stay free in parents' room. AE, MC, V.

Proprietor Jay Jones, who also owns 10th Mountain Sports, caters to adventure travelers who want to tie mountain-biking or river-rafting excursions into their travel plans. Most rooms here are bunkhouse style, but there are no more than six beds to a room; some private rooms with queen-size beds have private baths. There's a games and meeting room and a hot tub.

**DELAWARE HOTEL, 700 Harrison Ave. (P.O. Box 960), Leadville, CO 80461. Tel. 719/486-1418,** or 800/748-2004. 32 rms, 4 suites (all with bath). TV
**$ Rates** (including breakfast): $40–$60 single or double; $70–$80 suite. AE, CB, DC, DISC, JCB, MC, V.

This 1886 structure, originally a mercantile and apartment building, opened as a hotel on its centennial anniversary. The simple rooms display the antique furnishings and decor of the late Victorian period, including handmade quilts as wall hangings behind brass or iron beds. Though every room is a little different, each has a hardwood floor, cable color television, and modern bathroom (with a shower but no tub). Charlotte's restaurant (main dishes run $6.50 to $12.95) serves traditional American cuisine, including a house Stroganoff in a large second-floor room with historic photos; beer and wine are sold. Also on the premises are a hot tub, a ski and sports shop, an ice-cream parlor and deli, and an old-time photo shop.

**THE LEADVILLE COUNTRY INN, 127 E. Eighth St. (P.O. Box 1989), Leadville, CO 80461. Tel. 719/486-2354,** or 800/748-2354. 10 rms (all with bath).

**$ Rates** (including breakfast): $42–$67 single; $52–$77 double. AE, CB, DC, MC, V.

A stately 15-room Queen Anne Victorian built in 1893, this bed-and-breakfast inn has been restored to its past elegance with rich hand-rubbed woods and antique furnishings—including brass and iron beds, claw-foot bathtubs, and turn-of-the-century quilts. Half the rooms are in the old Carriage House, the balance in the main inn. Smoking is not permitted. A full gourmet breakfast includes frozen-fruit smoothies and caramel-pecan cinnamon rolls. Elaborate six-course dinners, with a sleigh or carriage ride and servers in period costume, are offered by reservation for $39 per person.

**THE NORRIS HOUSE, 120 W. Fourth St., Leadville, CO 80461. Tel. 486-2141.** 7 rms.

**$ Rates** (including breakfast): Summer, $35 single; $45–$65 double. Winter, $45 single; $55–$75 double. AE, MC, V.

An 1879 Victorian on Leadville's original "millionaires' row," the Norris House features the original handcrafted woodwork, detailed fireplace mantels, and crystal lights installed by its first owners. Rooms range from warm and cozy to large and sunny; a favorite is Estelle's Room, with a large fireplace, a brass bed, and a TV and telephone. Children are welcome; smokers and pets may be accommodated. Packed lunches ($4 to $12) and sit-down dinners ($5 to $12, by reservation) are offered.

**PAN ARK LODGE, 5827 U.S. 24, Leadville, CO 80461. Tel. 486-1063.** 44 rms, 4 suites (all with bath).

**$ Rates:** $49–$54 single or double; $69 suite. MC, V.

Located 9½ miles south of Leadville, this comfortable motel has spacious rooms, all with natural moss-rock fireplaces, electric kitchenettes, and beautiful mountain views. A handful have televisions. There's a coin-operated laundry for guests.

## CAMPGROUNDS

**THE SAGEBRUSHER R.V. PARK, 135 W. Second St., Leadville, CO 80461. Tel. 719/486-0679.** 28 sites.

**$ Rates:** $16 per site per vehicle (four people). MC, V.

All RV sites have electric hookups, picnic tables, and barbecue grills. The bathhouse has full shower facilities. The park is open year round.

**SUGAR LOAFIN' CAMPGROUND, 303 Colo. 300, Leadville, CO 80461. Tel. 719/486-1031** or 486-1613.

**$ Rates:** $8 tents; $16 RVs.

Located 3½ miles northwest of downtown Leadville out West Sixth Street, and near Turquoise Lake, this campsite has drive-through RV spaces and rustic tentsites. The center building has TV, phones, showers, and a laundry; there's also a general store (with fishing tackle and souvenirs) and a recreation room.

# WHERE TO DINE

**GARDEN CAFE, 115 W. Fourth St. Tel. 486-9917.**

**Cuisine:** ITALIAN/AMERICAN.

**$ Prices:** Breakfast $2–$6; lunch $3–$6; dinner $6–$12. No credit cards.

292 • THE NORTHERN ROCKIES

**Open:** Breakfast/lunch daily 7am–3pm; dinner Wed–Sun 5–9pm.

The "garden" label is a bit of a misnomer, because there's no garden at this small house west of Harrison Avenue. There are, however, healthy, filling breakfasts and lunches, and homemade Italian dinners. Beer and wine are served, and there's a children's menu.

**THE GOLDEN BURRO CAFE, 710 Harrison Ave. Tel. 486-1239.**
   **Cuisine:** AMERICAN.
   **$ Prices:** Breakfast $2–$5; lunch $4–$6; dinner $5–$12. MC, V.
   **Open:** Summer, daily 6am–10pm; winter, daily 7am–9pm.

Established in 1938, the Golden Burro serves up generous portions of old American favorites—like liver and onions, chicken-fried steak, a hot meatloaf sandwich, and rainbow trout grilled in butter. Breakfasts offer home-baked cinnamon rolls; lunches include soups like those out of grandma's kitchen.

**THE GRILL BAR & CAFE, 715 Elm St. Tel. 486-9930.**
   **Cuisine:** MEXICAN.
   **$ Prices:** $2–$9.50. MC, V.
   **Open:** Daily 11am–10:30pm.

Colorful sombreros and serapes cover the white-stucco walls of this south-end restaurant, which offers delicious south-of-the-border cuisine. Enjoy burritos, enchiladas, or stuffed sopaipillas (with chicken or beef, topped with green chiles). There's patio dining and, in the backyard, horseshoe pits!

**LA CANTINA. 1942 U.S. 24 South. Tel. 486-9927.**
   **Cuisine:** NEW MEXICAN.
   **$ Prices:** Lunch $3–$5; dinner $5–$7. MC, V.
   **Open:** Summer, daily 11am–10pm; winter, daily 4–10pm.

What is probably Leadville's finest regional Mexican food is served at this large restaurant, a mile south of downtown. Lean meat and fire-roasted green chiles, along with homemade tortillas and tamales, are typical of the cuisine. The restaurant features an antique bar, large wooden booths, and Hispanic music and dancing many weekends.

**THE PROSPECTOR, Colo. 91 N. Tel. 719/486-2117,** or toll free 800/748-2324.
   **Cuisine:** STEAK/SEAFOOD. **Reservations:** Recommended.
   **$ Prices:** Main courses $9–$15. MC, V.
   **Open:** Dinner only, Mon–Thurs 5–9pm, Fri–Sat 5–9:30pm.

Leadville's finest restaurant is lodged in a spacious log cabin with a stone entrance, 3½ miles north of the city in a lovely mountain setting. Dinners include aged prime rib, New York steaks, and deep-fried prawns. All meals include a salad bar and soup tureen; there's also a full cocktail bar.

---

# 7. ASPEN

172 miles W of Denver, 130 miles E of Grand Junction

**GETTING THERE   By Plane**   From mid-December to early April, visitors can fly directly into Aspen's **Pitkin County Airport** (also known as Sardy Field), 3 miles northwest of Aspen (tel. 303/920-5380). **United Express** (tel. 303/925-3400, or 800/241-6522) offers daily nonstops from Chicago's O'Hare, twice daily (except Wednesday) from Los Angeles, and direct flights from Dallas/Fort Worth four times weekly.

Charters to or from Aspen, including flights from Denver and scenic trips to Crested Butte, are offered by **Aspen Aviation** (tel. 303/925-2522).

Most visitors fly into **Denver's Stapleton International Airport,** and continue to Vail with either **United Express** or **Continental Express** (tel.

303/925-4350, or 800/525-0280). Both airlines have many flights to and from Denver each day, up to a dozen or more each during peak ski season. Courtesy vans, taxis, limousines, rental cars, and public buses are all available at the airport.

From Denver, it's possible to take the shuttle vans or taxis of either **Skier Connection** (tel. 800/824-1104) or **Aspen Limo** (tel. 303/925-2400, or 800/322-2112). Connecting ground transportation is also available from the airport in Grand Junction (see Chapter 10, "The Western Slope").

**By Train**  En route between San Francisco and Chicago, **Amtrak** (tel. 303/534-2812 in Denver, or 800/USA-RAIL or 800/835-8725) stops in Glenwood Springs, 42 miles northwest of Aspen. The Denver–Glenwood and Grand Junction–Glenwood segments are particularly scenic. Taxis and limousines, as well as rental cars, are available at the depot.

**By Bus**  Coaches of **Greyhound/Trailways** (tel. 925-8484) stop in Aspen at the Rubey Park Transportation Center, in the 400 block of East Durant Avenue (at Mill Street).

**By Car**  Aspen is located on Colo. 82, halfway between I-70 at Glenwood Springs (42 miles northwest) and U.S. 24 south of Leadville (44 miles east). In summer, it's a scenic 3½-hour drive from Denver: Leave I-70 West at Exit 195 (Copper Mountain); follow Colo. 91 south to Leadville, where you pick up U.S. 24; then turn east on Colo. 82 through Twin Lakes and over 12,095-foot Independence Pass. In winter, the Independence Pass road is closed, so you'll have to take I-70 to Glenwood, then backtrack up Colo. 82. In optimal winter driving conditions, it'll take about 4 hours from Denver.

**SPECIAL EVENTS**  The Aspen area hosts the following annual events: the **Wintersköl Carnival,** in the third week of January, in Aspen/Snowmass; the **Snowmass Mardi Gras,** in late February or early March, in Snowmass; the **International Design Conference,** the third week of June, in Aspen; the **Snowmass Hot Air Balloon Festival,** on the fourth weekend of June, in Snowmass; the **Aspen Institute for Humanistic Studies Lecture Series,** on Tuesday from late June to late August, in Aspen; the **Aspen Music Festival,** from late June to late August, in Aspen; the **DanceAspen Summer Festival,** from July 5 to mid-August, in Aspen; the **Aspen Writers Conference,** in the third and fourth weeks of July, in Aspen; the **Snowmass Children's Festival,** on the first weekend of August, in Snowmass; the **Snowmass Oktoberfest,** on Labor Day weekend, in Snowmass; and the **Aspen Filmfest,** in late September, in Aspen.

---

**S**ilver miners established the town of Aspen in 1879, first dubbing it "Ute City" after the Native American Ute tribe, but renaming it Aspen on its incorporation in 1880. When the Smuggler Mine produced the world's largest silver nugget (1,840 lbs.), prospectors headed to Aspen in droves. The city soon had 12,000 citizens—but just as quickly the population dwindled to one-tenth that number after the 1893 silver crash. Ranching and small mining enterprises kept the town alive as a supply center.

Shortly before World War II, three investors established a small ski area on Aspen Mountain with a primitive "boat tow." During the early 1940s, 10th Mountain Division soldiers training at Camp Hale near Leadville often weekended in Aspen, and were enthralled with its possibilities. An infusion of money in 1945 by Chicago industrialist Walter Paepcke, who moved to Aspen with his wife, Elizabeth, resulted in the construction of what was then the world's longest chair lift. The Aspen Skiing Corporation (now Company) was founded the following year; in 1950 the resort's status as an international resort was confirmed when it hosted the alpine world skiing championships. Aspen's scope as a ski destination grew with the opening in 1958 of Buttermilk Mountain and Aspen Highlands, and in 1967 with the establishment of Snowmass Village and ski area. (All but Highlands, which is under independent management, are operated by the Aspen Skiing Company.)

The Paepckes perceived Aspen as a year-round cultural center as well as a resort community. In 1949 they organized the Goethe Bicentennial Convocation, which established the Aspen Institute for Humanistic Studies and the Aspen Music Festival. In 1951 they started the first International Design Conference.

All three events, which continue today, have contributed to Aspen's appeal to cosmopolitan and sophisticated residents and visitors.

## ORIENTATION

Aspen has an elevation of 7,908 feet and a year-round population of about 6,000. (The city holds as many as 20,000, including visitors.)

**INFORMATION** For information on Aspen, contact the **Aspen Chamber Resort Association,** 303 East Main Street, Aspen, CO 81611, or drop by the **Aspen Visitor Center** at the Wheeler Opera House, Hyman Avenue and Mill Street (tel. 925-1940).

Transportation, hotel, and other reservations are handled by **Aspen Central Reservations and Travel** (tel. 303/925-9000, or 800/262-7736) or the **Snowmass Resort Association Travel Division** (tel. 303/923-2010, or 800/332-3245).

**CITY LAYOUT** Located in the heart of White River National Forest, Aspen is in the relatively flat valley of the Roaring Fork River, a tributary of the Colorado River. It's lodged at the northern foot of Aspen Mountain, facing Smuggler Mountain to its north and the peaks of the Elk Mountain Range to its east.

Entering town from the northwest on Colo. 82, the arterial jogs right (south) two blocks on Seventh Street, then left (east) at **Main Street.** "East" and "West" street numbers are separated by **Garmisch Street,** the next cross-street after First Street. Continuing east, you'll cross Aspen Street, Monarch Street (which essentially marks the western boundary of downtown Aspen), **Mill Street** (the town's main north-south street), Galena Street, Hunter Street, Spring Street, and **Original Street** (the east end of downtown). Colorado 82 turns south again on Original, crossing Hopkins Avenue and Hyman Avenue, continuing east again toward Independence Pass on Cooper Avenue. **Durant Avenue,** one block south of Cooper, sits at the foot of Aspen Mountain.

At this writing, there are no one-way streets in Aspen, but there are **pedestrian malls** on Cooper Avenue and Hyman Avenue between Mill Street and Galena Street, on Mill Street between Hyman Avenue and Durant Avenue, and on Galena Street between Cooper and Durant, which throw a curve into the downtown traffic flow.

Looking at the entire Aspen valley from an aircraft approaching from the north, you'd see the city of **Aspen and Aspen Mountain** on the left (east), followed in order by **Aspen Highlands, Buttermilk Mountain,** the Pitkin County Airport, and **Snowmass Village and ski area.** Main access to Snowmass, Aspen's "second city" 12 miles closer to Glenwood Springs than the more famous resort town, is off Colo. 82 via Owl Creek Road, just east of the airport, or Brush Creek Road, 3 miles northwest of the airport.

## GETTING AROUND

**BY BUS** The **Roaring Fork Transit Agency (RFTA),** 20101 West Colo. 82, Aspen (tel. 920-1905), provides free bus service within the Aspen city limits, and connections east as far as Carbondale, for continued transport to Glenwood Springs, for prices up to $3 for adults and $2 for children 6 to 16 and seniors 65 and older (children under 6 ride free). The fare is $1.50 (50¢ for children and seniors) to Snowmass Village. Exact fare is required. Normal hours are 7:15am to 12:30am daily. Further information can be obtained at the **Rubey Park Transit Center,** Durant Avenue between Mill Street and Galena Street, Aspen (tel. 925-8484). Schedules, frequency, and routes vary with the seasons; services include free ski shuttles in winter, shuttles to the Aspen Music Festival, and tours to the Maroon Bells scenic area in summer.

Free shuttle transportation within Snowmass Village is offered daily during winter, and on a limited schedule in summer, by the **Snowmass Transportation Department** (tel. 923-3777, or 923-3500 after 5pm).

**BY TAXI** Taxi service is offered by **Aspen Limo** (tel. 925-2400) or **High Mountain Taxi** (tel. 925-TAXI).

**BY RENTAL CAR** Auto-rental agencies include **Alamo** (tel. 303/925-8056, or 800/327-9633), **Avis** (tel. 303/925-2355, or 800/331-1212), **Budget** (tel. 303/925-2151, or 800/527-0700), **Eagle** (tel. 800/282-2128), **Hertz** (tel. 800/654-3131), **National** (tel. 303/925-1144, or 800/227-7368), and **Thrifty** (tel. 800/367-2277). **Mountain Express** (tel. 925-2880) specializes in four-wheel-drive vehicles.

## FAST FACTS

The **area code** is 303. In case of **emergency,** call **911.** For regular business, contact the Aspen Police, Galena Street and Hopkins Avenue (tel. 920-5400), the Snowmass Police (tel. 923-5330), or the Pitkin County Sheriff, Main Street and Galena Street (tel. 920-5300). The **Aspen Valley Hospital** is at 200 Castle Creek Road, near Aspen Highlands (tel. 925-1120). There are **hotlines** for **mental health** (tel. 920-5555) and **poison center** (tel. 800/332-3073). The **post office** is at 235 Puppy Smith Street, off Mill Street north of Main (tel. 925-7523); there's another in the Snowmass Center (tel. 923-2497). For **road reports,** call 920-5454 (or 303/639-1234 for statewide conditions). Sales **tax** of 7.2% and a civic assessment of 4% are added to hotel bills. Local cable **television** is Channel 12.

## WHAT TO SEE & DO

### ATTRACTIONS

**ASPEN MOUNTAIN, Aspen Skiing Company, Durant Ave. and Hunter St. (P.O. Box 1248), Aspen, CO 81612. Tel. 303/925-1220,** or 925-1940 for snow reports.

Aspen Mountain—known to locals as "Ajax," for an old miner's claim—is not for the timid. It is the American West's original hard-core ski mountain, with no fewer than 23 of its named runs "double diamond"—for experts only. One-third of the mountain's runs are left forever ungroomed, ecstasy for bump runners. There are mountain-long runs for intermediates as well as advanced skiers, but beginners should look to one of the other Aspen areas.

From the Sundeck restaurant at the mountain's 11,212-foot summit, numerous intermediate runs extend on either side of Bell Mountain—through Copper Bowl and down Spar Gulch. To the east of the Gulch, the knob of Bell offers a mecca for mogul mashers, with bump runs down its ridge and its east and west faces. To the west of the Gulch, the face of Ruthie's is wonderful for intermediate cruisers, while more mogul runs drop off International. Ruthie's Run extends for over 2 miles down the west ridge of the mountain, with an extension via Magnifico Cut Off and Little Nell to the base.

**Mid-mountain restaurants** include Bonnie's, at Tourtelotte Park near the top of Ruthie's Lift, and Ruthie's, at the bottom of said chair lift.

Aspen Mountain has a 3,267-foot vertical, with 75 trails on 625 skiable acres. Eight lifts—the high-speed Silver Queen gondola, three quad chairs, and four double chairs—serve up to 10,775 skiers per hour. Average annual snowfall at the summit is 300 inches (25 ft.).

Snowcats deliver advanced and expert skiers to an additional 1,500 acres of powder skiing in back bowls.

**Admission:** Tickets, $41 adults (as low as $37 per day for multiday, multi-area tickets), $23 children 7–12 and seniors 65–69, ($22 per day for multiday tickets), free for children under 6 and seniors over 69. Equipment rentals average $22 per day; full-day class lessons start at $40.

**Open:** Thanksgiving to mid-Apr, daily 9am–3:30pm.

**ASPEN HIGHLANDS, Maroon Creek Rd. (P.O. Box T), Aspen, CO 81612. Tel. 303/925-5300.**

Highlands has two major features going for it: the longest vertical drop (3,800 ft.)

of any area in Colorado, and the most balanced skiable terrain—novice to expert, with lots of intermediate slopes—in the Aspen valley.

It takes four lifts to reach the 11,800-foot Loge Peak summit, where most of the advanced expert runs are found in the Steeplechase area and 65 acres of glades in the Olympic Bowl. Kandahar, Golden Horn, and Thunderbowl give the intermediate skier a long run from top to bottom, and novices are best served mid-mountain on trails like Red Onion and Apple Strudel. There are three **restaurants:** Schwanie's at the base, Merry-Go-Round mid-mountain, and Cloud 9 picnic hut (for ski clubs only) atop the Cloud 9 chair.

Highlands has 78 trails on 552 acres, served by 11 lifts (nine double chairs and two Pomas). Uphill capacity is 10,000 skiers per hour.

**Admission:** Tickets, $40 adults (as low as $23 per day for multiday tickets), $20 children 12 and under or seniors 65–69 (as low as $13 for multiday tickets), free for seniors over 69 and children accompanied by parents purchasing regularly priced tickets. Full-day class lessons start at $40 per day.

**Open:** Thanksgiving to mid-Apr, daily 9am–4pm.

**BUTTERMILK MOUNTAIN, Aspen Skiing Company, West Buttermilk Rd. at Colo. 82 (P.O. Box 1248), Aspen, CO 81612. Tel. 303/925-1220,** or 925-1940 for snow reports.

Buttermilk is nominally a beginners' mountain. In fact, *Ski* magazine has rated it the best place in North America to learn how to ski. But there's plenty of intermediate and ample advanced terrain as well.

The smallest of Aspen's four mountains has three segments: **Main Buttermilk,** rising from the Inn at Aspen, with a variety of intermediate trails and the long, easy, winding Homestead Road; **Buttermilk West,** a mountaintop (9,900 ft.) novice area; and **Tiehack,** the intermediate-advanced section where Aspen town-league races are held. The Cliffhouse restaurant is atop Main Buttermilk, and there are cafés at the foot of the other two segments.

Seven lifts (six double chairs and a platter-pull) serve 45 trails on 410 acres, with a 2,030-foot vertical. Uphill capacity is 6,600 skiers per hour; average annual snowfall at the summit is 200 inches (16 ft. 8 in.).

Special features include the Vic Braden Ski College, which offers an intensive 5-day adult learn-to-ski program ($650); the Powder Pandas for 3- to 6-year-olds; and a 200-foot-long half-pipe for snowboarders, with a 23% grade.

**Admission:** Tickets, $41 adults (as low as $37 per day for multiday, multi-area tickets), $23 children 7–12 and seniors 65–69, ($22 per day for multiday tickets), free for children under 6 and seniors over 69. Equipment rentals average $22 per day; full-day class lessons start at $40.

**Open:** Mid-Dec to early Apr, daily 9am–4pm.

**SNOWMASS SKI AREA, Aspen Skiing Company, Snowmelt Rd. (P.O. Box 1248, Aspen, CO 81612), Snowmass. Tel. 303/925-1220,** or 925-1940 for snow reports.

A huge, ostensibly intermediate mountain with something for everyone, Snowmass has 33% more skiable acreage than the other three Aspen areas combined! Actually four distinct self-contained areas, each with its own lift system and restaurant, its terrain varies from easy beginner runs to the pitches of the Cirque and the Hanging Valley Wall, the steepest in the Aspen area.

Big Burn, site of a forest fire set by 19th-century Utes to discourage settlers, boasts wide-open advanced and intermediate slopes and the expert drops of the Cirque. Atop the intermediate Alpine Springs trails is the advanced High Alpine Lift, from which experts can traverse to the formidable Hanging Valley Wall. Elk Camp is ideal for early intermediates who prefer long cruising runs. Sam's Knob has advanced upper trails diving through trees, and a variety of intermediate and novice runs around its northeast face and base. All areas meet in the scattered condominium developments that surround Snowmass Village Mall.

Hungry skiers head for Ullrhof restaurant at the foot of Big Burn, High Alpine atop Alpine Springs, Café Suzanne at the base of Elk Camp, and Sam's Knob at that peak's summit.

All told, there are 2,100 skiable acres at Snowmass, with a 3,615-foot vertical drop. The mountain has 72 trails served by 16 lifts (3 quad chairs, 2 triple chairs, 9 double chairs, and 2 platter-pulls), with an uphill capacity of 20,535 skiers per hour. Average annual snowfall at the 11,835-foot summit is 300 inches (25 ft.).

The renowned Snowmass ski school has hundreds of instructors, as well as Snow Cubs and Big Burn Bears programs for children 18 months and older. The area also caters to snowboarders with a "half-pipe" 545 feet long, 55 feet wide, and a 22% grade.

**Admission:** Tickets, $41 adults (as low as $37 per day for multiday, multi-area tickets), $23 children 7–12 and seniors 65–69 ($22 per day for multiday tickets), free for children under 6 and seniors over 69. Equipment rentals average $22 per day; full-day class lessons start at $40.

**Open:** Thanksgiving to mid-Apr, daily 8:30am–3:30pm.

## Natural Attractions

### MAROON BELLS, Maroon Creek Rd., 10 miles west of Aspen.

These two sheer, pyramidal peaks are probably the most photographed mountains in the Rockies south of Wyoming's Grand Tetons. They're a beautiful scene in the winter, spring, or summer, but especially in the fall, when their reflection in Maroon Lake is framed by the changing colors of the aspen leaves.

## Museums

### ANDERSON RANCH ARTS CENTER, 5263 Owl Creek Rd., Snowmass Village. Tel. 923-3181.

This art colony, where visitors can mingle with working artists, has two nationally acclaimed programs. October to May, 20 American artists take part in an 8-month residency outside of professional or academic atmospheres, where they can create a body of work—be it ceramics, woodwork, textile art, photography, or painting—and receive critical feedback from their peers. In June, July, and August, 78 1- to 3-week summer workshops teach a wide range of artists' skills to novices and professionals in every imaginable medium. Meet-the-artist slide lectures are free and open to the public. Exhibitions in the center's gallery are rotated every 4 weeks, year round.

**Admission:** Free.

**Open:** Mon–Fri 9am–5pm; studio tours by appointment.

### ASPEN ART MUSEUM, 590 N. Mill St., Aspen. Tel. 925-8050.

Though it has no permanent exhibits, the Aspen Art Museum hosts major touring national shows in fine arts, design arts, and architecture. Recent shows have included works from the Whitney Museum of American Art and over a century of photographs from the pages of *National Geographic* magazine. Frequent lectures, films, discussions, and receptions are open to the Aspen community and visitors.

**Admission:** $2 adults, $1 students and seniors, free for children under 12, free for everyone Thurs evening.

**Open:** Tues–Wed and Fri–Sun noon–6pm, Thurs noon–8pm.

### ASPEN HISTORICAL SOCIETY MUSEUM, Wheeler-Stallard House, 620 W. Bleeker St., Aspen. Tel. 925-3721.

Silver baron Jerome Wheeler had this three-story Victorian brick home built in 1888. Its steeply pitched roofs, dormers, and gables have made it a landmark in Aspen's West End neighborhood. As museum and archives of the Aspen Historical Society since 1969, the house has been restored to its appearance in the heady days before the silver crash, with late 19th-century furniture, photos, clothing, and toys. Exhibits describe Aspen history from the Native American Ute tribe's culture through the mining rush, from railroads and ranching to the founding of the ski industry. The Carriage House presents temporary exhibits, and the gift shop offers a variety of interesting souvenirs. Inquire about information, maps, and guided walking tours of historic Aspen.

**Admission:** $1 adults, 50¢ children.

**Open:** Mid-June to Sept and mid-Dec to mid-Apr, Tues–Sat 1–4pm.

## SPORTS & RECREATION

**BALLOONING** **Aspen Balloon Adventures** (tel. 923-5749) and **Unicorn Balloon Company** (tel. 925-5752) fly high over the Roaring Fork Valley and surrounding mountain slopes, offering spectacular bird's-eye views. Inquire about the romantic champagne flights. The annual **Snowmass Balloon Festival** brings the colorful vessels into the air by droves the last weekend of June.

Visitors interested in other air sports can check with **Gliders of Aspen** (tel. 925-3418 or 925-3694) for sightseeing trips or instruction. Parasailing—popular in winter among adventurous skiers—is taught by the **Aspen Parasailing School** (tel. 925-7625 or 920-2449) and **Sky Center Aspen** (tel. 925-5044).

**BICYCLING** There are two bike paths of note. One connects Aspen with Snowmass Village; it begins at Seventh Street south of Hopkins Avenue, cuts through wilderness to Colo. 82, then follows Owl Creek Road and Brush Creek Road to the Snowmass Mall. Extensions link it with Aspen High School and the Aspen Business Park. The Rio Grande Trail follows the Roaring Fork River from near the Aspen Post Office, on Puppy Smith Lane, through Henry Stein Park to the community of Woody Creek, off Colo. 82 near Snowmass.

The best source of biking information is the **Aspen Bicycle Club** (tel. 925-7978). Backcountry mountain-biking tours and downhill road cruises from Independence Pass are offered by **Aspen Bike Tours** (tel. 920-4059), **Blazing Pedals** (tel. 925-5651 in Aspen or 923-4544 in Snowmass), and **Timberline Bicycle Tours and Cycle Center** (tel. 925-9237 or 925-5773).

For rentals and service, check with **Ajax Bike & Sports,** 635 East Hyman Avenue (tel. 925-7662); **Aspen Sports,** 408 East Cooper Avenue (tel. 925-6331) or Snowmass Mall (tel. 923-6111, or 800/544-6648); **Aspen Velo Bike Shop,** 465 North Mill Street (tel. 925-1495); **Hub of Aspen,** 315 East Hyman Avenue (tel. 925-7970); or **Sabbatini's,** 434 East Cooper Avenue (tel. 920-1180). All shops have full information to guide bikers.

**DOG SLEDDING** The only working dog-sled kennel in the lower 48 United States is ✪ **Krabloonik,** 4250 Divide Road, Snowmass Village (tel. 923-3953). Every day in winter, teams of 13 dogs pull people and provisions on handcrafted sleds into the Snowmass–Maroon Bells Wilderness Area. Half-day trips, departing at 9am and 1:30pm, include lunch at Krabloonik's fine restaurant.

**FISHING** Perhaps the best of a great deal of good trout fishing in the Aspen area is to be found in the Roaring Fork and Frying Pan rivers. Both are rated "gold medal streams." The Roaring Fork follows Colo. 82 through Aspen from Independence Pass; the Frying Pan starts near Tennessee Pass, northeast of Aspen, and joins the Roaring Fork at Basalt, 18 miles down-valley.

**Aspen Rod & Gun,** 525 East Cooper Avenue (tel. 920-2140), has a full rod-and-tackle shop with license sales, and offers year-round guided fishing trips. The **Taylor Creek Fly Shop,** next to City Market in Basalt (tel. 927-4374), is one of the nation's largest fly-fishing guide services.

**GOLF** There are two public 18-hole championship courses in the Aspen valley, both with pro shops, driving ranges, and PGA instruction. The **Aspen Golf Course,** Colo. 82, 1 mile west of Aspen (tel. 925-2145), 7,125 yards, also has a restaurant and a marvelous view of the Maroon Bells. The **Snowmass Lodge & Golf Course,** Snowmass Club Circle, Snowmass (tel. 923-3148), is a 6,900-yard course designed by Arnold Palmer and Ed Seay. It has a putting green and snack shop, and is adjacent to the Snowmass Club's full athletic facilities.

**HEALTH CLUBS** Aspen's only public downtown health club is the **Aspen Athletic Club,** 720 East Hyman Avenue (tel. 925-2531), with weights and exercise equipment, aerobics classes, racquetball courts, a lap pool, steam and suntan rooms, and a pro shop.

**HIKING & BACKPACKING**   Your best source of information is the **U.S. Forest Service** for White River National Forest (tel. 925-3445). Perhaps the favorite among many outstanding trails is the route past the Maroon Bells to Crested Butte; the trek would take 175 miles by mountain road, but it's only about 30 miles by foot—14 from the end of Aspen's Maroon Creek Road.

For maps and additional hiking information, as well as camping and hiking equipment, see **Ute Mountaineer,** 308 South Mill Street (tel. 925-2849). Hardy outdoors-lovers can join **Aspen Expeditions,** P.O. Box 2432, Aspen, CO 81612 (tel. 303/925-7625), for guided adventure-travel treks and peak ascents, or its adjunct **Rocky Mountain Climbing School** for rock- and ice-climbing courses.

**HORSEBACK RIDING**   Several stables in the Aspen valley offer everything from riding lessons to day rides, overnights to Crested Butte, and week-long pack trips into the Snowmass–Maroon Bells Wilderness Area. Some outfitters even package gourmet meals and country-and-western serenades with their expeditions.

Inquire with **Brush Creek Stables,** 1 mile south of Colo. 82 on Brush Creek Road, Snowmass (tel. 923-4522); **Capitol Peak Outfitters,** Maroon Creek Road opposite Aspen Highlands (tel. 925-6987 or 923-4402); **Moon Run Outfitters,** 8276 Snowmass Creek Road, Old Snowmass (tel. 923-4945); **Snowmass Stables,** 2735 Brush Creek Road, Snowmass Village (tel. 923-3075); or **T Lazy 7 Ranch,** Maroon Creek Road (tel. 925-7040). The T Lazy 7 also offers winter sleigh rides and summer stagecoach rides!

**ICE SKATING**   There's ice skating at the indoor **Aspen Ice Garden,** 233 West Hyman Avenue (tel. 920-5141). Call for public skating hours, admission fees, and rental rates.

**RIVER RAFTING**   In summer, several outfitters have booths set up opposite the Aspen Visitor Center in the Wheeler Opera House at Mill Street and Hyman Avenue. Sharing a toll-free phone (tel. 800/282-RAFT), they include **Blazing Paddles** (tel. 925-5651), **River Rats** (tel. 925-7648), and **Snowmass Whitewater** (tel. 925-5651 or 923-4544 at Snowmass Village Mall).

Another local rafting firm—**Colorado Riff Raft,** 555 East Durant (tel. 925-5405)—shares an address with the **Aspen Kayak School** (tel. 925-6248). Weekly kayak classes start on Monday; weekend classes are held on Saturday and Sunday. Private lessons and extended guided trips can be arranged.

**RODEO**   **Snowmass Stables,** 2735 Brush Creek Road, Snowmass Village (tel. 923-3075), hosts a western barbecue and rodeo every Wednesday night from late June through late August. Food service starts at 6pm, followed by a 2-hour rodeo at 7:30pm with bull and bronc riding, calf roping, and barrel racing. Prices for the combination barbecue-rodeo are $18 for adults, $13 for kids 12 and under; for the rodeo only, $7 for adults, $4 for kids. Reservations are advised for the barbecue.

**SKIING [NORDIC]**   The **Aspen/Snowmass Nordic Council** (tel. 925-2145) operates a free nordic trail system—supported by private and municipal donations—with nearly 50 miles of groomed double track extending throughout the Aspen-Snowmass area, and incorporating summer bicycle paths. Instruction and rentals are offered along the trail at the **Aspen Cross Country Center,** Colo. 82 between Aspen and Buttermilk (tel. 925-2145), and the **Snowmass Lodge & Club Touring Center,** Snowmass Club Circle, Snowmass Village (tel. 923-3148).

**Ashcroft Ski Touring** (tel. 925-1971), has 30km (18 miles) of terrain around the old ghost town of Ashcroft in the Castle Creek Valley, 12 miles up Castle Creek Road off Colo. 82. All services from rentals, to instruction, to guided backcountry day and overnight trips, are available—as is the popular Pine Creek Cookhouse restaurant.

Independent backcountry skiers should consult the **U.S. Forest Service,** White River National Forest (tel. 925-3445), and the **Avalanche Conditions Hotline** (tel. 920-1664). Two hut systems are especially significant—the 13-hut **10th Mountain Trail Association** (tel. 925-5775) toward Vail, and the 6-hut **Alfred A. Braun Hut System** (tel. 925-7345) toward Crested Butte. Call for hut reservations, or join a tour with **Aspen Alpine Guides** (tel. 925-6680), **Elk Mountain Guides** (tel. 925-9075), or **Paragon Guides** (tel. 949-4272). **Aspen Expeditions** (tel. 925-7625) offers ski-mountaineering expeditions as well as hut-to-hut tours.

**SLEIGH RIDES** These could include gourmet dinner rides or simple lunch trips and are offered by **Moon Run Outfitters,** 8276 Snowmass Creek Road, Old Snowmass (tel. 923-4945); **Snowmass Stables,** 2735 Brush Creek Road, Snowmass Village, (tel. 923-3075); and **T Lazy 7 Ranch,** Maroon Creek Road (tel. 925-4614 or 925-7040).

**SNOWBOARDING** Snowboarders are welcome at Aspen Highlands, Buttermilk, and Snowmass mountains (see above), where lessons are also offered. Buttermilk and Snowmass have "half-pipes" reserved for "shredders." For equipment rentals and information, see **The Alternative Edge,** 520 East Durant Avenue (tel. 925-8272), or **Hub of Aspen,** 315 East Hyman Avenue (tel. 925-7970).

**SNOWMOBILING** There's snowmobiling on 26 miles of groomed trails from the **T Lazy 7 Ranch** (above), all the way to the base of the Maroon Bells. Guided tours include a lunch tour to the ghost town of Independence, and a Gold Hill mine tour with lunch at the Sundeck Restaurant atop Aspen Mountain. Tours (including moonlight tours) are also offered by **Western Adventures** (tel. 923-3337).

**TENNIS** There are six public courts at **Aspen Meadows Tennis Center,** Meadows Road north off Eighth Street (tel. 925-7208), and 11 at the **Snowmass Lodge & Club Tennis Garden,** Snowmass Club Circle, Snowmass Village (tel. 923-5600, ext. 122). Both centers have pro shops with rentals and instruction.

## SHOPPING

It's hard to go wrong shopping in Aspen, provided you've got the cash or credit to pay for it. The quality of clothing, jewelry, art, sporting goods, and other retail items is universally high. Following are a few of my favorite shops:

**ART** **Aspen Grove Fine Arts** (internationally recognized artists), 525 East Cooper Avenue (tel. 925-5151); **Blue Corn** (New Mexico native art), 520 East Durant Avenue (tel. 920-3302); **Patrick Collins Gallery** (wilderness photography), 520 East Durant Avenue (tel. 920-4105); **Christy Lee Fine Arts** (impressionists and Taos school), 205 South Mill Street (tel. 925-8885); the **Omnibus Gallery** (vintage posters), 533 East Cooper Avenue (tel. 925-5567); **Shaw Gallery** (American Modernist paintings and Native American antiques), 525 East Cooper Avenue (tel. 925-2873); and **The World Collection** (international folk art), 525 East Cooper Avenue (tel. 925-8822).

**FASHIONS** **Aspen Eel Exotics** (leather goods), 205 South Mill Street (tel. 925-2552); **Aspen Kids** (children's casual), 400 East Hyman Avenue (tel. 925-4626); **The Freudian Slip** (lingerie), 416 South Hunter Street (tel. 925-4427); **Mark Justin** (men's and women's), 217 South Galena Street (tel. 925-1046); **Stefan Kaelin** (ski fashions), 447 East Cooper Street (tel. 925-2989); **Kristan of Aspen** (men's and women's), 602 East Cooper Street (tel. 925-7409); **Panache** (women's), 406 South Galena Street (tel. 920-2237); **Spurs** (western), 207 South Galena Street (tel. 925-6130); and **Suzanne's** (sweaters), 205 South Mill Street (tel. 920-2535).

**JEWELRY** **Aspen Leaf Jewelers,** 121 South Galena Street (tel. 925-5693); **The Golden Bough,** 433 East Hyman Avenue (tel. 925-2660); **HWR Jewelry,** 318 South Galena Street (tel. 925-4610); and **MacMillan,** 425 East Hopkins Avenue (tel. 925-4797);

**SPORTING GOODS** **Great Stuff** (collectibles), 402 South Galena Street (tel. 290-BATS); **Pomeroy Sports,** 614 East Durant Avenue (tel. 925-7875); and **Gene Taylor Sports,** Snowmass Village Mall (tel. 923-4336).

## EVENING ENTERTAINMENT

**THE PERFORMING ARTS** The focus of the performing arts in Aspen is the 1889 ✪ **Wheeler Opera House,** 328 East Hyman Avenue (tel. 920-2266, or

925-2750 for the box office). Built in the heyday of the mining era by silver baron Jerome B. Wheeler, this stage—meticulously restored in 1984—hosts a year-round program of music, theater, dance, film, and lectures. The box office is open Monday through Saturday from 10am to 5pm, and in summer, also on Sunday from 10am to 3:30pm; guided backstage tours by appointment.

The ✪ **Aspen Music Festival** (tel. 925-3258, or 925-9042 after May 15 for the box office) has been held annually since 1949. Lasting 9 weeks from late June to late August, it offers classical music, opera, jazz, and choral works. Most concerts take place in the 1,700-seat Music Tent at Third Street and Gillespie Street, but there are free events around the Aspen area, matinees and other programs at the Wheeler Opera House, and Saturday "Music on the Mountain" concerts atop Aspen Mountain. About 100,000 music lovers visit Aspen for the festival, so plan ahead: Write P.O. Box AA, Aspen, CO 81612. Most individual event tickets are $14 to $25, with some events as high as $30. If you plan a longer stay, inquire about subscription tickets.

The ✪ **DanceAspen Festival** (tel. 925-7718, or 925-2750 after June 1 for the box office) has taken its place with Jacob's Pillow in the Massachusetts Berkshires and the American Dance Festival in Durham, N.C., as the nation's leading summer dance festivals. Lasting 6 weeks from July through the second week of August, it features a broad spectrum of dance forms. In 1992 the festival is scheduled to move from Aspen High School to the new 550-seat Aspen School District Auditorium. For tickets, write P.O. Box 8745, Aspen, CO 81612. Most individual tickets are $7 to $22 for evening performances, $7 to $16 for matinees; subscription tickets are discounted. Running concurrently is a summer dance school for 200 teenagers selected during a 28-city winter audition tour.

The **Aspen Theatre Company** (tel. 925-2750) performs two Off Broadway plays during a short summer season at the Wheeler Opera House. The **Snowmass/ Aspen Repertory Theatre** (tel. 923-3773) offers three musical comedies or mystery productions between late June and mid-August, plus a children's matinee show at the Snowmass Performing Arts Center, Snowmass Mall.

**NIGHTCLUBS   Club Paradise,** 450 South Galena Street (tel. 925-5886), has attracted such rock stars as Stevie Nicks and Neil Young; Tuesday through Saturday nights in season, you may find any sort of live music from rock and reggae to jazz and blues. **The Paragon,** 419 East Hyman Avenue (tel. 925-9811), glitters with raised, mirrored dance platforms, three bars, big-screen videos, and nonstop discs. **Ebbe's,** 312 South Galena Street (tel. 925-6200), has three floors: a piano bar in the basement, a *karaoke* (video sing-along) bar, and live music for dancing beneath a top-level skylight. **The Tippler,** 535 East Dean Street (tel. 925-4977), near the gondola base, draws après-skiers as well as late-night dancers. Its counterpart in the Snowmass Village Mall is **The Timbermill** (tel. 923-4774). Country music lovers appreciate **Shooters Saloon,** 220 South Galena Street (tel. 925-4567), and **Cowboys,** at the Silvertree Hotel in Snowmass (tel. 923-3520).

The best place to find celebrities is the elegant **Caribou Club,** inspired by Annabelle's of London, in the remodeled basement of an old hardware store at 405 East Hopkins Avenue (tel. 920-1800). You'll have to pull strings to get in. A one-time, 2-week temporary membership, with a current member's recommendation, is $200.

**THE BAR SCENE**   It seems the fashion to do one's drinking at a historic bar. The **Hotel Jerome Bar** (the "J Bar"), Main Street and Mill Street (tel. 920-1000), has universal appeal. **Bentley's at the Wheeler,** 328 East Hyman Avenue (tel. 920-2240), is an elegant English-style pub. The **Red Onion,** 420 East Cooper Avenue (tel. 925-9043), is Aspen's oldest bar. The **Ute City Banque,** 501 East Hyman Avenue (tel. 925-4373), is a former silver miners' bank, and the **Smuggler Land Office,** Hopkins Street and Galena Street (tel. 925-8624), is just that—a 19th-century land office.

Aspen's requisite **Hard Rock Café,** 210 South Galena Street (tel. 920-1666), opened in 1991, as did **Legends of Aspen,** 325 East Main Street (tel. 925-5860), a sports bar. **Shlomo's,** in the Little Nell Hotel, 675 East Durant Avenue (tel. 920-6333), draws scores of après-skiers, though those of better means prefer to tipple before dinner at **Mezzaluna,** 600 East Cooper Avenue (tel. 925-5882). **Boogie's,** 534 East Cooper Avenue (tel. 925-6610), attracts a late-night crowd.

# WHERE TO STAY

Forty hotels or lodges and a like number of condominium complexes provide beds for some 10,000 Aspen visitors at any given time. Standards range from dorm bunks to exclusive presidential suites. Despite the range, or perhaps because of it, occupancy rates run 90% or higher during peak winter and summer seasons, so it's essential to make reservations as early as possible. The easiest way to do so is to call **Aspen Central Reservations** (tel. 800/262-7736), or if you're planning to stay in Snowmass Village, **Snowmass Central Reservations** (tel. 800/322-3245).

Most hotels and condos offer sharply differing rates according to the "season." That means more than just winter and summer. Depending upon the lodge, there are either three or four winter seasons. "Value season" (from the opening of ski season in November to the beginning of the Christmas holidays, and the last few weeks of ski season in April) is the least expensive. The Christmas–New Year holiday period is the most expensive. Relatively high "regular" or "peak" ski-season rates may be posted the entire ensuing January to March period, although many lodges reduce rates during the less-busy weeks of January and early February. Summer rates are low compared to those of ski season. Many accommodations close during the spring and fall; if they're open, rates during those months are typically the lowest of any time during the year.

## ASPEN

### Very Expensive

**HOTEL JEROME, 330 E. Main St., Aspen, CO 81611. Tel. 303/920-1000,** or 800/331-7213, 800/423-0037 in Colorado. Fax 303/920-1040. 79 rms, 15 suites. TV TEL

**$ Rates:** Value season, $179–$199 single; $199–$219 double; $289–$399 suite. Pre-Christmas and Jan–Mar, $319–$349 single; $349–$379 double; $399–$549 suite. Christmas holidays, $419–$449 single; $449–$479 double; $499–$649 suite. Mid-Apr to mid-Nov, $159 single; $159–$199 double; $269–$379 suite. AE, CB, DC, MC, V. **Parking:** Underground.

Jerome B. Wheeler, made rich by silver and anxious to tell his friends in New York (he was president of Macy's) that Aspen had a hotel the equal of the Ritz in Paris, had the Jerome built during the peak of the silver boom. It opened in 1889 as Colorado's first hotel with electricity and indoor plumbing, and the first west of the Mississippi with a hydraulic elevator. For 4 years the Jerome was indeed a showpiece. Then came the silver crash—but the hotel lived on. The Jerome is on the National Register of Historic Places, its Eastlake Victorian architecture lovingly preserved and furnished with $1 million in period antiques.

Each guest room is different. All are elegant, with one-of-a-kind antiques (like writing desks and settees) and objets d'art. Lace curtains adorn the tall windows, floral paper covers the walls, and the floors are fully carpeted. Ornate headboards and down comforters grace the king-size or double beds. There are concessions to modern luxury, of course: remote-control color TVs, direct-dial phones, and refrigerators. Bathrooms, finished with white Carrera marble and reproduction 19th-century octagonal tiles, contain hairdryers and oversize Jacuzzi tubs.

**Dining/Entertainment:** The Jerome Grille serves hearty portions of meat, fish, poultry, wild game, and pasta, with à la carte dinner main courses ranging from $17 to $28. Fresh Florida stone crab is a specialty from mid-October to mid-May. A more casual breakfast and lunch are also served here. Lighter appetites can visit the Jerome Pizza Co. in the basement, or opt for some "pub grub" in the Jerome Bar.

**Services:** Room service, concierge, 24-hour front desk, valet laundry, complimentary van, daily newspaper delivered to room, business and secretarial services.

**Facilities:** Heated swimming pool with sundeck, Jacuzzi, massage; sundry shop; meeting space for 400.

# ASPEN

N

Anderson Ranch Arts Center ❶
Aspen Art Museum ❷
Aspen Center for Environmental Studies ❸
Aspen Highlands ❹
Aspen Historical Society Museum ❺

Aspen Mountain ❻
Buttermilk Mountain ❼
Maroon Bells ❽
Snowmass Ski Area ❾
Wheeler Opera House ❿

Post Office ⊠    Information ⓘ

## Map labels

Eastwood Rd.
Roaring Fork River
Westview Dr.
McSkimming Rd.
Midland Ave.
Park Ave.
Riverside Ave.
Riverside Dr.
Cleveland St.
West End St.
Waters Ave.
Spruce St.
Walnut St.
Lone Pine Ave.
Hunter Creek
Gibson Ave.
Spring St. N. St.
St. Francis St.
Bay St.
King St.
Neale Ave.
Queen St.
Original St.
Ute Ave.
Spring St.
Hunter St.
Post Office
Galena St.
Bus Station
Puppy Smith St.
Red Mtn Rd.
Lake Ave.
Hallam Lake
City Hall
Mill St.
Monarch St.
Wagner Park
Gilpin Ave.
Cooper Ave.
Durant Ave.
Dean St.
Juan St.
Aspen St.
Paepcke Park
Hyman Ave.
Garmisch St.
Willoughby Wy.
Roaring Fork Rd.
1st St.
2nd St.
3rd St.
4th St.
Castle Ave.
Gillespie St.
Pearl Ct.
Lake Ave.
North St.
Francis St.
Hallam St.
Bleeker St.
Main St.
5th St.
6th St.
Hopkins Ave.
DRG & WRR
7th St.
Smuggler St.
8th St.
Meadows Rd.
Castle Creek
City Hospital
Power Plant Rd.
82
Black Birch Dr.
Overlook Dr.
Bunny
Castle Creek Dr.
Cemetery Ln.
Maroon Creek Rd.

COLORADO
Denver
Aspen

**THE LITTLE NELL, 675 E. Durant Ave., Aspen, CO 81611. Tel. 303/920-4600,** or **800/525-6200,** or **800/525-6200.** Fax 303/920-4670. 79 rms, 13 suites. A/C MINIBAR TV TEL

**$ Rates:** Summer, $200–$275 single or double; $325–$1,250 suite. Spring and fall, $160–$225 single or double; $275–$975 suite. Pre-Christmas and early Jan to Mar, $300–$400 single or double; $450–$1,800 suite. Holiday period, $425–$510 single or double; $600–$2,500 suite. AE, CB, DC, DISC, JCB, MC, V. **Parking:** Valet parking.

The Aspen Skiing Company opened its showcase hotel for the 1989–90 ski season, and today rooms here may be the most sought-after of any in the resort. Located 17 paces (yes, it's been measured) from the base terminal of the Silver Queen gondola, the Little Nell deserves every plaudit it receives for its location, its design, and its highly professional and friendly staff. Here's a hotel that not only has a full-time ski concierge to handle ski storage and complimentary nightly waxing, tickets, rentals, and lessons, it even has a snow-melt system built into the sidewalks.

Because of the hotel's innovative architectural design and variations in decorating, no two guest rooms are exactly alike. All have working gas fireplaces, Belgian wool carpeting, alderwood furniture, custom-woven chenille lounge chairs and love seats, and Audubon bird prints on the walls. A remote-control television (with built-in videocassette recorder) and refrigerator are contained in a wall unit. Closets are large enough to have separate dressing and storage areas. Telephones carry two lines. Marble-finished bathrooms contain two vanities, Jacuzzi tubs, hairdryers, steam irons, telephones, and Crabtree & Evelyn toiletries. Standard suites have separate Jacuzzi tubs and steam showers, big-screen TVs, stereos, cellular phones, and private living-room safes. Five executive apartments have all this and more, including their own fax machines.

**Dining/Entertainment:** The restaurant (see "Where to Dine," below) serves "American alpine cuisine" in an artsy atmosphere with large windows looking toward the hotel courtyard. The Living Room Bar is just that—a plush living room—with lots of greenery, a two-sided sandstone fireplace, and outdoor terrace seating. Shlomo's deli offers ski-in/ski-out casual dining three times a day, and is a popular haunt for after-ski tipplers.

**Services:** 24-hour room service, full-service concierge, winter ski concierge, same-day valet laundry, complimentary shuttle, full accessibility for the disabled.

**Facilities:** Year-round outdoor heated swimming pool and Jacuzzi; fitness club with Nautilus equipment, steam room, and spa services, including massage; ski technician on staff; specialty arcade with eight shops; meeting space for 200; temporary membership to Snowmass Lodge & Club (racquet sports, golf, cross-country skiing, etc.).

## Expensive

**ASPEN CLUB LODGE, 709 E. Durant Ave. (at Spring St.), Aspen, CO 81611. Tel. 303/925-6760,** or **800/882-2582, 800/443-2582** in Colorado. Fax 303/925-6778. 90 rms. TV TEL

**$ Rates** (including continental breakfast): Summer, $115–$135 single or double; $165 suite. Spring and fall, $70–$100 single or double; $100–$115 suite. Early/late ski season, $120–$145 single or double; $175 suite. Christmas, $250–$275 single or double; $305 suite. Jan–Mar, $195–$235 single or double; $260–$275 suite. Children 12 and under stay free in parents' room. AE, CB, DC, MC, V. **Parking:** Free, underground.

The special attraction about the Aspen Club is, well, the Aspen Club. It's *the* athletic club for Aspen residents. You're as likely to see Michael Douglas lifting weights or John Denver taking a swim as you are to see Chris Evert Mill or Martina Navratilova on the tennis courts—in fact, Chris's sister, Clare Evert, is the resident tennis pro. The club's Fitness and Sports Medicine Institute is of major importance to professional athletes in rehabilitation. The club is about a mile out of town, but guests at the Aspen Club Lodge—or any of the various condominiums and private homes rented by Aspen Club Realty—become temporary members of the Aspen Club.

The lodge is adjacent to the Little Nell, near the foot of the Aspen Mountain gondola. The spacious lobby has a large central lounge with big picture windows on the slopes. Rooms are comfortable and crisply decorated, with nice use of light woods. All have a king-size or two queen-size beds, a private balcony, a TV tucked away in an armoire, and a coffee maker.

**Dining/Entertainment:** The Primavera restaurant features gourmet Italian cuisine for dinner only, including an outstanding antipasto buffet.

**Services:** Room service, concierge, valet laundry, airport shuttle.

**Facilities:** Heated outdoor swimming pool, Jacuzzi, saunas, meeting space for 80. The Aspen Club, 1450 Crystal Lake Rd. (tel. 925-8900), offers indoor and outdoor tennis, racquetball, squash, basketball, indoor golf, swimming, aerobics, weights, exercise equipment, Jacuzzis, saunas, steam rooms, cold plunges, massage rooms, and more. The Fitness and Sports Medicine Institute offers fitness evaluations, conditioning sessions, and nutritional analyses.

**THE SARDY HOUSE, 128 E. Main St. (at Aspen St.), Aspen, CO 81611. Tel. 303/920-2525.** 14 rms, 6 suites. TV TEL

**$ Rates** (including breakfast): Early/late ski season, $120–$175 single or double; $225–$300 suite. Pre-Christmas and Jan–Mar, $220–$285 single or double; $350–$500 suite. Holiday period, $295–$360 single or double; $425–$575 suite. Summer, $135–$200 single; $145–$210 double; $250–$350 suite. AE, CB, DC, MC, V. **Parking:** Free.

A red-brick Victorian mansion built in 1892, the Sardy House stands opposite Paepcke Park where Colo. 82 enters downtown from the west. Majestic spruce trees rise above the inn's landscaped grounds. Inside, lace curtains, rose-filled carpets, and period antiques lend a delicate elegance. An enclosed gallery bridges a private brick mews, joining the Sardy House to its Carriage House wing.

The well-kept rooms combine antique Victorian and modern furnishings: cherrywood beds and armoires, wicker chairs and sofas. There are Jacuzzi tubs in all but two, which have antique clawfoot tubs. Other touches include clock radios, down comforters, terry-cloth robes, and heated towel racks. All rooms have entertainment centers with VCRs, wet bars, and hideaway sofas. Three have private entrances; one has a private balcony and sitting room; one has a fireplace. The Carriage House Suite features a winding, wrought-iron staircase to its second floor.

**Dining/Entertainment:** The Sardy House restaurant presents candlelit continental dinners with silver service, in a plush fireplace room. Main courses of filet mignon, lamb, lobster, and salmon run $18.75 to $27.75. It's also open to the public for breakfast ($6.25 to $10.25). Jack's Bar is open from 4pm daily.

**Services:** Room service morning and evening, valet laundry.

**Facilities:** Heated outdoor swimming pool, hot tub, sauna; private ski storage and heated boot lockers.

### Moderate

**ASPEN COUNTRY INN, Colo. 82 at Tiehack Rd. (P.O. Box 1368), Aspen, CO 81612. Tel. 303/925-2700,** or 800/525-4012. Fax 303/920-4412. 49 rms, 1 suite. TV TEL

**$ Rates** (including breakfast in winter): Single or double, $65–$90 spring and fall, $78–$115 summer, $100–$130 early/late ski season, $180–$235 Christmas, $120–$165 Jan, $150–$200 Feb–Mar. AE, CB, DC, MC, V. **Closed:** Mid-Apr to mid-June and mid-Sept to mid-Dec. **Parking:** Free.

This delightful inn, located between the Tiehack and Buttermilk base facilities at the foot of Buttermilk Mountain, offers a touch of country elegance. Operated by Village Resorts, it has a sitting area and library around a big stone fireplace. Rooms have a view of either the Rockies or the Roaring Fork valley. Most have a king-size or two double beds and handsome vanities; 15 poolside and fireplace rooms have Jacuzzi tubs or bidets.

The inn's restaurant serves elegant dinners ($14–$25) on Wedgwood china and Lennox crystal nightly during ski season (or for parties by reservation in summer), featuring game, beef, seafood, and pasta dishes.

Services and facilities include complimentary ski shuttle, valet laundry, 24-hour desk, no-smoking rooms, facilities for the disabled; heated outdoor swimming pool and year-round Jacuzzi.

**HEARTHSTONE HOUSE, 134 E. Hyman Ave. (at Aspen St.), Aspen, CO 81611. Tel. 303/925-7632.** Fax 303/920-4450. 18 rms (all with bath). TV TEL

**$ Rates** (including breakfast and afternoon tea): Summer, $94–$110 single; $98–$128 double; $148–$158 suite. Winter, $158–$168 single; $168–$188 double; $190–$210 suite. AE, MC, V. **Parking:** Free.

Small and sophisticated in the tradition of European luxury inns, the Hearthstone House is located just two blocks west of the Wheeler Opera House. Guests share a large, elegant living room with teak and leather furnishings, a wood-burning fireplace, a dining room with bright flowers, and an extensive library. Most of the rooms are bright and homey but relatively small, with queen-size, double, or twin beds, original abstract art, small TVs, and vanities. Three "king" rooms feature Jacuzzi tubs, full-wall mirrors, and much more space.

Special touches include valet laundry and an Austrian herbal steam.

**HOTEL ASPEN, 110 W. Main St. (at Garmisch St.), Aspen, CO 81611. Tel. 303/925-3441,** or 800/527-7369. Fax 303/920-1379. 37 rms, 8 suites (all with bath). TV TEL

**$ Rates** (including continental breakfast): Early/late ski season, $69–$89 single or double; $135–$155 suite. Holiday period, $200–$220 single or double; $275–$295 suite. Early Jan to early Feb, $99–$119 single or double; $155–$175 suite. Early Feb to late Mar, $165–$185 single or double; $225–$245 suite. Mid-Apr to mid-June and late Sept to late Nov, $64–$79 single or double; $100–$115 suite. Mid-June to late Aug, $90–$105 single or double; $130–$145 suite. Late Aug to late Sept, $74–$89 single or double; $105–$120 suite. AE, CB, DC, DISC, MC, V. **Parking:** Free.

Bridging the geographical gap between Aspen's Victorian West End neighborhood and its bustling downtown is this pleasant modern hotel, located just three blocks west of the Hotel Jerome. Above the small lobby, a second-floor living room with a fireplace and library doubles as a breakfast and après-ski party room. All rooms are upscale and well lit, making attractive use of light woods and strong pastels. Standard one-bedroom units have a king- or queen-size beds; deluxe units have a terrace or balcony. Solarium suites include enclosed sitting porches overlooking Aspen Mountain. Many rooms, including the penthouse suites, have private Jacuzzi tubs. All rooms have a wet bar.

Services and facilities include valet laundry, an outdoor swimming pool, two outdoor Jacuzzis, and meeting space for up to 60.

**INDEPENDENCE SQUARE HOTEL, 404 S. Galena St., Aspen, CO 81611. Tel. 303/920-2313,** or 800/882-2582, 800/443-2582 in Colorado. Fax 303/925-6778. 28 rms (all with bath). TV TEL

**$ Rates** (including continental breakfast): Single or double, $95–$200 early/late ski season, $200–$285 holiday period, $115–$225 Jan to mid-Feb, $135–$250 mid-Feb to Mar. 5-night minimum in winter. AE, CB, DC, DISC, MC, V. **Parking:** Free.

A renovated historic property on the downtown mall opposite the Rubey Park bus station, this hotel is one of the Aspen Club group. Light breakfasts and après-ski drinks are served in the second-floor atrium lounge with a large fireplace and the ground-floor library with books, newspapers, and board games. Colorful photographs adorn the hallways. Guest rooms can dazzle with colors alone—purple doors and peach trim—but decor is otherwise simple, with lots of light woods and good use of modern and historic photos. All rooms have double beds (some of them Murphys) with down comforters, ample closet space, refrigerators, and modern but cramped bathrooms.

Services and facilities include concierge, airport shuttle, individual ski lockers, rooftop Jacuzzi and sun deck, and complimentary use of the Aspen Club.

**THE INN AT ASPEN, 38750 Colo. 82, Aspen, CO 81611. Tel. 303/925-1500,** or 800/952-1515, 800/826-4998 in Colorado. Fax 303/925-9037. 120 rms, 4 suites (all with bath). A/C TV TEL
**$ Rates** (including breakfast): Early/late ski season, $110–$155 single or double; $200 suite. Holiday period, $225–$300 single or double; $600 suite. Jan to mid-Feb, $130–$180 single or double; $350 suite. Mid-Feb to Mar, $155–$210 single or double; $400 suite. Mid-Apr to Mid-Nov, $65–$90 single or double; $115 suite. AE, CB, DC, DISC, MC, V. **Parking:** Free.
Nestled at the foot of Buttermilk Mountain, this ski-in/ski-out hotel offers views of either the slopes or the Roaring Fork valley. Studios are neat and cozy, with private balconies, queen-size Murphy beds, double sleeper sofas, easy chairs, dining tables, and vanities. Kitchenettes (stocked for four people) have microwave ovens, refrigerators, toasters, and coffee makers. Executive studios are larger but furnished the same; all rooms have mauve or pale-lilac color schemes. Most guests prefer to pay a little extra for the mountain view.
Dining facilities include: Barrington's Fireside Dining Room and Barrington's Café. The hotel lounge has a sunken section that enables indoor/outdoor Jacuzzi bathers to imbibe. The hotel also offers a heated outdoor swimming pool, fitness center, masseuse, gift shop, private ski lockers, meeting space for 225, room service, concierge, shuttle service, valet laundry, and safety-deposit boxes.

**LIMELITE LODGE, 228 E. Cooper Ave. (at Monarch St.), Aspen, CO 81611. Tel. 303/925-3025,** or 800/433-0832. Fax 303/925-5120. 60 rms, 3 suites (all with bath). TV TEL
**$ Rates** (including continental breakfast): Early/late ski season, $68–$98 single or double; $130 suite. Holiday period, $148–$168 single or double; $225 suite. Jan, $102–$118 single or double; $170 suite. Feb–Mar, $138–$158 single or double; $215 suite. May–June, $58–$98 single or double; $130 suite. July–Aug, $88–$118 single or double; $170 suite. Sept–Oct, $68–$98 single or double; $130 suite. AE, CB, DC, DISC, MC, V. **Parking:** Free.
A unique barbed-wire sculpture stands outside this motel catty-corner from Wagner Park. The lodge has two separate buildings facing each other across Cooper Avenue—one three stories, the other two—each with its own heated outdoor swimming pool and Jacuzzi. Rooms are very well kept. Most have two double beds with down comforters, a large pinewood dresser and other furnishings, floral wallpaper, and a small private bath on the other side of a walk-through closet/vanity. Jacuzzi rooms are available.
The Columbine Room offers breakfast every morning and a warming fire every night. On Monday and Thursday nights in winter, there are hot-spiced-wine après-ski parties. Hot beverages are available 24 hours.
Services and facilities include a 24-hour desk, rooms for the disabled, two heated outdoor swimming pools, Jacuzzis, sauna, guest laundry, and ski lockers.

## Inexpensive

**ST. MORITZ LODGE, 334 W. Hyman Ave., Aspen, CO 81612. Tel. 303/925-3220.** 12 dorm rms (shared bath), 13 standard (all with bath). TV TEL
**$ Rates** (including continental breakfast): Peak summer season, $29 dorm bed; $55 standard room (single or double); $125 condominium. Peak winter season, $36 dorm bed; $125 standard room; $275 condominium. AE, MC, V.
A friendly European-style lodge with a large fireplace in its lobby, the St. Moritz appeals to budget watchers with dorm rooms (small but sufficient) and low-priced standard rooms with cable color television and private tiled bathrooms. The lodge also operates several fully equipped (but outdated) condominium apartments. Some units have fireplaces. There's also a heated outdoor swimming pool, Jacuzzi, and sauna. Breakfast and après-ski refreshments are served daily in the lower lounge.

**THE SKIER'S CHALET, 233 Gilbert St. (P.O. Box 248), Aspen, CO 81612. Tel. 303/920-2037.** 18 rms (all with bath). TV TEL

**$ Rates** (including continental breakfast): Summer, $55 single; $60–$75 double. Winter, $90 single; $100–$120 double. MC, V. **Parking:** On street.

Howard Awrey built this lodge and restaurant at the foot of Lift 1A at Gilbert Street and Aspen Street in 1952, and he has run it ever since. He added a second building in 1965. Combining European style with old-time Aspen ambience, it's popular with folks who come to ski and don't need frills, for instance, international ski racers. Basic rooms have two double beds with down comforters, a desk/dresser, refrigerator, and ski photos on the walls. Breakfast is served in the family room, which also boasts a fireplace and piano. Adjacent, at 710 South Aspen Street, is the Skier's Chalet Steak House, serving large portions at reasonable prices. The outdoor swimming pool is heated to 104° in winter.

## SNOWMASS

Snowmass lodges about 8,000 guests in seven lodges and 22 condo complexes. Call **Snowmass Central Reservations** (tel. 800/322-3245).

### Very Expensive

**THE SNOWMASS LODGE & CLUB, Snowmass Club Circle (P.O. Drawer G-2), Snowmass Village, CO 81615. Tel. 303/923-5600,** or 800/525-0710. Fax 303/923-6944. 76 rms, 65 suites. A/C MINIBAR TV TEL

**$ Rates** (including breakfast): Early/late season, $125–$175 single or double; $180–$340 villa. Pre-Christmas and Feb–Mar, $225–$295 single or double; $340–$600 villa. Holiday period, $275–$375 single or double; $405–$690 villa. Jan, $175–$225 single or double; $225–$390 villa. Spring and fall, $125–$175 single or double; $180–$340 villa. Summer, $150–$200 single or double; $200–$360 villa. Children 12 and under stay free in parents' room. AE, CB, DC, DISC, JCB, MC, V. **Parking:** Free.

A mile below the ski lifts at Snowmass Village sprawls this 567-acre sports resort and conference center. Despite its distance from the slopes, this is indeed a skiers' hotel: All room prices include lift tickets! Surrounded by a golf course that converts in winter to a nordic ski center, and near 11 outdoor tennis courts and two swimming pools, the three-story building of stone and cedar shakes is ideal for the sports lover. Within, a massive rock fireplace dominates a living room of plush couches and pinewood floors. A reading nook has out-of-town papers and current magazines, and a handcrafted piano bar highlights an intimate cocktail lounge.

Guests are greeted in their rooms by a complimentary bottle of champagne. The lodge itself has 76 rooms, including nine premium units and four deluxe rooms. Each has a queen-size bed and sofa bed, reproduction antique pine furniture including a desk, cable television hidden in an armoire, direct-dial phones, radio, humidifier, terry-cloth robes, wet bar, refrigerator, coffee maker, and a private patio or balcony with mountain or poolside view. Sixty-five adjacent villas of one to three bedrooms have all these amenities and more, including full kitchens, a bath per bedroom, and full living/dining areas. Most also have wood-burning fireplaces.

**Dining/Entertainment:** The Four Corners dining room serves three meals daily in a two-level garden atmosphere. Gourmet American food is priced in the high moderate range. From May to September, casual lunches are served in the Summerhouse restaurant by the tennis courts. There's a snack bar in the golf/cross-country clubhouse, and a cocktail lounge/piano bar in the main lodge.

**Services:** 24-hour room service and valet laundry, full-service concierge, ski concierge slopeside, ski and golf equipment storage, nursery and child care, foreign exchange desk, morning newspaper and fresh coffee in room, business services, room for the disabled.

**Facilities:** 18-hole championship golf course converts to nordic ski center in winter, with seasonal pro shop/ski-rental shop; two indoor and 11 outdoor tennis courts, with pro shop; racquetball and squash courts; heated outdoor lap pool and recreational swimming pool; bicycle rentals; full athletic club (including weights, aerobics, hot tubs, saunas, steam rooms, massage, and facials); guest laundry; games room; meeting space for up to 225.

## Moderate

**HOTEL WILDWOOD, 40 Elbert Lane (P.O. Box 5037), Snowmass Village, CO 81615. Tel. 303/923-3550,** or 800/445-1642, 800/833-1603 in Colorado. Fax 303/923-4844. 145 rms, 4 suites (all with bath). TV TEL
**$ Rates** (including continental breakfast): Early/late ski season, $86–$96 single or double; $135 suite. Holiday period, $175–$185 single or double; $245 suite. Jan, $127–$137 single or double; $200 suite. Feb–Mar, $161–$171 single or double; $221 suite. Mid-Apr to May and mid-Sept to mid-Nov, $70 single or double; $110 suite. June to mid-Sept, $84–$95 single or double; $130 suite. Children 12 and under stay free in parents' room. AE, MC, V. **Parking:** Free.
Located next to the Snowmass Village Mall and adjacent to the ski slopes, the Wildwood likes to call itself "a small hotel with grand hospitality." The lobby and rooms are nicely appointed, with southwestern motifs and burgundy color schemes. Colorful framed posters are a trademark of the guest rooms, some of which have private balconies. Others overlook the courtyard heated swimming pool and Jacuzzi. All rooms have refrigerators, coffee makers, and remote-control televisions.

Pippin's Steak & Lobster Restaurant serves gourmet family-style dinners nightly, with main courses priced $11.95 to $27.95. Children staying at the hotel get a 50% discount off the children's menu. Après-ski drinks are also served in the bar here.

Services and facilities include evening room service, 24-hour desk, valet laundry, courtesy van to airport and around Snowmass, saunas, ski lockers, exchange library, and meeting rooms.

**MOUNTAIN CHALET, 132 Daly Lane (P.O. Box 5066), Snowmass Village, CO 81615. Tel. 303/923-3900,** or 800/843-1579. 64 rms. TV TEL
**$ Rates** (including full breakfast): Single or double, $85–$110 early/late ski season, $150–$190 holiday period, $125–$157 Jan, $144–$175 Feb–Mar, $80–$100 June–Sept. Minimum 7 nights in holiday period and Feb–Mar. AE, DISC, MC, V.
**Closed:** Mid-Apr to May and mid-Sept to Thanksgiving. **Parking:** $6 per day.
A small but elegant European-style ski hotel, the four-story Mountain Chalet is a ski-in/ski-out accommodation on the slopes below the Snowmass Village Mall. Rooms are simple but nicely kept, with light-wood furnishings, including a desk, plus cable TV, AM/FM radio, and small refrigerator. Many rooms have a fireplace or private balcony.

Hot beverages are available 24 hours on the third floor. Winter Sundays, there's always an après-ski party. Services and facilities include limited airport shuttle, valet laundry, heated outdoor swimming pool, hot tub, saunas, guest laundry, games room, and ski storage.

## Inexpensive

**SNOWMASS INN, Daly Lane (P.O. Box 5640), Snowmass Village, CO 81615. Tel. 303/923-4202.** 44 rms (all with bath). TV TEL
**$ Rates** (including continental breakfast): Single or double, $80 Thanksgiving to mid-Dec, $100 pre-Christmas period, $140 Christmas, $115 Jan, $125 Feb–Mar, $90 end of Mar to mid-Apr, $70 mid-May to mid-Oct. MC, V. **Parking:** Free.
**Closed:** Mid-Apr to mid-May and mid-Oct to Thanksgiving.
Located opposite the north side of the Village Mall, the Snowmass Inn has a large stone fireplace in its lobby and four floors of guest rooms. Queen-size Murphy beds lower electronically from the walls, and large sleeper sofas enable each room to sleep four. All rooms have mini-refrigerators, wet bars, cable TV, full bathrooms with vanities, and coffee and tea each morning. Facilities include a year-round heated swimming pool, king-size Jacuzzi, sauna, guest laundry, and courtesy airport shuttle.

# WHERE TO DINE

There are more than 100 restaurants in the Aspen-Snowmass area to cater to every kind of hunger pang. Most are open nightly during the winter (Thanksgiving to early April) and summer (mid-June to mid-September) seasons. Between seasons, however, most close their doors and give their staffs a vacation. Call ahead if you're visiting at these times.

## ASPEN

### Very Expensive

**PINE CREEK COOKHOUSE, 11399 Castle Creek Rd., Ashcroft. Tel. 925-1044.**
> **Cuisine:** CONTINENTAL. **Reservations:** Recommended at lunch, required at dinner.
> **$ Prices:** Lunch $12–$18; fixed-price dinner $50 ($60 including sleigh ride). AE, MC, V.
> **Open:** June 15–Oct 1 and Dec 15–Apr 15, lunch daily noon–2:30pm; dinner daily 6–9pm.

A cross-country ski center was established near the mining ghost town of Ashcroft, 13 miles from Aspen at the foot of the Elk Mountain Range, and this restaurant followed soon after. Surrounded by 13,000-foot peaks, the cookhouse can be reached by road in summer, by sleigh or cross-country skis only in winter. Skiers put on miners' headlamps and follow a guide for 20 minutes to reach the rustic restaurant, while sleigh riders huddle under fur rugs as mules pull them to dinner.

Lunch is served on an outdoor deck, weather permitting. Dinner is always an event. It starts with a steaming mug of hot mulled cider, then continues with a hearty homemade soup and a main course that might be baked trout, lamb, or guinea hen. Brownies in chocolate-hazelnut sauce, if they're on the menu, are a wonderful conclusion to the meal.

**PIÑONS, 105 S. Mill St. Tel. 920-2021.**
> **Cuisine:** CREATIVE REGIONAL. **Reservations:** Recommended.
> **$ Prices:** Appetizers $8–$12; main courses $22–$32. AE, MC, V.
> **Open:** Dinner only, daily 6–10pm.

Tremendous attention to detail went into creating the contemporary western ranch setting of Piñons, with its aged stucco walls and braided whip leather around the stairwell. New Age music soothes the nerves, as do such appetizers as the justly famous venison dumplings, smoked-duck quesadillas, and seafood chowder. Main dishes range from prime rib of buffalo to mesquite-grilled tuna, sautéed in crushed macadamia nuts and cloaked in lime butter. If you're not macadamia-ed out, the chocolate macadamia-nut tart is "to die for."

**RENAISSANCE, 304 E. Hopkins Ave., at Monarch St. Tel. 925-2402.**
> **Cuisine:** CREATIVE AMERICAN. **Reservations:** Required.
> **$ Prices:** Appetizers $10–$26; main courses $26–$35; six-course "menu dégustation" $85. AE, MC, V.
> **Open:** Tues–Sun 6–10pm. **Closed:** Mid-Apr to mid-June and mid-Sept to mid-Dec.

Chef-owner Charles Dale has covered much ground in his 30-odd years, from an expatriate childhood in southern France to an art-history degree from Princeton and a master's in political science from New York University to a position as chef saucier at the Big Apple's noted Le Cirque. It has all come together at Renaissance. The art history is manifested in the decor: A Chagall original graces the front entrance, and ceramic sculptures brighten niches in the lime-and-peach pastel decor. The poly-sci is evident in his management of an international staff.

The rest, of course, is clear in the cuisine. The menu changes frequently, depending on what fresh foods are available, but might feature such appetizers as carpaccio of tuna with essence of black truffle or sautéed foie gras with poached pears and pomegranate seeds. A la carte dinner dishes might include grilled striped bass with fennel-and-tomato marmalade, saddle of venison with stuffed cabbage gourmand, or ravioli à la Monégasque with pistachio-nut pesto. You can't miss on the desserts, either, with crème brûlée Le Cirque or hot chocolate soufflé in the offing. The exquisite wine selection is small but hand-picked. Renaissance does not have full cocktail service, nor does it permit smoking.

### Expensive

**THE GOLDEN HORN, 320 S. Mill St. Tel. 925-3373.**

**Cuisine:** SWISS. **Reservations:** Highly recommended.
$ **Prices:** Appetizers $5.50–$9.50; main courses $13–$29. AE, CB, DC, MC, V.
**Open:** Dinner only, daily 5:30–10:30pm. **Closed:** Early Apr to mid-June and Labor Day–Thanksgiving.

An Aspen favorite since 1949, and the town's longest continually operating restaurant, the Golden Horn features the friendly alpine atmosphere of chef-owner Klaus Christ's native Switzerland. Named for the golden horn on the dark-paneled wall near the fireplace, it's famous for its hearty Swiss cuisine—Wiener Rostbraten (a thick steak), venison, and fresh fish—and more recently for "cuisine minceur."

The latter is a low-calorie style of cooking developed in the spa town of Eugénie-les-Bains, France, that keeps three-course dinners to less than 450 calories. A serving of tomato-basil soup, a main course of free-range chicken breast sautéed with rosemary and white wine, and a dessert of fresh berries steamed in parchment paper fills the bill. All items are fat-free and salt-free. The Golden Horn's 260-bottle wine list has earned it a place on *The Wine Spectator*'s "top 100" list of U.S. restaurants.

## THE LITTLE NELL, 675 E. Durant Ave. Tel. 920-4600.

**Cuisine:** CREATIVE REGIONAL. **Reservations:** Highly recommended.
$ **Prices:** Appetizers $6–$12.75; main courses $7.50–$12.75 at lunch, $18.75–$26.25 at dinner. AE, CB, DC, DISC, JCB, MC, V.
**Open:** Breakfast daily 7–10am; lunch daily 11:30am–2pm; dinner daily 5:30–10:30pm.

Dinner here usually begins with a cocktail in the Living Room Bar, with its plush chairs and couches spaced around a massive, two-sided sandstone fireplace. Then it moves into the spacious restaurant, its big windows gazing toward the Little Nell hotel courtyard, its walls hung like an art gallery.

The cuisine bears the moniker "American alpine cooking," focusing on innovative preparations of wild game and fresh seafood. Breakfast has numerous egg specialties; lunch focuses on pasta creations and one-pot dishes like black bean and venison chili pie. At dinner, you can start with a corn and wild-rice chowder or trout cakes with cabbage-and-apple slaw. Main dishes, all served à la carte, include oven-roast antelope and bobwhite quail with peach-and-mint chutney, smoked duck with plum mustard and Portobello mushrooms, or for lighter eaters, rosemary chicken with lemon and garlic, or mushroom strudel and eggplant ratatouille. For dessert, try the cinnamon-brioche bread pudding with spiced rum sauce.

## SYZYGY, 520 E. Hyman Ave. Tel. 925-3700.

**Cuisine:** CREATIVE INTERNATIONAL. **Reservations:** Requested.
$ **Prices:** Appetizers $7–$14; main courses $18–$25. MC, V.
**Open:** Dinner only, daily 5:30–10:30pm (lounge open to 2am Mon–Sat, to midnight Sun). **Closed:** Mid-Apr to May and Oct to mid-Nov.

In scientific terms, a "syzygy" is an alignment of heavenly bodies or a union of biological organisms. In culinary terms it's a perfect fusion of food, service, and presentation. At least that's the claim of this second-story restaurant, a casually elegant establishment with "water walls" accenting an otherwise gray decor.

The menu blends elements of French, Italian, Asian, and southwestern cuisines. One popular appetizer, for instance, is sushi rolls of veal carpaccio, avocado, and chipotle. Likewise unique are celery-root pancakes with corn, crème fraîche, and smoked salmon. For a main dish, consider oysters, broiled with pancetta and chipotle-creamed spinach, or spicy Asian-style lobster in rice paper. Pear tarte tatin is a delectable dessert.

Light rock music is presented, sometimes by nationally known performers, nightly from 10:30pm to closing.

## Moderate

## ASPEN GROVE CAFE, 525 E. Cooper Ave. Tel. 925-6162.

**Cuisine:** INTERNATIONAL. **Reservations:** Recommended at dinner.

**$ Prices:** Main courses $3.50–$6.95 at breakfast, $3.25–$6.75 at lunch, $9.95–$16.95 at dinner. AE, MC, V.
**Open:** Breakfast/lunch daily 7am–3pm; dinner daily 5–10pm.

This garden restaurant in the heart of downtown Aspen offers a bright, airy atmosphere during the day, a more elegant mood in the evening with pink linen and candlelight service. Luncheon specials include the ménage à trois salad (curried chicken, tuna, and carpaccio), pastas, and hot and cold sandwiches. For dinner, consider the blackened halibut, Cajun duck, pistachio schnitzel, spinach ravioli, or beef Stroganoff.

**THE CHART HOUSE, 219 E. Durant Ave., at Monarch St. Tel. 925-3525.**
**Cuisine:** STEAK/SEAFOOD. **Reservations:** Recommended.
**$ Prices:** Main courses $10.95–$19.95. AE, DC, MC, V.
**Open:** Dinner only, daily 5:30–10pm.

The first Chart House in the United States was established here in Aspen in 1961. Contemporary rustic decor—rough-hewn wood walls with sports-action photos, planter boxes beside marble-top tables, polished brass around the 60-item salad bar—suits the alpine location. The menu emphasizes steaks, prime rib, and seafood.

**THE GRILL ON THE PARK, 307 S. Mill St. Tel. 920-3700.**
**Cuisine:** AMERICAN. **Reservations:** Not accepted.
**$ Prices:** Breakfast $3–$6.50; lunch $3.50–$8.50; dinner $10.50–$23.50. AE, CB, DC, DISC, MC, V.
**Open:** Daily 11:30am–11pm.

It's not the view toward the Wagner Park soccer field across the street that makes the Grill so popular among Aspen residents. It's the open mesquite grill, generous portions, and friendly service. Barbecued ribs and chicken, fresh fish, thick steaks and chops highlight the dinner menu. Pasta is always a midday hit, along with half-pound burgers, Chicago-style hot dogs, and imaginative salads. Dine at the bar if you're in a hurry and can't wait for a table.

**OMI, 415 E. Main St. Tel. 920-1084.**
**Cuisine:** CREATIVE CONTINENTAL. **Reservations:** Recommended.
**$ Prices:** Appetizers $5.95–$8.95; main courses $11.95–$18.95. AE, MC, V.
**Open:** Dinner only, daily 5–10:30pm.

Sitting near the corner of Mill Street opposite the Pitkin County Courthouse, this casual restaurant offers modern preparations of French, German, Italian, and American cuisine. It's a favorite of pre- and posttheater-goers. House salad accompanies such dishes as poached salmon with ginger-and-lime sauce, lamb chop with cream and chives, or breast of chicken Hunter. Desserts and cappuccino are served until midnight.

**SMUGGLER LAND OFFICE LTD., 415 E. Hopkins Ave. Tel. 925-8624.**
**Cuisine:** CAJUN/SEAFOOD. **Reservations:** Recommended.
**$ Prices:** Appetizers $5–$9; main courses $12–$19. AE, CB, DC, MC, V.
**Open:** Dinner daily 6–10:30pm; food service daily 4:30pm–midnight (bar open to 2am Mon–Sat, to midnight Sun).

The historic Brand Building, which indeed housed the company that controlled the late 19th-century Smuggler Mine, has been restored in grand Victorian style. From its casual ground-floor bar to the two upper dining levels, there's a feeling of old-time elegance. In summer, dinner is served in an outdoor sculpture garden. Oysters on the half-shell are a favored appetizer. Rack of lamb, fresh seafood, pasta, and Créole and Cajun specialties—including tasty blackened snapper and pepper steak—highlight the menu.

**TAKAH SUSHI, 420 E. Hyman Ave. Tel. 925-8588.**
**Cuisine:** JAPANESE. **Reservations:** Recommended.
**$ Prices:** Appetizers $5–$12; main courses $15–$21. AE, CB, DC, MC, V.
**Open:** Dinner only, daily 5:30–11pm.

This lively sushi bar and Japanese restaurant has been praised by the *New York Times* for its sushi being "some of the best between Malibu and Manhattan." No fewer than

50 varieties of sushi are sliced and rolled here, from *uni* (sea urchin) to *tako* (octopus), flying-fish roe to freshwater eel. If raw fish isn't your style, try the softshell crab, deep-fried and wrapped inside a California roll. Or go for more traditional steak teriyaki or tempura-fried shrimp.

**UTE CITY BANQUE, 501 E. Hyman Ave., at Galena St. Tel. 925-4373.**
   **Cuisine:** AMERICAN/CONTINENTAL. **Reservations:** Recommended.
   **$ Prices:** Appetizers $4.50–$8.50; main course $4.95–$9.95 at lunch, $10.95–$18.95 at dinner. AE, CB, DC, MC, V.
   **Open:** Lunch daily 11:30am–2:30pm; dinner daily 6–10pm (bar-café daily 4:30–11pm; bar open until 2am).

A financial institution (the Aspen State Bank) in the 1890s and a popular restaurant in the 1990s, the Ute City features Victorian decor and the longest solid-oak bar in town. The menu specializes in such dishes as rack of lamb, roast duckling, veal, and fresh fish. A light bar menu is served from 4 to 11pm daily.

**WIENERSTUBE, 633 E. Hyman Ave., at Spring St. Tel. 925-3357.**
   **Cuisine:** AUSTRIAN. **Reservations:** Recommended at dinner.
   **$ Prices:** Breakfast $3.50–$7.50; lunch $5–$11; dinner $9–$17. AE, CB, DC, MC, V.
   **Open:** Tues–Sun 7am–10pm.

Boyhood friends Gerhard Mayritsch and Helmut Schloffer, natives of the Tyrolean village of Villach, opened this restaurant in 1965. One tradition they preserved from the old country was the *stammitsch,* a large community dining table that Aspen locals quickly found to their liking. Today, behind the stained glass of this beautiful garden establishment, you'll find the shakers and movers of this bustling community talking in animated tones over breakfast, lunch, and dinner. There are private tables and booths for everyone else, where they enjoy Viennese pastries in the morning and at teatime (3 to 5pm daily), Austrian sausages for lunch, and Sauerbraten or Rindsrouladen for dinner.

### Inexpensive

**ASIA, 132 W. Main St. Tel. 925-5433.**
   **Cuisine:** CHINESE. **Reservations:** Recommended.
   **$ Prices:** Appetizers $3.95–$7.95; main courses $8.95–$20.95. AE, CB, DC, MC, V.
   **Open:** Daily noon–midnight.

Lodged in an opulent century-old Victorian manor, this is probably Aspen's finest Chinese restaurant. Chef Steve Ko, who cooked for two decades in Taipei and New York before moving to the Rockies, makes Cantonese, Mandarin, Hunan, and Szechuan dishes to individual order. House specialties include Shan-tan beef (with a crispy orange skin), shrimp and scallops in spicy Yu-shan sauce, Peking duck, and an upscale combination of stir-fried lobster tail and beef tenderloin.

**BAHN THAI, 308 S. Hunter St. Tel. 925-5518.**
   **Cuisine:** THAI. **Reservations:** Recommended.
   **$ Prices:** Appetizers $5.95–$12.95; main courses $6.95–$10.95. AE, MC, V.
   **Open:** Mon–Sat 11:30am–10:30pm, Sun 5:30–10:30pm.

Got a taste for something spicy . . . really spicy? Start with a bowl of *tom yum goong* (hot-and-sour lemongrass soup), then follow it with a red or green chicken curry, *pahd Thai* (fried noodles with pork and ground peanuts), or a variety of other Southeast Asian dishes. The restaurant is on the lower level of the Centennial Building, between Cooper Avenue and Hyman Avenue.

**BENTLEY'S AT THE WHEELER, 328 E. Hyman Ave. Tel. 920-2240.**
   **Cuisine:** AMERICAN. **Reservations:** Not accepted.
   **$ Prices:** Lunch $4.95–$9.75; dinner $9.95–$13.50. AE, MC, V.
   **Open:** Lunch daily 11:30am–3pm; dinner daily 5:30–11pm.

A Victorian pub in the 19th-century Wheeler Opera House, Bentley's has a classic bar made from an old English bank counter. Luncheon sandwiches (including "Bentley's burger") and other light dishes such as chicken quesadillas, Caesar salad, and grilled trout are served throughout the day. Generous dinners—served with vegetables, potatoes or rice, rolls and butter—range from pasta provençal to barbecued ribs and grilled swordfish.

### THE CANTINA, 411 E. Main St., at Mill St. Tel. 925-FOOD.
**Cuisine:** MEXICAN. **Reservations:** Not accepted.
**$ Prices:** Lunch $5.75–$8.95; dinner $8.95–$13.95. AE, MC, V.
**Open:** Daily 11am–11pm (bar open to 2am Mon–Sat, to midnight Sun).

"The last time anything this enjoyable came up from Mexico, it was confiscated by the sheriff." That's the claim of this restaurant, one of Aspen's most popular taco-and-enchilada joints. The decor is simple—hardwood floors and tables—with lots of greenery around, and courtyard seating in summer. Portions are huge: They fill a plate that's a foot in diameter. Try the chimichangas, a house specialty.

### LITTLE ANNIE'S EATING HOUSE, 517 E. Hyman Ave. Tel. 925-1098.
**Cuisine:** AMERICAN. **Reservations:** Not accepted.
**$ Prices:** Lunch $3.50–$8.95; dinner $9.50–$14.95. MC, V.
**Open:** Daily 11:30am–11:30pm (bar open to 2am).

Like an Old West saloon, Little Annie's is a rustic bar that attracts working folk, ski bums, families on a budget, and jet-setters looking for a change of pace. It seems there's always a line to get in—for oversize sandwiches, homemade soups, and the best burgers in town at lunch; for barbecued pork ribs, Rocky Mountain trout, and "veg-head" lasagne at dinner. Evening dishes are served with Annie's famous potato pancakes.

### POUR LA FRANCE! CAFE & BISTRO, 413 E. Main St., at Mill St. Tel. 920-1151.
**Cuisine:** INTERNATIONAL. **Reservations:** Not accepted.
**$ Prices:** Breakfast $1.95–$6.95; lunch $3.95–$6.95; dinner $5.95–$11.95. MC, V.
**Open:** Summer, daily 7am–9pm; winter, daily 7am–10pm.

This pleasant European-style sidewalk café—known for its freshly baked croissants and pastries in the morning, its quiches and homemade soups midday—undergoes an evening metamorphosis to a quiet bistro. Nightly specials might include such eclectic dishes as chiles rellenos françaises or Thai crab cakes, or any number of interesting beef or tenderloin dishes. Wines, including champagne, are served by the glass.

### Budget

### LA COCINA, 308 E. Hopkins Ave. Tel. 925-9714.
**Cuisine:** MEXICAN.
**$ Prices:** Main courses $5.95–$9.95. No credit cards.
**Open:** Dinner only, daily 5–10pm. **Closed:** Mid-Apr to May and Oct to mid-Nov.

*Ski* magazine calls La Cocina "one of the unmissables" in Aspen. A free basket of corn chips and spicy-hot salsa have greeted diners here for more than two decades. Start with the green-chile soup, then slide into a platter of blue-corn chicken enchiladas with a side of posole. Top it off with homemade "chocolate velvet" dessert. The bar keeps hopping until the wee hours.

### MAIN STREET BAKERY & CAFE, 201 E. Main St., at Aspen St. Tel. 925-6446.
**Cuisine:** INTERNATIONAL.
**$ Prices:** $2.95–$8.95. MC, V.
**Open:** Mon–Sat 6:30am–9:30pm, Sun 7:30am–4pm.

This old-time Aspen bakery beside Paepcke Park serves three meals a day to hungry locals, and pastries, teas, and espresso drinks in between. Stuffed French toast is a morning favorite; homemade soups, sandwiches, and salads set the tone at lunch. The dinner menu changes nightly, but typically includes meat or vegetarian lasagne, home-style pot pies, pizzas, and stir-fries.

### THE RED ONION, 420 E. Cooper St. Tel. 925-9043.
**Cuisine:** AMERICAN/MEXICAN.

**$ Prices:** Lunch $4.95–$6.50; dinner $5.95–$8.95. AE, MC, V.
**Open:** Daily 11:30am–10pm (bar open until 2am Mon–Sat, to midnight Sun).
Aspen's oldest surviving bar changes with the times: It has an indoor ski "corral" for folks just off the slopes. Burgers and Philadelphia steak sandwiches are big favorites at lunchtime; Mexican cuisine holds forth at night, with the likes of burritos, fajitas, and taco salads. Daily specials feature traditional American fare. Appetizers are half price during happy hour (3:30 to 5:30pm daily).

## SNOWMASS

### Expensive

**KRABLOONIK, 1201 Divide Rd., off Brush Creek Rd., Snowmass Village. Tel. 923-3953.**
   **Cuisine:** WILD GAME/SEAFOOD. **Reservations:** Recommended at lunch, essential at dinner.
**$ Prices:** Appetizers $3.50–$8.50 at lunch, $9–$11 at dinner; main courses $8.95–$27.95 at lunch, $21.50–$49.50 at dinner. DC, DISC, MC, V.
   **Open:** Winter, lunch daily 11am–2pm; dinner seatings daily at 6 and 8:30pm. Summer, dinner seatings daily at 6 and 8:30pm; brunch Sun 10am–2pm.
There's something very wild, something that harkens to Jack London, perhaps, about sitting in a long cabin watching teams of sled dogs come and go as you bite into a caribou stew or wild-boar sandwich. That's part of the pleasure of Krabloonik. A venture of the largest dog kennel in America's lower 48 states, this rustic restaurant has huge picture windows with mountain views and seating around a sunken fire pit. Framed posters and photographs on its walls portray the Iditarod race, Alaska's "granddaddy" of all modern sled-dog races, in which Krabloonik owner Dan MacEachen is an annual competitor.
   Skiers can drop into the restaurant from the Campground lift for winter lunch, or visitors can dine before or after an excursion with the dogs. The stew and the barbecued Swedish boar are popular midday meals, as is smoked Cornish game hen. In the evening, begin with Krabloonik's wild-mushroom soup or a "waffle" of smoked elk and pecans. Then try moose loin grilled with juniper-and-madeira glâce, pheasant breast stuffed with mozzarella cheese, or rainbow trout with crayfish tails and lemon beurre blanc.

### Moderate

**COWBOYS, in the Silvertree Hotel, Elbert Lane, Snowmass Village Mall. Tel. 923-5249.**
   **Cuisine:** CREATIVE REGIONAL. **Reservations:** Accepted only for groups of eight or more.
**$ Prices:** Appetizers $5–$8; main courses $12–$23. AE, CB, DC, DISC, MC, V.
   **Open:** Après ski daily 2:30–5:30pm, dinner daily 5:30–9pm.
Country-and-western music fans, exalt: This may be your ultimate restaurant. Not only can you dance to your favorite swing when dinner is over, but you can get two-step instruction as well. That is, of course, after you've sampled the self-labeled "contemporary cowboy cuisine." Typical appetizers include spiced chicken empañadas with cheese and tomatoes, and a terrine of smoked trout on jicama and tomatillo relish. Main dishes include mesquite-grilled porterhouse steak, a wild-game-and-smoked-duck sausage with roasted garlic-and-pecan pudding, and onion-crusted salmon with fried corn and asiago cheese.

**IL POGGIO, Elbert Lane, Snowmass Village Mall. Tel. 923-4292.**
   **Cuisine:** ITALIAN. **Reservations:** Recommended for the Ristorante.
**$ Prices:** Appetizers $6–$9; main courses $9–$18. AE, MC, V.
   **Open:** Dinner only, daily 5:30–10pm.
Actually two eateries in one, Il Poggio consists of the Ristorante—an elegant fine dining room with an extensive wine list—and a livelier and more casual Caffè, with its huge pizza oven and pasta menu. The Ristorante focuses on "authentic food from

Italy's small towns." Those dishes include such appetizers as prosciutto e frutta, pasta courses such as fettuccine al zafferano (with rabbit and wild mushrooms), and main courses such as fagiano arrosta (whole roasted baby pheasant), vitello ai carciofi (veal with artichoke), and fresh fish specials.

**THE TOWER BAR AND RESTAURANT, Snowmass Village Mall. Tel. 923-4650.**

**Cuisine:** AMERICAN. **Reservations:** Recommended at dinner.
**$ Prices:** Lunch $4.95–$9.95; dinner $12.95–$21.95. AE, CB, DC, MC, V.
**Open:** Lunch daily 11:30am–3pm; dinner daily 5:30–10:30pm.

Three features, besides its central location in the heart of the Snowmass Village Mall, make the Tower special. First is the tower for which it's named, a valley landmark. Second is the fact that it's owned by popular singer John Denver, an Aspen resident who frequently drops by. Third, there's no telling what its bartenders may have up their sleeves: They're amateur magicians who help maintain the food of a family-oriented restaurant. Main dishes include traditional favorites such as prime rib, New York steak, and barbecued shrimp, as well as creative dishes such as salmon Mediterranean, balsamic chicken, mussels with sweet basil, and fettuccine primavera.

## Inexpensive

**LA PIÑATA, Daly Lane, Snowmass Village. Tel. 923-2153.**

**Cuisine:** MEXICAN. **Reservations:** Not accepted.
**$ Prices:** Appetizers $4.95–$7.95; main courses $7.95–$14.95. AE, CB, DC, MC, V.
**Open:** Winter, dinner only, daily 5–10pm; summer, dinner only, daily 5–11pm (bar daily 3pm–2am).

Festive decor, a roaring fire, and a spacious deck make this a favorite Snowmass dining spot. Margarita specials highlight après-ski beginning at 3pm, and dinner specials such as Mr. Murphy's Kitchen Sink Chimichanga keep things hopping all evening. Standard combination meals—burritos, enchiladas, and chiles relleños—are prepared Sonora style. There are nightly fresh fish dishes (often including a crabmeat enchilada), and a few "gringo" dinners such as steak and chicken.

**MOON DOGS, Village Shuttle Depot, Daly Lane, Snowmass Village. Tel. 923-6655.**

**Cuisine:** AMERICAN.
**$ Prices:** $1–$5.25. No credit cards.
**Open:** Daily 8am–midnight.

An antique San Francisco cable car beside the Snowmass bus center houses this self-proclaimed "gourmet fast-food stand." Moon dogs—slow-grilled beef frankfurters—are the house favorite, but you can also get hero sandwiches, Coney Island knishes, egg McMoonDogs for breakfast, and popcorn all day long.

**WOODY CREEK TAVERN, Upper River Rd., Woody Creek. Tel. 923-4585.**

**Cuisine:** AMERICAN. **Reservations:** Not accepted.
**$ Prices:** $3.50–$14.95. No credit cards.
**Open:** Daily 11:30am–10pm (bar open until 2am Mon–Sat, to midnight Sun).

Woody Creek has become as much a hangout for celebrities, including maverick writer Hunter S. Thompson and actor Don Johnson, as for locals. Probably the only old-time, rustic tavern left in the Aspen area, its walls are covered with a variety of news clippings and other paraphernalia. Grilled buffalo beer sausage, barbecued pork ribs, and thick steaks are the most popular menu choices, along with burgers and Mexican food.

To get there, drive three-quarters of a mile west of Brush Creek Road (the Snowmass Village turnoff) on Colo. 82, turn north on River Road, take a left at the first fork, and continue 1¼ miles.

# CHAPTER 10

# THE WESTERN SLOPE

**1. GRAND JUNCTION**
**2. GLENWOOD SPRINGS**
**3. MONTROSE**

Westward-flowing rivers like the Colorado, Gunnison, and Yampa are the lifeblood of the vast, semidesert Western Slope of the Colorado Rockies. These streams support the region's largest communities (Grand Junction and Glenwood Springs on the Colorado, Montrose on the Uncompaghre, Delta on the Gunnison, Craig on the Yampa), irrigate the fertile soils for agriculture and ranching, and enable exploitation of rich mineral resources, including oil, coal, and uranium.

From the tourist standpoint, though, the rivers are much more. Over tens of thousands of years their ceaseless energy has gouged stunning canyons now encompassed by three national monuments: Colorado, Dinosaur, and Black Canyon of the Gunnison. Colorado National Monument, west of Grand Junction, is remarkable for its landforms and prehistoric petroglyphs. Dinosaur National Monument, in the state's northwestern corner, preserves a stunning wealth of fossil remains, along with the spectacular canyons of the Yampa and Green rivers. The Black Canyon, east of Montrose, is a dark, narrow, and virtually impenetrable chasm that draws adventurous rock climbers and rafters from throughout the West.

---

## 1. GRAND JUNCTION

251 miles W of Denver, 169 miles N of Durango

**GETTING THERE** **By Plane** On the north side of Grand Junction, **Walker Field,** 2828 H Road (tel. 244-9100), is less than a mile off I-70's Horizon Road exit. A dozen or more commercial flights arrive each day nonstop from Denver, Phoenix, Salt Lake City, Las Vegas, and Durango, with connections to cities nationwide.

The airport is served by **American West** (tel. 303/245-3460, or 800/247-5692), **Continental** (tel. 303/241-4200, or 800/525-0820), **SkyWest** (for Delta; tel. 800/453-9417), and **United Express** (tel. 800/241-6522).

**By Train** **Amtrak,** First Street and Pitkin Avenue (tel. 800/USA-RAIL), is firmly established in Grand Junction. The *California Zephyr* stops once daily, in each direction, on its main route from San Francisco and Salt Lake City to Denver and Chicago.

**By Bus** The coaches of **Greyhound/Trailways,** and **TNM&O,** 230 South Fifth Street (tel. 242-6012), connect Grand Junction with communities throughout the United States and Canada.

**By Car** Grand Junction is located on I-70. U.S. 50 is the main artery from the south, connecting also with Montrose and Durango.

**Information** Contact the **Grand Junction Visitor & Convention Bureau,** 360 Grand Avenue, Grand Junction, CO 81501 (tel. 303/242-3214, or 800/962-2547). There's a **Tourist Information Center** (tel. 243-1001) on Horizon Drive north of I-70, and a **Colorado Welcome Center** at I-70 Exit 19 (Colorado National Monument), 12 miles west of Grand Junction.

**Getting Around**  **Sunshine Taxi** (tel. 245-9013) will whisk you around town.
**Car rentals** are available in the airport area from Avis (tel. 244-9170), Budget (tel. 244-9155), Hertz (tel. 243-0747), National (tel. 243-6626), and Thrifty (tel. 243-7556).

**Fast Facts**  The **area code** is 303. In case of **emergency, call 911; St. Mary's Hospital** is on F Road at Fourth Street (tel. 244-2273). The main **post office** is at 241 North Fourth Street. For **road conditions,** call 245-8800.

**SPECIAL EVENTS**  The Grand Junction area hosts the following annual events: **Daffodil Days,** in the second and third weeks of March; **Cinco de Mayo,** on May 5; the **Colorado Stampede Parade and Rodeo,** on the third full weekend of June; **Dinosaur Days,** during the fourth week of July; the **Mesa County Fair,** in the first full week of August; and the **Peach Festival,** in Palisade in mid-August.

---

**L**ocated at the confluence of the Gunnison and Colorado rivers, Grand Junction was founded in 1882 where the spike was driven to connect Denver and Salt Lake by rail. It quickly became the primary trade and distribution center between the two state capitals, and its mild climate, together with the fertile soil and irrigation potential of the river valleys, helped it grow into an important agricultural area. Soybeans, and later peaches and pears, were the most important crops; recently, its profile as a wine-producing region has increased. The city also was a center of the western Colorado uranium boom in the 1950s and the oil-shale boom in the late 1970s.

# WHAT TO SEE & DO
## ATTRACTIONS

**COLORADO NATIONAL MONUMENT, off Colo. 340, Fruita. Tel. 303/ 858-3617.**

Eons of erosion by water and wind created this spectacular landscape along the northern rim of the Uncompahgre Plateau. Red-rock canyons and sandstone monoliths, some towering more than 2,000 feet above the Colorado River and its intermittent tributaries, dominate a wilderness of 32 square miles. Bighorn sheep, mountain lions, and golden eagles are among the semidesert denizens of the monument, which was established in 1911.

The east entrance is only 5 miles west of Grand Junction off Monument Road. But the best way to explore is to begin at the west entrance, following the signs off I-70 from Fruita, 15 miles west of Grand Junction. It's here that the 23-mile **Rim Rock Drive** begins, snaking up dramatic **Fruita Canyon** and offering panoramic views across the Colorado River valley to the Grand Mesa and Book Cliffs. At 4 miles it reaches the national monument headquarters and **Visitor Center** near the Saddlehorn Campground. Exhibits on geology and history, and a slide show, introduce the park year round; guided walks and campfire talks are frequently scheduled.

Rim Rock Drive offers access to hiking trails throughout the national monument, varying in length from 400 yards to 8½ miles. Most of the park's canyons are accessible to hikers, often following well-trodden deer trails as they crisscross north-facing slopes. Strange formations such as **Window Rock,** the massive rounded **Coke Ovens,** the boulder-strewn **Devils Kitchen,** the barely touching **Kissing Couple,** and the free-standing **Independence Monument**—all of which can be viewed from the road—are easily reached by foot. Ancient Native American petroglyphs are frequently seen.

Entombed within the rock layers throughout the national monument are the fossil remains of dinosaurs, fish and shellfish, early mammals, and other creatures that lived over a span of 100 million years. A combination of upward lifts, erosion, and volcanic eruptions caused the chaos of formations here. Each layer visible in the striations of the canyon walls marks a time in the land's history. The fossils permit scientists to date these rocks back through the Mesozoic Era of 225 million to 65 million years ago.

**Admission:** $3 per vehicle and $1 per person.
**Open:** Memorial Day–Labor Day, daily 8am–8pm; the rest of the year, daily 8am–4:30pm.

## CROSS ORCHARDS LIVING HISTORY FARM, 3079 F Rd. Tel. 434-9814.

Considered the finest remaining site from the early 20th-century Grand Valley agricultural boom era, Cross Orchards (a division of the Museum of Western Colorado) has re-created a life-style now usually found only in history books. On its 4.4 acres are a blacksmith shop, barn and packing shed, workers' bunkhouse, and former farm manager's residence, as well as an extensive collection of vintage farming and road-building equipment, a railway exhibit, a farm activity area, and a country store and gift shop. Living-history demonstrations are offered several times daily in summer, and various special events are held throughout the year. The original Cross Orchards Farm (1896–1923) covered 243 acres and boasted 22,000 apple trees.

**Admission:** $2 adults, $1.50 seniors 60 and older, 50¢ children 2–12.
**Open:** Mid-May to Nov 1, Wed–Sat 10am–4pm, and other days for special events.

## DINOSAUR VALLEY MUSEUM, 362 Main St., at Fourth St. Tel. 243-DINO or 241-9210.

The animated replicas (complete with sound effects) of such dinosaurs as stegosaurus, triceratops, corythosaurus, and pteranodon thrill youngsters at the Dinosaur Valley Museum. Adults can study regional paleontological history, examine a model of a dinosaur dig, and look at plaster casts of dinosaur prints. On the premises are a working "paleo lab" and a gift shop.

**Admission:** $3.50 adults, $2 children 2–12.
**Open:** Memorial Day–Sept, daily 9am–6pm; the rest of the year, Tues–Sat 10am–5pm.

## DOOZOO CHILDREN'S MUSEUM, 635 Main St. Tel. 241-5225.

Children 1 to 12 get hands-on experience in a variety of activities, from play-acting a grownup profession to performing scientific experiments and testing their creative artistic horizons. The toy store here specializes in educational items.

**Admission:** $2 adults and children.
**Open:** Mon–Sat 10am–5:30pm, Sun noon–5pm.

## MUSEUM OF WESTERN COLORADO, 248 S. Fourth St., at Ute St. Tel. 242-0971.

Exhibits on regional geology, history, and culture are the highlights of this small but eminently worthwhile museum. Of special interest is the Western Colorado Timeline, with photographs and artifacts from every decade since the 1880s. Natural history, prehistoric Native American artifacts, pioneer items, Old West–style paintings, and a Guinness World Record 40-foot-tall unicycle—built by Grand Junction's own Jim Petty—are other highlights.

**Admission:** Free (donations appreciated).
**Open:** Memorial Day–Labor Day, Mon–Sat 10am–4:45pm; the rest of the year, Tues–Sat 10am–4:45pm.

## WESTERN COLORADO CENTER FOR THE ARTS, 1803 N. Seventh St., at Orchard Ave. Tel. 243-7337.

The works of cowboy artist Harold Bryant are featured in the permanent collection of this modern-art museum, which also hosts many temporary exhibits.

**Admission:** Free.
**Open:** Tues–Sat 10am–5pm.

## SPORTS & RECREATION

**BICYCLING** Grand Junction has become important to mountain bikers as the eastern terminus of **Kokopelli's Trail** to Moab, Utah. Winding for 128 miles through sandstone and shale canyons, it has an elevation differential of about 4,200 feet. There are primitive campsites at intervals along the trail. The Colorado gateway is at the Loma Boat Launch, 15 miles west of Grand Junction off I-70.

Another popular route is the **Tabeguache Trail,** running 142 miles from Shavano Valley, near Montrose, to No Thoroughfare Canyon, near the Colorado National Monument west of Grand Junction. For information on either trail, contact the **Colorado Plateau Mountain-Bike Trail Association,** P.O. Box 4602, Grand Junction, CO 81502 (tel. 241-9561), or the **Bureau of Land Management,** 764 Horizon Drive, Grand Junction (tel. 243-6561).

There's also a bike route through and around **Colorado National Monument** (see above); covering 33 miles, it follows Rim Rock Drive through the park and 10 additional miles on rural South Camp Road and South Broadway at the base of the canyons. The national monument publishes a descriptive brochure.

**GOLF** The 18-hole **Tiara Rado Golf Course,** 2063 South Broadway (tel. 245-8085), is at the base of the Colorado National Monument canyons. The 9-hole **Lincoln Park Golf Course,** 12th Street and North Avenue (tel. 242-6394), is in the center of town.

**HIKING** Hikers need look no further than **Colorado National Monument** (see above) for a wide choice of excellent day and overnight trips. A variety of descriptive brochures can be obtained at the park Visitors Center.

**HORSEBACK RIDING** Trail rides of 1 hour ($12) to a full day ($50) are available through **Rimrock Deer Park & Outdoor Center,** on the Colorado River near the west entrance to the Colorado National Monument (tel. 858-9555). Hayrides and cookouts can also be scheduled.

**RIVER RAFTING** Colorado River raft trips of 1½ hours to 2 days or longer are offered by **Adventure Bound River Expeditions,** 2392 H Road, Grand Junction (tel. 241-5633, or 800/423-5668), and **Rimrock Deer Park & Outdoor Center,** P.O. Box 604, Fruita CO 81521 (tel. 858-9555). Prices start at $13 ($11 for children under 13) for the shortest trips, up to $135 ($125 for children) for 2-day trips. One-day trips usually take in the Walter Walker Wildlife Sanctuary. Longer journeys may shoot the Class III and IV rapids of the Ruby, Horsethief, and Westwater Canyons.

Adventure Bound also takes experienced rafters down the Yampa and Green rivers through Dinosaur National Monument, and down the Colorado through Utah's Canyonlands National Park.

**SKIING** The **Powderhorn Resort,** Colo. 65, 7 miles west of Mesa (tel. 245-1140, or 800/8-POWDER), is located 35 miles east of Grand Junction on the north face of the Grand Mesa. A favorite of powder skiers of all ability levels, it offers 255 acres of skiing, with an overnight lodge, two restaurants, a lounge, shops, and full equipment rentals. Full-day tickets are $22 for adults ($19 Monday through Friday) and $11 for children 12 and under ($9 Monday through Friday); kids 6 and under ski free with adults on Monday through Friday.

The resort also offers 18km (11 miles) of groomed cross-country trails (trail pass $7), ice skating (rentals $2.50), and snowmobile tours ($35 per person). The resort office in Grand Junction is at 744 Horizon Drive (tel. 245-5343).

# WHERE TO STAY
## MODERATE

**GRAND JUNCTION HILTON, 743 Horizon Dr., Grand Junction, CO 81506. Tel. 303/241-8888,** or 800/HILTONS. Fax 303/241-8888, ext. 160. 248 rms, 16 suites (all with bath). A/C TV TEL

**$ Rates:** $65–$105 single or double; $94–$225 suite. Weekend rate $59 single or double. Children stay free in parents' room. AE, CB, DC, DISC, MC, V. **Parking:** Free.

A modern eight-story hotel just off I-70, the Hilton is memorable for its bright pastel decor and fine display of artwork in the lobby. The spacious guest rooms have a king-size or two double beds, full-length curtains to separate the entranceway and bathroom from the bedroom area, and contemporary furnishings like clear-glass lamps and full-mirror closet doors.

Dining and entertainment facilities include the Rocking Horse Cattle & Seafood Company, Christie's Restaurant, the Beer Garden, the Observations Lounge off the lobby, and Charades nightclub. There are occasional summer concerts on the lawn.

Room service, valet laundry, no-smoking rooms, and facilities for the disabled are available, as are an outdoor swimming pool and Jacuzzi, three tennis courts, weight and exercise room, volleyball court, horseshoe pits, children's playground, games room, travel agent, meeting space for 600; and vending machines with microwave ovens on some floors.

**HOLIDAY INN, 755 Horizon Dr. (P.O. Box 1725), Grand Junction, CO 81502. Tel. 303/243-6790,** or 800/HOLIDAY. Fax 303/243-6790, ext. 2233. 278 rms, 14 suites (all with bath). A/C TV TEL
$ **Rates:** $46–$51 single; $51–$56 double; $60–$65 suite. AE, CB, DC, DISC, JCB, MC, V. **Parking:** Free.

A spacious central garden courtyard and a skylit indoor garden-style HoliDome—both with swimming pools and other facilities—make this property a delight for recreation lovers. Most mauve-and-green floral-decorated rooms face one pool or the other. Most have two double beds, but many have queen-size or king-size beds, and some also have sofa sleepers or working desks.

Cinnamon's restaurant serves three meals daily, and Errett's Lounge features a large dance floor.

The hotel offers room service, valet laundry, courtesy shuttle, no-smoking rooms, facilities for the disabled, indoor and outdoor swimming pools, Jacuzzi, sauna, exercise room, games room, video arcade, guest laundries, gift shop, liquor store, and meeting space for 500.

**THE ORCHARD HOUSE, 3573 E½ Rd., Palisade, CO 81526. Tel. 303/ 464-0529.** 3 rms (1 with bath, 2 with shared bath). A/C TV
$ **Rates** (including breakfast): $45 single; $60 double. MC, V.

Situated in the midst of the Grand Valley orchard and wine country, this pleasant country homestead is more than just a bed and breakfast. Hosts Bill and Stephanie Schmid have created a true home environment, with a living room connecting to an upstairs master bedroom (complete with king-size brass bed) and a second downstairs bedroom (this one with twin beds). Guests have a private entrance and their own kitchen, and can use the washer and dryer. Gourmet home-cooked candlelight dinners, complete with wine, are a nightly option at $45 per couple.

**RAMADA INN, 2790 Crossroads Blvd. (at Horizon Rd.), Grand Junction, CO 81506. Tel. 303/241-8411,** or 800/2-RAMADA. Fax 303/241-1077. 139 rms, 17 suites (all with bath). A/C TV TEL
$ **Rates:** Mon–Fri, $55 single; $60 double. Sat–Sun, $45 single or double June–Aug, $42 single or double Sept–May. Suite $110–$170. Children under 18 stay free in parents' room. AE, CB, DC, DISC, JCB, MC, V. **Parking:** Free.

There's an elegant, country-style feel to the Ramada lobby, with its parquet floors and reproduction antique furnishings. Guest rooms are more modern in appearance. Most have two double beds and standard hotel furnishings, including clock radios and vanities. Executive Choice rooms have working desks and Jacuzzi baths.

Oliver's, built to resemble a Victorian library, serves three meals daily. Bailey's Lounge features free hors d'oeuvres from 5 to 7:30pm nightly and a disc jockey playing dance music nightly. Services and facilities include room service, free shuttle van, no-smoking rooms, facilities for the disabled, 24-hour heated indoor pool and whirlpool, health-club privileges, video arcade, and meeting space for 300.

## INEXPENSIVE

**HOWARD JOHNSON HOTEL, 752 Horizon Dr., Grand Junction, CO 81501. Tel. 303/243-5150,** or 800/654-2000. Fax 303/241-1512. 99 rms (all with bath). A/C TV TEL
$ **Rates** (including continental breakfast): Single or double, $38–$58 mid-June to Labor Day, $36–$44 Apr to mid-June and Labor Day to mid-Nov, $30–$40 mid-Nov to Mar. AE, CB, DC, DISC, MC, V. **Parking:** Free.

Ideal for business travelers, this franchise features Executive Section rooms with special amenities, including morning newspapers and temporary membership in an adjacent health club. All rooms are comfortable, although those on the north side (with two double beds) are more spacious than those on the south side (with one queen-size bed). All have indoor entrances and coffee makers. Adjacent to Starvin' Arvin's Family Restaurant, the hotel offers courtesy shuttle service, no-smoking rooms and rooms for the handicapped, and a guest laundry.

**JUNCTION COUNTRY INN,** 861 Grand Ave., Grand Junction, CO 81501. Tel. 303/241-2817. 4 rms (2 with bath, 2 with shared bath). A/C
**$ Rates** (including breakfast): $25–$34 single; $30–$59 double. AE, MC, V.

Not many bed and breakfasts welcome children, but this is one that does. The 1907 Victorian former home of Dr. Edward Eldridge, a pioneer physician, it features bright antique-filled guest rooms, each with its own individual features. One of them even has a playhouse under the stairs. Children are glad to know there's a TV in the inn's common room, and that no smoking is permitted indoors.

**TWO RIVERS INN,** 141 N. First St., Grand Junction, CO 81501. Tel. 303/245-8585. 42 rms (all with bath). A/C TV TEL
**$ Rates:** Single or double, $35–$42 summer, $30–$35 winter. AE, DISC, MC, V.
**Parking:** Free.

A two-story orange-brick building just two blocks from the downtown pedestrian mall, this is the nicest of several motels off the I-70 corridor. Every room is identical, clean, and comfortable, with two queen-size beds, standard furnishings, a double vanity, and a full bathroom. There's an outdoor swimming pool and Jacuzzi, and courtesy-car service.

## WHERE TO DINE
### MODERATE

**G.B. GLADSTONE'S,** 2531 N. 12th St., at Patterson Rd. Tel. 241-6000.
**Cuisine:** STEAK/SEAFOOD. **Reservations:** Recommended.
**$ Prices:** Appetizers $2.95–$4.95; main courses $3.95–$6.95 at lunch, $6.95–$24.95 at dinner. AE, CB, DC, DISC, MC, V.
**Open:** Mon–Sat 11am–10pm, Sun 11am–9pm (bar open later).

Nostalgia dominates the mood of this popular restaurant. The Croquet Room, for instance, is decorated with early 20th-century sports regalia. The Library would delight an old-book collector. The Sun Room has huge windows to let in the light of day. The sunken central bar is most nostalgic (and most packed) on Friday nights, when '50s rock 'n' roll records blast patrons.

Local businesspeople enjoy the lunches here: hot and cold sandwiches, soups, salads, quiche, fish and chips, and more. Dinners include everything from pastas, teriyaki chicken, and fresh fish specials to succulent prime rib and Australian lobster tail. Favorite appetizers are peel-and-eat shrimp and crab-stuffed wontons.

**THE WINERY,** 642 Main St. Tel. 242-4100.
**Cuisine:** STEAK/SEAFOOD. **Reservations:** Not accepted.
**$ Prices:** Appetizers $4–$6.50; main courses $9.50–$29.90. AE, CB, DC, MC, V.
**Open:** Dinner only, daily 4:30–10pm.

A dimly lit restaurant with a modern rustic decor of unfinished wood and brick, the Winery looks the part. Reached off an alleyway between Sixth Street and Seventh Street, it has beautiful cut-glass windows and oil paintings of regional or classical interest. The food is of *everyone's* interest. You can start with stuffed mushrooms or oysters on the half shell, then dive into one of the house-special combo meals: steak or prime rib, matched with lobster or crab legs.

### INEXPENSIVE

**LOS REYES,** 811 S. Seventh St. Tel. 245-8392.
**Cuisine:** MEXICAN. **Reservations:** Not accepted.
**$ Prices:** $1.75–$7.50. No credit cards.

**Open:** Daily 11am–9pm.

This authentic, family-operated Mexican restaurant is in a less attractive part of Grand Junction, near the railroad tracks—but it's definitely the right side of the tracks! The simple white-stucco building with tile floors serves diners in two large rooms; a third room, at the entrance, is a waiting room for hordes who wait patiently for tables. Most folks find it worthwhile to experiment with house variations on standard favorites like tacos, tamales, and enchiladas, such as the avocado-and-pork tortilla.

## OMA'S GERMAN DELI, 317 Main St. Tel. 245-8229.

**Cuisine:** GERMAN. **Reservations:** Not accepted.
**$ Prices:** $2.25–$4.45. No credit cards.
**Open:** Mon–Fri 10am–3pm, Sat 10am–2pm.

Lederhosen-clad servers greet you in this tiny restaurant, which features German-language newspapers and magazines and a wall map of Germany, with pins placed by European visitors marking their hometowns. The menu includes Bratwurst, Knackwurst, and other German sausages, with Sauerkraut and potato salad; cabbage rolls and homemade soups; sandwiches and salads; and delicious pastries.

## PANTUSO'S RISTORANTE, 2782 Crossroads Blvd. Tel. 243-0000.

**Cuisine:** ITALIAN. **Reservations:** For large parties only.
**$ Prices:** Appetizers $4.50; main courses $3.25–$13.25 at lunch, $5.75–$13.45 at dinner. AE, CB, DC, MC, V.
**Open:** Lunch Mon–Fri 11:30am–1:45pm; dinner Mon–Thurs 5:30–9:30pm, Fri–Sat 5:30–10pm.

Located behind the Holiday Inn and Ramada hotels, off Horizon Drive, Pantuso's has casual garden-style decor and a simple but imaginative menu. There's pizza, pasta, and sandwiches for lunch; homemade ravioli and lasagne for dinner. House specialties include eggplant parmigiana, baked bacala (codfish), and stuffed bell peppers.

## RIVER CITY CAFE AND BAR, 748 North Ave., at Seventh St. Tel. 245-8040.

**Cuisine:** INTERNATIONAL. **Reservations:** Recommended.
**$ Prices:** Appetizers $1.50–$5.75; main courses $4.95–$7.95 at lunch, $4.95–$13.95 at dinner. AE, MC, V.
**Open:** Mon–Sat 11am–midnight.

Colorful stained glass and poster-size photos of old-time sports figures inject a party atmosphere in the restaurant. (It's considerably quieter than the bar, which has live bands—playing everything from bluegrass to infusion jazz to reggae—Wednesday through Saturday nights.) Pasta, pizza, and Mexican food are popular at lunch. At dinner, unusual sauces such as Thai peanut, Indian tandoori, and lemon pepper spice-up steaks, chicken, and seafood specials. The andouille sausage–and-garlic fettuccine is unique and delicious.

## SWEETWATERS UPTOWN, 336 Main St. Tel. 243-3900.

**Cuisine:** ITALIAN. **Reservations:** Recommended.
**$ Prices:** Appetizers $3.75–$6.50; main courses $4.50–$6.25 at lunch, $6–$11.95 at dinner. AE, MC, V.
**Open:** Mon–Thurs 11am–9pm, Fri–Sat 11am–10pm.

Sweetwaters offers casual dining in a streetside lounge and espresso bar, and more elegant garden-style dining in upholstered wooden booths at the rear of the restaurant. Art photography and light jazz help attract a cultured crowd. Daily luncheon specials include the likes of hamburger Italiano or vegetarian cannelloni. Dinners include pasta, meats, and fresh seafood dishes. Try veal or chicken saltimbocca, Bresciana steak, shrimp or scallops Alfredo.

# EASY EXCURSIONS
## PALISADE VALLEY

Heading east from Grand Junction, eschew I-70 for U.S. 6 through the Palisade Valley. Famous for its fruit orchards and vineyards, the area produces outstanding peaches, pears, apples, cherries, apricots, plums, and grapes, most of them between late June and mid-September, when you'll find the roadsides speckled with fruit stands.

The area recently has earned formal designation as Colorado's first official viticultural area—which means that it has been recognized as a viable winemaking district. Tours and tasting are offered by several wineries, including **Colorado Cellars,** 3553 E Road (tel. 464-7921); **Carlson Vineyards,** 461 35th Road, Palisade (tel. 464-5554); and **Plum Creek Cellars,** 3708 G Road (tel. 464-7586). The wineries are open most afternoons in summer, on Friday and Saturday afternoons only in winter, but it's best to call ahead to confirm. The Colorado Cellars 1988 Grand Gamé is a particularly good drop.

## GRAND MESA

If you take I-70 Exit 49, 18 miles east of Grand Junction, and turn east on Colo. 65, you'll climb nearly 6,000 feet to the crest of ✪ Grand Mesa, the largest flat-top mountain in the world. Forty miles across, and averaging 10,500 feet in elevation, it is largely encompassed within Grand Mesa National Forest. Atop the mesa are more than a dozen campgrounds and countless picnic sites in rich pine forests, and more than 200 tiny lakes stocked with rainbow trout. You can follow Colo. 65 south some 70 miles through Cedaredge to Delta, or follow the all-weather gravel Land's End Road down 55 hairpin curves (it sometimes seems you're falling off the edge of the earth) to Whitewater, on U.S. 50 south of Grand Junction.

## DINOSAUR NATIONAL MONUMENT

The main attraction in these precincts is ✪ Dinosaur National Monument, off U.S. 40, Dinosaur (tel. 303/374-2216). Straddling the Colorado-Utah border, the national monument encompasses 325 square miles of stark canyonland at the confluence of the Yampa and Green rivers.

About 145 million years ago this region was a suitable habitat for dinosaurs, including vegetarians such as diplodocus, brontosaurus, and stegosaurus, and sharp-toothed carnivores like allosaurus. Most of their skeletons decayed and disappeared, but in at least one spot, floodwater washed dinosaur carcasses onto a sandbar, where they were preserved in sand and covered with sediment. This **Dinosaur Quarry,** 7 miles north of Jensen, Utah, off U.S. 40, has revealed many long-vanished species, including fossils of sea creatures two to three times older than any land dinosaurs.

The main park headquarters and **Visitor Center** are 2 miles east of the community of Dinosaur on U.S. 40, 20 miles northwest of Rangely and 95 miles from Grand Junction. Exhibits and a short slide program provide an orientation to the canyon country, reached via the 31-mile **Harpers Corner Scenic Drive.** There are several turnouts en route for canyon overlooks, and a 1½-mile hike from Harpers Corner itself, at the end of the road, to an even more spectacular viewpoint. Several four-wheel-drive roads branch off Harpers Corner Drive. Also accessible by car are **Deerlodge Park,** where the Yampa River drops into its canyon, about 50 miles east of Dinosaur off U.S. 40; and the **Gates of Lodore,** at the head of the Green River's Canyon of Lodore, about 80 miles west of Craig off Colo. 318.

The park is open daily from Memorial Day to Labor Day, daily from 8am to 4:30pm; the rest of the year, Monday through Friday from 8am to 4:30pm. Admission is $3 per vehicle and $1 per adult.

# 2. GLENWOOD SPRINGS

169 miles W of Denver, 84 miles E of Grand Junction,
41 miles NW of Aspen

**GETTING THERE** **By Train** There's **Amtrak** (tel. 800/USA-RAIL) service to

Glenwood Junction daily aboard the *California Zephyr,* direct from Denver and Salt Lake City. The depot is on South River Street at Cooper Avenue, opposite the hot springs.

**By Bus**　The coaches of **Greyhound/Trailways** (tel. 945-8501) stop next to the Village Inn at Laurel Street and West Sixth Street, just off I-70.

**By Car**　**I-70** follows the Colorado River through Glenwood Springs. Colo. 82 (the **Aspen Highway**) links the city with Aspen, 41 miles southeast.

**ESSENTIALS Orientation**　Glenwood Springs's population is about 6,000. The northward-flowing **Roaring Fork River** joins the **Colorado River** at a T junction in the heart of Glenwood Springs. Streets follow the valleys carved by the two streams. Downtown Glenwood is south of the Colorado and east of the Roaring Fork, with north-south **Grand Avenue** (Colo. 82) its main thoroughfare. **Old Glenwood,** including the hot springs and Hotel Colorado, is on the north side of I-70 and the Colorado.

**Information**　The **Glenwood Springs Chamber Resort Association,** 1102 Grand Avenue, Glenwood Springs, CO 81601 (tel. 303/945-6589), maintains a visitor information center on the south side of downtown, en route to Aspen.

**Getting Around**　There's daily commuter service to and from Aspen, and east on I-70 as far as Rifle, via **Aspen Limousine,** 330 Seventh Street (tel. 303/945-9400, or 800/222-2112). **Yellow Cab** (tel. 945-2225) is good for shorter hops.

**Fast Facts**　The **area code** is 303. In case of **emergency,** call **911. Valley View Hospital** is at 1906 Blake Avenue (tel. 945-6535), a block east of Colo. 82 at 19th Street. The main **post office** is on Colorado Avenue at Ninth Street.

**SPECIAL EVENTS**　Annual events in the Glenwood Springs area include the **Ski Spree Winter Carnival,** from late January to early February; the **Strawberry Days Festival,** in the second full week of June; and the **Fall Art Festival,** in the fourth week of September.

---

**U**te tribespeople visited the Yampah (big medicine) mineral springs on the banks of the Colorado River for centuries. They came from miles around to heal their wounds, or to use nearby vapor caves as a natural sauna. The first white party to find the springs was a geological expedition led by Capt. Richard Sopris in 1860. But it wasn't until 1882 that the springs were developed by three Devereux brothers, who had made a small fortune in silver at Aspen. They built the largest hot-springs pool in the world in 1888, added a red sandstone bath house, then built the Hotel Colorado in 1893, soon attracting everyone from European royalty to movie stars to President Theodore Roosevelt.

The springs supported the town until the outbreak of the Great Depression and World War II caused a business decline. But after the war, with the growth of the ski industry at nearby Aspen, Glenwood began to emerge as a tourist resort town. Today it's a popular recreational center. The hot-springs complex underwent a total renovation in the 1970s. In the early 1990s a major attraction was the spectacular highway engineering work in narrow Glenwood Canyon, just east of town.

## WHAT TO SEE & DO
### ATTRACTIONS

**GLENWOOD HOT SPRINGS POOL, 401 N. River Rd. Tel. 945-7131.**
　In business for more than a century, this pool—created in 1888 when enterprising developers diverted the course of the Colorado River—is fed by one of the world's hottest springs. Yampah Spring flows at a rate of 3.5 million gallons per day, with

temperatures measuring between 124°F and 130°F. Its content is predominantly sodium chloride, but there are significant quantities of lime, potassium, and magnesium, and traces of other therapeutic minerals.

The two open-air pools together are nearly two city blocks in length. The larger pool, 405 feet long and 100 feet wide, holds more than a million gallons of water, and is maintained between 86°F and 90°F. The smaller pool, 100 feet square, is kept between 102°F and 104°F. There's also a children's pool with a water slide, and a miniature golf course.

The red sandstone administration building overlooking the pools was the Hot Springs Lodge from 1890 to 1986, when a new hotel and bath house complex were built. An athletic club was also opened at that time.

**Admission:** $5.75 adults, $3.50 children 3–12; reduced night rates. Suit and towel rentals available. Athletic club nonmember use charge is $9.50.

**Open:** Summer, daily 7:30am–10pm; Winter, daily 9am–10pm. **Closed:** Second Wed of each month, Oct–May.

## YAMPAH VAPOR CAVES, 709 E. Sixth St. Tel. 945-0667.

The hot Yampah Spring water flows through the floor of nearby caves, creating natural underground steam baths. Utes once used the chambers to take advantage of their curative powers. Today the cave has an adjacent spa where such treatments as massages, facials, herbal wraps, and body "muds" are offered.

**Admission:** $6.75 for caves; spa treatments start at $22.

**Open:** Daily 9am–9pm.

## FRONTIER HISTORICAL MUSEUM, 1001 Colorado Ave. Tel. 945-4448.

The highlight of this museum, which occupies a late-Victorian home, is the original bedroom furniture of Colorado legends Horace and Baby Doe Tabor, brought here from Leadville. The collection also includes other pioneer home furnishings, antique dolls and toys, historic photos and maps, Native American artifacts, minerals, and a walk-through coal mine.

**Admission:** $1.50 adults, free for children 12 and under.

**Open:** Memorial Day–Labor Day, daily 1–4pm; the rest of the year, Thurs–Sat 1–4pm.

## SPORTS & RECREATION

**BICYCLING** A bike trail runs from the Yampah Vapor Caves into Glenwood Canyon, and four-wheel-drive roads in the adjacent White River National Forest are ideal for mountain bikers. Rent from **Alpine Bicycle,** 109 Sixth Street (tel. 945-6434), or **Ski Sunlight Bike Rental,** 1315 Grand Avenue (tel. 945-9425).

**FISHING** Get licenses, equipment, and advice from **Roaring Fork Anglers,** 2022 Grand Avenue (tel. 945-0180), or **Scott's Outdoor Specialists,** 1022 Grand Avenue (tel. 945-5761).

**GOLF** Glenwood Springs has two nine-hole courses: **Glenwood Springs Golf Club,** 193 Sunny Acres Road (tel. 945-7086), and **Westbank Ranch Golf Club,** 1007 Westbank Road (tel. 945-7032). Some 27 miles west, near Rifle, is the championship 18-hole **Battlement Mesa Golf Course,** North Battlement Mesa Parkway (tel. 295-PAR-4).

The best of three minigolf courses in Glenwood is **Johnson's Park Miniature Golf,** 51579 U.S. 6 and 24, West Glenwood Springs (tel. 945-9608), with two 18-hole water-obstacle courses.

**HIKING** There are many trails in the Glenwood area; ask at the **White River National Forest** office, Ninth Street and Grand Avenue (tel. 945-2521), for the "Hiking and Biking Trails" map. Perhaps the most convenient walk for day-hikers is the **Doc Holliday Trail,** which climbs about half a mile from 13th Street and

Bennett Street to an old cemetery that contains the grave of notorious gunslinger Doc Holliday. There's a panoramic view across the town from here.

**HORSEBACK RIDING**   Trips by the hour, the day, or the week, including pack expeditions and sunset barbecue rides, are offered by **Canyon Creek Outfitters,** 444208 U.S. 6 & 24, West Glenwood Springs (tel. 984-2000); **Dawson's Guide Service,** P.O. Box 87, New Castle, CO 81647 (tel. 984-2136); and **Sunlight Inn Horseback Rides,** 10252 County Road 117 (tel. 945-5225).

**RIVER RAFTING**   Travel down the Colorado River through spectacular Glenwood Canyon in rafts or inflatable kayaks with **Rock Gardens,** 1308 County Road 129 (tel. 945-6737), or **White Water Rafting,** I-70 Exit 114, West Glenwood Springs (tel. 945-8477).

**SKIING**   **Ski Sunlight,** 10901 County Road 117 (tel. 303/945-7491, or 800/445-7931), is located 10 miles south of Glenwood in the White River National Forest. Geared toward families and intermediate skiers, Sunlight has a 2,010-foot vertical, from the day lodge to the 9,895-foot summit of Compas Mountain. Served by three chair lifts and a ski-school surface lift, it has 350 acres of skiable terrain and 33 trails. Full-day tickets are $28 for adults, $15 for children 6 to 12 and seniors 60 to 69; under 6 and over 69 ski free. For equipment rentals and repairs, see the **Ski Sunlight Ski Shop,** 1315 Grand Avenue (tel. 945-9425).

Nordic skiers can try the 14km (8¾ miles) of track laid out in the **Spring Gulch Trail System** by the Mount Sopris Nordic Council. There's a parking area and rest rooms 7 miles south of Carbondale (20 miles from Glenwood Springs) on County Road 108. Get directions and cross-country equipment from **Summit Canyon Mountaineering,** 1001 Grand Avenue (tel. 945-6994).

**SNOWMOBILING**   The **Sunlight to Powderhorn Trail,** running 120 miles from Glenwood's local ski area to Grand Junction's, on the Grand Mesa, is the longest multi-use winter recreational trail in Colorado. It is fully marked and continuously groomed. Numerous other trails—a total of 300 miles—can be accessed from the end of Country Road 11, 2 miles beyond Ski Sunlight and 12 miles south of Glenwood Springs. For information and rentals, contact **Rocky Mountain Sports,** 2177 300th Road (tel. 945-8885).

# WHERE TO STAY

## MODERATE

**HOTEL COLORADO, 526 Pine St., Glenwood Springs, CO 81601. Tel. 303/945-6511,** or 800/544-3998. Fax 303/945-2030. 103 rms, 25 suites (all with bath). TV TEL
**$ Rates:** $60–$75 single; $67–$95 double; $130–$250 suite. AE, CB, DC, DISC, MC, V. **Parking:** Free.

Scheduled to celebrate its centennial of operation in June 1993, the stately Hotel Colorado is a truly remarkable building. Constructed of sandstone and Roman brick, this registered National Historic Landmark was modeled after Italy's Villa de Medici. Two American presidents—William Howard Taft and Theodore Roosevelt—spoke around the turn of the century to crowds gathered beneath the orators' balcony in a lovely landscaped fountain *piazza.* In fact, this was the home of the "Teddy Bear": When a disappointed Roosevelt returned to the hotel in May 1905 after an unsuccessful bear hunt, hotel maids made him a small bear from scraps of cloth, and a reporter coined the phrase.

Today's guest rooms have been fully redecorated and furnished with period antiques. No two are alike. Most have double beds and the usual hotel furnishings; parlor suites are much more spacious than standard rooms, with upgraded decor and amenities. Fifth-floor penthouse suites have wet bars and refrigerators to go along with outstanding views. Two bell-tower suites, reached by stairs only, have double Jacuzzis and private dining balconies. They also have private staircases into the ancient bell towers, where 19th-century graffiti can still be deciphered!

The Devereux Room, with its vaulted ceiling, serves gourmet continental fare in a formal turn-of-the-century atmosphere. The Palm Court Bar and Grill offers casual dining in a garden atmosphere beneath the hotel's original 19th-century skylight.

Services and facilities include valet laundry, courtesy van to and from the train station, 24-hour desk; European-style health spa with sauna, Jacuzzi, massage, Nautilus and free weights; chiropractor; gift shop; sports center with rental equipment; and meeting space for up to 200.

**HOT SPRINGS LODGE & POOL, 415 Sixth St., Glenwood Springs, CO 81601. Tel. 303/945-6571,** or 800/537-SWIM in Colorado. Fax 303/945-6683. 107 rms (all with bath). A/C TV TEL

**$ Rates:** Mar 15–Sept and Christmas holidays, $59–$75 single or double; Oct–Mar 14 except Christmas, $49–$62 single or double. AE, CB, DC, DISC, MC, V. **Parking:** Free.

Heated by the springs that bubble through the hillside beneath it, this handsome modern motel overlooks the Glenwood Hot Springs Pool complex. The handsome blues and roses of the high-ceilinged lobby extend to the spacious guest rooms, 75% of which have private balconies or patios. Rooms have two queen-size or one king-size bed and light-wood furnishings, as well as coffee makers and safes for valuables. Larger rooms have hideabeds, refrigerators, and double vanities.

The poolside Hot Springs Restaurant serves coffee-shop-style meals, and there's a small lounge. The hotel also offers no-smoking rooms, facilities for the disabled, guest discounts for hot springs pool and athletic club (see "What to See & Do," above), Jacuzzi, video arcade, guest laundry, sportswear shop, and meeting space for 60.

**RAMADA INN, 124 W. Sixth St., Glenwood Springs, CO 81601. Tel. 303/945-2500,** or 800/228-2828, 800/332-1472 in Colorado. Fax 303/945-2530. 121 rms, 4 suites (all with bath). A/C TV TEL

**$ Rates:** High season (Mon–Fri, Mar, mid-May to mid-Oct, Christmas holidays), $65–$79 single or double; low season (all other times), $59–$68 single or double; high-season Sat–Sun and holidays, $74–$88 single or double. Children under 18 stay free in parents' room. AE, CB, DC, DISC, MC, V. **Parking:** Free.

The only true full-service hotel in Glenwood Springs, the Ramada offers spacious guest rooms with bright decor. All have one king-size or two queen-size beds and standard motel furnishings. Studio suites have kitchenettes and hideaway sofas to accommodate families; larger suites also have fireplaces and steam Jacuzzis.

The Rosegarden Restaurant serves three meals daily. A seafood buffet is served every Friday night. The Celebrations Lounge has live country-and-western entertainment Wednesday through Saturday nights, with free dance lessons Tuesday through Thursday. The hotel also offers room service, valet laundry, free shuttle service, no-smoking rooms, facilities for the disabled, an indoor swimming pool, hot tub, guest laundry, and meeting space for 500.

## INEXPENSIVE

**ADDUCCI'S INN BED & BREAKFAST, 1023 Grand Ave., Glenwood Springs, CO 81601. Tel. 303/945-9341.** 5 rms.

**$ Rates** (including breakfast): $28–$55 single; $38–$55 double. MC, V.

A lovely turn-of-the-century Victorian on Glenwood's main street houses this B&B. Furnished with period antiques, it also has a games parlor, a hot tub, and complimentary pickup from train and bus depots. Rooms have private baths, but showers are shared.

**GLENWOOD SPRINGS HOSTEL, 1021 Grand Ave., Glenwood Springs, CO 81601. Tel. 303/945-8545.** 24 beds.

**$ Rates:** International Youth Hostel Association members and students $9.50, weekly $55; nonmembers $11.50, weekly $65. No credit cards.

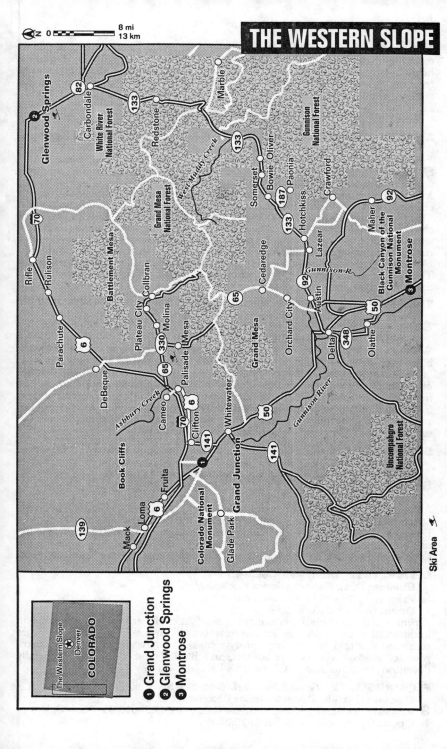

THE WESTERN SLOPE

8 mi
13 km

Glenwood Springs
Carbondale
White River National Forest
Redstone
Marble
Gunnison National Forest
Bowie
Oliver
Somerset
Paonia
Crawford
Maher
Hotchkiss
Lazear
Black Canyon of the Gunnison National Monument
Montrose
Cedaredge
Gunnison R.
Austin
Olathe
Delta
Grand Mesa National Forest
Grand Mesa
Orchard City
Battlement Mesa
Collbran
Plateau City
Molina
Mesa
Rifle
Rulison
Parachute
DeBeque
Palisade
Cameo
Clifton
Whitewater
Gunnison River
Uncompahgre National Forest
Book Cliffs
Fruita
Grand Junction
Colorado National Monument
Glade Park
Mack
Loma
Ashbury Creek
West Muddy Creek

Ski Area

The Western Slope
Denver
COLORADO

❶ Grand Junction
❷ Glenwood Springs
❸ Montrose

A plus for this hostel is its large record library, from which guests are encouraged to record their own cassette tapes. Otherwise, it's similar to many others: dormitory bunks, a large (modern) shared kitchen, common toilets and showers, guest laundry facilities, and other common areas. Linen is provided, and bus or train pickup can be arranged with advance notice.

# WHERE TO DINE

**ANDRE'S RESTAURANT, 51753 U.S. 6 & 24, West Glenwood Springs. Tel. 945-5367.**
    **Cuisine:** AMERICAN. **Reservations:** Not necessary.
    **$ Prices:** Lunch $5.25–$8.65; dinner $5.95–$10.50. AE, MC, V.
    **Open:** Wed–Mon 11:30am–9pm.
Model trains circle the dining room on an elaborate track system suspended from the ceiling of this family-oriented restaurant, located midway between I-70 Exits 114 and 116. Guests sit in wrought-iron chairs and enjoy home-style cooking including chicken pot pie and beef stew. Portions are huge, especially the combination dinner, which includes a meatballs or Italian sausage appetizer, soup or salad, and a choice of *two* pasta dishes—lasagne, ravioli, spaghetti, or gnocchi. Homemade desserts include New York–style cheesecake and ice cream home-churned in a wooden bucket. There's a children's menu, but no alcohol is served. Andre's candies and a variety of decorative items are sold in a small gift shop.

**THE BAYOU, 52103 U.S. 6, West Glenwood Springs. Tel. 945-1047.**
    **Cuisine:** CAJUN/CREOLE. **Reservations:** Suggested for large parties.
    **$ Prices:** Appetizers $4.50–$5.75; main courses $6.90–$12.95. AE, MC, V.
    **Open:** Dinner only, daily 4–10pm.
Western Colorado's classic New Orleans–style eatery can't be mistaken: Frog eyes bulge from the green awning over its deck, which looks toward I-70 near Exit 114. Harlequin masks hang on the walls and Zydeco music filters through this very rustic, often rowdy restaurant. Come for down-home Cajun cuisine—including sautéed frogs' legs, deep-fried catfish, shrimp lagniappe, chicken étouffée, or swamp and moo (redfish and ribeye)—and stay for the staff-provided entertainment, including "dumb waitron tricks," birthday specials (ask if you dare), and the Frog Leg Revue. On summer Sunday afternoons there's live music on the deck.

**BUFFALO VALLEY INN, Colo. 82, 3½ miles south of Glenwood Springs. Tel. 945-5297.**
    **Cuisine:** STEAK/SEAFOOD. **Reservations:** Recommended.
    **$ Prices:** Appetizers $3.95–$4.95; main courses $8.95–$16.95. AE, DC, MC, V.
    **Open:** Dinner only, daily 5–10pm.
An oversize log cabin with country-style decor, right down to the red-checkered tablecloths, the Buffalo Valley Inn specializes in steaks, seafoods, and barbecues. Diners can start with Rocky Mountain oysters, then dive into prime rib, buffalo steak, or Rocky Mountain rainbow trout. Barbecue beef, chicken, and baby back ribs are slow-smoked over apple wood and include soup or salad, potatoes or beans, and rolls.

**DELICE, 1512 Grand Ave. Tel. 945-9424.**
    **Cuisine:** DELI. **Reservations:** Not accepted.
    **$ Prices:** $1.95–$4.70. No credit cards.
    **Open:** Mon–Sat 10am–3pm.
Aspenites still talk about European immigrant Walter Huber's Swiss Pastry Shop, an institution for three decades after it was opened in 1957. Huber's family has continued that tradition, serving deli-style croissant sandwiches, homemade soups, gourmet salads, Swiss sausage platters, and Black Forest cakes at this friendly downtown luncheon stop in Glenwood's Executive Plaza.

**FLORINDO'S, 721 Grand Ave. Tel. 945-1245.**
    **Cuisine:** ITALIAN. **Reservations:** Recommended.
    **$ Prices:** Appetizers $4.50–$7.95; main courses $8.95–$15.95. AE, MC, V.
    **Open:** Dinner only, Mon–Sat 5–10:30pm.

The extensive menu at Florindo's caters to aficionados of all Italian cuisine, but especially Florentine. Here's where to come for a Mediterranean feast. Start with clams Posillipo or eggplant Rollatini, and follow with baked lasagne fiorentina or gnocchi alla marinara. Then it's time for the main course: veal dolce vita, pollo Valdostana, or perhaps delizie di mare—a seafood combination served in a red sauce over linguine. Vegetarians are also catered to.

**RESTAURANT SOPRIS, Colo. 82, 7 miles south of Glenwood Springs. Tel. 945-7771.**

   **Cuisine:** CONTINENTAL. **Reservations:** Recommended.

**$**  **Prices:** Appetizers $2.50–$4.95; main courses $9.95–$25.95. AE, DC, MC, V.

   **Open:** Dinner only, daily 5–10pm.

Luzern, Switzerland, native Kurt Wigger spent 17 years as chef at Aspen's Red Onion before opening his own restaurant. In 1991 he celebrated his 17th year at the Sopris. Amid red-lit Victorian decor, accented by reproductions of classic oil paintings, Wigger serves up generous portions of veal and seafood dishes, as well as steaks and other meats. House specialties include wienerschnitzel, rack of lamb, filet mignon chasseur, and lobster scampi in a garlic sauce.

# EASY EXCURSIONS

## REDSTONE

Traveling south from Glenwood Springs, Colo. 82 follows the Roaring Fork River as far as Carbondale, an old coal-mining town. Colo. 133 branches off south from Carbondale, following the Crystal River Valley toward Paonia and Delta. And 17 miles south of Carbondale and 30 miles from Glenwood, it passes through the historic community of Redstone. In 1900, coal and steel baron John Cleveland Osgood, one of the wealthiest industrialists of his day, built this model company village for the men who worked in his coal mines. The brightly colored chalet-style family cottages still line the streets today.

**WHERE TO STAY & DINE**   The  **✪ Redstone Inn,** a handsome bachelors' residence with a Tudor-style clocktower, is now a hotel-restaurant. (Write 0082 Redstone Boulevard, Redstone, CO 81623; tel. 303/963-2526. Rates are $48 single or double with shared bath, $65 to $90 with private bath.)

   Osgood's own  **✪ Cleveholm Manor,** 0058 Redstone Boulevard, Redstone, CO 81623 (tel. 303/963-3463), was a 42-room mansion that quickly became known as "The Redstone Castle." The red sandstone walls were carved by stonecutters from Austria and Italy; the elegant interior was furnished with Tiffany chandeliers, Persian rugs, Chinese urns, and a backdrop of leather, silk, damask, and velvet wall coverings. Roosevelts, Rockefellers, Goulds, Morgans, and other turn-of-the-century notables were entertained here. The manor is now a bed and breakfast, with three suites ($134 to $159), five upscale rooms ($104), and eight former servants' rooms that share three bathrooms ($74). And the entire castle can be rented for 24 hours for private functions—for just $3,390. For nonguests, tours are conducted by reservation Monday through Friday from the adjacent **Redstone Country Store** (tel. 963-3408); the cost is $10 for adults, $5 for children 5 to 12.

## CRAIG

Some 47 miles north of Meeker—115 miles from Glenwood Springs—is Craig, with 10,000 people the largest town in Colorado north of I-70 and west of the Front Range. Located in the Yampa River Valley, it's a popular center for river rafters and big-game hunters. Of particular interest in town are the **Museum of Northwest Colorado,** 590 Yampa Avenue (tel. 824-6360), with colorful historical exhibits open Monday through Saturday, and the **Sand Rock Nature Trail,** Alta Vista Drive at Ninth Street, accessing prehistoric petroglyphs and a panoramic view of Craig.

**WHERE TO STAY & DINE**   A good place to stay is the **A Bar Z Motel,** 2690 U.S. 40, Craig, CO 81625 (tel. 303/824-7066), with rates of $28 to $40 single or double.

Hungry? Try **Desperado Restaurant,** 2045 U.S. 40 (tel. 824-6900), or **Mather's Bar & Grill,** 420 Yampa Avenue (tel. 824-9946). For more information, consult the **Moffat County Visitor Center,** 360 East Victory Way (tel. 303/824-5689).

# 3. MONTROSE

61 miles S of Grand Junction, 108 miles N of Durango

**GETTING THERE   By Plane**   The **Montrose County Airport,** 2100 Airport Road (tel. 303/249-3203), off U.S. 50 2 miles northwest of town, is served daily by **Continental Express** (tel. 303/249-1399, or 800/525-0820) and **United Express** (tel. 303/249-8455, or 800/241-6522).

**By Bus**   TNM&O coaches arrive and depart from the **Montrose Bus Depot,** 50 North Townsend Avenue (tel. 303/249-6673).

**By Car**   Montrose is an hour's drive southeast of Grand Junction via U.S. 50, 2½ hours' drive north of Durango via U.S. 550, and 5½ hours' drive west of Colorado Springs via U.S. 50 through Salida and Gunnison.

**ESSENTIALS   Orientation**   Montrose has a population of about 10,500. The city sits on the east bank of the Uncompahgre River. Its main street, **Townsend Avenue** (U.S. 50 North/U.S. 550 South), parallels the stream in a northwest-southeast direction. **Main Street** (U.S. 50 East/Colo. 90 West) crosses Townsend in the center of town. Numbered streets extend north and south from Main.

**Information**   Contact the **Montrose Visitors & Convention Bureau** (tel. 800/873-0244) or the **Montrose County Chamber of Commerce** (tel. 303/249-5515), both at 550 North Townsend Avenue, Montrose, CO 81401.

**Getting Around**   **Western Express Taxi** (tel. 249-8880) provides round-the-clock cab service.

   **Car rentals** are available in the airport area from Budget (tel. 249-6083), Dollar (tel. 249-3770), Hertz (tel. 249-9447), and National (tel. 249-3453).

**Fast Facts**   The **area code** is 303. In case of **emergency,** call 249-9611. The **Montrose Memorial Hospital** is at 800 South Third Street (tel. 249-2211). The main **post office** is at 321 South First Street (tel. 249-6654). For **road conditions** or **weather,** call 249-9363.

**SPECIAL EVENTS**   Each year Montrose hosts the **Air Rendezvous** in April, the **Lighter Than Air Balloon Affaire** in July, the **Montrose County Fair** in August, the **Elk Hunters Ball** in September, and **Colorfest** in September and October.

**W**ith just 9 inches of average annual precipitation, the valley of the Uncompahgre River is semidesert. Ute tribespeople were its original inhabitants; in fact, the great Chief Ouray settled and ranched here in the 1860s and 1870s. After the Utes were forced to migrate to Utah in 1881, the town of Pomona—later to become Montrose—was established at this site.

   Surrounded by the Uncompahgre, Gunnison, and Grand Mesa national forests, and within a short drive of Black Canyon of the Gunnison National Monument and Curecanti National Recreation Area, Montrose has become a major outdoor recreation center.

## WHAT TO SEE & DO
### ATTRACTIONS
**BLACK CANYON OF THE GUNNISON NATIONAL MONUMENT, Colo. 347, 7 miles north of U.S. 50. Tel. 303/249-1915.**

"No other canyon in North America combines the depth, narrowness, sheerness, and somber countenance of the Black Canyon." These words were penned by geologist Wallace Hansen, who mapped the canyon in the 1950s and probably knew it better than anyone else. The deepest and most spectacular 12 miles of the 53-mile canyon are located within the national monument. The walls are almost always in dark shadows, the rays of sunlight penetrate to the Gunnison River at the canyon floor only for brief periods at midday.

The Black Canyon ranges in depth from 1,730 to 2,700 feet. Its width at its narrowest point ("The Narrows") is only 1,100 feet at the rim . . . and 40 feet at the river. This deep slash in the earth took two million years of erosion to form it, a process that's still going on—albeit slowed by the damming of the Gunnison above the park.

The Black Canyon is one of the few remaining unspoiled areas of its kind in the United States. Although a summer-only access road winds to the bottom of the canyon at the East Portal dam, in the adjoining Curecanti National Recreation Area, only foot trails permeate the wilderness of the canyon floor through the national monument. Few visitors make that trek. Most view the canyon from the **South Rim Road,** site of a Visitor Center open year round, or the less-accessible **North Rim Road,** open summers only. Short paths off both roads lead to viewpoints with informational signs explaining the unique geology of the canyon. Printed brochures describe several hikes.

Float trips are dangerous and are blocked in many places by rocks; rafters who have tried it agree that they spend more time scrambling over rocks than running the river. Accomplished rock climbers, however, adore the sheer canyon walls.

There are campgrounds on both rims, with a restricted water supply hauled in by truck. To reach the south rim, travel east 8 miles from Montrose on U.S. 50 to the well-marked turnoff. To reach the north rim from Montrose, you must drive north 21 miles on U.S. 50 to Delta, east 31 miles on Colo. 92 to Crawford, then south on a 13-mile access road. **National Park Service** headquarters are at 2233 East Main Street (P.O. Box 1648), Montrose, CO 81402 (tel. 303/249-7036).

**Admission:** $3 per vehicle.

**Open:** South rim, summer, daily 8am–8pm; winter, daily 8am–4:30pm. North rim, summer only, daily 8am–8pm.

## MONTROSE COUNTY HISTORICAL MUSEUM, W. Main St. and Rio Grande Ave. Tel. 249-2085 or 249-6135.

Late 19th- and early 20th-century pioneer life is highlighted by the small museum, which includes a walk-though homesteader's cabin, country store, and children's room. Artifacts of mining, farming, railroading, and water engineering are also displayed, and a library houses the region's historical archives.

**Admission:** $1.50 adults, 50¢ children 5–12, free for children under 5.

**Open:** May–Oct, Mon–Sat 9am–5pm, Sun 1–5pm.

## UTE INDIAN MUSEUM, 17253 Chipeta Dr. Tel. 249-3098.

Located on the site of the final residence of southern Ute Chief Ouray and his wife, Chipeta, this interesting museum—3 miles south of town off U.S. 550—offers the Colorado Historical Society's most complete exhibition of Ute traditional and ceremonial artifacts, including clothing. Several dioramas depict mid-19th-century life-styles. Also on the grounds are Chipeta's grave and tiny, bubbling Ouray Springs. The adobe structure in which Ouray lived at the time of his death in 1881 burned to the ground in 1945.

**Admission:** $2 adults, $1 seniors (over 65) and children 6–16, free for children under 6.

**Open:** Memorial Day weekend–Labor Day, Mon–Sat 10am–5pm, Sun 1–5pm; Sept, modified hours.

## SPORTS & RECREATION

**BICYCLING** The **Tabeguache Trail**—142 miles from Shavano Valley, near Montrose, to No Thoroughfare Canyon, near the Colorado National Monument west of Grand Junction—is a popular and challenging route for mountain bikers. For information, contact the **Colorado Plateau Mountain-Bike Trail Association,** P.O. Box 4602, Grand Junction, CO 81502 (tel. 303/241-9561). Bikers can also use the **Uncompahgre Riverway;** it is eventually scheduled to connect Montrose with Delta (21 miles north) and Ouray (37 miles south). For rentals, see **Montrose Sporting Goods,** 219 West Main Street (tel. 249-9292).

**BOATING   Morrow Point Reservoir** is 20 miles east of Montrose via U.S. 50. Boat tours lasting 1½ hours leave the **Pine Creek Boat Dock** near the Cimarron Visitors Center (tel. 249-4074) daily, Memorial Day to Labor Day. Boats can also be rented from the **Elk Creek Marina** (tel. 641-0707) and the **Lake Fork Marina** (tel. 641-3048) in Curecanti National Recreation Area; and at **Ridgway Reservoir** (tel. 626-5822) in Ridgway State Recreation Area, 20 miles south of Montrose off U.S. 550.

For information on canoe and kayak trips and rentals, consult the **Montrose Outdoor Center,** 2500 North Townsend Avenue (tel. 249-4486).

**FISHING   For** starters, you can drop a line into the **Uncompahgre River** from Riverbottom Park, reached via Apollo Road off Rio Grande Avenue. Most anglers seek rainbow trout here and at **Chipeta Lake,** behind the Ute Indian Museum south of Montrose. About 20 miles east via U.S. 50 is the **Gunnison River,** which produces trophy-class brown and rainbow trout. Kokanee salmon can also be caught in **Morrow Point Reservoir,** 35 miles east via U.S. 50. There are numerous other fishing spots in the region. For information, or to enroll in a fly-casting class, visit the **Montrose Outdoor Center,** 2500 North Townsend Avenue (tel. 249-4486), or book a trip with **Gunnison River Expeditions** (tel. 249-4441).

**GOLF   The** 18-hole **Montrose Golf Course,** 1350 Birch Street (tel. 249-8551), welcomes visitors.

**HIKING   Important** hiking trails in the area include the 4½-mile **Ute Trail** along the Gunnison River, 20 miles northeast of Montrose, and the 17-mile **Alpine Trail** from Silver Jack Reservoir in Uncompahgre National Forest, 35 miles southeast of Montrose via Cimarron on U.S. 50. For a wide choice of hiking options, consult the **U.S. Forest Service,** 2505 South Townsend Avenue (tel. 249-3711), or the **Bureau of Land Management,** 2465 South Townsend Avenue (tel. 249-7791).

**HORSEBACK RIDING**   Stables in the region include **Montrose Dressage** (tel. 249-4441); **Needle Rock Ranch,** 4345 F Road, Crawford (tel. 921-3050); and **Hyatt Guides & Outfitter** (tel. 249-9733).

**RIVER RAFTING   Gunnison River Expeditions** (tel. 249-4441) runs frequent trips down the Gunnison and other streams.

## WHERE TO STAY

**RED ARROW MOTOR INN, 1702 E. Main St., Montrose, CO 81402. Tel. 303/249-9641,** or 800/468-9323. Fax 303/249-8380. 58 rms, 2 suites (all with bath). A/C TV TEL
**$  Rates:** Sept–June, $52–$69 single or double; $140 suite. July–Aug, $82–$99 single or double; $160 suite. AE, CB, DC, DISC, MC, V.
A Best Western property, the Red Arrow is a large two-story near the east end of town, on the way toward the Black Canyon. Rooms, most of which have queen-size beds, are very spacious. Small refrigerators, hairdryers, and makeup mirrors are found in every room. A handful of "spa rooms" have large Jacuzzi tubs and additional amenities. Motel facilities include a solarium with a hot tub and fitness center, an outdoor swimming pool, a children's playground and picnic area, a guest laundry, and conference space for up to 350 people. The adjoining Sizzler Buffet Court & Grill restaurant serves three meals daily.

**RED BARN MOTEL, 1417 E. Main St., Montrose, CO 81401. Tel. 303/249-4507.** 70 rms (all with bath). A/C TV TEL
**$  Rates:** June–Sept, $40 single; $43–$50 double. Oct–May, $30 single; $33–$40 double. AE, CB, DC, DISC, MC, V.

The barn isn't red—it's white, with a red roof. Neither is the barn a motel—it's a restaurant and lounge, under separate ownership from the motel. The motel is built of brick, and it's orange. But it does share a parking lot with the barn, and thereby, I suppose, the name. At least there's no such confusion in the motel rooms. Furnished with either double or queen-size beds, they are simple and comfortable. Most have desks, coffee makers, and vanities, though furnishings vary some from room to room. The motel boasts a swimming pool, hot tub, sauna, and fitness center.

**WESTERN MOTEL, 1200 E. Main St. (at Stough Ave.), Montrose, CO 81401. Tel. 303/249-3481,** or 800/445-7301. 28 rms (all with bath). A/C TV TEL
**$ Rates:** Memorial Day–Labor Day, $28–$32 single; $30–$44 double. Labor Day to mid-Nov, $28–$30 single; $30–$40 double. Mid-Nov to Memorial Day, $24–$28 single; $28–$36 double. Family units $8 additional. AE, DISC, MC, V.
A one-story red-brick building with a two-story annex, this pleasant and inexpensive motel is ideal for budget-watchers. Rooms are cozy, clean, and comfortable, with bright earth-tones decor, full baths, good-size desks, and other standard furnishings. A few family rooms and waterbed rooms are available. Facilities include a heated swimming pool, open seasonally, and a Jacuzzi.

## WHERE TO DINE

**GLEN EYRIE RESTAURANT, 2351 S. Townsend Ave. Tel. 249-9263.**
   **Cuisine:** CONTINENTAL. **Reservations:** Recommended.
**$ Prices:** Appetizers $3.95–$7.75; main courses $5.95–$7.50 at lunch, $10.75–$17.95 at dinner. AE, CB, DC, MC, V.
   **Open:** Lunch Tues–Fri 11:30am–2pm; dinner Tues–Sun 5–8:30pm; brunch Sun 11am–2pm.
Montrose's finest restaurant is lodged in a large colonial home on the south end of town. In summer, guests can dine outdoors in the wine garden beneath apricot trees; in winter, folks seek tables nearest the large central fireplace. The luncheon menu focuses on soups, salads, sandwiches, and light dishes. Gourmet dinner choices include chateaubriand bouquetière, veal forestière, duck à l'orange, salmon en papillote, and bouillabaisse.

**MARY'S RESTAURANT & LOUNGE, 1519 E. Main St. Tel. 249-3910** or 249-0915 (after 5pm).
   **Cuisine:** AMERICAN. **Reservations:** Recommended at dinner.
**$ Prices:** Breakfast $1.95–$5.75; lunch $2.50–$4.55, dinner main courses $4.75–$15.50. AE, MC, V.
   **Open:** 7am–10pm daily.
A popular local hangout, Mary's serves breakfast and lunch in its downstairs café, dinner and drinks in a more elegant upstairs dining room. Steaks, chops, chicken, and seafood dinners are accompanied by a trip through the soup-and-salad bar.

**RED BARN RESTAURANT & LOUNGE, 1413 E. Main St. Tel. 249-9202.**
   **Cuisine:** AMERICAN. **Reservations:** Recommended at dinner.
**$ Prices:** Appetizers $2.95–$5.95; main courses $3–$5.95 at lunch, $7.95–$16.95 at dinner. AE, CB, DC, MC, V.
   **Open:** Lunch Mon–Fri 11am–3pm; dinner daily 3–10:30pm; brunch Sun 9am–3pm.
A homey restaurant with a big fireplace and bigger portions, the Red Barn serves up Montrose's best steaks (including a 16-ounce top sirloin), prime rib, jumbo shrimp, and a popular beef stew pot. A salad bar comes with every main dish. Lighter meals and gourmet burgers are available day or night.

**THE WHOLE ENCHILADA RESTAURANTE, 44 S. Grand Ave., near W. Main St. Tel. 249-1881.**
   **Cuisine:** MEXICAN. **Reservations:** Not necessary.
**$ Prices:** Appetizers $1.95–$5.50; main courses $2.50–$5.95 at lunch, $2.50–$9.95 at dinner. AE, MC, V.

**Open:** Daily 11am–10pm.
Come for the expected—burritos, tostadas, fajitas, chimichangas, and so forth—or the unexpected, such as enchiladas Acapulco (filled with chicken, olives, and almonds), crab enchiladas, or the El Paso chimichanga (filled with beef and jalapeño peppers). A full-service outdoor patio is open in summer.

# EASY EXCURSIONS

## DELTA

Between Montrose and Grand Junction lies Delta County, bounded on the south by the Black Canyon of the Gunnison and on the north by the Grand Mesa. Its county seat is Delta, a town of 4,000 people, 21 miles north of Montrose on U.S. 50. Delta is sometimes called "the city of murals" because many of its fine historical buildings display colorful murals on their outer walls, with themes ranging from Native American legends to wildlife to apple labels.

The highlight of a visit here is **✪ Fort Uncompahgre,** in Confluence Park at the west end of Gunnison River Drive (tel. 874-8349), just north of Delta off U.S. 50. The original fort was built in 1826 at the confluence of the Gunnison and Uncompahgre rivers as a small fur-trading post; it was abandoned in 1844 after an attack by Utes. Today it has been replicated as a living-history museum, with four hand-hewn log buildings—a trade room, store room, and living quarters—facing a courtyard. Costumed traders, trappers, and laborers describe their lives, and zealous history buffs can arrange weekend stays to temporarily assume 19th-century lifestyles. The fort is open year round: Memorial Day to Labor Day, Tuesday through Saturday from 10am to 5pm; the rest of the year, Wednesday through Sunday from 10am to 5pm.

Also in Delta is the **Delta County Museum,** 251 Meeker Street (tel. 874-9721). It's best known for its world-class butterfly collection; other exhibits include the historic Delta County Jail and the Jones Gallery of large dinosaur bones. Open Monday through Friday from 10am to 4pm.

**WHERE TO STAY & DINE** If you're planning to stop in Delta, a good place to stay is the **Best Western Sundance Motel,** 903 Main Street, Delta, CO 81416 (tel. 303/874-9781). Eat at **The Last Chance,** 420 Main Street (tel. 874-9355). For more information, contact the **Delta County Tourism Council,** 301 Main Street, Delta, CO 81416 (tel. 303/874-8616, or 800/228-7009).

## ON FROM DELTA

If you follow Colo. 92 east out of Delta and up the Gunnison, you can turn north off Colo. 92 just 4 miles east of Delta, onto Colo. 65. This route leads through **Cedaredge,** 14 miles from Delta, and on across the Grand Mesa. The **Pioneer Town Historical Museum,** south of downtown Cedaredge on Colo. 65 (tel. 856-3006), is a re-creation of an 1880 western town, complete with Wells Fargo stagecoach depot, jailhouse, general store, saloon, newspaper office, one-room schoolhouse, church, and many other buildings of the times. It's open Memorial Day to Labor Day, Monday through Saturday from 9am to 5pm and on Sunday from 1 to 5pm.

**WHERE TO STAY & DINE** If you're in this neck of the woods, so to speak, you might enjoy staying at the unique **✪ Cedars' Edge Llamas Bed and Breakfast,** 2169 Colo. 65, Cedaredge, CO 81413 (tel. 303/856-6836), whose guest rooms have private decks overlooking pastures of llamas. Farther on, atop the Grand Mesa at 10,200 feet, is the **Alexander Lake Lodge,** Colo. 65 (P.O. Box 93), Cedaredge, CO 81413 (tel. 303/856-6700), a turn-of-the-century log building with a full-service restaurant and lounge, cabins, an RV park, summer stables, and winter snowmobiling.

# CHAPTER 11

# SOUTHWESTERN COLORADO

1. DURANGO
2. CORTEZ
3. TELLURIDE
4. OURAY
5. PAGOSA SPRINGS

Southwestern Colorado is a land apart from the rest of the state. The spectacular mountain wall of the San Juan Range formed a barrier between cultural regions, with the result that residents of this area traditionally have more in common with the Native American tribes of New Mexico and Arizona than with those of the greater Rocky Mountain region. The prehistoric Anasazi cliff dwellings of Mesa Verde National Park are a case in point, and there are many more similar but less-well-known sites throughout this corner of the state, focused primarily around Cortez.

Durango is the main city of the region. Its vintage-1880 main street and narrow-gauge railroad harken back to the Old West days of the late 19th century, when it boomed as a transportation center for the region's rich silver and gold mines. Telluride, at the end of a box canyon surrounded by 14,000-foot peaks, has capitalized on its highly evident mining heritage in its evolution as a major ski and summer resort. And those who drive the Million Dollar Highway—down U.S. 550 from Ouray, over 11,008-foot Red Mountain Pass, through Silverton, and on past the Purgatory resort to Durango—can't miss spotting the remains of turn-of-the-century mines scattered over the mountainsides.

## 1. DURANGO

332 miles SW of Denver; 169 miles S of Grand Junction;
50 miles N of Farmington, N.M.

**GETTING THERE   By Plane   La Plata Field,** 18 miles southeast of Durango off Colo. 172, has direct daily nonstop service from Grand Junction and Denver; Phoenix, Arizona; Albuquerque and Farmington, New Mexico; and Dallas/Fort Worth, Texas; with connections to cities throughout North America. The airport is served by **America West** (tel. 303/247-9597, or 800/247-5692), **Continental Express** (tel. 303/259-3466, or 800/525-0280), **Mesa** (tel. 303/259-5178, or 800/637-2247), and **United Express** (tel. 303/247-9735, or 800/241-6522).

**By Train**   There's no direct passenger service from out of town, unless you're coming in from Silverton, 49 miles north. In that event, you can ride the **Durango & Silverton Narrow Gauge Railroad** (tel. 247-2733). See "What to See & Do," below.

**By Bus**   Coaches of **TNM&O** (Texas, New Mexico, & Oklahoma) arrive and depart from the **Durango Bus Center,** 275 East Eighth Avenue (tel. 303/259-2755).

**By Car**  Durango is located at the crossroads of east-west U.S. 160 and north-south U.S. 550. From I-70, turn south at Grand Junction on U.S. 50, which joins U.S. 550 at Montrose. From I-25, turn west at Walsenburg on U.S. 160. The most direct route from Denver, when snow conditions allow, is via U.S. 285 south to Del Norte, then west on U.S. 160 across Wolf Creek Pass to Durango. From Santa Fe, N.M., follow U.S. 84 north to Pagosa Springs, Colo., and turn west on U.S. 160 to Durango. From Farmington, N.M., take U.S. 550 north. From the Grand Canyon area, follow U.S. 160 northeast through the "Four Corners" of Arizona, New Mexico, Utah, and Colorado.

**SPECIAL EVENTS**  Annual events in the Durango area include **Snowdown!,** in Durango and Purgatory, from late January to early February; the **North American Speed Skiing Championships,** in Silverton, during the first week of May; the **Durango Fine Arts Festival and Songwriters Rendezvous,** in Durango, on the first weekend of May; the **Sky Ute Stampede and Rodeo,** in Ignacio, on the first weekend of June; the **Animas River Days,** in Durango, on the last weekend of June; the **State Mountain Bike Championships,** in Purgatory, during Fourth of July week; **Music in the Mountains,** in Purgatory, during the last week of July and the first week of August; **Fiesta Days,** in Durango, on the last weekend of July; the **La Plata County Fair,** in Durango, during the second week of August; and **Hardrockers Holidays,** in Silverton, on the second weekend of August.

---

**D**urango was founded in 1880 when the Denver & Rio Grande Railroad line was extended to Silverton to haul precious metals from high-country mines. Within a year 2,000 new residents had turned the town into a smelting and transportation center. Although more than $300 million worth of silver, gold, and other minerals rode along the route over the years, the unstable nature of the mining business gave the town many ups and downs. One of the "ups" occurred in 1915, when southern Colorado boy Jack Dempsey, then 20, won $50 in a 10-round boxing match at the Central Hotel. Dempsey went on to become the world heavyweight champion.

Durango remained a small center for ranching and mining into the 1960s. With the opening in 1965 of the Purgatory ski resort, 25 miles north of Durango, a tourism boom began. When the railroad abandoned its tracks from Antonito, Colo., to Durango in the late 1960s, leaving only the Durango-Silverton spur, the town panicked. But from that potential economic disaster blossomed a savior. The Durango & Silverton Narrow Gauge Railroad is now Durango's biggest tourist attraction, hauling more than 200,000 passengers each summer.

# ORIENTATION

**INFORMATION**  Contact the **Durango Area Chamber Resort Association,** 111 South Camino del Rio (P.O. Box 2587), Durango, CO 81302 (tel. 303/247-0312, or 800/525-8855, 800/358-8855 in Colorado), or the **Durango Area Reservation and Information Service,** P.O. Box 666, Durango, CO 81302 (tel. 303/247-3220, or 800/525-8855). The chamber's **Visitor Center** is just south of downtown, on U.S. 160/550 opposite the intersection of East Eighth Avenue; it's open Monday through Friday from 8am to 7pm, on Saturday from 10am to 7pm, and on Sunday from noon to 7pm.

**CITY LAYOUT**  The city is situated on the banks of the Animas River, which flows south to join the San Juan River at Farmington, N.M. U.S. 160 brushes the south side of downtown Durango; U.S. 550 branches north at the river as **Camino del Rio,** turning northeast to intersect **Main Avenue** at 14th Street. Downtown Durango is built around Main Avenue, from **5th Street** north to **14th Street;** the numbered streets continue north beyond 32nd. **Sixth Street,** from Camino del Rio to East Eighth Avenue, is the principal downtown cross-street. Numbered avenues parallel Main to the east and west; East Third Avenue becomes Florida Road after 15th Street, winding eventually to Vallecito Reservoir; East Eighth climbs a mesa to the campus of Fort Lewis College, a 4-year liberal-arts school.

# GETTING AROUND

The **Durango Lift** (tel. 259-LIFT) is the city bus, providing transportation throughout Durango May to August, daily from 8am to 5:30pm; and September to April, daily from 7am to 6:30pm; closed major public holidays. The fare is 75¢ per ride. There are bus stops on Main Avenue at 6th, 9th, and 12th Streets, and at Rotary Park, East Second Avenue and 15th Street; otherwise, you must "wave enthusiastically at the driver if you want him to stop," as the official route map urges.

In summer, horse-drawn **Carriages for Hire** (tel. 247-5699) and bicycle-drawn **Colorado Carriage** (tel. 385-7817) operate throughout downtown.

**Taxi** service in Durango is provided 24 hours by Durango Transportation (tel. 259-4818).

**Rental Cars**   Several car-rental agencies, including **Avis** (tel. 247-9761), **Hertz** (tel. 247-3933), and **National** (tel. 259-0068), have outlets at the airport; in town, you can get a vehicle from **Rent-a-Wreck**, 21698 U.S. 160 West (tel. 259-5858), or **Thrifty**, 20541 U.S. 160 West (259-3504).

# FAST FACTS

The **area code** is 303. In case of **emergency,** call **911;** for other law-enforcement business, call the Durango Police (tel. 247-3232) or the La Plata County Sheriff (tel. 247-1155). The **hospital,** Mercy Medical Center, is at 375 East Park Avenue (tel. 247-4311). For **road conditions,** call 259-2366. For **weather** call 247-0930.

# WHAT TO SEE & DO

## ATTRACTIONS

### DURANGO & SILVERTON NARROW GAUGE RAILROAD, 479 Main Ave. Tel. 303/247-2733 or 247-9349.

Colorado's most famous train—and rightfully so—has been in continual operation since 1881. In all that time, its route has never varied: up the Rio de las Animas Perdidas (the River of Lost Souls) and through 45 miles of mountain and San Juan National Forest wilderness to the tiny mining town of Silverton and return. America's only regulated 100% coal-fired locomotives pull strings of Victorian coaches on the 3,000-foot climb, past relics of mining and railroad activity from the last century.

The trip takes 3¼ hours each way, with a 2-hour stopover in Silverton (see "Easy Excursions," below) before the return trip. (It's also possible to overnight in Silverton and return to Durango the following day.) Stops are made for water, and may also be made for hikers and fishermen at trailheads inaccessible by road. Refreshments and snacks are available on all trains; there's a bar in the first-class Alamosa Parlor Car. Several private cars are available for charter, including the 1878 *Nomad*—the oldest operating private car in the world, host of U.S. presidents from Taft to Ford—and the *Railcamp.* The latter is a boxcar refurbished as a recreational vehicle; it's "spotted" on a siding in secluded Cascade Canyon each Monday and then picked up and returned to Durango each Friday. Inquire for rates and other information.

**Admission:** Round-trip fare, $37.15 adults and children 12 and older, $18.65 children 5–11; $63.85 parlor car (minimum age 21). Advance reservations advised. Railroad yard tours (45 min.) $5 adults, $2.50 children 5–11.

**Open:** First Sat of May through last Sun of Oct. At the peak of the summer season, trains depart at 7:30, 8:30, 9:30, and 10:15am, with a shorter run to Cascade Canyon at 4:30pm, July to mid-Aug. (The 8:30 and 9:30am trains have extended seasons.)

**ANIMAS MUSEUM, 3065 W. Second Ave., at 31st Street. Tel. 259-2402.**

An old stone schoolhouse is the home of the La Plata County Historical Society museum, so it's appropriate that a turn-of-the-century classroom is one of its central displays. Local history, Native American prehistory, and natural history are unveiled in a variety of exhibits.

**Admission:** $1.50 adults, free for children under 12.
**Open:** Late May to late Sept, Mon–Fri 10am–6pm, Sat–Sun 11am–4pm.

## SPORTS & RECREATION

**AIRBORNE SPORTS**   You can get a quiet, airborne look at Durango and the San Juan Mountains if you go aloft with **Blue Horizon Balloon Adventures** (tel. 247-5096), or **Val Air Glider Rides,** U.S. 550 (tel. 247-9037 or 247-2628), 2½ miles north of Durango.

**ALPINE SLIDE**   The **Purgatory Alpine Slide** (tel. 247-9000) is open weekends, Memorial Day to mid-June, then daily to Labor Day, weather permitting. Enthusiasts ride the chair lift up, then come down the mountain in a chute, on a self-controlled sled.

**BICYCLING**   The varied terrain and myriad trails of San Juan National Forest have made Durango a nationally important center for mountain biking. The **Colorado Trail** (see "Hiking," below), **Hermosa Creek Trail** (beginning 11 miles north of Durango off U.S. 550), and **La Plata Canyon Road** (beginning 11 miles west of Durango off U.S. 160) are among the favorite jaunts for locals. More enthusiastic bikers can tackle the 236-mile **San Juan Skyway** loop from Durango through Cortez, Telluride, Ouray, Silverton, and back to Durango.

The **Purgatory/Durango** resort, 25 miles north of Durango on U.S. 550 (see "Skiing," below), is the site of the Colorado state mountain-biking championships each Fourth of July week. Rentals and maps are available at the resort from **Mountain Bike Specialists** (tel. 247-9000, ext. 5102, or 800/255-8377), open from June 15 to Labor Day, daily from 9am to 5pm.

For more complete information on routes, guided tours, and bicycle rentals in Durango and vicinity, contact the **Durango Sports Company,** 3101 Main Avenue (tel. 259-4600); **Hassle Free Sports,** 2615 Main Avenue (tel. 259-3874); or **The Outdoorsman,** 949 Main Avenue (tel. 247-4066).

**BOATING**   There are two large lakes in the Durango area. **Vallecito Lake,** 22 miles east via County Roads 240 and 501, has numerous marinas with boat and fishing-equipment rentals. Marinas on the 11-mile-long lake include **Angler's Wharf,** 17250 County Road 501 (tel. 884-9477), and **Mountain Marina,** 14810 County Road 501 (tel. 884-9450), both on the lake's west shore.

Forty miles southeast of Durango on Colo. 151, the village of Arboles is the northern gateway to **Navajo Lake,** a 37-mile-long reservoir that spans the Colorado–New Mexico border. The **Arboles Marina** (tel. 883-2343) has rental boats and a marine-equipment store.

**FISHING**   Vallecito Lake (see "Boating," above) is a prime spot for rainbow and brown trout, kokanee salmon, and northern pike. The **Animas River** is good for trout through Durango, and it's even better 20 miles north of the city, in the **Devils Falls** area at Takoma power plant. Savvy anglers also recommend the **Piedra River,** 38 miles east of Durango via U.S. 160. Don't forget to get your Colorado fishing license first.

But you won't need a license if you drop a line in a private trout pond. Tackle and bait are provided free, and all the angler pays is $3 a pound (until inflation drives the price up) for fish caught. Try the **Twin Buttes Trout Ranch,** Lightner Creek, 3 miles west of Durango on County Road 207 off U.S. 160 (tel. 259-0479); the **Silver Streams Lodge,** County Roads 500 and 501, Vallecito Lake (tel. 884-2770); or the **Trapper's Den,** 37101 U.S. 160 West, Mancos (tel. 533-7147).

Fly-fishing expeditions are offered by **Duranglers** (tel. 385-4081).

**GOLF** Two 18-hole golf courses open in May, weather permitting. In Durango, the **Hillcrest Golf Course,** 2300 Rim Drive (tel. 247-1499), is adjacent to Fort Lewis College. Eighteen miles north on U.S. 550 is the challenging **Tamarron Resort Golf Course,** nationally renowned for its narrow fairways. Golfers will find that accuracy on the drive is more important than distance.

**HIKING & BACKPACKING** Durango is at the western end of the 469-mile **Colorado Trail** to Denver. The trailhead is 3½ miles up Junction Creek Road, an extension of 25th Street west of Main Avenue. There are numerous other trails in the Durango area, including paths into the **Weminuche Wilderness Area** reached via the Durango & Silverton railroad. For full information, contact the **Animas Ranger District,** San Juan National Forest, 701 Camino del Rio, Room 301 (tel. 247-4874). "Be on top by noon." Though precipitation averages under 20 inches a year, thunderstorms are frequent on summer afternoons.

**HORSEBACK RIDING** Hourly, all-day, and overnight rides, as well as hunting and fishing expeditions, are arranged by a variety of stables and outfitters throughout the Durango area. If you're interested only in the ride, check out **Bar D Riding Stables,** 9 miles north of Durango on East Animas Road (tel. 247-5755); or **Meadowlark Ranch,** 19786 County Road 501, Vallecito Lake (tel. 884-2966). For longer expeditions, talk to **Rapp Guide Service,** Bear Ranch, 20 miles north of Durango on U.S. 550 (tel. 247-8923 or 247-8454); **Silverado Outfitters,** 7575 County Road 203 (tel. 247-1869); or any of several guest ranches in the Vallecito Lake area.

Llama hikes with gourmet lunches, or overnight expeditions accompanied by Andean beasts of burden, are the specialty of **Buckhorn Llama,** 1843 County Road 207 (tel. 259-5965), and the **Turnbull Llama Company** (tel. 259-3773).

**HOT SPRINGS** **Trimble Hot Springs,** 6 miles north of Durango on U.S. 550 (tel. 247-0111), at the junction of County Road 203 and Trimble Lane, is a national historic site. Facilities include an Olympic-size natural hot springs pool and therapy pool, massage and therapy rooms, private tubs, a snack bar, a park, and gardens. It's open daily from 7am to 10pm.

**ICE SKATING** Ice skating is available at Chapman Hill and at several locations around Vallecito Lake.

**MOUNTAINEERING** Guided tours and instruction in standard mountaineering, rock- and ice-climbing, backcountry skiing, avalanche awareness, and other arduous pursuits are offered by **Southwest Adventures,** 780 Main Avenue (tel. 259-0370).

**RIVER RAFTING** The three stages of the Animas River provide excitement for rafters of all experience and ability levels. The churning Class IV and V rapids of the upper Animas mark its rapid descent from the San Juan Range. The 6 miles from Trimble Hot Springs into downtown Durango are an easy, gently rolling rush. Downstream from Durango, the river is mainly Class II and III, promising a few thrills but mostly relaxation.

Most of the many outfitters in Durango offer everything from quick 1½-hour river trips to overnight guided excursions. They include **Durango Rivertrippers,** 720 Main Avenue (tel. 259-0289); **Flexible Flyers Rafting,** Ninth Street and Roosa Avenue (tel. 247-4628); **Mountain Waters Rafting,** 108 West Sixth Street (tel. 259-4191); and **Southwest Adventures,** 780 Main Avenue (tel. 259-0370). The **Four Corners Marine & Kayak School,** 360 South Camino del Rio (tel. 259-3893), not only runs raft trips, but offers daily lessons in kayaking and canoeing.

**RODEO** From the second week of June through the third week of August, the **Durango Pro Rodeo** takes place every Tuesday and Wednesday night at the La Plata County Fairgrounds, Main Avenue and 25th Street (tel. 247-2308).

**SKIING** Some 25 miles north of Durango on U.S. 550, **Purgatory/Durango,** operated by the Durango Ski Corporation, P.O. Box 666, Durango, CO 81302 (tel. 303/247-9000, or 800/525-0892 for reservations), has a reputation of getting more sunshine than any other Colorado resort. Surprisingly, the sun doesn't come at the expense of snowfall: More than 250 inches a year (over 20 ft.) falls here. The 630 acres of skiable terrain are predominantly intermediate, but there are ample expert runs on the mountain's Backside, and plenty of easy runs for beginners. Sixty-two trails are served by nine chair lifts (four triples and five doubles), providing an hourly uphill capacity of 12,700 skiers on a vertical of 2,029 feet (base elevation 8,793 ft.; summit elevation 10,822 ft.).

Two on-mountain restaurants—Dante's and the Powderhouse—complement the facilities of Purgatory Village, which include a hotel, condominiums, several restaurants and taverns, shops, and activity centers. All-day tickets are $34 for adults, $20 for seniors 65 and over, $17 for children 12 and under. The area usually is open from Thanksgiving to mid-April, daily from 9am to 4pm.

The **Purgatory Cross-Country Ski Center** offers 16km (10 miles) of trails for nordic skiers. Trail fees are $5 for adults, $3 for children and seniors.

There are small local ski areas at **Chapman Hill,** adjacent to the Fort Lewis College campus overlooking Durango, with night skiing Monday through Friday from 6 to 8pm and day skiing on Saturday and Sunday, snow permitting; and at **Hesperus,** with one lift rising above U.S. 160, 12 miles west of Durango.

**SLEIGH RIDES & SNOWMOBILING** Sleigh rides and snowmobiling from Purgatory can be arranged with a quick phone call to **Purgatory/Durango Central Reservations** (tel. 800/525-0892).

**SWIMMING** The **Durango Municipal Pool,** 2400 Main Avenue (tel. 259-9988), is open summers only. Year-round indoor public swimming is available at **Fort Lewis College** (tel. 247-7184).

## EVENING ENTERTAINMENT

During the summer season, two stage shows draw Durango visitors. The ✪ **Diamond Circle Theatre,** in the Strater Hotel, 699 Main Avenue (tel. 247-4431), presents turn-of-the-century melodrama and professional vaudeville. The **Durango Jamboree,** in the Abbey Theatre, with an alley entrance near Sixth Street and Main Avenue (tel. 259-1290), presents a musical comedy show with a western theme.

Dinner shows, including cowboy-style barbecues and live western-music revues, are offered by **Bar D Chuckwagon,** 8080 County Road 250 (tel. 247-5753), 9 miles north of Durango, and **Trapper's Den Chuckwagon Dinner & Western Show,** U.S. 160, Mancos (tel. 533-7147), 1¼ miles east of the entrance to Mesa Verde National Park. Reservations are necessary; both operations are open Memorial Day to Labor Day only.

Back in town, there's entertainment and dancing nightly, year round, at many of Durango's bars and restaurants. **Farquahrts,** 725 Main Avenue (tel. 247-5440), is the top venue for live rock bands, while the **Sundance Saloon,** north side of Sixth Street between Main Avenue and East Second Avenue, is the place to dance to country-and-western music. For jazz music, visit **The Continental,** 658 Main Avenue (tel. 259-2888). The **Diamond Belle Saloon,** in the Strater Hotel, 699 Main Avenue (tel. 247-4431), has an unforgettable Victorian ambience, complete with ragtime piano player.

Other popular bars are the **Carvers Bakery & Brew Pub,** 1022 Main Avenue (tel. 259-2545), Durango's only commercial custom brewery; **Father Murphy's Pub and Gardens,** 636 Main Avenue (tel. 259-0334), an Irish pub; **Francisco's,** 619 Main Avenue (tel. 247-4098), a Mexican cantina with a big-screen TV for sporting events; and **Olde Tymer's,** 1000 Main Avenue (tel. 259-2990), a favorite local hangout.

# WHERE TO STAY

The following selections are categorized according to their high-season rates—generally Memorial Day to Labor Day, though the mid-winter ski season is most expensive at the Purgatory ski resort. Lodging at other times of year is considerably cheaper.

## VERY EXPENSIVE

**THE WIT'S END GUEST RANCH & RESORT, 254 County Rd. 500, Vallecito Lake, CO 81122. Tel. 303/884-4113.** 21 cabins. TV TEL
**$ Rates** (for two guests, including all meals and activities): $290–$335 one bedroom, $390–$485 two bedrooms. Additional adults $145; children's discounts. Rates effective Memorial Day–Labor Day, Thanksgiving and Christmas holidays, and "Spring Break," with minimum stay of 4–7 days; 20% less with no minimum stay at other times. AE, MC, V.

What a lovely place this is! Encompassing 365 acres in a narrow valley at the head of Vallecito Lake, surrounded by the 12,000- to 14,000-foot peaks of the Weminuche Wilderness, the Wit's End offers guests a unique combination of rustic outdoors and sophisticated luxury. Its main focus is a beautiful three-story hunting lodge, a memorable structure (dating from the 1870s) of hand-hewn logs, with a huge stone fireplace and walls mirrored with cut glass from London's 1853 Crystal Palace.

Log cabins, some of them 120 years old, have retained their rustic outer appearance but have been totally renovated with knotty-pine interiors and modern luxuries. The cabins all have fully equipped kitchens, stone fireplaces, queen-size beds, full bathrooms, French doors, porches and/or decks, and invariably striking views. Largest of all is the utterly charming, two-story John Patrick Cabin, built by hand in the 1870s. Many cabins are on the ranch ponds; others are located on Vallecito Creek.

**Dining/Entertainment:** Dinner and drinks are served in the Old Lodge at the Lake Restaurant and Colorado Tavern. The evening meal is included in all packages for resort guests, and is open to the public as well, by reservation, from 5 to 9:30pm nightly in summer, Thursday through Saturday in winter. Fixed-price dinners, including choice of appetizer and main course of prime rib, filet mignon, roast duckling, or chicken Culbertson, are $20; other hearty American dishes are priced $13 to $19. On Sunday, brunch is served from 11am to 2pm, and a family-style dinner (priced $7 to $12.95) from 3 to 8pm. The Tavern, on the second floor, has an antique billiards table; above it is a library loft. Breakfast and lunch are served daily at the Café at "D" Creek, adjacent to the Wit's End General Store; meal hours are 7am to 4pm in summer, 10am to 2pm in winter.

**Services:** Room service (additional charge).

**Facilities:** Swimming pool, four spas, tennis courts, volleyball, horseshoes, trout fishing (five spring-fed ponds); some packages also include horseback riding, cross-country skiing, ice skating, snowmobiling, and other activities. Additional charge for hunting and fishing packages. Facilities for large groups (up to 120) and conferences. General store, sporting-goods store, rodeo arena.

## EXPENSIVE

**GENERAL PALMER HOTEL, 567 Main Ave., Durango, CO 81301. Tel. 303/247-4747,** or 800/523-3358. Fax 303/259-0536. 34 rms, 5 suites. TV TEL
**$ Rates** (including breakfast): May–Oct and Christmas holidays, $75–$90 single; $85–$125 double; $145 suite. Nov–Apr except Christmas, $45–$60 single; $50–$85 double; $90–$95 suite. AE, CB, DC, DISC, MC, V. **Parking:** Free.

As you enter the lobby of this elegant Victorian hotel built in 1898, you'll see two rooms: a library to your left, testifying to the property's sophistication; and a Teddy Bear room to your right, indicative of its charm. In fact, guests aren't allowed to go to sleep at night without Hugs and Kisses on their beds. (They're Hershey's Kisses, and the bears are all nicknamed "Hugs.")

Staircases or old-time elevators ascend to narrow turn-of-the-century corridors. Guest rooms are all individually decorated, each with a character of its own. All have unique beds: brass, pewter, wicker, or perhaps a wooden four-poster with hand-crocheted canopies. Brass lamps and other handsome appointments add to the mood, along with Caswell & Massey amenities in the bathrooms. Specialty rooms include studios with queen-size Murphy beds, refrigerators, and wet bars; family suites with adjoining rooms; and a pair of bridal suites with Jacuzzis for two and champagne in the refrigerator.

**Services:** Room service, concierge, valet laundry, complimentary morning newspaper, no-smoking rooms.

**PURGATORY VILLAGE HOTEL, Purgatory/Durango Resort, U.S. 550 (P.O. Box 666), Durango, CO 81302. Tel. 303/247-9000,** or 800/525-0892. 140 units. TV TEL

**$ Rates:** June–Sept, $59–$70 double; $90–$140 suite. Apr–May and Oct to mid-Nov, $49–$60 double; $75–$120 suite. Mid-Nov to early Mar except Christmas holidays, $89–$110 double; $165–$275 suite. Christmas, $129–$160 double; $240–$400 suite. Early–end Mar, $109–$135 double; $205–$340 suite. Weekly rates available Apr–Nov. AE, CB, DC, DISC, MC, V. **Parking:** Free, covered lot.

The main hotel at the Purgatory/Durango Resort, 25 miles north of the city of Durango, is as pleasant a hotel as you're likely to find at any small ski resort. It's ski-in/ski-out in winter, mountain bike-in/bike-out in summer—and what outdoors lover could ask for more?

A variety of room types are available, both in the hotel building itself and in adjacent condominiums under resort management. Every room, regardless of size, has a kitchen, fireplace, and private deck, as well as a "snow room" with a ski locker in the entry. Standard one- and two-bedroom suites have Jacuzzi baths and/or steamer showers, classic furnishings, and microwaves and dishwashers in their kitchens. The efficiency unit makes ultimate use of space: Its Murphy bed doubles as a dining table, and its room divider is also a sleeper sofa.

**Dining/Entertainment:** Mesquite's restaurant offers fine continental dining, evenings during the winter and summer seasons. Sterling's cafeteria and lounge serves three meals daily. Farquahrt's pub, adjacent to the hotel, serves up pizza and live music for dancing.

**Services:** Concierge.

**Facilities:** Sports shop (with rentals), indoor/outdoor pool and hot tub, two rooftop hot tubs, guest laundry.

**RED LION INN/DURANGO, 501 Camino del Rio, Durango, CO 81301. Tel. 303/259-6580,** or 800/547-8010. Fax 303/259-4398. 152 rms, 7 suites. A/C TV TEL

**$ Rates:** May to mid-June, $79–$89 single; $89–$99 double; $175 suite. Mid-June to Sept, $98–$108 single; $108–$118 double; $188 suite. Oct, $85–$95 single; $95–$105 double; $175 suite. Nov–Apr, $71–$81 single; $81–$91 double; $171 suite. AE, CB, DC, DISC, MC, V. **Parking:** Free.

Not all of Durango dates from the 19th century. This expansive modern hotel, stretched along the banks of the Animas River at the intersection of U.S. 160 and U.S. 550, is a case in point. The lobby, restaurant, and lounge separate two four-story wings of guest rooms, with views of either the river or downtown Durango.

Typical rooms are handsomely appointed in earth tones with rich dark-wood furnishings. They have a king-size or two queen-size beds, a clock radio, a working desk with a telephone *or* a sofa and chair beside a coffee table, and a TV hidden away in an armoire.

**Dining/Entertainment:** The Edgewater Dining Room serves three meals daily overlooking the Animas River. Breakfast ($2.50 to $5.50) features an omelet bar; lunch includes sandwiches, salads, and light dishes ($4.25 to $8.95). Steak, seafood, and pasta dinners run $10 to $21.95. The adjacent lounge has live entertainment. In summer, the River Rat Café offers outdoor riverside dining.

**Services:** Room service, concierge, complimentary shuttle to airport and skiing.

**Facilities:** Indoor swimming pool, spa, sauna, fitness center, ski rental and storage, meeting space for up to 420, gift shop.

**STRATER HOTEL, 699 Main Ave. (P.O. Drawer E), Durango, CO 81302. Tel. 303/247-4431,** or 800/247-4431, 800/227-4431 in Colorado. Fax 303/259-2208. 93 rms. TV TEL

$ **Rates:** May to mid-Oct, $70–$91 single; $83–$105 double. Mid-Oct to Apr except holiday periods, $49–$72 single; $56–$93 double. Christmas and Presidents Day holidays, $64–$82 single; $75–$93 double. AE, CB, DC, MC, V.

Durango's most famous hotel, a four-story red-brick structure, is an exceptional example of American Victorian architecture. Built in 1887 by Henry H. Strater, a prominent druggist of the mining-boom era, the hotel boasts its original ornamental brickwork and white-stone cornices. Crystal chandeliers and a variety of ornate woodworking styles can be seen in the public areas, along with intricately carved columns and anaglyptic ceiling designs. The hotel has been in the family of current general manager Rod Barker for three generations.

Spread throughout the guest rooms is one of the world's largest collections of American Victorian walnut antiques. They help assure that every room is a museum. Great care was taken in the velvet drapery and upholstery, which varies in color from greens to dark mauves. Many mattresses had to be custom made to fit the nonstandard sizes of century-old beds. Even the wallpaper is authentic to the 1880s. You may think twice before reserving Room 222, at the corner of Seventh Street and Main Avenue and directly over the Diamond Belle Saloon, but it was good enough for author Louis L'Amour, whose prolific typewriter often drowned out the noise of the ragtime piano below.

**Dining/Entertainment:** Henry's restaurant serves gourmet international cuisine in an elegant atmosphere. Three meals are served daily, 6:30am to 2pm and 5:30 to 9pm (to 10pm on Friday and Saturday). Dishes like chicken piccata and pepper steak Herbert run $11.95 to $17.95, and locals enjoy the Sunday brunch buffet ($9.95), served from 10:30am to 2pm. The Diamond Belle Saloon has live ragtime piano Monday through Saturday nights and bluegrass on Sunday; and the Diamond Circle Theatre (see "Evening Entertainment" in "What to See & Do," above) presents a summer melodrama.

**Services:** Room service, valet laundry, no-smoking rooms.

**Facilities:** Large Jacuzzi, meeting space for 180.

**TAMARRON RESORT, U.S. 550 (P.O. Drawer 3131), Durango, CO 81302. Tel. 303/259-2000,** or 800/678-1000. Fax 303/259-0745. 250 rms, 50 suites. A/C TV TEL

$ **Rates:** Apr, $67 single or double; $94–$134 suite. May and Oct, $94 single or double; $154–$188 suite. June–Sept, $146 single or double; $209–$292 suite. AE, CB, DC, DISC, MC, V. **Parking:** Free.

There's no denying the commitment to nature at this quiet year-round conference resort 18 miles north of Durango. Spread across 650 acres in the midst of San Juan National Forest, Tamarron was specially designed to fit its beautiful natural setting, on a rocky cliff near the Animas River, with the least intrusion possible. The championship 18-hole golf course becomes a nordic ski course in winter, and there's a family orientation in activities from horseback riding to fishing. The Main Lodge, on which most activities center, maintains a feeling of western elegance with its use of stone and natural woods, picture windows, cathedral ceilings, and regional artwork.

Guest rooms are in the Main Lodge or in three separate town-house clusters (Pinecone, Gamble Oak, and High Point) spread across nearly a mile of land. Most have fully equipped kitchenettes and private balconies. Many have lofts with vaulted ceilings. Guests can choose between spacious studio units; one-, two-, and three-bedroom town-house units; and executive suites.

**Dining/Entertainment:** Tuxedoed waiters offer candlelight service and gourmet continental cuisine in Le Canyon Room, where a pianist plays dinner music from a mezzanine deck from 5:30 to 9:30pm daily. Three meals daily are served in the San Juan Dining Room (from 7am to 2pm and 6 to 9pm), with its strong southwestern decor. Afternoon and evening snacks can be garnered in the Caboose Café. Bands play light contemporary rock Monday through Saturday nights in the San Juan Lounge.

**Services:** Concierge; shuttle service (fee) between Purgatory, Durango, Mesa Verde, and La Plata airport.

**Facilities:** Indoor/outdoor swimming pool, hot tubs, saunas, steam rooms, fitness club, golf course/nordic ski course, tennis courts, stables, other summer and winter activities; children's recreational program (includes stocked trout pond, miniature train, and mile-long nature trail); general store; gift, clothing, and sports shops; guest laundries; meeting facilities for up to 500.

## MODERATE

**BEST WESTERN MOUNTAIN SHADOWS, 3255 N. Main Ave., Durango, CO 81301. Tel. 303/247-5200,** or 800/528-1234. 63 rms, 2 suites (all with bath). A/C TV TEL
**$ Rates** (including continental breakfast): Jan–Mar, $45 single; $50 double. Apr–Memorial Day, $31–$41 single; $38–$48 double. Memorial Day–Labor Day and Christmas holidays, $68–$75 single or double. Labor Day–Christmas Eve, $37–$58 single; $41–$63 double. AE, CB, DC, DISC, MC, V. **Parking:** Free.
You can't miss this two-story motel on the north end of town: Its geodesic plexiglas dome, housing its swimming pool and hot tub, is one-of-a-kind in Durango. Equally unusual is the cigar-store cowboy standing at the lobby entrance. The spacious and colorful guest rooms have small refrigerators, microwave ovens, and coffee makers, and the motel also offers a guest laundry, a games room, free airport pickup, and a ski bus in winter.

**COMFORT INN, 2930 N. Main Ave., Durango, CO 81301. Tel. 303/259-5373,** or 800/228-5150. 48 rms (all with bath). A/C TV TEL
**$ Rates:** Memorial Day–Labor Day, $52.80 single; $67.10 double. Christmas holidays, $45 single; $65 double. Rest of the year, $38.50 single; $38.50–$45 double. Children under 18 stay free in parents' room. AE, CB, DC, DISC, MC, V. **Parking:** Free.
Built in modern pueblo style, with flat roofs and stuccoed walls, this Comfort Inn has a swimming pool and two hot tubs at the top of a hillside overlooking the Animas River. Bright, comfortable rooms are in three separate buildings, and feature standing furnishings as well as tiled bathrooms and vanities. Complimentary coffee and juices are available 24 hours in the lobby.

**IRON HORSE INN, 5800 N. Main Ave. (U.S. 550 North), Durango, CO 81301. Tel. 303/259-1010,** or 800/748-2990. Fax 303/385-4791. 138 suites. A/C TV TEL
**$ Rates:** May–Oct, $50–$61 single suite; $55–$69 double suite; $88–$95 deluxe suite. Nov–Apr except Christmas, $42–$48 single suite; $52–$58 double suite; $62–$68 deluxe suite. Christmas holidays, $68 single; $78 double; $88 deluxe suite. AE, CB, DC, DISC, MC, V. **Parking:** Free.
Located a mile north of Durango beside the tracks of the Durango & Silverton Narrow Gauge Railroad, the Iron Horse can honestly declare that every room is a bilevel suite. Upstairs is the master bedroom. Downstairs, there's a fireplace, television, wet bar and sink, dining table, and either a sleeper sofa or a queen-size bed. The Depot Restaurant serves three meals daily in a hunting-lodge atmosphere, with emphasis on steak and seafood dishes; the adjoining Rendezvous Lounge has a big-screen TV for sporting events. The motel also features a large indoor pool and hot tub, two games rooms, two guest laundries, and meeting space for up to 600 people.

**SILVER SPUR MOTEL, 3416 N. Main Ave., Durango, CO 81301. Tel. 303/247-5552,** or 800/748-1715. 31 rms, 2 suites (all with bath). A/C TV TEL
**$ Rates:** May–Oct, $58 single; $65 double; $85 suite. Nov–Apr, $28 single; $32 double; $42 suite. AE, CB, DC, DISC, MC, V. **Parking:** Free.
Junipers and pine trees not only surround this motel but go right through it! A crudely cut hole in the wood-shake roof allows one large ponderosa to survive quite nicely. That's just one of the special touches you'll find at the Silver Spur, one of the older hostelries along north Durango's motel row. Rooms are clean and comfortable, with standard furnishings. There's a coffee shop and lounge, and an outdoor swimming pool, open seasonally.

# WHERE TO DINE
## MODERATE

**ARIANO'S, 150 E. Sixth St. Tel. 247-8146.**
**Cuisine:** ITALIAN. **Reservations:** Not accepted.
**$ Prices:** Appetizers $3.95–$6.25; main courses $8.50–$15.95. AE, MC, V.
**Open:** Memorial Day–Labor Day, dinner only, daily 5–10:30pm; the rest of the year, dinner only, Mon–Sat 5:30–10pm.

Enter this restaurant through its sports bar, with old photos and news clippings of great boxers and baseball players. Then proceed past the open kitchen into the dining room, where chains of garlic hang from the columns. Pasta is made fresh daily here; veal is hard-carved and pounded. And everything is made to order, from the spicy fettuccine Napolitano to the veal Zingara, the Italian baked trout to the chicken Vincent. The wine list is dominated by Italian imports, and cappuccinos complement fine desserts.

**FRANCISCO'S RESTAURANTE Y CANTINA, 619 Main Ave. Tel. 247-4098.**
**Cuisine:** MEXICAN/AMERICAN. **Reservations:** Not accepted.
**$ Prices:** Breakfast $3.25–$5.95; lunch $3.75–$8.95; dinner $6.50–$15.50. AE, CB, DC, DISC, MC, V.
**Open:** Memorial Day–Labor Day, daily 7am–10:30pm; the rest of the year, daily 8am–10:30pm.

This enormous come-as-you-are family restaurant, 8,000 square feet in area, maintains a festive Mexican atmosphere. Imitation adobe bricks, carved wooden pillars, a traditional *viga-latilla* ceiling, and the Hispanic dress of the servers make it feel like a courtyard in Guadalajara. The menu ranges from south-of-the-border specialties such as enchiladas Durango (two blue-corn tortillas over a bed of beef and green chiles) and carne adovada burritos (marinated pork in a hot chile Caribe sauce) to steaks, trout, and chicken Navajo style (roast with a cilantro-cream sauce). There's a children's menu, and the bar manufactures excellent margaritas.

**ORE HOUSE, 147 E. Sixth St. Tel. 247-5707.**
**Cuisine:** STEAK/SEAFOOD. **Reservations:** Not accepted.
**$ Prices:** Appetizers $2.50–$4.50; main courses $9.50–$18.95. AE, MC, V.
**Open:** Dinner only, daily 5:30–11pm.

The decor in this dimly lit restaurant is nearly equal to the food, and that's saying a lot. Everything from antique spurs to old skis to kitchen cannisters decorates the walls, along with handsome western oils and Navajo sand paintings. A full-wall mural by artist John Grow depicts turn-of-the-century Durango at the corner of Sixth and Main, with various citizens of modern Durango and Hollywood stars in the surrealistic set. The menu, on the other hand, is *realistic*—though generous. More than a dozen steaks are offered, including steak Ore House—a filet wrapped in bacon, stuffed with crabmeat, and topped with béarnaise sauce. Other specials include chicken Sonora and shrimp Hawaiian. All dishes come with salad bar, baked potato, and sourdough bread. The double-chocolate mousse cake has won local awards.

**THE PALACE GRILL, 2 Depot Place. Tel. 247-2018.**
**Cuisine:** STEAK/SEAFOOD. **Reservations:** Accepted only for Sun brunch.
**$ Prices:** Appetizers $4.25–$6.50; main courses $10.50–$26. AE, CB, DC, MC, V.
**Open:** Memorial Day–Labor Day, lunch daily 11am–2pm; Dec–Mother's Day, brunch Sun 10am–2pm; year round, dinner daily 5:30–10pm.

With its Victorian drawing-room atmosphere, adjacent to the Durango & Silverton Narrow Gauge Railroad terminal, this may be Durango's finest restaurant. Tiffany lamps hang over the tables, graciously positioned near a large fireplace, in an ambience of historical photos and classic oil paintings. The menu is noted for its mesquite grills and daily fish specials. Frequent diners rave about the duck, roasted with a honey-and-almond sauce, and steak McMahon, a New York sirloin on hash browns, with a brown sauce and sautéed onions. Fish of the day may be salmon, swordfish, ahi (Hawaiian tuna), or something entirely different. The Quiet Lady Tavern, named for the headless female sculpture at its entrance, is a beautiful lounge, complete with library and British pub-style darts.

**THE RED SNAPPER, 144 E. Ninth St. Tel. 259-3417.**
   **Cuisine:** SEAFOOD. **Reservations:** Not accepted.
$ **Prices:** Appetizers $2.95–$5.95; main courses $12.50–$30. AE, MC, V.
   **Open:** Dinner only, daily 5–10pm.
The atmosphere at this fine restaurant, occupying the first floor of the 1905 Colorado Heritage Plaza, is truly exotic. Silk orchids and birds-of-paradise flowers hover over tropical aquariums, where clownfish coddle themselves in sea anemones between the smoking and no-smoking rooms. Etched-glass seashore designs separate the quiet bar from the rest of the establishment. The restaurant boasts a superb salad bar, but diners come for the fresh seafood, flown in three or four times a week from the Atlantic, Pacific, and Gulf of Mexico. You can start with fresh oysters on the half-shell, then move into one of the fresh catches (grilled or baked as you like it); or try the scallops dijonaise or—of course—the red snapper, prepared Monterey, Puerto Vallarta, or Cajun Créole style. For non-seafood eaters, there is "landfood" on the menu, too. The pumpkin-and-walnut cheesecake makes a delightful conclusion to the meal.

### INEXPENSIVE

**CARVERS BAKERY/CAFE/BREWERY, 1022 Main Ave. Tel. 259-2545.**
   **Cuisine:** AMERICAN. **Reservations:** Not accepted.
$ **Prices:** Appetizers $1.75–$4.95; main courses $3.25–$6.50.
   **Open:** Mon–Sat 6:30am–10pm, Sun 6:30am–2pm.
In the front of this small restaurant is a bakery and gift counter, with seating at booths and tables. In the rear is a tiny brewpub, the only one in Durango, open daily from 4 to 10pm. Sandwiches like hamburgers and vegetarian Reubens dominate the menu, but evening brewpub specials include barley-glazed almond chicken, sirloin strips in a gravy of mushrooms, onions, and stout, and "brew-jitas"—fajitas pan-fried in tequila and salsa.

**OLDE TYMER'S CAFE, 10th St. and Main Ave. Tel. 259-2990.**
   **Cuisine:** AMERICAN. **Reservations:** Not accepted.
$ **Prices:** $2.95–$6.50. DISC, MC, V.
   **Open:** Mon–Sat 11am–10pm, Sun 11am–9pm.
"We're a little tacky," said the bartender, "but we're proud of it." Perhaps that's why this ever-popular local hangout is packed 7 nights a week. A mountain bike belonging to world-champion racer Greg Herbold, a Durango native, is suspended from the ceiling, and antique bottles and tins from this early 20th-century Wall Drug store are filed away in mezzanine-high shelves. The local newspaper voted hamburgers here—7 ounces of meat in an onion roll—as the best in Durango. The menu also features homemade chili, salads, and daily specials, including fried chicken on Tuesday and Mexican meals on weekends.

**SHELBY'S NEW YORK BAKERY, 750 Main Ave. Tel. 247-3936.**
   **Cuisine:** DELI. **Reservations:** Not accepted.
$ **Prices:** $2.25–$5.50. MC, V.
   **Open:** Daily 7am–4pm.
A comfortable delicatessen with hardwood floors and plants hanging from a central skylight, Shelby's will entice you with the pies and cakes in its display case near the front door. But you can also get delicious omelets and blueberry blue-corn pancakes here, as well as a variety of soups, salads, and sandwiches at lunchtime.

# EASY EXCURSIONS
## SAN JUAN SKYWAY

No visitor to southwestern Colorado should miss a drive around the    ✪ San Juan Skyway, a 236-mile circuit that crosses five mountain passes and takes in the spectacular best of the San Juan Mountains, as well as the cities and towns of the region. It can be accomplished in a single all-day drive from Durango, or can be divided up into several days, incorporating stops in such communities as Cortez, Telluride, and Ouray—all of them subsequently discussed in this chapter.

The route can be driven either clockwise (heading west from Durango on U.S. 160) or counterclockwise (heading north from Durango on U.S. 550). The former choice passes through the village of **Hesperus,** 11 miles west of Durango, from which a county road runs 10 miles north up the **La Plata Canyon,** with its mining ruins and ghost towns. Farther west, U.S. 160 passes the entrance road to **Mesa Verde National Park** and on into the city of **Cortez,** 46 miles west of Durango.

Turn north here on Colo. 145, which passes through the historic town of **Dolores,** site of the **Anasazi Heritage Center and Museum,** then proceeds up the Dolores River Valley, a favorite of trout fishermen. Sixty miles from Cortez, the route crosses 10,222-foot **Lizard Head Pass,** named for a startling rock spire that looms above the alpine meadows beside the road. It then descends 13 miles to the resort town of **Telluride,** set in a beautiful box canyon 4 miles off the main road.

Follow Colo. 145 west from Telluride, down the San Miguel River valley to **Placerville,** then turn north on Colo. 62, across 8,970-foot **Dallas Divide,** to **Ridgway,** a historic railroad town and home of a new state recreation area. Turn south here on U.S. 550 to the scenic and historic hot-springs town of **Ouray.** Here begins the remarkable **Million Dollar Highway,** so named for all the mineral wealth that once passed over it.

The 23 miles from Ouray over 11,008-foot ✪ **Red Mountain Pass** to Silverton is one of the most gorgeous drives anywhere on earth. It shimmies up the sheer sides of the Uncompahgre Gorge, through tunnels and past cascading waterfalls, then follows a historic toll road built in the 19th century by Otto Mears, "Pathfinder of the San Juans." Various mining apparatus and log cabins are in evidence everywhere on the slopes of the iron-colored mountains, many of them over 14,000 feet in elevation.

From Silverton, U.S. 550 climbs over Molas and Coalbank passes, both above 10,000 feet, then more-or-less parallels the track of the Durango & Silverton Narrow Gauge Railroad as it follows the Animas River south to Durango, passing en route the **Purgatory/Durango** ski resort (see "Skiing" in "Sports & Recreation," above) and the impressive **Tamarron Resort** complex (see "Where to Stay," above).

## SILVERTON

Silverton calls itself "the mining town that never quit." Situated at an altitude of 9,318 feet, at the northern terminus of the Durango & Silverton Narrow Gauge Railroad, the town has a year-round population of 750, perhaps twice that many in summer. The entire town is a National Historic Landmark District. Founded on silver production in 1871, it boomed after the rail spur from Durango was built a decade later. Even today, the **Sunnyside Mine,** which opened in 1874, is Colorado's largest active gold producer. **Blair Street** was such a notorious area of saloons and brothels a century ago that no less a character than Bat Masterson, fresh from taming Dodge City, Kansas, was imported to subdue the criminal elements. Today the original false-fronted buildings remain, but they now house restaurants and galleries, and are frequently used as Old West movie sets.

**WHAT TO SEE & DO** The **San Juan County Historical Society Museum,** in the turn-of-the-century jail on Greene Street at 15th Street (tel. 387-5838), displays memorabilia of Silverton's boom days daily from Memorial Day weekend to mid-October. The adjacent **San Juan County Courthouse** has a gold-domed clock tower, and a National Park Service grant has helped in the restoration of the **Town Hall,** at 14th Street and Greene Street. An outstanding gallery is **Silverton Artworks,** 1028 Blair Street (tel. 387-5823), featuring the work of weaver-ceramicist Ruth A. Darr and watercolorist Michael Darr.

You can get walking-tour maps and other information from the **Silverton Chamber of Commerce,** Greene Street (Colo. 110) off U.S. 550 (P.O. Box 565), Silverton, CO 81433 (tel. 303/387-5654, or 800/752-4494).

**WHERE TO STAY** For overnight stays, consider the **Grand Imperial Hotel,** 1219 Greene Street, Silverton, CO 81433 (tel. 303/387-5527), an opulent showcase dating from 1883 that houses the Hub Saloon, where the old song, "There'll Be a Hot Time in the Old Town Tonight," was penned. A stone facade, tin mansard roof, and pressed-tin ceilings usher guests into 40 Victorian-style rooms with private baths. Rates are $45 to $60 double. The hotel is open May through October only.

Year-round lodging is available at the **Prospector Hotel,** 1015 Greene Street, Silverton, CO 81433 (tel. 303/387-5466), with rates of $30 to $40; and the **Teller House,** 1250 Greene Street, Silverton, CO 81433 (tel. 303/387-5423), a bed-and-breakfast with rates of $29 to $45.

**WHERE TO DINE** Leading restaurants open year round include the **Buffalo Grill,** 1303 Greene Street (tel. 387-5515), serving three meals daily; and the **San Juan Café & Saloon,** 1129 Greene Street (tel. 387-5794), with lunch and dinner in an 1893 building.

### IGNACIO

This small community, 24 miles southeast of Durango via Colo. 172, is the headquarters of the **Southern Ute Indian Reservation.** The 15- by 75-mile reservation, home to 1,150 tribe members, has an economy based on wood products, coal, and natural gas. The ✪ **Southern Ute Indian Cultural Center** at the Sky Ute Lodge displays two centuries of native bead- and leatherwork along with prehistoric artifacts, and its gift shop is of special interest for souvenir hunters. Tribe members lead tours of the **Chimney Rock archeological site,** 30 miles east of Ignacio off Colo. 151.

**WHERE TO STAY & DINE** The tribe owns and operates the **Sky Ute Lodge,** Colo. 172 (P.O. Box 550), Ignacio, CO 81137 (tel. 303/563-4531). There's a restaurant here, an indoor and outdoor swimming pool, and shuttle service to and from La Plata Field airport. The 38 clean, pleasant rooms have private baths, TVs, and telephones. Nightly rates are $30 to $42 double.

# 2. CORTEZ

46 miles W of Durango, 203 miles S of Grand Junction

**GETTING THERE** **By Plane** Cortez Airport, off U.S. 550 (tel. 303/565-9510), is served by **Mesa Airlines** (tel. 800/637-2247), with daily flights from Denver and Colorado Springs; Albuquerque and Farmington, New Mexico; Phoenix, Arizona; and Laramie, Wyoming.

**By Car** Cortez is located at the junction of U.S. 666 and U.S. 160. U.S. 666 runs north to Monticello, Utah (and on to Salt Lake City), and south to Gallup, New Mexico (on I-40); U.S. 160 runs east through Durango to Walsenburg, on I-25, and west through the Four Corners to the Grand Canyon region of Arizona. Colo. 145, north to Telluride and Grand Junction, intersects U.S. 160 at the east end of town.

**ESSENTIALS** **Orientation** U.S. 160 from Durango crosses north-south Colo. 145 (**Dolores Road**) as it enters Cortez from the east, then runs due west through town for about 2 miles as **Main Street.** Easily the city's main thoroughfare, Main Street eventually intersects U.S. 666, which runs roughly southwest-northeast as **Broadway** at the west end of town.

Cortez has a population of about 8,000 and elevation of 6,200 feet.

**Information** The best source is the **Colorado Welcome Center at Cortez,** Cortez City Park, 928 East Main Street (P.O. Box 968), Cortez, CO 81321 (tel.

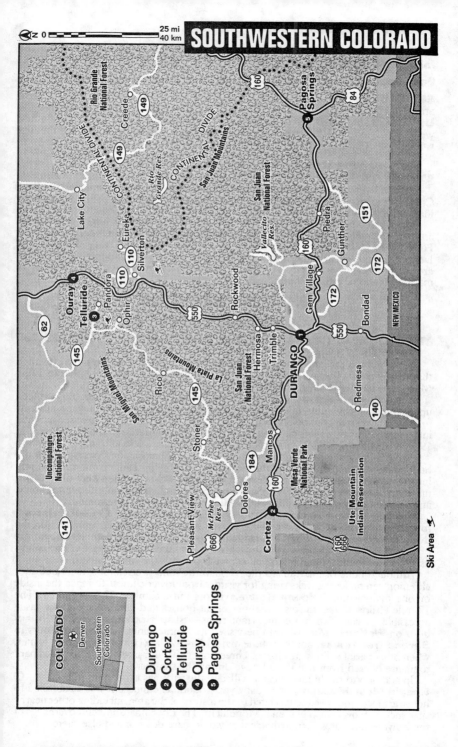

303/565-3414, or 800/346-6528). Also consult the **Mesa Verde–Cortez Visitor Information Bureau,** P.O. Drawer HH, Cortez, CO 81321 (tel. 800/253-1616).

**Fast Facts** The **area code** is 303. In case of **emergency, call 911.**

**SPECIAL EVENTS** Cortez's annual events include the **Indian Dances,** at Main Street and Market Street, Monday through Thursday nights from June to August; the **Ute Mountain Tribal Bear Dance,** in the American Legion Arena on the first weekend of June; the **Montezuma County Fair,** at the Fairgrounds on the first weekend of August.

---

**S**ometimes called "the archeological center of the United States," Cortez is surrounded by a vast complex of ancient Anasazi villages that dominated the Four Corners region—where Colorado, New Mexico, Arizona, and Utah's borders join—1,000 years ago.

Mesa Verde National Park, 10 miles east, is certainly the most prominent nearby attraction, drawing some 800,000 visitors annually. In addition, ruins such as those of Hovenweep National Monument, Sand Canyon Pueblo, Lowry Pueblo, the Dominguez and Escalante Ruins, and the various sites of Ute Mountain Tribal Park are an easy drive from the city. And San Juan National Forest, just to the north, offers many recreational opportunities.

# WHAT TO SEE & DO
## THE MAJOR SITES

**MESA VERDE NATIONAL PARK, P.O. Box 277, Mancos, CO 81328. Tel. 303/533-7731.**

Mesa Verde is the largest archeological preserve in the United States. It's estimated that there are 10,000 to 12,000 ruins in its canyons, dating from A.D. 600 to 1300. Many sites have never been excavated.

The area was unknown until ranchers Charles and Richard Wetherill chanced upon some of the ruins in 1888. More-or-less uncontrolled looting of artifacts followed the discovery until a New York newspaper reporter's stories aroused national interest in protecting the site. The 52,000-acre site was declared a national park in 1906, and is the only U.S. national park devoted to the works of man.

The earliest-known inhabitants of Mesa Verde (Spanish for "green tableland") built subterranean pit houses on the mesa tops. During the 13th century they moved into caves and constructed complex cliff dwellings. These homes were obviously a massive construction project. Yet the Anasazi lived in them for only about a century, and abandoned the site around A.D. 1300 for reasons never determined.

The largest and most elaborate ruin in the Southwest is the ✪ **Cliff Palace,** a four-story apartment complex with stepped-back roofs forming porches for the dwellings above. Reached by a self-guided quarter-mile downhill path, its assemblage of towers, masonry facades with square windows, and *kivas* (large circular rooms used for spiritual ceremonies) are all set back beneath the rim of a cliff.

Although none of the trails to the Mesa Verde ruins is strenuous, the 8,000-foot elevation can make the treks tiring for visitors from lower climes. To reach the inside of one major ruin, **Balcony House,** visitors must climb a 32-foot ladder. The 12-mile **Ruins Road** makes a number of pit houses and cliffside overlooks easily accessible by car. Two more important ruins—**Step House** and **Long House,** both on **Wetherill Mesa**—can be visited in summer only. Rangers lead tours to **Spruce Tree House,** another of the major cliff-dwelling complexes, only in winter, when other park facilities are closed. Three-hour ($10) and six-hour ($12) guided park tours are offered from Far View Lodge during the summer.

In addition to the hidden cliffside villages, the park has other treasures in the ✪ **Chapin Mesa Museum,** open daily year round. The museum was established to house artifacts and specimens related to the history of the area, including other nearby sites such as Hovenweep National Monument. The dry climate and cliff overhangs of the canyons have preserved artifacts that would have deteriorated elsewhere.

**Chapin Mesa,** site of the park headquarters, the museum, and a post office, is 21 miles from the park entrance on U.S. 160. **Morefield Village,** site of Mesa Verde's 477-site campground, is 4 miles in from U.S. 160. The **Far View Visitor Center** (open in summer only), site of the 150-unit Far View Lodge (see "Where to Stay," below), a restaurant, gift shop, and other facilities, is 15 miles off U.S. 160. In summer, rangers organize nightly campfire programs on various subjects. In winter, the Ruins Road and museum remain open, but other facilities are closed.

**Admission:** $5 per vehicle, or $2 per passenger for motor coaches; free for seniors (62 and over), children (12 and younger), and the disabled.

**Open:** Park, 24 hours a day, year round; ruins, daily 8am–sunset; museum, daily 8am–6:30pm in summer, daily 8am–5pm the rest of the year. Food, gas, and lodging available May–Oct; full interpretive services available mid-June to Labor Day.

**HOVENWEEP NATIONAL MONUMENT, 43 miles west of Cortez via Colo. 10 or McElmo Canyon Rd. Tel. 303/529-4461.**

Located along the Colorado-Utah border, this national monument—consisting of six separate groups of ruins (four of them in Colorado)—contains some of the area's most striking and isolated Anasazi sites. It's noted for its mysterious, 20-foot-high sandstone towers, some of them square, others oval, circular, or D-shaped.

The towers have small windows up and down their masonry sides, and remain very solid today. Archeologists have suggested their possible function as everything from guard or signal towers to celestial observatories or ceremonial structures, to water towers or granaries. The ranger on duty keeps a collection of visitors' guesses.

Headquarters are located at the **Square Tower Ruins,** the most impressive and best preserved of the sites; the Tower Point Loop Trail here winds past the ruins and identifies desert plants used by the Native Americans for food, clothing, medicine, and other purposes. Also in Colorado are the **Holly Ruins, Horseshoe Ruins,** and **Cutthroat Castle Ruins;** across the line in Utah are the **Brush Arbor Ruins** and the **Cajon Ruins.**

*Hovenweep* is the Ute word for "deserted valley." The Anasazi abandoned it about A.D. 1300, and even today it's often overlooked by tourists, in sharp contrast to Mesa Verde. Even the campground is nearly vacant during the peak summer season, perhaps because there are no firewood, camping supplies, gasoline, or telephone service available at the monument. Moreover, access is by graded dirt roads that become muddy—sometimes impassably so—during rainstorms.

**Admission:** Free.

**Open:** Daily 8am–sunset.

## OTHER ANASAZI SITES

**ANASAZI HERITAGE CENTER, 27501 Colo. 184, Dolores. Tel. 303/ 882-4811.**

When the Dolores River was dammed and McPhee Reservoir created in 1985, some 1,600 ancient Anasazi sites were threatened. Because the U.S. Congress acted with foresight and set aside 4% of the project costs for archeological work, many of them were saved: a stunning two million artifacts, samples, and other prehistoric records were rescued. The largest share are displayed in this museum, which opened in 1989. Located 10 miles north of Cortez, just over a mile west of Colo. 145, it is set into a hillside near the remains of the 12th-century Dominguez and Escalante ruins.

Operated by the Bureau of Land Management, the Anasazi Heritage Center emphasizes visitor involvement in its exhibits. Children and adults are invited to examine corn-grinding implements, a loom and other weaving materials, and a re-created pit house. There's an opportunity to touch artifacts 1,000 to 2,000 years old, to examine samples through microscopes, to research using interactive computer programs, and to engage in video lessons in archeological techniques.

A separate gallery houses temporary exhibits. The center also has a theater and a superb bookshop with a national mail-order catalog. A trail leads from the museum half a mile to the Escalante Ruin, atop a low hill with a spectacular view across the Montezuma Valley.

**Admission:** Free.

**Open:** Apr 15–Oct, daily 9am–5pm; Nov–Apr 14, Thurs–Mon 9am–5pm (days and hours may vary). **Closed:** New Year's Day, Thanksgiving, Christmas.

**CORTEZ CENTER AND MUSEUM, 25 N. Market St., Cortez. Tel. 303/ 565-1151,** or 800/346-6528.

The center is a clearinghouse for information on various Anasazi sites and participation in Native American cultural experiences in Colorado's southwestern corner. It also features interpretive exhibits from various Anasazi sites and the modern Ute reservation, as well as a laboratory for University of Colorado archeologists. In summer, an evening series of lectures on archeology and other cultural topics is offered here.

The center also is headquarters for Anasazi Tours, a privately operated service that offers half-day and full-day guided tours of archeological sites in the area, many of them otherwise inaccessible. Among them is the Yellow Jacket Pueblo, a University of Colorado dig believed to have been a large regional ceremonial center for the Anasazi. It contains a great *kiva* and numerous multistoried buildings and towers.

**Admission:** Free.

**Open:** Memorial Day–Labor Day, Mon–Sat 10am–4pm; the rest of the year, Tues–Sat 10am–4pm.

**CROW CANYON ARCHEOLOGICAL CENTER AND SCHOOL, 23390 County Rd. K, Cortez. Tel. 303/565-8975,** or 800/422-8975.

It's rare to find a research facility that actively encourages the participation of lay outsiders. Here, even if you've never turned a trowel of dirt, you can work side-by-side with professional archeologists in an important dig. Programs at this independent center also include laboratory analysis, artifact classification, and other insights into methods used to unravel the mysteries of the Anasazi.

The center's main excavation is at the **Sand Canyon Pueblo,** a 300-room Anasazi community 13 miles northwest of Cortez. It contains 14 towers and 90 *kivas,* and may have served as a ritual center for the Four Corners region.

Day programs are open to short-term Cortez visitors, with a minimum 1-day advance reservation; lunch is included. Participants in extended programs live on site, either in the dormitory-style lodge or in one of 10 four-bed hogans.

In addition to its excavations, Crow Canyon sponsors several field seminars, specialized programs for teachers and students of all ages, and the Anasazi Symposia, a series of 1-week, nondigging introductions to archeology.

**Admission:** Day programs, $25 adults, $12.50 children under 12.

**Open:** Last week of May through second week of Oct, Tues and Thurs 9am–4pm.

**LOWERY PUEBLO RUINS, County Rd. CC, 9 miles west of Pleasant View. Tel. 303/247-4082.**

An excavated 12th-century Anasazi village, 26 miles from Cortez via U.S. 666, Lowery Pueblo may have been a medieval ritual center. A self-guided interpretive trail leads past a great *kiva,* or circular spiritual chamber, to the remains of a painted *kiva* at 54 feet in diameter, one of the largest ever found. The Bureau of Land Management, which maintains this designated National Historic Landmark, also operates picnic grounds and rest-room facilities here.

**Admission:** Free.

**Open:** Daily 8am–sunset, year round (except when winter weather conditions close the gravel access road).

**UTE MOUNTAIN TRIBAL PARK, Towaoc. Tel. 303/565-3751, ext. 282,** or 303/565-4684.

If you liked Mesa Verde, but would have enjoyed the ruins more without the company of so many fellow tourists, you'll *love* the Ute Mountain Tribal Park. Set aside by the Ute Mountain Indian Reservation to preserve its Anasazi heritage, the 125,000-acre park—which abuts Mesa Verde National Park to the south and west—includes hundreds of surface ruins and cliff dwellings that compare in size and complexity with those in Mesa Verde, as well as wall paintings and ancient petroglyphs.

Accessibility to the Ute park, however, is strictly limited to guided tours by confirmed reservation. Full- and half-day tours begin at the Ute Mountain Pottery factory on U.S. 666, 15 miles south of Cortez; mountain-bike and backpacking trips are also offered. No food, lodging, gasoline, or other services are available within the park. Be sure to bring your own food and drinking water; and because you're expected to use your own vehicle for transportation within the park, make sure your gas tank is full: The main ruins are 40 miles off the paved roads. There's one primitive campground on the Mancos River for overnight stays.

**Admission:** Tours start at $25 per person.

**Open:** Full-day tours begin at 8am, half-day tours at 8am and noon, by confirmed reservation.

## WHERE TO STAY

**ANASAZI MOTOR INN, 666 S. Broadway, Cortez, CO 81321. Tel. 303/565-3773,** or 800/972-6232. Fax 303/565-1027. 85 rms, 2 suites (all with bath). A/C TV TEL

$ **Rates:** Memorial Day–Sept, $55 single; $61–$68 double. Oct–Memorial Day, $40 single; $44–$48 double. AE, DISC, MC, V.

A large motel on U.S. 666 south out of Cortez, the Anasazi boasts rooms with queen-size or double beds and standard motel furnishings. There's a large outdoor pool, a covered hot tub, a coffee shop (open daily from 5:30am to 10pm), and a lounge with live country-and-western entertainment Thursday through Saturday nights year round. The motel also has a gift shop.

**ARROW MOTEL, 440 S. Broadway, Cortez, CO 81321. Tel. 303/565-7778.** 30 rms (all with bath). A/C TV TEL

$ **Rates:** Memorial Day–Labor Day, $38 single; $48 double. Labor Day–Memorial Day, $24 single; $32 double. Children under 12 stay free in parents' room. AE, CB, DC, DISC, MC, V.

A small Ma and Pa–style motel, the Arrow is perfect for families on a budget. Flower boxes decorate the buildings, and facilities include an outdoor swimming pool, Jacuzzi, guest laundry, and picnic area with fenced playground. Twelve rooms have refrigerators and microwave ovens.

**CORTEZ INN, 2121 E. Main St., Cortez, CO 81321. Tel. 303/565-6000.** 99 rms, 1 suite (all with bath). A/C TV TEL

$ **Rates** (including continental breakfast): May–Sept, $47–$49 single; $58–$60 double, suite $66–88. Oct–Apr, $37–$39 single; $45–$47 double; suite $85. Children under 17 stay free in parents' room. AE, DISC, MC, V.

This handsome motel near the east (Mesa Verde) end of town is Cortez's largest. It has a spacious lobby and a large indoor swimming pool and Jacuzzi. Guest rooms typically have queen-size beds, with wood furnishings and regional decor. VCRs and videotapes are available for rental by guests.

**FAR VIEW LODGE, Mesa Verde National Park, ARA Mesa Verde Co., P.O. Box 277, Mancos, CO 81328. Tel. 303/529-4421.** Fax 303/533-7831. 150 rms (all with bath).

$ **Rates:** Mid-Apr to Memorial Day and first 3 weeks of Oct, $69 single or double; Memorial Day–Oct 1, $89 single or double. Additional person in same room, $6. Early May and Oct, second night free. **Closed:** Mid-Oct to mid-Apr. AE, CB, DC, MC, V.

Fourteen miles from the national park entrance, in the heart of Mesa Verde National Park, this facility lodges guests in 17 separate buildings spread across a hilltop. Rooms are cozy, with private balconies and southwestern decor, including original sand paintings. There's no TV or telephone, only the spirits of the Anasazi to keep you awake at night.

**Dining/Entertainment:** The Metate Room serves steak, seafood, and game specialties nightly from 5 to 9:30pm. Main courses range in price from $7.95 to $16.50. The Far View Lounge is open from 4 to 11pm. Multimedia shows are presented nightly at 6:30, 7:30, 8:30, and 9:30pm. The Far View Terrace, half a mile from the lodge, serves breakfast, lunch, and dinner from 7am to 9pm daily.

**Services:** 24-hour desk, complimentary morning coffee and newspaper.
**Facilities:** Gift shop, tour desk.

# WHERE TO DINE

**ANTONIO'S, 104 E. Main St. Tel. 565-9066.**
   **Cuisine:** MEXICAN.
   **$ Prices:** Appetizers $3.25–$5; main courses $4.95–$7.95 at lunch, $4.95–$13.95 at dinner. MC, V.
   **Open:** Daily 11am–10pm.
A wall-size mural of a Mexican mountain village dominates one wall, while a garden trellis beckons diners to a rear room. Hispanic music sets the mood for hearty portions of tacos, tostadas, enchiladas, chimichangas, "gringo burgers," or *chimeritos*—fried eggroll skins, stuffed with ground beef and topped with green chiles. A variety of steaks are also available.

**HOMESTEADERS RESTAURANT, 45 E. Main St. Tel. 565-6253.**
   **Cuisine:** AMERICAN/MEXICAN. **Reservations:** Recommended in summer.
   **$ Prices:** Appetizers $2–$4.30; main courses $3–$4.60 at lunch, $5.30–$11 at dinner. AE, MC, V.
   **Open:** Breakfast/lunch Mon–Sat 7am–3pm; dinner Mon–Sat 5–9pm.
A rustic barn provides the atmosphere for this popular family restaurant. A big waterwheel greets guests at the entrance, while throughout the dining room hang harnesses, skillets, and other pioneer artifacts. The menu ranges from tacos to chicken-fried steak, rainbow trout to barbecued spareribs.

**MILLWOOD JUNCTION, U.S. 160 and Main St., Mancos. Tel. 533-7338.**
   **Cuisine:** STEAK/SEAFOOD.
   **$ Prices:** Appetizers $3.25–$10.50; main courses $8.95–$22.50.
   **Open:** Dinner only, daily 5:30–10:30pm.
The atmosphere at this restaurant, 7 miles east (toward Durango) of the Mesa Verde National Park entrance, recalls a turn-of-the-century sawmilling industry that supported the Mancos-area economy. The food, though, is decidedly modern. House specials include the likes of steak au poivre and beer-battered catfish with pecan butter; you can also get pastas, pork ribs, and a variety of other steaks and seafood. On Friday night a seafood buffet draws folks from miles around.

**NERO'S, 303 W. Main St. Tel. 565-7366.**
   **Cuisine:** ITALIAN. **Reservations:** Recommended.
   **$ Prices:** Appetizers $3.75–$5.95; main courses $5.75–$13.95. AE, MC, V.
   **Open:** Dinner only, daily 5–10pm.
A small, quaint restaurant with a wrought-iron and stained-glass decor, Nero's doubles its capacity in summer when its outdoor patio opens up. Main courses—which include soup or salad and garlic bread—feature chicken Florentine, veal marsala, shrimp parmesan, and a variety of homemade pastas. Creative nightly specials include the likes of fresh marlin with a spicy garlic sauce and pork tenderloin with bourbon-cream sauce.

---

# 3. TELLURIDE

126 miles N of Durango, 127 miles S of Grand Junction

**GETTING THERE  By Plane**  The **Telluride Regional Airport,** atop a 9,000-foot plateau 5 miles west of Telluride, is served by **Continental Express** (tel. 303/728-3194, or 800/525-0280) year round from Denver, Grand Junction, and Montrose; and during the winter season by **United Express** (tel. 800/777-3980) from Denver, **Mesa Airlines** (tel. 303/728-4868, or 800/637-2247) from Albuquerque and Phoenix, and **SkyWest** (Delta) (tel. 800/453-9417) from Los Angeles. Visitors can also fly into airports in Montrose, Grand Junction, Durango, and Cortez, and travel by ground transportation to Telluride.

Limousine service to and from all these airports is provided by reservation by **Telluride Transit Company** (tel. 303/728-6000).

**By Car**   Telluride is reached via Colo. 145. From the north (Grand Junction) or south (Durango), turn west off U.S. 550 at Ridgway, onto Colo. 62. Proceed 25 miles to Placerville, and turn left (southeast) onto Colo. 145. The road junction to Cortez is 13 miles ahead; Telluride is another 4 miles, at the end of a box canyon.

**ESSENTIALS   Orientation**   Telluride has a population of about 1,300 and an elevation of 8,745 feet. The city is located on the **San Miguel River** where it flows out of a box canyon formed by the 14,000-foot peaks of the San Juan Mountains. Colo. 145, which enters town from the west, is known as **Colorado Avenue,** and is Telluride's main street. The main part of historic downtown runs five blocks west from Aspen Street to Willow Street; beyond here is the **Town Park**, site of many summer festivals. Columbia Avenue parallels Colorado Avenue to the north, Pacific Avenue to the south.

**Telluride Mountain Village,** some 750 feet higher than the historical town at 9,500 feet, is reached by ski lift (a gondola is planned) or by **Mountain Village Boulevard** off Colo. 145, a mile south of the Telluride junction.

**Information**   Contact the **Telluride Chamber Resort Association,** 666 West Colorado Avenue (P.O. Box 653), Telluride, CO 81435 (tel. 303/728-3041); or **Telluride Central Reservations,** P.O. Box 1009, Telluride, CO 81435 (tel. 800/525-3455).

**Getting Around**   In winter, the **San Miguel Transit Service** (tel. 728-4191) provides free daily bus service from November 20 to April 10. Buses run five times an hour in the town of Telluride; during peak ski season, shuttles operate to Telluride Mountain Village twice an hour from 7:30am to 4:30pm, and hourly until 9:30pm.

**Skip's Taxi** (tel. 728-6667) and **Telluride Transit** (tel. 728-6000) provide taxi service.

**Budget** (tel. 303/728-4642, or 800/221-2419) and **Hertz** (tel. 303/728-3163, or 800/654-3131) have car rentals at the airport.

If you're out drinking late at night and realize it's best not to drive, call the Telluride Marshal's Office for the **Tipsy Taxi** (tel. 728-3818), a free community service.

**Fast Facts**   The **area code** is 303. In case of **emergency,** call 728-3081. The **hospital,** Telluride Medical Center, is at 500 West Pacific Avenue (tel. 728-3848).

**SPECIAL EVENTS**   Telluride's annual events include **Surf the Rockies Week,** the first week of April; **Mountainfilm,** the weekend after Memorial Day; the **Bluegrass, Country & Acoustic Music Festival,** the third full weekend of June; the **Mid-Summer Music Festival** (contemporary), the third weekend of July; the **Jazz Celebration,** the first weekend of August; the **Chamber Music Festival,** for 11 days in mid-August; the **Mushroom Festival,** the fourth weekend of August; the **Film Festival,** Labor Day weekend; and **Torchlight Parades,** at the Telluride Ski Resort on Christmas Eve and New Year's Eve.

For information on events throughout the year, call Telluride's **festival hotline** (tel. 728-6079).

---

❚ncorporated in 1878 as the mining town of Columbia, Telluride took its modern name in the 1880s. Some say it was named for tellurium, a gold-bearing ore; others insist it was pidgin for "to hell you ride." This was a seriously rowdy town a century ago. In fact, Butch Cassidy robbed his first bank here. A gold boom followed on the heels of the silver crash of 1893, and lead, copper, and zinc were mined as late as 1978.

But after 1930, when the Bank of Telluride closed and the town's population had dwindled to 500 from a high of 3,000, Telluride was a dying town.

In 1968 entrepreneur Joe Zoline set to work on a "winter recreation area second to none." The Telluride Ski Company opened its first runs in 1972, and Telluride was a boom town again. Telluride's first summer festivals (bluegrass in June, film in September) were celebrated the following year. Today Telluride is a major summer and winter destination resort.

# WHAT TO SEE & DO
## HISTORIC TELLURIDE

As a National Historic District, Telluride has many fascinating historic buildings. A walking tour described in the seasonal *Telluride Vacation Guide* suggests a detailed route.

Start at the **San Miguel County Courthouse,** at Colorado Avenue at Oak Street. Built in 1887, it remains in use today. A block north and west, at Columbia Avenue and Aspen Street, is the **L. L. Nunn House,** home of the late 19th-century mining engineer who created the first high-voltage alternating-current power plant in the world. George Westinghouse provided the generators, Nikola Tesla designed the motor, and by 1894, the entire town of Telluride and most nearby mines were electrically lighted.

Walk two blocks east on Columbia Avenue and two blocks north on Fir Street to the **San Miguel County Historical Museum,** 317 North Fir Street (tel. 728-3344). Photographs and artifacts here recall Telluride's mining heyday. The museum is open from Memorial Day to mid-October, daily from 10am to 5pm.

Two blocks east of Fir Street, on Galena Avenue at Spruce Street, is **St. Patrick's Catholic Church,** built in 1895. Its wooden Stations of the Cross figures were carved in Austria's Tyrol region. Ironically, the church wasn't far from Telluride's red-light district, known as **Popcorn Alley,** three blocks south around Spruce and Pacific.

Perhaps Telluride's most famous landmark is the **Sheridan Hotel and Opera House.** Located opposite the County Courthouse (the starting point of this tour) at Colorado and Oak (tel. 728-4351), it was built in 1895 and in its early days rivaled Denver's Brown Palace Hotel in service and cuisine. The exquisite Opera House was added in 1914, and boasted a Venetian scene painted on its roll curtain. Both establishments are still in business today.

## OTHER ATTRACTIONS

**BRIDAL VEIL FALLS, Colorado Ave. (Colo. 145).**
Colorado's highest waterfall (365 feet) can be seen from almost any point in Telluride, but most readily from the east end of Colorado Avenue. The falls freeze in winter, then slowly melt in early spring, creating a dramatic effect. Perched at the top edge of the falls is a national historic landmark, a hydroelectric power plant that served area mines at the turn of the century. Accessible by hiking or driving a switchback, four-wheel-drive road, the plant is currently under restoration by a private entrepreneur who hopes to once again supply power to Telluride.

**TELLURIDE SKI RESORT, 562 Mountain Village Rd. (P.O. Box 11155), Telluride, CO 81435. Tel. 303/728-3856,** or 728-3614 for snow reports.
Two separate communities—Victorian Telluride at its base and the European-style Mountain Village Resort at midslope—offer an atmosphere not found elsewhere in North America. With the Doral Telluride Resort and Spa, the largest ski-resort spa on the continent, having opened in 1992, Telluride is becoming more than just an alpine lookalike.

The mountain has four divisions. The **Front Face,** which drops sharply from the mountain's summit to the town of Telluride, is characterized by steep moguls, tree and glade skiing, and challenging groomed pitches for experts and advanced intermediates. **Gorrono Basin,** which rises from the Mountain Village Resort, caters to intermediate skiers. The broad, gentle slopes of **The Meadows** stretch beneath

Gorrono Basin to the foot of **Sunshine Peak.** This mountain, with trails over 2½ miles long devoted entirely to novice skiers, is served by the world's longest high-speed quad chair. There are seven on-mountain restaurants, including **Gorrono Ranch,** a historic homestead in the middle of Gorrono Basin.

In all, Telluride offers 656 acres of skiable terrain. The vertical drop is an impressive 3,165 feet from the 11,890-foot summit. The mountain has 43 trails served by 10 lifts (one quad chair, two triples, six doubles, and a Poma) with an uphill capacity of 10,000 skiers per hour. There are an additional 40km (24 miles) of nordic trails, and helicopter skiing is also available. Average annual snowfall is 300 inches (25 ft.).

For summer visitors, the **Coonskin Scenic Chair Lift** operates mid-June through mid-September, Thursday through Sunday from 10am to 2pm. The base facility is at Mahoney Drive and Pacific Street in downtown Telluride.

**Admission:** $36 adults, to as low as $31 per day for multiday tickets; $20 children 6–12, $22 per day seniors 65–69, free for children under 6 and seniors over 69. Class lessons start at $35.

**Open:** Thanksgiving to early Apr, daily 9am–4pm.

## SPORTS & RECREATION

**BALLOONING** You can get a lift aloft with **San Juan Balloon Adventures,** 516 South Amelia Street, Ridgway (tel. 728-5104).

**BICYCLING** Telluride is a major mountain-biking center. The **San Juan Hut System** links the town with Moab, Utah, via a 215-mile-long network of backcountry dirt roads. Every 35 miles are primitive cabins, each with bunks and cooking gear. System offices are at 224 East Colorado Avenue (tel. 728-6935).

Bicycle sales, rentals, and repairs are handled by **Olympic Sports,** 150 West Colorado Avenue (tel. 728-4477), and **Paragon Sports,** 213 West Colorado Avenue (tel. 728-4525). Guided tours are offered by **Telluride Outside,** 666 West Colorado Avenue (tel. 728-3895).

**FISHING** There's good fishing in the **San Miguel River** through Telluride, but even better in nearby alpine lakes, including **Silver Lake,** reached by foot in Bridal Veil Basin, and **Trout and Priest Lakes,** 12 miles south on Colo. 145.

Equipment, licenses, and fly-fishing instruction are offered by **Olympic Sports,** 150 West Colorado Avenue (tel. 728-4477), and **Telluride Outside,** 666 West Colorado Avenue (tel. 728-3895).

**GOLF** The new 18-hole **Telluride Golf Club** is located at Telluride Mountain Village (tel. 728-8000).

**HIKING & MOUNTAINEERING** Sporting-goods stores have maps of trails in the Telluride area. Especially popular is the 1-mile **San Miguel River Corridor Trail** through Telluride, and the 1½-mile walk to the foot of **Bridal Veil Falls,** at the east end of Telluride Canyon.

Guided mountain expeditions can be arranged through **Antoine Savelli Guides,** 335 North Willow Street (tel. 728-3705), or **Fantasy Ridge Mountain Guides,** 205 West Colorado Avenue (tel. 728-3546).

**HORSEBACK RIDING** See **Many Ponies** on Silver Pick Road (tel. 728-6278) or **Telluride Outfitters,** 666 West Colorado Avenue (tel. 728-3895).

**ICE SKATING** There's ice skating daily in winter, and from 7 to 10pm on Wednesday nights, at the Town Park (tel. 728-3851). Skate rentals are available.

**SKIING [NORDIC]** Nordic skiers will also find rentals and instruction at the **Telluride Nordic Center** in Town Park (tel. 728-3404).

**SNOWMOBILING** Tours are offered by **Telluride Outside,** 666 West Colorado Avenue (tel. 728-3895).

**SWIMMING** There's a public pool, as well as tennis courts, at **Telluride Town Park,** Maple Street at Colorado Avenue (tel. 728-3071).

# WHERE TO STAY

## EXPENSIVE

**DORAL TELLURIDE RESORT & SPA, 624 Mountain Village Blvd., Mountain Village Resort, Telluride, CO 81435. Tel. 303/728-3741.** 177 rms. TV TEL
**$ Rates:** To be announced.
Scheduled to open at Mountain Village Resort in April 1992, this hotel will be the largest ski-resort spa in North America. Located at the foot of the Gorrono Basin slopes, with an 18-hole championship golf course on its flank, the Doral promises to be one of Colorado's premier properties.

**PENNINGTON'S MOUNTAIN VILLAGE INN, 100 Pennington Court (P.O. Box 2428), Mountain Village Resort, Telluride, CO 81435. Tel. 303/728-5337,** or 800/543-1437. 12 rms (all with bath). TV TEL
**$ Rates** (single or double, including breakfast): $150 Jan to early Feb, $175 early Feb to early Apr, $120 early Apr to early June, $150 early June to early Sept, $140; early Sept to Thanksgiving week, $235 Thanksgiving and Christmas hols, $150 weeks between hols. AE, CB, DC, DISC, MC, V.
Located just off Colo. 145 at the entrance to Telluride Mountain Village, high above the San Miguel River valley, Pennington's is indeed a luxurious getaway. This is the ultimate in bed and breakfasts, with French country decor throughout. Every room has king-size or queen-size beds, private decks, and refrigerators stocked with alcoholic beverages—included in the price of the room. Breakfast can be served in your room (if you so choose) at your convenience. There's a daily happy hour (actually two hours); a library lounge with books, games, and a large fireplace; an indoor Jacuzzi and steam room; guest laundry facilities; and lockers for ski and golf equipment.

## MODERATE

**CIMARRON LODGE, 568 W. Pacific Ave. (P.O. Box 756), Telluride, CO 81435. Tel. 303/728-3803,** or 800/233-9292. Fax 303/728-5236. 52 units (40 suites). TV TEL
**$ Rates:** Summer season, $55–$65 single or double; $80–$85 suite. Summer festival weekends, $100–$110 single or double; $120–$134 suite. Peak winter season (Feb–Mar), $120–$130 single or double; $150–$161 suite. Christmas hols, $160–$170 single or double; $200–$207 suite. The rest of the ski season, $90–$95 single or double; $110–$115 suite. AE, MC, V. **Parking:** Free, underground.
A luxury lodging with a premier location at the foot of the Coonskin chair, the Cimarron offers a dozen charming bed and breakfast–style hotel rooms and a wide choice of one-, two-, and three-bedroom condominiums. Each hotel room is like a small studio apartment with a queen-size bed, sleeper sofa, and kitchenette (with microwave oven and mini-refrigerator). Condo suites include full living rooms and kitchens (complete with dishwashers) and private decks.
Within the lodge complex is Cassidy's Restaurant & Bar and a conference center that seats 120. Other facilities include ski shops and boutiques, a guest laundry, swimming pool, sauna, and a beautiful tile spa overlooking the San Miguel River.

**ICE HOUSE LODGE, San Juan Ave. and Fir St. (P.O. Box 2909), Telluride, CO 81435. Tel. 303/728-6300,** or 800/544-3436. 50 rms (all with bath). MINIBAR TV TEL
**$ Rates** (single or double, including continental breakfast): $70–$95 summer season, $100–$125 summer festival weekends, $115–$140 peak winter season (Feb–Mar), $140–$175 Christmas hols, $85–$110 rest of the ski season. AE, CB, DC, DISC, MC, V. **Parking:** Free, covered lot.
A full-service hotel just half a block from the Oak Street chair lift, the Ice House

offers casual luxury in the European alpine style. Stairs or an elevator ascend from the ground-floor entrance to the lobby, where bright furnishings and southwestern motifs prevail. The decor carries to the guest rooms, each of which has a king-size bed and sleeper sofa or two queen-size beds, European comforters, an oversize tub, and a gorgeous mountain view from a private deck. Room service from La Marmotte French restaurant next door is available in season, and there are a hot tub and steam room in the basement.

**MANITOU HOTEL, south end of Fir St. (P.O. Box 756), Telluride, CO 81435. Tel. 303/728-3803,** or 800/233-9292. Fax 303/728-5236. 11 rms (all with bath). TV TEL
$ **Rates** (single or double, including breakfast): $70–$80 summer season, $95–$115 summer festival weekends, $105–$115 peak winter season (Feb–Mar), $125–$150 Christmas hols, $85–$95 the rest of the ski season. AE, MC, V.
A hideaway for devoted skiers just steps from the Oak Street chair lift, this bed-and-breakfast hotel keeps things cozy—and friendly. Larger rooms sleep six, with two double beds in a loft and a sleeper sofa downstairs, plus a small kitchen. Most rooms have queen-size beds with sleeper sofas and three-quarter baths, or two double beds and a separate bathroom and toilet. Furnishings are basic; guests spend more time in the hotel hot tub than in their rooms when they're not sleeping. The hotel serves breakfast in the morning, complimentary wine and cheese in the afternoon (after skiing).

**RIVERSIDE CONDOMINUMS, 450–460 S. Pine St. (P.O. Box 276), Telluride, CO 81435. Tel. 303/728-4311,** or 800/852-0015. 70 rms.
$ **Rates:** Summer, $85 one-bedroom; $110 two-bedroom; festival weeks, $170–$205. Winter, $95–$125 early/late ski season, $192–$355 Christmas hols, $125–$185 Jan, $185–$245 Feb–Mar. AE, MC, V. Minimum lengths of stay may be required at busy times.
A luxury condo on the south bank of the San Miguel River, literally on the lower slopes of Telluride Mountain, rooms at the Riverside are among the best available in the town of Telluride. Decor varies, but rooms typically have fireplaces, entertainment centers, private decks or balconies, steam showers, and hot-water heaters. Upper-story rooms are especially spacious, with posh furnishings and fully stocked kitchens, complete with microwave ovens and dishwashers.

## INEXPENSIVE

**THE DAHL HAUS, 122 S. Oak St. (P.O. Box 695), Telluride, CO 81435. Tel. 303/728-4158.** 9 rms (1 with bath).
$ **Rates** (including breakfast): Summer, $32 single, $40 double; festival weeks, $60 single or double. Winter, $40–$45 single, $50–$55 double; hol period, $60 single or double. MC, V.
A century ago this was a boarding house for miners; today it's one of downtown Telluride's best lodging bargains. With Victorian antique furnishings, handmade quilts and curtains, and a TV room/library, it maintains a homey atmosphere. Adjoining condominiums, priced $55 to $110 in summer, higher in winter and during festival weeks, have private baths and kitchens, plus a common Jacuzzi and guest laundry.

**NEW SHERIDAN HOTEL, 231 W. Colorado Ave. (P.O. Box 980), Telluride, CO 81435. Tel. 303/728-4351.** 23 rms (about half with bath), 1 suite. TV TEL
$ **Rates** (single or double): Spring and fall seasons, $29 without bath, $49 with bath. The rest of the year, $39–$59 Memorial Day–Labor Day, $39–$69 early ski season, $79–$139 Christmas hols, $52–$99 Jan, $89–$109 Feb to early Apr. Children under 14 stay free in parents' room. MC, V.
The pride of Telluride when it was built in 1895, the New Sheridan reached the peak of its fame in 1902 when presidential candidate William Jennings Bryan delivered a famous speech from a platform outside. The hotel closed in 1925 and didn't reopen until 1977. Now it has been extensively renovated, and returned to the Victorian era

with brass beds, oak furniture, and stained-glass lamp fixtures. About half the rooms are without private baths. The Continental Room restaurant and Sheridan bar—with its Austrian-made cherrywood bar—are on the first floor.

**THE VICTORIAN INN, 401 W. Pacific Ave. (P.O. Box 217), Telluride, CO 81435. Tel. 303/728-6601,** or 800/537-2614. 26 rms (20 with bath). TV TEL
**$ Rates** (including continental breakfast): Spring, summer, and fall, $35 single without bath; $42–$46 single with bath; $39 double without bath, $49–$53 double with bath. Festival weeks, $63–$80 single; $69–$86 double. Winter except Christmas, $47–$62 single; $47–$66 double. Christmas holidays, $76–$95 single; $82–$104 double. AE, MC, V.

Built in 1976 in keeping with the turn-of-the-century flavor of the town of Telluride, the Victorian is a budget guest lodge offering rooms with either private or shared baths. Rooms are fully carpeted, with individually controlled heating. The hotel has a sauna and hot tub for sore skiers.

# WHERE TO DINE
## EXPENSIVE

**CAMPAGNA, 435 W. Pacific Ave. Tel. 728-6190.**
   **Cuisine:** ITALIAN. **Reservations:** Recommended.
**$ Prices:** Appetizers $6.50–$7.95; main courses $13.50–$25. Prices discounted 30% off-season. AE, MC, V.
   **Open:** Memorial Day–Labor Day and late Nov to early Apr, dinner only, daily 5–10pm.

Recalling his parents' home in Tuscany, chef Vincent Esposito has converted an old miner's house into an open, friendly, country-style Italian restaurant. He changes the menu nightly, but it always includes wild game. Boar is a favorite, along with pheasant and quail. The pollo e salsiccia in umido (chicken and spicy sausage in broth, served over grilled polenta) is especially tasty. There's a good selection of antipasti and pastas to start, and home-cooked desserts to finish.

**LA MARMOTTE, 150 W. San Juan Ave. Tel. 728-6232.**
   **Cuisine:** FRENCH. **Reservations:** Recommended.
**$ Prices:** Appetizers $4.75–$10.75; main courses $13.50–$23.95. AE, MC, V.
   **Open:** June–Sept, dinner daily 6–10pm; brunch Sun 10am–2pm. Dec to early Apr, dinner only, daily 6–10pm.

In a tiny house of exposed brick and weathered wood beside the Ice House Lodge—in fact, this building *was* Telluride's ice house at the turn of the century—Bertrand and Nöelle Lepel-Cointet have fashioned a memorable dining experience. This is country-style French cuisine at its finest. Start with le feuilleté d'huitres au champagne (oysters in puff pastry with a champagne sauce) or salade de faisan fumé (a smoked-pheasant salad with mango, avocado, and grapes). Then enjoy a main dish, which could be a daily special, côtes d'agneau aux noisettes (lamb chops in a hazelnut crust with a cranberry-and-pepper coulis), or canard aux framboises (grilled duck with a raspberry demiglace and vegetable mousses).

## MODERATE

**THE ATHENIAN SENATE, 123 S. Spruce St. Tel. 728-3018.**
   **Cuisine:** GREEK. **Reservations:** Recommended.
**$ Prices:** Appetizers $3.25–$9.95; main courses $6.95–$18.95. AE, MC, V.
   **Open:** Late May to late Sept and late Nov to early Apr, daily 5pm–3am.

Located in the heart of Popcorn Alley, Telluride's historic red-light district, the Senate was the home in the early 20th century of "Big Billy," perhaps the town's best-known madam. It closed in 1935 and reopened as a restaurant in 1967. Especially noted for its late-night menu, it offers a full slate of such Greek favorites as spanakopita (spinach pie) and saganaki (flamed kasseri cheese), gyro sandwiches and kefthethes (meatballs), as well as such filling dishes as moussaka (both meat and vegetarian), dolamathes (stuffed grape leaves), and lamb Stroganoff.

**EXCELSIOR CAFE, 200 W. Colorado Ave. Tel. 728-4250.**
   **Cuisine:** INTERNATIONAL. **Reservations:** Recommended.
 $ **Prices:** Breakfast $2.75–$6.95, lunch $4.75–$6.95; dinner appetizers $5.95–$7.50, main dishes $9.75–$17.95. MC, V.
   **Open:** Memorial Day–Labor Day and late Nov to early Apr, breakfast/lunch daily 7:30am–2:30pm; dinner daily 5:30–9:30pm.

The building occupied by this charming restaurant was a bowling alley in the 1890s; now it's so charming with its brick walls, pressed-tin ceilings, and spiral staircase, you could still hear a pin drop. Breakfast features eggs Benedict, Florentine, and Excelsior (scrambled with smoked salmon and hollandaise); lunches include pasta Sicilia (penne with broccoli and pine nuts in a tomato sauce) and a variety of deli-style sandwiches. Dinner is more upscale: Start with venison terrine or lobster and Brie, then move on to Annamese grilled shrimp, vegetable strudel, cheese fondue, or beef tenderloin stuffed with crabmeat and vegetables. The espresso machine is always active.

**SILVERGLADE, 115 W. Colorado Ave. Tel. 728-4943.**
   **Cuisine:** CREATIVE AMERICAN. **Reservations:** Recommended.
 $ **Prices:** Appetizers $6.95–$8.50; main courses $12.95–$16.95. MC, V.
   **Open:** Late May to mid-Sept and mid-Nov to mid-Apr, dinner only, Mon–Sat 5:30–10:30pm.

This new addition to the Telluride dining scene has been welcomed by locals, especially those who love fresh seafood. Sushi (the only sushi in over 100 miles) is an overwhelmingly popular appetizer. Main courses vary nightly, according to what seafood is available. They might include a linguine with smoked salmon, asparagus, mushrooms, and lemon cream; shrimp grilled in a garlic black-bean sauce or curried à la Thai; or veal with roasted red peppers, marsala, and mushrooms.

## INEXPENSIVE

**DELI DOWNSTAIRS, 217 W. Colorado Ave. Tel. 728-4004.**
   **Cuisine:** DELI.
 $ **Prices:** $1–$7.25. MC, V.
   **Open:** Daily 8:30am–midnight.

This pleasant basement delicatessen has a loyal local following for its sandwiches, like the Logpile (German sausage and sauerkraut), the Dewdrop (crab salad), and the Plunge (ham, roast beef, turkey, avocado, and two cheeses). It also serves a variety of burritos (including the breakfast burrito) and tacos, as well as delicious milkshakes and ice-cream sundaes.

**EDDIE'S, 300 W. Colorado Ave. Tel. 728-5335.**
   **Cuisine:** PIZZA/PASTA. **Reservations:** Not necessary.
 $ **Prices:** $5.80–$22. AE, MC, V.
   **Open:** Lunch Mon–Fri 11:30am–2pm; dinner daily 5:30–10pm.

One of the few Telluride restaurants that doesn't close during the slow periods between summer and winter visitor seasons, Eddie's specializes in New York–style pizza and gourmet pasta in a casually elegant atmosphere. The build-your-own pizza menu offers 26 different toppings; typical of the choices is the California Dreamin' blend of artichoke hearts, sun-dried and fresh tomatoes, avocado, and mozzarella and Gorgonzola cheeses. Pasta includes spinach and chicken canneloni, and a tortellini with smoked salmon.

**FLORADORA, 103 W. Colorado Ave. Tel. 728-3888.**
   **Cuisine:** AMERICAN/SOUTHWESTERN REGIONAL. **Reservations:** Recommended.
 $ **Prices:** Appetizers $3.25–$5.50; main courses $4.75–$7.25 at lunch, $10.95–$13.95 at dinner. MC, V.
   **Open:** Daily 11am–10pm. **Closed:** Mid-Apr to mid-May and mid-Oct to mid-Nov.

A Telluride dining institution for decades, this rustic saloon was named for two "working girls" of the mining era, Flora and Dora. Their images grace the menu and other decor. House specialties, including the Floradora burger, chicken sandwich, and fajitas, are topped with grilled onions, green peppers, and cheese. Steaks and seafood, including local trout and Alaskan halibut, highlight the dinner menu.

**GREGOR'S BAKERY AND CAFE, 217 E. Colorado Ave. Tel. 728-3334.**
   **Cuisine:** VEGETARIAN.
$ **Prices:** Breakfast $2.75–$5.25; lunch $3.95–$5.80; dinner $5.50–$9.90. MC, V.
   **Open:** Mon–Fri 6:30am–1pm, Sat–Sun 5–9pm.
The atmosphere here is simple, with wooden tables in a rustic building, but the cuisine is elaborate, and geared toward natural-foods lovers. Breakfast dishes include raspberry granola and macadamia-nut oatmeal pancakes. Lunches include a black-bean chile soup and a "Number Seven" sandwich—hummus, tomato, and spinach on seven-grain bread. But dinners are the real production, with dishes such as chiles relleños (with pecans and raisins), vegetarian lasagne, and uppma bhara bandghobi (cabbage leaves stuffed with quinoa, peppers, and onions, served on zucchini pancakes, and topped with tomato sauce). Wine and beer are available.

**T-RIDE COUNTRY CLUB, 333 W. Colorado Ave. Tel. 728-6344.**
   **Cuisine:** STEAK/SEAFOOD. **Reservations:** Not necessary.
$ **Prices:** $7.95–$14.95. MC, V.
   **Open:** Dinner only, daily 5–10pm.
There's no golf course at this country club, on a second story overlooking Telluride's main street. Instead, there's a large, essentially nondescript room where diners are encouraged to cook their own steaks, chicken, or seafood and indulge themselves at the town's largest salad bar. Hungry guests order their cut from a counter, throw it on a grill, then watch and wait for it to be ready.

---

# 4. OURAY

73 miles N of Durango, 96 miles S of Grand Junction

**GETTING THERE   By Bus**   Coaches of **TNM&O,** U.S. 550 (tel. 303/259-2755), stop in Ouray on their run between Durango and Grand Junction.

**By Car**   U.S. 550 runs through the heart of Ouray, connecting it with Durango to the south and—via U.S. 50, which it joins at Montrose—Grand Junction (and I-70) to the north.

**ESSENTIALS   Orientation**   Ouray is basically a one-street town. As you enter from the north on U.S. 550, which parallels the Uncompahgre River, the highway passes the Ouray Hot Springs Pool and becomes known as **Main Street.** Most civic buildings are a block east of Main, on Sixth Avenue at Fourth Street; several motels are three blocks farther south on Third Avenue, and west on First Street. Above Third Avenue, U.S. 550 begins its climb up switchbacks to the Million Dollar Highway. Ouray has an elevation of 7,800 feet and a population of about 700.

**Information**   Stop in the **Ouray Visitor Center** beside the Hot Springs Pool, on U.S. 550 at the north end of town; or contact the **Ouray County Chamber of Commerce,** P.O. Box 145, Ouray, CO 81427 (tel. 303/325-4746, or 800/228-1876).
   The **Ouray Historical Museum** (see "What to See & Do," below, has self-guided walking tour maps.

**Getting Around**   Ouray is so small—about eight blocks long and five blocks wide—that the only practical way to travel around the community is on foot.

**Fast Facts**   The **area code** is 303. In case of **emergency,** dial 0 (zero) for the operator. There's a **medical clinic** on the south side of town, on Third Avenue at Second Street. The **post office** is on Main Street, between Sixth Avenue and Seventh Avenue.

**SPECIAL EVENTS**   Annual events in Ouray include **Cabin Fever Days,** in mid-February; the **Top of the Rockies Draft Horse Pull and Western**

**Celebration,** on the weekend following July 4; the **Ouray County Fair,** the last weekend of August; and the **Imogene Mountain Run,** the first weekend of September.

---

**N**amed for the greatest chief of the Southern Ute tribe, whose homeland was in this area, Ouray got its start in the 1880s as a gold- and silver-mining camp. Today Ouray is a major center for exploring the ghost towns of the San Juan Mountains.

## WHAT TO SEE & DO

**BOX CANYON FALLS, Oak St. above Third Ave. Tel. 325-4464.**
Located at the southwest corner of Ouray, these falls are among the most impressive in the Rockies. The Uncompahgre River tumbles 285 feet through—not over, *through*—a solid cliff: It's easy to get a feeling of vertigo as you study the spectacle. The trail to the bottom of the falls is easy; to the top it is strenuous.
**Admission:** $1.25 adults, 75¢ children and seniors.
**Open:** Mid-May to mid-Oct.

**OURAY HISTORICAL MUSEUM, Sixth Ave. at Fifth St. Tel. 325-4576.**
Lodged in the original Miners' Hospital, built in 1887 by the Sisters of Mercy, this three-story museum is packed to its rafters with fascinating exhibits from Ouray's past. Displays include pioneer and mining-era relics, memorabilia of Chief Ouray and the Utes, Victorian hospital equipment, and photographs and other archival materials. Ask here for a walking-tour guide to the town's many historic buildings.
**Admission:** By donation.
**Open:** May–June 14 and Sept–Oct 15, Mon–Sat 10am–4pm, Sun 1–4pm; June 15–Aug, Mon–Fri 9am–6pm, Sat 9am–5pm, Sun 1–5pm; Oct 16–Apr, Wed–Sun 1–4pm.

**OURAY HOT SPRINGS POOL, U.S. 550, at the north end of Ouray. Tel. 325-4638.**
This pool, 250 feet long and 150 feet wide, holds nearly a million gallons of odorless mineral water. Spring water is cooled from 150°; the pool here is normally 80°, but there's a hot soak of 104°.
**Admission:** $4 adults, $3.50 students 13–17, $2.75 children 5–12 and seniors.
**Open:** Summer, Mon–Sat 9am–10pm, Sun 9am–7pm; winter, Wed–Mon noon–9pm.

## WHERE TO STAY

**THE MAIN STREET HOUSE, 334 Main St. (P.O. Box 87), Ouray, CO 81427. Tel. 303/325-4317.** 3 suites.
**$ Rates:** $50–$60 single or double. MC, V.
A turn-of-the-century home that has been fully restored, this house offers quiet and privacy just a few steps from the center of downtown. The Hayden Mountain Suite, which occupies the entire upstairs, has private decks on both sides of the house. The Oak Creek Suite includes a greenhouse, and both it and the adjacent Cascade Suite have futon sofas that convert to second beds.

**OURAY VICTORIAN INN, 50 Third Ave. (P.O. Box 1812), Ouray, CO 81427. Tel. 303/325-4064,** or 800/443-7361, 800/233-0392 in Colorado. 34 rms, 4 suites (all with bath). TV TEL
**$ Rates:** June 15–Sept, $46 single; $48 double; $68–$72 suite. Apr–June 14 and Oct–Jan 15, $32 single; $34–$36 double; $46–$54 suite. **Closed:** Jan 16–Mar. AE, DISC, MC, V.
A pretty two-story motel with gabled windows just below Box Canyon Falls, the Victorian also has two outdoor hot tubs and a sun deck. Rooms have a king-size bed and sofa sleeper or two queen-size beds, and standard furnishings. A guest laundry and a games room are bonuses.

**ST. ELMO HOTEL, 426 Main St. (P.O. Box 667), Ouray, CO 81427. Tel. 303/325-4951.** 9 rms (all with bath).
$ **Rates:** June 14–Sept, $68–$78 single or double; Oct–June 13, $50–$62 single or double. MC, V.
An 1898 town landmark that has been restored in art deco style, the St. Elmo has an old-fashioned lobby that's a meeting place for locals and guests alike. Its rooms, all with private baths, contain many original furnishings. Throughout are stained glass, polished wood, and brass trim. There's a television in the parlor, and an outdoor hot tub and sauna for guests. In the basement is the Bon Ton Restaurant (see "Where to Dine," below).

**WIESBADEN HOT SPRINGS SPA & LODGINGS, Sixth Ave. and Fifth St. (P.O. Box 349), Ouray, CO 81427. Tel. 303/325-4347.** 18 rms, 3 suites (all with bath). TV
$ **Rates:** $70–$90 double; $95–$110 suite. Rates discounted Sun–Thurs in winter. JCB, MC, V.
Built over a continually flowing hot-springs vapor cave, the Wiesbaden need never worry about artificial heating. The swimming pool, though outdoors, is open year round and heated to between 95° and 102°; massages, facials, and other spa services are always available. There's also a weight and exercise room, a sauna and a "flow-through" Jacuzzi. The original structure here was built in 1879. Today's rooms have an "old country" ambience with old photographs on the walls. Some rooms with outside entrances have small refrigerators and coffee makers; the Hill Cottage has its own wood stove; and the Sun Room, built into the natural rock above the vapor cave, has a piano and fireplace.

## WHERE TO DINE

**BON TON RESTAURANT, in the St. Elmo Hotel, 426 Main St. Tel. 325-4951.**
**Cuisine:** ITALIAN. **Reservations:** Recommended.
$ **Prices:** Appetizers $2.25–$5.50; main courses $8.75–$17. MC, V.
**Open:** Dinner daily 5–9pm; brunch Sun 10am–1pm.
A fixture in Ouray for more than a century—it had another location before moving into the St. Elmo Hotel basement in 1898—the Bon Ton is Ouray's finest. With stone outer walls, hardwood floors, and reproduction antique furnishings, it carries a Victorian rustic appeal. The menu includes a variety of pasta dishes, from tortellini carbonara to ravioli pesto; a "miners medley" of sautéed veal, sausage, and chicken on fettuccine; and various beef, veal, chicken, and fresh seafood dishes. There's a children's menu, too.

**SILVER NUGGET CAFE, 746 Main St. Tel. 325-4100.**
**Cuisine:** AMERICAN/MEXICAN. **Reservations:** Not necessary.
$ **Prices:** Breakfast $2.50–$5.75; lunch $3.25–$5.25; dinner $4.95–$11.95. No credit cards.
**Open:** Daily 7am–7pm. **Closed:** Christmas Day.
A clean, contemporary eatery, the Silver Nugget occupies a historic building at the north end of Ouray. You can get a Denver omelet or huevos rancheros for breakfast, and a wide variety of deli-style sandwiches for lunch. The dinner menu runs the gamut from liver and onions to fish and chips, ribeye steak to steak fajitas.
Alamosa and points east. It's also at the junction of U.S. 84, which runs south from here to Santa Fe, New Mexico.

# 5. PAGOSA SPRINGS

55 miles E of Durango, 89 miles W of Alamosa

**GETTING THERE  By Car**  U.S. 160 connects Pagosa Springs with Durango and points west, and Alamosa and points east. It's also at the junction of U.S. 84, which runs south from here to Santa Fe, New Mexico.

**ESSENTIALS** **Orientation** Pagosa Springs has a population of about 1,400 and an elevation around 7,000 feet. The city is located on the banks of the **San Juan River,** which flows southwest from Wolf Creek Pass through Farmington, New Mexico, eventually joining the Colorado River in Utah. **Pagosa Street** (U.S. 160) parallels the river through downtown until the river turns south. **Lightplant Road,** which crosses the river opposite the Town Park, passes the Pagosa hot springs. U.S. 84 intersects U.S. 160 at the eastern edge of the town.

**Information** Consult the **Pagosa Springs Chamber of Commerce,** P.O. Box 787, Pagosa Springs, CO 81147 (tel. 303/264-2360, or 800/252-2204). The chamber has a new visitor center on the south bank of the San Juan River at Lightplant Road.

**Fast Facts** The **area code** is 303. In case of **emergency,** dial 911. The **hospital,** Pagosa Clinic, is next to the town hall and police station on Pagosa Street near Fifth Street. The **post office** is at the corner of Lightplant Road and Lewis Street, a block north of the highway.

**SPECIAL EVENTS** The **Red Ryder Roundup** is held on the Fourth of July weekend.

---

**P**agosa (Ute for "healing waters") took its name from the thermal springs that spurt from the ground at 153°. There was no major white settlement here, however, until 1878, when Fort Lewis was constructed to help control the Utes. The town was incorporated in 1891, and although the spa never became a great commercial success, Pagosa Springs grew as an important lumbering center. Today it's a major recreational center, with hunting and fishing in summer, skiing at nearby Wolf Creek Pass in winter.

## WHAT TO SEE & DO

**FRED HARMAN ART MUSEUM, U.S. 160, 2 miles west of Pagosa Springs. Tel. 731-5785.**
The original works of Fred Harman, originator of the "Red Ryder" and "Little Beaver" comic strips and a great deal of rodeo and western movie art, are on exhibit.
**Admission:** $2 adults, $1 children.
**Open:** Mon–Fri 10:30am–5pm, Sat 10am–4pm, Sun noon–4pm.

**PAGOSA HOT SPRINGS, Lightplant Rd. south of the San Juan River.**
There's not much to see at the springs themselves, but interpretive signs describe their history and mineral content, and a path leads to an overlook. You wouldn't want to swim in these 153° waters anyway. A nearby motel has a hot-springs pool (see "Where to Stay," below). The water is high in sulfur, bicarbonate, sodium, chloride, potassium, silica, and magnesium. There are also significant parts fluoride, lithium, and boron, and tiny percentages of manganese, arsenic, iron, and zinc.

**WOLF CREEK SKI AREA, U.S. 160, 25 miles east of Pagosa Springs (P.O. Box 1036, Pagosa Springs, CO 81147). Tel. 303/731-5605.**
Wolf Creek is famous throughout Colorado as the area that consistently has the most snow. In fact, its annual average of 465 inches (almost 39 ft.) of powder exceeds any other resort in the Rocky Mountains. The region's topography is just right to capture cold fronts from all directions.
One of the state's oldest ski areas, Wolf Creek has terrain for skiers of all ability levels, but especially intermediates. Expert skiers often leave the lift-served slopes to dive down the powder of the **Water Fall Area,** then await pickup by a snowcat shuttle that returns them to the base area. Backcountry tours are offered by appointment.
In all, the area boasts 700 acres of terrain, with a vertical drop of 1,425 feet from the 11,775-foot summit. The mountain has 31 trails served by six lifts (two triple

chairs, three doubles, and a Poma). Two chairs are reserved for beginners. The **Wolf Creek Lodge** has restaurant and bar service, and ski sales and rentals.

**Admission:** Tickets, $26 adults, $15 children (12 or under) and seniors (65 or older); discounts for 3 or more days. Full-day class lessons start at $25; rental packages begin at $10.

**Open:** Thanksgiving to mid-April, daily 9am–4pm.

## WHERE TO STAY

**FAIRFIELD PAGOSA, U.S. 160 (P.O. Box 4040), Pagosa Springs, CO 81157. Tel. 303/731-4141,** or 800/523-7704. 100 rms, 138 suites (all with bath). A/C TV TEL

**$ Rates:** Single or double, $80–$85 June–Sept, $65–$70 Oct–May, $90–$95 major holidays. AE, CB, DC, DISC, MC, V.

Located 3½ miles west of Pagosa Springs, this major four-seasons resort complex not only has 27 holes of golf and seven tennis courts, but also boasts a marina (which becomes a skating rink in winter), a cross-country ski and snowmobile center, a complete health spa, and organized activities for every kind of outdoors lover. Appointed in southwestern regional decor, rooms vary in size from studios to three-bedroom suites. All suites have kitchens; there are a few fireplaces. The resort has a fine restaurant (The Great Divide) and lounge, and a heated indoor swimming pool, sauna, and whirlpool.

**THE SPA MOTEL, 317 Lightplant Rd. (P.O. Box 37), Pagosa Springs, CO 81147. Tel. 303/264-5910.** 18 rms (all with bath). TV TEL

**$ Rates:** June–Sept, $28–$30 single; $35–$40 double. Oct–May, $25–$30 single; $32 double. AE, DISC, MC, V.

The only remaining property in Pagosa Springs to take advantage of the hot mineral springs here, the Spa has two pools—one heated to 90°, the other to 106°—plus a steam room for the hard-core heater. Rooms have kitchens and queen-size beds; because they're family oriented, pets are permitted.

## WHERE TO DINE

**ASPEN RESTAURANT, 170 San Juan St. Tel. 264-2783.**

**Cuisine:** AMERICAN. **Reservations:** Not required.

**$ Prices:** $2.65–$11.95. MC, V.

**Open:** Daily 7am–9pm.

Located across from the U.S. Forest Service offices, this restaurant appeals to the entire family. The menu features great pancakes for breakfast and burgers for lunch; at dinner, there are steaks, seafood, and the great southern-style barbecues.

**OLE MINER'S STEAKHOUSE, U.S. 160, 3½ miles east of Pagosa Springs. Tel. 264-5981.**

**Cuisine:** STEAK/SEAFOOD. **Reservations:** Recommended.

**$ Prices:** Dinner main courses $8.50–$22.50. AE, MC, V.

**Open:** Summer and winter high seasons, dinner only, daily 5:30–10pm; rest of the year, dinner only, Mon–Sat 5:30–10pm.

This looks like an old mine shaft beside the highway on the way to Wolf Creek Pass, but the low lighting and attentive service inside quickly convince you otherwise—as does the food. The menu lists nearly a dozen char-broiled steaks, as well as shrimp, lobster, crab, chicken teriyaki, and pork kebabs. You'll have to leave your vices behind, though: The restaurant doesn't permit smoking, and doesn't serve alcohol.

# CHAPTER 12

# THE SOUTHERN ROCKIES

**1. GUNNISON**
**2. CRESTED BUTTE**
**3. SALIDA**
**4. ALAMOSA**

If Colorado is the rooftop of America, then the southern Rockies region is the rooftop of Colorado. Some 30 of Colorado's "14-ers"—14,000-foot peaks—ring the area, and from Monarch Pass, at 11,312 feet, rivers flow in three directions: the Gunnison west toward the Colorado, the San Luis south toward the Rio Grande, and the Arkansas east toward the Mississippi. Isolated from the rest of Colorado by these high mountains and rugged canyons, the region developed in a way that bred proud, independent-minded people.

The Spanish took several hesitant steps north, up the Rio Grande valley from Taos, in the late 18th century; the Hispanic influence remains stronger in the San Luis valley than in any other part of Colorado. Captain Zebulon Pike's party of U.S. Army explorers wandered through the mountains of this region in the winter and spring of 1807, and fur trappers knew it well in subsequent decades. San Luis was established in 1851, the first incorporated community in Colorado, and other farming settlements followed. Settlement of the northern mountains didn't begin until the 1870s.

Today the mountain and river towns of the north have earned a reputation as recreational capitals: Gunnison for fishing and hunting, Crested Butte for skiing and mountain biking, and Salida and Buena Vista for river rafting. Alamosa, hub of the San Luis Valley, is within easy reach of numerous scenic and historic attractions (including the Cumbres & Toltec Scenic Railway) as well as the remarkable Great Sand Dunes National Monument on the western flank of the Sangre de Cristo Range. In the foothills of the San Juan Range, which demarcates the western boundary of this region, are the fascinating old mining towns of Creede and Lake City.

## 1. GUNNISON

196 miles SW of Denver, 161 miles W of Pueblo, 65 miles E of Montrose

**GETTING THERE** **By Plane** The **Gunnison County Airport,** Rio Grande Avenue at 11th Street (tel. 641-0526), is just off U.S. 50, a few blocks south of downtown Gunnison. **Continental Express** (tel. 800/525-0820) and **United Express** (tel. 800/241-6522) provide daily year-round service from Denver and Grand Junction. During nearby Crested Butte's winter ski season, **United** (tel. 800/241-6522) flies direct from Chicago, **American Airlines** (tel. 800/433-7300) direct from Dallas/Fort Worth, and **Delta** (tel. 800/453-9417) direct from Salt Lake City.

**By Bus** Buses of **Greyhound/Trailways** (tel. 800/528-6055) and **TNM&O** both pass through Gunnison twice daily—once eastbound, once westbound. The station is at 303 East Tomichi Avenue (tel. 303/641-0060).

**By Car** Gunnison is located on U.S. 50, midway between Montrose and Salida. From Denver, the most direct route is U.S. 285 southwest to Poncha Springs (near Salida), then west on U.S. 50. From Grand Junction, follow U.S. 50 through Montrose.

**ESSENTIALS** **Orientation** The town is built on the southeast banks of the westerly flowing Gunnison River. **Tomichi Avenue** (U.S. 50) runs due east-west through town; many civic buildings are on **Virginia Avenue,** one block north. **Main Street** (Colo. 135) intersects Tomichi Avenue in the center of town, and proceeds north to Crested Butte. The campus of **Western State College,** a 4-year liberal arts school, is three blocks north of Tomichi Avenue and four blocks east of Main Street.

Gunnison has a population of 6,000 and an elevation of 7,700 feet.

**Information** Contact the **Gunnison Country Chamber of Commerce,** 500 East Tomichi Avenue (P.O. Box 36), Gunnison, CO 81230 (tel. 303/641-1501, or 800/274-7580).

**Getting Around** There's a **Budget Rent-a-Car** (tel. 641-4403) agency at the Gunnison County Airport.

**Fast Facts** The **area code** is 303. The **climate** in winter can become extremely cold—the average January low is –8°F, with occasional forays into the –30s—but midsummer temperatures frequently climb into the 80s. In case of **emergency,** call **911;** for normal business, contact the Gunnison County Sheriff (tel. 641-1113). **Gunnison Valley Public Hospital** is at 214 East Denver Street (tel. 641-1456), two blocks east of Main Street and six blocks north of U.S. 50. The main **post office** is at Virginia Avenue and Wisconsin Street (tel. 641-1884). For **road conditions,** call 641-2896. Total local **sales tax** is 7%.

**SPECIAL EVENTS** Annual events in Gunnison include the **Hottest Cold Spot in the Nation,** on the first weekend in February; the **American Indian Festival,** on the last weekend of June; **Cattlemen's Days and Rodeo,** Colorado's oldest continually held rodeo, in the third week in July; and the **Parade of Lights,** in late November or early December.

---

**U**te peoples began hunting in this area around the middle of the 17th century. Hispanic explorers probably never penetrated this isolated region, but mountain men, pursuing pelts, certainly had done so by the 1830s. It was first mapped by U.S. Army Capt. John Gunnison and his party of surveyors in 1853. A town platted near the confluence of Tomichi Creek and the Gunnison River in 1874 grew as a ranching center and transportation hub for nearby silver and gold mines. Western State College was established in 1911; now with an enrollment of 2,500, it is the only college in the United States with a certified technical-evacuation mountain-rescue team. Today ranching remains important to the region, but the leading economic stimuli are tourism and outdoor recreation: skiing, fishing, and hunting.

# WHAT TO SEE & DO
## ATTRACTIONS

**CURECANTI NATIONAL RECREATION AREA, 102 Elk Creek Rd. (U.S. 50), west of Gunnison. Tel. 303/641-2337.**

The Blue Mesa, Morrow Point, and Crystal dams on the Gunnison River, just below Gunnison, have created a series of three very different reservoirs, extending 35 miles to the mouth of the Black Canyon of the Gunnison (see "Montrose" in Chapter 10). **Blue Mesa Lake** (elevation 7,519 ft.), the easternmost of the three (beginning 9 miles west of Gunnison), is the largest lake in Colorado when filled to capacity, and is a water-sports paradise, popular for fishing, motorboating, sailboating, board sailing, and other activities. Fjordlike **Morrow Point Lake** (elevation 7,160 ft.) and **Crystal Lake** (elevation 6,755 ft.) fill long, serpentine canyons accessible only by precipitous trails, and thus are limited to use by hand-carried boats.

The **Elk Creek Visitor Center,** 15 miles west of Gunnison off U.S. 50, presents numerous exhibits and audiovisual programs, as well as maps and publications. Nature hikes and evening campground programs are presented throughout the season. The 90-minute **boat tours** leave from the marina here, daily Memorial Day to Labor Day, to explore Blue Mesa Lake's 96 miles of shoreline and three separate basins; there's a second major marina at **Lake Fork** at the reservoir's west end. At

**Cimarron,** 45 road miles west of Gunnison, there's an information center with a historic train exhibit and a road to the **Morrow Point Dam** powerplant, where free public tours are offered daily from Memorial Day to Labor Day.

U.S. 50 follows the north shore of Blue Mesa Lake, crossing to the south shore on a bridge between Sapinero and Cebolla basins. At Lake Fork, Colo. 92 to Crawford crosses to the north shore of Morrow Point Lake; it traces the canyon rim west for the next 30 miles, offering numerous spectacular views of the western lakes and canyons.

Fishermen visit Curecanti year round—there's ice fishing in winter—but the main season is May to October, when rainbow, brown, and Mackinaw trout, and kokanee salmon are caught in large numbers. Hunting, especially for elk and deer, is popular in season in the adjacent West Elk Mountains. Numerous day-hike trails, including a 2½-mile path to the volcanic Dillon Pinnacles, are located in the recreation area. There are 10 campgrounds in Curecanti and 21 picnic areas.

**Admission:** Free; fee for camping ($8 per vehicle per day) or boat tours ($7 adults, $4 children; by advance reservation).

**Open:** Recreation area, daily 24 hours. Elk Creek Visitor Center, mid-May to September, daily 8am–6pm; the rest of the year, intermittently.

**PIONEER MUSEUM, S. Adams St., at Tomichi Ave. Tel. 641-9963,** or 641-0943 in summer.

A narrow-gauge railroad engine, a flatcar, caboose, watertank, and an old post office are among the machines and structures on display at this local historical-society museum on the east side of town. A highlight is the 19th-century one-room Paragon School House, its desks and blackboards still in tact.

**Admission:** $1 adults, 50¢ children.

**Open:** Memorial Day–Labor Day, daily 9:30am–5pm.

## SPORTS & RECREATION

**BOATING** The lakes of Curecanti National Recreation Area (see "Attractions," above) offer some of Colorado's best boating; rentals can be arranged at the **Elk Creek Marina** on Blue Mesa Lake, 15 miles west of Gunnison off U.S. 50 (tel. 641-0707). There's another small marina on Taylor Reservoir, 30 miles north of Gunnison on the Taylor Canyon Road; contact the **Taylor Park Boat House** (tel. 641-2922).

**FISHING & HUNTING** The Gunnison River, both above and below town, and the tributary Taylor River, which joins the Gunnison at Almont, 11 miles north of town, are outstanding trout streams. In addition, the region's lakes are also rich in fish (see "Curecanti National Recreation Area" in "Attractions," above). Throughout the surrounding Gunnison National Forest, hunting for deer, elk, and other game animals is extremely popular. For fishing or hunting equipment, licenses, and information in Gunnison, visit **Berfield's Stage Stop,** 519 West Tomichi Avenue (tel. 641-5782), or **Gene Taylor's Sporting Goods,** 201 West Tomichi Avenue (tel. 641-1845). **Willowfly Anglers,** at the Three Rivers Resort, Almont (tel. 641-1303), offers fly-fishing instruction, rentals, and guide service. Inquire at the chamber of commerce about other guide services.

**GOLF** The 18-hole **Dos Rios Country Club,** Cama-Del Road, off U.S. 50 southwest of town (tel. 641-1482), is well regarded by many golfers. In addition, **Woods' Golf Range,** 2 miles east of Gunnison off U.S. 50 (tel. 641-0451), has a driving range, 9-hole putting green, and golf school.

**HIKING** There are endless opportunities for backcountry experiences in the **Gunnison National Forest,** which surrounds the town. For trail maps and other information, contact national forest headquarters at 216 North Colorado Street (tel. 641-0471).

**RIVER RAFTING** For trips on the Gunnison and other rivers, check with **Three Rivers Resort and Outfitting,** 11 miles north of Gunnison on Taylor Canyon Road, Almont (tel. 641-1303).

**SKIING**  The two major winter-sports centers in the area are **Crested Butte Mountain Resort,** 32 miles north on Colo. 135 (see "Crested Butte," below), and **Monarch Ski Resort,** 44 miles east on U.S. 50 (see "Salida," below).

# WHERE TO STAY

**BEST WESTERN TOMICHI VILLAGE INN, U.S. 50, 1½ miles east of Gunnison (P.O. Box 763), Gunnison, CO 81230. Tel. 303/641-1131,** or 800/528-1234. 48 rms, 1 suite (all with bath). A/C TV TEL
**$ Rates** (including continental breakfast): Jan–Mar and Labor Day–Oct, $34–$38 single; $44–$48 double. Apr–May 9 and Nov–Dec 19, $32–$36 single; $42–$46 double. May 10–June 15, $36–$44 single; $50–$58 double. June 16–Labor Day and Dec 20–31, $58–$64 single; $62–$68 double. AE, CB, DC, DISC, MC, V.
An alpine appearance characterizes this motel at the east end of Gunnison, across the highway from Tomichi Creek. The exterior is of wood and flagstone, with green decorative trim. The spacious guest rooms are appointed in shades of peach and slate, with rich wood furnishings; all have either two queen-size beds or a king-size bed and sleeper sofa. An outdoor swimming pool is open in summer; an indoor sauna and whirlpool are open year round. Next door is Josef's restaurant.

**MARY LAWRENCE INN, 601 N. Taylor St., Gunnison, CO 81230. Tel. 303/641-3343.** 4 rms, 1 suite (3 with bath).
**$ Rates** (including full breakfast): $46 single or double without bath, $55 single or double with bath; $68 suite. DISC, MC, V.
Children are welcome at this renovated Victorian bed-and-breakfast home, located in a quiet neighborhood two blocks east of Colo. 135 near Western State College, at Ruby Street. The downstairs of this big green house is shared by all guests: a living room, dining room, kitchen, sun room, and large outdoor deck. Steep stairs climb to the charmingly cluttered guest rooms, which include a two-room suite. All have antique furnishings, but otherwise they vary: for instance, the Chipeta Room reflects the region's Native American heritage; the Galloping Ghost Room has a country-style ambience and a well-stocked library; the Mullin Patch has stenciled walls and a hand-appliquéed quilt. All rooms have radios, but only the suite has a TV. A telephone and piano are available for all guests' use.

**WILDWOOD MOTEL, 1312 W. Tomichi Ave., Gunnison, CO 81230. Tel. 303/641-1663.** 11 rms, 2 suites (all with bath). TV
**$ Rates:** $32–$42 single or double; $48 suite. Fishing and hunting packages available. MC, V.
Built in 1928 as a summer refuge for members of the Chicago underworld, the Wildwood today is a favorite hideaway for budget-conscious outdoor sports lovers. Rooms here aren't fancy, but they're clean and well maintained, and all include a kitchen nook with refrigerator. Decor varies from regional art to nature themes; furnishings range from two queen-size beds, to one queen-size plus a table and chairs, to a double and two singles. All rooms have cable TV, but there are no phones except the pay phone beside the fish-cleaning station. The grounds contain a playground area, horseshoe pit, picnic tables, and two duck ponds, where Tasmanian rainbow trout are raised for release into the Gunnison River. Pets may be accepted by prior arrangement.

# WHERE TO DINE

**THE BEEF & BARREL, at the Cattlemen Inn, 301 W. Tomichi Ave. Tel. 641-1061.**
    **Cuisine:** STEAK. **Reservations:** Not necessary.
**$ Prices:** Appetizers $1.75–$3.75; main courses $4.75–$21.95. DC, MC, V.
    **Open:** Dinner only, daily 5–11pm.
A visit here will quickly remind you that you're in ranching country: Brands representing every local cattle operation are burned into the wall behind the salad bar. This popular restaurant has a rustic feeling with its low ceiling, dim lighting, and unfinished wood construction. Beef is the specialty here, and all steaks are hand-

cut—try the Delmonico. Fresh and deep-fried seafood and chicken are also on the menu, and there are children's offerings as well. The adjoining lounge has a big-screen TV for sports fans.

### EPICUREAN RESTAURANT, 110 N. Main St. Tel. 641-2964.

**Cuisine:** EUROPEAN DELI. **Reservations:** Not necessary.
**$ Prices:** Breakfast $2.95–$6.95; lunch $3.95–$6.95. MC, V.
**Open:** Mon–Sat 7am–5pm, Sun 7am–2pm.

Proprietress Ina Gerkey, a native of East Prussia, has created a tranquil island of continental culture in the Wild West. Classical music, oil paintings, and fresh flowers on every table have established a little bit of Europe between the rough-hewn log walls of this downtown café. If you're here for breakfast, don't miss the *ebelskiver*—ball-size Danish apple pancakes. You can also get soufflés, omelets, and wild-rice pancakes. For lunch, consider the Reuben (with sauerkraut and Swiss cheese on rye, of course) or the homemade soup with muffins. Catered continental-style dinners are served to large groups by reservation only.

### JOSEF'S, U.S. 50, 1½ miles east of Gunnison. Tel. 641-5032.

**Cuisine:** CONTINENTAL/AMERICAN. **Reservations:** Recommended at dinner.
**$ Prices:** Appetizers $4.95–$6.95; main courses $9.95–$15.95; lunch $4.95–$7.95. AE, CB, DC, DISC, MC, V.
**Open:** Lunch Mon–Sat 11am–2pm; dinner Sun–Thurs 5–9pm, Fri–Sat 5–10pm; brunch Sun 10am–2pm.

An Old World atmosphere pervades this fine restaurant adjacent to the Best Western Tomichi Village at the east end of town. The menu features a variety of steaks, chops, poultry, and seafood dishes, but the house specialties are German: beef Rouladen, served with egg noodles and red cabbage; Jaeger Schnitzel champignons, a rich preparation of traditional wienerschnitzel; Kässler Ribchen, a pork loin charbroiled with an apple, brandy, and honey glaze; and more. Lunch visitors enjoy Josef's burger, on a homemade Kaiser roll, or a lighter meal of coffee with Austrian pastries.

### RAMBLE II, Colo. 135, 2 miles north of Gunnison. Tel. 641-1207.

**Cuisine:** STEAK/SEAFOOD.
**$ Prices:** Appetizers $1.50–$4.95; main courses $4.95–$19.45. MC, V.
**Open:** Dinner only, Mon–Wed 4–11pm, Thurs 4pm–midnight, Fri–Sat 4pm–1am, Sun 2–9pm.

You can't miss this turquoise-painted building beside the road north toward Crested Butte. A family restaurant in the early evening, a country-and-western dance club later at night, it has pleasant tavern-style decor, with stained-glass windows casting a touch of elegance across the booths and tables. The menu features a variety of steaks, from chopped sirloin to a 20-ounce T-bone, and tasty local catches, including trout and walleye. Early-bird specials (starting at $4.95) are served from 5 to 6pm nightly; the restaurant also features excellent burgers and a good dessert menu. On Sunday afternoons from 2 to 5pm ballroom dancers can waltz and polka between sips of tea and bites of finger sandwiches.

# EASY EXCURSION

## LAKE CITY

The most interesting day trip for visitors to Gunnison is to the historic mining town of ✪ **Lake City,** 55 miles southwest via Colo. 149 (turn south off U.S. 50, 9 miles west of Gunnison). Founded in 1874, this former silver and gold town is set against a backdrop of 14,000-foot peaks in three different national forests—the Gunnison, Uncompahgre, and Rio Grande.

Today Lake City is Colorado's largest national historic district, with more than 75 buildings that date from the 19th century. Tour the **Hinsdale County Courthouse** (1877), site of the trial of the notorious Alferd Packer, who allegedly killed and ate five members of his mining party. Packer was sentenced to hang, but a technicality commuted his crime to manslaughter, and he wound up serving only 5 years. The fascinating geological area north of Lake City is known as the Cannibal Plateau (and in an instance of bad taste that can only be ascribed to college students, the University of Colorado has named its student cafeteria in honor of Packer).

Lake City is an important recreational center, especially for hiking and fishing in summer, cross-country skiing and snowmobiling in winter. **Lake San Cristobal,** just south of town, is Colorado's second-largest natural lake.

For information, contact the **Lake City Chamber of Commerce,** P.O. Box 430, Lake City, CO 81235 (tel. 303/944-2527).

# 2. CRESTED BUTTE

224 miles SW of Denver, 28 miles N of Gunnison

**GETTING THERE By Plane** The **Gunnison County Airport** (see "Gunnison," above) serves Crested Butte. Continental Express and United Express provide year-round service; American Airlines and Delta fly during winter ski season.

**By Bus** The **Alpine Express** (tel. 303/641-5074, or 800/822-4844) provides transportation between Gunnison Airport and Crested Butte hotels. The charge is $14 each way, with children 12 and under half price.

**By Car** Crested Butte is 28 miles north of Gunnison on Colo. 135. The only year-round access is via Gunnison (see "Gunnison" above). In summer, the gravel-surface Kebler Pass Road links Crested Butte with Colo. 133 at Paonia Reservoir, to the west; and four-wheel-drive vehicles can negotiate a difficult route south from Aspen, around the Maroon Bells.

**SPECIAL EVENTS** Crested Butte's annual events include the **Wildflower Festival,** in early July; the **Fat Tire Bike Week,** the second week of July; the **Mountain Man Rendezvous,** in mid-July; **Aerial Weekend,** in late July; the **Festival of the Arts,** in early August; the **Chamber Music Festival,** in mid-August; and the **Vinotok Slavic Fall Festival,** the third week of September.

The town of Crested Butte was born in 1880 as the Denver & Rio Grande line laid a narrow-gauge rail track from Gunnison to serve the gold and silver mines in the area. But coal, not the more "precious" minerals, sustained the town for six decades after its discovery in the late 1880s. Only in 1952 was the last of the mines operated by the Colorado Fuel and Iron Company forced to close. The economy languished until the Mount Crested Butte ski area was developed in 1961. The resort community followed in 1976.

Throughout the 1970s and 1980s young people moved to the town and renovated the old buildings as homes and businesses. An architectural review board ensured that all construction was true to the town's heritage, with the result that Crested Butte is one of the most authentic Victorian towns in Colorado today. You won't find any rich miners' mansions here: This was and is a working-man's town, without the ostentation seen elsewhere in the state.

Crested Butte has a permanent population of about 1,100 residents; Mount Crested Butte has another 350. The town is located at an elevation of 8,885 feet, with the resort village at 9,350 feet.

## ORIENTATION

**INFORMATION** Consult the **Crested Butte–Mount Crested Butte Chamber of Commerce,** Elk Avenue at Colo. 135 (P.O. Box 1288), Crested Butte, CO 81224 (tel. 303/349-6438). For specific resort information, contact **Crested Butte Mountain Resort,** 12 Snowmass Road (P.O. Box A), Mount Crested Butte, CO 81225 (tel. 303/349-2281; fax 303/349-2250).

**TOWN LAYOUT** There are actually two separate communities here: the old mining town of **Crested Butte,** and the modern resort village of **Mount Crested Butte,** 3½ miles away. Colo. 135 enters Crested Butte from the south and is intersected by **Elk Avenue,** which runs west-east as the town's main street. Numbered streets run north-south beginning with Fifth Street to the west of the highway. Beyond Elk Avenue, the highway is known as **Gothic Road,** which leads to the winding condominium-speckled roads surrounding the Mount Crested Butte village.

## GETTING AROUND

**Mountain Express** (tel. 349-5616) provides free shuttle-bus service between Crested Butte, Mount Crested Butte, and area condominiums, in winter daily from 7:15am to midnight, with shorter hours in summer. Local **taxi** service is also available.

## FAST FACTS

The **area code** is 303. In an **emergency,** dial **911.** The **Crested Butte Medical Clinic,** Gothic Road at Emmons Road, Mount Crested Butte (tel. 349-2121), can handle most health needs; emergency service evacuates patients to **Gunnison Valley Public Hospital,** 214 East Denver Street, Gunnison (tel. 641-1456). The **post office** is on the north side of Elk Avenue between Second Street and Third Street. Local **sales tax** is 8%.

## WHAT TO SEE & DO

**CRESTED BUTTE MOUNTAIN RESORT, 12 Snowmass Rd. (P.O. Box A), Mount Crested Butte, CO 81225. Tel. 303/349-2222,** or 800/544-8448; 303/349-2323 for snow reports. Fax 303/349-2250.
    Crested Butte may be Colorado's best-kept secret. Although it has never been placed in the same ranks as other resort towns, it may have more to offer than any of them. Situated at the intersection of two overlapping winter storm tracks, it's guaranteed outstanding snow. More than one-quarter of its terrain is devoted to beginners, yet it has what many experts consider the most challenging runs—"Extreme Limits" skiing—in the Rockies. Couple that with a town rich in Victorian heritage, and with "more fine restaurants per capita than any other town in America," according to the *Denver Post,* and you're left with a remarkable resort community.
    From the Grand Butte Hotel at the foot of the mountain, the **Silver Queen Lift** ascends to the top of the skiable peak, serving a series of advanced runs. The **Keystone Lift** departs from the same location and serves an expansive beginner area off Keystone Ridge. Over the backside of the ridge, the **Teocalli and Paradise Lifts** serve a predominantly intermediate series of trails. The **North Face Poma,** which climbs above Paradise Bowl near the top of the mountain, offers access to the extreme skiing of the North Face, the Glades, and Phoenix Bowl, which *Skiing* magazine has called "Expert skiing with a capital E."
    The resort has 817 acres of lift-served skiable terrain, not including an additional 395 acres of "Extreme Limits." The vertical drop is 2,300 feet from a summit of 11,400 feet. Mount Crested Butte has 81 trails served by 12 lifts (3 triples, 6 doubles, and 3 surface lifts) with an uphill capacity of 13,550 skiers per hour. Average annual snowfall is 229 inches (19 ft.) at the base, 300 inches (25 ft.) at the summit.
    **Admission:** Lift tickets, $36 adults ($26 in early and late season), $21 children 12 and under ($15 early and late), $18 seniors 65–69 ($13 early and late), free for seniors 70 and over, and free for children 12 and under when an adult buys a lift ticket, except during the Christmas holidays and the last half of March. Class lessons start at $24; adult rental packages, at $11.
    **Open:** Thanksgiving to early Apr, daily 9am–4pm.

## SPORTS & RECREATION

**BALLOONING**    The highest-altitude balloon company in North America is **Bighorn Balloon** (tel. 349-6335), offering year-round flights over the Rockies surrounding Crested Butte.

**BICYCLING**  Crested Butte has established a firm reputation as the mountain-biking capital of Colorado. From Jeep roads to hiking trails, there's something here to please every ability level. Popular rides include the challenging 25-mile ride over 10,707-foot Schofield Pass to the village of Marble, off Colo. 133; and the shorter Cement Creek Trail to the base of Italian Mountain.

For information on rentals or guided tours, contact **Flatiron Sports,** Treasury Center, Emmons Road, Mount Crested Butte (tel. 349-6656), or other sporting-goods stores. There's even a ☉ **Mountain Bike Hall of Fame Museum** at Elk Avenue and Fourth Street (tel. 349-7482), open summer, daily from 4:30pm to midnight.

**GOLF**  Robert Trent Jones II designed the 7,200-yard, 18-hole **Skyland Resort & Country Club** course, 385 Country Club Lane (tel. 349-6129), 2½ miles south of Crested Butte. Considered one of Colorado's best, the course has water hazards on each of the first 9 holes, rolling hills and knolls on the back 9.

**HIKING**  There are rich opportunities for hiking and backpacking in the Crested Butte area. Ask the chamber of commerce for trail suggestions, or contact the **Gunnison National Forest** office, 216 North Colorado Street, Gunnison (tel. 641-0471).

**HORSEBACK RIDING**  Guided rides are offered year round by **Fantasy Ranch** (tel. 349-5425), **Rendezvous Guides & Outfitters** (tel. 349-6593), and **Teocalli Outfitters** (tel. 349-7118). Perhaps the most popular trips are into the Irwin Lodge or Lost Lake Lodge, a pair of wilderness hideaways that prepare gourmet home-cooked lunches for riders.

**RIVER RAFTING  Crested Butte Rafting** (tel. 349-7423) and **American Adventures Expeditions** (tel. 349-2409) lead trips down the Gunnison or Taylor rivers, or for the more adventurous, the Arkansas.

**SKIING**  The **Crested Butte Nordic Center,** based at the Crested Butte Athletic Club, 512 Second Street (tel. 349-6201), is open in winter daily, from 9am to 4pm. The center maintains 29km (18 miles) of groomed trails, and organizes backcountry tours into more than 100 miles of wilderness trail. Tickets for track skiing are $5 per day for adults, $3 for children; rentals are $10 per day; all-day tours run $45 per person, with a two-person minimum.

**TENNIS**  There are more than 20 outdoor tennis courts between Crested Butte and Mount Crested Butte, including several in **Town Park** on Seventh Street at Elk Avenue. Inquire at the chamber of commerce about others.

# WHERE TO STAY

**GRANDE BUTTE HOTEL, Emmons Rd. (P.O. Box 5006), Mount Crested Butte, CO 81225. Tel. 303/349-7561,** or 800/833-8389. Fax 303/349-6332. 210 rms, 52 suites (all with bath). TV TEL

**$ Rates:** Thanksgiving to pre-Christmas, $95–$125 single or double; suite $165–$300. Christmas hols, $150–$190 single or double; suite $250–$550. Jan 4–31, $125–$155 single or double; $195–$400 suite. Feb–Mar, $145–$185 single or double; $240–$500 suite. Last week of season, $90–$120 single or double; $160–$300 suite. Early June to late Sept, $75–$90 single or double; $130–$300 suite. Children 17 or under stay free with parent. **Closed:** Early Apr to early June and late Sept to late Nov. AE, CB, DC, DISC, MC, V. **Parking:** Free valet service.

A luxurious property at the foot of the Silver King and Keystone lifts, this is the Crested Butte Mountain Resort's showcase hotel. Some 40,000 square feet of red cedar went into its construction, and an impressive collection of original oil paintings is hung throughout the hotel. Every guest room has a private balcony, wet bar and refrigerator, Jacuzzi bath, cable TV with in-house movies, and direct-dial phone. Standard rooms have a queen-size bed and sleeper sofa or two double beds.

**Dining/Entertainment:** Fine continental dinners are served in the Grande Café, which boasts a 160° wall of windows facing the ski slopes. The Roaring Elk coffee shop serves three meals daily; its outdoor barbecue deck is especially popular with skiers. In the evening, the Roaring Elk becomes an après-ski saloon with live dance music. Quieter conversations take place at the Fireside Lounge.

**Services:** Room service, concierge, valet laundry, complimentary shuttle service, ski valet and storage, no-smoking rooms, facilities for the disabled.

**Facilities:** Indoor swimming pool, Jacuzzi, sauna, games room, guest laundry, ski shop, ice-skating rink (with rentals), meeting space for 400.

**THE CLAIM JUMPER, 704 Whiterock Ave. (P.O. Box 1181), Crested Butte, CO 81224. Tel. 303/349-6471.** 6 rms. TV

**$ Rates** (including full breakfast): $55–$75 single or double; hol seasons, $75–$85 single or double. MC, V.

A huge log home packed with a museum-full of eclectic antiques and family heirlooms, this bed-and-breakfast inn easily qualifies as Crested Butte's most unusual accommodation. Each of the guest rooms has a particular theme, and is decorated accordingly. The Rough and Ready Room, of course, is dedicated to cowboys; Prospector's Gulch, to miners; and Commodore Corrigan's Cabin, to seafarers. The Sportsfan Attic is packed with baseball and football memorabilia. Fifties nostalgia buffs will enjoy Ethyl's Room (complete with restored gas pump) and Soda Creek ("Things go better with Coke"). The common living room has a turn-of-the-century hunting-lodge motif, complete with wood-burning stove; and the inn also features a redwood hot tub, full sauna, and antique games room.

**CRESTED BUTTE CLUB, 512 Second St. (P.O. Drawer 309), Crested Butte, CO 81224. Tel. 303/349-6655,** or 800/782-6037. 7 suites (all with bath). TV TEL

**$ Rates** (including continental breakfast): Single or double, $80–$110 early and late ski season, $170–$225 Christmas hols, $95–$125 Jan and early June to late Sept, $115–$155 Feb–Mar, $60–$85 early Apr to early June and late Sept to late Nov. AE, MC, V.

This is perhaps Crested Butte's most elegant lodging. The building, a national historic landmark that houses the town's athletic club, dates from 1886—though it didn't become an "inn" until 1989. The guest suites have captured the Victorian era and moved it into the late 20th century. All rooms have rich antique furnishings of oak, walnut, or cherry; four-poster king- or queen-size beds; gas fireplaces; copper-and-brass clawfoot bathtubs; his-and-hers pedestal sinks; and other 19th-century touches. The inn is entirely smoke-free, by the way. Guests have full athletic club access, including use of the lap pool, racquetball court, weight and exercise room, Jacuzzis, steam rooms, and aerobics studio. The Crested Butte Nordic Center is also located here, as is the sophisticated Club Pub, a turn-of-the-century establishment with a marble-top piano bar.

**ELK MOUNTAIN LODGE, Second and Gothic Sts. (P.O. Box 148), Crested Butte, CO 81224. Tel. 303/349-7533.** 20 rms (all with bath). TV TEL

**$ Rates** (including continental breakfast): Single or double, $44–$63 Apr–Thanksgiving, $49–$65 Thanksgiving to pre-Christmas, $79–$95 Christmas hols, $59–$75 Jan 2–Mar. Discounts for 3 or more nights in summer, 5 or more nights in winter. AE, DISC, MC, V.

Built in 1919 as a coal miners' boarding house, this lodge is one of the budget bargains of Crested Butte. Located two blocks north of Elk Avenue near the center of town, it's a three-story structure whose rates rise with the views. But even if you opt for the first floor, with neither a view nor a balcony (as third-floor rooms have), you'll be greeted with a bottle of champagne on arrival. Each room features a queen-size bed, private bath, TV, phone, and wood furnishings. A Jacuzzi and ski-storage area are open to all guests.

**THE NORDIC INN, Emmons and Treasury Rds. (P.O. Box 939), Mount Crested Butte, CO 81225. Tel. 303/349-5542.** 23 rms, 2 suites (all with bath). TV

**$ Rates** (including continental breakfast): Early and late ski season, $53 single; $58 double; $94 suite. Christmas hols, $101 single; $106 double; $142 suite. Early Jan to early Feb, $68 single; $73 double; $109 suite. Early Feb to Mar, $82 single; $87 double; $123 suite. Early Apr to late Nov, $48 single; $53 double; $89 suite. Children stay free in parents' room. AE, MC, V.

When the Nordic Inn was built in 1970, it was the only overnight accommodation at the foot of the Crested Butte ski slopes. The charming Norwegian-style inn is still going strong, its big fireplace the focus of attention for breakfasts and late-afternoon hot-wine and cider gatherings. Each guest room has two double beds, cable TV, and a private bath. A sundeck and outdoor Jacuzzi tub are shared by everyone. Some kitchen units are available. Families are especially welcome.

# WHERE TO DINE

**THE BAKERY CAFE, Elk Ave. and Third St. Tel. 349-7280.**
   **Cuisine:** DELI. **Reservations:** Not accepted.
   **$ Prices:** $2.70–$4.25. No credit cards.
   **Open:** Mid-June to Sept and Thanksgiving to early Apr, daily 7am–8pm; off-season, daily 7:30am–3:30pm.

Large picture windows and a sunroom give this popular café a bright, spacious atmosphere. All food is made fresh daily, including savory pastries, creative deli-style sandwiches, soups, salads, and desserts. You can also fill up on pizza, lasagne, or pot pies. Espresso coffees and juices are always available.

**KAROLINA'S KITCHEN, 127 Elk Ave. Tel. 349-6756.**
   **Cuisine:** AMERICAN. **Reservations:** Not accepted.
   **$ Prices:** Appetizers $4.95–$6.95; main courses $4.25–$13.95. No credit cards.
   **Open:** Daily 11:30am–10pm.

A former blacksmith's shop has been transformed into one of Crested Butte's most popular budget restaurants. Come for genuine home-cooking like pork chops with applesauce, T-bone steak, Appalachian turkey melt sandwiches, chili, or fish and chips. There are blue-plate specials daily, and breakfasts are served until 4pm. At night, Karolina's preparations are served in the adjoining Kochevar's Saloon and Gaming Hall, a popular tavern that displays a roulette wheel and slot machine from the Butte's rowdier days.

**LE BOSQUET, Elk Ave. and Second St. Tel. 349-5808.**
   **Cuisine:** CREATIVE CONTINENTAL. **Reservations:** Recommended.
   **$ Prices:** Dinner, appetizers $5.95–$7.95; main courses $12.95–$24.95; lunch $3.95–$6.50. AE, CB, DC, MC, V.
   **Open:** Late May to late Sept, lunch daily 11:30am–2pm; dinner daily 6–9pm. Late Nov to early Apr, lunch daily 11:30am–2pm; dinner daily 5:30–10pm. **Closed:** Early Apr to late May and late Sept to late Nov.

Green plants peek through the lace curtains of this popular garden-style restaurant, well known for its imaginative menu. Choices change weekly, but always include fresh seafood dishes and a chateaubriand. You might also find Colorado lamb shank, grilled duck breast, tournedos au Bosquet, hazelnut chicken, or any number of other hearty meals. Early diners can get a break in price on Le Bosquet's twilight menu.

**OSCAR'S BAR & CAFE, 229 Elk Ave. Tel. 349-6107.**
   **Cuisine:** INTERNATIONAL. **Reservations:** Not necessary.
   **$ Prices:** Appetizers $1.95–$7.50; main courses $4.95–$8.50 at lunch, $8.95–$16.95 at dinner. AE, MC, V.
   **Open:** May 15–Oct, lunch daily 11:30am–4pm; dinner daily 5–10pm. Thanksgiving–Apr, lunch daily 11am–3pm; dinner daily 5–10pm. **Closed:** Early Oct to late Nov and early Apr to mid-May.

This old building has had more incarnations than Crested Butte itself: Once a bank, it was later a drugstore, then a funeral parlor, before taking shape as this popular family restaurant. Prime rib, hand-cut steaks, and half-pound hamburgers are specialties, but you can also find a choice of southwestern fare and pastas, as well as a handful of

Asian and continental preparations. Kids have their own menu. In the evening, Oscar's has become known as the Butte's "official high-altitude adjustment center," with full bar service, five big-screen televisions, and nightly disc-jockey or karaoke entertainment. A patio bar is packed in summer.

**THE SLOGAR BAR & RESTAURANT, Second St. at Whiterock Ave. Tel. 349-5765.**
   **Cuisine:** AMERICAN. **Reservations:** Recommended.
$ **Prices:** Fixed-price dinner $10.95. MC, V.
   **Open:** Dinner only, daily 5–9pm.
If you do something right, why mess around with anything else? That's the way the Slogar feels about its skillet-fried chicken. Bird highlights the one-and-only fixed-price menu every night, accompanied by tangy cole slaw, mashed potatoes and gravy, biscuits with honey butter, creamed corn, and ice cream. You'll have to choose between coffee, tea, milk, and an alcoholic beverage, but unless you put in a special request for a family-style steak dinner, come for the chicken—it may be the best you've ever had! The atmosphere here, incidentally, is 1880s Victorian. The Slogar was the Slogar then, too, but nowhere near as elegant as it is today.

**SOUPÇON, in the alley off Second St. between Elk and Maroon Aves. Tel. 349-5448.**
   **Cuisine:** CONTINENTAL. **Reservations:** Highly recommended.
$ **Prices:** Appetizers $6.95–$8.95; main courses $17.95–$22.95. AE, MC, V.
   **Open:** Dinner only, daily 6–10pm.
This tiny log cabin with rough-hewn log benches, hidden in an alley behind Kochevar's Saloon, is hardly a place you'd expect to find candlelit, white-linen service and gourmet cuisine. But many big-city folks consider Soupçon to be Crested Butte's finest restaurant. In a casual, smoke-free atmosphere, diners pick their menu choices off a chalkboard that's changed nightly. You might start with scallops in caviar cream or duckling mousse, followed by a main dish of fresh swordfish with béarnaise sauce, roasted tenderloin of beef with green peppercorn sauce, or perhaps a colonial-style chicken curry. Desserts are sinful.

# 3. SALIDA

138 miles SW of Denver, 96 miles W of Pueblo, 82 miles N of Alamosa

**GETTING THERE By Plane** Small planes and charters can land at **Harriet Alexander Airport,** 2 miles west of downtown off Monarch Avenue. The nearest airport with commercial service is at Gunnison, 65 miles west (see "Gunnison," above).

**By Bus** Coaches of **Greyhound/Trailways** (tel. 800/528-6055) and **TNM&O,** 1147 Rainbow Boulevard (U.S. 50) (tel. 719/539-7474), serve Salida.

**By Car** U.S. 50 connects Salida with Grand Junction, 193 miles west on I-70, and Pueblo, 96 miles east on I-25. U.S. 285 runs north-south 5 miles west of Salida (through Poncha Springs); it extends northeast 138 miles to Denver, and south 255 miles to Santa Fe, New Mexico. Colo. 291 provides a vital 9-mile link through Salida, completing a triangle that ties the two U.S. highways together. About 23 miles north of Salida, and 2 miles south of Buena Vista, U.S. 24 branches north off U.S. 285, connecting Salida with I-70 at Vail, via Leadville.

**SPECIAL EVENTS** Annually, Salida sponsors the **FIBArk Festival** ("First in Boating on the Arkansas"), in mid-June; the **Chaffee County Fair,** in early August; and the **River Rendezvous,** the third week of September.

**W**ith a strategic location on the upper Arkansas River, near the headwaters of the Colorado River and Rio Grande tributaries, it was natural that Salida should become an important farming and transportation center for the central Rockies. Various Native Americans made it a part of their annual migration routes for millennia before Spanish explorers breached the wilderness in the early 18th century. Zebulon Pike opened the area for Americans 100 years later, and trappers and miners followed, the latter after the discovery of gold in 1859. When Leadville boomed on silver in the late 1870s, the Denver & Rio Grande Railway built a line up the Arkansas from Pueblo, and the town of Salida was founded at a key point on the line. The downtown core has kept its historic ambience alive to the present day. The railway no longer carries passengers, but it still operates up the Arkansas today as a freight line.

With the recreation boom of the past two decades, Salida and the neighboring community of Buena Vista, 25 miles north, have emerged as the white-water-rafting capitals of the Rockies. They're the principal centers of the **Arkansas Headwaters Recreation Area,** a 148-mile stretch of river from Leadville to Pueblo Reservoir. No fewer than 11 different rafting outfitters operate in the greater Salida area, and all have more business than they can handle during the May-to-September season.

Salida has a population of about 4,700 and an elevation of just over 7,000 feet.

## ORIENTATION

**INFORMATION** Consult the **Heart of the Rockies Chamber of Commerce,** 406 West Rainbow Boulevard, Salida, CO 81201 (tel. 719/539-2068).

**TOWN LAYOUT** Salida sits on the southwestern bank of the Arkansas River, just above its confluence with the South Arkansas. U.S. 50 (**Rainbow Boulevard**), which follows the north bank of the South Arkansas, marks the southern edge of the town. At the eastern city limit, Colo. 291 (**Oak Street**) turns north off U.S. 50, and six blocks later, turns northwest as **First Street** through the historic downtown area. Though the southeastern quadrant of the city is platted north-south, most of Salida is oriented at a 45° angle: lettered streets (A through O) run southwest-northeast, and numbered streets (1st through 17th) run northwest-southeast. The heart of town is around First through Third Street, where they are intersected by D Street and E Street.

## GETTING AROUND

**Chaffee County Transit,** 132 West First Street (tel. 539-3935), provides low-cost public transportation throughout the Salida–Buena Vista–Monarch area. Call for schedules.

Ford rental cars are available at **Salida Motors,** 6250 U.S. 50 (tel. 539-6633).

## FAST FACTS

The **area code** is 719. The **climate** ranges in temperature from an average July high of 84° to an average January low of 12°. In case of **emergency,** call 539-2596, or contact the Chaffee County Sheriff, Crestone Avenue off Third Street. Health care is provided by the **Heart of the Rockies Regional Medical Center,** First Street and B Street (tel. 539-6661). The main **post office** is at 310 D Street (tel. 539-2548). For **road conditions,** call 539-6688.

## WHAT TO SEE & DO
### ATTRACTIONS

**THE ANGEL OF SHAVANO, Mount Shavano, 15 miles west of Salida on the Continental Divide.**

In May and early June, this unusual feature is easily discerned on the slopes of 14,239-foot Mount Shavano. Created by spring snow lingering in open meadows, it resembles a woman, her arms outstretched, guarding the Arkansas Valley below her. Native American legend says her body melts away to nourish arid farmlands in the summer months, only to reappear the following spring.

**MONARCH AERIAL TRAMWAY, Monarch Pass, U.S. 50, 22 miles west of Salida. Tel. 719/539-4789.**

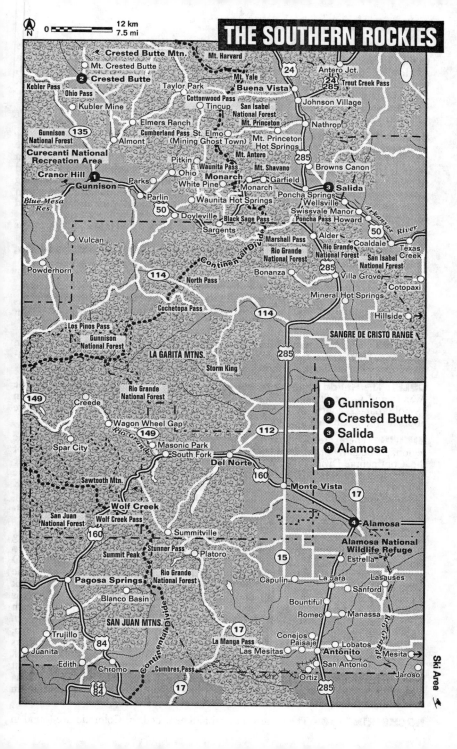

Open in summer only, this scenic tramway climbs from 11,312-foot Monarch Pass to the Continental Divide Observatory at an altitude of 11,921 feet, where there is a spectacular 360° view of the southern Colorado Rockies. When visibility is perfect, you can see for about 75 miles in any direction. The tram consists of six four-passenger gondolas.

**Admission:** $4.50 adults, $2.50 children.
**Open:** May 15–Oct 15, daily 9am–4pm.

### SALIDA HOT SPRINGS, 410 W. Rainbow Blvd. Tel. 539-6738.

Colorado's largest indoor hot springs have been in commercial operation since 1937, when the Works Progress Administration built the pools as a Depression-era project. Ute tribes considered the mineral waters, rich in bicarbonate, sodium, and sulphate, to be sacred and medicinal. Today, a lap pool, shallow pool, and wading pool are kept around 96°F year round; private hot baths are also available. A museum of Salida-area history is associated. In adjacent Centennial Park are tennis and volleyball courts and other recreational facilities.

**Admission:** $4 adults, $2 students 6–17, $1 children 5 and under, $1.50 seniors (60 and older).
**Open:** Memorial Day–Labor Day, daily noon–9pm; Labor Day–Memorial Day, Tues–Fri 4–9pm, Sat–Sun 1:30–9pm.

## SPORTS & RECREATION

**BICYCLING** The **Colorado Cyclery, 111** North E Street (tel. 539-BIKE), has information on bicycling throughout the region. The shop itself specializes in custom work and unusual bicycles.

**FISHING** The **Arkansas River** is considered by many as the finest fishing river in Colorado. There's also trout fishing in numerous **alpine lakes,** including Cottonwood Lake, Twin Lakes, Rainbow Lake, and O'Haver Lake.

**GOLF** The **Salida Golf Club,** an 18-hole, par-70 municipal course at Crestone Avenue and Grant Street (tel. 539-6373), and the **Collegiate Golf Course,** an 18-hole, par-72 course at 28775 Fairway Drive, Buena Vista (tel. 395-6622), are popular among Chaffee County residents and visitors.

**HIKING** There are outstanding trails for all experience levels throughout the region, particularly in the **San Isabel National Forest,** along the eastern slope of the Continental Divide west of Salida. Of particular interest are hikes into the Collegiate Range (Mounts Harvard, Columbia, Yale, Princeton, and Oxford) off the Cottonwood Creek road west of Buena Vista, and trips from the ghost town of **St. Elmo** up the Chalk Creek road from Mount Princeton Hot Springs.

For maps and other information, visit the offices of the **U.S. Forest Service,** 230 West 16th Street, Salida (tel. 539-3591).

**RIVER RAFTING** As previously mentioned, this region is the white-water-rafting center of the Rockies. The biggest reason is the ✪ **Arkansas Headwaters Recreation Area,** with headquarters on Colo. 291 (P.O. Box 126, Salida, CO 81201; tel. 719/539-7289). The recreation area has created 14 new sites along the river—4 of them above Salida, 10 below—offering everything from raft and kayak access to fishing, hiking, camping, and picnicking. The busiest stretch of the river is **Browns Canyon,** a pink-granite wilderness between Buena Vista and Salida, with Class III to V rapids focused on an 8-mile stretch from Nathrop to Hecla Junction.

For a full listing of all rafting companies operating in the Chaffee County area, check with the Heart of the Rockies Chamber of Commerce. Leading outfitters include **Dvorak's Kayak & Rafting Expeditions,** 17921 U.S. 285, Nathrop (tel. 719/539-6851, or 800/824-3795); **Moondance River Expeditions,** 310 West First Street, Salida (tel. 539-2113); and **Wilderness Aware,** P.O. Box 1550, Buena Vista, CO 81211 (tel. 719/395-2112, or 800/462-7238). Half-day excursions can run as low as $25 per person.

**ROCKHOUNDING** The richest mineral and gem beds in Colorado are found in the upper Arkansas River valley and the eastern slope of the Continental Divide, just west of Salida. For information, contact the **Columbine Gem and Mineral Society,** 525 West 16th Street, Salida (tel. 539-6196).

**SKIING** The **Monarch Ski Resort,** 20 miles west of Salida at Monarch Pass on U.S. 50, is among the finest of Colorado's smaller ski areas. It not only serves all levels of skiers, but also boasts the 100-room overnight **Monarch Mountain Lodge** (with very moderate prices) and gourmet restaurant. For information on either, write 1 Powder Place, Monarch, CO 81227 (tel. 719/539-2581, or 800/332-3668).

Monarch's four chair lifts serve distinctly different areas. The short **Tumbelina Lift** is ideal for beginners and early intermediates. The **Breeze Way Lift** serves predominantly intermediate terrain. The **Garfield Lift** is popular among advanced skiers, who can tango down the Kanonen and Cleanzer runs, but the long, winding Sleepy Hollow and Roundabout trails are ideal for novices. Less adept skiers can also take the **Panorama Lift** to the mountaintop and return to the bottom via Ticaboo or Sky Walker, but headwall runs like High Anxiety appeal to experts, and a recent expansion has added 30 acres of upper-level glade and powder skiing in the **Curecanti Bowl.**

All-day tickets cost $24 for adults, $15 for juniors (age 7 to 12), $12 for seniors (age 62 to 69), with discounts for multiday tickets and free skiing for all those under 7 or over 69. Group ski lessons cost $20. The area is open from Thanksgiving to early April, daily from 9am to 4pm.

# WHERE TO STAY

**ECONOMY 9 MOTEL, 7350 W. U.S. 50, Salida, CO 81201. Tel. 719/ 539-6733,** or 800/759-0338. 17 rms (all with bath). A/C TV TEL
**$ Rates:** Single or double, $24.50–$32.50 Apr–Memorial Day, $34.50–$46.50 Memorial Day–Labor Day, $30.50–$40.50 Mar and Labor Day–Oct, $26.50–$34.50 Nov–Feb. AE, CB, DC, DISC, MC, V.
A central park strip with paths through a forest of small evergreens, focused around a hot-tub pavilion, gives this small budget motel a friendly feel right from the start. Besides, coffee is always on in the office in the morning. Single rooms have a king-size bed, desk with a phone, nightstand, table and chairs, and large bathroom. Doubles are more spacious, and contain two queen-size beds. No-smoking rooms are available.

**THE POOR FARM COUNTRY INN, 8495 County Rd. 160, Salida, CO 81201. Tel. 719/539-3818.** 5 rms (2 with bath), 14 dormitory beds (shared bath).
**$ Rates** (including full breakfast): $41 single or double without bath, $51 single or double with bath. Children under 5 stay free in parents' room. JCB, MC, V.
Built by Chaffee County in 1892 as a home for the indigent, this building—about 2 miles northwest of town—served that purpose for half a century. Since 1983, however, it has been a charming bed and breakfast, and is listed on the National Register of Historic Places. The grounds cover 11 acres, including a quarter-mile stretch along the Arkansas River, as well as a fishing pond and play area for children. The downstairs contains a TV and games parlor with a piano, a large dining room, and an open kitchen. Guest rooms, appointed in country-style floral decor, are furnished with turn-of-the-century antiques. Two downstairs rooms have private baths; three second-story rooms share two baths. A dormitory loft sleeps another 14.

**RED WOOD LODGE, 7310 U.S. 50, Salida, CO 81201. Tel. 719/539-2528,** or 800/234-1077. 25 rms, 3 suites. A/C TV TEL
**$ Rates:** May 15–Sept 15 and hol periods, $48–$58 single; $58–$68 double or suite. Other times, $40–$44 single; $44–$58 double, $52–$58 suite. AE, CB, DC, DISC, MC, V.
Red cedar is used throughout this very nice property, from construction to custom furnishings to the two outdoor hot tubs. Every room is different, but each typically has king-size or queen-size beds, original artwork on the walls, a desk with phone, a TV on a credenza or tucked away in an armoire, pedestal sinks, clock radios, and other touches. Family suites have two full bedrooms, each with its own own remote-

control TV and phone. No-smoking rooms and facilities for the disabled are available; complimentary coffee and newspaper are offered in the lobby each morning. Besides the hot tubs, there's a heated outdoor pool, and a changing room, also heated, for those cold winter nights.

## WHERE TO DINE

### COUNTRY BOUNTY RESTAURANT & GIFT SHOPPE, 413 W. Rainbow Blvd. (U.S. 50). Tel. 539-3546.

**Cuisine:** AMERICAN/MEXICAN. **Reservations:** Not accepted.

**$ Prices:** Breakfast $2.25–$6.75; lunch $3.25–$6.95; dinner $4.25–$10.95. MC, V.

**Open:** Daily 7am–10pm.

It's hard to determine if this is more a gift shop than a restaurant or vice versa. Each seems to pervade the other, with all manner of country-style crafts, southwestern Native American jewelry, books, postcards, and more items on display almost spilling over into the dining booths. The fare on the menu is equally traditional: hotcakes, Denver omelets, and ham and eggs for breakfast; cheeseburgers and hot turkey sandwiches for lunch; chicken-fried steak and Rocky Mountain trout for dinner. There's also a Mexican menu and a variety of salads, along with locally famous pies for dessert. A children's menu is priced $2.25 to $2.95.

### FIRST ST. CAFE, 137 E. First St. Tel. 539-4759.

**Cuisine:** AMERICAN. **Reservations:** Not accepted.

**$ Prices:** Breakfast $1.25–$5.25; lunch $2.95–$7.95; dinner $6.25–$16.95. AE, DISC, MC, V.

**Open:** May 15–Sept, Mon–Sat 8am–10pm; Oct–May 14, Mon–Sat 8am–8pm.

A brick building dating from 1883, in the heart of historic downtown Salida, is the home of one of the city's most popular restaurants. The hardwood floor and many tables were once part of the stage at the Red Rocks Amphitheater west of Denver; less historic are the regional paintings and photographs on the walls, which give the café a gallery feel. Indeed, the establishment is a focal point for the artists, musicians, and social activists of the central Rockies. The kitchen turns out gourmet home-cooking: meals such as French toast, stuffed with cream cheese and walnuts, for breakfast; vegetarian casseroles and Monte Cristo sandwiches for lunch; steak Gardenier, barbecued ribs, and halibut filets for dinner.

---

# 4. ALAMOSA

216 miles SW of Denver; 149 miles E of Durango;
173 miles N of Santa Fe, New Mexico

**GETTING THERE By Plane** The **Alamosa Municipal Airport,** 3 miles south off U.S. 285 (tel. 589-2593), has daily service to and from Denver via **Continental Express** (tel. 719/589-3804, or 800/525-0820).

**By Bus** **SLV Van Lines,** 513 Sixth Street (tel. 719/589-4948), connects Alamosa with Greyhound/Trailways and TNM&O lines at Walsenburg.

**By Car** Alamosa is at the junction of U.S. 160, which runs east 73 miles to I-70 at Walsenburg and west to Durango and beyond; and U.S. 285, which extends south to Santa Fe, New Mexico, and north to Denver via Monte Vista and the upper Arkansas River valley. Because of a jog in U.S. 285, however, a more direct route into the city from the north is to take Colo. 17 the last 50 miles.

**SPECIAL EVENTS** Annual area events include **Cabin Fever Daze,** in mid-February, in Creede; the **Crane Festival,** in mid-March, in Monte Vista; the **Sunshine Festival,** on the first weekend of June, in Cole Park, Alamosa; **Cotton-**

wood Capers, on the Fourth of July weekend, in Alamosa; the **Colorado State Mining Championships,** on the Fourth of July weekend, in Creede; **Fiesta Days,** on the last weekend of July, in San Luis; and **Covered Wagon Days,** on the first weekend of August, in Del Norte.

---

**F**ounded in 1878 with the extension of the Denver & Rio Grande Railroad into the San Luis Valley, the town was named for the cottonwood (*alamosa*) trees that lined the banks of the Rio Grande. Soon rails spread out in all directions from the community, and it became a thriving transportation center for farmers and supply depot for miners. Today, with a population of about 7,000, Alamosa remains a center for farming, especially of vegetables. It is also the tourism hub for south-central Colorado, and an educational center: Adams State College, a 4-year institution, was founded here in 1921.

## ORIENTATION

**INFORMATION** The **Alamosa County Chamber of Commerce,** Cole Park (Chamber Drive at Third Street), Alamosa, CO 81101 (tel. 719/589-3681), can provide information on the entire six-county San Luis Valley region.

**TOWN LAYOUT** Located on the southwestern bank of the Rio Grande River, Alamosa is the center of the San Luis Valley—a vast basin, 7,500 feet in elevation, surrounded on the west by the San Juan Mountains and on the east by the sharp-ridged Sangre de Cristo Range. As you enter by car from the east, **U.S. 160** crosses a bridge over the Rio Grande; immediately ahead, on **Fourth Street** at Chamber Drive, are the city hall, police station, and chamber of commerce office. The arterial, however, runs south a block, then extends west as **Main Street.** Two blocks farther, Main is crossed by **State Avenue,** the principal north-south byway. Another six blocks ahead is the intersection of **West Avenue,** which runs south as U.S. 285. U.S. 160 continues in a northwesterly direction. **First Street,** four blocks north of Main, bisects the campus of **Adams State College** on the west side of town; numbered streets parallel First all the way south through 20th Street.

## FAST FACTS

The **area code** is 719. The **climate** averages in temperature from about 65°F in summer to 15°F in winter. In case of **emergency,** call 589-5807, or contact the Colorado State Patrol (tel. 589-2939). **San Luis Valley Regional Medical Center** is at 106 Blanca Street, at First Street (tel. 589-2511). The **post office** is at 505 Third Street, just off State Avenue (tel. 589-4908). Local **sales tax** is 7%.

## WHAT TO SEE & DO

### ATTRACTIONS

**GREAT SAND DUNES NATIONAL MONUMENT, Colo. 150, 38 miles northeast of Alamosa (Mosca, CO 81146). Tel. 378-2312.**
One of the most startling sights in North America is this 55-square-mile expanse of fine sand, piled nearly 700 feet high against the western edge of the Sangre de Cristo Mountains. The tallest sand dunes on the continent, they seem totally incongruous in this location, far from any sea or major desert. Explore them on foot: Although the surrounding mountain ranges are within view, it's easy to feel as if you are in the middle of nowhere.

The dunes were formed over thousands of years by winds blowing northeasterly across the San Luis Valley. They began forming at the end of the last Ice Age, when streams of water from melting glaciers carried rocks, gravel, and silt down from the mountains into the valley. Even today the winds are changing the face of the dunes, returning to the monument the sands that Medano Creek takes from the dunes' leading edge and carries into the valley.

So-called "reversing winds" from the mountains pile the dunes back upon themselves, building them higher and higher. Though it's physically impossible for sand to be piled steeper than 31°, they often seem more sheer because of deceptive shadows and colors that change with the light: gold, pink, tan, sometimes even bluish. Climbing dunes is fun, but it can be tiring at this 7,500-foot altitude. The sand can get as hot as 140°F in summer, so visitors must wear shoes to protect their feet.

Among the specialized animals that survive in this weird environment are the Ord kangaroo rat, a creature that never drinks water; and two insects found nowhere else on earth, the Great Sand Dunes tiger beetle and the giant sand-treader camel cricket. These animals and the flora of the adjacent mountain foothills are discussed in evening programs and guided walks during the summer season. A self-guided nature trail is open year round. Pinyon Flats Campground is open from May to October.

From Alamosa, there are two main routes to the national monument: east 14 miles on U.S. 160, then north on Colo. 150; or north 14 miles on Colo. 17 to Mosca, then east on Six Mile Lane to the junction of Colo. 150.

**Admission:** $1 per car.

**Open:** Monument, daily 24 hours. Visitor center, Memorial Day–Labor Day, daily 7am–8pm; the rest of the year, daily 8am–5pm.

**ADAMS STATE COLLEGE MUSEUMS, Richardson and Third Sts. Tel. 589-7151.**

There are two significant museums at Alamosa's higher-education institution. The **Luther E. Bean Museum,** on the second floor of Richardson Hall, has one of the Southwest's most complete collections of Hispanic *santos,* or religious icons, and a priceless collection of European porcelains and furniture. The **E. S. Museum** of archeology and anthropology, in the Education and Social Sciences Building, focuses on Anasazi artifacts.

**Admission:** Free.

**Open:** Bean Museum, Mon–Fri 1–5pm; E. S. Museum, afternoon tours by appointment.

**ALAMOSA–MONTE VISTA NATIONAL WILDLIFE REFUGE COMPLEX, El Rancho Lane, 6 miles southeast of Alamosa (P.O. Box 1148, Alamosa, CO 81101). Tel. 589-4021.**

At a time when wetlands conservation is a leading cause of environmentalists, these refuges have conserved nearly 25,000 acres of vital land for a variety of marsh birds and waterfowl, including many migrating and wintering species. Sandhill and whooping cranes visit in October; at other times of the year there may be egrets, herons, avocets, bitterns, and other avian species. A wide variety of ducks are year-round residents. The Alamosa unit, east of Alamosa via U.S. 160, straddles the Rio Grande and is the site of the refuge office; there's excellent wildlife viewing from the Bluff Overlook Road. The Monte Vista unit, 5 miles south of Monte Vista (22 miles west of Alamosa) off Colo. 15, has a self-guided loop drive along the Avocet Trail.

**Admission:** Free.

**Open:** Refuge, daily sunrise–sunset; refuge office, Mon–Fri 7:30am–4pm.

**RIO GRANDE ART MARKET, Main and State Sts. Tel. 589-5557.**

Traditional and contemporary works by artisans from throughout the San Luis Valley are sold daily at this fascinating market, a nonprofit project of the San Luis Valley Economic Development Council.

**Admission:** Free.

**Open:** Jan–Mar, Mon–Sat 10am–6pm; Apr–Dec, Mon–Sat 10am–8pm.

## SPORTS & RECREATION

**BICYCLING** Rentals, repairs, and full information on mountain biking in the upper Arkansas River valley can be obtained from **Kristi Mountain Sports,** Villa Mall, U.S. 160 (tel. 589-9759).

---

**FISHING**  The Rio Grande is an outstanding stream for trout, walleye, and catfish, and there are numerous reservoirs around the San Luis Valley. For licenses, tackle, and advice, visit **Spencer Sporting Goods**, 616 Main Street (tel. 589-4361).

**GOLF**  The **Cattails Golf Club**, on Country Club Circle off State Avenue (tel. 589-9515), is a new 18-hole course on the north side of Alamosa. The **Great Sand Dunes Country Club**, at Zapata Ranch, 5303 Colo. 150 (tel. 378-2356), is a championship 18-hole course, 26 miles northeast of Alamosa. There are two 9-hole courses in the San Luis Valley: the **Monte Vista Golf Course**, Monte Vista (tel. 852-9995), 17 miles west of Alamosa, and the **Los Cumbres Golf Course**, Crestone (tel. 256-4856), 50 miles northeast of Alamosa.

**HIKING**  The best opportunities in the region are found in the surrounding **Rio Grande National Forest**, with district offices at 1803 West U.S. 160, Monte Vista (tel. 852-5941). One of the most popular hikes with easy access is **Zapata Falls**, reached off Colo. 150 about 20 miles northeast of Alamosa. This cavernous waterfall on the northwest flank of 14,345-foot Mount Blanca freezes in the winter, turning its cave into a natural icebox that often remains so past July 4.

**HUNTING**  The national forest and surrounding public lands welcome hunters seeking deer and elk, upland game birds and waterfowl. Many enjoy stays at **Mt. Blanca Game Bird & Trout, Inc.**, P.O. Box 236, Blanca, CO 81123 (tel. 719/379-DUCK). This full-board lodge, reached by traveling 21 miles east from Alamosa on U.S. 160 and southwest about 5 miles on well-marked county roads, requires no license for guided hunting (September to April) or fishing (year round). Half-day expeditions for pheasant, chukkar, quail, and other game birds run $99, with lower prices for ducks, geese, or doves. Trout fishing is offered in five fully stocked ponds, at a cost of $35 (full day, catch-and-release). Rod and gun rentals and sales are available as well. Rooms run $58, double occupancy; three full meals is $27 additional per person.

**SWIMMING**  **Splashland Hot Springs**, Colo. 17 (tel. 589-5151), 1½ miles north of Alamosa, has a geothermally heated outdoor pool and wading pool; it's open Memorial Day to Labor Day, Thursday through Tuesday.

## WHERE TO STAY

**ALAMOSA LAMPLIGHTER MOTEL, 425 Main St., Alamosa, CO 81101. Tel. 719/589-6636,** or 800/359-2138. Fax 719/589-3831. 70 rms (all with bath). A/C TV TEL
**$ Rates:** May–Labor Day, $36–$46 single; $41–$52 double. Early Sept to Apr, $30–$38 single; $34–$44 double. AE, CB, DC, DISC, MC, V.
This downtown motel, of concrete-block construction, actually consists of two separate properties: the original building and an annex four blocks west. If some maintenance problems are conquered, this can be a very nice lodging. Guest rooms have king-size, queen-size, or double beds, with some waterbeds available; three rooms have kitchens. Furnishings include a desk, table and chairs, and vanity outside the bathroom area. No-smoking rooms are available. There's shuttle service to the Alamosa Airport, and valet laundry service at the desk. The motel has an indoor swimming pool and sauna, as well as a hot tub at the annex. A coffee shop is open from 6am to 9pm, serving standard American cuisine.

**THE COTTONWOOD INN, 123 San Juan Ave., Alamosa, CO 81101. Tel. 719/589-3882.** 5 rms (3 with bath).
**$ Rates** (including breakfast): $40–$61 single; $46–$65 double. MC, V.
This 1908 Edwardian bungalow, three blocks north of Main Street, has a distinct arts-and-crafts orientation. Hosts Julie Mordecai and George Sellman have decorated the common areas and guest bedrooms as a gallery of regional art, much of which is for sale. Each room is a little bit different: The Rosa Room, for instance, has queen-

size and single beds to accommodate small families, along with children's books and stuffed animals. The Blanca Room weds southwestern decor with art deco motifs, while the Verde Room features old prints and a hand-loomed coverlet. A television and video library are located in the living room.

**GREAT SAND DUNES COUNTRY CLUB & INN, Zapata Ranch, 5303 Colo. 150, Mosca, CO 81146. Tel. 719/378-2356.** Fax 719/378-2428. 14 rms, 1 suite (all with bath).

**$ Rates** (including breakfast): May–Labor Day, $150 single or double; $180 suite. Labor Day–Oct, $130 single or double; $160 suite. AE, DISC, MC, V. **Closed:** Nov–Apr.

Beautiful cottonwood trees surround and shade this lovely resort, which occupies the grounds of a former cattle ranch established by Spanish land grant in the early 19th century. The cattle aren't there anymore, but buffalo are raised on the ranch, and mule deer frequently browse the fairways of the 18-hole championship golf course. Guest rooms are intentionally rustic, with furnishings made by hand right on the ranch; but private baths, individually controlled heating, and quilted comforters take much of the raw edge off. This is a getaway spot: There's no smoking in the rooms, TVs are available by request only, and the only phone is one shared by all guests. A gourmet restaurant serves creative American cuisine, with lunches priced at $5.25 to $6.50 and dinner dishes running $10.95 to $15.50. Besides the golf course, facilities include a swimming pool, sauna and Jacuzzi, exercise and weight room, and horseback-riding stables.

The inn is located 26 miles northeast of Alamosa: Take U.S. 160 14 miles east; turn north on Colo. 150 as if to Grand Sand Dunes National Monument. Then 4 miles before the monument gate, turn onto a gravel road (signposted ZAPATA RANCH) and proceed three-quarters of a mile to the inn.

# WHERE TO DINE

**LARA'S SOFT-SPOKEN RESTAURANT, 801 State St. Tel. 589-6769.**
   **Cuisine:** MEXICAN/ITALIAN/AMERICAN. **Reservations:** Not necessary.
**$ Prices:** Appetizers $2.25–$3.25; main courses $2.50–$5.50 at lunch, $3.95–$11.95 at dinner. No credit cards.
   **Open:** Mon–Sat 11am–8pm.

As the name would suggest, the decor here is subdued and simple: white plastic chairs at wooden tables, local artwork on the walls, classical music piped through. The food, however, is worth shouting about. The Mexican-American dishes are particularly good, including sirloin steak verde (with a green-chile sauce) and arroz con pollo (a chicken-and-rice dish). Mark and Marian Lara serve a wide-ranging menu of steaks and ribs, crab legs and baked fish, Italian pastas, chicken Parmesan, and standard Mexican favorites such as enchiladas, burritos, and fajitas.

**ST. IVES PUB & EATERY, 719 Main St. Tel. 589-0711.**
   **Cuisine:** DELI. **Reservations:** Not accepted.
**$ Prices:** Appetizers $2.35–$4.95; lunch/dinner $2.75–$5.95. MC, V.
   **Open:** Mon–Sat 11am–midnight.

You'll find the "eatery" in front, with plants hanging above green-cloaked tables and big windows gazing upon pedestrians on Main Street; the "pub" in the rear, with a jukebox, sports TV, and simple wooden tables. The fare focuses on New York deli sandwiches, like the Reuben and the Empire State: roast beef, ham, turkey, corned beef, Swiss cheese, and cole slaw wedged between three slices of rye bread. Soups, salads, and hamburgers satisfy most other visitors.

**TRUE GRITS STEAK HOUSE, 100 Santa Fe Ave. Tel. 589-9954.**
   **Cuisine:** STEAK/SEAFOOD. **Reservations:** Recommended summer nights.
**$ Prices:** Appetizers $1–$3.50; main courses $5–$14; lunch $3.50–$5.90. DISC, MC, V.
   **Open:** Daily 11am–10pm.

Actor John Wayne is, beyond question, the star of this popular local restaurant just off U.S. 160 on the east side of the Rio Grande bridge. A movie poster of his Oscar-winning *True Grit* greets visitors near the entrance, while various photos and paintings of the Duke are interspersed with contemporary western decor elsewhere in the restaurant. Most folks come here for the mesquite-grilled steaks, like the Big Jake (a 20-ounce sirloin) or the Sons of Katy Elder (a tender filet mignon). You can also order a Rio Lobo (jumbo fantail shrimp) or other movies, *er,* meals by name. There's a children's menu and a large soup-and-salad bar, as well as a full lounge.

## EASY EXCURSIONS

Each of the other counties (besides Alamosa County) that make up the San Luis Valley has interesting attractions of its own.

### SAN LUIS

In the heart of Costilla County lies ✪ **San Luis,** the oldest town in Colorado. Located 42 miles southeast of Alamosa via U.S. 160 east and Colo. 159 south, the community (pop. 850) was founded in 1851 by Hispanic settlers moving north from Taos, New Mexico. Today the Spanish influence is still strong in the area.

A leading attraction is the **Shrine of the Stations of the Cross,** consisting of 15 Huberto Maestas bronzes that recount the story of Christ's death and resurrection, along a three-quarter-mile trail that winds around a hillside in the center of town. Also in San Luis are the **Sangre de Cristo Church** (Church of the Most Precious Blood), on Church Place, in continuous use as a place of worship since the early 1860s; the **San Luis Museum, Cultural and Commercial Center,** 402 Church Place (tel. 672-3611), with memorabilia of the area's rich Hispanic heritage; and the **Centro Artesano,** 512 Church Place, a cooperative venture of some 70 San Luis Valley artisans.

Sixteen miles north of San Luis and 26 miles east of Alamosa, on Colo. 159 just south of its junction with U.S. 160, is **Fort Garland State Museum** (tel. 719/379-3512), a re-creation of the 1858 fort that protected the San Luis Valley from attacks by natives and outlaws for 25 years. Col. Kit Carson was among the commandants of the fort, which consists of six flat-roofed adobe buildings. Exhibits portray life at the frontier post. It's open Memorial Day weekend to Labor Day, Monday through Saturday from 10am to 5pm and on Sunday from 1 to 5pm, with off-season tours by appointment.

**WHERE TO STAY & DINE** The Centro Artesan in San Luis is a part of **El Convento Bed and Breakfast,** 512 Church Place, San Luis, CO 81152 (tel. 672-4223). Built as a school in 1905, it now houses four handsome guest rooms with handcrafted furnishings and southwestern motifs. Rates are $40 single, $50 double. Good Mexican food is available at **Emma's Hacienda,** Main Street (tel. 672-9902).

### ANTONITO

South from Alamosa, U.S. 285 cuts a nearly straight line through the heart of Conejos County. The best-known attraction in this part of the state is the ✪ **Cumbres & Toltec Scenic Railroad,** P.O. Box 668, Antonito, CO 81120 (tel. 376-5483). The depot is 28 miles south of Alamosa, just off the highway. Built in 1880 to serve remote mining camps, the train follows a spectacular 64-mile narrow-gauge track through the San Juan Mountains from Antonito to Chama, New Mexico, and is considered the finest remaining example of a once-vast Rocky Mountain rail network. The *Colorado Limited* weaves through groves of pine and aspen, and past strange rock formations, before ascending through the spectacular Toltec Gorge of the Los Piños River. At the rail junction community of Osier, passengers picnic or have a catered lunch while the *Limited* stops to change engines with the *New Mexico Express.* Then round-trip passengers return to their starting point in Antonito, while onward passengers continue a climb through tunnels and trestles to the summit of 10,015-foot Cumbres Pass, then drop down a precipitous 4% grade to Chama.

A through trip from Antonito to Chama (or vice versa), traveling one way by van, runs $45.50 for adults, $23 for children 11 and under. A regular round-trip, without transfers, is $29, but this omits either the gorge or the pass. Either way, it's an all-day adventure, leaving between 8 and 10:30am, and returning between 4:30 and 6:30pm. Write or phone ahead for reservations: The train operates daily from Memorial Day weekend to mid-October. Jointly owned by the states of Colorado and New Mexico, it's a registered National Historic Site.

Also in the town of Antonito (pop. 1,100) is **Our Lady of Guadalupe Church,** the oldest church in the state of Colorado, built in the late 1850s.

## MANASSA

Seven miles north of Antonito on the highway back toward Alamosa, and 3 miles east on Colo. 142, is the village of Manassa (pop. 950), best known as the hometown of heavyweight boxing great Jack Dempsey. The former world champion (1919–26) was born here in 1895, and began his fighting career at the age of 14, earning $1 a bout in mining camps. He went on to international acclaim, and was an elder statesman of the sport until his death in 1979. The **Jack Dempsey Museum,** 401 Main Street (tel. 843-5207), open from Memorial Day to Labor Day, Monday through Saturday from 9am to 5pm, has many photographs and memorabilia of Dempsey and his family.

## CREEDE

Another 17 miles beyond Del Norte (48 miles west of Alamosa), Colo. 149 forks north off U.S. 160 at South Fork, and follows the Rio Grande nearly to its source in the San Juan Mountains. It's 23 miles from the junction to ✪ **Creede** (pop. 600), one of the best-preserved of all 19th-century Colorado silver-mining towns. Founded in 1889, it had a population of 10,000 by 1892, when a balladeer wrote, "It's day all day in the daytime, and there is no night in Creede." Over $1 million in silver was mined *every day.* But the Silver Panic of 1893 eclipsed Creede's rising star. For most of the next century area mines produced just enough silver and other minerals to sustain the community, until the 1960s when tourism and outdoor recreation became paramount.

**WHAT TO SEE & DO** The former Denver & Rio Grande Railroad depot is now the **Creede Museum,** Sixth Street and San Luis Street (tel. 658-2374), which tells the story of the town's wild-and-woolly heyday. There were dozens of saloons and gambling tables, and shootouts were not uncommon: Bob Ford, the killer of Jesse James, was murdered in his own saloon and is buried here. Bat Masterson and "Poker Alice" Tubbs were other notorious early residents. Photographs and exhibits on mining, gambling, and other activities are among the museum's collection. It's open Memorial Day to Labor Day, daily from 10am to 4pm; off-season, by appointment.

You can obtain a walking-tour map of historic Creede from the **Creede– Mineral County Chamber of Commerce,** north of the county courthouse on Creede Avenue about North First Street (P.O. Box 580), Creede, CO 81130 (tel. 658-2374). The chamber will also give intrepid travelers directions to the **Wheeler Geologic Area,** a region of bizarre natural rock formations accessible only by Jeep, horseback, or 5-hour hike; the ghost town of **Bachelor,** a rugged drive or hike north from Creede; and **North Creede Canyon,** where remnants of the old town of Creede still stand near the **Commodore Mine,** whose workings seem to keep a ghostly vigil over the canyon. Don't miss the **Creede Firehouse,** hewn out of solid rock; tours are offered twice daily, Monday through Saturday, in summer, by the Mineral County Extension Office (tel. 658-2848).

Of special interest is the ✪ **Creede Repertory Theatre,** P.O. Box 269, Creede, CO 81130 (tel. 658-2540), established in 1966 by a small troupe of young actors from the University of Kansas. Now a nationally acclaimed repertory company, it will celebrate its 27th year in 1992, with performances from mid-June through Labor Day in its theater on Creede Avenue at North First Street. Tickets for most performances run $8 and $9.

**WHERE TO STAY & DINE** Next door to the Rep Theatre is the **Creede Hotel & Restaurant,** Creede Avenue, Creede, CO 81130 (tel. 658-2608). A bed-and-breakfast establishment, it has four rooms, two with private bath, priced at $30 and $40. Reservations are suggested for the gourmet dinners served here.

Outside of Creede, the **Wason Ranch,** a hunting and fishing lodge 2 miles southeast on Colo. 149 (P.O. Box 220, Creede, CO 81130; tel. 658-2413), has modern, two-bedroom log cabins available for $40 per day, for up to four people.

## LA GARITA

Saguache County, north of Alamosa and Del Norte, is nearly as large as the other five San Luis Valley counties combined. One of its most interesting communities is La Garita, a quaint hamlet 43 miles northwest of Alamosa, 8 miles west of U.S. 285. Located here is the historical ✪ **San Juan Art Center** (tel. 719/734-3191), which offers a rare opportunity to see Hispanic artisans turning out works of traditional design in the old La Sapilla de San Juan Bautista Church. The craftspeople include weavers, potters, sculptors, and *colcha* embroiderers, all members of the Artes del Valle cooperative. The center is open from Memorial Day to Labor Day, Monday through Saturday from 10am to 5pm and on Sunday from 1 to 5pm; call for winter hours.

West of La Garita in the Rio Grande National Forest are several interesting sites, including **La Ventana Natural Arch** and the sheer cliffs of **Penitiente Canyon,** internationally famed among rock climbers. Both are reached via County Road 38A. Inquire locally for directions.

## CRESTONE

One of Colorado's most intriguing communities is remote Crestone, isolated at the foot of the Sangre de Cristo Range, 12 miles east of Colo. 17 on Colo. 117, about 50 miles north of Alamosa and 30 miles east of Saguache. Originally part of a 17th-century Spanish land grant, it has become an upscale community for New Age refugees of urban centers, under the aegis of the **Baca Grande Corporation,** P.O. Box 126, Crestone, CO 81131 (tel. 256-4864). Dine at **The Bistro,** in the Baca Meadows Townhouse Complex (tel. 256-4114).

# CHAPTER 13

# SOUTHEASTERN COLORADO

**1. PUEBLO**
**2. TRINIDAD**
**3. LA JUNTA**

**C**olorado's southeastern quadrant is dominated by the Arkansas River system. This mighty stream forges one of the world's most spectacular canyons—the deep, narrow Royal Gorge—as it wends its way down from the Rocky Mountain foothills. As it runs through Pueblo, the state's third-largest city, it supplies water for a major steel industry. Then it rolls across the Great Plains, providing life-giving water to an arid but soil-rich region that produces a wide variety of vegetables and fruits. Bent's Old Fort, a national historic site that has re-created the west's most important trading post of the 1830s and 1840s, also rests beside the river on the plains. South of Pueblo down I-25, the towns of Trinidad and Walsenburg are the centers of a century-old coal-mining district.

---

## 1. PUEBLO

111 miles S of Denver; 42 miles S of Colorado Springs;
317 miles N of Albuquerque, New Mexico

**GETTING THERE    By Plane**    The **Pueblo Memorial Airport,** Keeler Parkway off U.S. 50 East (tel. 948-3355), is served daily by **America West** (tel. 542-6989), **Continental Express** (tel. 948-2254), and **Trans World Airlines** (tel. 543-6100).

**By Bus**    Buses of **Greyhound/Trailways** and **TNM&O** serve Pueblo several times daily. The station is at 116 North Main Street (tel. 719/544-6295).

**By Car**    I-25 links Pueblo directly with Colorado Springs, Denver, and points north; and Santa Fe, Albuquerque, and other New Mexico cities to the south. U.S. 50 runs east to La Junta and west to Cañon City, Gunnison, and Montrose.

**SPECIAL EVENTS**    Major annual events include the **Governor's Cup Regatta,** at Pueblo Reservoir, in May; the **Rolling River Raft Race,** in July; the **Colorado State Fair,** in late August; the **Christmas Posada,** in December; and the **Yule Log Festival,** in Beulah, in December. The chamber of commerce has a recorded listing of weekly events (tel. 542-1776).

---

**A**lthough Zebulon Pike and his U.S. Army exploratory expedition camped at the future site of Pueblo (elevation 4,695 ft.) in 1806, there was no white settlement here until 1842, when Fort El Pueblo was constructed as a fur-trading outpost. It was abandoned following a Ute massacre in late 1854, but when the Colorado gold rush began in 1859, the town of Pueblo was laid out on the north side of the Arkansas River, at the site of the former fort. Other towns were platted in close proximity. Four communities—Pueblo, Central Pueblo, South Pueblo, and Bessemer (Minnequa)—grew together, each with its own street configuration, to become the modern city of Pueblo.

In the early 20th century the city grew as a major center for coal mining and steel production. Although its importance has waned somewhat, the CF&I Steel Corporation remains Pueblo's single largest employer. Job opportunities drew large immigrant populations, especially from Mexico and eastern Europe. Modern Pueblo has diversified, with many high-technology industries based here, as well as the University of Southern Colorado. As the largest city in southeastern Colorado, Pueblo is the market center for a 15-county region extending to the borders of New Mexico, Oklahoma, and Kansas. It's population is just under 100,000.

## ORIENTATION

**INFORMATION** Contact the **Pueblo Chamber of Commerce Convention and Visitors Council,** 302 North Santa Fe Avenue (P.O. Box 697), Pueblo, CO 81002 (tel. 719/542-1704), for most tourism needs. In summer, a **Visitor Information Center** is lodged in a caboose off I-25 Exit 101, in the K-Mart parking lot on Elizabeth Street at U.S. 50 West (tel. 719/543-1742); it's open May to September, daily from 8am to 5pm.

**CITY LAYOUT** The city of Pueblo is situated on the eastward-flowing Arkansas River at its confluence with Fountain Creek. The downtown core is located north of the Arkansas and west of the Fountain, immediately west of I-25. **Santa Fe Avenue** and **Main Street,** one block to its west, are the principal north-south thoroughfares; the cross streets are numbered (counting northward), with **Fourth Street** and **Eighth Street** the most important. Paralleling Main Street four blocks to its west is **Elizabeth Street,** another arterial that intersects U.S. 50 at I-25, opposite Pueblo Mall, at the north end of the city. U.S. 50 runs west from here toward Cañon City; U.S. 50 East exits I-25 about a mile farther south, and proceeds past the airport toward La Junta. Main and Fourth both cross the Arkansas to the **Mesa Junction** residential district, where several fine restaurants and bed-and-breakfasts are located. **Pueblo Boulevard** circles the city on its south and west sides, with spurs leading to the Nature Center and Pueblo Reservoir.

## GETTING AROUND

Public transportation is provided on a citywide network by **City Bus** (tel. 542-4306). For taxi service, call **City Cab** (tel. 543-2525).

Car rentals are available at the airport from **Budget** (tel. 948-3363), **Hertz** (tel. 948-3345), and **National** (tel. 948-3355).

## FAST FACTS

The **area code** is 719. In case of **emergency,** dial **911.** Medical services are provided downtown by **Parkview Episcopal Medical Center,** 400 West 16th Street (tel. 584-4000), or on the south side by **St. Mary–Corwin Regional Medical Center,** 1008 Minnequa Avenue (tel. 560-4000). The main **post office** is downtown at 421 North Main Street. For **road conditions,** call 545-8520. State and local **taxes** on rooms total 11.2%.

## WHAT TO SEE & DO

### ATTRACTIONS

**EL PUEBLO MUSEUM, First and Main Sts. Tel. 564-5274.**

Scheduled to be reconstructed at this downtown site in spring 1992, this museum presents a full-size reproduction of the original 1842 fort after which Pueblo was named. Previously occupying a former airport hangar at 905 South Prairie Street, its new location is where the El Pueblo fur-trading post stood for 12 years. Other permanent historical exhibits include artifacts from Native American tribes of the region and a description of the steel-making process.

**Admission:** $2 adults, $1 children.

**Open:** Memorial Day weekend–Labor Day, Tues–Sat 10am–5pm; the rest of the year, Wed–Sat 11am–3pm.

**THE GREENWAY AND NATURE CENTER, 5200 W. 11th St. Tel. 545-9114.**

A major recreational center, this park area comprises more than 20 miles of biking and hiking trails along the Arkansas River, along with a fishing dock, volleyball courts,

horseshoe pits, an amphitheater, tepees, reptile exhibit room, picnic areas, and a restaurant, the Café del Rio. Located here is the **Raptor Center of Pueblo,** where injured eagles, owls, hawks, and other birds of prey are nursed back to health.
**Admission:** Free.
**Open:** Daily 9am–5pm.

## HISTORIC WALKING TOUR, Union Ave. Tel. 542-1704.

Historic Pueblo runs along Union Avenue north from the Arkansas River to Elizabeth Street, a distance of about five blocks. More than 40 buildings here are listed on the National Register of Historic Places, including the **Vail Hotel,** headquarters of the Pueblo County Historical Society museum and library (open Tuesday through Saturday from 1 to 4pm), and **Union Depot,** which is slowly being converted into a historical showpiece—someday, perhaps, along the lines of Denver's Larimer Square. Walking-tour maps can be obtained from the chamber of commerce, 302 North Santa Fe Avenue.
**Admission:** Free.
**Open:** Daily 24 hours.

## PUEBLO ZOO, City Park, Goodnight Ave. Tel. 561-9664 or 561-8686.

More than 70 species of animals are displayed here, many of them in a herpetarium, Colorado's largest reptile facility. There are farm animals, a discovery room, children's rides, an antique carousel, and a gift shop.
**Admission:** 75¢ ages 12 and over, 25¢ children 5–11, free children under 5.
**Open:** Memorial Day weekend–Labor Day, daily 10am–5pm; the rest of the year, daily 9am–4pm. **Closed:** New Year's Day, Thanksgiving, and Christmas.

## ROSEMOUNT VICTORIAN HOUSE MUSEUM, 419 W. 14th St. Tel. 545-5290.

Pueblo's single leading attraction is this 37-room mansion, considered one of the finest surviving examples of Victorian architecture and decoration in North America. Built in 1891 for the pioneer Thatcher family, the three-story, 24,000-square-foot home is entirely of pink rhyolite stone in Richardsonian Romanesque style. Inside are exquisite oak, maple, and mahogany woodwork; remarkable works of stained glass; hand-decorated ceilings; exquisite Tiffany lighting fixtures; and 10 fireplaces, each with a unique character. Nearly all the furnishings are original to the mansion. On the upper floor is the early 20th-century McClelland collection of archeological curiosities from 67 countries, including an authentic Egyptian mummy.
**Admission:** $2 adults, $1 children and seniors.
**Open:** June–Aug, Mon–Sat 10am–4pm, Sun 2–4pm; Sept–Dec and Feb–May, Tues–Sat 1–4pm, Sun 2–4pm. **Closed:** Jan.

## SANGRE DE CRISTO ARTS AND CONFERENCE CENTER, 210 N. Santa Fe Ave. Tel. 543-0130.

Pueblo's cultural hub is a two-building complex that contains a 500-seat theater; two dance studios; four art galleries, one of which houses the Francis King Collection of Western Art; and the Pueblo Art Works Children's Museum, a hands-on participatory museum.
**Admission:** Varies.
**Open:** Times vary; children's museum, Mon–Sat 11am–4pm.

## SPORTS & RECREATION

**BICYCLING  The Greenway and Nature Center** (see "Attractions," above) includes more than 20 miles of bicycle paths along the Arkansas River. Bicycles can be rented at the **Nature Center of Pueblo,** 5200 West 11th Street (tel. 545-9114).

**BOATING  The Pueblo Reservoir,** also known as Lake Pueblo, is just minutes from downtown Pueblo. It features more than 60 miles of shoreline, and is rated as Colorado's single most popular recreational site. Boat rentals are available both from the **North Shore Marina,** off McCulloch Boulevard, Pueblo West, or the **South Shore Marina,** off Colo. 96, west of Pueblo Boulevard via Thatcher Avenue. Call 561-9320 for information. Waterskiing, sailing, board sailing, and jet sailing are among the popular activities. Boats and canoes can also be put into the Arkansas River at the **Greenway and Nature Center,** 5200 West 11th Street (tel. 545-9114).

**DOG RACING** There's racing at **Pueblo Greyhound Park,** Lake Avenue at Pueblo Boulevard (I-25 Exit 94; tel. 566-0370). Grandstand admission is 50¢. Call ahead for schedules.

**FISHING The Greenway and Nature Center,** 5200 West 11th Street (tel. 545-9114), boasts a 150-foot dock on the Arkansas River for fishing. Angling for rainbow trout, brown trout, kokanee salmon, and other fish is popular from shore or boat at **Pueblo Reservoir.**

**HIKING** Pueblo is the headquarters of the **San Isabel National Forest,** 1920 Valley Drive (tel. 545-8737). Information on hiking and backpacking opportunities throughout southern Colorado is available from its U.S. Forest Service office there (see the address and telephone number above).

**ICE SKATING** Public skating, lessons, hockey, figure skating, broomball, curling, and other rink activities take place at the **Pueblo Plaza Ice Arena,** 100 North Grand Avenue (tel. 542-8784). Skate rentals and sharpening are available at the arena's pro shop.

**MOTOR SPORTS** Nationally sanctioned drag-racing and dirt-truck competitions take place on a more-or-less regular basis at the **Pueblo Motorsports Park,** U.S. 50 and Pueblo Boulevard (tel. 547-9921).

Top stock-car races are held at the **Beacon Hill Speedway,** 400 Gobatti Place (tel. 545-6104).

**SWIMMING** The most popular area locally is the **Rock Canyon Recreation Area** at the east end of Lake Pueblo, 640 Pueblo Reservoir Road (tel. 561-9320). The area has a beach (50¢ admission), a water slide ($7 for all day), and bumper boats ($1 for 5 minutes).

## WHERE TO STAY

**ABRIENDO INN, 300 W. Abriendo Ave., Pueblo, CO 81004. Tel. 719/ 544-2703.** Fax 719/542-1806. 7 rms (all with bath). A/C TV TEL
   **$ Rates** (including breakfast): $43–$80 single; $48–$85 double. AE, DC, MC, V.
Built in 1906 as the mansion of brewing magnate Martin Walter, his wife, and his eight children, this house—built in traditional Foursquare architectural style—is Pueblo's finest bed-and-breakfast establishment. Located in the Mesa Junction neighborhood, just three blocks north of historic Union Avenue at the corner of Jackson Street, it has seven guest rooms, each decorated with antique furniture, quilts, armoires, and crocheted bedspreads on brass or four-poster beds. All rooms have TVs and Touch-Tone telephones with modem jacks. Two rooms are reserved for smokers. A gourmet breakfast is served in the oak-wainscoted dining room or on an outside patio in summer. Complimentary drinks are served daily from 5:30 to 7pm.

**HAMPTON INN, 4703 N. I-25 (at Eagle Ridge Rd.), Pueblo, CO 81008. Tel. 719/544-4700,** or 800/HAMPTON. Fax 719/544-6526, ext. 155. 112 rms (all with bath). A/C TV TEL
   **$ Rates** (including continental breakfast): $45–$55 single; $53–$63 double. During the State Fair, $60 single; $70 double. AE, CB, DC, DISC, MC, V.
A two-story beige concrete structure just off I-25, this motel at the north end of Pueblo is a solid representative of this reputable national chain. About half the guest rooms are geared for business travelers, with a king-size bed, sofa sleeper, and desk; the others have two queen-size beds and a table and chairs. All rooms have remote-control cable TVs with in-house movies, clock radios, and hairdryers. No-smoking rooms and facilities for the disabled are available. There's a guest laundry, and an outdoor swimming pool (open seasonally).

**RAMBLER MOTEL, 4400 N. Elizabeth St., Pueblo, CO 81008. Tel. 719/543-4173.** 28 rms, 2 suites (all with bath). TV TEL

**$ Rates:** May 15–Labor Day, $25 single; $29–$32 double; $48–$52 suite. Labor Day–May 14, $21 single; $25–$28 double; $45 suite. AE, CB, DC, DISC, MC, V.
A good choice for budget travelers, this white-brick motel surrounds a parking lot and central swimming pool (open seasonally). Twelve older rooms are wood-paneled, and have showers only (no tubs) in the bathrooms. Eighteen more spacious newer rooms have bright floral decor and modern furnishings. Every room has a queen-size bed or two double beds, a coffee maker, and free local telephone service. No-smoking rooms are available.

## WHERE TO DINE

**IRISH PUB & GRILLE, 108 W. Third St. Tel. 542-9974.**
 **Cuisine:** ITALIAN/AMERICAN. **Reservations:** Not necessary.
 **$ Prices:** Appetizers $2.50–$5.50; main courses $4.75–$8.95 at lunch, $4.95–$12.95 at dinner. AE, MC, V.
 **Open:** Mon–Sat 11am–11pm (bar open to 2am).
The clientele is American, the owners Italian-American, but there's a huge Irish flag draped from the ceiling, and therein lies much of the ambience of this downtown tavern. The Calantino family, which established the pub in 1933 and has never let it go, draws locals and visitors alike with the solid wood decor and memorabilia on the walls. Chef Jack Curry, former executive chef for Westin and Rock Resort hotels all over the world, prepares everything from pub fare—Philly cheese-steak sandwiches or buffalo burgers, for instance—to Australian lobster salads and a wide variety of linguine dishes and other pastas. Dinner choices range from chicken Picatta and New York strip steak to swordfish steak au poivre.

**LA RENAISSANCE, 217 E. Routt Ave., Mesa Junction. Tel. 543-6367.**
 **Cuisine:** STEAK/SEAFOOD. **Reservations:** Recommended.
 **$ Prices:** Appetizers $2–$7.50; main courses $4.95–$9.40 at lunch, $9.50–$23.80 at dinner. AE, CB, DC, DISC, MC, V.
 **Open:** Lunch Mon–Fri 11am–2pm; dinner Mon–Sat 5–9pm.
Housed in an old Presbyterian church building that dates from the 1880s, La Renaissance has stubbornly refused to make any major structural changes in becoming a restaurant. Instead, the pews are still used for seating, and the sanctuary, chapel, and parish hall have become separate dining rooms—albeit with revamped decor! Dining here is an all-inclusive experience. A three-course lunch and five-course dinner begin with a tureen of soup and finish with a dessert, served at the table from a wooden cart. Pasta contrapuntal (with mushrooms and onions) and baked asparagus Virginia (wrapped in ham) are popular lunches; prime rib, New Zealand deep-sea filet, and roast duck apriquitte are delicious dinners. The restaurant features an extensive wine list as well. It's in Mesa Junction, two blocks southwest of Abriendo Avenue at the corner of Michigan Street.

**MICO'S, 1310 U.S. 50 W. Tel. 545-8770.**
 **Cuisine:** STEAK/SEAFOOD. **Reservations:** Recommended Sat–Sun.
 **$ Prices:** Appetizers $3.95–$7.95; main courses $8.95–$16.95. AE, MC, V.
 **Open:** Dinner only, Mon–Sat 5–10pm, Sun 4–10pm (lounge open to 1am).
This casual restaurant has two sections: a dimly lit, black-upholstered steakhouse in front, a brighter fine-dining area in the rear. Classic light rock music is piped in, and large picture windows look out toward the highway. Chef-owner Mike Nygo, a former railroad worker, keeps the menu simple . . . and successful. You can start with peel-and-eat shrimp or deep-fried mushrooms, then move on to a T-bone steak (30 ounces, if you're up to it) in Mico's secret marinade, a char-broiled shish kebab, shrimp scampi, or any of many other choices of seafood, from crab to halibut.

## EASY EXCURSION
### ROYAL GORGE

One of the most impressive natural attractions in the entire state—albeit a bit overwhelmed these days by commercialism—is the ✪ **Royal Gorge,** 50 miles west of Pueblo (tel. 719/275-7507). This narrow and spectacular canyon on the Arkansas River, 1,055 feet deep, was cut through solid granite by three million years of water and wind erosion. It is spanned by the world's highest bridge and by an aerial tramway, built for no other reason than to thrill tourists. And more than half a million of them visit every year.

When Zebulon Pike encountered the gorge in 1806, he predicted that man would never conquer it. But by 1877 the Denver & Rio Grande Railroad had laid a route through the canyon, and it became a major national tourist attraction. The quarter-mile-long bridge was built in 1929, suspended from two 300-ton cables; it was reinforced in 1983. A funicular railway, the world's steepest, was completed in 1931; it plunges from the rim of the gorge to the floor at a 45° angle. The tram opened in 1969. Owned by the city of Cañon City, the 160-acre park also includes a multimedia theater, miniature railway, children's play area, four restaurants, six gift shops, craft village, entertainment gazebo, trolley shuttle service, and herds of tame mule deer.

The gorge is open every day, year round, from dawn to dusk. Admission—$6.50 for adults, $4.50 for children 4 to 11—includes crossing the bridge and a choice of a funicular or tram ride, or theater show. For another $2 you can pick two of the three options.

Royal Gorge raft trips are organized over varying lengths of the river, some involving rough white-water passages. Full-day trips cost $40 and up and there are 2-day trips including cookouts along the way. Two outfitters are **Royal Gorge Rafting,** 45045 U.S. 50 (tel. 275-5161), west of Cañon City; and **Arkansas Adventures,** U.S. 50, 20 miles above Royal Gorge (tel. 275-3229).

Near the entrance to the park is ☼ **Buckskin Joe Park & Railway,** a living western movie set that opened in 1958 and has since provided the scene for some two dozen films, including *How the West Was Won* and *The Cowboys.* Built on 30 acres, Buckskin Joe is a realistic re-creation of a frontier town of the late 1860s. A population of 70, all in period costume, play the roles of citizens of the day—most of them law abiding, some of them not. (Watch out for the gunslingers!) The scenic railway skirts the edge of the Royal Gorge. There's also a huge gift shop, a stagecoach, a museum, and stables for horseback riding. An all-inclusive ticket costs $10, or pay $5.50 for Buckskin Joe alone, $3.95 for the train. Open May to September, daily from 8am to dusk. (The railway runs March to November, daily from 8am to dusk.)

---

# 2. TRINIDAD

197 miles S of Denver; 192 miles N of Santa Fe, New Mexico

**GETTING THERE   By Plane**   The **Trinidad Municipal Airport,** 10 miles east off U.S. 350 (tel. 719/846-6271), handles private planes and charters, but no commercial flights.

**By Train**   The **Amtrak** *Southwest Chief* passes through Trinidad twice daily—once eastbound, once westbound—on the main line between Chicago and Los Angeles. The depot is on Nevada Street north of College Street, beneath I-25 (tel. 719/846-9283, or 800/872-7245).

**By Bus**   Coaches of **Greyhound/Trailways** (tel. 800/528-6055) and **TNM&O** (Texas, New Mexico, & Oklahoma; tel. 800/528-0447) serve Trinidad. The bus station is on State Street north of College Street (tel. 846-7271), a block west of the rail depot.

**By Car**   If you're traveling from north or south, take I-25: Trinidad sits astride the interstate, halfway between Denver and Santa Fe, New Mexico. From the east, you can take U.S. 50 into La Junta, then turn southwest for 80 miles on U.S. 350. From Durango and points west, take U.S. 160 to Walsenburg, then travel south 37 miles on I-25.

**SPECIAL EVENTS** Area annual events include **Will Overhead Day,** in Walsenburg, on the Saturday preceding Memorial Day; the **Spanish Peaks Fiesta,** in Walsenburg, the first weekend of June; the **Santa Fe Trail Festival,** in Trinidad, the second weekend of June; **Concerts in the Park,** in Kit Carson Park, Trinidad, on Sunday from June to August; **Cowboy Days,** in Trinidad, the last weekend of July; the **Trinidad Roundup,** in Trinidad, on Labor Day weekend; and **Plaza de los Leones,** in Walsenburg, the third weekend of September.

---

Trinidad has a long and colorful history. The longest single trail of dinosaur tracks in the world was found just southeast of the city; Plains tribes roamed the area for centuries before the first 17th- and 18th-century forays by Spanish explorers and settlers. Traders and trappers made this location an important stop on the northern branch of the Santa Fe Trail between Bent's Old Fort and Fort Union. It was incorporated in 1876, and the Atchison, Topeka, & Santa Fe Railway soon followed. Bat Masterson was sheriff in the 1880s, Wyatt Earp drove the stage, Kit Carson helped open the trade routes, and even Billy the Kid passed through. Many historic buildings—handsome structures of brick and sandstone—survive from this era.

German, Irish, Italian, Jewish, Polish, and Slavic immigrants were drawn to the area around the turn of the century by extensive coal mining just west of town and large cattle companies on the plains to the east. Mining—along with agriculture and railroading—sustained the town for decades. But in 1982 the coal mines closed, sending unemployment in the region to a staggering level. Trinidad has never completely recovered, but an economic-development effort, strong on tourism, has helped the town of about 9,500 survive. The coal mines recently reopened on a reduced level.

## ORIENTATION

**INFORMATION** The **Trinidad Visitor Center,** 135 North Animas Street (I-25, Exit 14A), Trinidad, CO 81082 (tel. 719/846-7244), is housed in an old Colorado & Southern Railroad caboose in Riverfront Park. It's open Monday through Saturday from 9am to 6pm and on Sunday from 10am to 5pm. A free trolley ride around historic downtown Trinidad begins here.

The **Colorado Welcome Center,** 309 North Nevada Avenue (I-25, Exit 14A), Trinidad, CO 81082 (tel. 719/846-9285, or 800/748-1970), open daily, has information not only on southeastern Colorado, but on the entire state.

**TOWN LAYOUT** Trinidad is nestled in the foothills of the Rocky Mountains. To its west is the Sangre de Cristo Range; to its east, the Great Plains. El Rio de Las Animas en Purgatorio (the river of lost souls in Purgatory), better known as the Purgatoire River, an Arkansas River tributary, flows from southwest to northeast through the center of town, paralleling **Main Street** (U.S. 160/350). The historic downtown area is focused around Main and **Commercial Street** on the south side of the river. Main joins I-25 on the west side of downtown.

## GETTING AROUND

Trinidad lacks an efficient public transit system, so the best way to get around is by **taxi** (tel. 846-2237).

You can rent a car from **Hertz,** Circle Chevrolet-Buick, I-25 Exit 11 (tel. 719/846-9805, or 800/327-7607), or **National,** Hadad Motor Sales, 723 North Commercial Street (tel. 719/846-3318, or 800/227-7368).

## FAST FACTS

The **area code** is 719. In case of **emergency,** dial **0** (zero) for the operator or 846-2227 for the Colorado State Patrol. Medical services are rendered at **Mt. San Rafael Hospital,** 410 Benedicta Avenue off Main Street (tel. 846-9213). For **road conditions,** call 846-9262.

# WHAT TO SEE & DO
## ATTRACTIONS

**AULTMAN MUSEUM OF PHOTOGRAPHY, 136 E. Main St. Tel. 846-3881.**

In 1889, Oliver E. Aultman moved to Trinidad and established the Aultman Photography Studio. For the rest of the 19th century and much of the 20th, he and his son, Glenn, recorded southern Colorado history through their camera lenses. Their photographic record is exhibited at this museum, which also features displays of early cameras, darkroom equipment, hand-painted backdrops, and other studio props. The studio, incidentally, is still operated by Glenn Aultman himself—unretired at age 87 in 1992.

**Admission:** Free.

**Open:** Early May to Sept, Mon–Tues and Thurs–Sat 10am–4pm; off-season, by appointment.

**BACA HOUSE, BLOOM HOUSE, AND PIONEER MUSEUM, 300 E. Main St. Tel. 846-7217.**

Standing together overlooking the old Santa Fe Trail, these buildings rank as Trinidad's principal tourist attraction. The **Baca House,** built in 1869, is a two-story adobe in Greek Revival style, owned by sheep rancher Felipe Baca. His descendants lived here until the 1920s, and the house still has most of its original furnishings. Nearby stands the **Bloom House,** a rococo Victorian manor embellished with fancy wood carving and ornate ironwork. Built in 1882 for cattleman Frank G. Bloom and his family, it also contains fascinating period decor. The Colorado Historical Society operates both homes and the **Pioneer Museum** in outbuildings of the Baca House, with 19th-century ranch implements and transportation, and exhibits on the era.

**Admission:** $2.50 adults, $1.25 children and seniors.

**Open:** Memorial Day weekend–Labor Day, Mon–Sat 10am–4pm, Sun 1–4pm; off-season, by appointment.

**CORAZON DE TRINIDAD NATIONAL HISTORIC DISTRICT, Main St.**

Main Street was once part of the Santa Fe Trail, and many of the streets that cross it are paved with red brick. The Trinidad Historical Society distributes a booklet titled "A Walk Through the History of Trinidad," available at the visitor center and elsewhere. Among the buildings it singles out for special attention are the **Trinidad Opera House** (1882), **Columbian Hotel** (1880), both on Main Street, and the **Trinidad Water Works** (1879) on Cedar Street.

**A. R. MITCHELL MEMORIAL MUSEUM OF WESTERN ART, 150 E. Main St. Tel. 846-4224.**

More than 250 paintings and illustrations by western artist Arthur Roy Mitchell (1889–1977) are displayed here, along with works by other nationally recognized artists and a collection of early Hispanic religious folk art.

**Admission:** Free.

**Open:** Late Apr to Sept, Mon–Sat 10am–4pm; off-season, by appointment.

**OLD FIREHOUSE NO. 1 CHILDREN'S MUSEUM, 314 N. Commercial St. Tel. 846-6172** or 846-2024.

Two historic fire trucks, Trinidad's original 1930s-era alarm system, and a restored turn-of-the-century schoolroom are exhibited. Another section of the museum has hands-on displays for children.

**Admission:** 50¢.

**Open:** June–Aug, Tues and Fri 10am–2pm.

## SPORTS & RECREATION

**BOATING**   Located 3 miles west of town on Colo. 12, **Trinidad State Recreation Area** (tel. 846-6951) features a 900-acre reservoir on the Purgatoire River. Powerboating and sailing, as well as waterskiing and board sailing, are encouraged.

There's also a 62-unit campground here. About 34 miles west of Trinidad on Colo. 12, **Monument Lake Park** (tel. 868-2776) also offers a marina and boating.

**FISHING**  Largemouth bass, rainbow and brown trout, channel catfish, and walleye are caught in **Trinidad Reservoir** (see "Boating," above). Fishing is also good in the **Purgatoire River** and other area streams. Supplies and information are available at **Riverside Drug Store,** Commercial Street and Plum Street (tel. 846-3221).

**GOLF**  The 9-hole, par-36 **Trinidad Municipal Golf Club,** off the Santa Fe Trail adjacent to I-25 (tel. 846-9918), has a driving range and pro shop. Some 60 miles northwest of Trinidad, on Colo. 12 near La Veta, is the 18-hole, par-72 **Grandote Golf and Country Club** (tel. 742-3123), a championship course designed by pro golfer Tom Weiskopf.

**HIKING**  There are numerous fine trails in the **San Isabel National Forest** around Cuchara, off Colo. 12 some 50 miles west of Trinidad. Nearer town, the **Levsa Canyon Trail** extends 5 miles from Trinidad State Recreation Area (see "Boating," above) to historic Cokedale (see "Easy Excursions," below).

**SKIING**  The **Cuchara Valley Resort,** P.O. Box 3, Cuchara, CO 81055 (tel. 742-3163, or 800/227-4436), is one of Colorado's newest winter destinations. Located 54 miles west of Trinidad on Colo. 12, the ski area has a vertical drop of 1,562 feet from the summit of 10,810-foot Baker Mountain. Five lifts, including two double chairs and one triple chair, serve 20 trails of all ability levels. The mountain also has a ski shop, restaurant, and other facilities.

## WHERE TO STAY

**BEST WESTERN COUNTRY CLUB INN, 900 W. Adams St., Trinidad, CO 81082. Tel. 719/846-2215,** or 800/955-2215. Fax 719/846-2215, ext. 111. 55 rms (all with bath). A/C TV TEL
**$ Rates:** Jan–Apr and early Oct to Dec, $39 single; $43 double. May to early June and Labor Day to early Oct, $43 single; $47 double. Early June to July 1, $60 single or double. July 2–Labor Day, $65 single or double. AE, CB, DC, DISC, MC, V.
Situated on a hillside overlooking I-25, adjacent to the municipal golf course, this is arguably Trinidad's best accommodation. Its restaurant, an upscale coffee shop with an adjoining lounge, rates highly as well, with a full salad bar and dinners priced at $5.95 to $17.95. The spacious guest rooms, appointed in earth tones, have one king-size or two queen-size beds, table and chairs, dresser, and double vanity. Facilities include a seasonal outdoor swimming pool, Jacuzzi, fitness room, guest laundry, and gift shop; the motel also offers a 24-hour desk and courtesy shuttle service.

**TRINIDAD MOTOR INN, 702 W. Main St., Trinidad, CO 81082. Tel. 719/846-2271.** 62 rms. A/C TV TEL
**$ Rates:** Jan to mid-May and Labor Day–Dec, $36 single; $39–$41 double. Mid-May to mid-June, $40 single; $44–$48 double. Mid-June to Labor Day, $38 single; $42–$48 double. AE, CB, DC, DISC, MC, V.
The downtown historic district is only a short walk away from this property, located just off I-25 at Exit 13B. Rooms are spacious and have all standard furnishings, including queen-size beds in most units. There's a heated outdoor swimming pool and guest laundry; the Stagecoach Dining Room serves three meals daily, and has an adjoining lounge.

## WHERE TO DINE

**ARTURO'S, 400 E. Main St. Tel. 846-6060.**
**Cuisine:** STEAK/SEAFOOD. **Reservations:** Recommended in summer.
**$ Prices:** Appetizers $2.95–$6.95; main courses $5.95–$17.95. AE, MC, V.
**Open:** Dinner only, May–Sept, daily 5–10pm; Oct–Apr, Fri–Sat 5–10pm.
A stonemason-turned-parson built this massive stone building next to the Bloom House as the First Christian Church in 1922. It still features much of its original style

and elegant decor. Diners are serenaded by piped-in classical music as they choose from a menu that features a variety of steaks, lobster, king crab, oysters, frogs' legs, and the like. Full dinners include salad, potato, vegetable, roll, and coffee or tea. There's a full bar downstairs.

### HACIENDA DE SANTA FE, 220 Pine St. Tel. 846-8660.

**Cuisine:** SOUTHWEST REGIONAL. **Reservations:** Not accepted.
**$ Prices:** Breakfast/lunch $2.95–$5.95; dinner $4.95–$9.95. AE, MC, V.
**Open:** Daily 7am–9pm.

This festive café beneath the Interstate, between Nevada and Commercial, offers up generous portions of New Mexico–style cuisine every day of the week. Come expecting to fill up on blue-corn enchiladas, carne adovada, or chimichangas, and leave room for melt-in-your-mouth sopaipillas for dessert.

### NANA & NANO'S PASTA HOUSE, 415 University St. Tel. 846-2696.

**Cuisine:** ITALIAN. **Reservations:** Not accepted.
**$ Prices:** Lunch $3.50–$6.50; dinner $5–$12.50. AE, MC, V.
**Open:** Lunch Mon–Fri 11:30am–1:30pm; dinner Mon–Thurs 4:30–8:30pm, Fri–Sat 4:30–9pm. Deli, Mon–Fri 9am–5:30pm.

The decor is simple here—red-checked tablecloths and candles in chianti bottles— but that doesn't stop crowds from waiting outside the door for a table. Enjoy homemade hero sandwiches for lunch; a variety of pastas, pizzas, and daily specials (such as chicken cacciatore or eggplant Parmesan) for dinner.

## EASY EXCURSIONS

### SCENIC HIGHWAY OF LEGENDS

Unquestionably the most interesting day trip from Trinidad is the 77-mile ✪ **Scenic Highway of Legends.** Colo. 12 runs west, north, then northeast to Walsenburg, via Cuchara and La Veta, en route passing numerous historic locations and many points of great natural beauty.

Traveling west, the first site of special note is **Cokedale,** just off the highway 7 miles west of Trinidad. The best example of an intact coal camp in Colorado, Cokedale was built in 1906 by the Carbon Coal and Coke Co. as a self-contained company town. When the mine closed in 1947, it was home to 1,500 people. Many of today's handful of residents are descendants of those miners, or are retired miners themselves. The town and surrounding area are listed on the National Register of Historic Places.

As you proceed west, you'll pass several old coal towns, including **Valdez** and **Segundo,** and two active coal mines, the **Golden Eagle Mine** and **New Elk Mine,** before entering the **Stonewall Valley,** 29 miles west of Trinidad. Named for a striking rock formation, a vertical bed of lithified sandstone, Stonewall is both the site of a small timber industry and the location of many summer homes. At Stonewall, the highway turns north past the **Monument Lake Resort** and across 9,941-foot **Cucharas Pass** into Huerfano County.

Overlooking the pass are the **Spanish Peaks,** eroded remnants of a 20-million-year-old volcano. The native Arapahoe believed them to be the home of the gods, and they served as guideposts to early travelers. Legends persist about the existence of a treasure of gold in this area, but none has ever been found.

### EN ROUTE TO WALSENBURG

Numerous fascinating geologic features become prominent as the road descends toward Walsenburg. Among them are the **Devils Stairsteps,** one of a series of erosion-resistant igneous dikes that radiate out like spokes from the Spanish Peaks; **Dakota Wall,** a layer of pressed sandstone thrust vertically from the earth; and **Goemmer Butte,** sometimes called "Devil's Thumb," a volcanic plug rising 500 feet from the valley floor.

Fourteen miles west of Walsenburg is the foothills village of **La Veta** (pop. 600), founded as a ranching center in 1862. Its **Francisco Fort Museum,** on Francisco

Street at Colo. 12 (tel. 738-1107), occupies that original plaza building, and incorporates a saloon, schoolhouse, blacksmith shop, Presbyterian church, and mining museum to depict frontier life. It's open from Memorial Day to Labor Day daily from 9am to 5pm; admission is $1.50 for adults, 75¢ for children. You can stay in La Veta at the **1899 Bed and Breakfast Inn,** P.O. Box 372, La Veta, CO 81955 (tel. 719/742-3576).

### FARTHER AFIELD

Northwest of Walsenburg, Colo. 69 winds through the Sangre de Cristo foothills 65 miles to Westcliffe before proceeding another 25 miles to join U.S. 50 west of Cañon City. En route, it passes through **Gardner,** 27 miles from Walsenburg, a growing artists' community and home of **Mission Wolf,** a sanctuary and refuge for some 30 pure and hybrid wolves. **Westcliffe** (pop. 350) is a popular summer and winter recreational center, and the seat of Custer County.

At the eastern edge of the county, on Colo. 165 near Rye, 29 miles east of Westcliffe and 33 miles southwest of Pueblo, is the unique **Bishop Castle,** a three-story-high medieval castle singlehandedly built by laborer Jim Bishop, who has gathered and set more than 2,000 tons of rocks per year since 1969. Bishop, now 48, calls it a monument "to hard-working poor people everywhere." Admission is by donation only.

---

# 3. LA JUNTA

64 miles E of Pueblo; 80 miles NE of Trinidad;
274 miles NW of Amarillo, Texas

**GETTING THERE   By Plane**   The **La Junta Municipal Airport** is 4 miles north of town off Colo. 109 (tel. 384-8407). It handles private and charter flights, but has no commercial service. Pueblo is the nearest commercial airport.

**By Train**   Passenger service is available aboard **Amtrak,** with a depot on First Street at Colorado Avenue (tel. 719/384-2275, or 800/872-7245). The *Southwest Chief* passes through twice daily—once eastbound, once westbound—on the main line between Chicago and Los Angeles.

**By Bus**   Buses of **Greyhound/Trailways** and **TNM&O** serve the town several times daily from all directions. Coaches stop at My Car Wash, 619 East Third Street (tel. 719/384-9288).

**By Car**   La Junta is easily reached via U.S. 50. The highway, which runs east into Kansas, is linked in the west to I-25 at Pueblo. From New Mexico, take exit I-25 at Trinidad and take U.S. 350; from Durango and southwestern Colorado, take U.S. 160 to Walsenburg, and continue on Colo. 10 to La Junta.

**SPECIAL EVENTS**   Area annual events include **Fiesta Days,** in La Junta, the second weekend of June; the **Bent County Fair,** in Las Animas, the last week of July; the **Arkansas Valley Fair,** in Rocky Ford, the third week of August; the **Fur Trade Encampment,** at Bent's Old Fort, on Labor Day weekend in September; **Early Settlers Day,** in La Junta, the Saturday after Labor Day; **Oktoberfest,** in Rocky Ford, the last weekend of September; and **1846 Christmas,** at Bent's Old Fort, in mid-December.

---

**A**rapahoe, Cheyenne, and Ute tribes once made the Arkansas River Valley their hunting and fishing grounds. Spanish soldiers passed through in the 17th and 18th centuries, but not until Zebulon Pike led his exploratory expedition up the river in 1806 did it became known to white Americans. Trappers and traders followed, creating the Santa Fe Trail; brothers William and Charles Bent built Bent's Fort in 1833 as a trading post, the first American settlement in the region. As settlers moved in, and with them the railroad, Fort Wise and Fort Lyon were built in the 1860s to house cavalry troops and put down tribal uprisings.

La Junta was founded in 1875 as a railroad camp. First called Manszaneras, then Otero, it was renamed La Junta—Spanish for "the junction"—on completion of rail links to Pueblo and Trinidad in 1877. The town flourished as a farming and ranching center. Today, with a population of about 8,500, its highly irrigated land produces a wide variety of fruits, vegetables, and wheat.

# ORIENTATION

**INFORMATION**   The best source is the **La Junta Chamber of Commerce,** 110 Santa Fe Avenue (P.O. Box 408), La Junta, CO 81050 (tel. 719/384-7411).

**TOWN LAYOUT**   La Junta is located on the Arkansas River at an elevation of 4,100 feet. U.S. 50, which runs through town as **First Street,** follows the river's south bank. The highways from Trinidad and Walsenburg join it just west of town. The downtown core focuses around First Street, Second Street, and Third Street, crossed by north-south **Colorado Avenue** and **Santa Fe Avenue.** At the east edge of town, Colo. 109 (**Adams Street**) crosses the Arkansas into North La Junta (where it becomes Main Street); six blocks past the river, Colo. 194 (**Trail Road**) forks to the right and leads 5 miles to Bent's Old Fort.

# FAST FACTS

The **area code** is 719. In case of **emergency,** call 384-2525 for police, 384-2323 for ambulance or fire. Health services are rendered by the **Arkansas Valley Regional Medical Center,** 1100 Carson Avenue at 10th Street (tel. 384-5412). The **post office** is located at Fourth Street and Colorado Avenue. For **road conditions,** call 1-336-4326.

# WHAT TO SEE & DO

## ATTRACTIONS

**BENT'S OLD FORT NATIONAL HISTORIC SITE, 35110 Colo. 194 East. Tel. 384-2596.**

Once the most important settlement on the Santa Fe Trail between Missouri and New Mexico, Bent's Old Fort has been reconstructed exactly as it was during its reign as a major trading post, from 1833 to 1849. Located 7 miles east of modern La Junta, this adobe fort on the Arkansas River was built by brothers Charles and William Bent and partner Ceran St. Vrain. It was the hub of trade between eastern U.S. merchants, Rocky Mountain fur trappers, Hispanics and Navajos from New Mexico, and Plains tribes (mainly Cheyenne, but including Arapahoe, Ute, Apache, Kiowa, and Comanche).

A description written by a traveler in 1840 is still apt today:

*Although built of the simple prairie soil, made to hold together by a rude mixture with straw and the plain grass itself, the fort is constructed with all the defensive capacities of a complete fortification. The dwellings, kitchens, the arrangements for comfort, are all such as to strike the wanderer with the liveliest surprise, as though an 'air-built castle' had dropped to earth before him in the midst of the vast desert.*

As American settlement increased and drove off the buffalo that were the lifeblood of the Plains tribes, the Bents were caught between two cultures. Serious hostilities began in 1847 and trade rapidly declined. The fort burned to the ground in 1849 and was not rebuilt until modern times. But it is as faithful as possible to the original design. Antiques and reproductions furnish the 33 rooms, which include a kitchen with an adjoining pantry, a cook's room, and a dining room; a trade room with robes, pelts, and blankets in stock; blacksmith and carpenter shops; William Bent's office and bedroom; quarters for Mexican laborers, trappers, and soldiers; a billiard room; and the quarters of a merchant's wife who kept a meticulous diary during her stay here in 1846, en route to Santa Fe.

It's a quarter-mile walk on a paved path from the historic site's contact station to the fort itself, where hosts in period costume greet visitors year round. Start your visit by viewing a 22-minute video, *Castle on the Plains,* which describes the rise and fall of the Bent empire. Then wander through the fort, pausing to watch demonstrations of frontier ways—blacksmithing, adobe making, trapping, cooking, medicine, and survival skills. In summer, 45-minute guided tours begin at 9:30am, 11:30am, 1:30pm, and 3:30pm daily. Books on the Santa Fe Trail and fur-trade era are for sale at the fort, along with period goods in the trade room.

**Admission:** $1 per person or $3 per vehicle.

**Open:** Memorial Day–Labor Day, daily 8am–6pm; the rest of the year, daily 8am–4:30pm.

### COMANCHE NATIONAL GRASSLAND, south of La Junta around several highways. Tel. 384-2181.

Harsh, hot prairie and rocky canyons comprise these 419,000 acres of range lands managed by the federal government. Wildlife management, including habitat improvement and the protection of nesting areas, is a key reason for the establishment of the preserve. Some 275 species of birds have been sighted here, from upland game birds and waterfowl to bald and golden eagles, as well as many reptiles, amphibians, fishes, and mammals (bear, puma, antelope, fox, coyote, and bobcat among them). The region is a favorite of hikers, birdwatchers, hunters, and anglers. Amateur archeologists study strange petroglyphs in caves and on canyon walls, and rockhounds are bound to be pleased with their treasures.

There are two separate parcels. One flanks U.S. 350 and Colo. 109 5 to 35 miles south and southwest of La Junta; the other surrounds U.S. 160 and U.S. 287/350 south and southwest of Springfield, itself some 100 miles southeast of La Junta. Both offer camping and picknicking. For more information, contact Comanche National Grassland headquarters, 27162 U.S. 287 (P.O. Box 127), Springfield, CO 81073 (tel. 719/523-6591).

### KOSHARE INDIAN MUSEUM AND KIVA, Otero Junior College, 115 W. 18th St. Tel. 384-4411.

A $5-million collection of Native American art—featuring tribal members both as artists and as the subject of works of art—is the focus of this excellent museum. Clothing, jewelry, basketry, and other crafts are presented, along with western paintings and sculptures. The museum itself is an adobe building that resembles a Taos-area pueblo, one block west of Colorado Avenue.

But the highlight of a visit, if at all possible, is to view a performance by the Koshare Dancers. This nationally acclaimed troop of Boy Scout Explorers performs an average of 50 times a year, primarily in their own great *kiva,* a circular chamber traditionally used for religious rites. Dances are held at least weekly in summer, and the Koshare Winter Ceremonial Dances are a December tradition.

**Admission:** Museum, free; dances, $4 adults, $2 students and children.

**Open:** Memorial Day–Labor Day, daily 9am–5pm; the rest of the year, daily 12:30–5pm. Dancers perform mid-June to mid-Aug, Sat at 8:15pm, and other times; call for schedule. **Closed:** New Year's Day, Thanksgiving, and Christmas.

### OTERO MUSEUM, Second and Anderson Sts. Tel. 384-7406 or 384-7121.

The history of the La Junta area is told through the collection at this new museum, located one block south of U.S. 50 near downtown. Period buildings, railroad artifacts, and early settler items are displayed; items include an 1866 stagecoach and other 19th-century transportation. A herb garden contains plants once medicinally used.

**Admission:** Free.

**Open:** June–Sept, daily 1–5pm; off-season, tours by appointment.

# WHERE TO STAY

### QUALITY INN, 1325 E. Third St. (P.O. Box 1180), La Junta, CO 81050. Tel. 719/384-2571. 60 rms (all with bath). A/C TV TEL

**$ Rates:** $38–$53 single; $42–$57 double. AE, CB, DC, DISC, MC, V.

Spacious rooms and a variety of facilities make this motel the best choice in La Junta. All guest rooms have king-size or queen-size beds, satellite TVs, desk/dressers, and other standard furnishings. The property has an outdoor swimming pool and separate children's pool, a hot tub, meeting rooms, and shuttle service. The Capri Restaurant serves three meals daily, with room service available, and the adjoining lounge has live entertainment on weekends. Pets are accepted. The motel is situated at the junction of Colo. 109, on the principal route to Bent's Old Fort.

**STAGECOACH MOTOR INN, 905 W. Third St., La Junta, CO 81050. Tel. 719/384-5476.** 30 rooms. A/C TV TEL

**$ Rates:** Jan to mid-June and mid-Sept to Dec, $28 single, $32–$38 double; mid-June to mid-Sept, $32 single, $38–$42 double. AE, CB, DC, DISC, MC, V.

A Best Western property, the Stagecoach has clean, basic rooms with queen-size or double beds and other travelers' necessities. There's an outdoor swimming pool here, as well as an exercise and weight room.

## WHERE TO DINE

**EL PATIO, 315 Colorado Ave. Tel. 384-6787.**
   **Cuisine:** MEXICAN. **Reservations:** Not necessary.
**$ Prices:** Main courses $3.50–$8.50. AE, MC, V.
   **Open:** 11am–7pm Mon–Tues and Thurs–Fri, 11am–3pm Wed and Sat.

A small red adobe building with a wrought-iron gate atop its steps, El Patio is a great place to eat in fine weather, when its outdoor garden—the patio—is packed with locals. Enjoy chile rellenos, tostadas, burritos, and other south-of-the-border favorites.

## NEARBY EXCURSION
### LAS ANIMAS

Las Animas (pop. 2,800) is 20 miles east of La Junta on U.S. 50. Just 2 miles south on Colo. 101 is **Boggsville,** one of Colorado's earliest permanent settlements, now being restored. Among its historical buildings is the home of famed frontier scout Kit Carson. **Fort Lyon** (built 1867), 6 miles east on U.S. 50, is now a veterans' hospital; but it includes the Kit Carson Chapel, which occupies the building in which Carson died in 1868. The **Kit Carson Museum,** Bent Avenue and Ninth Street in Las Animas (tel. 456-2005), tells his story and that of the area's history, Memorial Day to Labor Day, daily from 1 to 5pm. For information, consult the **Las Animas/Bent County Chamber of Commerce,** 511 Llewellyn Thompson Boulevard, Las Animas, CO 81054 (tel. 456-0453). A good place to stay overnight or dine is the **Best Western Bent's Fort Inn,** 10950 U.S. 50, Las Animas, CO 81054 (tel. 456-0011).

# INDEX

## GENERAL INFORMATION

## DESTINATIONS

**KEY TO ABBREVIATIONS:** B = Budget; B&B = Bed & Breakfast; E = Expensive; I = Inexpensive; M = Moderate; VE = Very expensive; YH = Youth hostel; * = Author's favorite; $ = Super value choice

# NOW, SAVE MONEY ON ALL YOUR TRAVELS!
## Join Frommer's™ Dollarwise® Travel Club

Saving money while traveling is never easy, which is why the **Dollarwise Travel Club** was formed 32 years ago to provide cost-cutting travel strategies, up-to-date travel information, and a sense of community for value-conscious travelers from all over the world.

In keeping with the money-saving concept, the annual membership fee is low—$25 for U.S. residents and $35 for residents of Canada, Mexico, and other countries—and is immediately exceeded by the value of your benefits, which include:

1. Any TWO books listed on the following pages;
2. Plus any ONE Frommer's City Guide;
3. A subscription to our quarterly newspaper, *The Dollarwise Traveler;*
4. A membership card that entitles you to purchase through the Club all Frommer's publications for 33% to 40% off their retail price.

The eight-page **Dollarwise Traveler** tells you about the latest developments in good-value travel worldwide and includes the following columns: **Hospitality Exchange** (for those offering and seeking hospitality in cities all over the world); and **Share-a-Trip** (for those looking for travel companions to share costs).

Aside from the various Frommer's Guides, the Gault Millau Guides, and the Real Guides you can also choose from our Special Editions, which include such titles as *Caribbean Hideaways* (the 100 most romantic places to stay in the Islands); and *Marilyn Wood's Wonderful Weekends* (a selection of the best mini-vacations within a 200-mile radius of New York City).

To join this Club, send the appropriate membership fee with your name and address to: Frommer's Dollarwise Travel Club, 15 Columbus Circle, New York, NY 10023. Remember to specify which single city guide and which two other guides you wish to receive in your initial package of member's benefits. Or tear out the pages, check off your choices, and send them to us with your membership fee.

---

**FROMMER BOOKS**
**PRENTICE HALL TRAVEL**          Date_____
**15 COLUMBUS CIRCLE**
**NEW YORK, NY 10023**

Friends: Please send me the books checked below.

## FROMMER'S™ COMPREHENSIVE GUIDES
(Guides listing facilities from budget to deluxe, with emphasis on the medium-priced)

| | | | |
|---|---|---|---|
| ☐ Alaska | $14.95 | ☐ Italy | $19.00 |
| ☐ Australia | $14.95 | ☐ Japan & Hong Kong | $17.00 |
| ☐ Austria & Hungary | $14.95 | ☐ Morocco | $18.00 |
| ☐ Belgium, Holland & Luxembourg | $14.95 | ☐ Nepal | $18.00 |
| ☐ Bermuda & The Bahamas | $17.00 | ☐ New England | $17.00 |
| ☐ Brazil | $14.95 | ☐ New Mexico | $13.95 |
| ☐ California | $18.00 | ☐ New York State | $19.00 |
| ☐ Canada | $16.00 | ☐ Northwest | $16.95 |
| ☐ Caribbean | $17.00 | ☐ Puerta Vallarta (avail. Feb. '92) | $14.00 |
| ☐ Carolinas & Georgia | $17.00 | ☐ Portugal, Madeira & the Azores | $14.95 |
| ☐ Colorado (avail. Jan '92) | $14.00 | ☐ Scandinavia | $18.95 |
| ☐ Cruises (incl. Alaska, Carib, Mex, Hawaii, Panama, Canada & US) | $16.00 | ☐ Scotland (avail. Feb. '92) | $17.00 |
| | | ☐ South Pacific | $20.00 |
| ☐ Delaware, Maryland, Pennsylvania & the New Jersey Shore (avail. Jan. '92) | $19.00 | ☐ Southeast Asia | $14.95 |
| | | ☐ Switzerland & Liechtenstein | $19.00 |
| ☐ Egypt | $14.95 | ☐ Thailand | $20.00 |
| ☐ England | $17.00 | ☐ Virginia (avail. Feb. '92) | $14.00 |
| ☐ Florida | $17.00 | ☐ Virgin Islands | $13.00 |
| ☐ France | $15.95 | ☐ USA | $16.95 |
| ☐ Germany | $18.00 | | |

0891492

# FROMMER'S CITY GUIDES
(Pocket-size guides to sightseeing and tourist accommodations and facilities in all price ranges)

| | |
|---|---|
| ☐ Amsterdam/Holland . . . . . . . . . . . . .$8.95 | ☐ Minneapolis/St. Paul . . . . . . . . . . . . .$8.95 |
| ☐ Athens. . . . . . . . . . . . . . . . . . . . . . .$8.95 | ☐ Montréal/Québec City. . . . . . . . . . . .$8.95 |
| ☐ Atlanta . . . . . . . . . . . . . . . . . . . . . . .$8.95 | ☐ New Orleans. . . . . . . . . . . . . . . . . . .$8.95 |
| ☐ Atlantic City/Cape May . . . . . . . . . . .$8.95 | ☐ New York . . . . . . . . . . . . . . . . . . . .$12.00 |
| ☐ Bangkok. . . . . . . . . . . . . . . . . . . . .$12.00 | ☐ Orlando . . . . . . . . . . . . . . . . . . . . .$12.00 |
| ☐ Barcelona . . . . . . . . . . . . . . . . . . . .$12.00 | ☐ Paris . . . . . . . . . . . . . . . . . . . . . . . . .$8.95 |
| ☐ Belgium . . . . . . . . . . . . . . . . . . . . . . .$7.95 | ☐ Philadelphia . . . . . . . . . . . . . . . . . .$11.00 |
| ☐ Berlin. . . . . . . . . . . . . . . . . . . . . . .$10.00 | ☐ Rio . . . . . . . . . . . . . . . . . . . . . . . . . .$8.95 |
| ☐ Boston. . . . . . . . . . . . . . . . . . . . . . .$8.95 | ☐ Rome. . . . . . . . . . . . . . . . . . . . . . . . .$8.95 |
| ☐ Cancún/Cozumel/Yucatán . . . . . . . . .$8.95 | ☐ Salt Lake City . . . . . . . . . . . . . . . . . .$8.95 |
| ☐ Chicago . . . . . . . . . . . . . . . . . . . . . . .$9.95 | ☐ San Diego. . . . . . . . . . . . . . . . . . . . .$8.95 |
| ☐ Denver/Boulder/Colorado Springs. . . .$8.95 | ☐ San Francisco . . . . . . . . . . . . . . . . .$12.00 |
| ☐ Dublin/Ireland. . . . . . . . . . . . . . . . .$10.00 | ☐ Santa Fe/Taos/Albuquerque. . . . . . . .$10.95 |
| ☐ Hawaii . . . . . . . . . . . . . . . . . . . . . .$12.00 | ☐ Seattle/Portland . . . . . . . . . . . . . . .$12.00 |
| ☐ Hong Kong . . . . . . . . . . . . . . . . . . . .$7.95 | ☐ St. Louis/Kansas City . . . . . . . . . . . .$9.95 |
| ☐ Las Vegas . . . . . . . . . . . . . . . . . . . . .$8.95 | ☐ Sydney. . . . . . . . . . . . . . . . . . . . . . .$8.95 |
| ☐ Lisbon/Madrid/Costa del Sol . . . . . . .$8.95 | ☐ Tampa/St. Petersburg . . . . . . . . . . . .$8.95 |
| ☐ London . . . . . . . . . . . . . . . . . . . . . .$12.00 | ☐ Tokyo. . . . . . . . . . . . . . . . . . . . . . . .$8.95 |
| ☐ Los Angeles . . . . . . . . . . . . . . . . . . .$8.95 | ☐ Toronto . . . . . . . . . . . . . . . . . . . . . .$8.95 |
| ☐ Mexico City/Acapulco . . . . . . . . . . .$8.95 | ☐ Vancouver/Victoria . . . . . . . . . . . . . .$7.95 |
| ☐ Miami . . . . . . . . . . . . . . . . . . . . . . .$8.95 | ☐ Washington, D.C. . . . . . . . . . . . . . .$12.00 |

# FROMMER'S $-A-DAY® GUIDES
(Guides to low-cost tourist accommodations and facilities)

| | |
|---|---|
| ☐ Australia on $40 a Day . . . . . . . . . . .$13.95 | ☐ Israel on $40 a Day. . . . . . . . . . . . . .$13.95 |
| ☐ Costa Rica, Guatemala & Belize | ☐ Mexico on $45 a Day . . . . . . . . . . . .$18.00 |
| on $35 a Day. . . . . . . . . . . . . . . . . .$15.95 | ☐ New York on $65 a Day. . . . . . . . . . .$15.00 |
| ☐ Eastern Europe on $25 a Day . . . . . . .$16.95 | ☐ New Zealand on $45 a Day . . . . . . . .$16.00 |
| ☐ England on $50 a Day. . . . . . . . . . . .$17.00 | ☐ Scotland & Wales on $40 a Day . . . . .$18.00 |
| ☐ Europe on $45 a Day . . . . . . . . . . . .$19.00 | ☐ South America on $40 a Day . . . . . . .$15.95 |
| ☐ Greece on $35 a Day . . . . . . . . . . . .$14.95 | ☐ Spain on $50 a Day . . . . . . . . . . . . .$15.95 |
| ☐ Hawaii on $70 a Day. . . . . . . . . . . . .$18.00 | ☐ Turkey on $40 a Day. . . . . . . . . . . . .$22.00 |
| ☐ India on $40 a Day . . . . . . . . . . . . . .$20.00 | ☐ Washington, D.C., on $45 a Day. . . . .$17.00 |
| ☐ Ireland on $40 a Day. . . . . . . . . . . . .$17.00 | |

# FROMMER'S CITY $-A-DAY GUIDES

| | |
|---|---|
| ☐ Berlin on $40 a Day . . . . . . . . . . . . .$12.00 | ☐ Madrid on $50 a Day (avail. Jan '92) . . .$13.00 |
| ☐ Copenhagen on $50 a Day . . . . . . . .$12.00 | ☐ Paris on $45 a Day . . . . . . . . . . . . . .$12.00 |
| ☐ London on $45 a Day . . . . . . . . . . . .$12.00 | ☐ Stockholm on $50 a Day (avail. Dec. '91)$13.00 |

# FROMMER'S FAMILY GUIDES

| | |
|---|---|
| ☐ California with Kids . . . . . . . . . . . . .$16.95 | ☐ San Francisco with Kids. . . . . . . . . . .$17.00 |
| ☐ Los Angeles with Kids . . . . . . . . . . . .$17.00 | ☐ Washington, D.C., with Kids (avail. Jan |
| ☐ New York City with Kids (avail. Jan '92) $18.00 | '92) . . . . . . . . . . . . . . . . . . . . . . . .$17.00 |

# SPECIAL EDITIONS

| | |
|---|---|
| ☐ Beat the High Cost of Travel. . . . . . . .$6.95 | ☐ Marilyn Wood's Wonderful Weekends |
| ☐ Bed & Breakfast—N. America . . . . . .$14.95 | (CT, DE, MA, NH, NJ, NY, PA, RI, VT) . . .$11.95 |
| ☐ Caribbean Hideaways . . . . . . . . . . . .$16.00 | ☐ Motorist's Phrase Book (Fr/Ger/Sp) . . . .$4.95 |
| ☐ Honeymoon Destinations (US, Mex & | ☐ The New World of Travel (annual by |
| Carib). . . . . . . . . . . . . . . . . . . . . . .$14.95 | Arthur Frommer for savvy travelers) . . .$16.95 |

**(TURN PAGE FOR ADDITONAL BOOKS AND ORDER FORM)**

| ☐ Paris Rendez-Vous . . . . . . . . . . . . . . $10.95 | ☐ Travel Diary and Record Book . . . . . . . . $5.95 |
| ☐ Swap and Go (Home Exchanging) . . . . $10.95 | ☐ Where to Stay USA (from $3 to $30 a night) . . . . . . . . . . . . . . . . . . . . . . $13.95 |

## FROMMER'S TOURING GUIDES

(Color illustrated guides that include walking tours, cultural and historic sites, and practical information)

| ☐ Amsterdam . . . . . . . . . . . . . . . . . . . $10.95 | ☐ New York . . . . . . . . . . . . . . . . . . . . $10.95 |
| ☐ Australia . . . . . . . . . . . . . . . . . . . . $12.95 | ☐ Paris . . . . . . . . . . . . . . . . . . . . . . . $8.95 |
| ☐ Brazil . . . . . . . . . . . . . . . . . . . . . . $10.95 | ☐ Rome . . . . . . . . . . . . . . . . . . . . . . $10.95 |
| ☐ Egypt . . . . . . . . . . . . . . . . . . . . . . . $8.95 | ☐ Scotland . . . . . . . . . . . . . . . . . . . . . $9.95 |
| ☐ Florence . . . . . . . . . . . . . . . . . . . . . $8.95 | ☐ Thailand . . . . . . . . . . . . . . . . . . . . $12.95 |
| ☐ Hong Kong . . . . . . . . . . . . . . . . . . . $10.95 | ☐ Turkey . . . . . . . . . . . . . . . . . . . . . $10.95 |
| ☐ London . . . . . . . . . . . . . . . . . . . . . $12.95 | ☐ Venice . . . . . . . . . . . . . . . . . . . . . . $8.95 |

## GAULT MILLAU

(The only guides that distinguish the truly superlative from the merely overrated)

| ☐ The Best of Chicago . . . . . . . . . . . . . $15.95 | ☐ The Best of Los Angeles . . . . . . . . . . $16.95 |
| ☐ The Best of Florida . . . . . . . . . . . . . . $17.00 | ☐ The Best of New England . . . . . . . . . $15.95 |
| ☐ The Best of France . . . . . . . . . . . . . . $16.95 | ☐ The Best of New Orleans . . . . . . . . . . $16.95 |
| ☐ The Best of Germany . . . . . . . . . . . . $18.00 | ☐ The Best of New York . . . . . . . . . . . . $16.95 |
| ☐ The Best of Hawaii . . . . . . . . . . . . . . $16.95 | ☐ The Best of Paris . . . . . . . . . . . . . . . $16.95 |
| ☐ The Best of Hong Kong . . . . . . . . . . . $16.95 | ☐ The Best of San Francisco . . . . . . . . . $16.95 |
| ☐ The Best of Italy . . . . . . . . . . . . . . . . $16.95 | ☐ The Best of Thailand . . . . . . . . . . . . . $17.95 |
| ☐ The Best of London . . . . . . . . . . . . . $16.95 | ☐ The Best of Toronto . . . . . . . . . . . . . $17.00 |
| | ☐ The Best of Washington, D.C. . . . . . . $16.95 | |

## THE REAL GUIDES

(Opinionated, politically aware guides for youthful budget-minded travelers)

| ☐ Amsterdam . . . . . . . . . . . . . . . . . . . $9.95 | ☐ Mexico . . . . . . . . . . . . . . . . . . . . . $11.95 |
| ☐ Berlin . . . . . . . . . . . . . . . . . . . . . . $11.95 | ☐ Morocco . . . . . . . . . . . . . . . . . . . . $12.95 |
| ☐ Brazil . . . . . . . . . . . . . . . . . . . . . . $13.95 | ☐ New York . . . . . . . . . . . . . . . . . . . . $9.95 |
| ☐ California & the West Coast . . . . . . . $11.95 | ☐ Paris . . . . . . . . . . . . . . . . . . . . . . . $9.95 |
| ☐ Czechoslovakia . . . . . . . . . . . . . . . . $13.95 | ☐ Peru . . . . . . . . . . . . . . . . . . . . . . . $12.95 |
| ☐ France . . . . . . . . . . . . . . . . . . . . . . $12.95 | ☐ Poland . . . . . . . . . . . . . . . . . . . . . $13.95 |
| ☐ Germany . . . . . . . . . . . . . . . . . . . . $13.95 | ☐ Portugal . . . . . . . . . . . . . . . . . . . . $10.95 |
| ☐ Greece . . . . . . . . . . . . . . . . . . . . . . $13.95 | ☐ San Francisco . . . . . . . . . . . . . . . . . $11.95 |
| ☐ Guatemala . . . . . . . . . . . . . . . . . . . $13.95 | ☐ Scandinavia . . . . . . . . . . . . . . . . . . $14.95 |
| ☐ Hong Kong . . . . . . . . . . . . . . . . . . . $11.95 | ☐ Spain . . . . . . . . . . . . . . . . . . . . . . $12.95 |
| ☐ Hungary . . . . . . . . . . . . . . . . . . . . . $12.95 | ☐ Turkey . . . . . . . . . . . . . . . . . . . . . $12.95 |
| ☐ Ireland . . . . . . . . . . . . . . . . . . . . . . $12.95 | ☐ Venice . . . . . . . . . . . . . . . . . . . . . $11.95 |
| ☐ Italy . . . . . . . . . . . . . . . . . . . . . . . $13.95 | ☐ Women Travel . . . . . . . . . . . . . . . . . $12.95 |
| ☐ Kenya . . . . . . . . . . . . . . . . . . . . . . $12.95 | ☐ Yugoslavia . . . . . . . . . . . . . . . . . . . $12.95 |

## ORDER NOW!

In U.S. include $2 shipping UPS for 1st book; $1 ea. add'l book. Outside U.S. $3 and $1, respectively.

**Allow four to six weeks for delivery in U.S., longer outside U.S. We discourage rush order service, but orders arriving with shipping fees plus a $15 surcharge will be handled as rush orders.**

Enclosed is my check or money order for $_____

NAME _____

ADDRESS _____

CITY _____ STATE _____ ZIP _____

0891492